A Celebration of Young Poets

Ohio – Fall 2007

Creative Communication, Inc.

A Celebration of Young Poets
Ohio – Fall 2007

An anthology compiled by Creative Communication, Inc.

Published by:

CREATIVE COMMUNICATION, INC.
1488 NORTH 200 WEST
LOGAN, UT 84341

All rights reserved. No part of this book may be reproduced or transmitted in any form or by any means, electronic or mechanical without written permission of the author and publisher.

Copyright © 2008 by Creative Communication, Inc.
Printed in the United States of America

ISBN: 978-1-60050-160-9

Foreword

The poets between these pages are not famous...yet. They are still learning how language creates images and how to reflect their thoughts through words. However, through their acceptance into this publication, these young poets have taken a giant leap that reflects their desire to write.

We are proud of this anthology and what it represents. Most poets who entered the contest were not accepted to be published. The poets who are included in this book represent the best poems from our youth. These young poets took a chance and were rewarded by being featured in this anthology. Without this book, these poems would have been lost in a locker or a backpack.

We will have a feeling of success if upon reading this anthology of poetry each reader finds a poem that evokes emotion. It may be a giggle or a smile. It may be a thoughtful reflection. You might find a poem that takes you back to an earlier day when a snowfall contains magic or when a pile of leaves was an irresistible temptation. If these poems can make you feel alive and have hope in our youth, then it will be time well spent.

As we thank the poets for sharing their work, we also thank you, the reader, for allowing us to be part of your life.

Thomas Worthen, Ph.D.
Editor
Creative Communication

WRITING CONTESTS!

Enter our next POETRY contest!

Enter our next ESSAY contest!

Why should I enter?
Win prizes and get published! Each year thousands of dollars in prizes are awarded in each region and tens of thousands of dollars in prizes are awarded throughout North America. The top writers in each division receive a monetary award and a free book that includes their published poem or essay. Entries of merit are also selected to be published in our anthology.

Who may enter?
There are four divisions in the poetry contest. The poetry divisions are grades K-3, 4-6, 7-9, and 10-12. There are three divisions in the essay contest. The essay division are grades 4-6, 7-9, and 10-12.

What is needed to enter the contest?
To enter the poetry contest send in one original poem, 21 lines or less. To enter the essay contest send in one original essay, 250 words or less, on any topic. Each entry must include the student's name, grade, address, city, state, and zip code, and the student's school name and school address. Students who include their teacher's name may help the teacher qualify for a free copy of the anthology.

How do I enter?

Enter a poem online at:
www.poeticpower.com
or
Mail your poem to:
Poetry Contest
1488 North 200 West
Logan, UT 84341

Enter an essay online at:
www.studentessaycontest.com
or
Mail your essay to:
Essay Contest
1488 North 200 West
Logan, UT 84341

When is the deadline?
Poetry contest deadlines are August 14th, December 4th, and April 8th. Essay contest deadlines are July 15th, October 15th, and February 17th. You can enter each contest, however, send only one poem or essay for each contest deadline.

Are there benefits for my school?
Yes. We award $15,000 each year in grants to help with Language Arts programs. Schools qualify to apply for a grant by having a large number of entries of which over fifty percent are accepted for publication. This typically tends to be about 15 accepted entries.

Are there benefits for my teacher?
Yes. Teachers with five or more students accepted to be published receive a free anthology that includes their students' writing.

For more information please go to our website at **www.poeticpower.com**, email us at editor@poeticpower.com or call 435-713-4411.

Table of Contents

Poetic Achievement Honor Schools 1

Language Arts Grant Recipients 5

Grades 10-11-12 7
    Top Poems 8
    High Merit Poems 18

Grades 7-8-9 61
    Top Poems 62
    High Merit Poems 72

Grades 4-5-6 197
    Top Poems 198
    High Merit Poems 208

Index 321

Fall 2007 Poetic Achievement Honor Schools

* Teachers who had fifteen or more poets accepted to be published

The following schools are recognized as receiving a "Poetic Achievement Award." This award is given to schools who have a large number of entries of which over fifty percent are accepted for publication. With hundreds of schools entering our contest, only a small percent of these schools are honored with this award. The purpose of this award is to recognize schools with excellent Language Arts programs. This award qualifies these schools to receive a complimentary copy of this anthology. In addition, these schools are eligible to apply for a Creative Communication Language Arts Grant. Grants of two hundred and fifty dollars each are awarded to further develop writing in our schools.

Barrington Elementary School
    Upper Arlington
        Clay Bogart*

Birchwood School
    Cleveland
        Helene Debelak*
        Jennifer Jackson

Chardon Middle School
    Chardon
        Patricia Miller*
        Cindy Newman*

Cline Elementary School
    Centerville
        Nancy Carlsen
        Judy E. Rutherford*

Clinton Massie Middle School
    Clarksville
        Bunny Bradshaw*

Dobbins Elementary School
    Poland
        Elaine Morlan*

EH Greene Intermediate School
    Cincinnati
        Carol Belanger*
        Mrs. Brubaker
        Leslie Burklow
        Mrs. Carlton
        Andrea Garten
        Michelle LaCalameto*
        Angie Ryan*
        Rita Sexton

Frank Ohl Middle School
    Youngstown
        Donnamarie Polak*

Gahanna Middle School East
    Gahanna
        Diane Heinmiller*

Gesu Elementary School
    Toledo
        M.E. Peters*

Glenwood Middle School
    Findlay
        Cynthia Habegger*

Hamersville Elementary and Middle School
Hamersville
    Tracy L. Gibson
    Carla Waits
    Angela K. Yockey

Harmon Middle School
Pickerington
    Terri Smolewski*
    Jan Wild*

Hilliard Davidson High School
Hilliard
    Mrs. Burke*
    Trace Crawford

Holy Angels School
Sidney
    Jeanne L. Schlagetter*

Hopewell Jr High School
West Chester
    Mary Anne Fifarek*

Hylen Souders Elementary School
Galena
    Nicole Leinweber*

Immaculate Conception School
Port Clinton
    Connie Snyder*

Incarnation School
Centerville
    Paula Paprocki*

J A Garfield Middle School
Garrettsville
    Debbie Cross*

Jefferson Elementary School
Jefferson
    Julie Wright*

Kinsner Elementary School
Strongsville
    Christine Pasko*

Licking Valley Intermediate School
Newark
    Mrs. E. Fee*

Licking Valley Middle School
Newark
    Kathy R. Mehler*

Logan Hocking Middle School
Logan
    Kellie Hayden*

Loveland High School
Loveland
    Theresa Bosse
    Heather Jamison
    John Jones
    Aimee Noel*

Matthew Duvall Elementary School
Cincinnati
    Mrs. Knabb*

McNicholas High School
Cincinnati
    Meloney Feldkamp*

Melrose Elementary School
Wooster
    Marty Boyle*

Miller City-New Cleveland School
Miller City
    Mrs. Rieger*

Monroe Elementary School
Monroe
    Jo Ashworth
    Susan Cooper
    Stephanie Decker
    Tina Dirksen
    Kristy Flannery
    Sheri Gillespie
    Susan Hamilton
    David Hogan
    Sheilia Holbrock

Poetic Achievement Honor Schools

Monroe Elementary School
Monroe (cont.)
    Jennifer Kenneally
    Tammy Larison
    Vickie Marchetti
    Gayle Martz
    Theresa Morris
    Kate O'Hara
    David Osborne
    Rachael Rist

Northfield Elementary School
Northfield
    Wendy Bailey*
    Lisa Bass
    Jennifer Beck*
    Ms. Berkley*
    Jaime Hoon*
    Terri Javorsky*
    Pat Kecskemety*
    Mrs. Mileti
    Ms. Ventre

Pike Christian Academy
Waverly
    Charlotte Saltzman*

Pike Delta York Middle School
Delta
    Jane Foor*

Prospect Elementary School
East Cleveland
    Oretha Carpenter*

Rocky River Middle School
Rocky River
    Amanda M. Liskovec*

Roosevelt Elementary School
McDonald
    Debbie Crish
    Patty Gault

Sanderson Elementary School
Lancaster
    Melinda Kitsmiller*
    Cathy Trimmer

South Range Middle School
Salem
    Carol Goodwin*

Spaulding Elementary School
Goshen
    Lisa Drees*

St Brendan Elementary School
North Olmsted
    Elizabeth Colborn*

St Christopher Elementary School
Vandalia
    Cecilia Castellano*

St Clement Elementary School
St Bernard
    Sr. Carol Louise*

St John the Baptist School
Cincinnati
    Cecelia Ante*

St Michael School
Independence
    Jo Ellen Kyanko*

St Monica Elementary School
Garfield Heights
    Donna Przybojewski*

St Paschal Baylon School
Highland Heights
    Mary Connors*

Stanton Middle School
Hammondsville
    Alicia Hartman*
    Mary Ann Hoobler

Tippecanoe Middle School
Tipp City
    Karen Jackson*
    Andrea McKinney*

Tremont Elementary School
    Upper Arlington
        Pauline Endo*
        Debra Welch*

Trilby Elementary School
    Toledo
        Kathy Chaka
        Jan Ellenberger

Verity Middle School
    Middletown
        Joni Sexton*

Waterloo Middle School
    Atwater
        Christine Barkhurst*

West Branch Middle School
    Beloit
        Libbie S. Romigh*

Westview Elementary School
    Jackson
        Pam Steele*

Whitmer High School
    Toledo
        Donna J. Hook*

Woodward Park Middle School
    Columbus
        Carol Morris*

Wooster Christian School
    Wooster
        Karen Masowich*

Language Arts Grant Recipients 2007-2008

After receiving a "Poetic Achievement Award" schools are encouraged to apply for a Creative Communication Language Arts Grant. The following is a list of schools who received a two hundred and fifty dollar grant for the 2007-2008 school year.

Acadamie DaVinci, Dunedin, FL
Altamont Elementary School, Altamont, KS
Belle Valley South School, Belleville, IL
Bose Elementary School, Kenosha, WI
Brittany Hill Middle School, Blue Springs, MO
Carver Jr High School, Spartanburg, SC
Cave City Elementary School, Cave City, AR
Central Elementary School, Iron Mountain, MI
Challenger K8 School of Science and Mathematics, Spring Hill, FL
Columbus Middle School, Columbus, MT
Cypress Christian School, Houston, TX
Deer River High School, Deer River, MN
Deweyville Middle School, Deweyville, TX
Four Peaks Elementary School, Fountain Hills, AZ
Fox Chase School, Philadelphia, PA
Fox Creek High School, North Augusta, SC
Grandview Alternative School, Grandview, MO
Hillcrest Elementary School, Lawrence, KS
Holbrook School, Holden, ME
Houston Middle School, Germantown, TN
Independence High School, Elko, NV
International College Preparatory Academy, Cincinnati, OH
John Bowne High School, Flushing, NY
Lorain County Joint Vocational School, Oberlin, OH
Merritt Secondary School, Merritt, BC
Midway Covenant Christian School, Powder Springs, GA
Muir Middle School, Milford, MI
Northlake Christian School, Covington, LA
Northwood Elementary School, Hilton, NY
Place Middle School, Denver, CO
Public School 124, South Ozone Park, NY

Language Arts Grant Winners cont.

Public School 219 Kennedy King, Brooklyn, NY
Rolling Hills Elementary School, San Diego, CA
St Anthony's School, Streator, IL
St Joan Of Arc School, Library, PA
St Joseph Catholic School, York, NE
St Joseph School-Fullerton, Baltimore, MD
St Monica Elementary School, Mishawaka, IN
St Peter Celestine Catholic School, Cherry Hill, NJ
Strasburg High School, Strasburg, VA
Stratton Elementary School, Stratton, ME
Tom Thomson Public School, Burlington, ON
Tremont Elementary School, Tremont, IL
Warren Elementary School, Warren, OR
Webster Elementary School, Hazel Park, MI
West Woods Elementary School, Arvada, CO
West Woods Upper Elementary School, Farmington, CT
White Pine Middle School, Richmond, UT
Winona Elementary School, Winona, TX
Wissahickon Charter School, Philadelphia, PA
Wood County Christian School, Williamstown, WV
Wray High School, Wray, CO

Young Poets
Grades 10-11-12

Note: The Top Ten poems were finalized through an online voting system. Creative Communication's judges first picked out the top poems. These poems were then posted online. The final step involved thousands of students and teachers who registered as online judges and voted for the Top Ten poems. We hope you enjoy these selections.

Top Poem Grades 10-11-12

Suttons Bay Sunset

Here I am, chillin' like a three-toed in Suttons Bay.
Almost slipping into unconsciousness due to boredom.
At the moment, life is like a mortar without its pestle.
I look outside and nature is begging me to paint her.

I awaken my paints and delineate her gorgeous sunset.
The sunlight dances off the deep dark
Blue water of Lake Michigan.
The sun makes its final goodbyes and lays down behind the hill.

My watercolor weakens my stern face into a smile.
Now I may dive into another project in life.
I will present my masterpiece to the one
Who is this sunset to me.

Brad Bedacht, Grade 10
Summit Country Day School

Top Poem Grades 10-11-12

City

A desert, wet with confusion,
this spoiled metropolis of broken smoky skies,
and trees of withered madness.
Where steel giants cast shadows
on faces of melted wax,
and bodies lie selfishly in their shade,
bound in riches,
packed tightly into every corner.

Someone help us.
We're all so dirty, and far too busy choking.
We're all living, and we don't even know it.

This desert we've created, cracked from time and tear,
where shallow hearts don't mind stealing stars from eyes,
and breath from blackened lungs,
so barren of beauty, a surplus of sound.

It's pointless to pretend you're breathing
this rotten air.

Sidewalks crumble,
ashes beneath the feet that plague it,
and this spoiled metropolis falls.

Danna Boughner, Grade 11
Newbury High School

Top Poem Grades 10-11-12

Life Will Look Up

It all seems so hazy
Like a quickly fading dream
You watch your life fall into place
Then fall apart at the seams
Like running from an avalanche
Or swimming up a river
You're working and waiting
For your hopes and dreams to deliver
Don't get discouraged
You'll learn the way
To face the darkest shadows
And the dawn of each new day
The skies will clear
While your dreams come into view
And a single thread can sew the seams
Then let you start your life anew
The snow will melt
The river will calm
Sit back and watch
Luck fall into your palm
Life will look up

Angel Fantozzi, Grade 11
Jefferson Area Jr-Sr High School

Top Poem Grades 10-11-12

A Life of a Shadow

Beautiful shadows from the milky moon,
Stray around town near the coffee shop.
They drink from cups of serene solitude,
With chocolate-feigned attitudes swirling at the top.
Underneath the shaded sky, the shadows move to a park,
Where they stroll across rain-splattered sidewalks.
And saunter beneath artificial branches in the dark,
As they look past the lake, past the tattered swans, nestled amongst the rocks.
The shadows traipse across the town's concrete,
And walk through lawns of synthetic grass.
Their imitations spelled out by washed off sidewalk-chalk on the street,
As they gaze past windows of broken glass.
The duplicated actions of the shadows' great ennui,
Lead them to believe that there must be something else.
But what else could they do, who else could they be?
Certainly by doing what they wanted, they could not be themselves.

Irene Gallagher, Grade 11
Brunswick High School

Top Poem Grades 10-11-12

Reflections

The world's a stage or so they say
And life is just a game
The rules get twisted and thrown away
But we play it all the same

An eye for an eye
The only way
Morality and chivalry
Are things of yesterday

Vanity and arrogance
The ruling hands at play
Souls stained deep with blood red sin
It's just the world's way

The first to throw the stones of guilt
Are never in the wrong
Hypocrites and fabricators
Lead us all in song

Blindly do we follow
Like lambs without a guide
No matter where we turn
There is no place to hide

David Jones, Grade 12
Jefferson Area Jr-Sr High School

Top Poem Grades 10-11-12

Waiting on the Shore

I wait on the shore
Wafting the salty breath of the ocean
Listening to her whispering secrets
Gazing at the aurora painted across the sky
Tasting her endless sea of tears
Touching the infinite sand of fool's gold
Experiencing the season fade

I wait on the shore
Breathing in winter's chilling breeze
Hearing the gasp of the wind
Watching the dancing snowflakes
Savoring the sprinkle white from above
Feeling her frozen heart
Remembering all of the past

I wait on the shore
Smelling the aroma of early buds
Harkening to the melody of his voice
Seeing his shadow appear from the distance
Licking my trembling lips
Sensing the warmth of his hands
Welcoming him into my arms

Seolah Kim, Grade 10
Hilliard Davidson High School

Top Poem Grades 10-11-12

Journey Called Life

Life isn't always easy
We are taught that from the start
It may be lonely, filled with dissidence
Or seeming to fall apart
Why do bad things happen?
The reasons are unknown
At one point we all feel broken down
Inept, frightened, and alone
We all strive for goals in life
Even if they are completed with ease
When we persevere and reach our goal
Life may seem a breeze
Live each day to the fullest come excitement, sorrow, or strife
We all take part in the inconsistent journey that many of us call life

Megan Kuebler, Grade 11
Notre Dame Academy

Top Poem Grades 10-11-12

I Am Beautiful

I am not that smart.
My self-esteem is too low,
But take a look inside my heart,
And you will see that it glows,
Because I am beautiful.

I hate to make decisions,
And I'd rather follow than lead,
But please harbor no illusions
That mean words won't cut me.
I am beautiful.

People call me fat and ugly,
Yet I say nothing to contradict them.
And despite what they believe,
I have somebody to call my best friend,
Because I am beautiful.

I believe in Him,
And God believes in me,
So why listen to them?
Just open your eyes and see;
I am beautiful.

Cynthia Lynn Maurer, Grade 10
Life Skills Center of North Columbus

Top Poem Grades 10-11-12

Ode to Writer's Block

Writing poems is a task I do not like to do,
I hate the time it takes to sit and write and think it through.
The hardest part of all is coming up with decent rhymes,
This always takes forever, and I do not have the time.

So imagine my dismay when I was forced in Language Arts,
To sit and write a poem! My rage was off the charts.
"You have no choice," said Mrs. Burke, "It's for a grade, you see."
And thus my painful quest began: to write some poetry.

How should I start? Where to begin? These questions crossed my mind.
I realized that good ideas were really hard to find.
Several days had passed since then, and still my page was bare,
I racked my brain for something good, but I found nothing there.

As my struggle turned to anger and my anger turned to hate,
I looked through other people's work, for something good to take.
Plagiarism! I could not do it! I felt a stab of shame,
This simple thing called poetry was driving me insane.

The deadline, it grew nearer, yet my hate began to ebb,
And in its place a hopeless cloud of doom fell on my head.
I'll never write good poetry! It's clearly plain to see,
There's not a shred of writing skills anywhere in me.

Michael Stephens, Grade 10
Hilliard Davidson High School

Top Poem Grades 10-11-12

Story of the Heart

I sit here, something bothers me
An old scent of pine trees triggers my memory
My dear, I have a story to tell.
Do you remember, not long ago
When we played tag in the glistening snow?
Our nose and cheeks tinted with a hint of pink
Where peppermint cocoa filled the air?

The frosty branches and the shining icicles
Where the cardinals sang songs with glee
The moment you put your blades on
You moved like you were free
The second you fell and cried
Right from the start, you had my heart

My dear, the story has a point
Consumed by your beauty, astounded by your grace
I fell in love with the face of an angel
From that moment when we were young
Till now this story my heart has sung
Of peppermint cocoa and pine trees
Of an angel my eyes see

Jessica Vissing, Grade 12
St Rita School for the Deaf

The Report Card
The day I dreaded had finally come
the teacher said "They're here"
I smelt the air and I think
that what I smelt was fear

She passed them out one by one
starting off with Johnny
Got all the way to the last
And handed it to Tommy

All across the room
kids began to cheer and cry
Some were happy screaming "Yes"
Others shouting "Why?"

I looked at mine and thought I'd see
An F, two D's three C's
But going straight down in a line
Were nothing but all B's

Osman Ali, Grade 10
Hilliard Davidson High School

Resting Heart
The wind blowing,
Screen door slamming against its frame
Like a beating heart it thumps.
Soon it will be over
His life will soon end.
The wind ceased
The door came to an abrupt stop.
The old man now lies dead,
His turmoil now over
Along with his resting heart
He can forever be the closed door.

Emily Lockwood, Grade 10
Seton High School

Luxury
Walking bare foot
On your own two feet
Swimming all day
To beat the heat
Running marathons
Climbing up stairs
Barely worrying
About unanswered prayers
Biking through town
To your destination
Hiking new heights
With no limited duration
Simple things in life
We take for granted
Until the day
They become disenchanted

Shayla Egnor, Grade 12
Sebring Mckinley High School

Change
You can tell anyone they have to change.
You have to be a better person than you are being, but will they?
Anyone can give a speech,
Do this or do that,
But will they?
When will someone change for the better?
The truth is there is no speech that will change somebody!
There is nothing I can do to change someone else!
So what can be done to change our community?
Each and every person takes care of themselves.
If there is going to be change, people have to want it!
It has to start with one or two.
The community will never stand up together, but like the way a fire starts with a spark,
Change can start with one!

Joe Bennett, Grade 11
Life Skills Center of Youngstown

For It's Friday Night
A cold chill runs down my back, we all know what will happen next.
The lights flash on and the crowd grows dense,
I lace up my Adidas cleats and get in my last stretch.
My team and I wait at the beginning of the tunnel, people stomping their feet.
It's time to take victory. It's time for the fight.
We rush out with our Panther Pride,
We are about to kick some butt all over the field,
To show everyone the sweat and tears we yield.
Looking around at the crowd of Maize and Blue,
The fans are stuck to the stands like glue.
For tonight is Friday night!

Austin Perry, Grade 11
Whitmer High School

Regretful Past Over Shadows True Love
In the corner of the living room was an album of unbearable photos
that I could not handle to stare at
without a tear running down —
down my long, saddened face.
The photos show my past —
the past that I miss terribly.
I long for the past to come back
as if it never left in the first place.
I could be the person I once was,
to the extent of having a prestigious life
I take back my actions
and regret what I did.
If only I could tell you
why I did what I did,
then you would understand
what I went through
and why I don't deserve you.
I would take it all back
if I knew it would fix everything,
but it all started out good.
And then a small song, a little smile, and then nothing.

Mark Huelskamp, Grade 11
Fairlawn High School

Happiness Is Light

Originating from a tiny flame
With potential to fill the entire room,
Reflecting ever so brightly
Off the face of its beholder,
Bringing contentment and warmth
To all those nearby,

An energy, a power
To illuminate the way,
A spark, a fuel
To light the straw,
A sun, a fresh start
To replace all previous concerns,

Not meant to be left alone
Since it is brighter when joined by others,
Not meant to be extinguished
Just to make the water disappear,
Not meant to die out
But used to light a new wick instead.

Esther Fox, Grade 12
Yavne High School

Living Dead

Who are we all?
Just another society-possessed doll?
Who we are is what we're not supposed to be
Close our eyes to what we're not supposed to see
Do we have any say in our own life?
Do what we're told, or it's our throat against the knife
What is wrong, what is right?
What is love, what is spite?
Don't know what to believe in
Doesn't matter, as long as we win
Try to be different, but we're still all the same
Try to define ourselves, forgetting our names
Working so hard, just to work harder
Who is the tyrant? Who is the martyr?
Searching for happiness in all the wrong places
Speeding through life, blurring the faces
Doing anything to be evaluated and praised
Through it all everything is hazed
Just wanting so bad to be someone
But nothing really matters when we're gone

Lucksmi Ohana, Grade 10
Hilliard Davidson High School

Pain…

Shouting and yelling is never ending
Words that hurt always sending to each other's feelings
Fears and loneliness are abundant in a child's eyes
Bruises that were pounded is a bad vice
Emotional abuse kills a mind's soul
This is my life taking its tolls

Karene Stanley, Grade 12
Goshen High School

Master Duo

You two are the perfect puppeteers,
a master duo.
You both pull a different set of strings
to the same puppet,
and somehow make it look convincing.
You weave your plans full of deceit
as you play this hideous game of hearts
and clubs.
You believe revenge is so sweet,
not caring who you hurt to achieve it,
just that you do.
A perfect duo,
master puppeteers.
You never plan to cut the strings,
but what happens when it doesn't look convincing anymore?
When people see through your lies?
Your strings get jumbled up…
The puppet falls.

Crystal Zimmerman, Grade 10
Lynchburg Clay High School

Regrets

You were my best friend
Who I loved more than anyone could
You told me it was okay
So I did what you thought I should

Under a spell of chaos
I followed my supposed knight
You led me to my greatest fall
From an implausible height

Now a damsel in distress
You said it wasn't supposed to end like this
That we'd still be friends
Till the very death of a kiss

Now that we are strangers
I'm to full to swallow the pride
Alone when I need you the most
I never knew the regrets I'd have to hide

Caroline Mayo, Grade 11
Loveland High School

Teachers

You teach us everything you know.
Rain, hail, or snow,
You are always at school; you always come.
You make us feel right at home.
You care about what happens to us.
You help us without a fuss.
This is just a little appreciation,
For the teachers that give us an education.

Nicole Temple, Grade 12
Bucyrus High School

Rain

As the sky falls over,
Rain sprinkles down
Falling by the window pane
As if the world is crying

Rain sprinkles down
My eyes are awakened
As if the world is crying
By the amount of hurt in front of us

My eyes are awakened
With gloomy thoughts
By the amount of hurt in front of us
My eyes swell with tears

As the sky falls over,
With gloomy thoughts
My eyes swell with tears
Falling by the window pane
Disha Labhasetwar, Grade 11
Solon High School

Perfection

When I look into your eyes
I see someone who is trapped
In a world of confusion
I stand right in front of you
Yet I'm a million miles away
My feelings are trapped with me
A million miles away from you
Jessica Drummond, Grade 10
Goshen High School

True Love

Walking through the front door,
Saying the first hello.
Spilling my secret world,
With your look so soft and mellow.
Holding me in your arms,
Singing our favorite song,
Feeling your passionate aura,
Wanting to stay all night long.
Sharing our broken hearts,
Which mend from day to day,
Knowing we're meant for each other;
Knowing you're just a touch away.
You're my true love,
That I don't want to lose.
Knowing that God is with us,
And our fate He did choose.
From now on until forever,
I wish to be with you.
With true, never-ending love,
That the radiance still shines through.
Shala Morrow, Grade 12
Morgan High School

The Ballad of Silence

In the beginning there was silence   In the beginning there was silence
Tongues frozen in place   As we were torn from our homes

For we were human   For we were human
We couldn't believe
That there could be hell on earth

                                      The fire burned flesh from bone
                                      Eating the souls of the men who
                                      Shoveled coal into the mouth of silence
Never shall I forget   Never shall I forget
I could only stutter
I could only listen
I could only watch
Man destroyed man   Man destroyed man
He let the silence in   He let the silence in until

Until
In the end   In the end
There was only silence   There was only silence
Ava Carvour, Grade 10
Hilliard Davidson High School

Hero

My cheeks are rising to the sun the moment I enter the atmosphere.
The smell of laundry and cleaning being done and candles lit.
She never wants help but she is just too kind to not offer,
Waiting for the moment to rest in front of the television together,
Stroking through her hair with bristles from the heart.
Smiling and eating our famous meal for the night,
Loving her for every moment I spend in her arms.
Hearing the shocking news after the memories have been made,
Put me at my knees asking God a question that I wanted to know.
Why would He give something horrible to someone I love so deeply.
Never receiving an answer but she understood what she had to do,
She had to put things aside and be as strong as the wind.
Battling Cancer made her strong and proud to be who she is.
Holding her head high and letting the breeze take her through,
To a place where she knows she is honored for every breath she takes.
My friend, my family is her title and HERO is who she will always be.
Adriane Roach, Grade 11
Whitmer High School

To the Limit

So much is on my chest. I'm tryin' hard to be my best.
I guess it's not enough, 'cuz this life keeps gettin' tough.
I hold these tears for so long, my depression seems to prolong.
Damn the one who gave me this pain, playin' me like chess, a board game.
I want to make a livin', but I'm not gettin' much for what I'm givin'.
I've reached my limit, this life I'd rather skip it.
Because of my devotions, I'll try to anchor my emotions.
I do have something to live for, so I'ma close my eyes and pretend to soar.
Lie to myself and say everything's OK, until the pain comes back the very next day!
Nicole Briggs, Grade 10
Midview High School

Sweetened Tea

Our love
progressed like sweetened tea.
We started, bitter enemies.
Velvet covered steel, we
were (as of yet) unsweetened tea.
Truces formed, an awkward sea
of sugary uncertainty.
We were slightly sweetened tea.
A stolen kiss, our love unseen,
yet it progressed like sweetened tea —
Ah! This must be ecstasy,
a sip — the taste is heavenly,
for there never was such a delicacy
as love that tastes like sweetened tea.
How did I not know love could be
so precious, not know what it means
to want to dance, to sing, be free,
in love that tastes like sweetened tea?

Sarah Butler, Grade 10
South High School

One of a Kind

Nana you are very unique
Kind of like an antique

Your love knows no bounds
The world would not be the same without you around

No matter what happens you are always there
I think that's what make you so very rare

I love you so much can't you see
I'm glad God made you especially for me

Love

Eric Buettner, Grade 11
Delphos St John High School

Light Up the Sky

Dad I need to thank you.
For making me who I am today.
For making the sun shine
And the birds sing wonderful songs.
I hope that you will never leave me
And that you will always love me.
And when you are gone,
Know that I will carry on your memory.
For without you I am lost.
And I know that it kills you to see me struggle,
To waste all that I have,
But I will try to be better
So that you can look at me
And light up the universe with your smile.

Nate Christmann, Grade 10
McNicholas High School

The Camp

It was a long, cold day during the war
Russian soldiers came in from the eastern shore
the Germans were firing at them from nearby
smoke and ashes polluted the sky
we were told to run, or else we'd be shot
we ran on, until we were weary and hot
then we made it to another camp, one prison to the next
we were yelled at often and treated like objects
at last the allies came, and we were free
everyone left through the wreckage and debris
we were all excited that we were getting out of here
and could finally leave behind all our hatred and our fear
our paranoia, hunger, lies and regret
this is something I'll never forget

Mark Abrams, Grade 12
D Russel Lee Career-Technology Center

Hope

There is no chance now
No going back no going forward.
Darkness
Enveloping you as happiness seems to evaporate.
Heaviness
Settles over you like a blanket,
Suffocating you.
Despair
Why me?
What did I do to deserve this?
Wait.
A light.
A light that shines bright
Even in the darkest of times.
Hope.

Amanda O'Brien, Grade 10
Hilliard Davidson High School

Flight at Dawn

The country is still
And the world sleeps,
But we run.
Hearts bond together and beat together as one pulse
Soft breath swishes in sequence
In a darkness that does not smother
Does not hold fear
A darkness that is light
And cold atmosphere that does not freeze
But breaks boundaries and sets free.
Free to live, to love, to run, to fly.
There is no turning back,
There are no regrets.
Everything is beautiful, limitless, timeless.
It is unexplainable, irreplaceable, flight on earth.
Time pauses, and waits for a long, still moment
Until we pass.

Lauren Winters, Grade 10
Hilliard Davidson High School

Isolation

Isolation is the key you see
Because when I'm alone and isolated, I'm at peace and in serenity
I get to be who I want to be, which I'm not always the person that others see
In isolation I have the opportunity to get lost exploring my imagination and dream, dreams that may appear to be out of reach
Or remember past obstacles that I thought I'd never get through, or think on the inner conflicts I dealt with…but no one knew
When I'm alone, there's no one with which I need to compete, I'm always the tallest, smartest, prettiest, and most unique…of course because my only competition is me
In isolation I'm myself, I don't have to worry about trying to be a second rate version of someone else
Although being around others is always good, we all need our time to reflect and acknowledge our own inner good!

Jalisa Mixon, Grade 12
Eastmoor Academy High School

Dreaming

Touchdown!! Steelers win! After the game, we partied all night.
Today's our day, but we have another fight.
Hard work is what we have to do all week.
After practice, get a good night's sleep.
Morning comes, so I got to eat well.
They say if you eat well, you play well.
So, it's game day, I'm nervous a little.
Because I have to catch the ball across the middle.
The Cowboys have some good defense and we have a good offense.
This is the championship game. Winner takes all.
During the coin toss, the Cowboys choose the ball.
The game is going good until they catch a bomb for a touchdown to put them up by seven.
We drove all the way up…Davenport runs it in for a TD.
Newman at the 20…the 10…the 5…touchdown! just like that on the kick return.
The third quarter is coming to an end, as the Steelers are behind by seven again.
Next, Willie Parker breaks and scores a 77 yard run.
The game is all tied up…it's fourth and ten on the ten yard line.
This is for the win. Roethlesberger drops back, throws it up to Terrance…WAKE UP,
Terrance!! Wake up! Time for school.
Did I catch it? Catch what? Nevermind.

Terrance Edmonds, Grade 12
Life Skills Center of Youngstown

Where I'm From

I'm from dress-up clothes, Lincoln logs, Barbie dolls, and Legos
From Mom's cheesy potatoes and Meem's mac and cheese
From trying to learn how to draw by watching Pappyland on Saturday mornings
I'm from an old dog called Bear and our cats, Socks, Fluffy, and Lucky
I am from fighting with Emmy over who got to be the "waitress" that day
I am from spending evenings catching lightning bugs to use as a night light
I'm from "Are we there yet?" and "Remember, Santa's watching"
From berry pickin' with cousins and sour faces from our berry juice tea parties
I'm from cuddling up at night with my favorite blanket (from Pammy) and a book
I'm from family game nights and long afternoons by the pool
I am from half-eaten tomatoes my brother left hanging on the vine and getting sticky from climbing our pine trees
I'm from Pammy's potato salad, deviled eggs, and hot chocolate
From making sculptures out of mud in the burning sun and playing tag while we waited for them to dry
I'm from Jell-O desserts and suckin' on icicles in winter
From made up games like yellowball and mean lady that made up my own make-believe world
I keep my memories in photo albums and boxes full of pictures
They stay clear in my mind because there are just some things that I will always remember

Rachel Stevens, Grade 12
William Henry Harrison High School

High Merit Poems – Grades 10, 11, and 12

I Love You

I don't care what they say!

L iking you just isn't good enough.
O ver all the times we've had, the
V ery good ones are the ones to blame.
E ven though some people may think me insane, a

Y oung couple we may be, but
O ver the course of time, they will see,
U ltimately, I believe you are the one for me.

Allen Revels Jr., Grade 11
Springboro High School

Fighting Soldier

Laying in the dark, looking at the stars,
not in his yard, but from home very far.
Yearning to see loved ones back home,
ignoring the feeling of being alone.
A loud crack fires off far in the black night,
he's overwhelmed with memories of the last fight.

Anger begins to cloud all his thoughts
for some don't appreciate the reasons he's fought.
They take for granted all their freedoms and their rights,
and abuse all the reasons that our soldiers fight.
Soldiers put it all on the line in lands afar,
for if they don't the fight could be in our backyard.

Silently he lets the unnerving feeling fade,
for there are some who are faithful and for the troops they pray.
Loyal to the end to the red, white and blue,
and greatly appreciate all that they do.
He smiles as he gets up to start the new day,
and says to himself, "God bless the USA!"

Tina Stuart, Grade 12
Jefferson Area Jr-Sr High School

My Motivation

As I sit here and think about life
I think about everything I don't do right
The stress is building up
And I just keep messing up
I wanna change and get on the right track
But when I take two steps forward I get three steps pulled back
My life is full of clouds and it's raining and turning black
But I see a little bit of light
That makes me strive and feel like everything will be all right
I gotta get on my feet
I gotta get things right
You can judge me as you want
But you can never effect my life
And after all the clouds and rain that darken my life
You will see my rainbow and how much I shine bright
So until then, thanks for being a motivation in my life

Raymond Ramos, Grade 11
Carl F Shuler School

In Her Name

In her name, they did not know,
her feelings inside, she refused to show.
In her name they carved a stone,
for a heart, that was better left alone.
In her name, she showed no fear,
she wouldn't shed a single tear.
In her name, you could see her face,
but how she felt, you could not place.
In her name, you saw a heart,
you did not know, that it was torn apart.
In her name, we should have known,
from all the signs that were not shown.

Katelynn Elizabeth Carrington, Grade 11
Springfield Clark County Vocational Center

Autumn

When you were born we got scared you might not make it,
but then you fought.

Now, months later when you were doing so well,
God beckoned you to his side leaving voids in our hearts.
We will fill them with the joy and warmth you brought to us.

You are and always will be the sparkle in our eyes
and the sunshine on every summer day.

When you get scared and lonely
look deep inside your heart
and we will all be there
just as you will be in ours.

Melissa Baringer, Grade 10
BOSS Buckeye On-Line School for Success

Some Things Are Left Behind, But Never Forgotten

Opportunities, and the chances taken in life.
Possibilities of becoming husband and wife.
Friends stand by your decisions, which seem so right.
Yet, when that phone call comes late in the night.
On the other side of the phone is a mellow voice.
With little thought she had made up her choice.
From just across town, to another state.
Relationship of a friendship had changed with no debate.
Lessons she'd teach, you'd forever remember.
A job offer was taken in all to surrender.
Some friends and her parents who stay at home.
An independent adult travels to New Jersey alone.
Single life influenced in ways you'd never think possible.
A friend is where the heart feels all is capable.
Everyone is brought up in their own environment.
Money is all that can change through status of employment.
However long a friend may be in time or miles.
Somewhere in that sky a star shines for the while.
Friendship holds that distance together.
Promise. We'll always be friends forever.

Amanda Hinojosa, Grade 12
Edison High School

another chance
time goes by
and we realize what we miss.
the seconds, minutes, hours fly past
and we can never get them back.
but time keeps going
now and forever
and we will always get
another chance.

Maddie Herbert, Grade 10
Hilliard Davidson High School

Redemption
Happiness is overrated.
No one seems to care.
Honesty is outdated.
Hatred is everywhere.
Kindness is overdue,
Compassion is always lost.
Chaos constantly surrounds you,
And the world is filled with loss.
Children are lashing out,
Parents do not care.
Poverty, murder, depression.
Sadness is everywhere.
Families aren't what they used to be,
Nothing is the same.
The world needs to believe,
Or everyone's losing this game.
Some may think I'm naive,
Some may be appalled.
But all I know is this;
That love can save us all.

Ashdon Slone, Grade 11
Keystone High School

Migration Without a Compass
I twitter and chirp,
And I heave a sigh,
As I fly an unfortunate breeze,
And up and down,
The refulgent ground,
Is actually the stormy seas.
I leave and alight,
And I turn around,
As I wait for the midwinter air,
And all about,
The feeling of doubt,
Has grown almost too hard to bear.
I twist and I turn,
And I beat the wind,
As I look for my magnetic key,
And once more,
I come to a door,
Oh south! My destiny!

Chloe Donaldson, Grade 12
Home School

Morning
The air was warm like mid June
A gentle breeze tickled the leaves of the sleeping trees
Robins fluttered from tree branch to tree branch waking up the forest
Dragon flies buzzed around each other playfully
The forest gently awoke as the golden sun shined cheerfully
This is only the beginning of another beautiful day

Molly Kayser, Grade 11
Delphos St John High School

Peroxide
I know you're scared, but I'm scared to,
You're like Peroxide for my wounds.
I have never felt this way before,
A love that runs through us so honest and pure.
You seem to put my situations at ease,
You're helpful words come like a calming breeze.
Thank you for helping me with what I fear,
I never thought a friend could be so dear.
"You are the company you keep," at some point this must be true,
Because people keep telling me I'm just like you.
From most people I do detach,
But it was my trust you did catch.
You're wonderful, especially how much you care,
Even when the circumstances just aren't fair.
There is nothing in this world I would trade for you,
There is so much you've helped me overcome and do.
I'm here to help you and you're here for me,
It's nice how you let me be myself and see,
That you'll be there to brighten me when I'm blue,
You're my best friend and I love you!

Sarah Apple, Grade 12
Russia High School

Why Trees Lose Their Leaves
Many years ago, in time that never was,
There once was a sparrow, cold and lost, with few feathers and fuzz.
Winter was coming, the hour grew near,
And with the little bird lost, he had many things to fear.
So he flew upon a Maple tree and asked him, "May I stay?"
The Maple tree stuck up his nose and said, "Of course not! Go away."
Defeated and crushed, the sparrow flew, till he landed on an Oak.
He pleaded, "May I stay the night?" But the Oak laughed and thought it a joke.
The Sparrow flew to an Evergreen, and looked up with deep blue eyes.
The Evergreen asked, "What's the matter?" And the sparrow then replied,
"I asked the Maple and the Oak, but they just turned me down.
So now I come to ask of you, with a heavy heart and frown."
The Evergreen looked upon the sparrow, and said, "There's plenty room here!
Use my branches, my leaves, my trunk, until you lose all your fear."
And as the Evergreen said this, a Blue Spruce and Juniper looked on.
They cried, "You can stay with us! Our branches to sit upon."
So this is why a pine will never lose his leaves,
because he had a heart, to help a friend in need.
And other trees grow bare, when winter breathes his breath
For their heavy hearts of stone, are punished by the look of death.

Christine Mazzone and James Atkinson, Grade 12
Newark Catholic High School

High Merit Poems – Grades 10, 11, and 12

My Hero

Whenever I'm feeling down or low,
I always know of that one place to go.

She's always, always there for me,
Making all of life's dreams easy to see.

She has a way of keeping me on track,
If anyone hurts me I know she has my back.

I know that she will never be far,
That's why she's my guiding star.

To me she's second to zero,
That's why I call her my grandma, my hero.

Jessica Alt, Grade 11
Delphos St John High School

Please Listen

Do not label me because of my race or age,
Black and a teen, yes,
but I'm still aware of this outrage,
Please listen to these words I utter,
Instead of this ignorant violence lend a hand to
One another, for in a way he is your brother,
Learn respect because I'm sure that's what you expect…
Please find another way to protect.
Live life to the fullest like it's your last,
And try to look forward
but don't forget about the past.
Please listen I don't speak for my health.
Baby Daddy's please take care of your children,
because that's apart of you, I'm sure you don't or wouldn't
appreciate your father doing it to you.
I hope you've been listening!

Sam Taylor, Grade 11
Eastmoor Academy High School

What Might Have Been

I wish we could be what we use to be.
You know just you and me.
What we had was wonderful,
Or does believing that just make me a fool?
I always imagined you being in my life,
I even imagined myself being your wife.
Being around you is always fun,
But I want to walk with you, watching the setting sun.
Being yours was always a blast,
But it was all too good to last.
I'll still be a faithful friend,
And I'll stick around till the end
But there will always be times when,
I think about what might of been.

Kira Craft, Grade 10
Eastern High School

Swings

You are swinging on the swings
you go higher and higher.
When you are at the highest, you get scared that
you are going to fall
(even though you were happy that you finally
swung to the highest point)
but now you are scared and want to get down.

Doesn't that sound like life?
When you are at highest in life, you kind of
get scared and want to stop.
But why do you get scared?
The harder you swing, the higher you will go;
and, everyone around you is going to be happy
for the accomplishment you have made.
So, don't be scared.
Swing harder.
Go higher.

Wined Martinez, Grade 10
Carl F Shuler School

Battle Field

I'm sitting here too enraged to think
The thunder and rain is over me
The fire and torch is beneath me
The flesh and stupidity is beside me
The frustration and confusion is inside of me
The blame is moving towards me
The reputation has cyclones around me
The reoccurrence of anxiety never leaves me
Sin tempts me
Pleasure punishes me
Friends scold me
Teachers fail me
Family shuns me
Knowledge is my escape
I withhold a battle within myself

Deon Jones, Grade 12
Eastmoor Academy High School

Autumn

As the world turns around
And the seasons change once again
The cool wind starts to blow
And the earth bursts into color
Vibrant reds, greens, yellows, and oranges swirl around
Showing that which was hidden is now found
Even through the vivid colors
The joy of summer's freedom
Slips into autumn's melancholy routine
The cycle continues
The same every year
Autumn enters in with majestic beauty
But with the good comes the dark winter.

Deanna Drenten, Grade 10
Hilliard Davidson High School

Sleep

Lay down in bed
To rest our heads
No troubles
Or struggles
For the moment
We can dream for hours
Of things unreal
We can dream of flowers
We think we feel
Good times and bad can be had
In this crazy world
You have unfurled
Great adventure can lie ahead
Whichever way the path has lead
And if you wander off the trail
And it seems your dream is getting stale
Change the ground that you are on
Maybe change it to a pond
And in a boat you sleep and sleep
Waking up when morning falls
Your great adventure begins to call

Mike Chido, Grade 11
Westlake High School

Rob Me Blind

I do, but I don't.
I should, but I won't.
'Cause I don't want to be alone.
Knock on my door,
Before we run out of time.
Break into my heart
And rob me blind.
Just leave the pieces
Scattered on the floor.
Don't worry.
My heart has been broken before.

Kristen Espe, Grade 10
Hilliard Davidson High School

Paradoxes

I don't quite like this emptiness,
But fullness would bring destruction.
I don't enjoy the lack,
But to add would mean reduction.

I despise this loneliness,
But company brings heartbreak.
I don't like living for nothing,
But everything else brings hate.

I don't like being a loner,
But acceptance breeds regret.
I can't believe I did it,
But now there's nothing to forget.

J.T. Weir, Grade 10
McNicholas High School

The Future Arrives

A soul is waiting.
Growing, stretching, and soon came into this world;
I waited patiently to see this beautiful star
That I've always wanted in my life…
The wonderful time had finally arrived;
The star was finally born.
When I heard, I hardly sat still;
I was so happy…

I finally arrived home; in my sight, a moving infant held by a woman
I came close and stared in amazement…
This infant looked up to me;
The world stood still…
Those angelic eyes;
I felt like I was going to be sucked in.
Those hands, so strong, yet soft…

He grabbed my finger, held me tightly…
"I can't believe I've finally got a beautiful baby brother!" I said, tearfully.
The world finally spun again.
His legs kept kicking; what an energetic baby!
A new star was born;
A bright star for the future.

Tara Trimble, Grade 12
St Rita School for the Deaf

What Is the Meaning of Life?

Is it being born and dying…
Growing up and learning from mistakes…
Is it experiencing new things when you have the chance…
Is it making goals and achieving them and giving your all in everything you do?
Is life becoming successful and looking back over the years;
when you're old and gray, and seeing what you have accomplished…

What is the meaning of life?
Is it helping yourself to strive and live, to be the best you can be…
Is life depending on yourself because you're accountable for only you…
Is it the Golden Rule — "Do unto others, as you would have them do unto you."
Is life helping others in their time of need, even if they may not give back…

What is the meaning of life?
Is it living it to the fullest…
Is it living for the moment…
Is life all about finding true happiness; cherishing every moment you have left?

What is the meaning of life?
Life is too short, and you have one chance to live it.
What is life to you?
Find out!
Before you know it, it will be over.

Katy Roth, Grade 12
Cuyahoga Falls High School

High Merit Poems – Grades 10, 11, and 12

The Truck
I am the truck.
My owner drives me
Through the mud and snow.
I get him from point A to point B
And sometimes from job site to job.

I start for him every morning.
I start through the bitter cold and hot weather.
I pull trailers with construction equipment.
I pull his travel trailers from vacation to vacation
Where no one would go.

He takes care of me.
He changes my oils and fluids.
He washes me with love and care.
He puts chrome and power coated upgrades on me.
He is the one who drives me and takes care of me
Until he sells me.

Richard Kulakowski, Grade 11
Whitmer High School

Run Away
Sometimes we say things we don't mean.
We make things appear how we want them to seem.
Sometimes we hide things until the moment is heated.
And what you just said to me, man I can't believe it.
I don't wanna believe what you just said to me.
'Cause boy you mean the world to me.
So I'll just…
Run away from all the things you lied about.
Run away from all the things we screamed and shout,
Run away from all the things you just told me.
Good and bad 'cause it was never good for me.
Run away behind my tears.
Run away and hide behind my fears.
Run away from my love for you.
'Cause I don't know what it would make me do.
I wish this wasn't true.
Me being erased from you.
I know I gotta face it one day.
But until that day,
I'll just…
Run away…

Constance Lott, Grade 11
Akron Alternative Academy

John "Beatz" Holohan
October 31, 2005
A best friend, a brother, an icon
Didn't survive.
Strong hands and a strong mind,
That night, the meaning of loss was redefined.
A drummer whose beats will continue to sound.
John Beatz, although you are gone, you'll always be around.

Kelly Massa, Grade 11
Westlake High School

My Savior, Dear Savior
Nailed to the cross, thou art Jesus.
My Savior, dear Savior, will thou lead us?
By thy example, we do act
According to thy word, perfect and exact.
Bearing all our sins in pain,
For this reason thy word we proclaim.
For thou were perfect in every way,
And we remember thee on every Sunday.
Tempted and tried though without mistake.
His body whipped, a sacrifice to make.
A crown of thorns placed upon his head,
The king of the Jews pronounced to be dead.
Crucifixion was his cruel death.
Words of love muttered in his last breath.
The deed was done and Christ hath died.
His mother weeping, in agony she cried.
But Jesus overcame; yes he arose on high.
And the word of Christ dwells, for our sins he did die.

Kelly Morris, Grade 11
Bucyrus High School

Laugh a Little
Laughter is greater than a powerful blast
It is a light from above giving hope
An assuring grip telling us we are ok
Letting it all out is a cure-all
A sign of who we really are comes from laughing
We are sending magic to our souls
It is a moment in our lives where worrying is forgotten
Laughter makes us strong with understanding life inside and out

Lindsey Looser, Grade 11
Delphos St John High School

My First Race
Walking up to the blocks
Stretching my cap over my head like socks
Putting my goggles on everything seems so clear
I don't have one fear
I hear "step up, take your mark"
Then everything seems dark
I close my eyes and feel the strength within me
Then I dive in and I can see
I kick and pull as hard as I can
And I see my boyfriend as a fan
I reach the wall and do a flip
And the air I sip
As I stare down at the bottom of the pool
I know that I can rule
I swim into the wall
It was quite a haul
I find out that I have won
I realize that I love swimming and it is really fun

Jamie Puls, Grade 11
Normandy High School

Why…

Why must you tear me down, every time I try to make it work?
Why can't you give me a little respect, whenever I say one little word?
Why must you be harsh and condescending, to me every time I enter a room?
Why can I never get a straight answer, when I ask you a simple question?
Why can't you let go of your egotistical self, and become the nice person I know you are?
Why must you make a wrong, which causes me to suffer?
Why must you blame me, for everything that goes wrong in the world?
Why must you judge me, for expressing my crazy ideas?
Why must you pierce your icy glare into me, whenever I smile with a genuine hi?
Why is everything a competition, which you must win?
Why can't our lives go back to what they were, selling lemonade at a dingy stand?
But, most importantly, why can't you be the best sister that I once knew?

Aline Tabet, Grade 12
McNicholas High School

Predictability

Look at the color of life. Change your dull image to a vibrant picture.
You've become a replica of everyone else, you barely think with your own intelligence anymore.
In a world of color, how are you going to stand out?
When everyone else's hand is down, raise yours to show you fight for discrepancy,
Where you can shine for who you are.
And not only will you be beautiful on the outside, but your inside will glow with modesty.
You're capable of grasping new beginnings by yourself. I'll be by your side to lead you away
From the pretenders. You're able to attain more. And looking down on what you had,
It was a challenge to leave everything you built for yourself.
You can slowly release your melodramatic hymn for the rest of the world to hear now.
They can't try to blame you with honesty when the only thing you want to do is make a difference.
The only light that reflects them is judgmental controversies.
With their hypnotized and glass eyes, and blank faces of insecurity.
Everyone seems to be escaping at once, and the ladder to extricate has become too crowded
Fake lives and empty hearts contradict the means of society.
For there's no one that can truly be liked for their outside presence only.
Predictability is the one thing that we can assume from them.
Their lack of words is so cliché to everything we've built.
And even against all odds they're still trying to preach from the same blank book of inconsistency.
And their S.O.S. calls of help have faded. But you're an individual,
While the rest of the world is full of mirror images. All reflecting the same light and purpose.

Peggy Cook, Grade 11
McNicholas High School

Dream

Close your eyes. Think of me.
Imagine a place you would want to be. Just dream.
You see me walking. You see me talking, thinking of you, while haters plottin'. Just dream.
Jump into me and you will see what true, funny love is supposed to be. Just dream.
Think of a place far far away, hoping and thinking that's where you want to stay. Just dream.
Think of a bed where you want to lay. If it's mine, then girl you're safe. Just dream.
Dream up high and dream down low. Follow your heart. It knows the right road. Just dream.
Open your eyes, sit and think. Take a nice shower and know you just dreamed.

Dion Artis, Grade 10
Life Skills Center of Youngstown

My Paranoia

I walk the same path every day,
Knowing that everything will always be okay.
I walk with pride and not with fear,
Knowing my home is very near.
My four legged friend leads the way,
With him I follow, so closely I stay.
But today the air blows a bit eerie,
I suddenly begin to feel a bit weary.
Shadows and silence fill all around,
I quickly turn back, now homeward bound.
The strange feeling of being followed,
Overwhelms me and makes it hard to swallow.
I pick up my pace
Just to be safe.
The crunch of the leaves beneath my feet,
My heart rate increases to the point where I can hear each beat.
Faster and faster I move my feet,
As they pick up the pace and slap on the street.
I so much desire to be home in my safe bed.
Where worries are no longer formed in my head.

Rachel Neltner, Grade 10
McNicholas High School

Lost Heroes

A day that started like hundreds before
Was changed in an instant by a God-awful roar
Heads were raised to look at the sight
Some people were sad, some ready to fight.
Out of the chaos sprang a glorious few
That knew that they had a duty to do.
Into the terror, they faced it head on
So that strangers like you had a chance to live on.
To the bodies that were buried and the ones never found
Their souls we remember and to their hearts we are bound.
To the heroes who climbed so more could be saved,
We are eternally grateful for the sacrifices they gave.

Andrew Smith, Grade 12
Tri County North High School

Sports

Orange and brown are the colors of the day.
The Browns are in the stadium ready to play.
Mom and Dad are dressed for action.
Let's hope they get a lot of satisfaction.
We all watch the Cavs whenever we can.
LeBron is really quite the man.
My sister and I shoot hoops on the lawn.
She plays for her school till the season is gone.
My personal favorite is soccer today.
It's fun to watch and it's fun to play.
Now that the Force has gone.
We play for Normandy and carry on.
Can't forget baseball, the Tribe plays and we cheer.
My all sports family is busy all year.

Jennifer Strenk, Grade 12
Normandy High School

I Will Stand Proud

Tears filled my eyes with disgust and anguish.
My knees buckled under this nefarious pressure.
I will stand proud and will let no one put me down!
They will not repudiate all that I have accomplished.

My knees buckled under this nefarious pressure.
Why must they defame my ethereal reputation?
They will not repudiate all that I have accomplished.
I will ameliorate over this virulent act of terror.

Why must they defame my ethereal reputation?
How dare these callow people try to fathom who I am.
I will ameliorate over this virulent act of terror.
They will not sequester me back into their corner.

Tears filled my eyes with disgust and anguish.
How dare these callow people try to fathom who I am.
They will not sequester me back into their corner.
I will stand proud and will let no one put me down!

Robert Kirian, Grade 11
Solon High School

Red Light

The empty road beckons me,
And the silence itches,
But my conscience holds back the scratch.

In the quiet night I stay,
and bow before the luminous red emperor.
I obey his command.

David Cappa, Grade 12
Loveland High School

Karasu

At night the crow flies
with the stars in his eyes,
winging away from me.
He looks down at I
from so far up high
and says "Don't you wish you were free?
You could float in the sky
like a feather in the breeze.
You could soar on the wind
past all the plants and trees."
I woke up the next morn to see
that the crow had become me!
I unfurled my wings
and leapt from my perch,
letting the sky take me.
It lifted me high and I began to fly
above all the plants and trees.
At night the crow flies
with the stars in his eyes,
winging along beside me.

Zeb Wilson, Grade 11
Jefferson Area Jr-Sr High School

Hearts Broken
Heads rushing
Heart pounding
Lips touching
Arms surrounding

Knees weak
Can't speak
Barely sleep
Don't freak

Falling fast
No mask
Big blast
Won't last

Words spoken
Throats chokin'
Lost token
Hearts Broken

Courtney Netto, Grade 10
Hilliard Davidson High School

Whenever
Whenever I'm scared
I come to you
Whenever I cry
You wipe away my tears
Whenever I stumble
You give me a hand
Whenever I talk
You understand
You're always there
You're all I need
You help me go on
When I think I can't
I can lean on you
And know
That you'll be there for me
Because everything is possible
With you

Yanna Pitsul, Grade 11
Normandy High School

Bottles
Endless crying, restless nights,
Her voice answers his moaning.
The tunes of her heart calm him,
The savor of formula fills him.
His glossy eyes watch her every move,
He is amazed by her silly gestures.
No toy or blanket can replace her.
Women dream of this bond,
But she lives the dream every day.
She is truly an angel of his.

Ashley Moreland, Grade 11
Whitmer High School

Sunrise
Passionate eyes will see the sun's last rays.
The stranger awoke from his happy haze.
The heat of the pavement as I barreled down the road.
My feet driving into the concrete, my arms whistling through the wind.
Many pathways to travel, and faces I have always known.
Hands to hands.
An open assault at my humorous attempt to keep running.
Broken dolls clutter the road, and stars keep falling from the sky.
Only one pair of eyes,
Steer me into the blinding light.
Bury my selfish breathing into all the wreckage of our past.
Steel, flesh, blood, and glass.
I'm screaming to the heavens, as my lungs become heavy with salt.
I cannot find the correct ministrations of brain and tongue.
I can only keep my run, strides not showing, but continuing to accelerate.
As the earth shakes and rocks our souls.
Questions above our weary heads, as everything breaks down.
Shattered at my palms, and eyes turned around.
That's when I realized some small piece of me, maybe all, is lost.

Tara Edwards, Grade 11
Trotwood-Madison High School

The Search
I feel the wrath of your embrace.
Touching deeper within my soul.
Trembling forces take over my mind.
As I reach you once more.
I know you're there trying to reach me.
I feel the warmth of your breath running down my spine, can't you see?
Tortured with fear and anxiety, I try to rush to see your face,
But by the time I turn to seek you, you're gone without a trace.
Maybe this isn't fate, but I've felt you once before.
Maybe something better is in store.
I try to forget and go my separate way…
This may not be my night.
But *tomorrow* will be my day!

Tracy Mead, Grade 12
Life Skills Center of Youngstown

My Mother
Mother, don't fret, I will always be here.
Yes, I know I will soon be leaving because college is near,
But I will call and come see you as much as I can,
And I will tell you everything because I know you're my biggest fan.
You taught me how to care, to never give up, and to always be true.
All my accomplishments were because of you.
A thousand miles away and still my love for you will never regress.
Your eyes will fill with tears, at the stories of my success.
At my highest and lowest points you were always there,
And I will miss your love and care;
But I will hear your comforting voice in the wind at night,
Telling me everything will be all right.
So please stop crying because I love you Mom,
And always will.

Matthew Schlagheck, Grade 12
McNicholas High School

From Out of My Dreams

Late at night when day is done,
And all are fast asleep,
I sit and gaze up at the stars,
And think of the secrets I keep.

For when I close my eyes at last,
Visions make my heart beat fast,
A stranger, a love, with beautiful eyes,
Who haunts my dreams never comes alive.

In every dream he comes to me,
While sun shines gold or moonlight gleams,
But when the morning comes at last,
He's just a dream all in my past.

Jessica Carmosino, Grade 12
Mayfield High School

Jake Scott

What if things were different?
If you were still standing here
Things would be much easier
We would live a lot less fear

As I visit you from time to time
I know you aren't coming back
Since all of our lives have been altered
It's hard to adjust and keep mine on track

Thinking about you every day
Helps to keep your memory strong
I sometimes dream you're in the hall
When I awake I realize I'm wrong

You are like an angel
Sent from the heavens above
To influence and touch all of our lives
With your greatest lesson of Love
I miss you Jake.

Kyle Nannah, Grade 12
Sebring Mckinley High School

Tears

Every day a new tear falls,
But I look away so no one saw.
No one knows how I feel inside,
Where all my feelings collide.
How every day something new goes wrong,
But I smile and try to keep going on.
Like everything's okay,
When really it feels like everything's fading away.
I don't know who I am anymore,
Like an apple with no core.
But I'll be okay,
Because hopefully my tears will stop one day.

Megan Pettet, Grade 11
Morgan High School

Where?

You're nowhere near me
Although I can see you in my head.
You can't touch me
Although I can still feel you.
You can't see me
although I'm looking at you from afar.
I wish you could be near me
And touch me and definitely see me
But I've become blind to you
I wish I could rewind and fix it all
I just guess that was our timing
I want to cry but the pain is all too strong
I don't know what to think
I don't know what to do
All I know is you are far away from me
Where I can only see and feel you.

Katie Anderson, Grade 11
Westfall High School

Seventeen

Just because I'm seventeen
Doesn't make me a child
Doesn't mean I don't lie
Doesn't make me naïve
Just because I'm seventeen
Don't think I fall into peer pressure
Don't assume all I do is wrong
Don't believe what you see in the movies
Just because I'm seventeen
Doesn't mean I don't have feelings
Doesn't mean I can't fall in love
Doesn't make me a bad person
Just because you're my parent
Doesn't make you right

Jessica Scheidler, Grade 12
McNicholas High School

Friends

I look behind myself
And I see the old dusty shelf,
On which I've set all my old friends,
who helped me through life's twists and bends.

I feel a need to stay
With those old friends for all my days.
Those, who stayed with me, who I beloved,
who I grew to know and love.

Then I look ahead,
And see my new friends instead.
These, who I hope to love and trust.
Well, it's new friends or bust!

Jacob Medvick, Grade 10
Revere High School

Invisibility

I am a tree, I do not move,
I sit and wait for my prey,
There is silence, nothing in sight,

I slowly turn my head,
My target is now in view,
It does not see me,
It walks into peril territory,
With no knowledge of it,

I slowly pull back my bow,
Like a tree pulls on its branches,
I look my prey dead in the eye,
I release,
My prey drops in an instant,

And I go as I was, like a tree,
Perfectly still.

Caleb Yutzy, Grade 10
Hilliard Davidson High School

Liquid Death

Death
pitch black
the uninviting smell of flowers
ghostly placed on the casket
Pictures with smiling faces
cast tears in their families eyes
flashbacks of that night
implant memories in their minds
they drank too little
and drove too fast
while their classmates
walk the stage
and move the tassel to the side
They scream
from high above
don't ever
drink and drive

Brooke Skyllingstad, Grade 10
Ursuline Academy

With You

With you by my side,
there's so much I can do.
With your love as my wings,
I can fly so high
my troubles evaporate
and I feel so alive.
You make me feel beautiful,
you make my face flush
with you as my lover,
I can do so much
because I'm with you.

Kat Schuessler, Grade 11
Stow-Munroe Falls High School

Imagine

You're sitting at the window, staring into the storm
Drifting into thought
You get that sinking feeling, like mud under a boot
After the rain ceases to drip from the cracks in heaven's floor
You walk through the woods

You're surrounded by gray and a heavy feeling of silence
The trees look wise, gloomy in despise of the day
And the sun; clouds refuse to let it come
You're alone, only nature by your side
And the sad song of the wind pouring into your ears

You've been here before
In your dreams?
You know where you're heading
Everything welcomes you with different tunes of the same sad song
Birds sing from above
They tell the woods of the end of the storm and of your arrival

You look around to see rain drops clinging to leaves
Peacefully resting?
Holding on for their short lives?
You stop and realize that you get to be part of this art
And that's exactly what you set out to do; to be part of it all

Sarah Myers, Grade 10
Hilliard Davidson High School

The High School Identity Dilemma

High schoolers are like several die,
Many-sided dice.
All thrown at one.
They try to settle on sides that do not pay a price.
But there is so many to choose from.
What should one do?
Which one should I become?
   A jock?
   A nerd?
   A class clown?
   Or a scholastic renown?
The likelihood of the individual's right choice drops.
What works for one does not work for another.
What is right for me?
   The answer lies within the equation of identity and individual.
Do they add up?
Friendships change as dice are rolled,
Identities spin this way and that.
Looking for the one that matches the equation.
What are the chances that all will succeed
In finding their true match?

Nada Naiyer, Grade 10
Hilliard Davidson High School

My Horse
Horses are like spirits floating in the sky
prancing while clouds go by.
Racing through fields of dreams
while their sparkling coats gleam,
horses are like the fire burning in my soul.
While protecting their precious young foals
horses are our rare gold bars,
dashing through the fields like racing cars
finding things we would never uncover
acting like our favorite lover.
But there is only one I can choose
and this one I would never loose.
The only horse for me
is my horse named Dream.
Casey Hennessey, Grade 11
Jefferson Area Jr-Sr High School

Childless Smile
Deep in the soul under the smile,
There is a kid in denial.
Behind the scenes away from the crowd,
There is a kid wearing a frown.
Before the tears, yet after the trial,
There is a kid wishing not to be a child.
He wipes his cheeks to dry his tears,
So his momma doesn't see his fear.
He hides the pain, but it only hurts worse,
This child is hungry but has nothing to fill the thirst.
Maybe tomorrow he'll have clean clothes,
Or possibly a tissue to wipe his nose.
Alone, afraid, tired, and scared,
This child has no smile or is it a smile without a child.
No more soul and no more smile,
This child worries no longer about denial.
Markie Sparks, Grade 12
D Russel Lee Career-Technology Center

I Fear Not
I care, I laugh, I bleed, I cry,
I love, I live, I hurt, I die.
In living, we are human but in dreams, we are freed,
In happiness, in sorrow, in peril, in need.
Take my hand
Let us take flight
Heed not the worries
Nor fear the plight
Brave with me a forbidden dance,
That romance and chivalry once did chance
A boat upon an uncertain course we go,
Marked with both great joy and yet great woe.
Alas I fear not a single crashing wave,
For there is new reason for my soul to save.
Paul Schulze, Grade 12
Russia High School

Life.
Life is an adventure in itself;
completely unpredictable.
Always taking unexpected turns in one direction,
then the other,
leaving my mind a tangled web of emotions.

I try to interpret the events.
Losing a loved one,
falling in love,
failing a test,
being utterly confused.
I stop and think,
"Is there any sense in this?"

The moment I grasp an idea of
what it's all about,
I am knocked off my feet once again,
and thrown into the turbulent waters of life.
Lauren Cupito, Grade 11
Loveland High School

A Geisha
Covered in silk sashes and flowers
Always poised, being careful not to fall
Long raven mane, done up to perfection
I am a porcelain doll, fragile but unbreakable
Years of obedience and training,
To be a part of the exclusive, or to end up a servant
I'm an entertainer to men and the envy of women
I am like the wind, swift and calm
I'm as perfect as it gets there is no room for mistakes
I am a walking form of art always on display
Lindsey O'Connor, Grade 12
Brunswick High School

To Accept "Me"
We're struggling to find ourselves,
but it makes no sense
that the more we look,
our innocence
is lost, is captured,
devoured — dead.
Our hearts lose more the more we're led.

So why attempt the odyssey
to find the truth of me,
when the truth is in
our reality?
Who I really am
is what you see.
An attempt at change is not to be.

Somehow, I must learn to accept "me,"
or face my own shame and cruelty.
Natalie House, Grade 11
Glen Este High School

Greetings and Givings
Warm and together families hug
We wrap up tight in our winter gloves
Memories appear, as stories we share
With my family, they always care
We share our food, our bread so sweet
At my house what a pleasant place to meet
Laura Williams, Grade 12
Goshen High School

Us
I always wonder if you see
the thoughts I keep inside of me
If eyes are windows to the soul
I also wonder what they've told.
Some day I want you to know
the feelings that I cannot show
Yet, because I have to wait
to see if they are caused by fate
or if I just imagined them.

I never have felt them before
Each time I want them more and more
I'm almost certain they are real
not something that I try to feel
They'll always be here in my heart
reaching to the deepest part
I hope today will be the day
that you will turn to me and say
you want to turn you and me into us.
Stephanie Edge, Grade 11
Jefferson Area Jr-Sr High School

Power and Control
The sun has the moon
The ocean has the desert
With life comes death
With pain comes joy
What I have is power
Power to write what is true
Power to write what is not
The light has the dark
The water has the fire
With anger comes forgiveness
With tears comes smiles
What I have is control
Control of what happens
Control of what is to happen
The morning has the night
The winter has the summer
With reading comes power
With writing comes control
What I do have is both
Power to teach you
Control of what I do
Seth Graves, Grade 11
The Alternative Center of Knox County

Roller Coaster Ride
As I stood in line to wait my turn
I thought that I would die.
I prayed to God to get me through
And said my last good-byes.

We climbed into the very first car,
They strapped us in real tight.
And soon the cars began to move
And whisked us out of sight.

The click clack of the chain was heard,
We climbed the hill so slow.
Before I knew it I looked ahead
And saw the ground below.

Slowly jaunting toward the loop,
My heart began to race.
I turned my head and saw the look
Upon my partner's face.

As the ride began to slow
I loosened up my grip.
And started making future plans
To take another trip.
Brittany Miller, Grade 11
Delphos St John High School

The Night
The night I lost my life
I viewed it all too clearly
Enclosed by these faces
I once held so dearly.
I felt nothing.
Accusations spewed forth
Drowning mercilessly so
I clawed and clutched for air
But I sank in the undertow.
I felt nothing.
A bloodcurdling scream
Inhuman for its capacity
Emits wide from stained lips
And shakes the vicinity.
I felt everything.
Sinking to the ground fast
Breakdown so bittersweet
Comfort is foreign exchange
The strength is finally beat.
I felt nothing.
I am nothing.
Tashina Robinson, Grade 10
Orrville High School

The Human Heart
The night contains one thousand eyes
But one in clear day
And every pupil precious
Though we refuse to say
The day contains one thousand tasks
As time, our focus too much
We waste away those moments
Always acting out of touch
Your hands contain ten fingers
And your feet contain ten toes
For many this is not a fact
Yet, do we care for those?
Our world contains so many lives
Too many lives to count
How many of these, soldiers
Fighting on our own account?
Everyone contains a heart
Beating to survive
From this there should be
Compassion to care
For others still alive.
Megan Leever, Grade 10
Loveland High School

What You Can't Put in Words
You'll never know what it's like
Until it happens to you
Your heart is gonna break
It will tear your soul in two

It will make you scream with fury
It's going to make you cry
And you will never stop,
You know it's all a lie

'This isn't happening'
No matter how much you say it, it's real
You're breaking down now, aren't you
Tell me, do you know how it feels?

This is what it feels like
But words just aren't enough
This is what I've come to
Though I've tried hard to be tough

I'm breaking down now aren't I?
I'm sorry, it's not my fault
Listen to the torment
That is to have loved and lost.
Gina Pattison, Grade 11
Wooster High School

Love

Love…
   Is this thing that people claim they have
   Something they can have at first sight?
   They close their eyes,
   Then realize the future waits
   Filled with all kinds of emotions.
   They open their eyes
   To see that they are standing side by side.
   They reach across to take a hand
   That will be held together forever
   Now knowing that this is it.

John Bell, Grade 11
Whitmer High School

In the Darkness

Eyes so deep they go beyond wisdom,
Seeing past my smiles into my soul.
Tell me, what do you see in the darkness?
The shattered pieces that refuse to be whole.
I can't run away from the past, the present.
It never really worked for me,
And memories are simply stories of the mind,
To remind me of what I use to be.
Cry on the inside, the world doesn't need my tears.
Hold them in, move on and hope it's in the right direction.
Let everything build up, but don't dare let go.
Slowly letting the thoughts drown out the actions.
Breathe in, Breathe out please just don't explode.
Falling, I am falling into the dark abyss.
Reaching yet never grasping, I am alone
Breathing, falling, reaching in the darkness

Sarah Williams, Grade 10
Westerville South High School

I Remember When

I remember when…
When you used to smile,
You used to be so happy.
I haven't seen this in a while.

I remember when…
When you loved everything life brought.
Nothing could go wrong.
At least that's what we thought.

I remember when…
A sickness was found,
We thought your time was up,
We weren't sure how long you would be around.

I remember when…
When mom would cry,
But now all she does is smile,
Because you refuse to say Good Bye.

Katrina Helmke, Grade 11
Rossford High School

On the Antiquity of Nike

O muse of the past enlighten this scholar
The sight of Victory what a headless squalor.
Her alabaster neck arched and edged,
I wonder in fact, "O where is her head?"
The splinters of her flight leave no plume found.
Her capture in marble, her flight bound.
Boreas' breeze provokes such a tangle.
Her soft ivory against her stony raiment mangle,
She waxes and undulates into molten swirls.
Her stony feathers long for her once antique frills.
A trumpet held no more yearns for unity.
Spiteful of her lost hand, she strives for impunity.
With honor decayed and power lost,
A flitter and flutter of echoless wings defrost.
Into our hearts from the Danaans who made her,
She engulfs eternity with her victorious glamour.

Daniel Rachovitsky, Grade 12
Summit Country Day School

Spiders on the Wall

They march on to the worst of places
Stone cold men
With sand blown faces
There they stand
Steadfast and tall
Marching…
Like spiders on the wall

They fight wars in combat
And in their minds alone
Only hoping
For safe passage home
Soon they are picked off
One by one they fall
The rest still marching
Like spiders on the wall

Arielle Blankenship, Grade 10
Akron Alternative Academy

In a Spiral Notebook

I write it down in this spiral notebook
Stop to think and take another look
Wondering what it is about these little blue lines
That inspires me to write such poetic rhymes
Or if what I write is real or make believe?
Come to think again
It's me myself that uses this pen
Writing thoughts of what to speak
Imprinting my soul on to you through ink
Is that really so hard to conceive?
Why write in this spiral notebook?
So that someday after so long,
Someone else just might take a look
Then they could know me my song

Cody McGuire, Grade 12
D Russel Lee Career-Technology Center

Friendship

Friendship is like life support
After a deadly crash
Without it there isn't life
Just throw it in the trash

My friends pick me up when I am down
They make me myself
As life support would
Bring me back to health

Without it there is just an outline
Of a body on a bed
Without friends or life support
You are surely dead

Breanne Deile, Grade 11
Loveland High School

Voice of Mist

Around me there is the cloaking mist
That drapes across the trees ahead,
Clinging to their hidden hearts,
Speaking of their tears unshed.

It rises off the darkened paths
Secluding what it cannot show,
Drifting past like spirits lost
Beyond what trails I claim to know.

And now the way is all but gone,
Devoured in its lonely wake
As the rain begins again to fall,
Upon the fragile, doomed to break.

Abrielle Fuerst, Grade 11
OHDELA Academy

Life

A time and place
For joy and pain.
For love and gain
Or death and shame.
Life is filled with each,
Waiting to be set free.
Filled with hope,
Kindness and hospitality.
Filled with despair,
Rudeness and bitterness.
We live for hope,
Only to be let down.
When it ends,
We're ready to go.
We have lived,
And want no more.
A time and place
For joy and pain.

Brianna Ashford, Grade 10
Lynchburg Clay High School

Branching Out

Deep down inside of me I can picture a time
When I was roped to my friends like a grape to a vine.
The need to be different lurked down in my heart.
I knew I needed to do something that would set me apart.

Field hockey season started and the grape vine loosened its grip,
Allowing all of the little grapes to slip.
Except for one that held on tight,
Refusing to give up and lose the fight.

This decision was certainly worth it in the end.
I've met many new people and made many new friends.
My life has flipped the page and started a new chapter.
All because of a decision that will affect me now and forever after.

Alexandra Dober, Grade 10
Summit Country Day School

The Feeling of Love

Thinking out loud wondering what would happen.
What I would do without him,
Where my heart would drift.
He means love to me.
Those wondering eyes that look me eye to eye.
The big wide open arms around me whenever I need them.
The sweet touch of his lips on my cheek to cheer me up.
The sound of his voice when he says "I love you."

What would happen to me if that all disappeared?
Life without it would tear my heart.
Feeling of love could never be felt again.
Tears of hurt and pain fall down my face with no one to wipe them away.
My thoughts all tangled up in knots that could never be undone.
The feeling of being put behind and lonesome.
Happiness doesn't show on the face or inside, just one dark hole of nothing.
Nothing to depend on,
Just one little empty heart with no where to go.

Christine Wong, Grade 11
Goshen High School

Untitled

Crying, dying, saving, prying, flying, saying,
All these separate feelings pouring out in pen.
Contradicting, overheating emotions down within.
Grasping, mapping, waving, gasping, trapping, weighing,

Truth is found in one, but proved so wrong in another.
Either making you want to cry — or go and try.
Maybe it's here in these words; pain, frustration, yet, hope still lie.
Perhaps you can't truly have one without the other.

You may then say that you'd rather have none.
But if I can't feel my own heart race,
Then where and what is my nonexistent cracked base?
I'd prefer to read and search and keep a pace and run.

Shawna Hite, Grade 11
Home School

Together Forever

Every time I shake my dreads I think of you
Cause you got them too
Constantly I want to be with you
All these others can't
Won't and don't treat you like I do
Let's just make it official
Just like a referee with a whistle
Girl you are the one I've been waiting on

Me and you can create something beautiful
Let's just be like our hair
And lock up
Together forever

There's no one like you
You're so unique
I'm really feeling your style
You dig
We're that perfect match
You're the one I pray for every night
You're Mrs. Right
I swear you're the grease in my hair
Cause you're always shining

Tyler Erskin, Grade 11
Eastmoor Academy High School

One Last Shot

I have one last shot, one last chance
one opportunity to make things right.
Exams looming, pressure mounting,
all the anxiety climbing has me on a roller coaster
But I don't have a choice.

"It's got to be done," I tell myself,
"there's no other way out."
The last twelve weeks have me screaming from insanity;
my friends all laugh at me.
"You're so stupid," they say to me,
"why do all those honors classes?"

Well, to be honest, it really is simple.
It was monotonously slow.
Getting A's on my tests all the time without studying was great,
but colleges won't look at that.
They want to see passion, effort, and determination!

"Any C's and you're grounded," my parents exclaim.
Ironically, I have three.
So I have one week left, one last shot,
to make my grades go up. These next seven days, I believe,
will be the longest run.

Chris Rapp, Grade 10
Revere High School

Sometimes

Sometimes I wonder what would be
    If Moses hadn't parted the Red Sea,
    If God hadn't created Adam and Eve.

Sometimes I wonder where we'd be,
    If Hitler hadn't hated the Jews,
    If Rosa had given up her seat.

Sometimes I wonder who I'd be,
    If I'd been born in Africa with HIV
    If I was placed in Iraq instead of the land of the free.

Sometimes I wonder these things and more,
and they force me to appreciate
    who
        what
            and where
                I am.

Rebecca Peel, Grade 11
Goshen High School

Winter Fun

The snow is falling oh so fast
Children playing in the snow covered grass
Sledding down a giant hill
That's when I throw a snowball at Bill
The snowball fight has begun
Which team will win and have the most fun
When the fight is over and one team has won
We all go back to my house that's when the party has just begun

Cath Wells, Grade 10
Loveland High School

Almost Over

Senior year has been nothing short of a blast,
These first few months have gone by so fast.
Homecoming, prom, sports and new year's eve,
Bringing in the year during which we're finally going to leave.
Only a few more months until graduation,
None of us can wait for that congratulation.
Finally getting out there on our own,
Leaving the life we've all lived and known.
No more high school homework, drama or worries,
Next time we walk this hall, we'll be in our thirties.
Throwing parties and celebrating our success,
Finally letting go of four years of stress.
Telling our friends never to forget,
Our friendships; the good times and the times we may regret.
Promising to hang out, get together, keep in touch,
Even though that may be promising a little too much.
There will be things we won't miss and things we may,
All our minds will be spinning through these on graduation day.
High school is really almost over now,
Seniors, stand up, it's time for one last bow.

Caroline Kirker, Grade 12
Glen Este High School

I Miss You

You've captivated my heart.
I'm beginning to fall apart.
I've missed your touch.
This time apart hurts so much.
I wish this wasn't real.
This all feels so surreal.
You're gone and I'm still here
But you feel so near.
Yet you're so far away.
I hope that you're okay.
I only have our memories,
It's sad to think —
I'll never see you again!

Carolyn Mazzei, Grade 10
Seton High School

Message of War

Bounding over rock and stone,
Never falter, paths are known,
Dire messages to tell,
Reach the city, ring the bell,
Tell the people what is here,
Cry to them to show no fear,
Build defenses none can breach,
Urgency to all beseech,
Armies come and bring a war,
We must fight to end their tour,
Judgment comes upon us all,
Crashing down upon our wall.

Matt Dykstra, Grade 11
Loveland High School

A Boy That I Know

A boy that I know:
Bright, cheerful.
Taking everyone's pain away:
Collecting it, holding it.
But letting it eat him
From the inside out.
Trying to smile
While his world fell apart.
Trying to make
Everyone happy,
But every time he took
Someone else's away,
It added to
His own kind of pain.
But he stays strong…
Or so we think,
For he can't make it through a day
Without wishing
He never woke up
That very morning.

Marie Paquette, Grade 10
McNicholas High School

The Ruler of the Wind

The air flows down past the tranquil trees,
And flies above the rustling leaves.
The squirrels and rabbits that scamper below,
Look up to find a boy staring out his window.

The boy, who's quite young, believes that he will be,
The ruler of the wind and the holder of the key.
The key is an emblem that unlocks a power
That can create spectacular mountains in under an hour.

The boy looks to the eagles for the answers he seeks.
They possess a magic quality that allows them to speak.
As they fly through the air in the midst of the wind,
The boy opens his window to let the magic begin.

He jumps out the window and begins his long flight.
He has wings like the eagles, except they're enormous and bright.
The air became warm as he ascended in the sky,
And the eagles blew fire and became mean and spry.

A tornado came down and sucked the eagles in.
It gave all their magic to the boy with the grin.
The key is now his; he possesses all the power.
He can now rule the wind and live in Dark Tower.

Marcus Alan Edwards, Grade 12
Unioto High School

There's Been a Change in Plans

It was all a lie,
It was just a routine.
Now I'm stuck with the question, "Why am I in love with a fiend?"
I'm going crazy and I'm going insane,
I'm unhealthy and I have you to blame.
I used to be an open and caring person but you put a lid on me.
I hated you for what you did to me.
But I couldn't leave…
I loved you more than life itself and I still believed
I believed in what we had but pain is all I received.
But I can't be stuck in the same old place.
I'm on an emotional roller coaster and it's just not safe.
Now it's time to get off this bumpy ride
And put our past to the side.
Time to move on and let go
Time to realize that I'm not that little girl anymore.
I've grown up and I'm sweet to the core!
I'm big and bad and unlike anything you've ever seen.
Sorry to sound conceited or a little mean
But it's time to say bye to that teen,
And hello to the queen!

Olivia Pleasant, Grade 11
Eastmoor Academy High School

Seasons

Summer is the blazing sun,
   warm, calming, and so fun.

Fall is the leaves crumbling to the ground,
   Red, yellow, orange, and brown.

Winter is the glittering snow,
   With temperatures very low.

Spring is the blooming new life,
   Nothing else is alike.

Kaitlynn Napholz, Grade 10
Revere High School

Raindrops and a Beautiful Crybaby

As raindrops fall on a long awaited land,
The moistness of its touch nourishes the soil.
While a teenage crybaby locked in her high away tower
Feels a slight pain in her heart
Her need for refreshment is in high demand.
So she opens up to the stormy night,
She gets soaked by the cleansing rain.
As the cold drops fall upon her porcelain skin,
The tears begin to saturate her eyes.
The beautiful teenage crybaby finds her only medicine
Is the feeling of the emotion escaping her body
Really, raindrops and teardrops are one in the same,
Rain is nourishment for the soil while tears nourish the soul.

Staci Sizemore, Grade 11
Whitmer High School

I Believe in You Dad

He's not really my father
But oh, does he deserve the title
He's the only one I've had,
The only one I'll ever have
He's the one that's been there
Through all my ups and downs
He believes in me
And understands me
No real father could do any better

But the doctors tell us
He might be leaving soon
Oh how I pray and pray
That just maybe a miracle
Could change such a horrible thing
I've always knew he was stronger than anyone
I just need him to prove
He can take on anything
So go out now
And conquer it all
I know you can do it
I believe in you Dad.

Becky Deane, Grade 12
Glen Este High School

Acid Rain

I can't take it,
I can't do the task that I set for myself.
Do I keep trying or keep dying?
My goals aren't helping itself.

It's like a pain,
That caused an infection.
My goals burning inside of me,
Filling me up like a lethal injection.

But I must make a correction,
The distractions that caused the attention.
I'm screaming now when I speak in a sentence,
Which caused me to believe in redemption.

But for a second,
I thought my goals vanished from sight.
They're moving away from me,
Advancing in height.

It's like dancing.
I learn the steps to keep moving with my feet,
But the heat of these goals,
Keep me moving to its beat.

Anthony Rodriguez, Grade 10
Life Skills Center of Youngstown

3.1

Anxiety Builds as I step to the line
The officials shout "It's almost time"
Everyone's quiet, their breath steady, slow
the gun roars "bang," everyone goes

Sprinting, racing, running fast
Men pushing, shouting to get past
First hill comes relaxed up, tired down
First mile done, heart begins to pound

Trees whizzing, twirling from the corner of my eye
Coach shouts "too slow" as I pass by
My body begins to hurt, my muscles are tight
Second mile passes as the race turns into a fight

No more thinking, no more use of my mind
Run the last mile to catch up from behind
Half a mile left, now a quarter mile to go
I can see the finish, I'm feeling too slow

I begin to sprint, 100 meters left; pain and ecstasy start to flow
Finally cross the finish, six weeks, six races to go

Elliott Moore, Grade 10
Hilliard Davidson High School

I Remember

I remember counting sheep to fall asleep every night.
I remember helping build a house for someone and knowing I made a difference.
I remember playing baseball and seeing my parents so happy.
I remember listening to my first rock song and was hooked.
I remember going on vacation and never having a care in the world.
I remember my first day of H.S. I made many new friends.
I remember playing with friends until dark and my mom being steamed.
I remember my grandma always sweet and warm.
I remember coming home from kindergarten and telling my mom what a great day I had.
I remember going to big league games and aspiring to be just like them.

Michael Hain, Grade 11
McNicholas High School

The Part of Me That's Died

I ask myself if losing you is nothing more than fate
To take your heart away from me, leaving sadness in its place.
My body beats with the tempo of the clock beside your bed,
My throat is dry with dreams bygone And the stale sense of regret.
My mental state collapses, I quake with utter fear, and my head descends
To meet my knees, the same time as a tear.
I'm freezing as the draft I feel turns just a little colder,
Until I turn to see your face stand proud beside my shoulder.
You judge your dying body lying still upon the bed,
What made you who you are is gone; your heart's already fled.
A machine cries out, it sends a signal loud, seemingly proclaiming:
If I want to say good-bye, then I better do it now.
I bend to kiss her forehead, Like that should help somehow.
So nothing's left uncertain now, I'm lost inside my head.
There's nothing more synonymous with a lost one than with dead.
Never once had you stumbled, or faltered in your step, until old age took hold of you,
And soon by time was kept. You really meant so much to me; I missed the chance to say.
I see you in the sun sometimes, I feel you every day.
And even though you're missing in my story's favorite part,
You're always strong inside my head
And stronger in my heart.

Victoria Simokov, Grade 10
Loveland High School

Why Does It Have to Be This Way?

You've made me smile, you've made me cry.
You've said it was all worth the while, but it seemed like a lie.
You've hurt me, you've made me sad.
A lot of times it gets old because you act like my dad.
You're always controlling me and telling me what to do.
Our problems and fights keep rolling like every time I put on my shoe.
You make up every excuse and it makes me want to say "ferme la bouche."
I'm sick of your mind games and your anger, you're becoming another one of my past dated lames.
The days and nights seem to get longer while you sit back and tell me "it just makes us stronger."
All we do is fight and make up, but all it does is make my heart feel tight.
I'm starting to second guess why I'm with you, and every time I do I seem to need a tissue.
I don't know what to do anymore I'm so lost.
You've destroyed a lot that was me, and now that things are bad this just happens to be your cost!
You've made me smile, you've made me cry.
Now all you do make me is sick, to the point I feel I might die!

Tasha Ricco, Grade 10
Chippewa High School

The Battle's Cry

As the battle horn sounds the orange sun sets
As darkness falls you can hear the loud jets
Soldiers, they lie in trenches to hide
Watching and waiting as one has just died.

Shot by a jet that had come by unseen
He falls to the ground, his uniform green
Surrounded by comrades, watching him pass
Knowing that this breath was probably his last.

They lift his body that is limp like death
And carefully lie him down with the rest
A day that seemed to last one hundred years
That ended for some, just as they had feared.

He's a pale ghosts in a casket of stone
Large loss of life that is now heading home.

Jaimie Kover, Grade 12
Jefferson Area Jr-Sr High School

Why??

Why am I here? To lose or to win?
Why are we here in this life of sin?
Why do we eat the way we eat?
Why do we talk the way we talk?
Why are we too afraid to walk?
Tell Me Why

Why do we have pride? To degrade the things that we love?
Why do we have songs for those who passed on to the above?
Why do we fight the way that we fight?
Why do we do the things we do?
Why do you resent being called a fool?
Tell Me Why

Why do we take life for granted? Because we can?
Why are our egos bigger than the size of Japan?
Why do we live the way that we live?
Why do we write the way we write?
Why do we give up without putting up a fight?
Tell Me Why

Sam Haygood, Grade 11
Eastmoor Academy High School

Tragedy

My friends and I have gone through many tragedies.
Objects of life we lost such as these.
Parents, girlfriends and problems from the subject of other.
We usually never hide feelings from one another.
We help out each other and try our best.
Then later those feelings are put to the test.

Steven Creech, Grade 12
Goshen High School

Guided by the Perceptions of a Pure Heart

Guided by the perceptions of a pure heart,
With the weakness of an unforgiving sin.
Appreciate the eyes of protection,
Still nothing remains inside.
I'm all alone, with hope to find someone,
I look through the eyes of many,
I gaze through the soul of everything,
All the pain waiting for a release.
Humanity has fallen apart,
With no hope of turning around.
Pick up the pieces of a puzzle,
That cannot be put back together.
But I am still here…with the humbleness of pity.
Yet again finding myself…with nothing.
I'm all alone, with no one to search for.
I look through the hearts of no one,
I stare through the soul of nothing,
Waiting for the pain that will never be.
I scrape through the ashes,
Of a burnt society.
To look for something, that I cannot see.

Dustin Beery, Grade 12
Chalker High School

Clock

It counts down the breaths I have left to take
It adds up all the mistakes I have yet to make
It reminds me of where I have been
It shows me that life should not have any sin
It gives my heart a steady beat
It looks down upon me so life I do not cheat
It never changes no matter what it goes through
It will always be honest to you
It might tell you something that comes as a shock
It might remind you that it's just a clock.

Hillary Monnin, Grade 12
Russia High School

The Test

The evening sun sets
Frustration enters our mind
We are last in both eyes and ears
Your voice is dreaded
Yet welcomed at the same time
You question our devotion
Though yours should be the one questioned
Time is almost up
Though much is left to do
Many silent frustrating days await us
The mind stores anger
Where it must remain for good to come
Strength and will is to be tested
Surviving this test will bring happiness and success
Failing will bring nothing but regret

Heather Winterhalter, Grade 11
Loveland High School

The Scarlet One

Great columns of fire,
The abode for the liar.
Home with the scarlet one,
Who promises you fun.

Follow him if you dare,
Down into his lair!
His ghoulish grin,
His want for you to sin.

He shall show you the crooked path,
Where there is no mercy but only wrath.
Tears will you shed,
Even after you are dead!

Mohammad Alam, Grade 10
Westerville North High School

Three Words I Miss

I was told three words,
They were left unheard.
The words that made me strong,
They made me hang on

These words I once hand
I lost my love, that's why I'm sad
Lost these, lost is pain
You were my main

The three words still haven't come back
And that's a hard fact
But my life still goes on
I'll just listen to a love song

Maybe the words will come again
And it won't feel the same
The joy of my life is to learn
Then it will finally be heard
I love you.

Meeco White, Grade 11
Eastmoor Academy High School

The Feeling of Fall

Leaves falling from trees,
The crisp cool air blowing them,
The feeling of fall.
Apples, pumpkin pies,
A cornucopia of
colors and flavors.
Brimmed with holidays,
Halloween and Thanksgiving,
Celebrating life.
Scarecrows and turkeys,
The sweet smell of cinnamon,
The feeling of fall.

Caroline Sawicki, Grade 11
Westlake High School

The Journey Within

You gotta catch them all to become a true master
Training is the key to make pikachu faster
You will journey to the end to get even more
All the pikachus, charmanders, and even bulbasaurs
It is what you live for, it is your passion
Just because you only know one hundred fifty does not make you old fashioned
Friendship and love is the most important part
Train all your friends even your weakest magikarp
Fight your hardest and make it to the league
But always keep in mind all of your partners' fatigues
Your journey has begun and now it is on
Of course I am speaking of my beloved Pokemon.

Will Tolerton, Grade 10
Revere High School

Summer's Fleeting

The times we had will never be here again.
They were my joy. Now it comes to an end.

Being with her every day was my heaven.
I will never forget when I made the move on March the eleven.

She was with me everywhere this season, with my family, with my friends.
I love her so much! We have no dead ends.

We went to the beach. We walked in the sand.
We went to the lake where I held her hand.

I will miss these times, but I will not dwell.
For I know there will surely be a lot more as well.

I will stand by idly and stay with her.
Because I know we will share another summer.

Nick Daigle, Grade 12
Springboro High School

The Dream

I had this dream we were in happiness always stuck
And that I found my prince charming in my youth was just my luck

There was a smile on my face and a ring on my finger
After you left a sweet dizziness came from your scent that did linger

I was drunk on romance, from love quotes and false promises I choke
And regret my heart racing from lies of unconditional feelings you spoke

I had this dream that together you and I could do no wrong
And no matter what happened, we'd be together all along

However, every dream must end and every hope blossoms or dies
When a "match made in heaven" isn't exactly delivered from the skies

You jerked me from my joyful dream and my heart was screaming
Now you want to go back to it, and you've already started dreaming

Kelsey Ballew, Grade 12
Unioto High School

Hostage to Her Own Humanity
Wishing to be excellent,
Left crying on the floor.
Why is she so average?
Why can't she be something more?

She's that typical teen,
Not like the ones who live on screens,
But the girl who lives next door,
The girl who is all that she seems.

Why can't she be mysterious?
Why can't she find more depth?
She'll spend hours being who she's not,
Trying to make someone catch their breath.

It's hard being so ordinary,
So hard being like the rest.
Excellence left beyond her grasp,
She will never be the best.

Amy Ashworth, Grade 11
McNicholas High School

An Empty Seat
They lay you in the ground.
I never got to say goodbye.
Beside me is an empty seat,
And I wonder why.
Why did all this have to happen?
Why'd it have to be you?
And when you were just a teen,
We never had a clue.
Beside me is an empty seat.
Full of tears and pain,
Full of hurt and anger.
And beside me is your name.
You never got to graduate.
You only had a year to go.
Now the seat is empty,
And graduation is so slow.
But you we will remember.
Or at least I know I will.
For beside me is an empty seat.
And when they call your name everyone will be still.

Jessica Densmore, Grade 12
Beaver Local High School

Smile
Please, just smile for me,
let me see the sparkle shine through,
smile, for your happiness,
smile, because you know you are loved,
smile, for your mother and father who love you,
smile, for your younger brother who looks up to you so much,
smile, for the future you'll have, but, please just smile for me.

Jenna Kennard, Grade 11
Bloom-Carroll High School

Life
What is life if you do not live it out?
Is it just a temporary state?
Is it a meaningless waste of time?
Life is not meant for these.

Your life is meant to be lived out.
It is not meant to be wasted,
To be watching TV or playing video games.
It is not something meant to be wasted.

Life will always be hard and full of hard times.
It is work that makes it worthwhile.
It is work that makes you feel you are worthwhile.
What you put into your life is what you will get out of it.

What is life if you do not enjoy it?
Not just passing through it, but doing things worthwhile,
To create memories worth remembering.
It is your only life to enjoy this world.

How will you leave your life in the eyes of others?
Will they remember your kindness years from your death?
Have you put meaning into your life and shared it with others?
Your life will be measured by this.

Matt Winkler, Grade 10
Hilliard Davidson High School

Darkness
I woke up and couldn't move
It felt like I was tied down
I couldn't open my eyes or mouth
I was certain I was being kidnapped

I was hoping this would just be a dream
But it wasn't
There were voices in the background
I couldn't make out what they were saying
I was also wondering why someone would want
To kidnap me

The next time I woke up
There were lots of people standing around me
I was wondering if they were my kidnappers
And if they were
What were they going to do with me

Finally they told me they were doctors
And I was in the hospital
I had never been so relieved.

Dan Corrigan, Grade 10
Hilliard Davidson High School

Another's Last
A patch of dirt on a polished path
An innocence that could not last
A moment in time unable to take back
It came and went so fast…

One small slip up
One short rush
A simple trip turned to a deadly hush
One's fun night is another's last…

Hearts were broken and minds confused
Everything you have is what you lose
Many years have past, but none forgotten
It's the memories that last…

A patch of dirt on a polished path
An innocence that could not last
A moment in time unable to take back
And its time that hid the evidence.

Stephanie Myers, Grade 10
Hilliard Davidson High School

What Am I?
My balance is like one of a surfers
Stronger than a football player
My finger prints are only mine
Tree house is what I live in
Salad is all I eat
Joey lives in my pocket
Can see you from a mile away
Fur is as soft as a blanket
Sunset is when I awake
Mickey has nothing on my ears

Anthony Manco, Grade 12
Brunswick High School

Just for You
Near or far
Wherever you are.
When we're together or apart
The thought of you warms my heart.
When I doze off into space,
I can just picture your lovely face.
Every time I see your smile,
I hope we stay together for a while.
I can't see myself with anyone but you;
Thanks for all the things you do.
When I look into your beautiful eyes,
I hope our friendship never dies.
You're always there,
Because you really care.
I just want you to know,
I never want to let you go.

Evan Hebemann, Grade 11
McNicholas High School

Deceit
I can feel the lies burrow into my tender skin
You say you're all protecting me with smiles so thin
I know what you're all trying to do
But shut up, sit down let me explain something to you

Don't keep me from this world
I can take care of myself, I'm a big girl
I've seen more than most people will ever see
Let me have my space, just let me be

Don't try and tell me you know what I'm going through
Because in reality you weren't there, so how could you?
Say what you want, I don't care
'Cause now I know the honest truth and it's that you'll never be there

Go ahead tell me I'm wrong
I can take it, even though I'm not very strong
Funny thing is, is that I'm right
But you can't except losing the battle so you put up your guard and start to fight

I try so hard to keep your world right side up
But in return mine begins to go up side down
Emotions convey out of my heart
I can't take care of you anymore, because I'm falling apart
I can't help but just fall apart

Hannah Whelpley, Grade 11
Brunswick High School

Don't Leave Me
The world is spinning rapidly,
He is walking away from me.
I call out his name with desperation in my voice;
He pauses for a second but doesn't look back.
He keeps walking.

I am dizzy and disoriented
Up is down and down is up.
Salty tears prick my eyes and impair my vision
And the fountain in the square appears to sparkle more than usual.

He is leaving me
And as I fall to my knees I see him
Through a thick curtain of wet droplets
Make the turn at the end of the walk
That we made so many times together.

Never again will I make that turn with him
Because he is gone and I am
Alone.

Erin Randall, Grade 10
Loveland High School

Game Day

Two hours before the game and time passes by,
Excited and nervous, my emotions fly.

It's the big game we've been waiting for,
Just a couple hours 'til we hit the floor.

After loosening up and getting in our shots,
We run to the locker room and shake what we got.

In comes coach with an inspirational speech,
We listen intently before he gets out of reach.

With twenty minutes to go, both teams take the floor,
Competitive faces are given back and forth.

The buzzer sounds and teams take to their benches,
As we live up to all our pretenses.

With that, everyone lines up for the jump ball
Emotions are bouncing all off the wall.

If we played as a team,
Things would have gone well,
But disunited we stood, disunited we fell.

Rachel Voss, Grade 11
Loveland High School

Elementary

Life was so much easier when…
We didn't like boys.
There was indoor recess on rainy days.
Show and tell meant bringing in toys.
We got to skip class to practice Christmas plays.
There were no detentions,
Just ten minutes off recess.
Our biggest projects were book report presentations.
On picture day our parents told us how to dress.
The bus meant long, noisy rides,
With the older kids sitting in the back.
We'd fight over turns on the slide,
But share the lunches that we'd pack.
We would count down the days for a field trip.
Art was the easiest, mixing paint and clay.
The classes weren't so bad that we wanted to skip.
School didn't seem to take all day.
It was no big deal when we didn't change for gym class,
All we played was kick ball or Red Rover.
Spelling was the hardest test to pass.
Friday nights meant a sleepover.

Kylie James, Grade 12
Glen Este High School

My Wonderful Sister

My wonderful sister does a lot for me.
She makes it all seem so easy.
She brings me up when I am down.
She makes my frown turn around.

We have fun baking all kinds of goodies.
But my favorite has to be those chocolate chip cookies.
They are always warm and creamy,
But never hard and chewy.

My sister and I go shopping together.
When she is there things always turn out better.
When my sister is not here I always whine.
Because I'd like to have her with me all of the time.

My wonderful sister and I are very close.
We even wear each other's clothes.
We are always wearing fun things together.
And that will go on forever.

Brittany Mossing, Grade 11
Whitmer High School

Don't Miss Me!

After counting all the sheep in the world…
I'm still crying,
    Still thinking,
And asking why
I'm still wondering,
    Still day dreaming,
And asking what if
I'm still shaking,
    Still sweating,
And asking why me.
I still don't understand,
Why you left me.
I thought I was the best I could be,
But I guess not
I was just being me…

Kayla Hurford, Grade 11
Sebring Mckinley High School

Untitled

I gave you my heart.
I don't want you to do me the way I been done before.
My heart is so sick and sore.
I'm gonna give my heart to you
And I want you to stay true.
Don't play with my feelings or with me
Because you're the one who holds the key
To the way I feel.
If you hurt me, I'm not sure if I could deal
With another heartbreakin'.
Please be different than other guys.
Don't be fakin'.

Jasmaine Shepherd, Grade 10
Life Skills Center of Youngstown

My Angel*

The day you left, my soul had gone. They told me to stop crying and to be strong.
But visions of us all together dance in my mind.
Why did you have to leave? Lord was it her time?
I had a dream that you came and visited me last night.
You said "Man wipe up them tears everything's going to be all right.
Just because I'm not here physically doesn't mean a thing.
But when you call I'll come and comfort I will bring.
For I am flying high with God I have earned my wings.
For now I am playing the harp while my fellow angels sing."
I said "When will we meet again?"
She said "Only God would know.
But when you hear a voice say 'come my child it is time to go.'
For once you hear that voice I want you never to look back.
There I'll be standing smiling with my corn rolls to the back."
She turned and looked at me and said "I have to go home."
So I gave her a kiss and a hug and said "You wait for me I won't be long."
She said "Get yourself together and make sure you know God.
Because He's who I serve," and she left with a nod.

Marcheri Combs, Grade 12
Akron Alternative Academy
*In loving memory of ShawRica (Tuna) Lester

Poetry

A lot of people use poetry to convey the thoughts they think.
Some poetry will raise your spirits, and others will make them sink.
There are many uses for writing, the intention of the mind.
And each poem is different; to each is their own kind.
Some write in love while others write from rage.
There are many different reasons for the rhyming of the page.
But what is true poetry?
Where does it come from, and whose minds does it press?
If I wrote that I hate you, would it make you love me less?
If I said that I would kill myself, would you believe that which you see?
Or would you take it all as feelings, when it is something you can't see?
In essence, poems are like the eyes, a gateway to our soul.
A glimpse behind the mind, of what is so easily controlled.
Love, hate, peace, all feeling that no one can trust.
In the modern age we live in, when nothing seems as such.
These words are for nothing, nothing more than to prove the truth,
Trust your heart not your eyes, and it will lead you to the truth.
If this poem has brought some thought, then it has done what it should do.
The words of the page mean nothing; it's the heart that makes them true.

Ben Hayes, Grade 12
D Russel Lee Career-Technology Center

Jump

Large, luminous, lofting high above the water, the cliff towered. Little I stand beneath the barbarous beast. Alone and willing to take a chance. A large twisted, knotted, and moldy rope was the only thing between me and my jump. Escalating to the top, push by pull, my arms become like sea weeds swaying with each and every move. Wits and strength have gotten me to the top, but courage will end this. My spirit is free now, free like the ocean changes its tides when it pleases. My choice comes at the top of this cliff. A gentle breeze like God's hand guides me like a navigator of his ship. Slowly, slipping and sliding off the cliff my feet become like concrete blocks pulling me down towards the water. Splashing, successfully, in the water, I feel completed and whole. One jump can change your view of things, one choice can start a whole new beginning. Still splashing in excitement the feelings of splendid sweet success are lost, but now I know where to find them.

Clay Stein, Grade 10
Summit Country Day School

High Merit Poems – Grades 10, 11, and 12

Korean War

As I stood in front of that wall
And I couldn't believe the pain that I saw

In the pictures that seemed to come alive
As I looked deep into their eyes

They saved people that they may never meet
They trekked through a country with bare feet

As they fought for peace to let them be
They all soon learned freedom's not free

Raegan Haines, Grade 11
Delphos St John High School

Painless

The sounds.
The squealing tires,
The shattering glass,
The crunching of the colliding cars,
Metal scraping against metal.

The sights.
One car smashed against the other,
The bright, flashing lights,
The warm blood on your hands,
The fading figures standing over your body.

The feeling.
The angel's strong hands around your limp arms.
Painless.

Meghan Bush, Grade 10
McNicholas High School

Love Is in the Air

Their eyes unite from afar:
Strolling, whispering, and blushing.
Their hearts pulsate with affection;
Time stands still when they are together.

Strolling, whispering, and blushing,
Their hands are bonded with passion.
Time stands still when they are together;
Destiny and fate working together for the same cause.

Their hands are bonded with passion.
An everlasting promise,
Destiny and fate working together for the same cause,
Sealed with a kiss.

Their eyes unite from afar,
An everlasting promise,
Sealed with a kiss.
Their hearts pulsate with affection.

Alyssa Janezic, Grade 11
Solon High School

Life

Who…gives life?
Parents, God, demons, the devil.
Walk with me on the right road.

What…is life?
Despair, struggling, living, strength.
Show me through the broken path.

Where…will I die?
With family, in bed, alone, in public.
Be with me until the end.

When…will I die?
Now, unexpected, later, painfully.
Help me learn through a new set of eyes.

Why…do I die?
To make room, lose pain, escape reality, kill old stress.
Show me what it means to be loved.

How…will I live?
In darkness, unknowing, in peace, fully.
Teach me how to understand.

Joseph Hemsink, Grade 12
Elder High School

Departure

In the dream O'Hare
I have nothing to declare
(steps lightly across sensors
fades away into
the wind above myriad night lights).

Gone, slipped of the Earth
and can't decide whether I miss it or not.
The exhilaration of separation,
of nameless travelers with similar destinations.

Is this a flock of languid souls?
Or shall it be a coven
of weary witches in flight?

Oh, let us let things name themselves.
Up here there is nothing,
out there, nothing,
to solidify us.

Hello morning in the clouds.
I am real again and vaguely upset about it.

Nolan Burger, Grade 12
Lucas High School

Why I Like Her

Oh, she makes me laugh
she's in my dream
she lets me fly
With love's wide wings
She's beautiful
She sets me free
She makes me want to be me
She makes me tipsy
Like beer, rum and wine
When she laughs, I'll laugh
When she cries, I'll cry
The thing I fear most
Is our possible goodbye
She makes me so happy
When all is said and all is done
When the drums stop beating
And the song is done
I want to be there with her
To share our last breath
I'll love her always
Even after death
John-Christopher King, Grade 11
Libbey High School

Nobody Said

I sat there
Watching people go by
No one stopped to look
And nobody knew how
Lonely I was
In the noise and clatter
Nobody asked me
What is the matter
Through all the noise
Nobody said,
"Don't cry today"
Tomorrow will be better
Wipe away the tears
Nobody gave me
a word of cheer
Nobody said,
"I love you, dear"
Kayla Russell, Grade 12
Pike County Career Technology Center

Hope

In the darkness of colors
it's hard to find the truth.
in the emptiness of a heart
it's hard to find love.
In the loneliness of a soul
it's hard to find a goal,
but never give up, you can find
the good is not just in your mind.
Chantal Franz, Grade 11
Jefferson Area Jr-Sr High School

A New Day

Today's a new day, the times are changing
And it seems like our love is fading.
I told myself I was so done with all the denying,
And the tons of tears from crying.
But here we are again, tonight, constantly arguing and fighting.
I was told if you're in love, you can work it out.
And he says that we will without a doubt.
Being who I am, I believe every word he tells me.
I can't help it his touch sets me free.
I wonder when I am going to prove him wrong.
Show him that I am not weak, I've always been strong.
I guess it's just something about him I can't leave be.
I love him and I know he loves me.
But everything we've been through has been worth the while
We worked it out and both left with a smile.
He did the sweetest things for me, and when I asked why he said "just cuz."
I had no doubt in my mind that we could make it like it was.
The unconditional love is all I need.
I don't need the house, the cars, or even the jewelry.
Finally I gave him the key to my heart to keep forever.
I hope it is something he'll love and treasure.
Bree Lyons, Grade 11
Whitmer High School

Facade

These words that spill from my pen
Are the truth behind my eyes and
That ache in your heart that just won't disappear
Is the truth that flows through your veins
The feeling in your fingertips
That flows to your wrists,
Blue and bruised
And continues to your soul that was once painted a golden yellow
A tear falls around your lips, and the truth you hide, is hidden deeper
The facade you wear is the only thing you know
And you thought you knew them better than yourself, but check again
They've figured you out
All these un-sent letters, cloak the you trapped inside
The hidden tears, fake smiles, too strong emotion
You're the epitome of sin, but don't worry, it's not like we're much better.
Austin Bessey, Grade 10
Loveland High School

Love Lives On

Sometimes people don't realize,
What they have until it's gone,
But with you, that's not true.
For eighteen years, you've been my number one.

With each passing day,
My heart grows fonder of you.
Despite our trials and despite our tribulations, for many we've overcome.
You are my greatest asset in life and to you, I give you my love.
William Oliver, Grade 10
Life Skills Center of Youngstown

Things Gone Bad

want. want. want. want. want.
want you.
to talk with.
to think about.
to touch.
to greet.

words flew. hate grew.

wanted. wanted. wanted. wanted. wanted.
wanted you.
to talk with.
to think about.
to touch.
to greet.

do you? do you? do you love me?
or is it her? don't lie!

choose. choose. Choose!
I'm going to.
In fact — I have!

You had me once…then things went bad.

Hayley Raterman, Grade 10
Sidney High School

The Sad Good-bye

She said I was her friend
'Till her life had come to an end.
She was in a brown-black casket
And we put flowers for her in a pink basket.
As I looked at her lifeless face
Everyone walked by at a fast, steady pace.
Some people were so sad that they cried
When they found out that she had died.
Her three children would walk around
And cried so hard they fell to the ground.
There was a picture of them all together
Smiling outside in the freezing weather.
I realized then I was too weak to speak
As I stood up to give a heartfelt speech.
We drove to her final resting place
And found she would have a large enough space.
Then all of a sudden I sank to my knees
And begged God to bring her back to these young three.
As we all looked down and said our final good-byes
Everyone had tears filling their eyes.
There were no more words to say.

Erica Tournoux, Grade 10
Marlington High School

To and Fro

Reality is a conflict,
Wars have come and gone,
But there are wars being fought.
The world, is it due to eradication? No
But it's due to change.
The past doesn't repeat, but will for some.
The world spins, spins of difference each day,
Terror, yes, wars, yes, disasters, yes,
A change is due,
A change and hope for those who believe.
Reality is conflict,
But conflict is a process due to change.
The Only One, God is Reality,
Who doesn't endure conflict
But ends them.
Reality is yet to change.

Robert Okyere, Grade 11
Westerville North High School

Beholden to Nothing and Nobody

I thought it was ok,
I could deal with it,
I was wrong,
It's killing me so slow I just want to scream.
I want to be free of the mental torture being forced on me.
To be able to talk freely about what's happening to me.
I'm becoming such a lesser version of me,
getting harder and harder to see.
I'm fading away slowly but surely
beholden to nothing and nobody.

Kaitlin Frankart, Grade 10
Arcadia High School

The Day My World Fell Apart

So quiet no one said a word
The priest's sad voice was the only thing heard
I tried to be strong I didn't wanna cry
But faded images started to play in my mind
I sat in silence listening to the preacher speak
About my little brother, a couple of tears ran down my cheek
I saw the coffin with colorful flowers placed on top
Knowing what laid inside made my heart stop

As he was lowered into the soil I tried to be brave
But the thought made me sick of having to visit him at his grave
I felt my heart break and I put my hands in my hair
I looked up to the sun which seemed to hide in despair
I tried to speak but no words came out
I wanted to scream I wanted to shout
I thought of his body laying motionless and cold
As many years will pass it will slowly decompose
I ran my fingers along the name engraved in stone
I wonder what it feels like to be eternally and forever alone…

Leslie Santos, Grade 11
Carl F Shuler School

All for You

You may not understand
I don't expect you to
All the things I've ever done
All I'll ever do
It's all for you.
I try to be your girl
Everything you need.
But how can I
When I don't know what to do?
I know that I love you
And I'm doing it all for you.
I'm afraid of heartbreak
I'm afraid of pain
But I'm here anyway
Doing it all for you.
Tons of tears
And hours of hurt later
Everything I'm doing now
All the pain I'm causing myself
It's all for you.
Amber Holland, Grade 11
Licking Heights High School

I Hope

I hope she's all you ever wanted.
I hope she's everything you need.
I hope she makes you happy.
You deserve that much at least.
Stephanie Hammond, Grade 11
Shadyside High School

Never Gonna Find Me…

Crashing waves and soothing sounds,
Running fast I hit the ground.
Screeching gulls and falling rain,
No more strength to run again.
All my time has just run out,
Get away I scream, I shout.
Lying drained in falling rain,
All was lost and nothing gained.
Hold your hand but not for long,
The thought of "us" it all went wrong.
Screaming, slashing,
Thunder rolls as our hearts are clashing.
Working hard and working up,
Strength enough to just stand up.
Grabbing for your helpful hand,
As you leave me in the sand.
Waves are rolling, grabbing me,
Fingers fold to pull me out to sea.
You're so sweet but not profound,
Out to sea and never found…
Andy Pettibone, Grade 12
Bloom-Carroll High School

An Unheard Cry for Help

An abundance of rocks, on top of an overpass,
Once grew a single blade of grass,
Strong, and bold, it strived alone, wet and cold, but nevertheless, it prospered.

Emerald green with porcelain morning dew,
Sturdy to the rocks, while fragile to the world,
Not a soul noticed, because nobody cared how powerful was this blade of grass.

So bold it stood, solitary among silver rocks, and grew to be a skyscraper,
So proud and confident, but none of it mattered,
Because not many wandered upon this bridge.

It was a welcome mat for downtown nomads, a safe place to spend the night,
A waste of time that must be consumed, somehow, somewhere.
So why not cash it in here, on top of this stony forgotten overpass bridge,
Where there grows a wild inspirational grass.

The single blade cries emotional, transparent tears disguised as morning dew,
But nobody ever knew it screamed in solitude.
Its strength died as its hope for companionship weakened into one final breath.

I now sit where this tortured single blade of grass used to grow,
And I wish I could have shown him how much I cared,
And how inspirational he had been.
Naomi Grace West, Grade 11
Whitmer High School

Where I'm From

I am from school levies,
From ridiculous sports prices and strange clubs.
I am from the city with trailers outside of the middle school.
I am from the hackberry tree,
The Bartlett pear, that now stands in place of the tired old apple tree.

I am from a/c to heat in one day,
From thunderstorms to blizzards.
I'm from the people who think they know something, and the ones that really do,
From I don't know and I know exactly what the problem is.

I'm from McCormick and Creech,
Fast food and speeding tickets.
In the deepest part of my mind
Memories from way back when
A collection of all the good times
To remind me of everything that I once had.

I am from that place —
Still there however,
Still living free
Rob Finley, Grade 12
D Russel Lee Career-Technology Center

Winter Wonderland

W hirling snowflakes falling outside
I gloos made by little children clad in hats and gloves
N ewly fallen snow crunches under your boots
T rees glistening with decorations and lights
E vergreen smell drifting through your house
R eindeer carrying Santa through the night

Leah Lozen, Grade 11
Loveland High School

Airplane

I am fascinated by
A vacuous plate of dispassionate glass
That contains the world.
I press against it,
Leaving moist, misty marks
With my soft pink hands.
My breath races out
To blanket the gleaming night-face of the city
And draws back into me,
Cold and vital,
Wise with what it has seen.
My body,
Calm and uncomplaining,
Rushes east on the crest of a breeze,
Warm in anticipation,
Tight with readiness
To tear my eyes from this porthole to eternity
And follow with my feet
Where my breath has just gone.

Allison Heimann, Grade 11
Westlake High School

Principle Profession

The world turns,
the pendulum falls,
one more domino,
click, tick, click, tick.

Time fails to yield, time fails to heal,
no one sees the past,
no one can estimate the future.

Life continues onward,
coffee fuels the masses,
beauty reigns supreme,
the Bard reenacts truth with passion.

Faith grows impatient
with disciples who are ignorant,
children play games with ethics,
people fall in love,

the principle profession of life is consistency.

Matt Hersha, Grade 10
Hilliard Davidson High School

Thunderstorm

It all begins…

Slowly at first,
Pitter, patter, pitter, patter

The gray, uniformed troops approach.
The wind picks up and tension fills the air.
Persistent.

The clouds grow darker.
The rains keep up.

Charge!
Now black. The clouds collide like soldiers.

Boom!
The thunder sounds like shots.
Heaven seems unhappy

Lashing out!
The lightning slices through the darkness.
The dense water hangs motionless.

Will victory ever come?

Dawnelle Jewell, Grade 12
Badger High School

A Glimpse of a Girl

I remember once, a glimpse of a girl
Who held her dreams in her palm
And wore a smile that could light the sky.
She had the essence of an angel.
Her locks smooth as the sea.
Her eyes so mystical
One could leave all reality if gazing too deep.
She once had a love
Who swept her heart away.
Her lips quivered when he drew near
And her soul radiated with felicity.
She knew her destiny.
Each goal as clear as the midnight air.
Her course was set
And her journey had just begun.
The earth has turned
Seasons have come and gone
What has become of her?
The mirror reminds me of my past
And I realize that I am sailing away
Slowly fading from days of bliss.

Molly Lashner, Grade 11
Solon High School

invincible

driving with no destination
into the sunset
the moon visible
the radiant colors that blanket
across the never-ending fields
pure happiness is felt
in your heart and soul
your whole life brightens
and stops for a moment in time
a perfect moment
that can never be recreated
you understand everything
for this one tiny instant
in this instant
the world is yours
you are free
you are as golden
as the sun hits the land
and no one can stop you
you are invincible
Courtney Justine Murphy, Grade 12
Sylvania Northview High School

I Cannot Say 'Goodbye'

I love how you make me laugh
And how your baby blue eyes shine
As I begin to smile
And remember you are all mine
I love how you love me
And how your voice echoes in my ear
As you say "I need you"
So quiet that only I can hear
I hate you make me cry
And how your blue eyes become mean
As I start to turn away
And cry without being seen
I hate how you hate me
When I do not say "I love you"
And you begin to whine
Until I say I love you, too
Even though you make me laugh
You also make my cry
Even though you can be mean
I cannot say goodbye
Because I will always love you
Ariel Meighen, Grade 11
Jefferson Area Jr-Sr High School

Time

What happened to you?
You used to be happy.
You used to love me.
It seems that time has changed you.

What happened to you?
You used to be my confidant,
My battles became yours.
It seems the void between us is growing.

What happened to you?
You used to be real,
You criticized those you deem as fake.
It seems time has made you a hypocrite.

What happened to you?
You used to be proud of me,
You never used to belittle me.
It seems that time has changed you.

What happened to me?
I still love you,
I still try and make you proud.
Time may change you, but I am still me.
Halie Motter, Grade 11
Whitmer High School

The Swing

A knotted plank, a braided rope,
Slung high amidst the leaves,
Liquid sunlight spatters,
'Cross the earthen forest floor.

Eyes shut tight, I grasp the cord,
Breath heavy in my chest.
Kicking off into the breeze,
I leave this world behind.

Leaning this way, shifting that,
Moving with the wind,
A haven from the troubles, cares,
A pendulum of solace.

Twisting through the chilly air,
My hair swirls like a halo,
Watching colors coalesce,
Autumn's dusky palette.

A shard of time, a reverie,
Defying thought and wonder.
I close my eyes, cling tighter still,
To this peace, this moment,
This instant in which I can fly.
Julie Weiner, Grade 11
Shaker Heights High School

Forever 'Till the End

To shed a thousand tears
will not change those hateful
years when I spent my time
through agonies and fears.

To yell out all my pain
will not help me to contain
my heart which you
unknowingly have strained.

To shield away the light
won't help, 'cause I know you
might not return after
our unforgiving fight.

To say that I was wrong
may not fix our broken
song, but together is
where we truly belong.

I need you back, my friend.
Our love isn't hard to
mend, because I'll love you
forever 'till the end.
Victoria Recker, Grade 11
Delphos St John High School

The Lisp

It really must stink going through life
With a lisp stuck in your mouth,
You just don't sound right.

All of your S's sound so obscure,
And truthfully nobody knows of a cure.
I made a small list
Of words that don't sound right,
I'll name some to you now,
And try to rhyme them I might.

Starting at Sasquatch,
And ending with sisters
Your saliva is splashing
As you say these tongue twisters.
While slushie is quite a toughie to say
6 sphinxes were just added to the array.
So I hope you understand now
What I'm trying to convey,
Don't catch the lisp
And you'll be okay.
Luke Berry, Grade 10
Revere High School

Drowning Alive

The waves have drift'd me away
To a familiar and unwelcoming territory
Kisses me on the cheek
And consumes me entirely
leaving my heart to drift to shore
While this tidal wave feeds on my soul

These addictions I carry
And this mess that surrounds me
Only weighs me down
Closer to the fire
Away from the clouds
Blinded by darkness
Scorched by the light
I'm stuck in the middle
And nothing feels all right

Each time I struggle to escape
I get sucked further back in
The force to relapse in unknown
With nothing of my sanity left
I find it amazing my will to fight survives
Even though each day I run a chance of drowning alive

Renee Klausing, Grade 11
Delphos St John High School

Realizing

Why did I stick up for you?
When everyone else put you down,
was it true friendship or was it just courtesy?
Too bad it doesn't matter now!

Why is it that you could tell everyone else the truth,
but when it came to me it was all lies?
What were you thinking or weren't you?
Did it ever cross your mind that it would hurt me!
I didn't think so!

You took our friendship for granted.
Always thinking that I would be there to bail you out,
at a drop of a dime;
Never realizing I had my own life,
till the day I wasn't there.

As I look back now,
and wonder why;
how I did not see it coming.
I should have known,
it was just all a game to you!

Katie Neumeier, Grade 11
Delphos St John High School

In My Heart

Every time I think of you boy;
You make me hurt inside;
Why can't I just forget you;
Get lost, get out of my mind.
Every day there are reminders;
Of what there used to be;
I just can't seem to lose the thought;
Of you always with me.
Please get lost, just go away;
Please, just for my own sake;
For I have fallen way too hard;
For someone I cannot take.
All I want is someone;
To show me that they care;
To prove their love just for me;
Oh why can't life be fair.
I know this will never happen;
For that I really fear;
For being alone the rest of my life;
Is why I keep you there.

Ashley Koenn, Grade 11
Paulding High School

Wishing

Some nights in bed I lay
Wishing you would come to take me away
to a place where we can be alone
somewhere that they have never known
somewhere that we can just be us
and never listen to anyone fuss
but I am here
and you are there
my heart is now cold with fear
as my eyes let slip just one tear
I wonder what to do or say
all I can do is bow my head to pray.

Brittney Gibson, Grade 11
Sebring Mckinley High School

To the One I Love

I've tried writing this a hundred times
And every time it's never good enough

My dear this is for you

You are every breath I take
And let it be known that you are my everything

You and I are a jigsaw puzzle
We fit together so perfectly

I can't imagine a day going by without you by my side
And if that day is to come a part of me will die

Ana Fleisher, Grade 11
Loveland High School

Light

Darkness all around,
The end seems near
Yet it's so far away.
I'm feeling so bound;
It's been a year
Since I've seen light of day.

Suddenly there's hope,
A light so faint
That I can barely see.
Clutching to the rope
That holds my weight,
Keeps me from getting free.

I don't know the why
Behind the war —
Behind the endless fight.
I just know I'll die
And lose my soul
Before I lose this light.

Ryan Hoffman, Grade 12
Massillon Christian School

The Great White

Well, I lift my sword
To fight this great white beast
My cuts leave marks of black
Occasionally blue
Even rare is purple, green or red
Sometimes my sword leaves wounds
Of silvery grey
More often than not
I use blades of awesome colour
To hide the remains of a slaughter
The wounds I leave are small
Precise
And they always hit true
I need not, not ever
Ever run the beast through
The great white beast, leaf-like and thin
Never, never, never fights back
I always triumph, I always conquer

Joe Scheidenberger, Grade 12
McNicholas High School

Empty Victory

Our buildings now are all destroyed,
as completely as the people.
Our country's houses don't exist,
except some here, abandoned
The one thing in this country left,
Is a squadron of long range bombers.
And now you tell me on this day,
that we now are the victors?

Alex Lieb, Grade 10
Hilliard Davidson High School

My Brother's a Marine

My brother is a Marine.
He can sneak around and never be seen.
He can stand up really quick.
He can take someone out with just a flick.
He is proud of what he has become.
They talk about the few and the proud, I jump to say my brother's one.

Laura Schaffner, Grade 12
D Russel Lee Career-Technology Center

Musical High

Notes swaying and swirling smoothly through my head.
Hypnotizing me with their tempting tunes,
Making me lust for more.

Notes dance and twirl in front of my eyes,
Like ballroom dancers before a king.
As the beats bound and leap within my mind,
I reach a musical high.

My body becomes a marionette to a musical puppeteer.
And with every trill I receive a thrill.
And in the heart of every beat I see beauty.
And still my movements rise and fall to the dynamic of the piece,
As a leaf will imitate the movements of an autumn wind.

So many ways of expression,
No limits but your mind.
So many inspirations,
Just never enough time.

Kayla Slomski, Grade 10
Hilliard Davidson High School

A Serviceman

Dearest of the night,
Our loving embrace was not meant to be forever good-bye.
Just a promise to my country to do or die.
'Tis because of this country that we are now separated.
For long ago when from England this country was freed,
Children and wives and mothers all had a need.
For many a father and husband and son were lost in this strife,
But for this great cause they were willing to give up their life.
We know that we must keep this freedom which we have wrought,
That is why we have fought.
For our children and wives we will make these wrongs right,
We will cure this great plight.
That is why, my love, I am not there with you now,
But remember always our everlasting vow.
I volitionally gave myself for you, and for all mankind,
"Greater love hast no man than to give his life for a friend,"
This was said and portrayed by one great man,
Now I have followed His plan.
To be able to be a Service to Man,
One must be a Serviceman.

Leah Johanni, Grade 11
Sacred Heart of Jesus Academy

Growin' Up

Life is goin' so fast,
Leavin' the past in the past,
I think of the time when I was born,
Seeing that I've grown up,
Put up and never gave up,
Made it through the worst,
So now they say I'm goin' to turn out great,
How does that happen when I'm goin' at this rate,
Don't want to discriminate,
Yet I still have a lot to face,
In my life that hasn't ended,
Even the many times I have got double crossed,
Still making it through, it's true,
Livin' today every day like it's my last day,
It's just that I'm growin' up.

Michael Moore, Grade 12
Champion High School

Storm on a Fleeting Moment

You can feel it.
The exhilarated feeling deep in the pit of your soul
When the trees sing their subtle song of rain
You can feel it.
When a tower of rising cloud slides across the trees
You can feel it.
The low bass of coming thunder echoes off the sky
When the first wet dew caresses your face
You can feel it.
As the first rains come down
And the soft patter patter of a million splatters are heard
You can feel it.
When the song bird sings shrilly from a tree
And the flash of lightning streaks overhead
It is done.
One soft, quiet calm is heard
And Nature's finale crashes around you
In a fleeting moment,
Nature's song is done,
Storm on a Fleeting Moment.

Kevin T. Smith, Grade 10
Hilliard Davidson High School

What Am I?

I come in different shapes and sizes,
but I always taste the same.
Most people eat me when they feel down,
thinking I will make them feel better.
I am shaped like a bunny on Easter,
and a Santa Claus on Christmas.
I am like a sweet person,
that helps others at time of need.
People of all ages adore me,
and I will always be around.
What am I?

Nataliya Shtyrkalo, Grade 12
Brunswick High School

Poetry

Shall I compare thee to a summer's day?
Is what the great Shakespeare once said
In the times of romance and drama.
But to say it now?
What would it mean to anyone who heard?

Why would I be a summer's day?
One person might ask.
Summer is too hot,
Another might say.

The times we live in now would never say such a thing.
Does that mean poetry has lost its meaning?
No.
Poetry has only evolved into something new.

This new age brings on new meanings to poetry.
In some ways it makes it more open.
Just like in lyrics where they say whatever they want

So is poetry now something totally different than it was then?
No.
It will always be the way it is.
So I shall say, Shall I compare thee to a summer's day?

Denver Coulson, Grade 10
Loveland High School

Just Another Bad Dream

Emptiness…
Like a world with no life
It hit me
So fast and hard
I'm falling
Deeper and deeper into that dark hole
The more and more I try to bear it
The more it drains my life away
I can feel my heart falling into my stomach
Like I am on a rollercoaster
Falling faster and faster
I'm scared
Boom!
Hard, cold, and rough surface underneath me
I can hardly see the four walls around me
I feel trapped, alone
Turning my head
I see the dim light
Someone walks towards me
Grabs me, shakes me
"Blake wake up! It's time to get out of bed!"

Blake Kellum, Grade 10
Eastmoor Academy High School

My Harlequin

Steps echo in my mind
The echoing reaches my soul
I search for her, blind
Endlessly seeking my goal

I wake, eyes dripping
Once more I have failed
To remove the guise
She undoubtedly wore

Mouth open to scream
No sound comes
She haunts my dreams
My mind fills with doubt

Wishing for the one I seek
My eyes bleed
My heart bleak
Desiring the love I need

Will I ever find her
The elusive harlequin
Who in this hour
Is my heroine

Rickey Larkin, Grade 12
D Russel Lee Career-Technology Center

I See

I see a mirror
In front of me.

Through the mirror
I see me…

Through me I see
A person of fear…

Through me I see
A person that will soon tear…

Through me I see
A person that is mad…

Through me I see
A person that is sad…

Through me I see
A person in pain…

Through me I see
A person that has no where to drain…

Autumn Bender, Grade 10
Life Skills Center of Youngstown

A Winter's Eve

Firelight upon my face
Soft calm carols sung with grace,
White as snow
The twinkling lights begin to glow,
The tinsel draping shines
As thoughts of mistletoe fill my mind,
I settle in blankets away from the winter breeze
From the window I can see the ice frosting upon the trees,
The December moon glistens
It would be a blessing if we could all just listen,
The magic of the night is in the air
So mystical a heart can hardly bear.

Anna Pieper, Grade 10
McNicholas High School

Cold Hearted

A certain pain fills my heart and I could not tell if it was him
Being with somebody else or him not loving me?
The pain fills my body, soul and heart.
Every breath I take it hurts even more.
Even in my dreams, my heart is cold and filled with ice
That won't melt away for real love to warm up my heart.
The voice in my dream is laughing at me,
Telling me I am a fool for trying to fall in love with him.
Every time my heart beats, it gets colder and colder.
I wake up looking at him, and there goes that pain again
Just beating me up until I can't breathe.
I'm gasping and pulling on him to help me.
He takes one look at me with his cold dark eyes and presses on my heart.
My body feels cold with no love for him.
I open my eyes and he is gone.
I feel a sharp pain in my heart.
I look down, and there was a knife causing that certain pain in my heart.

Sherri Roberts, Grade 10
PACE High School - North

Until the End

You were the cool one, and I was the new girl.
I didn't know befriending you would change a part of my world.
Sometimes I get jealous, when I hear you giving praise,
For a job I have done better, on some different days.
There's so much tenacity, built inside of you.
But through your stubborn storm, I can find my way through.
I can see through the act, yes I can see through it all.
I know how fierce you'd fight with your back against a wall.
Many times I've pondered, and this may sound wrong,
But sometimes I find myself wishing I had someone like you as my mom.
Maybe someone just like you, in whom I can confide.
Someone who always challenges me, but in the end is on my side.
Someone who knows to push which buttons, when, and where.
Someone who I can be myself with, and doesn't find me too much to bear.
You're a great mom, and a most valued friend.
The toughest boss I've ever had,
But someone I'd stick it out with until the end.

Jacqueline Newnam, Grade 12
Eastern High School

Where I Am From

I am from princess wands,
From tiaras and feather boas,
I'm from pink sparkle dust and chipped fingernail polish

I am from puppy kisses
Best Friends giggling to sunrise
And fun filled trips to Grandma's house

I am from long drives,
From getting sick in the mountains
I am from airplane rides
From getting lost in the airport and missing the plane

I am from trips to the hospital,
Ambulance rides that seem to last forever,
Time standing still…

I am from banging on pianos
Endless clarinet squeaks
From dreaming I AM Mozart

I am from laughter,
From unconditional love
And all the memories contained in my heart

Kate Brown, Grade 10
Hilliard Davidson High School

Painting the Portrait of Life

Paintings of accomplished artists
Passed before the young student's eyes.
Mixtures of bright colors, bold streaks,
Or faint whispers from the paint brush.
Framed expressions of thought, beauty.
What quality! What brilliance!
He studied each piece and began to appreciate.
Sitting in silence at his desk,
He traced his pen over the page.
Measuring his level of skill
Drawing objects once, twice, three times.
He trained his hand to capture shapes
Ever perfecting his talents.
He practiced every day and began to succeed.
After years of effort and work,
The painter knew that it was time
To choose the hues from his palate
And begin his own masterpiece.
With the canvas stretched before him
And a soft brush poised in his grasp,
He envisioned his future and began to paint.

Orly Covitch, Grade 12
Beatrice J Stone Yavne High School

Play Hearts

All my streets halt at an infinite wall
I'm just a handful of clay too hard to mold
You can't play hearts until they fall
And everything that is warm, eventually grows cold.

Midnight in a foreign cafe, well beyond neon
I feel lost in an unusual place, alone in a desert
Perhaps I'll just sit here until the loneliness has gone
Finding different emotions to overexert.

Give me a furnace that does not work
Give me a law that I'm allowed to break
Every fading smile slices time with a smirk
And the thing-called-love takes a long time to make.

Take me out under a star that will not crash
Teach me to dance in the flowers like you know it all
Let's begin a game, something rough and rash
But you can't play hearts until they fall.

Lindsay Cameron, Grade 11
Chalker High School

Maybe

I walked home alone on that midsummer's day,
thinking about you and how I loved you so.
Smiling to myself and thinking about us.
Maybe it was your laugh,
that had me from hello.
Maybe it was how you drove your car,
leaning back and humming to the radio,
or maybe how you smiled at me,
with that little look in your eye;
teasing yet so mysterious.
Maybe, just maybe, it was all just a dream.
And you weren't my fairy tale,
but that can't be, because to me,
maybe doesn't mean a thing.

Ashley Moore, Grade 10
Oak Hills High School

Big Mistake

This world is just a big mistake.
All we ever do is fight, then love, then fight again.
This world has made us crazy.
Peace breaking and countries dividing,
And still nothing seems to matter;
Except you and I.
This world is falling apart.
Every living thing still;
Everything except our love.
Is this a dream?
Has the world made a big mistake,
Or have I?

Riley Hatcher, Grade 10
Hilliard Davidson High School

The Tragedy of a Leaf

As I look out on an autumn day, I see the wind caressing the tree tops making them sway to music only they can hear, the music is the very fabric of the universe, beautiful and eternal, the lyrical undertones resting faintly on the edges of our minds, but never making past our subconsciousness. The golden rays of sunshine softly kissing their leaves, making them burst into a myriad of colors ranging from golden brown to a lustrous red. Now, close your eyes, picture the leaves falling from the trunks of their mothering trees, the cold, viscous and bitter, stealing the life and ripping the warmth from the fleshy greenery, drying it out and making it brittle, a massacre so beautiful and brutal you have to be like nature to appreciate the ordeal thoroughly, soaking in the brilliance and beauty while dwelling in the knowledge of their screams while they're separated from their life-giving organ, the cold laughter silently with the breeze. Its amazing how everything intertwines.

Joey Niehoff, Grade 12
The Alternative Center of Knox County

Heroes

The alarm sounds at three o'clock in the morning, you were sound asleep but now you are prepared for the job,
You receive the call for a fire at the corner of Ninth and Elm streets, you pack up your gear and you pull away from the station.

The sirens of the truck break up the silence of night, the bright red lights seem to awaken the streets,
Three blocks away you can see the bright glow of the flames, you know just what to do.

It is well below freezing but you are determined, the high rise seems to never end,
Six stories up and only ten to go, the sixteenth floor is your destination.

The higher you get the hotter the air, the smoke continues to get darker,
The hose roll is getting heavy but nothing can stop you now, the door is the only thing holding you back.

You charge the hose line and swing open the door, smoke and flames billow out surrounding you,
It is hot, impossible to see.

As flames begin to die down you can see the destruction, a family apartment now turned to ash,
Memories lost and pictures saved, no lives were lost or injured.

Another night on the job, no two are ever the same,
You do not think of yourself as a hero, you are just doing a job that you love.

Nicole Taylor, Grade 12
D Russel Lee Career-Technology Center

I Am the Keeper of My Goal

He sits, stooping on the sideline, scathing at every save.
At night his face dances beneath my eyelids, his words reverberating in my ears.
My fists clench, my teeth grind as I remember his echoing sneer.
And my mind races in pursuit of that everlasting, peaceful sleep.

A new man appears, his feathered wings visible only in the new found light
And knocks. I open the door to two new teams but it is hard to close it behind me.
Looking back, I find comfort in the familiar darkness, yet the light before me is so appealing.
Loyalty and longing rage within me, splitting me from the inside, outside.

I wake in the morning to discover the storm within subsided.
Looking in the mirror, I see my eyes sparkle, lighting my face and casting away yesterday's sorrows.
My hands relax, and my face tightens in a way long lost,
A smile.

Anna Albi, Grade 10
Summit Country Day School

Feel Please
Never have you heard my cries
Never have you seen my eyes
All you ever say are lies
This is where my stomach ties.
And in my throat my heart brakes
All your gives turn into takes
Your beautiful smiles were only fake
Now your true self begins to wake.
The thought of you is implanted in my brain
My feelings are messed up, it's like a hurricane
Crying myself to sleep, I've truly gone insane
How could you put me through all this pain?
Can you find it in you heart to make this go away?
Please wait for me to be stronger some other day
How can you be fine, how can you be okay
Isn't there anything left you want to say?
Carly Pearce, Grade 10
McNicholas High School

The Game I Play
The game I play is never simple
But it is very rewarding.
Under pressure, I never cripple
But is it very stressful

What is the game that I speak?
It is the game of life.
Can I ever reach the peak?
Sure, but I have to strive.

Striving, a force based on self trust and personal gain
Never can I have enough of it, but always can I look for it
Like an explosion in the heart, like storms full of rain
Through striving, I have won the game I play.
Jeff Pejsa, Grade 11
Normandy High School

The Mask That's Hiding Me*
The mask in me hides my fears,
When the mask is on I shed no tears.
The mask I wear shows no feelings,
When I wear it there will be no healing.
The mask that's hiding me controls my thoughts,
Through tough times I have always fought.
The mask is invisible as you see,
The only person who can see this mask is me.
When I wear the mask, sometimes I wish I would die,
When the mask is off I am not shy.
The mask is hiding the real me,
I want to take it off so I can feel free.
When the mask is on please let me be,
I cannot feel because of the mask that's hiding me.
Summer Fowler, Grade 12
Westerville Central High School
*Go Warhawks

Never
I will never forget your face,
I will never forget your love,
Even though you're not here,
I still feel your presence from above.

I will never let memories fade,
I will keep them freely in mind,
I will never let them go,
I'll think of you all the time.

Nothing will ever be the same,
But change is always good,
You're better off up there,
Where you will never be judged.

All I want to ask,
Is that you watch me close from heaven,
Please just know that I won't forget you,
Not today, not tomorrow, never!
Jazmine McCaleb, Grade 11
Eastmoor Academy High School

Growing Up
Red roses gradually fade as the sun sets,
And time ticks on just as before.
My whole existence a series of regrets,
Something I have always tried to ignore.

So many unspoken feelings build up inside,
As I struggle to forget what happened long-ago.
Others attempting to help only to be denied,
I am not interested in your selfish quid pro quo.

True friends almost impossible to acquire,
With compassionate gestures absent from the days.
For someone to care becomes my greatest desire,
But I am dismissed as "going through a phase."

Growing up becomes a feasible task,
For no longer am I so desperate and alone.
Nevermore will I hide behind a misread mask,
My true self prepared to appear and be shown.
Sarah Shifflett, Grade 12
McNicholas High School

Ideal of My Life
Memories of my past haunt me now
I try to block them out but I don't know how
Tears leave my eyes as I stay in silence
Dealing with my life, nothing but violence
Scared to say how I feel
Hating my life, wishing it wasn't real
Waking up in the morning, wishing I was still asleep
I'm sick of my life, all I do is weep
I get judged by people who don't even know me
No need to explain my life, you can already see!
Felicia McKenzie, Grade 11
Carl F Shuler School

Tennis

He walks up to the line
With a determined look on his face
He bounces the ball three times
And winds up for his serve

Pulling the racket behind his head
Then snapping it forward striking the ball
The ball travels at an incredible speed
But hits the top of the net and falls

"Fault one" calls the official in a loud voice
The man gets another ball ready to try again
Bouncing the ball only two times he pulls his racket back
Extends his arm and the ball is hit

It flies in the air at a decent speed
Just making it over the net
The ball hits in the corner of the box
And the official calls out,
"ACE!"

Olivia Reaney, Grade 10
Loveland High School

A Friendship Lost

Riding bikes in the summer, snowball fights in the winter.
We played all day, and stayed up all night.
We had fun together, we got in trouble together.
We swore to be friends forever.
What happened?
We used to be happy.
But we went our different ways.
I wish you would change the way you live.
And maybe again, we could be friends.
If we tried, it just might work.
But for now we could use our space.
I may see you from time to time,
At the mall, in a grocery line.
I can't help but hate the way you act,
It's not really you, and you know that.
I'll always hope that we could ride bikes in the summer,
Have snowball fights in the winter,
Have fun together, get in trouble together.
Again…

Michael Gregory, Grade 12
Scarlet Oaks Career Development Campus

Young Poets
Grades 7-8-9

Note: The Top Ten poems were finalized through an online voting system. Creative Communication's judges first picked out the top poems. These poems were then posted online. The final step involved thousands of students and teachers who registered as online judges and voted for the Top Ten poems. We hope you enjoy these selections.

Top Poem Grades 7-8-9

Moonlit Night

The crickets sang their soothing song
As the moon climbed into the night,
Smiling down with its glow,
A grinning, luminous crescent.
The last of the sun's brilliant rays
Were engulfed by an inky blackness
As the Earth pulled up its blanket of stars.
They danced way above the clouds
With so much energy that some leapt,
Twinkling o'er the many hills and plains.
Fireflies floated carelessly around,
Whispering to each other as they buzzed about.
The creatures of the night happily played,
Waiting for the earth to wake in the morning.

Erin Clepper, Grade 7
Gahanna Middle School East

Top Poem Grades 7-8-9

My Christmas Wish

The Christmas music,
I can hear,
Makes me completely filled,
With holiday cheer.

I dance and prance,
And sing all the time,
What really troubles me,
Is a Christmas wish of mine.

I wrote to Santa,
That jolly old man,
But the sad thing is,
I don't think he can help the crisis at hand.

The Christmas spirit is all being lost,
And the funny thing is,
It's all about commercialism,
And it's mostly the kids.

Their pleading and begging, and making huge lists,
Their pushing their parents away from their bliss,
Can't we go back to a simpler time?
And that, only that is the Christmas wish of mine.

Claudia Giuffre, Grade 7
St Gertrude School

Top Poem Grades 7-8-9

The Guard Dog

Sitting up straight and proud as can be, I watch and I wait protecting the tree.
Won't Santa be scared when he sees me growling?
Frightened as can be I interrupted his prowling?
I can see it now, my wonderful prize: a vision of Santa running before my eyes.
Wait, what's that whisper, that disturbance, that noise?
Could it be the thump of boots, the rustle of toys?
I wag my tail, and I bare my teeth.
I fix my eyes on the hearth under the wreath.
Down the chimney bearded Santa scurries and slides.
He appears happy and jolly with the sack that he hides.
Spotting me he comes over saying, "Good dog" and "Nice boy."
I snarl and growl ending Santa Claus' cheerful joy.
A flicker of fear crossed the big man's face.
He scurries back up the chimney as I start to chase.
Mission accomplished and job well done, I settle back down knowing I've won.
The respect of the family is all that matters to me
Won't they be glad to see how well I've guarded the tree?

Audrey Goddard, Grade 8
Chardon Middle School

Top Poem Grades 7-8-9

Teen Life

Teen life is amazing
Everywhere you turn.
And if you are not careful,
Sometimes you will burn.
Children we are no longer,
Adults we will become.
For now we're in the middle,
Our growing is not done.
Some days will be easy,
Others might not be.
We'll make it through each one of them,
With the help of family.
Lessons will be learned,
Decisions we will make.
Fears we will have some,
And risks we might just take.
One day when we're grown,
I hope that I can say:
My teen years were eventful,
In each and every way.

Chelsa Johnson, Grade 9
Washington Sr High School

Top Poem Grades 7-8-9

Scrapbook Memories

Remember the days when your biggest
obstacle was the monkey bars?
And you'd lay outside looking for shooting stars
wishing for something big
like to win at street hockey against the neighborhood kids.
The days when you'd call out to Mom,
"five minutes more!"
And there were the things you knew for sure
like to never step on a crack,
or trade a chocolate snack pack.
It was the days when your biggest hero was Tommy Pickles
and in your pocket was a wad of gum,
stickers and a few nickels.
The days when you had a Power Ranger band-aid for your boo boo
It was the times when you saved up for the last
Chuckie Cheese token,
and the only thing you had to protect
was your favorite crayon from being broken.

Jane Marshall, Grade 8
St Christopher Elementary School

Top Poem Grades 7-8-9

Lend a Hand

With trees bending in the wind,
I listen to nature's call.
The chirps of birds grow farther away
As leaves and petals begin to fall.

I don't understand what the world is telling me
Or anything it's trying to say,
But I do know that we're killing the Earth.
Can't there be another way?

Trees are cut down, one by one,
As all of the water is going to waste.
The Earth is being destroyed,
And to help it, we have to make haste.

If we know that we should fix our mistakes,
Why is there still corruption in our land?
Maybe all we really need
Is for everyone to lend a hand.

Jannatun Mohd-Amir, Grade 8
Ridgeview Middle School

Top Poem Grades 7-8-9

Strength

There is a windowfish in you
With transparent glass locking you inside
But within the glass lays a fighting Beta
It smacks against the glass, looking for an escape
It roars in impatience and only you can soothe
It with your calming ocean waters
It lives inside you, trying to break free
But that is your strength to move on

Jackie Mulay, Grade 7
Incarnation School

Top Poem Grades 7-8-9

Vending Machines

I really hate vending machines
They tend to make me mad
When those goodies won't come out
It tends to make me sad
I shake the machine…still no luck
Then I start to shout
People around me stop and stare
My goodies still won't come out
I look out the clear glass window
Then I see a man
My food's name is on his jacket
And he's driving a big white van
He walks up to me and stops
"What's the matter" he asks
"My food won't come out" I say
Then he starts to laugh
"Well lucky for you I have the key
That opens up that door
I'll open it up, get out your candy
And then you'll be sad no more"

Megan Nagy, Grade 7
Union Local Middle School

Top Poem Grades 7-8-9

The Staring Match

I look at the cat.
The cat looks at me.
I blink first.
He turns, whiskers trembling with glee.

"Now, wait just a moment!
A rematch," I plea.
He saunters back.
We'll play best out of three.

We go at it again.
Though we'd scarcely begun,
The cat smiles inside,
For he knows he has won.

I squint, I squirm.
How dry-eyed I became!
Though I stare with a vengeance,
The result is the same.

I am undaunted.
For victory will I strive!
What do you say, cat,
To best out of five?

Leandra Trudeau, Grade 8
St Michael School

Top Poem Grades 7-8-9

Let Them Be

Let them be as music boxes
Always playing perfectly
But always repeatedly, never changing

I'd rather be a majestic piano
Able to make mistakes, and still sound good
Always playing something new

I am free to make mistakes
To play a different tune
To play nonsense
Just to satisfy myself
They can be dainty
Always tinkling along
I can bang excitedly
Or whisper quietly
Always changing, never boring

I'd rather be completely tuneless
Than a wimpy music box
If I could be different, exciting
Magnificent, wonderful
Not always perfect —
I'd rather be a grand piano.

Valerie Weingart, Grade 7
West Branch Middle School

Inside This Box

Inside this box are magical
things. Inside this box are toys
from my childhood that will
stay in my heart for as long as
I live. Inside this box are
papers from past years that
remind me of how much I
have grown. Inside this box is
a different dimension and in
that dimension everyone
loves, no one hates and there
is no killing. Inside that box
are my memories that will last
for a life time.

Alvaro Pareja, Grade 7
Gahanna Middle School East

Life

it started out as a lump
in the perfect ocean
but it swelled and
became a wave
that gained power
as it rose and
then it fell back into
what it once
was.

that is life.

Sarah Lucas, Grade 8
Birchwood School

Over There

As we sleep in our beds,
Safe and sound,
Curled up in a blanket,
Dreaming peacefully,
We don't really think about,
Over there.

Many people lose their lives,
Many children lose a parent,
Many people go insane,
Never being able to forget about,
Over there.

One day a year,
We think about the brave,
Men and women,
Who risked their lives,
For me and you,
And we only celebrate,
Them one day a year,
Veteran's Day.

Laura Parilla, Grade 7
South Range Middle School

At the Drag Races!

I feel the rumbles of the engines in my toes.
I try to talk but all is just a mumble.
My nose notices the nasty stench of burnt rubber.
There sits the driver, silent and focused because he is the pilot.
As they pull up slowly she thinks, "This chance is a one and only!"
Now they are at the starting line the race fans wait to see
Who will have the fastest time.
Ready…set…GREEN!

Kelsi Lowther, Grade 8
Logan-Hocking Middle School

For My Grandmother

For my grandmother, who in the nineties…

Made anyone and everyone laugh
Inhaled cashew like there was no tomorrow
Traveled the world with me on her magic carpet
Invented stories that would have me laughing for hours
Allowed me to play with her turquoise necklace and never got annoyed
Observed me while I played, but usually joined in
Depended on her Scottish terrier for company
Provided the best hugs you could get
Walked frequently and loved it. Loved me unconditionally and let me know

For my grandmother, who in the two thousands…

Was diagnosed with Alzheimer's
Can't recognize her four sons
Remembers nothing of our magic carpet rides, or the stories she told me
Is cautious about her guests in her nursing home, to her we are strangers
Has kept her indestructible sense of humor
Is hurt when she knows she is hurting her loved ones, by her lack of recalling them
Trusts hesitantly, not easily, like she used to
Is lost in a world she used to know so well. Is present, but only physically
Is lucky; she has a family that visits her as often as they can, even if it kills them

Veronica Colborn, Grade 8
St Brendan Elementary School

My Wish

As I sit here alone in my room.
I listen to the rain slowly beating against my window.
And I wished…
That one day I can be loved.
Be loved for who I am instead of someone I am not.
For someone to hold me, to tell me everything will be all right.
For someone to wipe the tears from my eyes;
someone to listen to me and actually care about what I have to say.
For that one person who will never leave me, leave me alone in the darkness.
For someone to put a smile back on my face.
But what I want most of all. The thing I wish for most of all.
Is to love.
I wish for my heart to no longer be so cold and full of hate.
How can I ever be loved if I can't love someone in return?
How can I ever trust with my heat if it was hurt so many times before?

Ianna N. Wyatt, Grade 8
Labrae Middle School

Sense of Sorrow

I have lost someone.
That I really love.
I never got to say good-bye or sorry.
Sorry for asking for to much.
Sorry for making my little remarks.
Sorry for saying I hate you.
Sorry for not saying I love you more often.
Sorry for not wanting to talk.
My gut hurts every time someone says your name.
I feel as if your still here.
My heart tells me you are.
My heads tells me your not.
You've saved so many lives.
Lives of people you didn't even know.
So why couldn't someone do the same for you.
My heart has a big whole where you use to be.
My love for you is stronger.
You are my father.
You always will be.
And I will never forget you.

Natasha Hess, Grade 9
Western High School

My Sister

My sister can be annoying
She is always in my way
She has her bossy moods
They happen every day
She has this crazy boyfriend
He is weird in every way
I don't think their relationship will last another day
But then again they are perfect for each other
So maybe he can stay.

Katelynn Melrose, Grade 8
Licking Valley Middle School

Nature's Song

As I climb a tree, I look behind me,
Two trees sawing to the rhyme of nature's song.
I look forward, two pine trees tall and wise
Birds sit in them waiting until the time
Is just right to fly away.
They sing along with the trees,
Leaves flying through the air keeping the beat
Nature's song
The tree moves rapidly,
Keeping up with the leaves,
I jump down three branches.
I look back again.
The trees still dancing,
Nature's song
The birds sing happily while they fly
To their new beginnings
Nature's song.

Elizabeth Hope Johnson, Grade 7
Western Reserve Middle School

Three Glasses of Wine

He was afraid he wouldn't get home in time,
After having three glasses of wine.
He realized he would be home here soon,
But couldn't see anything in the light of the moon.

He was turning on a pretty sharp curve,
When all of the sudden there was a big swerve.
He was lying there for about an hour,
Right underneath the Eiffel Tower.

Soon people started to crowd around,
It seemed like so much more people than the whole town.
About the time the ambulance came,
Everything started to sound the same.

He soon died later that night,
Not long after he lost his sight.
It seemed like it took so much more time,
And all because of three glasses of wine.

Miranda Sams, Grade 7
Field Jr High School

The Teacher

I walk to the classroom,
in the back of my mind the rumors loom.
Had she killed her son?
Should she return to the loony bin from which she had come?

I was shaking as I approached,
arriving with my planner as I had been coached.
I entered the room with her at the door,
and flinched as she scolded, nearly leaving the floor.

"I hope you would not do something as elementary,
as bringing no paper, class time is not FREE!"
I flew out the door in a skittish mood,
my first impression had not been good.

I returned quite quickly,
feeling a little sickly.
The class had begun,
and I hoped I'd be alive when it was done.

David Geresy, Grade 8
Hopewell Jr High School

The Sunset

Magnificent strokes of orange painted across the sky
Mingle with pinks, reds, yellows
A watercolor painting
By a heavenly artist
Slowly the sun falls down toward Earth
As darkness approaches
The painting fades
And only the moon remains

Kristina Thompsen, Grade 8
St Christopher Elementary School

Water
crystal, clear, and blue
available to the world
refreshing, healthy
Andrew Kovich, Grade 8
Incarnation School

Terror
Terror
Fills my body.
My face turns white.
My hands get sweaty.
My knees start to knock.
Knock, knock, knock.

I hear noises
Everywhere.
I can't escape.
I see shadows,
Strange yet familiar.

Mist swirls at my feet.
I twist and turn.
Cacophonies of voices fill my head.
I start to run,
But can't get away.
I run faster and faster.

I sit up
As raindrops run like tears
Down my window.
Dream.
Haley Kurtz, Grade 8
Hopewell Jr High School

Autumn Is…
The sight of leaves falling from the trees.
They call out to us with crunch, crunch.
The Halloween candy is fun to munch.
Autumn smells of turkey, so good to eat.
And feels like leaves tickling my feet.
AUTUMN IS HERE!
Brian Hawthorne, Grade 7
West Branch Middle School

Soldier
Here we go again in a war,
Fighting for our rights,
Forced to leave our families,
Wondering if we'll live to see them,
Wondering if what we're doing,
Is going to improve lives,
Better stop that thinking,
And hope we'll live to see,
Yet another day.
Trent Bowers, Grade 7
Glenwood Middle School

Ode to My Heart
My heart is like bubble gum chewed and spit out of someone's mouth,
Sometimes my heart can be like a big teddy bear, cuddly and warm,
Sometimes my heart will be like a raging bull, mad and angry,
Sometimes it will act like beautiful butterflies, fluttering around inside of me,
Ode to my beautiful heart.
Amber Mishler, Grade 7
J A Garfield Middle School

The Perfect Christmas
As I woke up to the blanket of snow, over the sleeping ground,
I sprang out of bed and rushed down the hall.
For my eyes have not betrayed me,
Gifts and toys are piled high to the middle of the tree,
And I have a feeling they are all for me.
A new remote control car, and some new Lego sets, just to name a few.
But the more and more I opened,
I still wait for the perfect gift.
The soft brown fur of the small body.
The ears would perk up when you call its name,
Then come running to greet me at the door after school.
The wag of the tail, the warmness of the nose,
The eyes like a pool of water when you look into them.
Then I heard a soft bark and I jumped to surprise.
My mom and dad knowing their love,
Have gotten me a cute little dog,
That I loved forever and ever,
Still to this day, yet all the new gifts,
I have thought about and played with,
My cute little Christmas dog.
John Palumbo, Grade 8
Jackson Middle School

It
Something's always watching me, I can feel it in my spine.
Am I the only one who feels it?
It always seems to come when I wish my life was different,
when I can't stand my normal life anymore.
Is it the same for everyone else?
I've always stuck out of the rest,
like everyone else is water and I'm fire, and they can put me out.
Does anyone else feel that way?
Sometimes I can hear someone talking,
even when everyone else is silent.
Can anyone else hear it?
It tells me that there's something different about me,
something 'special' so to speak.
That I'm someone that is on this earth for a particular reason.
Should I listen to it? Should I ignore it?
Will it bring joy to my life? Will it bring horror?
I guess I'll know when the time comes,
when I'm courageous enough to listen to it.
Will I ever have the courage?
The answer will come when a silent moon glistens in the sky.
When will this happen? I may never know…
Haley Tolle, Grade 7
Fairfield Local Middle School

You

i'm not exactly sure
what love is
but i think i'm feeling it
every time you're around
i get these butterflies
and i could understand, if i got them 'cause
i just met you
but i've been having them for years now.
you've always been there
you're my best friend
and you make me feel different
all the time
you make me feel so
alive.
no one else
can make me feel
like the way you do
and i don't want to
ever love
another.

Katie Keaton, Grade 9
Glen Este High School

A Joyful Time of Year

Winter, winter it's finally here.
There is no longer anything to fear.
Gentle snow, bitter nights,
And all those great snowball fights.
When the temperature rises spring comes fast.
I know deep down winter will not last.
Winter is completely gone, as it seems.
The only snowstorms left are in my dreams.

Topher Garzony, Grade 7
Gesu Elementary School

I Am From

I am from celebrating holidays
From always cooking out
I am from friends and family
From hanging out on the weekends
From my mom and Ashley

I am from "live it, love it, learn it"
From laughing and sleeping all day
I am from music
From wanting and asking
From shopping

I am from "friends before guys always"
From having many best friends
From Cristina, Teny and Maggie
Walking around acting silly

From a lot of "you had to be there moments"

Christy Cowgill, Grade 8
Verity Middle School

A Night Called Halloween

Haunted, very haunted house,
Even scarier than a louse,
Away you'll be blown,
If you intrude all, all alone.
In a house or in a room,
You'll follow a path being scared into gloom.
On a night called Halloween.
You can run but they will catch you,
You can hide but they will find you,
You can scream but they'll still scare you,
On a night called Halloween.
Haunted, very haunted house,
Being hunted like a grouse,
At last you have reached the exit,
Frantically filled with glee,
You have made it through
This haunted, very haunted house alive
On a night called Halloween.

Molly Blomer, Grade 8
Hopewell Jr High School

Happiness

Happiness is the feeling you get,
When you know everything is ok.
It is like when you were a child,
And you lost your first tooth.
It always makes you feel,
Like you have just got an A+,
On your science test.
It is a feeling I will never forget.
And it is always the best the very first time,
And you know exactly what it is.
You are like the sunshine on a rainy day.
Without you the world would be dark and dreary.
Happiness

George Alexander Henderson, Grade 7
Gahanna Middle School East

In the Woods

A navy blue evening has fallen upon the woods
The emerald leaves get dull against the sky
The chirp of the day
Changes to a whisper in the night
And the atmosphere is sprinkled with light
From the shimmer of fireflies lining the sky
Fresh damp dew glazes the ground
Sticking to the mint blades of grass
The amber trees tower above
Giants in a small world
The smell of pine and oak engulfs the air
As the last light dims away
Everything turns still
And evening turns to night
In the woods

Tara Smith, Grade 7
Gahanna Middle School East

Winter

Wintertime is beautiful.
Dressed in white,
Like a bride on her wedding day.
It will bring us together,
All our friends and family.
There are lots of parties.
And many TV specials.
Wintertime is beautiful.

James Elekonich, Grade 7
Gesu Elementary School

What Is Our Flag?

A tattered cloth,
Of red, white, and blue.
With stars and stripes,
What does it mean to you.

What does it stand for,
Colonies and states.
Or much more,
Like war and fights.

How do we show our respect?
What does it represent?

From the War of 1812,
To 2007.
All the things that it shows,
What does it mean to you?

Ashley Goldacker, Grade 7
Glenwood Middle School

The Ride Down

Staring down a lonesome hill,
Wishing I could go uphill.
But nothing now can turn me back,
from the beckoning snowy track.
So I give in to the plea, to the dare,
Not caring about how I'll fare.
And I slide down.

Tottering down on an unstable board,
the wind against me as it roars.
I fear for my own safety now,
Scared of hitting a tree bough.
So I quicken my already speeding pace,
Until I'm breathless like running a race.
And I slide on.

I'm almost down to the end,
With no more bumps to apprehend.
So I don't worry about any sprawling.
And I fall face
down.

Serena Chang, Grade 7
Birchwood School

Facing the Fear

Sweat began to pour from my face like an avalanche.
My body felt cemented.
I awaited the hour when the whole universe would be watching.
A line was said, and I shook as I came out from behind the curtain.
The crowd stared me down as I missed the first line.
I flicked away the embarrassment like it was a fly resting on my flesh.
When I finished talking, the crowd began to roar.
I took a bow while my face was beaming.
I had finally conquered my stage fright!

Paige Barlow, Grade 8
St Christopher Elementary School

For My Older Sister

For my older sister who in the nineties...

Played with me all day long.
Swam in the inflatable pool in the back yard.
Cried when I pulled her hair when she was "exercising."
Blew out my birthday candles and made me cry about it.
Giggled for hours while we played with our puppy.
Sang Jim Croce with me in the car rides to day care
Danced for the video camera my dad always had in his hand.
Ran around playing tag and twirled her hair when she was tired.
Wouldn't sleep unless she knew I was in my bed.

For my older sister who in the two-thousands...

Wildly screams when I take her camera.
Throws a fit when I check her text messages.
Criticizes my sets and tells me they should be better.
Makes fun of me when I fall and annoys me when I want to be alone.
Talks to me all night about school.
Helps me through all my struggles.
Hates when I'm around her and her "high school friends."
Understands why I'm crying even if I don't tell her exactly what's wrong.
Loves me no matter what.

Sara Worthing, Grade 8
St Brendan Elementary School

My Daddy

I miss them, I miss them not. These are the feelings I've fought,
He ignored me most of my life, should I ignore him now?

He pays attention, but yet he doesn't, I used to cry for what he wasn't,
He left me alone but came back, happiness I should not lack.

I don't care anymore, but yet I do, when I was a child he made my dreams true,
But left so early not to return, in that spot grew a Red Fern.

I might be lying or telling the truth, how would you know about my youth.
The man left for he wasn't ready, so I cried he was my daddy.

He returned to my life after 9 years. He would never return, were my fears.
He welcomes me with a smile, I guess it's nice once in a while.

Victoria Ferrell, Grade 7
Meadowbrook Middle School

Tree

I twinkle and shine
Because a brightness is on me
The sun; it makes me look like a diamond star
My limbs twist turn bend
While kids hit and kick me
I am a twizzler; I twist, I turn, I bend
They say I am a beauty because of their hope
But to me I am just a death that has not died
My only beauty; my few leaves, dead, but a beauty to me
The tree
I become a nap with a gift
Having white fall on me
The white comes every year wrapped in crystals
Keeping me warm
In this battlefield of gusts
A wind comes
Whipping on my face
Blows my blanket off
Off to the ground
and sometimes blows it back up to me
The tree

Kayla Giuliani, Grade 7
Boardman Glenwood Middle School

Competition

Makeup, shirts and skirts,
is all part of the sport.
Chanting, dancing, smiling:
fun while it lasts.
But when it's all said and done,
everyone had a blast.
If we throw too hard or not enough
the flyer could end up in a cast.
The judges are watching, grading, and critiquing,
which make us nervous, but still we do our best.
When we are off the stage,
it's our time to rest.
We get a first place medal
and our stomachs can settle.
The excitement lasts a week or two,
and then it's time to travel.
We go to bordering states
and see cheerleaders with unique license plates.

Sara Gordon, Grade 8
Chardon Middle School

Mom

Mom
Heroic, creative
Amazing, loving, caring
Someone who is always there for her kids
Understanding, giving, motivating
Trustworthy, helpful
Mother

Haley Looney, Grade 7
St Jude School

I Am Water

I am water;
Cool, calming, rapid,
And steady.
I am rain; falling as a downpour.
Calming, gentle.
I am a pond;
Still, and quiet.
I am a river;
Rushing, but steady.
A flood;
Drowning, and rapid.
I am what's left on the window after a rain.
Silent and a blur.
I am water;
Cool, calming, rapid,
And steady.

Marina Loy, Grade 7
West Branch Middle School

Ode to My Basketball

Basketball
You are what makes my life perfect
When I go to sleep
I dream about you
When I am in the gym I look for you
So I can hold you close to my heart
Basketball
I dribble you down the court
I pass you then you get passed back to me
I shoot you in the hoop you make us 2 points
Then the other team rebounds you
I chase them to get you back
Basketball
I love you
I'll do anything for you
Whatever
Whenever
However
All I know is
I love you

Kiyara Kinser, Grade 7
West Branch Middle School

Childhood Is

Childhood is learning.
Childhood is growing.
Childhood is watching the bubbles go blowing.
Childhood is picking mom's flowers.
Childhood is building big towers.
Childhood is waiting for Santa for hours and hours.
Childhood is when boo-boos get kisses.
Childhood is when stars get wishes.
Childhood is bliss.
Childhood is waiting to grow up, not knowing what you'll miss.

Tyler McConaha, Grade 7
St Monica Elementary School

Scars

These scars I have,
Help me to remember.
To remember the ones I lost,
To remember the ones I loved.
To remember why I'm here,
To remember how I got here.
As I sit here,
I look at these scars.

These scars I have,
Help to show me where I've been.
To show me what I went through,
To show me what I missed.
To show me the pain,
To show me that I'm human.
As I sit here,
I look at these scars.
Matt Johnson, Grade 9
Badger High School

Today

Today I pray
All worries will be gone
Today I say
All worries will be lost
Today is the day
To forget
Get over
Let everything go
Today is the day
I am new
Don't even start to think
You can change me
Brooke McNeal, Grade 8
Aurora Academy

Harrowing Steps

Walking through the door of evil,
Plunging into the horrific,
Spine-tingling coldness,
My greatest fears awaken.
I am engulfed by
Many who mirror my panic.
I glance at the face
That will be my English Educator.
Harried was I,
When I heard the acuteness
Of her voice.
All that comes
To my quivering lips
Is a simple okay
To her demonic demands.
What a way
To start a terrifying day.
Alexa Brownfield, Grade 8
Hopewell Jr High School

This Last Letter

I sit here quietly writing to you, my dear,
I have tried to find you, I have walked so far,
But the fate of mankind has prevented me from finding you again.
I need you here, love, I need to feel the comfort of your arms.
I cannot go on, I cannot see through this darkness enveloping me.
The monsters, they will never leave,
They are keeping me from reaching you, love.
I cry out to this empty room, my mind filled with despair.
I cannot see anything but this vast darkness,
As outside, these monsters slowly destroy the human race.
There is nothing left that I can do,
For this darkness is surrounding my mind with every passing moment,
I cannot see anything, my dear, and I pray you are safe and warm.
No one can save me, I am alone, I am lost.
The monsters are looming nearer,
And I do not mean to frighten you, love, but never again will you hear my voice.
The fate of the world lingers over this room.
The monsters are here, here inside, they are coming for me,
But I have no strength left to hide.
I'll miss you, love, I'm sorry, I thought you were all I needed,
I'm sorry, you just weren't enough. And these last words are all I have left.
Lexi Perrault, Grade 8
Glenwood Middle School

Ode to the Stars

Each one tells a story and each one has a different meaning.
Whenever I get confused or I need help with something,
I just look up and all the answers are right there.
Sometimes, I think I am alone but then
I just look up and realize I'm never alone.
Stars are like people, each one has different and unique qualities.
If you ever feel like you are not loved or forgotten,
All you need to do is look up at the stars.
Kaitlynn Carr, Grade 7
St Brendan Elementary School

Where I'm From

I am from trampolines and singing all day.
I'm from the mud we were covered in from the creek.

I am from the glasses and funny faces when I was sad.
From the love and kindness of my family.

I am from the remember whens and you had to be theres.
From cheer up and smile.
I am from dancing and singing just to have fun.

I am from Lori and Bud.
Mashed potatoes and gravy.
From the life my uncle lost to the leg my grandfather lost.

Now I remember these moments of my life that then seemed like nothing
but now as I look back they are something very important.
Melinda Dotson, Grade 8
Logan Hocking Middle School

I Am

I am a crazy girl whose life is chocolate and friends.
I wonder how life will be 30 years from now
I hear birds singing and stream water trickling
I see a glorious world where songs don't get stuck in your head.
I want to be able to fly south with the birds in winter
I am a crazy girl whose life is chocolate and friends
I pretend that I am Mary Poppins flying with her umbrella
I feel sorry for all the forgotten eraser shavings
I touch the speaker of my iPod and it tickles my fingers
I worry about being in a small cage forever
I cry when my hot chocolate burns my tongue
I am a crazy girl whose life is chocolate and friends
I understand why snowmen are made
I say the chicken came before the egg
I dream that clouds are marshmallows and we live on them
I try to brush the night sky with my fingertip
I hope someday a woman will become president
I am a crazy girl whose life is chocolate and friends.

Alayna Rowell, Grade 7
Hopewell Loudon Local Elementary School

My Reflection

Where is my *reflection*? I looked into the mirror,
and I see no long shiny teeth
I see no long black coat
I see nothing.
And I wonder, am I real or am I *imaginary*?

Matthew Brown, Grade 8
Clinton Massie Middle School

Silent Night? Yeah Right

Such a fright,
upon my roof,
on a dark and scary night,
could it be just a spoof?

I try to see
what it could be.
It surely wasn't nice,
but could it be just ice,
slipping, falling, who knows where,
just to give me a scare?

Listening, waiting, concentrating.
What could that loud noise be?
Worrying, thinking, panicking,
hoping the object soon would flee.

Then a different sound comes to ear.
This one not bringing as much fear.
This time plop, splish, splash,
not causing as much of a crash.
Just ice we found,
slipping, breaking, melting to the ground.

Christian Roehm, Grade 8
Hopewell Jr High School

The Violet Moon

The violet moon
When it comes out I feel enchanted
It makes everything magical come out to live
You see the light of the magical beasts
You see fairies and witches and wizards all around
You see spell books and magic coming toward you
When the Violet moon comes out for a night light

Caitlyn Seger, Grade 8
Labrae Middle School

All About Me

I am an athletic girl who loves her friends
I wonder what I would do without my friends
I hear the crashing sound of waves
I see volleyballs and basketballs everywhere
I want our team to do well in basketball
I am an athletic girl who loves her friends

I pretend that I am a professional volleyball player
I feel happy when I am with my friends
I touch a basketball and I am excited
I worry about war
I cry when someone I love dies
I am an athletic girl who loves her friends

I understand that to win you have to try
I say that the war should end
I dream of becoming a singer
I try to always be a good friend
I hope me and my friends are friends forever
I am an athletic girl who loves friends

Erin Reinhart-Anez, Grade 7
Hopewell Loudon Local Jr/Sr High School

Tonight's Battle

Goodbye mother, goodbye father, goodbye family and friends.
For tonight is the night
When we'll leave our campsite
And our lives may very well end.

The nerves are winning the battle
In my body and my brain,
It's worse than the thought of the bomb and bullet's
Tough and screaming pain.

The bodies of my fellow soldiers
Will perish before my eyes,
A war is nothing but death and grief
And bloody dreadful lies.

We represent the red, white, and blue
And the eagle's soar,
Tonight I'll be heroic
Even though it's my very first war.

Lauren Alberti, Grade 8
Gesu Elementary School

Piles of Leaves

Piles of colored leaves,
Like sand dunes line the ocean,
Decorate tree lawns.
Matt Dagg, Grade 7
St Paschal Baylon School

The Day We Met

Heart of fire.
No pretending.
Thoughts go higher,
   never descending.
We can be just as beautiful I bet
   as the sun ascending on the lawn.
No, not a sunset.
I'm talking about the crack of dawn.
Oh how I think
   of the day we met.
How I bought you that drink
   on that boat, Silhouette.
I wish that that night
   could have lasted forever.
The City of Lights
   can't compare to your splendor.
Oh how I thank the One up above,
   that I have met you, the one I love.
Jonathan Decipeda, Grade 8
Chardon Middle School

Scareover

At my house for a sleepover,
We thought it would be fun.
Down in my basement,
With a door into darkness.
We were sitting there talking
In the pitch black that surrounded us.
We look over to that door and we hear
A scratching sound in the shadows.
Full of fear we sit there in the darkness,
So scared we could scream.
Behind the door, waiting, watching.
A shadow emerges.
It is a dark figure —
Looming, stalking.
It grows and moves toward us.
Suddenly, it bolts out at us.
We scream like we never have before.
It pounces — my cat.
Samantha Armes, Grade 8
Hopewell Jr High School

Autumn Leaves

The crisp, autumn leaves
Soar overhead like a hawk
Searching for its prey.
Ericka Pugel, Grade 7
St Paschal Baylon School

When I Am Old

When I am old I will take naps every day.
When I am old I will go to very fancy restaurants.
When I am old I will live in a small house.
When I am old I will let my grandkids come over
When I am old I will give my grandkids a lot of Christmas presents.
When I am old I will play with my grandkids if I am healthy
When I am old I will be very happy no matter what.
When I am old I will go on a cross country trip.
When I am old I will go on a lot of vacations.
When I am old I will be a loving husband.
When I am old I will care about how I look.
When I am old I will live in Ohio or Michigan.
When I am old I will take my grandkids to the zoo.
When I am old I will try to find a car that everybody would like.
Tommy Spader, Grade 8
Sacred Heart Elementary School

Childhood Is...

Childhood is playing all day without a care.
Childhood is running away when Mom tries to brush your hair.

Childhood is wanting sweets every day of the week.
Childhood is annoying your mother until her sanity went over its peak.

Childhood is making a new friend every day.
Childhood is being extremely shy, until the company's away.

Childhood is getting up early on Saturdays just to watch cartoons.
Childhood is acting just like a buffoon.

Childhood is going by way too fast.
Childhood is wanting the good times to last.
Maria Rimmel, Grade 7
St Monica Elementary School

World Series of Chess

It is midnight now, and I've been in a ferocious battle for seventeen hours.
Oh, the nervousness!
Millions of people are watching this very game on their televisions.
Should I move left?
Should I move right?
Does he have a bishop waiting to take my knight?
The pondering of every move ages me in hours that seem like years.
He has left his castle open for me to take him. Is this a trap?
Oh, the frustration!
The game must end sometime.
Okay, I think I will take his castle.
I move my piece; take my hand off my queen, but NO!
I had failed to see his knight waiting to take my piece.
What will I do?
I see an opening.
There is a hole in his defense where he moved his knight.
A drop of sweat rolls off my cheek as I carefully move my knight three spaces.
Proudly I declare, "Checkmate!"
Michael McGraw, Grade 8
St Christopher Elementary School

Guitar

Once again, I am here and ever present.
In my lap lays something very important to me.
An exquisite sunset.
Just lying there.
With a pick in my right hand, I am ready to play.

Jay Bryant, Grade 8
St Christopher Elementary School

Long Run

I stand and wait on the sideline,
While I'm waiting I'm stretching
Loosening my muscles
Hoping the defense will do their job
By stopping the other team from scoring, as they do so
The offensive players and I run
Out on to the field towards the huddle
I stand and listen to the quarterback
Tell us the play. I jog to my position, in my three point stance
Waiting and listening without moving
For the quarterback to yell "Hike"
As he does I fake the block
And sneak to the outside, I watch the ball
Come into my hands
I tuck the ball and I run
Running down the sidelines towards the end zone
Shaking defenders off me left and right
I finally reach the end zone with excitement
As the ref blows the whistle and throws his hands up,
I say to myself…I've just scored a TOUCHDOWN

Jared Dyer, Grade 8
St Aloysius Gonzaga School

A Painful Story

When I was just four years old
This painful story was told
It broke my heart I pushed it away
I did not want to hear
I did not want to speak
I did not want to see this painful part of me
What He went through just for us
It is worse than getting an eyeful of dust
How could this be true?
What He did for me and you
What He did for you and me
I cannot believe that painful story
How He died how He gave His pride
How He rose again that painful story
How He was placed upon the cross
With a crown full of thorns upon His head
How He sacrificed His life just for us
That painful story
How He died how He gave His pride
How He rose again
How He sacrificed His life for you and me.

Desiree Alexander, Grade 8
Chardon Middle School

I Miss You

I miss you
and I think about you day and night
I worry about you
but I know you'll be all right
I wonder how things would be if you didn't leave
but I remind myself there's no reason to grieve
I love you so much with all my heart
and I count the days 'till we're not apart
I respect you
No matter what I might say or do
I admire you
because you help our country too
You're what gives me hope, you make me so proud
but to everyone else, you're just a dad in the crowd
Despite what they say, it's all worth the fight
And my future and yours looks incredibly bright

Alyssa Villacres, Grade 9
Hilliard Davidson High School

What Is Sapphire?

Sapphire is the sky without a cloud
Makes people so proud
Sapphire is the ocean calm and still
Makes everyone watch upon a hill
Sapphire is cold
Like the winter which one likes to scold
Sapphire is a ring
When they see it they want to sing
Sapphire, blistering and screaming, too
But on winter mornings the dawns are blue.

Matthew Truex, Grade 7
West Branch Middle School

Beware of the Wolf

There is a wolf in me. With teeth.
Teeth like white-hot steel
Sabers straight out of the fire.
Ready to attack.
It howls like a soldier
Grieving for its lost troops.
It hunts you. It hunts all. To be alone.
It hides behind my joy.
Always waiting to leap out of the shadows.
Beware of the wolf.

Julie Howell, Grade 7
Incarnation School

The Falling Star

I watched a meteor streak through the sky
A blistering ball of light.
Scalding hot and bright as a star
And too beautiful for a price tag.
If wishes are for fools
Then meteors make us clowns.

George Bashour, Grade 8
Birchwood School

Fall

```
      F
       A
        L
         L
          I
           N
            G
```
Waiting
Swirling, twirling
Through air
Broken, ripped
Bang! There's ground
Raked again
Withered away
Wait…
Till next
```
        F
         A
          L
           L
```
To play

Sammy Crain, Grade 8
Licking Valley Middle School

Heroes

Heroes
Brave, courageous
Caring, helping, loving
Doctors, firefighters, policemen, teachers
Comforting, guiding, saving
Knowledgeable, strong
Idol

Erika Emling, Grade 7
St Jude School

City of Sin

My hands are burning
because the light I was holding
has burned down to ash
and now I'm learning
the card player's folding
because he's out of cash
and the things I'm beholding
won't come clear without a flash
There are too many layers
too many prayers and too many players
and the angel's work is so hard
to save all the lost souls
they get dealt one bad card
and they're dying
over something they could never control
they're lying, and good men are trying
but the angels aren't buying in
in the City of Sin

Kate Miller, Grade 8
New Albany Middle School

I Am

I am an outgoing air soft player who loves to play air soft.
I wonder what is going through other people's minds when I attack.
I hear the air soft BB whiz right past me.
I see a bunch of cowards standing in my way.
I want to win all the games that I play.
I am an outgoing air soft player who loves to play air soft.

I pretend that my opponents are weak and scared.
I feel defeat in the palm of my hands.
I touch victory since it is so close.
I worry about getting shot a lot.
I cry when we were so close to victory but then it gets taken away.
I am an outgoing air soft player who loves to play air soft.

I understand that my team can't always win every match.
I say if you don't give 100% then don't expect to succeed.
I dream about air soft guns all the time.
I try 110% when I play air soft.
I hope that my team and I will be the best team in Grove City.
I am an outgoing air soft player who loves to play air soft.

Jerrod Plumly, Grade 8
Jackson Middle School

He's My Homemade Soldier

Nick is a simple minded man, though he is very smart
I knew how his personality would be like, from the very start.

People were always around him, it was like he was in a cage.
But when I was always around him I felt very safe.

But now he's gone and he took that feeling with him,
As soon as he left, the bright lights in our house dimmed.

I still love him, because he's my brother.
But when I'm sad, I'll just think of him as Nick, my homemade soldier.

Racheal Forcier, Grade 7
J A Garfield Middle School

Christmas Morning

I am on the outside looking in.
Out in the cold looking at a fire radiant with red and yellow heat.
The wood crackling as it burns.
I am on the outside looking in.
I see an old dog sleeping comfortably and happy.
Children laughing and playing with their new toys.
I am on the outside looking in.
Mom and dad drinking fresh hot coffee.
I smell fresh breakfast with eggs and pancakes.
I am on the outside looking in.
I see a beautifully decorated tree with pretty ornaments.
I see gift wrapping torn to shreds and boxes opened.
Looking in I see the gold joy on each of their faces.
I wish I could be like them happy and full of joy.

Ken Brewer, Grade 8
Chardon Middle School

I Used to Wait

I used to wait for your call,
Now I don't want you at all.
I used to want you to want me,
Now I just wish you would leave.
I didn't think someone could change that fast
I guess I always knew we wouldn't be.

Megan Hadzinsky, Grade 7
J A Garfield Middle School

A Wonderful Fall Day

The leaves were waving in the wind,
On a crisp fall day.
The leaves were changing color as we spoke.
Crunch, crunch goes the leaves when you take each step.
The cool fall air was like a dream come true.
As I looked inside the TV was on an army commercial.
When I got inside I got warm fast, and took a deep breath.
I got a snack, and then jumped on the couch.
The cupcake I ate was lemony, and creamy like whip cream.
When I got back outside, it was much colder,
And the crisp air was gone.
It was now smoky!
I looked around and saw a fire in the neighbor's yard.
Once I got over there, we started making s'mores.
The s'mores were like cotton candy,
The marshmallow melted in your mouth,
And the chocolate was like a liquid miracle.
I wasn't careful next to the fire.
And I singed my pants.
And that was my fall day!!!!

Kyle Schockman, Grade 7
Incarnation School

Feeling of Accomplishment

I feel nice riding in an open field on my four-wheeler
with wind blowing in my frozen face.
Mud swooshing onto my wet, smelly face
makes me want to ride even harder.
I feel a feeling of great accomplishment
from the nice breeze and beautiful smell of the woods.
Seeing all the animals run and play makes me laugh
and smile a little bit.
Nothing in my mind can make me feel sad or rushed.
When I ride, I am a whole different person, I feel free from
everything around me.
I just know that I ride for the feel of pride,
fun and accomplishment of treating myself to something I enjoy.
Riding with people makes me feel like I am in a movie.
Racing to see who can go faster makes me get an urge to
Just ride the wind and go as fast as the four-wheeler can go.
As the sun sets, I know it's time for me to go back home,
and I get a little sad, but I know I'll be back for more riding.
When I get back, I smell like gas and mud
and that's the way it should be.

Gabrielle O'Donnell, Grade 8
Chardon Middle School

Wreck*

Happy, free,
Few of us know what they would come to be,
Drinks, joints — addicted to these,
We predicted, what others couldn't see.

They wouldn't stop the madness,
We would reply only with sadness.
One line of meth, reckless path,
They were on a horrible wrath.

Faithful night, as high as a kite, so stoned,
Eyes so bright, everyone moaned.
Drive home, what a fright.
People died that faithful night, 2 or 3,
Maybe more, death filled to the core,

A phone call awoken,
Many battered, hearts shattered,
Families broken.
Only a token left of what used to be so real,
Many see what other don't even feel.

Stephie Lollo, Grade 8
Licking Valley Middle School
*Dedicated to those who lost loved ones
because of drugs and alcohol.

Ode to Ketchup

Red,
Gooey,
Slimy,
And gross.
I love this substance more than most.
The ruby red looks,
The shiny, soft feeling,
Who knew something so nasty could be so appealing?
Of all the condiments, I love you the most,
I love your sweet taste when I spread you on toast,
With apples, oranges, hot dogs as well,
Why you taste so amazing, I never could tell.
My friends think I'm crazy, though I'm perfectly sane,
Because without you, food is simply too plain.

Elena Ross, Grade 8
Agnon School

Inside/Outside

Inside I am a rainbow parrot,
Speaking, singing, and squealing.
Outside I am a zooming Corvette,
Always on the move.

Inside I am a spotted Beagle,
Loyal, smart, and loving.
Outside I am dynamite on the Forth of July,
Ready to explode with laughter.

Deanna Gifford, Grade 7
South Range Middle School

An Interesting Sight

The phone rings
Ding-ding-ding
Finish the dishes please,
Says mom
As I walk over
To the sink
I see a very
Strange sight
There are two
Idiotic squirrels running
In circles
Around my backyard
They are chasing each other
Unexpectedly they change
The route they were taking
The reckless squirrels
Climb up the ladder
Leading to the slide
Astonishingly they glide down
The slide together
What an interesting sight.
Jami Aufderbeck, Grade 8
St Aloysius Gonzaga School

Dirt Bike Race

Dirt bikes go so fast
Fast a cheetah catching its prey
12 laps
Is all you need
Give it all you got
You go so high when you ramp
High as the sky
Don't look back
1 lap to go
You're catching the leader
Last turn
Pass them on the outside
Black and white flags
You see them
Getting closer and closer
Crossing the finish line in first place
You won
Hooray!!!!
Leigha Moran, Grade 8
Licking Valley Middle School

Dreams

Dreams
Imaginary, flattering
Sleeping, thinking, hoping
Fantasy, wishing, factual, critical
Unflattering, seeing, being
Actuality, authentic
Reality
Jessica Kaiser, Grade 7
Fort Recovery Middle School

The Traitors

Why does it always start on a cold and gloomy day?
Things never seeming to work your way,
When you have many friends who all but leave you
Just when you think the friendship will stay.

You thought you'd trust them forever,
But it turns out you'll see them never,
When they all but face up and leave you,
You're feeling under the weather.

Many years have gone by,
You remember those days and begin to cry,
For those who went and left you
The pain is as though you might die.

Slowly you drift to the past,
Remembering what a blast,
You and your friends had together before they went away
And now you know the sorrow won't last.

From elementary to high school you are now a young man,
You are full of knowledge and remember things usually don't go as you plan,
Forget those who up and left you, remember your family who will always be there
And make as many new friends as you can!
Mark Sitch, Grade 7
South Range Middle School

In the Barn

I am on the outside of a barn looking in.
I see horses hanging their heads outside of their stalls.
I can see hay being thrown down from the hayloft.

I am on the outside looking in and hear the warm, soft whinnies of little, fuzzy ponies.
I hear oats, sweet feed, and pellets being dumped into hungry horses' feed bins.
I hear horses swishing their tails at unwanted pesky little flies.

I am on the outside looking in, and I am able to smell washed, clean, happy horses.
I smell fresh sawdust being put into very clean stalls.
I can smell the fresh green hay.

I feel joy when I am looking into the barn.
Relaxation and calmness overcome me and all of my worries go away.
Looking into the barn, it seems like the happiest place on Earth.
I hope I never have to leave the barn once I go in.
Ashley Winters, Grade 8
Chardon Middle School

Where I'm From

I'm from the soaring bluebird that makes my heart go wild
I'm from looking out from my porch at the dew that the night brought, to the leaves
I'm from bumble bees buzzing in my ear in spring
I'm from the sweet sap that gets on my hand when I climb our tall pine trees.
I'm from the tulips that burst up in Spring
I'm from all nature.
Shiloh VanOss, Grade 7
J A Garfield Middle School

High Merit Poems – Grades 7, 8, and 9

A Veteran of the Korean War*
I hear bombs going off and fire rises around me.
Shots resound in all directions.
My fellow soldiers are screaming over distressing affliction.
And I, Paul Easton, am half buried under a crumbled wall,
legs distorted awkwardly at an 83 degree angle.

In the hospital with a broken leg and thumb, the pain comes.
I know I still need to keep a stiff upper lip while next to all the other soldiers.
Only three of my ten troops have survived;
I feel the utmost respect for those who died.

I exit my room in search of some fresh air.
I exhale slowly, sinking into a cushioned lounge chair.
Welcome thoughts of home permeate my brain.
I remembered muted voices and strangely familiar sounds.
I am transported back to my last Christmas at home; I was playing the organ.
My family members are convened in a circle; melodious carols ebb upward.

Two years later, standing in Flanders Field,
I visit my friends' graves, perusing the copious names on a wall.
I stumble across a war memorial plaque honoring those who have served and survived.
Next to the several comrades' engraved names,
my eyes fall on a more familiar etching: "Paul Easton."
I am proud and honored to be a veteran.

Evan Webr, Grade 7
South Range Middle School
*As told in part by my grandfather, Paul Easton, before he passed away.

I Am From
I am from the smoke of the burgers grilling.
The taste of grandma's noodles.
The sound of all the kids playing.

I am from the sound of crunching leaves in the woods.
The smell of nature.
The old apple trees in the backyard.
All the time we were hitting the apples with bats, never will miss the old yellow jackets though.

I am from funny and comedy like people.
And smart ones too.
Always a joke then sometimes a smart alec remark.
I'm from the building of demolition derby cars, and mushroom and deer hunting.

I am from the smell of pumpkin pie.
Turkey and stuffing.
From the torn knee my grandpa got.
To the back surgery my dad had.

Looking at old pictures.
Bringing back good and sad memories.
Keeping hold of these moments.
Seeing those faces I do not know.
But will always remember those good memories.

Codi Dennis, Grade 8
Logan Hocking Middle School

Cheetah
Cheetah
Fierce, fast
Sprint, prowling, pouncing
Fast runner, slow-moving
Hiding, walking, sleeping
Slow, creeping
Turtle
Chad Schroer, Grade 7
Fort Recovery Middle School

Reading
R eally
E xciting
A nd
D elightful
I n
N ew
G alaxies
Camilla MacKenzie, Grade 7
St Gertrude School

The Beat of My Heart
My heart
Is beating
With each breath
It's bleeding
You don't know
My pain
You never will
Understand
Don't lead me on
Just to
Tear me down
It's my heart
In your hands
Take care
Of it
I wouldn't do
You wrong
This is my
Heart
It's beating
For you
Mariah Mathes, Grade 9
Glen Este High School

Veteran
Veteran,
Brave, heroic,
Caring, serving, unwavering,
Marine, soldier, hero, defender,
Sacrificing, loving, protecting,
Courageous, honorable,
Grandpa.
Shelby Snow, Grade 7
St Jude School

Childhood Is…
Childhood is being immature.
Childhood is being with family and friends.
Childhood is only having school for a job.
Childhood is having fun.
Childhood is not being an adult.
Childhood is going to the movies with your friends.
Childhood is not having a care in life.
Childhood is being afraid of the dentist.
Childhood is waking up on Christmas morning and rushing
down the steps and seeing all of the presents.
Childhood is playing in the mud and having your mom clean your dirty clothes.
Marcus Murray, Grade 7
St Monica Elementary School

At the Corner
It sits, rumbling at the corner.
The scruffy, rundown being inside stares as if he is hypnotized.
A noxious scent surrounds the vicinity.

I walk slowly, shakily towards it.
Still, it idles, expecting a sudden getaway.
I can hear the engine running as clear as I can hear my fearful heart beating.
The man inside remains staring directly at me with the eyes of an eagle.

Mortified, I pause at a friendly neighbor's home.
I don't dare to cross the street.

Waiting…
Waiting…
Waiting…

Finally, the garbage truck speeds away, leaving a horrid odor behind.
A sense of relief and security fills the air.

The nightmare is over.
Tori Meyer, Grade 8
Hopewell Jr High School

A Cold Winter Night
The snow comes whispering
down to the cold winter ground.
The snowman that was built earlier
is now starting to catch more sparkling snow.
The snow sits quietly on the ground,
just like little kids getting ready to listen to a Christmas story.
On the roof you hear a big thump.
You look out the foggy window and see inches of snow.
When you walk into the living room
you see piles of gifts waiting to be opened.
You open the door and a swipe of cold air smacked you in the face.
It is Christmas!
The odor coming off the candle is very soothing.
You sit around the crackling fire opening gifts!
Kalene Kennedy, Grade 7
Gahanna Middle School East

Curse of Love

This crazy mixed up feeling,
That no one can control.
It makes your heart beat faster,
It flows throughout your soul.

This feeling makes you happy,
This feeling makes you sad.
This feeling makes you go insane,
This feeling makes you mad.

I feel this feeling quite a lot,
Sometimes I wish it would just stop.
This weird, wild emotion could drive
Anyone up a wall.

It's the curse called love that give everyone a pain.
It's brilliant, it's great, it's bad and it's horrible.
This curse has found me, and now I can't escape.

Kim White, Grade 8
Licking Valley Middle School

Without Me

You are gone
You are gone
You are gone
I can't do anything about it
My teardrops fall one by one
I didn't even get to tell you goodbye
Why did you leave?
I don't want you to leave this world without me

Laurna Curby, Grade 7
J A Garfield Middle School

Beautiful

I try so hard to lose weight,
But I guess it's my fate.
God wanted me big and beautiful,
And he gave me a good soul,
A good soul only good people can see,
Not the kind of people who want to judge me.
It used to hurt me on the in, what's on the out,
And now I see there's nothing to hurt about.
So big or small,
Thick or thin,
My man's gonna love me in the skin I'm in.

Jennifer Tejeda, Grade 9
Life Skills Center of Youngstown

My Grandma's House

It looks like a cottage in the 1800's
With the scent of freshly baked pumpkin pie
Breathing the aroma of the leaves outside
People talking in the kitchen
Feeling the smooth soft counter tops

Katie Baytos, Grade 7
South Range Middle School

For the Love of My Parents

If I lost them what would I do?
Who would I turn to when I'm down and blue?
I love my parents very much so
and they love me back for this I know,

We've been through it all, the rain and the snow,
and no matter what they have not let me go.
I know my parents care about me
because they will cross the widest ocean and the deepest sea.

We've had the worst times when we are apart
but they were still there and filled in my heart.
I am so apologetic for the pain that I caused
and yet they accept me with all my flaws.

We've had lots of love lost
but I'll pay it all back no matter the cost.
I can't explain the way I feel
but I'm very thankful for them and that is real.

We've overcome all the trials and tribulations
and at the end of the day we've all had a cheerful sensation.
If I lost them what would I do?
Who would I turn to when I'm down and blue?

Jasmine Cherry, Grade 9
Norwalk High School

Snowflakes

A snowflake falls on the ground
Until it is white all around
It happens this time every year
That is when people start with cheer
It signals the start of a season
When people are more thankful for a good reason
They are thankful for another great year
Of hope, happiness, and cheer

Eric Mihaly, Grade 7
Gesu Elementary School

Yes, That's Me

Yes, that's me, look and you'll see
My hair is blond
My eyes are blue
My arms are reaching out for you
My hands are soft as a soft teddy bear
My heart is very warm
I'm a person who can help
I will never let you down
My friends tell me I'm a nice person to be around
I live to have fun
I hope to have fun each and every day
I dream of happy things
It's all clear as can be.
That's positively, absolutely me.

Caitlin Stephenson, Grade 7
Waterloo Middle School

Green

Green is the color of
John Deere tractors
And the pasture
Green is the color of hay
That farmers feed to cows.
Green is the color of money
And my favorite NFL team
The Green Bay Packers.
Green is my favorite color.
Dustin Campbell, Grade 7
West Branch Middle School

Best Friends Forever

Wedding rings are to everlasting love as
BFF rings are to everlasting friendship

Filled with emotion
Tears and devotion
To make specialness grow
To see love show

Though such simple thing
Just a simple plastic ring
Best friends forever seems real
Nothing compared, it's a sealed deal

A person that's always there for you
In a lifetime, only a few
A shoulder to cry
Not ending till they die

Wedding rings are to everlasting love as
BFF rings are to everlasting friendship
Darci Gruenwald, Grade 8
St Clement Elementary School

Hunting

Gutting a deer
Shooting a turkey,
Bam!
Killing my first squirrel
That's what's fun about hunting,
Hiking a mile,
Man I'm beat!
Shooting a goose,
Bang!
That's what's fun about hunting,
Climbing up a tree stand,
I can see for a mile!
Finding my first deer rub,
The bark's scraped clean!
That's what's fun about
Hunting
Zach Ruggles, Grade 7
West Branch Middle School

The Woods

As I trudge
Through the woods
I stop and listen
To the murmur of the trees
Frozen in time
Even with life about it
The squirrels start running
As the hunters come through
The timid deer sighted
All is quiet
Aim is taken
All of the sudden
The bellow of the gun
The deer starts to slip away
The shot misses
The deer escapes into the trees
Nicholas Concilla, Grade 7
Gahanna Middle School East

Crunch

C rackling crescents
R estfully rotating
U nder umbrellas
N ear nature's
C reatively colored
H aven of leaves
Taylor Lintz, Grade 7
St Brendan Elementary School

It Will Have to Wait

My bare feet brush the
Cold rough stone porch
My ears and mind relax at the
Soothing sound of the crickets
Talking to each other

My eyes catch a golden leaf
Fluttering to the ground
My nose and lungs take in
And enjoy the crisp fresh air
Of the cool evening

I flinch at the rustling sound
Noise of the nocturnal animals
Scurrying in the treetops

Vroom — vroom — vroom!
A choppy sound of a leaf blower
Snaps me back to reality

Ugh! Dinner time
My perfect evening
Will have to wait
Alexandra Bohme, Grade 7
Incarnation School

There's My Ship

There's my ship,
She is out,
On the water,
The white mast,
Has been soaked,
By the sea,
The Captain,
Is standing,
On the deck,
Where would we be,
If there wasn't wind?
Even though,
It gets a little crazy,
Out at sea,
We can all be strong,
I'll make sure,
That we will make it through this,
We are strong and are free,
We can stand anything,
We can't back down,
We'll make it to the shore.
Laura Deall, Grade 7
Glenwood Middle School

Spiders Wait

In this dark corner
with long, silky strings
I wait longingly for a
wayward bug's wings!
Elissa Kuharich, Grade 7
St Michael School

Sailor's Love

Gone away, sail away,
Across a field of blue.
Away from my home,
And away from my girl Sue.

Eyes of true blue,
And a heart of true gold.
They both come sailing after me,
To her my heart was sold.

The sea of blue water,
Calls out my name.
I'm sorry my dear,
To the call of the sea, I came.

Sitting here above the sail,
The wind stirs my hair.
The love of the sea,
Wraps itself around me.
Jessica Blubaugh, Grade 7
Glenwood Middle School

High Merit Poems – Grades 7, 8, and 9

An Empty Bottle
Empty bottles lie on the table
making one thirsty
for what was in them before
All the fights and temper tantrums —
a relationship that is permanently damaged
by carelessness, selfishness, and stupid mistakes.
For this reason, the bottles are now empty.
One thinks that by making the bottles empty,
the relationship will heal.
It will only heal when the bottles are all gone
and you have changed your attitude and perspective
to please others.
The bottle will someday be full again
due to caring, compassion, and thoughtfulness.
Cassie Lipp, Grade 8
St Clement Elementary School

The Reef
As the clear-sky day turned into the storm of the century,
the sailors continued to their port in Miami.
As the wind started to blow, and the clouds started to blacken
a crew member asked, "Should we stop, Captain?"
"No we can make it!" the captain screamed back;
his words were lost with a loud smack
of a box falling from an uppermost cabinet,
which opened as it tipped back and forth with the ship.

The winds jolted the ship as they grew stronger.
The crew knew the ship wouldn't last much longer.
They knew they'd probably end up at the bottom of the ocean,
but they focused on working so that wouldn't be the end.
The wrecked ship started its slow descent,
and with it on its trip were its unfortunate men.
The ship had crashed silently into a hidden reef,
but no one noticed so now it sleeps in the deep.
Ann O'Brien, Grade 8
Chardon Middle School

Compass
If I were a compass
I'd lead your heart to mine
I'd make it so you always knew where I was to find
If I were a compass
I'd lead you on your way
To a happy life and happy kids
To die happy some day
If I were a compass
I'd tell you south from north
I'd tell you where not to go
And when to sally forth
If I were a compass
I'd show you left from right and
Lead you on your own way
In the darkest nights
Cloe Cooper, Grade 7
Gahanna Middle School East

For My Friend Who in The…
For my friend who in the nineties…

Enjoyed waking up and watching cartoons
Scarfed down eggs like no tomorrow
Who got in fights and forgot them after
Played video games for hours
Climbed trees and then jumped down
Jumped into leaf piles after running around the yard
Explored through the forest not scared of anything
Who found about the two-way phone when offline
Loved playing who wants to be a millionaire online

For my friend who in the two thousands…

Liked running around the beach
Ran around our house until he found something
Bought a new video game every week
Could not wait until Christmas
Never stop forgiving me after something
Was so happy after I beat a level on Mario
Bawled his eyes out when I moved away
Stop calling after I moved to Middle Burg Heights
Jacob Wallenhorst, Grade 8
St Brendan Elementary School

Last Lap
Adrenaline
Last chance to win
Roaring engines from quads are deafening
White flag out, last lap, last chance for glory
Battle turn for turn, jump for jump
No margin for error…mess up it's all over
You swing left he swings left, it's a battle till the end…
Never give up…blisters piercing your hands…
Two turns left…never letting up on the throttle…
Fifth gear pinned till the end…
The final turn he goes right…
Dive in left for all your might
You jump the finish line first…
Victory has never tasted so sweet…
Never give up…
Evan Cockrell, Grade 8
Licking Valley Middle School

The Promise
The promise forgotten in cloudy skies
The whistling wind never dies

I hope the clouds soon fade
Because the promise you promised has been on delay

The sun is now out and the promise has come about
And now you're with me, and I'm with you,
and that is something I would never doubt.
Abbie Brown, Grade 7
J A Garfield Middle School

Fall

I walk outside
to look around
and all I see
are leaves falling
down
down
down
all I know is
it won't be
long before
all the leaves
are all but gone

Stephanie Schnipke, Grade 7
Miller City-New Cleveland School

Orange Is

Orange is lava from a volcano,
Fiery flowers, and flames
Orange like a grapefruit
Orange is a fire burning bright
Like a sunset every night
Orange is rage, hot-tempered and angry
Orange reminds me of Halloween
The pumpkins, candy and decorations
He will commit arson
Burning everything
Orange is tough and uncontrollable,
Just like me.

Cade Neiser, Grade 7
West Branch Middle School

Knives

So cold so sharp
So alone
Where were we when
Your trust was
Ripped to pieces
Heartbroken?
We are but selfish mortals,
Cruel and vain.
Who are we to
Enslave your brethren
Look upon you and
Your ice eyes.
Gods and goddesses
Fallen from their sacred pedestal.
So unfeeling.

Caroline Bao, Grade 8
New Albany Middle School

Brown Leaf

The pretty brown leaf,
Is swaying in the fierce wind
Trying to hold on

Alyssa Snyder, Grade 7
St Paschal Baylon School

Angels

Tiny faces looking down on us and seeing around
for a place for us to stay
and be found
Tears in their eyes as they find a place for us to begin
our life
as they fly away and find their place
that is all that matters in this case
giving us love, hope and guidance
That will keep us out of trouble and anything that comes our way
Angels will always be there to help you find your way

Allie Gushura, Grade 7
J A Garfield Middle School

I…

I am a clever person who's fanatic about horses.
I wonder if there is another world, waiting to be explored.
I hear a buzzing sound when danger is in the air.
I see two fawns playing "chase" in the field.
I want a graceful horse that can run like the wind.
I am a clever person who's fanatic about horses.

I pretend I'm floating on a cloud with no weight on my shoulders.
I feel the faintest pounding of a mustang's hooves.
I touch the plush fur of a polar bear's back.
I worry about ill-treated children.
I cry when no one else is there for someone.
I am a clever person who's fanatic about horses.

I understand life is not fair.
I say nature should be left alone.
I dream of a black horse swiftly moving in the morning mist.
I try to make a difference in the world.
I hope I own a Quarter-Horse ranch someday.
I am a clever person who is fanatic about horses.

Logan Frank, Grade 7
Hopewell Loudon Local Jr/Sr High School

Open Your Mind to Nature

On a typical day I wake up to see,
the nature-popping out and looking at me.
I see the leaves all vivid and bright.
I think to myself what a beautiful sight.
I notice the trickle of snowflakes descending,
Which makes me realize that the leaves will soon be ending.
I get out of my bed to get ready but my thinking was steady.
All I could think about was the nature all beautiful and bright.
I also think about the beautiful cold winter night.
All of the leaves soon to be falling,
Which gives a hint that winter is calling.
Winter is for many a favorite part of the year,
Which makes me expect that the winter coats and hot chocolate are soon to be near.
I open my mind to nature that cold winter day.
I realize that details and beauties instead of just to lay.

Reilly Condon, Grade 8
Chardon Middle School

Imagination

In my imagination my mind blows *wild*,
And we are not talking about it being *mild!*
In my imagination, it is inside,
In my mind!
Not just any ordinary *kind!*
In my imagination, it's *a great* place to be.
In my imagination it is *ME!*

Nattalie Porcase, Grade 7
J A Garfield Middle School

For the First Time

For the first time he held my hand,
And made me feel like he was my only man,
For the first time he said "I Love You,"
And I knew in my heart I loved him too.

The first time he looked in my eyes,
I knew he'd be the one who'd never say "goodbye,"
For the first time…in a long time,
I found the one who makes me shine.

For the first time I've fallen in love,
And he made me rise above,
All that people said,
And I know our love won't shed.

For the first time I've done something right,
I found the one who'll hold me tight,
The one who'll be there every day,
And for the first time, I can finally stay

Ashley Jett, Grade 8
Fairfield Local Middle School

My Best Friend*

You died when I was just nine years old.
In the casket lay my father limp and cold.

His blank blue eyes staring back at me.
How could this be?

I know you have gone to bed with the Lord.
But sometimes I need you more.

Life has gotten really hard without you,
but I have to get through.

I really miss you, dad, I really do.
No one even has a clue,
of the love we shared
and how much you cared

You were my best friend,
But your life had to come to and end.

Aron Carver, Grade 7
J A Garfield Middle School
*Dedicated to my father Barry Carver 1960-2004

Where Happiness Is

One day we'll find a place where happiness is.
Yes, where the candy grows,
And where the chocolate river flows,
One day, one day.

One day we'll find a place where the happiness is.
Where the money trees give,
Where it is impossible to make a sin,
Yes, one day, one day.

Oh we'll find a place where the happiness is.
No children crying,
No drug buying,
The happiest place on Earth!

Chelsea Finney, Grade 8
Chardon Middle School

Death

I was right there by her casket crying
I missed her the next day
I used to go to her house almost every day
now, she watches over every move I make
tellin' me right from wrong
I hope someday I will see her again
then, we can talk all we want and watch over our loved ones
death is nothing to joke around with, death is serious
if you think death is cool
then think about people who love you and will miss you
death isn't fun
believe me I know

Aliesha Mills, Grade 8
Riverview East Academy

Darkness

Darkness,
crowding spaces,
it fills ever so fast,
creating the fear of the unknown.
Take it away I say.
Take it away.
No one hears me.
Darkness,
deep deep darkness.
I try to run from it,
I can feel the adrenaline.
Terror beholds me with its chilling arms like a tomb,
I run faster.
I hit something.
I stop dead in my tracks,
too scared to move
A beam of light suddenly appears,
stripping fear from my body
I see the figure
"Oh. Hi mom."

Katya Seitz, Grade 9
Magnificat High School

Autumn

Autumn Giants in the breeze
Leaves of gold, leaves of green
Colors of fall, present and past
Swaying in the wind

Autumn streams ever flowing
Spinning, twirling
Never ceasing
Running with the wind

Autumn sounds, voices of fall
Children are laughing, trees are stirring
Dogs are barking, birds are chirping
Carried by the wind

Autumn changes, Nature's breath
Chills both land and sky
Nature's hand stealthily moving
Making what? The wind

Chris Marino, Grade 7
Incarnation School

Lonely Purple

Purple is lonely
It's the color not most would think of
It sits in the crayon box
While red, blue, and yellow
Are always being used

Purple is lonely
When it is used
It's for the gentlest reasons
It feels like a soft silk gown

Purple is like lavender buds
Falling into a peaceful pond
Filled with water lilies

If you could taste purple
It would be as calming
And gentle as herbal tea
On a cool spring day

Tamara Bruening, Grade 8
Chardon Middle School

Winter

Winter signs are showing.
The leaves are all gone.
The wind is blowing,
With the snowfall at dawn.
The water is freezing.
Although it's hard to understand,
To some the winter weather is pleasing.
Winter is truly a wonderland.

Jordan Casper, Grade 7
Gesu Elementary School

Amanda, That's Me

Amanda Shepka, that's my name,
fulfilling my dreams is my game.
This poem is all about me, this is my life, this is who I am.
People may judge, they may stare,
but just being me is the main idea.
My life is mainly about family, friends, and education of course,
but without my faith I would be lost.
When I feel down and out of place, I turned to friends for advice.
My friends are very dear to me, Steph, Alexis, Angela, and Becca,
they are always there, they always care.
"Never give up, never let go, hold on tight," is what my parents always say,
and, of course, I always listen, which is why I'm where I am today.
Everywhere I go, I make a memory,
then I look back, laugh, and remember those times.
My advice for others is live your life the way you want,
life is a precious gift that doesn't last forever.
Now, when I look back, reread my poem,
thinking everything is perfect until I realize that this poem isn't over,
it's still going on, just like me,
still living my life.

Amanda Shepka, Grade 8
St Monica Elementary School

Victory

To be the best I can be
To be patient until you get your chance
To make peace with your opponent
To leave the race with dignity
To be successful at the finish line
To achieve is to believe
To thrive in other sports
To find the best in others
To find the best in yourself
To get down low and beat my cousin Ricky in the Soap Box Derby
This is a victory

Brittany Ann Schneider, Grade 7
South Range Middle School

The Best Set of Friends

From the second that I met you, I knew we had something special
You were there when I needed you
I was there for you too
Sometimes friends let me down but I could always turn to you
You never left me when others did
You stuck by me through thick and thin
Through fights and fun I took care of you and you took care of me
Whenever I needed a favor, a good laugh, or even just someone to talk to,
You always listened and helped in any way that you could
You could always make me laugh no matter what the situation was
Sometimes we picked on each other, but we never meant it
Basically whatever happened in the past or happens in the present or future
I'll stick with you and I know that you'll stick with me
We make the best set of friends

Emily Mason, Grade 8
Logan Hocking Middle School

Teachers

T he best way of learning is from a teacher. Teachers can be
E xciting and very outgoing. They can also be very, very
A nxious to see most of their students. They can be very
C heerful and can root for the class when there is a game. They
H elp students when they struggle with a class. Teachers
E ncourage us students to do our best and to
R espect our classmates, teachers and ourselves
S ome are strict but most are very, very wonderful!

Paige Stachowski, Grade 7
J A Garfield Middle School

Growing Up

Growing up has its ups and downs
It can be fun when you receive more privileges
And it can be tough when more is expected
It can be fun when you have more to do
And it can be tough when you are alone
Through the good, the bad, the happy, and the sad
Everyone must grow up
Problems will come and mistakes will be made
But soon it may come to an end

Taylor Swint, Grade 8
Gesu Elementary School

Sounds of Fall

Leaves crunch beneath our feet,
Animals scurry looking for their last harvest,
Pies baking in the oven,
Wind blowing through the trees,
Children playing in the leaves.

Mary Margaret Whitney, Grade 8
St Michael School

Friends Are Forever

Friends are forever
Boys are whatever.
This is a motto
Every girl should follow.
Your friends will always be there for you
For whatever you want to do.
They will cheer you on
They will make a smile from your frown.
Memories, movies
Sleepovers, parties…
…You're with your friends through it all.
You know there will always be someone you can call.
Through good times and bad,
Crying and laughing is to be had.
When I laugh, you laugh.
When I am hurt, and am embarrassed to cry,
You cry for me.
So now,
I just want you to *always* remember…
Friends *are* forever!

Olivia Burgei, Grade 7
Miller City-New Cleveland School

A Standing Ovation

Extremely tired
The banging of the crowd, hitting the bleachers
Confidence flowing away slowly
Yelling of my coach and teammates
Other team surging towards me
2 seconds later
The ball sinks into the net
Thunderous applause
the crowd erupts
Gasping for air
Heart beating faster and faster
Determination growing
WHOOSH
A standing ovation

Tyra Nichols, Grade 7
St Clement Elementary School

Black Out

Running fast, running slow, how fast will I go?
Going past foes, I know
Just how far will I go?
1 more mile now I know, this is the chance I just might blow
Getting darker…
Going slower…
Getting tired…
Legs on fire…
Will crushing…

I wake up
I found out
What I've done
Ran too hard, "Have I won?"
"I am sorry, you are done."
I blacked out
On the run.

Kevin Copley, Grade 8
Licking Valley Middle School

All About Me

I am a future firefighter who likes dogs
I wonder how many stars there are
I hear the sirens from miles away
I see the school burning down
I am a future firefighter who likes dogs
I pretend to rescue people from buildings
I feel the worry of people trapped in buildings
I worry for people's lives
I cry for the peoples lives lost in the line of duty
I am a future firefighter who likes dogs
I understand lives will be lost
I say 'If I can help, I will'
I dream of saving as many people as I can
I hope to make my dream come true
I am a future firefighter who likes dogs

Tyler Ruble, Grade 7
Hopewell Loudon Local Jr/Sr High School

Veterans' Day

To a veteran an American flag might say thank you for defending me
and your contribution will not be forgotten.
To a Red Cross volunteer an American flag might say thank you for
giving up your time to help those in need.
To a recruit it might symbolize what he is risking his life for.
To a draft dodger it might say what is your problem and why don't you fight?
To a small child it might not mean a thing.
But to an immigrant it will represent everything a new life, new friends, and a new job.
But to a veteran an American flag might say thank you for defending
me and your contribution will not be forgotten.

Scott Zilke, Grade 8
Western Reserve Middle School

Childhood Is…

Childhood is swimming on a beach without any sunscreen, then regretting it.
Childhood is writing on the walls even though you know better.
Childhood is making endless snow angels on a snow day.
Childhood is locking yourself in your room for the whole day because you're mad at your parents.
Childhood is wanting that brand new bike in the store window.
Childhood is building up the courage to finally take off your training wheels.
Childhood is waiting for the tooth fairy to take away your tooth to her castle of teeth.
Childhood is wanting to be everything like your dad.
Childhood is starting off eating clean, then it all ends up on your face.
Childhood is counting every moment till your birthday.

Jacob Katzenmeyer, Grade 7
St Monica Elementary School

Consideration

Consideration is
To show sportsmanship when you play football or baseball
To let ladies go first through a restaurant door on a date
To not leave your friends behind when you do something sweet and exciting
To help the younger 4th graders when they are being picked on by biggest stronger kids
To speak up for your best friend when they're getting in trouble by an authority for something they didn't do
To not speak when my favorite teacher Mrs. Goodwin is talking
To follow instructions that your parents give you even if you don't want to
To listen to your friend when they tell stories even if they're run-on sentences or just plain stupid
To stop annoying someone with a weird noise when they tell you to stop
This is to show consideration

Tim Nichols, Grade 7
South Range Middle School

Where I'm From

I am from rag dolls, Oxidol, and Vick's cough syrup.
I am from a log cabin with wooden floors surrounded by fields.
I am from the apple tree where we used to sit and eat apples all day long.
I am from the family picnics we had all the time, (rain or shine).
I am from the "Well I declares" and the "Quite a bits."
I am from the Baptist and having to go to church every Sunday.
I am from Cattlesburg, Kentucky, popcorn, and tomatoes.
I am from Sophie, my mom who was a very hard worker in the kitchen.
I am from the big maple tree in my backyard in Kentucky.
I am from working in the fields with my siblings, also bringing in wood and water to cook.
I am from the family keepsakes we had in a special place and most importantly my Bible.

Ashley VanCamp, Grade 7
West Branch Middle School

High Merit Poems – Grades 7, 8, and 9

What Time Is It!?

Scan your tickets in at the gate,
To watch the game you'll have to wait,
You have a sign and a glove,
You're here to cheer for the team you love,
Hot dogs ready on the grill,
Soon there will be stomachs to fill,
Popcorn, candy, a souvenir cup,
Everyone hopes their team won't give up,
A little longer and it will start,
Everyone can feel the beat of your heart,
Can you believe they made it this far,
Now every player will be a star,
You find your seat in the upper deck,
The field from there looks like a speck,
It doesn't matter you're here for the thrill,
Of watching your team show off its skill,
You look around and see that the stadium's full,
Fans know the game won't be dull,
The game's about to start, but don't have a cow,
What time is it!? It's game time now!

Gregory Kula, Grade 8
St Michael School

Snow Day

A snow day starts off by waking up at ten
Then you go downstairs and hang out in the den
You get breakfast, donuts and juice.

Call your friends, see what's happ'n
They'll ask their parents if they can go sledd'n
You'll get a ride from your mom
All the way, the park and back
Drop your friends on the way
You'll be tired after a long winter's day.

You wake up the next morning to see if you have a delay
Looks like you'll be staring at the chalkboard all day.

Sean Hickey, Grade 7
Gesu Elementary School

I Am on the Outside Looking In

I am on the outside of their group looking in.
They are all there for each other, I want that.
They have a friend "love" for each other, I want that.
They involve me but I know it's fake.
I am on the outside looking in.
They talk behind my back; they think I don't see it.
They think I don't see them, laughing at me.
They think I don't hear them, talking behind my back.
I am on the outside looking in.
I see the way they act around me.
I hear how fake they are to me.
I am on the outside looking in.
I want what they have.

Samantha Wagner, Grade 8
Chardon Middle School

Winter Time Again

Winter nights cold and snowy.
Christmas lights twinkling in the night.
Hot cider and cookies flow freely.
It is wintertime again.

Snow covers the ground while children are playing.
Snowballs flying and snowmen appearing.
Families gather around a glowing fire.
It is wintertime again.

Anthony Taylor, Grade 7
Gesu Elementary School

I Can't Write a Poem

I can't write a poem
No, this is insane!
I can't deal with this stress on my brain
Rhythm is impossible
Rhyming's confusing
Bet you think this is amusing
Wasted so much time,
Deadline's almost here!
Probably have this done by this time next year
No…I *can't* write a poem
It really isn't fair!
Why in the world should I really care?
I'd rather do other things
Like go out with my friends
Instead I'm stuck in her until this ends
Now I read this over,
I really feel dumb,
Turns out…I *can* write a poem!

Hayley Lavender, Grade 8
Licking Valley Middle School

The Call

The phone rang at night;
It gave me quite a fright;
My dad was in serious trouble;
My mom left to help on the double.

Nothing this bad should ever happen to me;
The situation gave me anything but glee;
My dad had gotten hit, and then he crashed;
His car was almost totaled and nearly smashed.

My dad was wearing his belt;
But much pain was probably felt.
It occurred at a nearby traffic light,
On this dreadful and horrific night.

Since he had hit his head;
My mom sent him straight to bed.
Just like that he could have been gone;
But he is still alive, and he lives on.

Billy Barren, Grade 8
Hopewell Jr High School

Forgotten and Broken

A broken doll
Hoping…
Waiting…
For a new friend
Collecting dust
Upon a high shelf
All alone
Quietly awaiting
Wearing her pink polka-dot dress
A crack on her face
Where all her teardrops pour
The old porcelain doll
Remembers her old friend
Once joyful
Once loving
Memories of all good times
Never to hear again
From her old friend
A broken doll
Hoping…
Waiting…

Hannah Ungruhe, Grade 8
St Clement Elementary School

Run Run Away

After a fight,
In the middle of night
I run, run away
Can't during the day
Running is like a flight
To my aunt's street and house
But neither she or her spouse
Answered the door
Twelve houses more
Quiet as a mouse
"Can I come in?"
Tears poke my eyes like a pin
"I need to call my dad,
Things are going bad."
She knows what has been
To the police station we go
Am I a run away? No!
I'm with my dad
Because I felt so mad
My step-dad is my foe.

Carly McLoskey, Grade 7
J A Garfield Middle School

Thunderstorms

Two tambourines smashing together
Rain pouring down my face
My shoes are drenched
My brain is rattled
An umbrella would help

Maci Anello, Grade 8
St Clement Elementary School

The Forest of Angels

Gliding through the forest the moon was a shining blue bubble glowing in the sky.
The forest around me was illuminated in a magical blue light.
The tree tops above green as emeralds and pure as light.
The small waterfalls like falling blue silk, rhyming in time to the fairies' dance.
The wind blowing in time with my soft, white, beating wings
that seemed an endless canopy of white feathers.
The song of the dragon rings clear and true like a lament, piercing the heart.
The diamonds in the white caves sparkle bright, true and valiantly.
This is the forest of angels.

Katarina Fiely, Grade 7
Incarnation School

The Side You Never See

You always wondered why I did, what I did that day,
But I've told you all I know, I've said what I have to say.
I was wrong what happened, it will never be right.
But you won't listen, you won't see the light.

It's not my way, it's not what I do;
So get over it, go cry, boo hoo, boo hoo.
I don't make fun of other people, I just don't like to try to bend,
Or break or crack their soul.

But of course you say, "It's all pretend!"
"A joke, a laugh, a game!" Until someone does it to your friend.
Then it's "What? How dare they! Do they wanna pick a fight?
They really shouldn't have messed with us. They're going down tonight."

But have you ever wondered, what it's like on the other end.
The side that can barely protect, the side that's not your friend?
So there you go, that's why.
And if you can't understand, then I guess it's good-bye.

I can't just stand around,
Doing nothing.
So I've started caring,
I'm doing something.

Molly Honecker, Grade 8
Clinton Massie Middle School

Winter Time

I'm on the inside looking out.
Looking out at the cold, windy, and very snowy night.
Being glad to be in my nice warm log cabin.
Drinking a cup of hot creamy dark chocolate.
I'm on the inside looking out.
Out at the white powdery snow blowing in the wind.
Out at the white covered pine trees.
Out at the snow glittering in the firelight from behind me.
I'm on the inside looking out.
Looking at the frost on the frozen window sill.
Looking at the fog on the window from my warm breath with the scent of hot cocoa.
Looking at my grandmother coming to the door with lots of presents.
I'm on the inside looking out.

Kyle Meier, Grade 8
Chardon Middle School

High Merit Poems – Grades 7, 8, and 9

Soldier

Click, clack goes his boots as he walks down the hall
He looks at his reflection in the clean polished wall
He had a rugged face with a scar on his jaw
It came from a knife, not a tooth or a claw.

He remembered a time, a special one,
When he patrolled a village in the hot desert sun.
And the blue-eyed girl,
And the blue-eyed girl.

She'd been kicking and screaming in the arms of a man,
A hooded fellow with a knife in his hand.
With courage the soldier leapt on his back
And freed the girl from his fiendish attack.

Unfortunately, on his cheek he had felt
A trickle of blood from a gaping welt.
He then slugged the man, who fell to the ground.
From behind the soldier came a tiny sound.

"Thanks for saving me from that man in the hood,
You can have dinner at my house, you really should."
The soldier took her hand and thought
You did good, man, you did good.

Alex Getz, Grade 8
Christ the King Catholic School

Through My Eyes

I see fake people walking,
I see hurt disappointed people,
I see fear, anger, and confusion,
I see different people everyday,
I see success to those who work,
I see nice personalities behind hard faces,
I see love in which no one knows,
I see through my eyes

Cassandra Hickey, Grade 8
Forest Park Elementary School

Beach

As you lay on the beach,
Hear the birds and the waves,
Feel the hot breeze running down,
When you surf in the water
And you wipe out, it's fun
No worries no responsibilities,
Just you, the quiet,
Just dream about being free to do whatever you want,
As you lay feel the sand in your hands and feet,
There is a turtle coming right up to you,
Doesn't run away just sits right next to you,
Beach a place to do whatever you want to,
Be open, don't worry

Alyssa Moore, Grade 8
Miller City-New Cleveland School

The Human Race

We all belong to a thing called the human race…
How fitting that name is.
We all race.
Constantly,
Subconsciously.
Forever, we're racing.
Isn't that new car, house, superficial item…
So glamorous?
Race for it.
Race to acquire —
Acquire status, tangible items, things that fade.
The only unfading thing is love.
We righteously race to attain love;
But what's the point when it ends in hatred; divorce?
Love is nothing more than an illusion now.
The media is breaking through to you,
Where people become objects and objects become people.
Racing to become beautiful. Plastic surgery galore.
Beauty is found in reality, not in plastic replicas.
Our lives represent the longest, toughest race in history.
We just don't realize it.

Emily Grieshop, Grade 9
Coldwater Jr-Sr High School

Love, Music, Passion

Love is a musical note,
played gently and smoothly
Love is the beat
to a slow moving song
played with ease

Passion is love and feeling
like the way you smile at him and those beautiful eyes
Passion is dancing
delicately and pleasurably

Love is passion, feeling, emotions
for that one special person
Love is the music in you
breaking free and dancing full heartedly
spreading to the one you secretly smile at from afar
Love is him finally returning that same smile

Jordan Carruthers, Grade 8
Clinton Massie Middle School

What Is Love?

Love is the care that parents give their children,
The trust friends have in each other,
The adoration that husbands give their wives and
The affection they return,
The devotion teachers give their students,
And the passion good leaders give their countries.
Love is when God sent His only Son to die in place of us.
That is Love.

A.J. Kmetz, Grade 8
Wooster Christian School

My Game

Homeruns, grand slams, and base hits
Helmets, visors, bats and mitts
Running, diving, making the catch
For us the opponent is no match.
Yes, yes, yes we win the game
Where's the trophy I can claim?

Emily Rybak, Grade 7
J A Garfield Middle School

Life

Life is too short
To live wrong.
You will have to live life right
As you live along.
It might be long
Or if not, short.
Don't lead yourself to pain,
And live life sore.
Life is like a game
Or a puzzle of pain.
Take your time
To finish the game.
Take one step,
Or just take two,
But take the right ones,
And lead yourself through.

Aykee Henderson, Grade 8
Hope Academy Cathedral Campus

Football

Stepping onto the field
Crowd going bananas
Heart pounding
Stomach boiling
First quarter
Scorching day

Game almost over
Fourth quarter
Heart like an extinct volcano
Tensions high
Setting the play
Hike
Long pass to the ten-yard line
Pass is good

Tackle
Ball on the ten-yard line
Touchdown Spartans
Field goal to end the game
Kick
The kick is good

Spartans win the game

Shawn Napier, Grade 7
St Clement Elementary School

Autumn

I am on the inside looking out.
I see the wonderful color changed leaves.
I feel the wind blowing through my open window.
I smell the fresh taste of apple cider coming from the orchard next to my house.
I am on the inside looking out.
I see little kids raking the leaves and then jumping in them.
I hear the laughter of little children screaming with their friends.
I listen to the wind trying to tell me a secret.
I am on the inside looking out.
I see most of the leaves getting bagged up.
I hope there are some leaves left for me to play in when I finish my homework.

Alyssa Fox, Grade 8
Chardon Middle School

The Veterans

They risk their lives
They risk some body parts
All to save America
And the people in it.
They come together
For what they believe
Working like a team
With people they might not like
All for the rights of Americans.

Eating only heated foods
And chewing gum
They only have letters
To connect to their family.
Many people may think they are crazy
We do not
We pray and pray
Hoping they live
Through the dangers that await them

Imagine if you were the one out there with a gun and armor
Millions of people depending on you imagine the stress
Also imagine the kids with their dads in the war, imagine the worry.

Sarah Sabol, Grade 7
South Range Middle School

Childhood Is

Childhood is when your parents give you nicknames.
Childhood is dancing like no one is watching.
Childhood is fries, hot dogs, hamburgers, and candy.
Childhood is making up games when you are bored.
Childhood is playing with Barbies.
Childhood is having sleepovers, and gossiping.
Childhood is not caring what you are wearing.
Childhood is drinking luke-warm hot chocolate on a cold winter day.
Childhood is bugging your brothers and sisters to play with you.
Childhood is learning how to add and subtract.
Childhood is special to me.

Jacqueline Brown, Grade 7
St Monica Elementary School

The Magnificence of a Brilliant Soul

The shining authenticity of a figure that lies only upon the fourth dimension,
    creates a masterpiece of sheet brilliance, otherwise known as a lovable soul.
Those spectacular few
    the defenders of a stability to our universe
    tend to cause a tremble, force the wind to utter a shutter and make the earth spin round.
For the sound
    that even dogs cannot hear.
For the smell
    that cannot even send a scent to a deer
From ear to ear
    there are eyes
    That could never visibly see such a thing.
For something so great
    that if it could be felt
    there would never be enough words among the universe to even start to describe
    how amazingly wonderful a simple touch can do.
For those who contain such effulgent structures have been, or will be praised with utmost
    enlightenment from the gods, or just the average being from any part of the world.
For souls are possessed
    as they hold the key to the not-yet discovered alternate universe called the fourth dimension,
    furthermore known as the most powerful beings of our time, or of time itself.

Lisa Radl, Grade 8
Chardon Middle School

Green Is…

Green is mistletoe
And blinking Christmas lights.
The color of Christmas trees.
The color of ornaments, wrapping paper, and bows.
It's the color you see when the grass is peeping through the snow.

It's the color of stockings, ribbons, teddy bears, and books.
The color of toys that make little kids smile.
The color you see when you sneak down the stairs on Christmas Eve to see what you got.

Green is gumballs, stocking stuffers, and skittles.
Color of fabric.
Green is the color of pine needles left in your carpet long after Christmas is gone.

TyAnn Gray, Grade 8
Clinton Massie Middle School

I Remember

I remember…
Like pages in a scrapbook signed by best friends
Words like fresh, swizz, and burn.
Two famous people Monica Abbot and Zac Effron
Anybody's iPods, cell phones, and colorful Rocketdog shoes
The place in the story where Count Olaf kidnapped the Baudalaires
The injury when I got four stitches from running into the wall in the dark.
Our house was "in the hood" my hometown in Youngstown
And outside it was surrounded by semi trucks and cars speeding like cheetahs.
The sound of my screeching siblings when they would attempt to aggravate me as I talk on the phone with my friends.
Anyone who was brave enough to ask for help, not caring about being embarrassed.

Carly DeRose, Grade 7
South Range Middle School

Vanishing Visitor

In my cousin's dark house,
It was late at night.
The doorknob turned,
And filled us with fright.

Who was this visitor,
Standing at the door?
Our fear was rising,
Like an ascending black balloon.

Everyone is asleep,
We sit here and weep.
Darkness is all around us,
And footsteps surround us.

Shaking with terror,
We go to the hall,
And downstairs to Grandma,
To find there was no one at all.

Lauren Haller, Grade 8
Hopewell Jr High School

Mosquitoes

annoying insect
buzzing pesky blood sucker
spray spray go away

Mitchell Haber, Grade 8
Incarnation School

Shroud of Black

There is a town
Shrouded in black
The ones who once lived here
Are not coming back
Debris has been scattered
Disaster has hit
And the souls of all lost
Will never forget

Devastated and hurt
By friend and foe
Of what reward
No one shall know
Alone sits a child
Tattered and worn
Tears soaked his face
As he sat and mourned

This lone little child
Puts out a hurt sound
His efforts are lost
No one's around

Remember the price of war

Julia Pullins, Grade 9
Berne Union High School

Veteran's Day

As night fell I lay in my hammock,
Worrying about what would happen to me that next day.
I think of my family at home,
How much they miss me and worry for my safety.

My sister and brother say that they dream about me,
Which makes me feel more pain inside.
I then think of my mom and dad,
How they miss holding me in their arms when I was younger.

Calling me their little girl, telling me that I will always be safe,
But tonight I sit in the darkness.
Waiting to be back home to be loved,
As my heart breaks into millions of pieces every waking moment.

Alexis Popa, Grade 7
South Range Middle School

Love

Love can be sweet
Love can be cruel
But sometimes love can be unpleasantly rude
You can feel joy
You can feel pain
It is not a game
Love can be real but only if you want it to
Love can be fake if you don't know what to do
Especially if you're with the wrong person
Believe me it's true!
I've been there and been back
Love is strong
You wouldn't want to come back
You can love, love so much you feel like you're on top of the world
When you fall out of love It's like you fell all the way to hell
You can do nothing but yell
Love is something everyone wants in life
It's just a game of give and take
Love don't come easy, and you don't want it to be fake
So wait for your love can be true
You might not find anybody, but somebody might find you.

Briel Ward, Grade 8
Riverview East Academy

My Memories

I remember,
Like a page in a Heartland book,
Words like thoroughbred, mare, and gelding,
Two famous people were Ty, and Amy Fleming,
Anybody's saddle, bridle, and blanket,
The place in the story where everyone is scared,
The injury in the Heartland book when the barn collapsed on Ty,
Our house was a two-story white farmhouse,
And outside it was two barns and pastures,
The sound of horses running as they play,
Anyone who sees a horse should want to ride.

Nicole Proverbs, Grade 7
South Range Middle School

High Merit Poems – Grades 7, 8, and 9

Two Paths, One Choice
Decisions, choices, and the emotions of others
Take the wrong path and you'll hurt another
Confusing? definitely but it's all in the game of life
Sometimes though the choice you make
Will just be like cutting a brick with a butter knife
Don't worry, you'll make it just follow your heart
If you make the right choice it will set you apart
From the others who came to this path not so long ago
But did not know which way to go
They attempted to go around
But soon found out that what goes up must always come down
Amy Miller, Grade 8
Pike Delta York Middle School

Troops
They live with no warmth
They can run out of food and lose their appetite
They can be split from their families
They won't see their families again for a while

Stay strong
Fight for freedom
Believe
I honor you one day a year
You have lived so we can too
I have a million thoughts about your safety

For us,
We thank you for serving,
And we appreciate the things you have done for us
I see the plane in the sky
Flying flying away
Is it leaving for Iraq?

Soldiers go away
Over night to fight
For what we call
Freedom!!!
Kylie Keller, Grade 7
South Range Middle School

On the Outside Looking into a Box
I am on the outside looking in.
I am looking at a box full of familiar faces.
I see backstabbers, guilt and regret.
I see fake tans and bleach blonde hair.
I am on the outside looking in a box full of unhappy souls.
I see fakeness and cowards worried about being accepted.
I hear gossip and the cries of those who it is about.
I see an outer shell that I wish I could break off of those people.
I see people trying to get out but being pushed back in.
I see people trying to get in but are pushed back out.
I am on the outside looking in a box.
I've never been so happy to be on the outside looking in.
Lizy Golias, Grade 8
Chardon Middle School

The Clumsy Ghost
One night when I was all alone,
Listening the TV's monotonous drone,
I heard a tap-tapping at my door.
The tap turned into a pound;
This noise it did confound
For no visitor did I expect
In my mind I did resurrect
Images of some fiendish host come to visit me!!!
Then there came a scratching
And what I feared was an unlatching
At a window near the door. As I ran to fetch a bat,
I stepped on the tail of my cat;
I jumped about a foot and saw something the color of soot
Run through my yard in the back
Into our trampoline this specter did smack.
It let out a yell, and as it fell
I caught sight of something familiar.
The top of this ghost's head
Was ever so red and I thought with a scoff
As it ran off
That my friends were rather uncouth!!!
Kyle Souders, Grade 8
Hopewell Jr High School

Football
Life is a football game.
Fans cheering on the players.
The game begins with the kickoff.
The start of a new adventure.
A time when the players hope to achieve that big move,
the many plays to follow.
To try and find a pathway to break into.
One wrong decision to make or break your chance at victory.
If you try your best, you can achieve many goals.
But every game must end with a win or a loss.
Jerry Jansen, Grade 7
St Brendan Elementary School

First Class Jerk
I love to talk during math,
I usually make people laugh.
And when the teacher turns around,
there is not a sound.
We continue on with my most hated class,
this is probably because I never, ever pass.
I begin to chatter,
and again the teacher looks.
I ask what is the matter.
He points at my closed books.
Somehow I am discovered,
and the class receives more work.
Then I am ignored and treated
just like a first class jerk.
Brandi Gerschutz, Grade 7
Miller City-New Cleveland School

The Sun

Light bright orange sphere
In the turquoise sky up high
Glaring towards Earth

Chris Rieser, Grade 8
Incarnation School

The Broken Key

Lying there
A broken key
Old but not rusted
A painted heart peeling
Broken in half never to be used again
The key is love
To love to open the hearts of others
To reveal the secrets of your life
Will it ever be fixed

Michael Turner, Grade 8
St Clement Elementary School

The Song

Super silly songs she sings…
Notes not noise now…
Lyrics sung so slowly…
Perfect pitch playing profoundly…
Words written while whistling…
About antelopes eating ants…
Beat-bopping toe-tapping,
Rhythm-moving sound…
Flowing freely, feeling fancy…
Pulling, prodding, pushing you
along…
Song slowing…
Quickly quieting…
Coming calmly to an end…

Kelsey Niehauser, Grade 8
St Jude School

Purpose

My soul purpose in life
I would have to say
is not to have everything I want,
but to make somebody's day.
To make people happy
is the best thing in the world,
but how many people can I make smile?

I try to make as many
people as I can smile,
but that's all I can do.
As many as I can.
I can't do more.
I can't do less.
No matter how hard I try
That's as good as it gets.

Beth Taphous, Grade 8
Chardon Middle School

With These Words

With these words
So fast and desperate,
I ask, no plead,
You do not speak one word
For it shall be tainted with the sounds
Of footsteps marching to the tune of our demise.
Give them not the satisfaction
Of hearing us in this fraction
Of a second that I make this wretched speech — no no!
Do not speak, for the word will be the bullet that destroys me,
Do not speak, lest it destroy us both.
We shall be silence, no, nonexistence,
There will be nothing here to find.
The metal in my hand can settle the clamor in my mind
And give them no example to make of me
But is it worth it, is it worth it
To wait for the agents of our destruction —
Or to take destiny and make my world fade by my own hand?
I do not know — I do not know, but for this second I do know one thing —
I ask, no plead,
You do not speak one word.

Andrew Boudon, Grade 9
St Edward High School

The Night Sky

The night sky is a vast and endless quilt
expertly sewn together by a master of his trade.
The stars are carefully stitched into a deep, velvet backdrop with a
single creamy drop.
Then
Suddenly, it all
Vanishes
To reveal the bright promising rays of tomorrow.
But do not worry for when the sun goes down a new creation will
reveal itself once again.

Elisabeth Beard, Grade 7
Gahanna Middle School East

Dreams

Dreams are wide,
    dreams are big.
Dreams are the imagination and creativity in someone's head.
It gets them jumbled up in fantasy worlds,
    especially little kids.
There're kings and queens and mystery lands that no one has been to.
There are fairies who fly on the night's sky.
They glow in the dark, with a yellow so bright,
    they could be your night light.
But then again kids get scared of the nightmares they had
    and the monsters under the bed.
Those monsters keep them from falling asleep.
Dreams could be whatever you want,
    just dig deep and wide and you'll find your fantasy world.

Stephanie Molnar, Grade 8
Chardon Middle School

Grandma's House

A speckled dog sprinting my way,
A warm greeting and how are you as I walk through her door.
The kitchen counters gliding beneath my fingers as I walk past,
The subtle creek of the stairs leading me to the top,
A sweet aroma of strawberries lingers through the house.

Jessie Bolen, Grade 7
South Range Middle School

Military

Darkness surrounds me, a new grunt,
Hearing the nonstop crying and screaming
Of wounded troops,
Once they were beloved by everyone

Grandpa stuck with it every day
He didn't know what to expect
It was not for his benefit
But for the freedom of others
In America

Everything is so loud
It hurts my ears
All I can hear is
Screaming,
Crying,
Explosions

The never-ending war of pain
Of tears
Of sadness
When is this going to end?
We want freedom
Not death

Rachel Coler, Grade 7
South Range Middle School

Back in Hamersville

When I was young in Hamersville
  I used to visit my grandma
    and stay with her all day and play.
When I was young in Hamersville
  my family would have a family reunion
    and we would spend the whole day together.
Later, I would go to my dad's and sit around the fire
  roasting marshmallows around back.
When I was young in Hamersville
  we would go swimming at my dad's
    and stay up late watching movies and eating popcorn.
Afterward, we would go outside and catch lightning bugs.
When I was young in Hamersville
  I always felt happy
    because I was around my family.
And that was always enough.

Jessica Young, Grade 7
Hamersville Elementary and Middle School

The Kid Across My Face

Number 97, the kid across my face
  has a mean face
  he thinks he's going over me
  I'm ready to stand and fight
  I put my mean face on, too
    look eye to eye
  ready for down…set…go
   the quarterback yelling
  hoping I protect him, I do too

He calls, "GO!"
  we go for each other
 both pushing with all our might
  dirt and mud flinging everywhere
quarterback moves around, look for his man
    I'm still stopping number 97
   fans cheering, hoping for a score
   quarterback throws, perfect pass
  thanks to the perfect protection I gave
the ball sailing in the air into the receiver hands
        SCORE, WIN
      because *I* blocked number 97

Drake McArtor, Grade 8
Licking Valley Middle School

Who I Am

I am just a girl who is almost fourteen,
  screaming and yelling is my thing.
I am a cheerleader, that's what I do best,
I do well in science, but not so well on tests.
Fergie is who I admire because she can sing,
  My favorite food is chicken wings.
  I resemble a Convertible Corvette,
    'cuz I'm cool and laid back.
If you're looking for me, I'll be at the mall,
 You can reach me by just giving me a call.
My mom calls me Megpie, my dad calls me Pumpkin,
  Sometimes my uncle calls me a Munchkin.
    Being kind and helpful is how I am.
   One kind of food I despise is lamb.
  I have a fear of bugs, especially spiders,
    I look up to heroes like firefighters.
My three best friends and I will be friends till we're old,
This is me, who I am, I'm just a girl whose story was just told.
        My name is Meghan!

Meghan Dikowicz, Grade 8
St Monica Elementary School

The Ocean

The smell of the ocean
Is a sweet but gentle potion
The warm sand melts softly between your toes
While being in your summer clothes
No noises not even a motion

Katie Boeckman, Grade 8
Incarnation School

One Single Rose
All I want
Is one single rose
And the guy
Who hands it to me.
Shelby Mae Baker, Grade 8
Labrae Middle School

Wide Ocean
I skipped a rock far
across the open ocean
and it sank real fast
Tommy Hollis, Grade 7
St Paschal Baylon School

Inferno Leaves
Red, orange, and gold leaves
Like inferno in the trees
Blazing throughout fall
Thomas King, Grade 7
St Paschal Baylon School

On the Inside
I am on the inside looking out
I see all these people around caving in
I don't have any space
I hear all this gossip
And feel in a rush
The bell is going to ring
And I will be late
I am on the inside looking out
Everything is going 'round
Left right, up down
I have no way to go
I have no one to listen
I need to go this way
To get my books?
To get to class?
I am on the inside looking out
I want to go I want to run
I want to be free of my responsibilities
Of my friends of my life
I am on the inside looking out
I wish I could be let out
Samantha Kuzmic, Grade 8
Chardon Middle School

Halloween/Christmas
Halloween
Gruesome, insane
Chilling, frightening, haunting
Goblins, ghouls, celebration, Santa
Snowing, giving, caroling
Fancy, glorious
Christmas
Becca Stricker, Grade 8
Incarnation School

What I've Learned
I've learned that being smart enough
won't help you when you really need it.
I've learned that if you have talent,
you should share it with others.
I've learned that if you play a sport well,
then you should teach others who aren't that good.
I've learned that the love your family has
won't ever change as you get older.
I've learned that if you have one friend,
you will be happy, and if you have two friends,
you will have a lifetime worth of laughs.
I've learned that happiness is the joy in life,
you should enjoy it while you can.
I've learned that hardships happen every day,
but you should make the most of the day any ways.
I've learned that time passes with every moment — good or bad—
time won't stop for anyone.
I've learned that with times comes responsibility,
you need to make the most of your time now.
I've learned that when life goes on,
you should make the most of life today.
Katie Stroup, Grade 8
Sacred Heart Elementary School

All About Me
I am 13 and an 8th grader at St. Monica School
Chinese is my favorite food
I am just one goofy girl that loves to make other people laugh
But hearing kids brag and seeing them cheat, just makes me sad
People say I resemble a money 'cause I act just funny
My dream is to be a doctor to help my fellow people
My walk is pretty sluggish, I'm usually in the back
Slimy snakes and crawling bugs make my skin tickle
People tell me I act blonde when I do something dumb
Playing sports is my passion and fast pitch is so fun
You can see my tongue sticking out when I concentrate too much
Drawing and writing are just not for me
My favorite colors are anything neon and orange
People say I am clumsy 'cause I am always tripping or dropping something
This is me, an ordinary teen, it's me Becca Bode
Rebecca Bode, Grade 8
St Monica Elementary School

My Sport
V ery real; and fun.
O utrageously tough; and hard work.
L oose feeling; like nothing else in the world matters.
L ike nothing could go wrong I bump, set, and spike.
E xhausting; but greatly appreciated.
Y ou have to be pushed in order to work towards that one word, pro.
B uilds confidence in my soul after a victory.
A n amazing energizer for kids.
L azy? Not a chance.
L ack of effort, means no win, which means no team work.
Johna Tigner, Grade 8
Licking Valley Middle School

Wind

The wind is so wondrous as it flows through the air.
I love the sweet feeling as it blows through my hair.
It whispers to me, about many things,
from the mountains, oceans, lakes and trees.
It's the feeling of hope,
Not the feeling of doubt.
It's a feeling I simply can't live without.
It cools me off like a nice cold drink,
like a simple glass of water from the sink.
It takes we away when I'm feeling bad.
It reminds me of times when I was glad.
The wind is a friend that blows at my back.
It fills me with the confidence that I lack.
It's a feeling that I can't quite describe,
but when I feel it I'm more than alive.

Shannon Dagg, Grade 8
Chardon Middle School

Teammates

A hand has five individual fingers
that close into one united fist,
Like five players on the basketball court
Battling and giving each other support.

Hours of practice, sweat and tears,
My team has developed over the years.
Achievements, trophies, and medals from the past
Appreciated, but it's our memories that will last.

Through all the wins and losses we share,
In the end, my teammates are friends who care.

Halle Herringshaw, Grade 8
Chardon Middle School

Sad Is Black

Sad is black like deep space filled with obsidian
It digs through my heart
It reminds me of the time my relative died
It makes me want to take a trip to heaven

DJ Wooten, Grade 7
Incarnation School

The Tear

That's what happened,
on that December day.
Not a single tear welled up in her eye,
not even her fear could make her cry.
She couldn't speak,
for everything she knew became so bleak
In the corner of her eye,
she could not see
the light she felt from her head to her feet.
In a single moment things would change,
that's when she knew things would never be the same.

Alexandra Merriman, Grade 8
Clinton Massie Middle School

Football

We were at our Lisbon game,
our record was two-for-0
our cheerleaders cheering
they were cheering go-go-go.

It was second quarter with us in the lead,
there was a fumble on the play so I pick it up and run
the whole team behind me, and cheering on the sidelines
while I think in my head "It's my turn to have fun."

In the end we won
with the score at thirty-zero
while the team eats cupcakes
we pick up our trash and go.

Scott Smith, Grade 7
South Range Middle School

We Thank Our Troops

We thank our troops for all the things they've done,
even if it was with a gun.
We thank our troops for freedom,
even though we are sometimes not free.
We thank our troops for going to Iraq,
but that was because we were under attack.
As I lie in bed and think about all that they've done,
I realize that they didn't do it for themselves,
but for the United States of America and America's citizens.

Karlie Lomax, Grade 8
Labrae Middle School

Pink Is a Smile

Pink is
A beautiful sunset
Filled with pink lemonade
And flamingos
And pink toes
But when day turns to night;
Pink becomes a summer night
Filled with emotion.

Pink is the feeling you get
The day your baby is born
When you wrap them up in the baby pink
Blanket, but baby turns to child
With a life full of smiles.

Pink is bubble gum
You embarrassingly get caught chewing
During class, but when your
Friend gives you a hug, everything is all right.

Pink is love, faith, and hope
That comes from the heart!

Tiffany Allen, Grade 8
Clinton Massie Middle School

Nature's Beauty
Eerie mist coming off the mountain side
Wind blowing off the trees
White, fluffy clouds in the sky
Red, blue, and yellow flowers
Cold snow lying across the grass
Freshness of the water
Sounds of birds chirping
Peaceful
Mysterious
Joey Anello, Grade 7
St Clement Elementary School

Panic
Breathe,
Breathe.
Wait!
I can't breathe.
PANIC!
Sets in.
The crying starts.
Trapped.
Feeling the pain of holding in.
But …
Can't let it out or else it will hurt worse.
Dizzy.
BLACK …
Starting to see,
Again.
Breathe.
Yes,
I CAN breathe.
Jessika Hall, Grade 8
Hopewell Jr High School

Fall
Leaves are falling
And the wind is blowing
And everything is changing

It is the season of color
And relaxing days
Raking the leaves
While the kids play

It is the season of eating turkey
On that Thanksgiving Day

It is the season of fall
The best season of all
This season of fall is the one I like best
The colors, turkey, and leaves
Are way better than the rest
Rachael Skedel, Grade 8
Chardon Middle School

Every Day
I die and die
Every day
Until you come
And take me away
So I wait
While I debate
Whether or not to go
And whether or not to stay
Anna Sauerwein, Grade 7
Aurora Academy

Rain
The season is cold
Temperature drops like rain
In a cloudy sky
Timmy Hollis, Grade 7
St Paschal Baylon School

Veterans' Day
V ictory for the Americans
E xpected peace forever
T he landing on the beaches on D-Day
E ight bombs
R ifles firing
A way from your family
N ever return home
S aving of the French

D ying for your country
A rriving in Germany
Y our freedom
Ted Nedzelski, Grade 8
Western Reserve Middle School

Snowflake
A snowflake falls down
from the sky. A small diamond
now on the white ground.
Thomas Manning, Grade 8
St Brendan Elementary School

Graves
Lonely graves call for
A visitor to come with
Old memories.
Kayla Jones, Grade 8
St Aloysius Gonzaga School

Lure of Leaves
The leaves in the lake
Floating like red, mad bobbers
Try to stay afloat.
Billy Grebenc, Grade 7
St Paschal Baylon School

Love's Young Dream*
I wait and wait for you to come.
You didn't come yesterday and
I fear you won't come.
You don't come again,
I cry for now I know
you aren't coming at all.
I still wait even though
I think you won't come.
Then, to my surprise you
arrive and you are very sorry.
I give you the drooping flowers
that I have been holding for days.
I'm overjoyed you came
I thought you wouldn't.
Now and forever I will
always believe you will come.
Ariel Burns, Grade 7
Pike Delta York Middle School
**Based on the painting*
by Jennie Augusta Brownescombe

Yellow
Yellow is like
The bright sun
In the late afternoon
Yellow is like
A dandelion
Swaying in the wind
Yellow is like
Fresh squeezed lemonade
Sitting in a cold, sweating glass
Yellow is like
A star at night
Gracefully resting in the sky
Emily McIntyre, Grade 7
Gahanna Middle School East

Veteran's Day
It starts out with a war
Then sometimes ends with death
Some people just have memories
Families are so sad

You can be a veteran
Or maybe a new recruit
But please be safe
For I want you to come home

Fight for our freedom
So we can be safe
For you won't come home tonight
And I will be crying
Alexis Kenney, Grade 7
South Range Middle School

High Merit Poems – Grades 7, 8, and 9

Where I Am From
I am from the country,
From the animals, the dirt, and the pond.
I am from the family horse rides.
I am from the days of baby sitting.
From the hugs, the kisses,
And the yummy pancakes early in the mornings.
To the forgetful memory of my great Aunt Joann.
I'm from the crazy costumes,
The candy and the long parades.
From the trick-or-treat to the scary spooks.
I'm from the mash potatoes and rolls,
My Grandma Kuhn made
From the open heart surgery on my dog
To the good byes we had to say
These memories make up
Who I am today
To the people I've lost
To the people I will meet.
The older I grow,
The new memories will form but,
I will never forget these memories.
Candice Kilbarger, Grade 8
Logan Hocking Middle School

White
White is the freshness of a soft summer air.
The quiet whistle of a white winter's wind.
The softness of a white glistening blanket of snow.
The white wake of an ocean's thundering waves
Crashing down on the white sands of a tropical beach.
The white radiance of the moon shining down on a calm pond.
The blinding white of a winter blizzard
The creamy whiteness of a sweet milkshake.
The minty taste of a white and red candy cane.
The white chill of winter's final snow.
Pat Quinn, Grade 8
Chardon Middle School

Neil Armstrong
Floating above Earth's big open sky,
Was one really brave, smart and cool guy.
We all know he's Neil Armstrong,
He was up there for so very long.

Towards the white clouds did he fly,
To be met with a pitch black sky.
One small step would change his life,
One happy person would be his wife.

Gray dirt, black sky was really all it was,
But man did that place cause quite a buzz.
Back in time on all TV's,
Was sure a spectacle for all to see.
Austin McHugh, Grade 8
Christ the King Catholic School

What I've Learned
I've learned that "good enough,"
is never your best in school or in life.
I've learned parents will and always love you,
no matter how bad you mess up.
I've learned how you play a sport,
can reflect on what kind of person you are.
I've learned that life is too short,
to ever waste a second of it.
I've learned I wish I had one more chance,
to say good-bye to my great-grandpa before he died.
I've learned when you play on a team,
you win and lose as a team not a single person.
I've learned things happen for a reason,
you just have to make the best of it.
I've learned grandparents always know how to cheer you up,
especially when you are having problems at home or school.
I've learned the harder you work for something,
the more you appreciate it.
Tori Reidling, Grade 8
Sacred Heart Elementary School

Veterans
Veterans
Brave, strong
Marching, saluting, leading
Doctors, firefighters, soldiers, police men
Loving, helping, caring
Intelligent, wise
Superheroes
Santiago Gutierrez, Grade 7
St Jude School

Orange
Orange is the autumn leaf
Falling from the tree
Orange is the brain freeze of
Sherbet ice cream on a summer day
Orange is the contagious aroma of
A freshly baked pumpkin pie
Orange is the gratitude we have
And the meals we eat on Thanksgiving Day
Orange is the crackle
And the smoky smell of a newly lit fire
Orange is the cooling relief
And satisfaction of a creamsicle
Orange is the tiny crunch
After we jump into an abundant pile of leaves
Orange is the first bite
Into the juiciest orange from the farm market
Orange is the refreshing feeling
Of making a new friend
Orange is the time we spend with
Our family huddled around the cozy campfire
Orange is everywhere…
Lauren Wells, Grade 8
St Christopher Elementary School

Halloween Night

I throw a sheet upon my head
cut out some eyes and tear the thread,
I scurry past houses with light
After all it's Halloween night

I offer all a dreadful fright
As I scream a boo into the night,
So on I hop from manse to manse
Spinning, twirling, doing my dance

I open my bag filled with treats
And feast upon my gooey eats,
The marshmallows are so sticky
Oh, I'm in heaven so icky!

Breslyn McCrory, Grade 7
Gesu Catholic School

Fire

Peaceful
Crackling
Hot
Gr
ow
in
g
Bright
Strong
Killing
Gr
ow
in
g
Bigger
Ash
Flaming
Gr
ow
in g
Destroying everything in sight

Vonnie Spaulding, Grade 8
Licking Valley Middle School

The Eagles

I fly with the eagles oh so high
In the middle of the desert
Or the middle of the ocean.
The softness of the wind in my face
And the wet sprays of the sea.
Looking for prey
If it be fish or rabbit
Whatever it may be.
A summer of hot days
Or winters with cold nights,
I'm looking for food wherever it may be.

Matt McBride, Grade 8
Chardon Middle School

Firehawk

A beast of rides, it seemed so sly, with all its twists and turns.
I stood aghast, against the blast, as my stomach began to churn.
No turning back now, I was amongst a crowd who seemed more fearless than I.
I took a step, as the line crept, and approached my flying doom.
I felt myself quiver as the ride sent a shiver racing down my spine.
I wanted to quit, just get out of it, but I was out of time.
I approached the line, as my fears aligned, and I began to shake.
Another ride out of sight, and we were almost there.
I wouldn't dare to ever bear
My feelings of distress, but inside I was a mess
As I stepped onto my biggest fear — The flying roller coaster.
We were up the hill, the clicking in my ear beginning to dissipate.
We flew through the air! The hill — the loop —
The triple corkscrew!
The ride stopped, and I was caught with a smile on my face.
I stepped, my heart hurriedly beating
As my fears forever forever rolled away.

Laura Shrake, Grade 8
Hopewell Jr High School

Love

Love is a fluffy, purple-like magenta.
It sounds like a slow, romantic, Luther Vandross song.
It tastes like juicy strawberries dipped in warm, melted milk chocolate.
It smells like a succulent, Guatemalan roast, mocha coffee.
It looks like a bundle of bright pink, light red, crimson orange,
and vivid yellow daisies arranged like a beautiful sunset.
It feels like a refreshing splash of cold water in your face the moment
you wake up in the morning making your heart jump.

Sean Reck, Grade 8
Chardon Middle School

The Perfect Team

My cousin is great in many ways,
She is nice and funny and always brightens up my day.
When we are together the sky's the limit. Any situation that is a boring one,
You can bet we will find a way to make it more fun.
Cheerful, bright, and feeling free,
The two of us make a perfect team.
La, la, la, we sing songs in delight.
We laugh at one another, our singing notes aren't quite right.
Splashes of water as we jump into the lake,
And, screams of delight as we crash into the waves.
Our entertaining experiences never stop.
Cheerful, bright and feeling free,
The two of us make a perfect team.
Our laughs and our shouts of joy continue to roll on.
We continue to grow older but we will never part.
Her bright blonde hair and my dark brown locks
Sway in the wind as we run along the docks.
We will stick together, forever as one, cousins by blood, sisters at heart.
Cheerful, bright, and feeling free,
Facing the world, a perfect team.

Carly Bonfiglio, Grade 8
Christ the King Catholic School

Voting

In the month of December
Inside the voting booths
On the shelf, the book lays
To be opened for your key punch
Since your favorite nominee is running
For Election Day.
Upon him you must vote
With the hopes he will be one of the elect.
Throughout the night,
Beside the TV, we wait patiently
For the final count.

Michelle Marchese, Grade 7
Wooster Christian School

Privation

I watch the golden sun rise above me
And ponder why I should go and tarry.
Cold passersby at me only stare,
And burn me with their lethal glare.
So why should I, over others, worry?
I am the poorest of the population.

As the forgotten of a rapid city;
I work for me-myself only.
To help others like me would be a waste.
Yet, I see others who with haste
Attend to wretches just like me.
They give themselves this obligation.

I ponder this then I suppose
The Samaritan does have his pros.
That helping each other is where it will start,
To improve the world with my small part.
To those that have nothing, my talents I shall dispose.
Anyone can help to stop privation.

Sarah Cunningham, Grade 8
Chardon Middle School

Just Chocolate

Creamy,
    Rich,
        And sensationally yummy.
Smooth,
    Delightful,
        And in my tummy.

It makes my mouth
    Water
        While my jaw opens wide
It tingles my
    Taste-buds
        As it enters inside,

It's really nothing special…just chocolate.

Eddie Ruff, Grade 8
St Christopher Elementary School

Christmas Will Be Lonely

Getting up at four in the morning,
Going to bed at twenty-two hours.

Seeing the fire glowing in their eyes,
Seeking the pain of the left behind.

Looking for the missing men,
Loving the smiles in the picture frame.

Trying to remember the faces, telling them I'm home to stay,
Not realizing what will happen the next day.

Wrinkling up a letter, telling me I can't go home,
Risking the pain of them to mourn.

Writing up a storm, not knowing when another
Chance for these to arrive at home.

Because this Christmas will be just like another day,
Not able to go home with the family and stay.

Underneath the Christmas tree, lie the presents of that soldier
Who can't come home.

Hannah Mowery, Grade 8
Western Reserve Middle School

The Long Lost Have Returned

They experienced the blood
They experienced the great explosions
Of the huge bombs being fired
They ran through the forest getting shot at
Fighting hard, long, and proud
To be an American
Some had been sick
Some had been shot
But the fact they were fighting to be free
Kept them going
They were looking to go home
To be a free country
As they got back off that ship
The country roared with joy
Because of their hard effort
We were free

Dalton Kurtz, Grade 7
South Range Middle School

Dances

Booming music, amassed with teenagers
Crazy boys, flirty girls
Supervising parents watching every step you take.
Fast songs, slow songs
Lights of different shades,
And cute outfits.

Nicole Dona, Grade 8
Incarnation School

The Picture

See this picture on my wall?
It tells the future of us all.
We can't escape our fate,
for we all die on a certain date.
Two paths heaven and hell;
we the dead hear the bell.
Passionless eyes, without dreams,
for that's the way that it seems.
We hate and kill,
but we have no free will.
Our leaders lie.
The followers die.
The rich stand.
The poor fall.
The high walk.
The low crawl.
Are you the one who will crawl?
See this picture on my wall?
It tells the future of us all;
We will all eventually fall.

Shane Lash, Grade 8
Indian Creek Jr High School

Windshield

As white as new fallen snow
The clouds crowd my body
Like white sheets of slender paper
Trees as charismatic as roses
Shine to the sky like the radiant sun
So soft like silk on a lustrous day
The wind exposed on my face
Sharp as a blade skin's me as
I walk like a mouse.

Ciera Chaffee, Grade 7
Wooster Christian School

Sisterly Love

Sisterly love is…
An unbreakable bond,
A hug when you're sad,
An endless circle of love,
But we sometimes get mad.

Sisterly love is…
Never-ending love and compassion,
A warm feeling inside,
A kiss on the cheek,
There are no secrets to hide.

Sisterly love is…
A safe to lock all of your secrets in,
A person to fight,
A lifetime of memories,
A comforter through the night.

Mary DiGeronimo, Grade 8
St Michael School

Purple

Purple is
Lovable and silky like a baby.
The fresh smell of a purple rose, its fragrance filling the air.
The bright purple sky illuminating the entire sky.
The purple sweetness of a sweet grape.
The silky softness of a purple cashmere sweater.
The warm fluffy purple collar worn on a cold, winter day.
The crackling purple leaves as they leave the tree at the first sign of fall.
The purple trees bloom when spring comes.
The gentle purple touch of a nice, caring friend.

Holly Sobole, Grade 8
Chardon Middle School

The Soldier's Pocket

A crinkled and worn photograph of my bright eyed little boy
Sits quietly in my pocket, near my heart.

Gun shots go off, bombs blow up.
I feel the heat on my face,
I run to take cover and wait.
My heart pounds so loud,
Inside my pocket my little boy must hear it too.

High above the clouds my journey is soon about to end,
I reach for my pocket, yes, he's still there.

The plane touches down, I take giant steps scooping up my bright eyed little boy,
He presses against my pocket.
And I hold him close to my heart.

Erica Wagner, Grade 8
Chardon Middle School

Godzilla the Almighty

Crash, bang, BOOM!!!
The people of Hong-Kong are now doomed.
The creature can destroy this city like a piece of pie
And that's no lie.
His size describes his name
And his name is beyond fame.
Who am I talking about?
He is bad inside and out.
He is GODZILLA the Almighty
And he is totally not tiny.
He destroys everything in his way
So don't get in his way, okay.
He is the eighth wonder of the world
And some say he came from the underworld.
He can cause a 100.8 EARTHQUAKE!!!
And to him it is a piece of cake.
The biggest city in the world is his jungle gym
So really nothing can stop him.
Not even the Air Force, Navy, or the US Army
Because it isn't like taking out Barney.
So if you hear him, you better move your hinny because he is GODZILLA the Almighty.

Adam Hart, Grade 8
Incarnation School

High Merit Poems – Grades 7, 8, and 9

What I Like About Autumn
The blazing hot summer's rays
Turn into breezy, cool autumn days
The trees turn bare
And color fills the air
With reds, oranges, yellows and browns
The fallen leaves fill the towns
I hear a crunch with each step I take
This is what I like about autumn

The food is plentiful
Fresh and crisp
The walks through the parks
Are pleasant and brisk
The weather is just right
The changes through the towns are a wonderful sight
Decorations are hung
There are many festivities to be found
This is what I like about autumn

Elizabeth Larkin, Grade 7
Incarnation School

Beauty of a Shell
From the depth of the ocean to the palm of my hand,
There lay a shell of beauty.
The porcelain mirror's roughness
Is softened by the pink hill of color.
The deep valleys on my shell are filled with orangish-brown
Rivers flowing freely between each hill.
Now I take care of this wondrous shell
As the ocean did before me.

Carmen Ramos, Grade 7
Western Reserve Middle School

Signed with a Tear Drop
Writing a letter, trying to feel better
Don't know what to say about what happened that day
Signed with a tear drop

Spent that day, trying to find a way,
Those big brown eyes weren't a disguise
Signed with a tear drop

My mind will say, cry the heart ache away
As my tears are falling, my heart is calling
Signed with a tear drop

Goldie Lox, you're like chicken pox
I try to scratch you away, but the heart ache is hear to stay
Signed with a tear drop

Writing a letter, trying to feel better
Don't know what to say about what happened that day
Signed with a tear drop

Katie White, Grade 8
Licking Valley Middle School

Writing a Poem
Writing a poem is a hard thing to do
Writing a poem that comes from you.
Writing a poem that speaks your mind
Hoping that readers to you will be kind.
Writing a poem on a big open space
Knowing full well it isn't a race.
Writing a poem can be easy it seems
but writing a poem has no ounce of ease.
So here I am writing this poem
Sitting at school wishing I could be home.
So this poem ends as the bell's 'bout to ring
I guess writing a poem isn't such a hard thing.

Danica Smith, Grade 8
Nordonia Middle School

Wars
Why do we fight in wars,
There is so much blood and horror,
Why is there so much suffering,
Why are we always fighting,
One war ends, another begins,
Why do so many lives end,
Why do the U.S., Korea, Japan, Iraq, and Iran
Always fight in wars

Patrick Enoch, Grade 7
J A Garfield Middle School

The Beauty of Nature
Glistening water coming down the stream,
Birds singing in the air
Not a creature seeming to care.
Swimming, flying, walking, all seeming to get along.
Now just listen, do you hear it?
It's nature's beautiful song.
It goes on-and-on,
It's the never ending song.
Now look around you,
Leaves falling, nuts disappearing,
What's happening?
Nature's rhythm is changing.
It's adding on to nature's never ending,
Beautiful song.

Ariel Berger, Grade 7
Miller City-New Cleveland School

Mountain
M egaton creature of God.
O riginal existence from the beginning of the world.
U nbelievable bulk.
N ervous bomb.
T remendous nature.
A wesome beauty.
I naccessible top.
N o one can conquer it.

Jooheon Yoon, Grade 8
Incarnation School

Unpredictable

Sometimes you go out of your way
To try and make things okay
Your thoughts and dreams
Can spiral out of control
And in the end you'll fall apart
Just like a broken heart
But try to make it through
Because...
It's something unpredictable
But in the end it is the way it is.

Morgan Harper, Grade 8
Chardon Middle School

Big Buck Down

Buck in range
60 yards
Heart hammering
Breath lost
Hands trembling
Deep breath...
Click!
Safety off
A second seems
To be an hour
Closer
Closer
Closer
Finger glued
To trigger
Gentle pull, POW!
Deer runs
Deer staggers
Deer collapse
To the ground
Big buck down

Roy Zimmerman, Grade 8
Licking Valley Middle School

In Our Lives

Trees are turning,
Hearts are yearning,
To grow older, quickly now!

'Til in the days
Of misty haze
We sit and wonder "How?"

How did we,
So young and free,
Get trapped in this undertow?

We never guess why
Through life we fly
Until, to death, we bow.

Hannah Randolph, Grade 8
Gesu Elementary School

Sitting the Bench

I made the team but here I sit. I'm wondering if I should quit.
The coach must think I need more work. Sometimes I think he's a jerk.
I wish that he would just ease up.
It's pee-wee, not the Stanley Cup.
Can't he see how hard I try?
I do all the positions that he says.
I know I have a ways to go, but not playing doesn't flow.
Now the coach is coming towards me.
He knows I'm bummed and really angry.
"Look, I know you want to play."
The stupid coach starts to say.
"You know what to do. The others do too.
That's why at practice I push you so hard.
You have what it takes to go far.
I already know what you can do. I have to see for you.
Now, try to help the team by being a supreme leader and all you can be."
He pats me as he walks away. Leaving me speechless — what could I say?
The coach is a good guy after all.
I feel pretty stupid, I feel kind of small.
But, wow, he thinks that I'm not a pest. He actually likes me!
Who would of guessed?

Peter Klausner, Grade 8
Christ the King Catholic School

My Family Is a Car

My family is a candy apple red Mustang.
My father is the v8 engine that keeps us all going.
My mother is the steering wheel that guides us all.
My brother is the Goodyear tires that keep us from falling.
My sister is all of the slightly tinted windows that let the sun shine in.
My dog Ginger is the horn because of her deep thundering bark.
My dog Maddie is the heater because of the warmth from her loving heart.
My grandparents are the doors that open to all of our hearts.
My aunts and uncles are the leather interior luxuries that spoil us.
My cousins are the radio that makes a lot of wild music.
And I, I am the nuts and bolts that keep us all together by caring for others.

Kraig Dexter, Grade 7
Waterloo Middle School

Childhood Is...

Childhood is saying "I want that" to everything you see.
Childhood is playing in the leaves.
Childhood is eating what you want to eat.
Childhood is trying to understand what you can't.
Childhood is mocking or trying to be just like the person you look up to.
Childhood is thinking that everyone is your friend.
Childhood is thinking and believing you can do anything.
Childhood is loving every animal you see.
Childhood is being disobedient when it's time to leave.
Childhood is playing dress up.
Childhood is not knowing any of the dangers.
Childhood is playing at Swings'n'Things.
Childhood is all of these things.

Elizabeth Russell, Grade 7
St Monica Elementary School

The Nightmare That Is My Life

Boom! Boom! Boom! The lightning was intense, chronic
The phone rang, Ring! Ring! Ring!

I answer, but no one is there, when I try to hang up,
I hear a voice, loud, low, lurid.

It asks questions — I know the answers, but I don't say
They creep me out, that is not okay!

They threaten to come and get me, I hang up the phone,
And run away into the dark and storm; cold, wet and terrified I arrive at my neighbor's house.

I knock on the door, I walk inside.
I'm comforted, I do not cry.

For I am scared of the threat they made —
I was elusive of the place I had been, now I am safe.

Amy Ng, Grade 8
Hopewell Jr High School

Basketball

I remember...
Like pages in a winter sports program
Words like shoot, pass, and dribble
Two famous people were Michael Jordan and Julius Erving
Anybody's jersey, basketball, and basketball shoes
The place where Derek Fisher made the game winning shot at the buzzer
The injury when you vault to get a rebound and you land on someone's foot and sprain your ankle
Our house was a gray-sided house on a road where no one obeys the speed limit
And outside it was a court where the basketball hoop toppled down in a thunderstorm and snapped into two pieces
The sound of basketballs smacking the concrete
Anyone who has a basketball hoop should shoot hoops frequently.

Cole Krumpak, Grade 7
South Range Middle School

I Am in Love

I am in love.
I melt like a popsicle in Florida every time I look into his gorgeous eyes.
I wonder if I even exist in his world.
I envy his girlfriend, who is much prettier than me.
I understand that life isn't a romance novel, so I doubt that I will ever even get to talk to him.
I am curious.
I want to be cured of this awful feeling that most people claim to be the most precious feature of life.
When I think of him, I can feel my heart pounding on my ribs, like a prisoner in a jail cell, crying for help.
I cry because I don't understand why love just drops on us in the most unpleasant time, like a bomb.
I dream I could at least have a whole conversation with him without blushing and forgetting my name.
I tell my friends everything about this curse and they look clueless. Is it love, or am I just sick?
I am confused.
I think back to the good days when boys were just good friends.
I hate myself for what I let my life turn into. Is it normal?
I need love more than anything, and more than ever. No one understands.
I try to become the girl I once was but this is life, not a movie with a rewind and fast forward button.
I have to take charge of my life, I am older now.
I am in love.

Kristina Cain, Grade 8
Western Reserve Middle School

I Am From

I am from open skies and green grass
Surfing, swimming, and catching bass
Running, playing making friends
That last forever to the end

I am from the roads abroad
Stretching long and far
Cooped together like peas in a pod
All in that old musty car

I am from all the sports
Running up and down the court
Kicking, throwing, catching ball
Playing until I hear a call

I am from reading books
Of many many genres
Harry Potter and sci-fi
Are some I can't deny

I am from writing stories
Writing until I reach the glory
Get me started and I will not stop
Going until I hit the dot.

Katie Hosler, Grade 7
Logan Hocking Middle School

More Than Friends

We started out as friends
   Talking, laughing, sharing
Before I even knew
   My feelings turned to caring

As I came to know him
   My emotions began to grow
Then one day I accidentally
   Let my feelings show

I told him what was in my heart
   Only to hear him say
That he had always felt
   Exactly the same way

So now we are more than friends
   He's someone I've come to treasure
The love that is in our hearts
   Is more than we can measure

Lakota Boetcher, Grade 7
Logan Hocking Middle School

Graceful

The beautiful leaf
Blew gracefully through the wind
On a cool fall day

Caroline Tyler, Grade 7
St Paschal Baylon School

Goodbye

People don't stay forever.
Some leave because they are moving away.
Others leave because they want change.
And some might leave because they are taken away by death.
The ones that leave might wish they never left
Others might not understand why they left
But I know when people leave it hurts.
It's not something that's easy. It's really hard
Especially when it's death that takes them away.
They don't choose to leave and others don't want them to leave.
It's going to hurt when you think that they are gone.
But then we all have to remember God has a reason for everything.
And we all have to accept that death is at the end of each of our lives.
We might not want it but hopefully later then sooner it will happen to all of us.

Colleen Connolly, Grade 8
St Brendan Elementary School

Heroes of the War

For the veterans of the war I write for thee.
You fought so hard to protect the U.S.A.
Seeing so many comrades and enemies die.
Most would be phased by bombs being dropped onto the ground.
But you kept on fighting.
Dodging bullets at every turn.
You pull the trigger of your gun.
Just to save our country.
You risk your lives.
Going into enemy territory.
Whether you are in the Army, Navy, Air Force, or paramedics
You are all heroes to us.

Jonathan Chef, Grade 7
South Range Middle School

I Am From

I am from playing hide-and-seek and tag.
I am from rock and roll filling my ears 'til they pop.
I am from the comedy and horror movies watched late at night,
And the piles of Coca Cola and Pepsi cans.
I am from eating way too much chocolate.
I'm from my truly evil dad,
and my scary yet nice mom.

I am from fist fights with my sister,
And yelling from my brother.
I'm from watching and laughing at my baby sister eat dirt.
And from jumping for joy about getting my dog.
I'm from reading manga and watching anime.
I am from watching my grandma who's hurt from some sort of brain damage.

I am from my school filled with a few good friends
I'm from fighting with my mom for no reason.
I'm from good friends, and surrounded by a few backstabbers.
I am from watching too much TV and unpaid cell phone bills.
And from watching movies at the drive-in with friends and family.

Jade McIntosh, Grade 8
Verity Middle School

A Flower

A seed we start in the ground we lay
All for people to enjoy us some way
Water and sun we grow so tall
For most of us we will die in the fall
In a pot a garden our colors are so bright
An odor of smell some of us might
Our life so short given to thee
Hope everyone will see how pretty we can be

Amanda Burris, Grade 8
St Christopher Elementary School

Peace

Calm, soft, clean
No war can be seen

Peace is comfortable and warm
peace may come in many a form

Relieved, serene, still
No men about to kill

War is finished, war is done
Dance with your wife, dance with your son

Celebration, rejoicing, delight
No more terror, fear, or fright

Nathan Harley, Grade 8
Wooster Christian School

My Life in the Country

I love my life in the country,
with fields so far and wide,
where birds fill the air with sweet songs of joy,
and trees reach for the sky.

I've lived out here all my life,
and I hope I never leave.
Just give me a home in the country,
that will be good enough for me.

The horizon is lined with hills and trees,
and the air is crowded with birds and bees.
Please, just give me a home in the country,
that will be good enough for me.

The fields are full of wheat and corn,
and the trees are stuffed with apples and acorn.
Please, just give me a home in the country,
That will be good enough for me.

I love my home in the country,
now I know I'll never leave.
Just give me a home in the country,
that is the home for me!

Kristie Hammond, Grade 7
Sheridan Middle School

I Sit Down

I step onto my hard square porch
Finishing my warm buttery snack of bread
Walking towards the various colored flowers
Freezing on the hard cold step
I sit down
The icy winds beating against me
As I caught a whiff of fresh cut grass
With the birds
Singing their lovely morning song
I glance at the street
As I am blinded by the bright headlights
I begin to move toward a sappy scent
Only to be startled by a meow
I run inside with my cat

Bryan Roth, Grade 7
Incarnation School

Dejection, Interpretation of Poe's Life

Hear the novel baby cry —
As the doctors give a sigh,
Born with a happy mind,
Finest of its kind,
When his mom begins to die,
They hand him to his father,
Now his life's become a lie.
But the boy has a plan,
He will become a man,
But he lost his way,
And he will pay,
In dismay he tries a drink,
He does not even think,
His life is now on the brink.
Forever he is alone,
His life has gone unknown,
His heart cannot be sewn,
Of this life he cannot fight,
He'll try to live with all his might,
Forever he will write,
And live on.

Savannah Stark, Grade 8
Glenwood Middle School

Childhood Is…

Childhood is walking like a penguin in snow suits.
Childhood is dying Easter eggs and eating them.
Childhood is taking a cookie when Mom's not looking.
Childhood is building snowmen in the snow.
Childhood is building forts from Legos.
Childhood is playing with Barbie dolls.
Childhood is watching *Teletubbies* in the morning.
Childhood is playing tag in the yard.
Childhood is eating mac and cheese for lunch.
Childhood is everything good in life.

Allyson Hamlin, Grade 7
St Monica Elementary School

Football

In the game
Having no shame

Breaking tackles left and right
Catching balls out of sight

Floating through the air
Like a bee without a care

Throwing the ball
Hoping not to fall

It's the one big pass
Wishing you won't fall in the grass

Cody Lang, Grade 8
Licking Valley Middle School

The Forgotten

Lost, left behind, forgotten
They are always excluded
Shunned by the others
Sad and lonely
Not cared for, not noticed, not loved
For things they have done
And for things they have not done
Things they have done wrong
Or things that were not liked
They are forever lost
Forever unloved
They are forgotten

Blake Wilimitis, Grade 8
St Christopher Elementary School

Lonely Valley

Looking at this scene
It seems so lonely,
As if it were a dream,
Of me and the lake only.
The sun is setting low,
The clouds are up high,
Hills arising in the dark,
Looks like shadows in the sky.
I'm feeling kind of sad,
I need someone to walk with me,
We'll be best friends forever,
Come with me and you'll see.
We can walk this whole valley,
From dawn until night,
And we'll keep on walking,
'Till the valley is no longer in sight.
We'll remember,
How neatly everything was laid,
And we'll be together forever,
So our friendship will never fade.

Torez McGee, Grade 7
Islamic School of Greater Toledo

Them

I'm just like them or do I just think that, obviously I do.
When they look they laugh and don't care who they hurt.
They talk about me behind my back and nobody seems to care but me.
When I walk toward them they walk away.
When I try to talk they don't want to.
You know who I'm talking about.
Their name I won't say.
Though the people I'm talking about should know they've done wrong.
They might stop, for a week or two.
After that they will do what they do best and do it all over again.
The looking, the laughing, hurting people's feelings.
I need to stop caring as all of you do too.
Looks or popularity does not matter but what do I know.
You all have a brain, a heart, and feelings.
I know you're all saying whatever and who cares but the people that get picked on do.
I'm tired of coming home crying or crying at school.
Everyone is tired of getting laughed at, everyone but them.
I can't change myself and I don't want to either.
I'm myself no one will ever change that.
When you laugh at me for being different I'll laugh at you because you're not.
Stop laughing at me and leave me alone I'm unique so what?

Tearna Freeman, Grade 7
Waterloo Middle School

Lightning

Lightning powerful rushing energy.
Free spirited energy of nature taking beauty from its surroundings.
Showing us the wondrous night as day.
Blazing colors of white, pink, blue, and purples,
shining through the darkness as a beacon for hope
for people in the darkest storms of fear.
Providing glimpses of the wonders around us.
Creating light through the darkest storms,
Lighting up the whole sky for all to see.
Showing judgment and force of nature
that repels all from wrong.
A power that is forever continuing.
Lightning powerful rushing energy.

Eddie Neumeister, Grade 8
St Clement Elementary School

Want

Wealth sees poverty sitting in the cold street
Eyeing him with envy
Poverty sees wealth driving past
Spotting him with greed
Wealth wants poverty for the freedom from his suit
Forgetting that there is no freedom on the streets
Poverty wants wealth for the freedom from his daily rhythm of begging
Overlooking the fact that there is no freedom in the business world
Both want the other side
Not knowing what it holds

Seth Panning, Grade 7
Gahanna Middle School East

High Merit Poems – Grades 7, 8, and 9

Love for Now
I know that we're just friends,
And that's where our relationship ends.
I just want you to know,
I'll never let you go,
As more or just a friend,
Because I love the way you look in the wind.
Your hair moves gently,
To smile, I always tend.
You whisper in my ear,
The things I dream to hear.
I think about you day and night,
Especially your strength and might.
But I'm sick of all this drama,
I don't want to hear it,
Your sick of all this drama,
But your in the middle of it,
I want it all to end,
So find a new future girlfriend.
Jessica Jones, Grade 8
South Vienna Middle School

America
Land of the free,
Home of the brave;
Fought for freedom,
And gave us our name;
Honored to be a citizen,
Have so many rights;
Sleep with peace and security,
Every day and night
Today troops are in fight;
So brave and courageous,
Grants us our protection and each of our rights
Look upon the flag with reverence;
The red, white, and blue,
Each symbol represents freedom,
For me and you
Alison Lammers, Grade 8
Miller City-New Cleveland School

God Sent Me an Angel
Precious and loving, a gift from above,
God has given me a sister to love,
Claire Elizabeth is her name,
Our lives since haven't been the same.
She is adorable as can be,
I see quite a resemblance to me,
Blue eyes and light brown hair,
Her nickname to us is Claire Bear.
An angel from heaven as you can see,
If you knew her, you would agree,
I was sad at first that I wasn't given a brother
Now I wouldn't trade her for any other.
Christen Westphal, Grade 8
St Michael School

At the Lake
As I step outside the icy wind whips around me
Midnight black and football brown dogs racing around me
Fighting for attention
Tickle of grass beneath me sends me to a trance
A fierce call of geese, a soft howl of dogs, soft licks
Honeysuckle drifts through the air
Awakens bees
Soft hum grows nearer
Run!
Paige Buchenroth, Grade 7
Incarnation School

The Flame
Panic overflows and the pain begins to sting.
Your lip begins to tremble; next up comes a scene.
Drowning in hateful air, the emotions begin to tear.
Your eyes get wet, and the coldness comes…
The wild fire that once burned inside begins to flicker,
Then, in a flash, turns into embers.
Now the flame is gone and there is only fear.
Then you tell yourself you never really cared.
Heather Cooper, Grade 9
Washington Senior High School

Sweet Taste
I step out on my back porch and sit down
On a chair as everything surrounds me.
The windy air chills me.
The sun shines down on my face.
Birds sing softly; leaves fall silently.
The road is noisy with cars speeding fast.
Shouts and whispers come from down the street.
Pine trees and freshly cut grass are around me.
The scent of morning air swirls around.
Colorful trees sway in the breeze.
Grass covers the yard in a wave of green.
Blue is over my head with puffs of white.
Something leaves a sweet taste in my mouth.
Suddenly, a door shuts and awakens me,
I am back in reality…
Emily Nolan, Grade 7
Incarnation School

Grandpa
September 28th 2007
was the day you had to leave us and go up to heaven.
You went through so much and most of it was bad
but you still had a smile on your face even when you were sad.
There are so many memories we have in our hearts
of you wearing hats and loving to play cards.
We all loved you so much and wish you didn't have to go
but everyone's time comes and you were up to go.
I miss you so much but I'll never see you here again
until it is my time to go up to heaven I'll see you then.
Amanda Kindle, Grade 7
Miller City-New Cleveland School

Not Enough Time

Six years was not long enough,
There was so much love to yet be given.
Given to the one we all miss the most,
To the one who is now our loving ghost.
There are times where I wish you were still here,
But now I understand that where you are you have no fear.
Memories surround me of what used to be,
And looking at your pictures you look so happy and free.
All of the sorrow takes me back to your coffin,
And how the family was filled with pain not looking what there was for tomorrow,
We all sat there left to shame taking the blame that we had no control over.
That night we had heard you have been hit by a driver who was not paying attention to the road,
It was minutes before every family member had arose to the hospital.
It was crazy I was only eight and yet my heart still takes the blame.
Even though it's no one's fault,
There was so much to be taught.
But God never makes mistakes,
I guess you were the next angel He wanted to take.

Catherine Stankiewicz, Grade 9
Norwalk High School

Hatred

I hate you. The strongest words I'll ever say.
But do I really hate you?
I ask myself that question
every day since I bellowed those same words at you.

This day is different. I've realized that I don't hate you.
I hate what you've become.
My so-called best friend is now a green-eyed monster.
How could you get so jealous? How could I be so oblivious and not see this coming?

I guess you were right. Two hearts can't share one dream.
You thought he was yours for the taking.
I know I intervened with your plan
but you didn't have to be so malicious.

We were the best of friends before, two peas in a pod.
Now my body overheats even when I think of you and the rude remarks you made about me.
I cruise under the radar, unnoticed like the tears of hatred that still fall today.
I hate what you've become.

Caitlyn Adams, Grade 7
South Range Middle School

Memories

It was a rainy night. As she shook with fright.
In her attic all alone, remembering of her parents and of her little home.
She still remembers the memories of that day. Knowing that the memory will never go away.
It was also a rainy day when her parents died. They died in a car accident and she wasn't by their side.
She thinks, "It's all my fault for letting them go out." She thought it was a nightmare, but it didn't go away.
She thought, "It isn't real. I know it isn't true. But if it is what am I going to do?"
She knows deep down inside God will always be her guide.
As she looked into her trunk, and then her heart just sunk.
From the picture of her own family.

Emily Wright, Grade 7
Pike Christian Academy

High Merit Poems – Grades 7, 8, and 9

Ode to Snow

Snow
You fell down from the sky one day
Each in your own fragile flake
All different and special
Like the children of the earth
When you landed on the ground
Children ran and played around you
Packing you down tight
But when it gets warm
You melt away
Like the water on the outside of a cup
In the middle of summer
The children are sad to see you go
But you'll come back next year
Just as magnificent, if not better
And give pearly white joy to the world again

Morrisa Cohen, Grade 7
Gahanna Middle School East

The 2nd Time Around

I'm still trying to figure out what to do.
You said you love me but like her too.
I don't know if I should stay or go.
I can't see how you like her and me both.
I know she's from your past,
but I can't resist to ask,
who would it be if you had to choose,
her or me?
Just to let you know, if I leave I won't be back.
So don't think about dialing my digits and ask!
Really, I shouldn't have heard what I heard,
but I did.
Well, now I'm going to get out your picture,
so you and her can be together.
I guess we weren't meant to be.
I'm shocked that it took that long for me to see.
Now I know not to give anybody a second chance,
because all they do is throw your heart on the ground.

Dii'Azia Brown Hicks, Grade 8
Jackson Jr High School

Fall Is Coming

Everyone hates to hear
that fall is growing near
it will be such a bummer
after such a great summer
throwing frisbees, playing ball
making sand castles really tall
and on the roller coasters wee
now all there is are leaves
but wait this can be fun
rake the leaves and when you're done
take a jump and shout with glee
"This is going to be the best fall ever yes-sir-ree!"

Kylie Hardin, Grade 7
Hilliard Weaver Middle School

I Seem To…

I seem to take life day by day,
but I'm always looking at my future.
I seem to have things figured out,
but really I don't know where to begin.
I seem to be brave,
but a lot of the time I'm scared.
I seem to be strong,
but I have my weaknesses.
I seem to be quiet,
but I love to talk.
I seem not to care what people think about me,
but really I do.
I seem to take life as a reality,
but I do dream.
Life seems to be a lot of things,
but anything is possible if you just believe.

Kayla Yeckley, Grade 8
Sacred Heart Elementary School

Trust

Trust is a fan,
breaking, ending the feeling of comfort it supplies

Trust is a book,
turning pages to see if you will love it or hate it

Trust is an unmarked trail,
wishing you knew what lies behind the dark, weary pathway

Trust is a pair of dice,
testing your luck against fate

Christopher Groh, Grade 8
St Clement Elementary School

Where I'm From

I am from the fender on the
side of the John Deer tractor.

From the fun time at Nan and Pop's old sheep farm
I am from the Cope Sister's Sweet Corn Patch in our
field behind the barn.
From the branches of the surrounding maple trees.
And the nonstop barking throughout the night.
I am from a long Gator ride around the farm!
And the cold snowflakes that fall in the winter time.
From an apple that falls off the apple tree during fall.
I am from the gun stock to the deer.
The bullet flies during deer season.
I am from the shelves at Cope Farm Equipment.

From the dusty hay and straw mows.
I am from the fender on the side of a John Deere tractor
and I like it.

Alex Cope, Grade 7
West Branch Middle School

Christmas Nigh

Snowflakes falling,
outside your window,
carolers knocking on your door,
while they sing a Christmas carol
you drink your tasty hot cocoa,
then walking by your fireplace
you hear a ho-ho-ho,
running to your window to look,
you see not only snowflakes,
but you see Santa gliding across the sky,
to excite the little girls and boys.
What a wonderful Christmas nigh.

Allison Kitchens, Grade 7
Waterloo Middle School

Me You're Seeing

I'm starting to disappear,
Watch me fade away.
The world itself, so black and white,
Takes the pain away.

The hurt is how unending,
ripping through my emotion.
Hiding is the only way,
to seize all this commotion.

To people all around me,
I am a girl, corrupted.
But those who truly see me know,
My life's been interrupted.

I try each day, to fake a smile,
to be a happy being.
But it all comes down to just one thing,
It is not me you're seeing.

Chelsea Quinones, Grade 9
Badger High School

I Tried

The sky is filled with hatred
The ground soiled in blood
Explosions going everywhere
But I just have to sit here

Someone has got to stop it
But there is nothing I can do
I mean I am only 13
But this bloodshed has to end
I would help if I could but I can't

I can try and try
But my heroes are sure to perish
And their families are sure to cry
But there is nothing I can do

Jake Mitchell, Grade 7
South Range Middle School

Snow White Queen

Be scared, as though you've seen a ghost.
The words haunt you, like an old abandoned house.
Every word you read, your eyes follow like a dog chases after a ball.
You can't escape the melody, it swims through your veins like a fish in a waterfall.

My love rings in your ears like a wind-chime on a windy day.
You want to run away, but she hangs onto you like the gallows above.
Your heart is twisted, like the strings being played on a harp.
Frozen fear stuck in time with icicles.

Your mind twists with the strings on a violin.
Your hope is a black well.
Fear is found, in front of your soul.
Your dreams are daring and dangerous.

Everyone is staring, as though you're a stranger.
You don't understand why they can see you, but can't hear you.
As you sink to the ground, just remember all she wants is you.
Sleep soundly, my sweet love.

Chelsea Miles, Grade 8
Western Reserve Middle School

Him

A smile
A wave
A simple hello
His hellos
His good-byes
His simplistic stride
The way he holds me at night when I'm cold
His hand locked with mine
Our feet entwined
A smile spreads across my face
The fact that I know I'm safe
He's my hero from day to night
He's the one that's the light of my life
When he calls me I grin from ear-to-ear
When he walks me to my bus I wave good-bye
There's a possibility that tomorrow I might see him again
All I can do tonight is think of his smile, his wave, his simple hello

Kaitlyn Emery, Grade 9
Badger High School

My Angel

My angel breaking my tears.
Washing away all of my fears.
Her beautiful face impressing all that stand before her.
Making all problems disappear that occur.
Always there when I'm in need.
Forever my very best friend indeed.
Though she thinks she is just a failure I hate to see her tears fall.
She needs to know she's the best mom of all.
Viewing the world upon God's angle.
Forever being my angel.

Breanna Roush, Grade 8
Central Middle School

Why Did You Leave?

Why did you have to leave us,
before our very eyes?
I never knew you very well,
that I do despise.

I wish we could have grown up on the farm,
I bet all my family does, too,
playing around on the farm,
and hear the cows go "Moo."

It's O.K. that you have left us,
because someday I'll leave, too.
I'm happy the way it is right now,
but believe me big brother I miss you.

Alaina Deepe, Grade 7
Miller City-New Cleveland School

Where I Am From

I am from medicines, from Clorox and clothespins.
I am from the dirt outside.
I am from tree houses, from my good friend that died
of cancer, to churches and cornstalks on Halloween.

I'm from the hot fudge cake and sunglasses,
from Mount Everest and the Grand Canyon.
I'm from the Einsteins and pass-it-ons, from pull up
and tear down.
I'm from my soul and a golden lamb plus
Ten Commandments I know not to do.

I'm from mad bulls and muddy branch,
fried potatoes and strong onions.
From the sugar in sweet tea to the carbonated water in pop,
and the dog my dad had to put to sleep.
In my memories are pictures with lost faces, to make
me think of people when I get in trouble.
I am from snapshots before I left the family tree.

Robbie Snowden, Grade 8
Verity Middle School

Bus Ride

For people of a different race,
To be together in the same place.
On a bus, in a plane,
It doesn't matter, we're all the same.
From city to city, from town to town,
You'll find different ethnicities all around.
No matter the difference from skin to skin,
The only person that matters is the one within.
It doesn't matter, the time of day,
People will always feel one way.
To love or to hate is your choice,
But from us, ethnicity needs a voice.

Rachael Schumm, Grade 8
Glenwood Middle School

I Remember

I remember…
Cars rumbling and thunderous from my red mustang
Foods and dishes from family gatherings filled and luscious
Items found around your home like novels and chairs
Neighboring buildings like a post office
People wailing, dozing, watching TV
Names of relatives like Anna, Brad, and Jason

Tyler Fitzgerald, Grade 7
South Range Middle School

Veterans

They go to battle,
Some will not come back,
Some will receive a purple heart,
Many will lose a friend,
Many will lose a son, a dad, a brother, and an uncle,
All this for little pay.

The battle is tough,
The fear is tremendous,
The sacrifice is humongous,
All this for little pay.

One day a year we celebrate,
The brave,
The mighty,
The ones who protect us,
The veterans we celebrate.

Parker Winkel, Grade 7
South Range Middle School

Love

Love is the most precious thing in life,
It's the sweetest thing you'll ever hear,
The mushy feeling when they're near,

Love is something you can't replace,
It's your family and friends…
Yet, love never ends!

Renae Haynes, Grade 7
Hamersville Elementary and Middle School

The Power of Love

You know love is so strong,
it makes you do things you never, ever
thought you would do.
It hurts, it heals,
then wounds again.
It's the center of all relationships,
It's a bond, yet true,
It's family, friends, neighbors, it's people
of the past, today and tomorrow.
Just remember,
never take the people you love for granted!!!

Aleisha Kramer, Grade 8
St Ann Elementary School

Halloween

It's Halloween
Best time of the year
You get free candy
And go through haunted houses
Sometimes just for laughs
The costumes are always different
Every single year
I go out
And the candy
So sweet and so delicious
I get more and more
Each year I go out
Costumes can be scary
And yet others
Can be cool
And still others are funny
That is why
I love Halloween

Ryan Schoenung, Grade 8
St Aloysius Gonzaga School

Drumming on to Wisdom

Will I live to age eighteen?
Will I die tomorrow?
I look into my future now,
And I am filled with sorrow.

Battle takes over my mind,
I quiver at the thought,
Is this the life I ran away for?
Is this the life I sought?

War will make me stronger,
Wiser, nonetheless,
If I live tomorrow,
I'll straighten out this mess.

I know I must be brave,
This is something I must do,
I need to be strong,
For myself and my country too.

Jackie Miesle, Grade 8
Gesu Elementary School

Curly Hair

Daughter with curly hair
Your eyes are cinnamon color
Your heart beats like brother rabbit
Your cry is a sharp whistle

Daughter with curly hair
Your eyes are walnut brown
Your heart thumps like a galloping horse
Your whine is a wolf howling

Allison Oliver, Grade 7
South Range Middle School

The Roamers

"The roamers are coming! The roamers are coming!"
screams the town crier as he ran
through town to alert his people.
"Run or they will eat you!"
The town crier screams as
people flood into nearby houses.
CRASH! Something has been thrown through a window
nobody dares move. The crier thinks it's safe; to his misfortune the roamers
trick him
One
of the boys peek through a hole just in time to see the crier's contorted face
fading into
the night.

Tyler Bourst, Grade 8
Licking Valley Middle School

Sophia

A little girl who loves to tap,
sitting on a piano as she taps, taps, taps.
I run downstairs to see what is wrong,
and all I see is a cute little girl playing the piano as she sways along.

She looks and smiles with her light brown hair,
and waves to me with her big black teddy bear.
She runs around the house, thump, thump, thump,
and returns to the piano, to tap and sway all day long.

She giggles and laughs with her light green eyes,
that sparkle in the sunlight when she says bye-bye.
If you don't let that little girl tap her little rough annoying tone,
you'll hear a lot of thumping and crying pretty soon.

When the day is over, she runs to the piano and taps, taps, taps,
to avoid her nightly bath and final nap.
This little girl is my baby sis,
whose annoying and unexpected piano taps I will always remember and miss.

Eva Antypas, Grade 8
Christ the King Elementary School

At War While Growing Up

Being at war this young is never easy
Always having to get to the other man's level
Always feeling nervous thinking that you've done something wrong
Not knowing who to talk to
Afraid you might say the wrong thing
Afraid you might step on the wrong foot while marching
Afraid you might fire the gun at the wrong person
Afraid you might lose your life
Afraid that you might get your limbs cut off because of a bullet
Worried about what other people might say
Challenged by the obstacles thrown at you
That's why being at war young is never easy

Israelle Nelson, Grade 8
Gesu Elementary School

I Remember…
Like pages in a math text book, full of fractions
Words like divide, multiply, fractions
Two famous people Einstein, and Madame Curry
Anybody's calculator, pencil, eraser
The place in the story where no one can figure it out
The injury when my head hurt from studying
Our house was noisy and confusing
And outside it's hot and sunny in September
The sound of my pencil breaking in frustration
Anyone who dislikes math is my hero

Camden Molnar, Grade 7
South Range Middle School

Ode to Bart
Ode to you Bart Simpson,

You are what I do after school
I read your books and watch your television show.
I join your clubs and your organizations.
I wear your clothes and hats.
"Quoth the raven, eat my shorts"
Thank you Matt Groening
For inventing the Simpsons
Ode to you Bart Simpson.

Matthew Binius, Grade 7
West Branch Middle School

First Snow
First snow can hardly wait
Heart racing, can't wait
I think I see it
  f
   a
    l
     l
      i
       n
        g
Race outside, waiting watching
Cold chills sliding down my back as I stand
Alone waiting, watching
Snow flakes fall…wind blows…
I'm screaming, "Snow finally came"

Monica Appleman, Grade 8
Licking Valley Middle School

The Arrival of Winter
From clouds that can't get any grayer,
    fall finally calls a truce,
    surrendering to winter by releasing the snow
    it won't hold any longer.
Winter settles in slowly.
    Soft white flakes fall tentatively,
    oblivious to the angst of the city that lies below.
Mere background noise to the honking
    of horns, smoke, and exhaust,
    the snow continues its journey silently,
    offering simple pleasure to those
    who have the time to watch.
The snow lies peacefully, a frozen world set apart
    from reality but its own perfection.

Hannah Goddard, Grade 8
Chardon Middle School

The Battlefield
The pain and weakness all around them.
Families losing the ones they love.

Guns firing.
Bombs exploding.
The screaming.
The yelling.
The horror.

Everywhere is tragedy and death.
Everyone is dedicating their lives.
There is no peace.
No happiness.
Tears stream down their faces as they cry.

Soldiers are scared,
But won't back down.
They show their bravery.
They fight for freedom.
The battle is over.
To them we honor today.

Jon Kenney, Grade 7
South Range Middle School

Why?
Why do you do these things?
Why do you scream and yell
And make my life a living hell?
Sitting there day after day,
Yelling your words
And my mind a stray.
Thinking of the words I would say,
If only I had the chance.
They would pierce you like a broken lance.
Why do you sit there and punish me
For things that are not my fault?
That is when my life comes to a halt.
My home is like a prison,
Unhappy and locked up like an animal,
And I am not allowed to think.
Why do you say writing and dreaming are a waste of time?
When it is what keeps me sane
And keeps me from causing you pain?
To those around
Who don't make a sound
I stopped wondering why.

Jacob Wood, Grade 9
Washington Sr High School

Football

On the football field
You'll never yield
Juking left
Juking right
Running the ball
Tucking it in so tight
Breaking tackles
Throwing blocks
Linebackers tackle
Like A. J. Hawk
Safety hit
Like John Lynch
Right now
I'd much rather be pinched
Still giving 100 percent
Even though team is starting descend
You put point on the board
Hoping you'll win when the game is over
The coach is proud
You know you won
When the crowd is so loud

Jake Lagace, Grade 8
Licking Valley Middle School

Monster Buck

Big deer
Going to shoot it
Drew my gun
Safety off
Finger on the trigger
It saw me and lingered
Walked a little bit farther
Now…no shot
Waited…waited…
Finally it walked out into the open
Bang!!!!!!
Ran about 5 ft and dropped
Alive
Shot again
Dead
Field dressed
Loaded
Tagged
And processed
Glad

Derek Lee, Grade 8
Licking Valley Middle School

An Ant's Working Day

An ant walks slowly
Carelessly doing his work
Trying to survive.

Jason Kilbane, Grade 8
St Brendan Elementary School

Snowy Christmas

It's snowing, it's snowing.
The snow shimmers like diamonds.
The winter wind howls.
The world is slowly turned white.
Like a blanket, it wraps up the Earth.
Finally, it's what we are waiting for.
We can't believe it's here.
It's a white Christmas.

Eric Ragan, Grade 7
Gesu Elementary School

Dancing

I carefully
Place my tiny white flats
On his shiny square toed shoes
His suit smells of cologne and
Wedding flowers. I hug him as
We sway back and forth
And I feel
As though I am floating
With his smile,
That warm loving smile
I flash him a wide grin,
With my missing tooth
As the music tempo speeds
He swoops and swings
Me around until,
He hugs me
I don't want him to ever let go
But I know,
He will soon set me down

Gabby Pangallo, Grade 8
St Aloysius Gonzaga School

Line

A line is like a boundary
Between friends

A line is like a barrier
Around our emotions

A line is like a telephone wire
Going in and out of houses

A line is like a separation
Of the human race

A line is like meeting someone new
For the first time

A line can be a lot of things
But a line will always be a line

Hannah Garber, Grade 7
Gahanna Middle School East

Sun

Bright beam of glimmer
Immaculate rays that shine
Intense global heat

Garrett Wolking, Grade 8
Incarnation School

Day to Night

During the day the sun smiles at you
While playing in the grass
The grass dancing to the wind
It's time for lunch…
Your stomach speaks to you
And tells you what to eat

Night soon falls
Night…
When the world blinks
Everyone fast asleep
Dreaming, of who knows what
Sleep
When the whole world slows down

The alarm clock sounds
Time for another day

Katie Mackall, Grade 7
Gahanna Middle School East

I Am Wind

I am wind, strong,
but soothing, harsh,
but good to have around.
I am like the stubborn wind
when a kite is trying to fly.
A gentle breeze,
a fierce rush,
so powerful that you can't win.
I am cooling and relaxing,
but a tornado
that picks things up
and throws them
because they are in my space.
I am the angel in the wind…
but a wolf in the woods!

Olivia Polverine, Grade 7
West Branch Middle School

Football

Football
Hard, exciting
Running, tackling, scoring
Michigan versus Ohio State
Sport

Brian Friley, Grade 7
Pike Delta York Middle School

High Merit Poems – Grades 7, 8, and 9

Frozen Whispers
December is a wonderful time.
It is a time for winter,
For Christmas and for friends.
It's a time of joy and happiness, and of love and romance.

As the snow falls to the ground,
You look up and laugh.
You laugh at your many thoughts,
Thoughts of your wonderful life;
Your friends, your joy and happiness,
Your love, and all your romance.

Snowflakes remind you of your friends.
Each one is different,
They're never the same.
Some with many traits and virtues,
Others with nothing to give, but
Everything to take

Enjoy your snowflakes before they melt away.
Savanna Ross, Grade 8
Clinton Massie Middle School

Winter
little white flakes, falling down slow
little white flakes, called snow
sparkling, shimmering in the light
looking at them is such a delight.

making snowmen, snow angels too
in the snow there's so much to do
going outside every single day
my friends and I just love to play.

before you know it, it's gone 'til next year
so you might as well enjoy it while it's here
have fun playing outside in the snow
hurry! before winter decides to go.
Ashley Corley, Grade 7
Labrae Middle School

Farm Music
Cows mooing,
Tractors roaring,
Dogs barking,
Four wheelers riding back and forth to barns,
Birds chirping in the silo,
Combines dumping grain into the grain truck,
Smack, the wood getting thrown in the truck,
cats meowing in the barn,
The blade of the 8n scraping the floor in the barn,
The zero-turn mowing the grass.
And that's farm music.
Derek Delp, Grade 7
West Branch Middle School

The Chains
Slowly I chisel
Little by little: day by day
Slowly my chains fall away
They are little and big too
All are mistakes that no one should do
There are so many chains
I have rid of so few
It is not my fault
Most are from you
You who mock me
You who tease
You who tempt
And do what you please
Don't you understand?
If I fight back it's a chain on my hand
So I stay silent: my mouth stays closed
And you my friend, you go to show
While some always seem to get away
Their chains are building every day
And while our chains are little, theirs grow long
And together we will sing justice's fair song
Emma Wahl, Grade 8
St Gertrude School

When Will It End?
O, how I am disgusted, with this war going on,
Why can't we just get along?
What is wrong with us, all being together,
In a wonderful world with no fighting ever.

O, how I wish, there was no fighting or violence,
No more deaths or screaming, just silence.
I can't wait for this war to be done,
So we can go back to having fun.
Jacob Brookover, Grade 7
J A Garfield Middle School

A Young Girl's Story
Her name is Linda, intelligent and bright;
Darkness and spiders, her biggest fright.
The color blue is her favorite, and volleyball's her game;
She might have some flaws, but there's no one to blame.
There's some times in her life that aren't so perfect,
But with family and friends, every day is worth it.
She's friendly and helpful, loving and kind;
She's determined and strong, in spirit, body and mind.
Her animal resemblance is a horse you see;
Wild and fast, and ever so free.
She's polite and quiet, but outgoing at times,
Passionate for music, and making up silly rhymes.
Her car, a Corvette, stylish and fast;
The skip and spunk in her step is an ever last.
This is Linda, this is her story.
Laid back and loving life, not needing any glory.
Linda Niedermeyer, Grade 8
St Monica Elementary School

Seasons Go By
Fall is here!
Winter is near!
I know what that means.
It means later sunrises,
And earlier sunsets.
Shorter days,
Less time to play.
People raking leaves,
On every street.
Kids out trick-or-treating 'til 7 p.m.
Like their candy bags have no bottom.
As winter ends,
Spring begins.
Now that spring is here,
We know summer is near.
Seasons go by,
But the fun will always adhere.
Shayna Stolte, Grade 8
Licking Valley Middle School

Autumn Freeze
The harsh, howling wind
Swept through crisp autumn leaves like
An unwanted guest
Terry Mooney, Grade 7
St Paschal Baylon School

Wind
Relaxing, peaceful
Feeling of God's great presence
Cleansing troubled mind
Abby Fath, Grade 8
Incarnation School

99705
The snow is always falling
The quiet slue so still
Ducks always on it
But the mosquitos are so annoying
The flower beds so gorgeous
Fresh raspberries always good to eat
The wonderful neighbors
Annoying chickens clucking
My cute bunny hopping
Our sledding hill is always icy
Moose in the backyard
So we can't go out to play
My house is always the center of fun
It's the best place to be
It's peaceful
And every now and then, quiet
A place I always want to be
I was there for 7 years
And, I miss it
Megan Stainer, Grade 7
West Branch Middle School

A Broken Heart
A broken heart is more than just pain,
And we tend to blame that one heartbreaker.
The smile on his face
Is a part of you that is hard to replace.
You don't realize what you have until it is gone,
So hold it tight with
All of your might.
As much as we wish to always be together, there will come a
day when we can no longer endeavor,
Seeing as nothing lasts forever.
Wherever you are,
Beware of the people that you trust,
And even the people that you love,
Because in the end you may just end up with another broken heart.
Sarah Yehl, Grade 8
Chardon Middle School

The Storm
The rain kissed my cheek as it fell from the puffy clouds
The thunder screamed as loud as possible
The shutters clapped against my house
The lightning started yelling back at the thunder
Big bolts came from the sky
The wind cried as the thunder and lightning continued fighting
The trees danced in the wind
The storm was bad, but I ran through it as though nothing was wrong
I just had to get out of my house
It was trapping me
I ran through the storm
It was better than my fighting house
All I wished was that no one would come after me
Running through rain made me feel like nothing could go wrong
It comforted me
The rain drenched me as I stood in the middle of my court
The rain was a good friend to me
A good friend would tell me not to run away, no matter how bad things go
As I stood in the street, the rain told me how lucky I was to have my family
As I walked back into my house, it welcomed me
Beth Coccia, Grade 7
Gahanna Middle School East

Young Roses
I realize I have been ungrateful of these quick past eight years,
the things I've done, the people I've met and all their listening ears,
the stories that cheer me up on the slow moving Monday mornings
and the jokes they crack to make life fun and keep it from being ever so boring
I know the memories we've shared will last until the end
but who'd have thought I'd have to leave my very best of friends
from all these years spent together I have come to recognize,
that life here is short and to stop hiding in disguise but
to just sing out loud, laugh a lot, and show everyone your smile
because God needs young roses too, and no one knows if you'll be here awhile
most importantly you've taught me to love and forgive
thank you for that, I'll remember you all for as long as I live.
Mary Switala, Grade 8
Incarnation School

My Savior

To leave is to say goodbye,
but to leave you my love there are no words,
and when you left me I said nothing,
just stared after your empty footsteps with tears streaming down my face.

Finding the strength to move on seemed impossible,
but days turned into weeks,
and weeks into months;
then finally I found my salvation.

Faith is so often the child of fear,
and I feared my never-ending pain that dragged me farther and farther into the darkness.
It was suffocating; stealing my every breath as I desperately gasped for air.
That is when I found the Lord, my ever so precious Savior.

With Him I found happiness and joy.
My mind and heart began to sing in perfect harmony,
instead of stealing my breath, He give me the sweetest air to breath.
With Him I have everything so I cling to Him like a child clings to its mother,
refusing to let go.

Kristi Gockel, Grade 8
Chardon Middle School

When Christmas Comes

When winter comes it's time to sled, and time to sleep in cozy beds.
You know once it reaches here, you get the first snow of the year.
Snow days come and they go, but you can't wait till snowball fights.
Snow angels and snowmen made, when you get done you celebrate.
Hanging lights on Christmas trees, that soon under will have presents for me.
You make cookies and milk too, for Santa to eat, and thank you.
When Christmas comes the next day, you wake up happy because presents await.
Family and friends swing on by, to make conversations, or just say hi.
At the end of the day you don't want it to end, you can't wait till next year to do it again.

Taylor Hartfield, Grade 7
Gesu Elementary School

A Surprising Snake

My lips were smiling as I walked back calmed by the coastal waves
Unaware of the waiting and beguiling creature nearing with every movement my legs gave.

No fear was in my head. No worries crossed through my mind.
Until I saw that creature lying as still as a piece of lead, ready to put my family in a bind.

Diamonds down its back, the sly snake there sat,
The sound of a rattle was all it lacked, how I wished I could fly away like a bat!

My family stood stone still, this reptile did the same,
So we waited there until, we were sure the snake would be tame.

Back at the condo, my anxiety was gone. Yet every time I went outside, I must have looked like a hawk,
Searching for diamonds, hoping to not see a single one, while on that day's walk.

Now I have returned to my house, my fears have stopped piling,
Perhaps, next time, the snake will instead scare a mouse, freeing me to keep on smiling.

Sara Rayburn, Grade 8
Hopewell Jr High School

Imagination

I am bored,
as a board.

I am a knight,
in the night.

I am anything,
you are anything.

A man
with nothing,
nothing but his
imagination,
is rich.

A man,
with everything,
everything but an
imagination,
is poor.

Gregory Tewksbury, Grade 8
Riverview East Academy

This Is My Life

The name is Stephanie,
there's a brightness that
Shines through me,
like a bright yellow daisy
I'm loved, I'm forgotten,
I'm frightened, and I'm forgiven
I'm like a dog, loving, loud, and proud
Give me a drum roll,
With those drums
Blue eyes, blonde hair, light skin,
You can catch me anywhere,
from volleyball to family
It won't stop me, volleyball's my game,
family's my life
Nursing is where I'm headed,
in my yellow Mustang,
Being popular, cool, and smart
is pretty great,
but what I'm going for
Is being Stephanie

Stephanie Marie Wisniewski, Grade 8
St Monica Elementary School

Difference

Friends
Friendly, caring
Playing, talking, chatting
Delightful, funny, rude, dumb
Mean, uncaring
Bullies

Eric Brackman, Grade 7
Fort Recovery Middle School

Dawn

On a hot summer morning
I lie
Watching the sunrise on the beach
I erase all memories
I watch
The seagulls fly in circles around the sun
I listen
To each call as they squawk to each other
I watch
The sunrise with yellow rays
And as the sky turns from pink to orange to purple
I listen
To the clear blue waves crashing against the rocks then bouncing off
I watch
I listen
I lie

Krystal Dudas, Grade 8
St Brendan Elementary School

This Is Going Out to You

Stop all this frustration, you have given me
I can't stand this anymore, I just have to let go from the past and present
We were just friends and this is how it end?
I just don't understand why? But I guess all good things come to an end
I'm just tired of this broken heart so let me be,
So I don't have to suffer this any longer thanks for all the times and memories
But I believe it's mine and your time to move on now?
Don't you agree? All the rumors we believed in and we finally gave in
Wow, who knew that words can tear a person apart?
From the outside in those three words that you tossed around
But I keep condescending, everything we spoke
Just all the memories filled up in my mind trying to release, to stop this broken heart.
There's nothing that can compare to you
But if you want to play it like a game then let's play a never ending game
How did we get to this?
A broken heart, a mess of tears how did we come to this?
But I'm going to rock n' roll baby because I got a lot of things to do
So just remember this you're my never ending mess

Mariah Peake, Grade 8
Christ the King Catholic School

Love on the Field

You are the beat of my heart and the blood in my veins
you're the deer that roams in the woods as it rains.
You're the one that is there that obviously cared when I was right next to you.
You were the only one on my team that made my heart scream out your name.
You were my only shield out on that soccer field, what made you go?
You are the friend that I thought I could have 'till the end,
but my dream just went around that bend,
and has never came back.
You'll always be the one I love or loved that made my heart scream
that shielded me on the field and who will bring my dream back to me one day.

Alexia Stalnaker, Grade 7
J A Garfield Middle School

High Merit Poems – Grades 7, 8, and 9

The Hippo Revolution
There was a crocodile. He was big and mean.
He ruled over the Nile and was a killing machine.

Also in the river, there were hippos galore.
They only had a sliver, and they wanted more.

It was the hippos who started the fight.
They formed rows and charged with all their might.

The king croc first saw the enemy's rows,
and yelled, "Come gnaw on our hippo foes!"

Neither croc nor hippos showed signs of fright,
as they exchanged blows all through the night

At the first light of day the lead hippo said,
"We've made them pay; they're all wounded or dead.

But this I must, to the king crocodile.
I am going to be just and give you half of the Nile."

Luke Miller, Grade 8
Incarnation School

Last Shot
4th quarter…one chance…5 seconds
Legs trembling…
Here we go!
Ball in, dribbles fearlessly
3 seconds between the legs
1 second…half court shot
Swish!!!
Crowd cheering, "Hooray!!!"
Humongous, shiny trophy
Best feeling of them all — *TRIUMPH!*

Nathan Bauer, Grade 8
Licking Valley Middle School

I Once Knew a Sister*
I once knew a sister who adored the outdoors.
She loved riding her horse.
She believed in magic.
She loved collecting baby dolls.
She loved early mornings.
She knew no evil…
Now…
She's away driving her car to unknown places
Her horses waits for her in the pasture.
Magic no longer exists for her.
Her baby dolls are nowhere to be seen.
She sleeps late.
She now knows evil.

That other sister is gone…

Emilee Strong, Grade 7
West Branch Middle School
*Dedicated to my sister, Brittany Strong. Keep shining…

A Mix of Hope
'Tis the day that everybody waits for
The snow is falling and there is hope in the air
The snow is falling lightly
And like a prayer, it's near
Many people have the spirit
Yet, some just pass by
The snow is glistening like a diamond
Falling to the Earth from the angels up high
Many people have an idea,
Yet, some don't even care.

Connor Melms, Grade 7
Gesu Elementary School

The Thief
Cookie crumbs on the floor,
Fingerprints on the door,
The cookies had been stolen indeed.
But no fear! I'm in the lead.
Detective Jamie Cook will soon uncover the crook!
I went to my evil brother's lair,
And said, "Hey! That's no fair!
The cookies were not meant for you —"
He interrupted with a "Hee-Hoo!
I ain't no stealing thief,
So scram you bit of beef!"
I scurried to my sister's room,
Knowing I would meet my doom.
She carefully combed out her hair,
Before answering my questionnaire.
"Jamie, how could you dare,
Think I am a bit unfair!
Please, do not grief,
When I announce that you're the thief!"
I smiled a losing grin,
Well, maybe I committed that sin…

Lynn Daboul, Grade 8
Sylvania Timberstone Jr High School

If…
If I am not me, then who am I?
If you are not yourself, then who are you?
If you do not try, how can you succeed?
If we don't make mistakes, how can we learn?
If we take the easy paths, will we be challenged?
If we never take our time, where will we be?
If we're all the same, how can life differ?
If we all do our work, how can we fail?
If no one speaks up, could we have debates?
If we don't debate, how could we have opinions?
If we don't have control, could all hope be lost?
If no one works together, will all be lost?
If you do not believe me, look around.
If no one wrote this poem, how would we improve?

Natalie Schoen, Grade 7
Bellevue Jr High School

Mask of Tears
I hide behind a mask,
that holds all my fears.

I hide behind a mask,
a mask that's made of tears.

This mask holds all my secrets,
that haunts my thoughts and dreams.

This mask is colorful and bright,
just how I seem.

But underneath this mask,
is a crumbled wall.

Each crack stands for a tear,
that I let fall.

So each tear that I have cried,
makes up part of my mask.

So if this mask should break,
you'd see my tears at last.
Megan Massingill, Grade 8
Springboro Jr High School

Does He...?
I love him.
Does he love me?
Does he know what I feel?
Does he know what I see?
Does he see me when I'm not there?
Does he wish he was here?
Does he get the urge to call me?
Does my voice ring in his ear?
Will we ever be together?
Can it ever happen?
Does he want me with him forever?
Soon it will happen.
We belong together,
you know it's true.
Like peanut butter needs jelly
or a screwdriver needs a screw.
We'll be together soon.
I promise we will.
Because without you
time stands still.
Becca Kinman, Grade 8
Clinton Massie Middle School

Lord of the Storm
It sounds like gun shots
It looks like bright flashing lights
It's a thunder storm!
John Brownlee, Grade 7
St Paschal Baylon School

Turkey Day
I eagerly wake up early every Thanksgiving morning,
to help my mom cook delicious pumpkin pies.
I walk into the brightly lit living room and turn on the blank television screen,
then my entire family watches the Macy's Thanksgiving Day Parade.
After it is all over,
my mom starts to finish cooking.
As soon as she is done,
We order out to eat.
After we've thrown away every bit of the black burnt remains of my mom's food,
we eat our pizza.
This is one of our most favorite holidays,
for this is our Turkey Day.
Amanda Bushnell, Grade 8
Chardon Middle School

A Jacket with a Hood
Dear Santa, I don't want a lot this Christmas
I have been pretty good,
All I want is a pair of mittens and a jacket with a hood.
Mommy and Daddy just sold the car,
Please Santa it's getting quite cold.
All I want is a pair of mittens and a jacket with a hood.
I would like them to wear this winter.
Hey, big guy, are you listening?
I just don't get why it's so snowy this Christmas.
Please Mr. Claus, can you just slide them down the chimney this Christmas Eve?
I know you're a bit wide, but it'd sure make me smile
If I could just have a pair of mittens and a jacket with a hood.
Pretty please Santa, I sure have been good!
I could sit by the fire with little Joey but gee Santa
How I'd love a pair of mittens and a jacket with a hood.
So please, I hear you're a miracle worker,
I will take their word and hope, you'll grant me my
Pair of mittens and jacket with a hood.
You see Santa; I'm only seven and have my whole life
To live, I'd like to get through this Christmas please.
All I want is pair of mittens and a jacket with a hood.
Melissa Schmuhl, Grade 8
Chardon Middle School

Adventure of a Neanderthal
I briskly made my way out to the wide, wooden porch
I strolled gradually to the backyard where I had a seat
The grass resembled a green sea and was prickly against my skin
The trees hovered over me like huge green giants starting to turn brown
The birds and bugs produced a wonderful harmony between their chirps
The beautiful sound was quickly overpowered by loud rumbles of
lawn mowers and the rushing sounds of cars
A little while later, I found my hands feeling the rough,
jagged bark of many varied trees to fragile, green leaves
In the next moment, I felt myself become a Neanderthal
I was sticking my tongue to the earthy, spicy grass and woody sticks
Then a very unique aroma flew up my nose
My adventure was over, I silently returned inside
Sean Brown, Grade 7
Incarnation School

Twin Towers Attacked

The towers had come down, the plane had hit
Everyone was paralyzed with shock.
Nobody knew what was going to happen next,
But everywhere in the U.S. our people were on guard.

The citizens in the towers were screaming,
Louder and louder, another plane passed,
As the tower came, tumbling to the ground.

There was an explosion the fire fighters rushed there.
To save everyone they could from the monstrosity,
But most were lost along with the fighters.

Everyone knew it was the end of the towers,
And the beginning of terrorism

Now our military is in Iraq,
As many die every day,
We are fighting to prevent more terrorism,
Thank you for fighting for the U.S.

Shaun Jenkins, Grade 7
South Range Middle School

Life

Life is only what we live up to,
Many people believe in a non-playful way,
Those people may not understand,
That life if only lived once,
Not three times and not even twice,
This is recognized by many,
But put into play by few,
So those of which that want,
A fast paced or too serious of a life,
Can live their life without the enjoyment,
But not me,
Oh no not me,
I think that I'm going to sit back and relax,
Possibly take a nap or play my guitar,
And then,
I'm going to party!

David Niese, Grade 8
Miller City-New Cleveland School

The Beach

Hear the waves pounding hard against the sandy shore
Feel the HEAT from up above
See the dolphins soaring up high through the sky,
Hear the laughter of happy children
Feel the sand between your toes
See the shadows of the swaying palm trees
Be with your family
Spend time with your friends
At the beach is where all the fun is.

Kayla Kirkendall, Grade 8
Licking Valley Middle School

My Kind of Music

My kind of music is where there is a
theme to the song,
Where there is a person that has a voice
that stands out.
My kind of music makes my heart sing
along with my mouth,
The kind where the song is enough to
make my thoughts come to life.
My kind of music is the kind where I can
understand every word the singer is saying,
That I can imagine myself with the
passion and energy that the song is
trying to tell me.
My kind of music has its own heart.

Emmy Mays, Grade 8
Incarnation School

The Beach

The breeze passes through my hair
The tips of each lock tickles my face and neck
Sounds of relaxation and memories being made
Puts a smile upon my face
Sea gulls sawing to find their mate
Is satisfaction to my ears
Smells of salty water brushes my nose
I remember how aged the water is
And it makes me feel significant
I walk to the shore
Sizzling sand under my exposed feet
Finally I placed myself in the ocean
The water is a nice gateway
Waves of life crash upon my shins
The sun tanning my pale skin
Sends prickles of warmth throughout me
Everything is so calm
Peacefulness is all around me
The feeling is so marvelous
I never want to leave

Monica Neal, Grade 8
St Aloysius Gonzaga School

My Dog

My dog is spotted like a cheetah
With light brown legs like chocolate ice cream
He is as playful as a puppy
He is like socks, lays over my feet at night
My dog is like a tick, he doesn't like to leave

I always will take care of him
I will give him a Little People food
I will give him love and care
I will keep him warm
I will share my home with him
"I'm glad I rescued you, Biscuit!!"

Kara Williams, Grade 7
West Branch Middle School

Friends No More

This is just like starting from scratch;
I should not have gotten so attached
To the things we had.
It just makes me sad.

I don't want to cry;
I don't need to lie.
I made the biggest mistake
That I could ever make.

Please forgive me now;
I just can't see how
Our friendship can come to an end;
All I want is to be your friend.

I remember those days;
It seems like a different phase;
I'm sorry for the things I've done;
I guess you've won.

Being your friend is what made me glad,
But now all I'm doing is getting mad;
I'm guessing we aren't friends anymore,
Even though my heart is sore.

Amanda Roseberry, Grade 9
Seton High School

Winter's Wait!

Winter smiles as it
Patiently waits for autumn
To come to an end.

Johnathan Mangelluzzi, Grade 7
St Paschal Baylon School

Childhood Song

Sitting by the fireside,
My mother starts to play.
A song I know from childhood,
I'd listen every day.

With such a sweet melody,
It softened all my fears.
Mother broke into my thoughts,
"Quiet down my dear."

As she began to play her song,
And I began to listen.
I wondered how such a simple song,
Could shine and shimmer and glisten.

The notes fell down like raindrops,
Splash in puddles of my thoughts.
They bind me, twine, unwind me.
Penetrate me, I am caught.

Brialyn Hassett, Grade 8
Incarnation School

About Me

Alexis born January 6th, this is who I am,
At least what I am told.
But what is the real me, not just looks or when I'm born.
My personality, my feelings, that's who I really am.

Right now at this exact moment in time, I feel I can't write a poem,
But in my heart somewhere I know I can do it and achieve success.

As you know already my name is Alexis,
And I am thirteen.
I love ice skating the way music fills my heart and soul,
The way it makes me feel,
I forget my fears and worries when I'm on the ice.

My favorite color is pink because it reminds me of cotton candy.
I want to be an interior designer when I grow up.
I am creative that's why I think I would be good at this job.
My classmates tease me for being quiet.
I'm not nervous it's just the way I am,
But when I'm around my friends I am so loud.

Alexis Garnek, Grade 8
St Monica Elementary School

Cheyenne

The first time I laid eyes on you, my heart filled with love.
The first night you licked me good night, I laughed.
The next day when you barked your deep-toned bark, I smiled.
The day you raced me around the deck, I was joyful.
The night you couldn't move your body, I wondered.
The next day when I heard that you passed away, I was sad.
The day we buried you and said a prayer, I cried.
Whenever I think of you, I cry about all the good times we had.
I will always remember the times we had running and playing.
I will remember your bark, your whine, and the beat of your heart.
I will remember the tears I cried when we buried you.
I will remember your cute face and the color of your fur.
And most of all, I'll remember your name Cheyenne,
And the day you passed away, November 10, 2002,
The day when the clouds were dark,
But the sky was still as blue as blue.

Jessica Barth, Grade 8
Albion Middle School

On Top of the Tree

Climbing up onto a curling branch
Wanting to take a break, but I couldn't
A HEAVY load on your shoulders pulls me down, but I still continue on
Finally sitting on the top of the tree, unraveling my book bag taking out a
piece of sweet apple pie, a reading book, and a guinea pig in an old shirt.
Making a canopy holding the guinea pig in absolute safety while sharing a salad,
I read the half wooden smelling pages.
Ya, that is summer

Krista Dona, Grade 7
Incarnation School

High Merit Poems – Grades 7, 8, and 9

Faded
On a muggy day on a place called Earth
Something strange yet magnificent happened
Color tiptoed up the creaking stairway to the sky
And left the universe
Leaving scattered traces of white, black, and faded gray
No more blue skies, hazel eyes, bright red colored cherry pies
The sun was either up in the pale sky
Or down in the dark barrier between man and the stars
The moon was either sleeping in the hazy mountains
Or dimly sparkling in the soft heavens
Life was blank without color
Like peanut butter without jelly
Allie McMahon, Grade 8
St Christopher Elementary School

This Is Me
Maria is my name.
Dance is my game.
Hazel eyes, brown hair,
I really want a panda bear.
Being messy drives me crazy,
Some say I'm like a daisy.
Special Ed teacher is what I want to be.
Graceful, loving, and friendly best describe me.
Ghosts are my worst fear,
I have wide feet when I look in the mirror.
I wish pink was everywhere.
I'd chicken out if you gave me a dare.
Math is the worst thing,
Until I hear the bell ring.
I eat with my pinkie up,
Especially, when I drink from a cup.
I'm like a cruise ship, smooth and plain.
Marmar is my best nickname.
This is what I can be;
I hope that you remember me.
Maria Falorio, Grade 8
St Monica Elementary School

My Heart
My heart is a place where I've been before
With miles of glistening blue water and a bright yellow sun
A part of me used to be there
It's back with me again
I still love to visit there
To bring back all the memories
To bring back all the feelings
When I'm there I know who I am
I don't have to worry about anything
So I go there one last time
I remember everything
But it's time for me to go now
And everything is forgotten
I still miss that place in my heart
Kristen Prahl, Grade 9
St Ursula Academy High School

Penalty Rush
You're there, you see the QB running free
Hit him low, hit him high, he wonders, why me? Why?
Pick him up, drop him down, crowd makes no sound
Coaches scream, holler, and cheer, first big hit of the year
Then you see…on the ground it rolls free
The ball rolling at our team,
Linemen try picking it up, once, twice, three times
It is a lot of trouble, ball slips like a bubble.
No chance, you scoop it up
Off you go, diving into your end zone
You did it, you scored…
What is that down the field? I think it's coming back
Touchdown counts, only win of the year.
Zane Mealick, Grade 8
Licking Valley Middle School

Dream
I wander through a void in the deepest of my mind,
searching for that magnificent place to behold itself.
A place where the floor shines brightly as if crystals,
and the clouds can be touched be the sweetest of hands.
Flowers bloom a fragrance of the sweetest perfume,
and stars sing to the most beautiful of melodies.
A place that water reflects the most perfect of images,
and even a rock is as soft as resting on a pillow.
The air entangles all in the aroma of fresh morning dew,
and people say the most empowering things.
A place where the sky reaches beyond the heavens,
and love expands into the hearts of everyone.
Success reaches all who pursue its magnificent path,
and birds chirp to the melodies sang by the stars.
I wonder how this place will ever come to be,
searching all day and night it'll never come to me.
Somehow I long to touch this incredible world I dream of,
but deep inside I know what I already love.
I've longed for this imagined world but now I see,
my world's already the best for me.
Oliver Wang, Grade 8
Olentangy Hyatts Middle School

Favorite Pair of Jeans
That old pair of jeans
Ragged and ripped
Worn at the seams.
Faded and soft
Full of old memories,
Watching from the lifeguard loft
Sunsets on the beach.
Hoping for wonderful dreams
That I could finally reach
While wishing on dancing stars in the West.
I know whenever I slip them on
The possibilities are ENDLESS…
Suzanne Courter, Grade 8
St Christopher Elementary School

Orange

Orange is a carrot
or a feather on a parrot
Orange is a fire
and the color of a tiger
It's a falling leaf
and the color worn by a thief
It's the smell of a fire burning
or the color of the sun in the morning
Orange is the color of fall
and the best color of all

Brandon Buratti, Grade 7
West Branch Middle School

Love

I woke up one morning
And I never knew,
Today was the day
I would fall in love with you,
The touch of your lips the
Feelings that are true,
The comforting sound of your voice
When you say "I love you,"
When you hold my hand
Or even hug me,
When I look at the world
You're all I can see,
The feelings that are forever
Are feelings I have for you,
These feelings are love
And I hope you feel them to.

Ashlynn Seitz, Grade 8
Fairfield Local Middle School

The Gift of Life

Lets live life to the fullest
And not waste a single second
Soon we'll be gone
And we will regret it.
Our lives will pass,
Within a blink of an eye
We must enjoy it
Because soon we will die.
Don't get me wrong
Life can be tuff
And most of our days
Can be very rough.
Instead of making enemies,
Why not make friends?
To make our days brighter
Until the end
We're running out of time
To set things right
To make things better
Lets end the fight.

Jasmine Griffin, Grade 7
Waterloo Middle School

I Remember

I remember…
Like pages on a road map
Words like lol, swizz, and idk, on the computer
Two famous people like Fergie, and Mimz
The place in the Harry Potter book where it gets suspenseful
The injury when I twisted my wrist by falling off the monkey bars
Our house was like a bomb shelter from all the messes I made
And outside was perfectly mowed from my father
The sounds of the radio blaring in my ear
Anyone who knew me thought I was crazy

Tori Volpe, Grade 7
South Range Middle School

Remember When?

Remember when you first saw the ocean?
Those white capped waves and the sand in between your toes.
I remember

Remember that big pile of leaves?
All those colors that never seemed to end.
I remember

Remember your first snow?
It was just so cold outside, but you couldn't resist playing in it.
I remember

Remember your first Easter?
The bright colors of the flowers and the eggs hidden everywhere.
I remember

Andrea Sheller, Grade 7
J A Garfield Middle School

I Am From…

I am from the cold sand between my toes
From the waves crashing against the shore
I am from the salty air of the beach
From the fun family vacation
I am from those big glasses he wore
From the wheelchair he used all the time
I am from the hospital visits while he was sick
From his blue eyes that went with his dark brown hair
I am from David's warm hugs that were so great
I am from those many Christmas Eves at Grandma's house
From the delightful food, as Lucy put it, and many gifts and presents
I am from a loving family full of care and joy
From the many times "Santa Claus" would visit us
I am from the snowy evening my uncle passed away from many cries and sobs
I am from the long service and cold burial
From the many people passing by and paying their respects to our family
I am from accidents and apologies
From happiness, joy, and comfort
I am from fun and boring times
From many family events and tragedies
I am from many things good and bad

Laura Leffler, Grade 7
Logan Hocking Middle School

In the Middle of Fall

I was lying on my trampoline,
stressed out about homework,
But tired from school
The fresh pine aroma from my tree nearby
The squirrels prancing around my backyard
And the wind rushing in my face
The sun was setting
And it was getting cooler outside
My dog barking at the next door neighbor's dog
I called my dog over
And then we rested on the trampoline in the middle of fall

Maddy Miller, Grade 7
Incarnation School

Friends Forever

My friends are very special to me
They help me be who I want to be
We share many good times, day after day
Best friends always and forever…we say
Friends…more like sisters from the start
Sharing and caring, from the heart
Long talks, laughter, and advice
Everything that makes a relationship nice
Birthdays, slumber parties, shopping at the malls
Passing notes, IM-ing, and lots of phone calls
Boys, make-up, and of course clothes
Every subject, that only a girl knows
Rumors, gossip, secrets…not us
Facts and honesty, it's a must
Together we've experienced many laughs and cries
And we dread the day of saying our good-byes
Friends forever, tried and true
No one can ever compare to you
Through all the good times and the bad
By far, you're the best friends, I've ever had.

Meagan Giblin, Grade 7
Miller City-New Cleveland School

It's Not My Fault

It's not my fault we are in the war
And the Twin Towers were attacked

Thousands of people died in the rubble,
Some wanted to stay in their bubble

Soldiers are fighting for our freedom
And we know they will eventually beat em'

I don't know why peace is such a hard, hard thing!
I know the joy of living in America can bring

So when the flag waves to and fro,
I know my cousin died a "HERO."

Jamie Willis, Grade 7
Waterloo Middle School

My Summer Memory

As I glimpsed up into the air,
I began to remember about last summer,
how we went to Canada for vacation,
and the kids we met up there.

I brought a friend to keep me company,
and we went out on Miners Bay Lake.
We brought a couple of inner tubes,
which could have been our mistake.

We then experienced war tubing
on the cool two foot waves,
My friend had the best time ever,
flipping most kids out of the way.

When we were coming in,
and I thought we were done,
my friend Zack jumped onto my tube,
just trying to have some fun.

I will never forget that day,
on Miners Bay Lake.
For it was the most fun I've had in a long time,
and wonderful memories to make.

Nathan Pohl, Grade 8
Chardon Middle School

Opportunity

Opportunity is black
It is a panther waiting to attack its prey
It is a brave crow ready to fly higher than ever before
It runs through our veins
It reminds me of my life
Full of opportunities
It makes me want to always be the best that I can be.

John Urbanic, Grade 7
Incarnation School

The Storm

The wind pushes with all its might
Knocking over the rocking chair on the porch
Causing it to make a loud thud
The porch creaks as it sways
The radio bellows trying to be heard
Over the loud roaring storm
The wind chimes clang
Making the poor frightened cat jump
With a terrifying screech
The car doors slam
The plants dance with joy
Raising their heads up to the clouds
Trying to catch a drink
Thunder and lightning clash together
Like warriors fighting for their lives

Mandy Paez, Grade 7
Gahanna Middle School East

My Mind
The last few months
My mind has been engulfed
CONSUMED
With every thought
Every emotion
That has ever run through
My train of thought
I keep my composure
When people are around
I break down when they aren't
The tears
They run down my face
As a raindrop on a hillside
They never
STOP
I have no one
All I have is my conscience
The scariest place
To be alone in
Is in your own
MIND

Sierra Kleinmann, Grade 9
Glen Este High School

Veteran
Veteran
Courageous, honorable
Protecting, suffering, saving
Soldiers, surgeons, officials, firemen
Sacrificing, life-giving, representing
Proud, freedom-givers
Father

Ryan G. Saunders, Grade 7
St Jude School

Dreams
A dream is something,
that will take you away.
Just a few hours,
it may stay.
I have had many thoughts,
but dreams are the greatest.
But sometimes I can't remember them,
not even the faintest.

A dream is something,
that will take you away.
Just for a few hours,
it may stay.
I have had many dreams,
I can try to share them all.
Dreams about fairy tales,
Or King George the III's fall.
Dreams are your hopes and thoughts!

Ashley Schnupp, Grade 8
Home School

Where I'm From
I'm from the city longing to live in the country
I'm from the warmth of the dryer
to the sound of the washing machine
from summers at girl scout camp
to family vacations to the beach as well as daily visits to Kings Island

I'm from tree climbing from endless hours on the trampoline
to trips to the city pool
I'm from the lake where we seadoo from dawn until dusk
where shells are aplenty where sand in your toes feels like heaven
I'm from the beach where seagulls and children cry where we chase the birds

I'm from family where love never runs low
where laughter is aplenty
hugs and kisses are always
where tears of sorrow are rare
where when things go wrong I run to
I'm from, love

Sadie Slamka, Grade 8
Verity Middle School

The Emotion in Between
When a problem defeats me,
My feelings fall in a place,
That is between anger and sadness.
It is an emotion that is neither one nor the other,
But rather, something that lurks in the sea of desperation,
And haunts the mansion of self-pity.
When I experience this emotion,
I feel nothing else,
Just my mind clearing the semblance of fog away.
I think about the situation,
Its negative outcome, the failure,
But the positive side as well.
The emotion is peculiar,
Like a feeling of white-nothingness,
That allows many thoughts to roam free.
Other sentiments float by,
Outside the protective aura of my present state,
Trying to find a cranny in my soul where they can find a home at last.
Then slowly, as all emotions do,
The trance almost fades away,
Like a peaceful dream disturbed.

Jacques de Villiers, Grade 8
Birchwood School

SR Playoffs
Fans dressed in their team's colors for the big game.
The beat from the SR band playing the fight song.
Footballs being thrown on and off the muddy field.
Terrible mud flavored in my mouth from the cleats of the players.
Football players sweat around me that terrible stench.

Brad Phillips, Grade 7
South Range Middle School

Childhood Is…

Childhood is spending endless days in the sun.
Childhood is playing baseball with friends.
Childhood is sleepovers every weekend.
Childhood is staying up late and watching your favorite cartoon.
Childhood is watching the fireworks on the Fourth of July.
Childhood is jumping in the big pile of leaves during the fall.
Childhood is waking up early on Christmas Day.
Childhood is looking for Easter eggs around the house.
Childhood is sleeping in as long as you can.
Childhood is swimming with your friends in the heat.

Tina Horvath, Grade 7
St Monica Elementary School

Veteran's Day

Veteran's day is a serious day
A dedication to the dead soldiers
Or soldiers who are still shooting

Vietnam, Korea, World War II
These soldiers fought to protect all of us

My father, Dennis Erdel, a Navy veteran
My uncle Daniel Erdel was in the Air Force
To protect a nation called the USA

All those soldiers made a sacrifice
With the risk of getting killed

They leave no one behind in the field of battle
They take care of each other

They have a whole nation to watch and protect
Not to leave it behind when it's in trouble

So thank the soldiers for making your life the fullest
Without them our nation would fall
So thank all the soldiers

Dylan Erdel, Grade 7
South Range Middle School

Grandma

Your touch, your hug
I miss making Christmas
Dinner with you. The sweet
Smell of honey backed ham
Collard greens and home made rolls
I miss your company
From playing dolls together
To watching sad movies and crying together
You are the best grandma
I ever had in my life
I miss your hugs
I miss your touch
And I definitely miss your cooking
But most of all, I miss you

Maya Dandridge, Grade 7
Gahanna Middle School East

Laughter

Laughter: something that expresses emotion,
Loud giggles made by a friend.
You can hear it among many,
The smile on one's face ready to burst!

Laughter: something that roars with joy behind it,
A noise people love to hear.
Squeaks heard at surprise parties,
The never ending feeling!

Laughter: something you cannot hold in,
The moment you never want to end.
Little munchkins making mischief,
The best feeling in the world!

Laughter: something that expresses emotion,
The smile on one's face ready to burst!!

Sheridan Zumwald, Grade 8
St Christopher Elementary School

Swimming Pool

Inside this pool is a world of opportunity,
It's a chance for play, friends, practice,
And competition
Inside this pool is a mind
Ready to challenge anyone ready to win
Inside this pool is a loud cry
It gets louder with each painful dive
Piercing bodies coming through one after another
Inside this pool is a secret place where you cannot stay long
But when you are there you are safe
You are in a new world where you won't be harmed
Inside this pool lies a family though not all are related
A family of teammates
To help each other,
And cheer each other in races,
Even when the competition is tough
Nothing can tear us apart,
We are a family,
A family away from our own,
Inside this pool,
Is a wonderful place.

Emily Demjanenko, Grade 7
Gahanna Middle School East

G-d

How do I find out if You're really there?
Do I look into heaven and stare?
You'll peek out of the cloud, give me a reassuring wink.
Reality will hit me once I blink.
Or was that reality?
I'll never know
If that was really You G-d, popping out to say hello.

Evette Yedid, Grade 8
Agnon School

Night Before Battle

Wrapped up in my thoughts,
I sit here by myself
Thinking of war
And thinking of my future health.

Will I die?
Will I survive?
Will I only get a few cuts,
Or barely make it out alive?

Thoughts trail to my family.
Mother, father, and sister, too.
I wish that I could see them now
And say to them "I love you."

But I have to be brave
And I have to be strong.
After all, I knew what I was
Getting myself into all along.

So I'll enter this battle
With my head held high
And I know I won't be forgotten
Even if I do indeed die.

Devon Ertle, Grade 8
Gesu Elementary School

Birthday Scare

My friends and I cannot wait
For my big party in December
We're planning out what will be done
So it's a party we will remember

Finally the party day comes
Rushing, hurrying, preparing all the food
Lighting the fire, setting up the chairs
Giving the bonfire a creepy mood

Cars pull in, the party has begun
Friends wishing me a happy birthday
We gather around the bonfire
With many scary stories on the way

Nervously sitting there in the darkness
Awaiting the story's end
We hear a rustle in the woods behind us
We scream, in someone we send

Out jumped a large dark figure
Scared us half to death
Although it was my brother in a mask
That birthday turned out to be the best

Jacquelyn Oddo, Grade 7
South Range Middle School

My Cat

Ally the cat
Is a little bit fat,
Like a pillow all soft and furry,
Like an engine and quite purry.
Running and jumping,
And constantly bumping,
Rocking and knocking things over.
Rolling and falling,
Like a newborn he is always bawling.
What kind of cat could he be?

Rory McFaul, Grade 8
Chardon Middle School

The Tiger

Look at the tiger,
And what do you see?
A haunting creature?
No — not me.

I see a beast
Ready to be tamed.
A wild creature
On the road to fame.

You may see a predator
That must be locked in a cage.
For it is a beast
That is full of rage.

But I see an angel
A striped beauty you may say.
I believe it's a wonder,
And I know you will too — someday.

I know you see the piercing teeth,
And the eyes that seem so cold.
But can you look past the eyes,
And dig deep into the soul.

Kevin Froimson, Grade 8
Agnon School

Home

It's cold outside
Everything's moving
Trees flailing
Grass swaying
Cars rushing past
Footsteps, it's raining
The wind flows violently
It's raining harder
The door lock clicks
Silence…

Chris Goydich, Grade 7
Incarnation School

Firecrackers

On a late July night,
When bugs start to bite.
You look in the sky and see,
Firecrackers falling on you and me.
Oh what a sight.

Sadie Collins, Grade 7
Westfall Middle School

My Secret of Life

Reading a book,
No homework,
Riding my bike,
Listening to music,
Ice cream,
Watching a movie,
Helping people,
Summer vacations,
Working hard,
Playing sports,
Pizza,
Making the team for volleyball,
Snow days,
Sleeping in,
The smile on someone's face,
Making the team for basketball,
That's the secret of life.

Kimberly Sposetta, Grade 7
West Branch Middle School

Open Field

Open space
Trees higher than the hills
More colors than a rainbow
Birds singing a beautiful song
Stars shining so bright at night

Nick Cox, Grade 7
St Clement Elementary School

Soccer

Soccer is fun to play,
Even though you may lose,
Don't go astray,
Every day of the week.
Even though your bones may creak,
Practice often while running in the sun,
And don't forget to have lots of fun.
Game after game,
Team after team,
Listening to the crowd scream,
Thinking of my dream,
The feeling of it in my soul,
Hoping to score the winning goal.

Jared Kern, Grade 8
Miller City-New Cleveland School

High Merit Poems – Grades 7, 8, and 9

My Secret of Life

The secret of life is…
Getting a hug before you go to school
Saying "HI" to your friends
Putting a smile on someone's face

The secret of life is…
Cooking with your grandma
The last day of school
Playing with Diamond, Tink, Tigger, and Jasmine

The secret of life is…
Holding your mom's hand
Playing with babies
Making your family laugh
Helping your sister in hard times

The secret of life is…
Seeing your dad coming home from the airport
Believing in God
Getting a hug and kiss before you go to bed
That's the secret of life!

Jessica Sands, Grade 7
West Branch Middle School

The Fate

Stick around, wait and see
The fate that is haunting me.
My faith alone is no good,
For it hides in the wood.
Stick around, wait and see
The fate that is haunting me.
I hold my breath and don't make a sound,
But it seems to know when I'm around.
Stick around, wait and see
The fate that is haunting me.
A scream enters the dark, cold night —
A scream to try and save my life.
The fate that has now taken my life
Floats away into the night.

Ashley Webb, Grade 8
Indian Creek Jr High School

My Surroundings

All these people around me, I just don't feel safe.
I feel like I'm being tortured in my own space.
The noise, the drama, it's all a disgrace.
I feel like I don't belong in this place.
People tell me that it's gon' get better.
But they don't know what I'm going through.
Thoughts run through my head like I don't know what to do.
The faces, the places, all these racist.
The pain, the game, it's all so insane.
I don't know what to do.
I guess I got to move on with my life like I've been doing.

Arnisha White, Grade 8
Alexander Graham Bell Academy

Words

Words are like a sword,
that may stab or touch your heart.
A decision,
in which may change the way a person may act or think.
If thinking is a rough draft of what to say,
then a word is like a final copy,
That has been turned in and remembered for life.
Hurtful words are the nasty flavors in a pack of suckers,
with an after taste that won't go away.
A word of kindness is as beautiful as a rose,
taken like a souvenir,
marking the event.

Zeenet Ahmed, Grade 7
Gahanna Middle School East

The Rain

The rain falls on the roof
Pitter patter
It is a drum stick
It moves with a beat
The rain is like a bunch of ants crawling across the world
They never stop
Until they are forced to stop
By the roof tops in the city
The rain falls on the roof
And wakes everyone up
It is so calm and peaceful
Until the thunder and lightning come
Then it is not so calm
It frightens many children
They think
Why is something so calm like the rain
Paired with something so destructive like thunder and lightning

Becca Scowden, Grade 7
Gahanna Middle School East

Granny

Through it all you stood tall
And I love you for that
Eleven years ago you took me in
And I love you for that
Never once did you give up on me always you believed in me
And I love you for that
You raised me you loved me
And I love you for that
Never have you failed me always you forgave me
And I love you for that
By you raising me you made me a better me
And I love you for that
Always got what I deserved good or bad
And I love you for that
You would go without so I could have what I wanted
And I love you for that
Through it all you stood tall
And I will always Love you for that!

Lauren Wilson, Grade 8
St Clement Elementary School

Sleepy Leaves
Sleepy leaves
As the sun goes down
the leaves will lie down and sleep
Tired from falling
Kendra Zbinovec, Grade 7
St Paschal Baylon School

A Dark Red Rose
A dark red rose,
smells so sweet to the nose.
It lies so cold,
forgotten and bold.
A dark red rose.
It floats down river wild,
so cold so mild.
The snow is high,
the icy river is not dry.
It floats down river wild.
You can hear the winter water,
as it grows and becomes hotter.
The dancing waves,
entering dark, lonely caves.
You can hear the winter water.
The river fills with dark, dark red,
but no blood has been shed.
There is a dark rose so sweet,
it makes winter cold to heat.
The river fills with dark, dark red.
A dark red rose so sweet.
Anna Cook, Grade 9
Badger High School

Fallen Warriors
Clutching to the lifeline,
 holding on for dear life,
 trying to survive.
Twisting, turning, twirling,
 letting go, the leaf falls.
Reluctantly, it dances down
 to join the ranks below.
Thousands of its comrades
 have already fallen.
Casualties of the war against winter.

Staring up at the sky,
 wondering how things were going
 for its numerous friends.
Suddenly, out of the sky come
 snowflakes, drifting down.
One by one they cover the leaf,
 until it is no longer exposed.
Yet another leaf has been buried
 under a white, frosty grave.
A casualty in the war against winter.
Anna Parker, Grade 8
Chardon Middle School

Spring
Spring is bright yellow with a soft rosy pink,
When flowers bloom, they sound like popcorn popping
 as they emerge from the ground popping up and blossoming
Spring tastes like fluffy scrumptious peep marshmallows
 assorted in a variety of colors
It smells like a fresh new beginning in front of my feet
 as I step outside into the luscious air
Spring looks like a new world covered in bright vivid colors
 with happiness surrounding it
Spring makes me feel revitalized, as the fresh crisp air nips at my skin
Megan Marshall, Grade 8
Chardon Middle School

Order My Steps Lord!
"ORDER MY STEPS LORD"
For I have again come 2
LOSE MY WAY!
As try so hard from "DA PAIN" I do 2
FOREVA STRAY!
While simply desirin' 2 secretly deep within "MYSELF"
To finally "BETTA MYSELF"
Yet Lord oh so silently I find myself whisperin' aloud
Dat is "MY LIFE" simple pain
Dat deep within tears me "APART" da most
Yea. It's "MY" secret pain
Which come 2 "STAIN" my hands da most
As I try 2 "WIPE AWAY" life misery-filled tears
Dat fall secretly from "MY FACE"
And as I come 2 shield "MYSELF" from da rain year after year
So suddenly "REVEALED" upon my stained hands Lord stand 2 be
"MY LIFE UNTOLD TRUTH ABOUT ME"
N da truth hurts me so "DEEP"
Dat nightly I "WEEP"
While upon my moment of weakness scream "I DO"
ORDER MY STEPS LORD!
Destynee Allen, Grade 9
Youthbuild Columbus Community School

The Path to Growing Up
It is difficult to come to grips with the path to growing up,
To take on the responsibilities that you have,
And to act more mature around others.
We are still like a child inside,
But some days we will have to live up to the adults that we will become,
And throw away the child that is in us.
Growing up leads to professions, parenthood,
And even leads us closer to death.
Growing up can be difficult,
But it makes us strong,
And prepares us for the future.
So come on, take the first step, lead the pack,
And take us down the path.
Not everyone wants to grow up,
But we will all have to do it.
Nate Steingass, Grade 8
Gesu Elementary School

No More Suffering

The bright and joyful day was falling into a dark, heart-racing night as, your body started to fall asleep.
My heart beating fast and rivers of tears.
I looked at you lying there, I felt helpless and scared.
I said, "I love you Uncle Herman."
As you were leaving this world, I prayed that you could stay just one more day, one more minute, one more second but, if you were tired I would let you sleep.
I heard loud cries and sad words, fearful you left me in this world lonely and cold.
You told of your love and through all the troubles, you knew I never left your side.
You told me you had a minute left.
I hugged you goodbye, you kissed my forehead and told of how you'd carry my presence with you at all times.
I seen the angels surrounding you at the bedside, I said goodbye.
There it was, it was done, no more pain and no more suffering.
It was time for you to go, I heard the Lord calling.
I let go of your hand and knew you held on just for us.
I'll be seeing you one day Uncle Herman.
I love you!

Monique Bais, Grade 7
Jefferson Jr High School

Who I Am

A poem about me, wow! what to say
My name is Danny and I am 13 years old.
I love art, any kind, and I love to write oh, how I love to write
Right now, I am writing a book called *Locked In School*
In that short start, that's most of my life.
When not writing or drawing, I watch TV or listen to music
Musicals are my favorite *Rent, Grease,* and *Hairspray*.
To describe me in one word…Clumsy…I trip over everything.
My favorite color is blue, although I like orange and green.
I love adventure Indiana Jones is great.
Between my friends and family I am Danielson, Zeke, and Nate
I've got a big family and many cousins, but mostly hang out with Katie and Hannah, they rock.
We all love art but to be more specific Interior Design
I would some day hope to pursue a career in it.
I am fascinated with the ocean, fish, and seashells.
It's just so mysterious and really cool.
Don't even get me started on school.
Well that's my life I never said it was interesting
I know you're thinking, that is a weird kid, but that's who I am…Danny Likar

Daniel Likar, Grade 8
St Monica Elementary School

I Remember

I remember…
Like pages in an American Girl book by Valerie Tripp
Words like sweet, awesome, swizzle
Two famous people Zac Efron and Miley Cyrus
Anybody's purple Adidas sandals, long, thick chapter books, black stretchy hair ties
The place in the story where Princess Emeralda turned into a bull frog when she sneezed
The injury when I cracked my head open playing basketball at my friend's house
Our house was a small log cabin in the middle of 100 acres
And outside it is an open area with fields of golden corn, baby deer roaming, blue birds chirping, and trees 15 feet high
The sound of my acoustic guitar playing "Let Her Cry"
Anyone who loves fast scampering deer and soaring, singing birds would love my beautiful backyard

Carly Siclari, Grade 7
South Range Middle School

Childhood Is

Childhood is trying to count all the snowflakes as they fall.
Childhood is playing games with your sisters because Mom would say it's too wet outside.
Childhood is having Mom check your closet and underneath the bed before going to sleep.
Childhood is wanting to be tall enough to ride all the rides at Cedar Point.
Childhood is looking out your window on Christmas Eve trying to find Rudolph's nose.
Childhood is watching Mom and Dad cook and wanting to help.
Childhood is playing dolls with your sisters for hours and then getting bored.
Childhood is sleeping in late and having the dog come in and lick your face.
Childhood is sleeping with a stuffed animal and then finding it on the floor in the morning.
Childhood is counting the days until your birthday.

Jessica Heigl, Grade 7
St Monica Elementary School

Mozart's Master Symphony: Family

My family is a symphony,
Performing in front of thousands.
Father is the brass,
Strong, foundation of the everlasting song, filling the ears of his fans with wisdom.
Mother is the frail strings.
Her uplifting sounds bring a smile to your saddened face. Joyful moods follow her every transition.
My younger brother is the woodwinds.
He follows triumphantly the footsteps of the strong brass and causes conflict between the sweet sounds of the strings and the strong, commanding voice of the brass.
I, myself, am the conductor of the never-ending symphony that is my loving family; I lead my family through hardships and bring them home.

Alexandria Bennett, Grade 7
Waterloo Middle School

I Am From

I am from two younger brothers and one younger sister, who sometimes drive me crazy
I am from technology — all electronics, laptops, cell phones, MP3's and Play Station games
I am from doing my best, being respectful and having good character
I am from exercise — a healthy body and spirit
I am from Las Vegas
I am from a house with no sky lights, that my father built himself
I am from the summer with warm, sunny and endless carefree days
I am from steak and a trip to Cici's Pizza with Aunt Lou and Uncle Goofy Dave
I am from Idora Park with everyone who enjoys wooden roller coasters and the good ol' days
I am from a snowy day, in a house warm and cozy from a crackling fire in the family room
I am from "It's a great day to be a Raider!"

John Fromel, Grade 7
South Range Middle School

Please Don't Think This Is Stupid

When it rains it touches everything, pouring real life down on me. I see you in my dreams love, and then think of you when I wake. I long to hear those words come from your lips again. This loss of you has brought me to a level of despair I have never yet known. My chest now feels so empty at the loss of my heart, but worry not dear heart I wish not to feel you at my chest again. Now I sit by the river and watch how the water rushes by and washes my tears away with it. I only hope that now you smile and laugh. I wish for your happiness. I hope that even time does not trouble you in this moment of what I hope is only a temporary absence. Oh how I wish I could open the door to see only you standing there to hold me in your arms to shelter me from this cruel world. And now I can only weep and have my vision blur before me. Only one thing remains clear and that my dear is my love for you is still undying. If only you knew how strong this love remains. As the sun now rises I wish you were here to see this beauty with me, but you may only be in my thoughts, which makes tears drip from the eyes you once said you could swim in. So now I must go live another day without you, good-bye my love.

Sarah Radley, Grade 9
Fairfield Freshman High School

High Merit Poems – Grades 7, 8, and 9

Remember Veteran's Day

Sixty-two lengthy years ago,
Our courageous soldiers fought
Abandoning their few loved ones,
To save us and thousands more.

Today, we reserve but one day
For remembering their valiant fight.
I take time to envision how fortunate I am,
Though that one day of my time,
Remains infinitesimal to the six years
Our courageous soldiers fought.

I may forget from day to day
The sacrifices made for my safety,
However on Veteran's Day I do remember,
How blessed we are to have such people in the world.

Elise Kogelnik, Grade 7
South Range Middle School

My Best Friend

The two of us always together,
Never for the bad but for the better,
She was great I loved her,
Always polite saying "Yes ma'am and sir."

That was then this is now,
Always wondering why he took her and how,
I wish she was here,
I miss her more and more each year.

Now she is an angel,
Watching over me,
My best friend,
Will now live forever in eternity.

Ashley Archer, Grade 8
Licking Valley Middle School

Through Two Pairs of Eyes

A soldier thinks…
Risking my life every day,
It is such a dangerous task,
But I am proud to fight,
To serve,
To help my country,
And win.

A wife ponders…
I am sick with worry every day.
When will you come back?
Will you come back?
Will we win?
You shouldn't have gone to help in the war,
And leave me here to endure the pain and the loneliness
If you don't come back.

Kayla Arnold, Grade 7
South Range Middle School

Finally Fall

The trees tenderly sway
In the calm, cool breeze.
The air is crisp, but breathtaking,
You feel quite at ease.

The vivid red, orange, and golden leaves,
Add a splash of color to the open, blue sky.
They tumble off the trees,
And through the air they fly!

How magnificent!
It's that time of year.
Everything is just perfect!
Fall is finally here!

Kara Ruffolo, Grade 8
Incarnation School

The Picture

The oil painting in a silver frame,
Hanging on the wall by a metal nail.
The picture is that of a small, wood house,
Whose brick gleams in the midsummer's day light.
The grass is green; the sky is light blue,
The tree's bark envies the rose's color.
You see a small, white cat in the window,
It's blank expression smiles back at you.
You see the dog sleeping on a red mat,
Dreaming of a warm, perfect paradise.
The caretaker is in the front planting,
The flowers almost reflect the sun's rays.
The front door bids you welcome to come home,
You realize that home is your own home.

Lindsey Massa, Grade 8
St Aloysius Gonzaga School

Who I Am

I am from my family and my friends.
I am from peewee football,
And playing for the Verity Vikings.
I am from my church
Where I play the drums
From Gospel hip-hop and R&B music.
I am from burning up at school
Because it's so hot
From the movies Stomp the Yard and Drum Line.
I'm from cell phones and computers around me.
From being born in Middletown
From my house and my grandpa's house.
I am from falling and getting hurt
I am from getting sick
And going to the hospital.
I am from watching TV
From playing sports.
I am from eating and collecting cards.
I am from learning in school

Quinten Hughley, Grade 8
Verity Middle School

Up North

Up North,
where the old ganders
mesh inevitably well.
Up North,
where old houses of Christ
toll their bells.
Up North,
where the young and restless
romp tan-coated.
Up North,
where the job of an accurately planned
field is noted.
Up North,
where the horse spirits run free
and the fireside is the place to be.
Up North,
the love for the land
shall not die.
Up North,
the love for the land
shall only thrive.

Megan Connolly, Grade 8
Chardon Middle School

My Sister

It was so long ago
People say it shouldn't hurt badly
But it does
Some people say they "understand"
But they really don't
Unless it happens to them
Sometimes it is hard to get over it
But I take it day by day

Paige Weakley, Grade 8
Licking Valley Middle School

Laughter

Laughter is joy in a child's eyes.
Funny in a humorous heart.
Tummies ache as it fills the air.
Contagious in a cheery way.
Smiles come with this chronic illness.
An epidemic that can't be cured.
When no one pouts, cries, or complains.
They can't hold back their silly chuckles.
Laughter causes happiness for all.
So why live without it?

Brynn Hagenbuch, Grade 7
Incarnation School

The Leaves' Dance

The leaf blowing near,
Acts like a ballerina,
Twirling on Earth's stage.

Nicole Flaugher, Grade 7
St Paschal Baylon School

Just One More Day

I'm awakened by the Sergeant's commands
It is time to face another battle
As I glance at my calendar, I cross off another day
Just one more day.

I march outside, trailing behind the Sergeant
Making sure that all my equipment is in its place
We head for the old jeep
All of a sudden, glass starts to shatter and the loud screech of a missile flies by.
I was lucky it missed me.

I'm awakened by the Sergeant's commands
It is time to face another battle.
I am surprised that I have lived through yesterday.
Just one more day.

It's almost time to go home
I'm glad I'm alive.
I'm packing up for today.
I have completed my mission.
Proud and happy, I'm flying home.

Nicole Hodgson, Grade 7
South Range Middle School

Flying Across the Field

Breakaway, they will never learn, no one can handle the way I twist and turn
Boom! Is all I hear, as my crowd screams and cheers
Launch the ball low or high, believe it or not I never jump or dive
Scoop down low run wild, I am just an average child
I'm like a bird, that's the lead of a flock, I'll always lead because of what I got
Touchdown! Sprinting so fast, now I'm home, cheering for myself in the end zone
Now they see…Who can handle a guy like me?
Call me vain, but I'm not, you just don't have what I've got.
Yes I brag, especially in front of you!
Make people mad, love you too, it's all fun and games
Till I step on the field, make your father proud, you know how it feels
Once again I fly across the field, stooping low jumping high, some I believe I'll fly
Try to catch me if you can, but remember, "I'm da the man!"

Trayvon Moore, Grade 8
Licking Valley Middle School

I Remember

Like pages in a Sports Illustrated issue
Words like victory, Steelers, Seahawks
Two famous people Hines Ward and Jerome Bettis
Anybody's number, position, or face
The place in the story where it says Steelers demolish the Seahawks
The injury when I broke my elbow
Our house was filled with pleasure
And outside it was peaceful and chilly
The sound of the howl of the Steelers fan
Anyone who performed for the Steelers that year has a Super Bowl ring

Mason Miller, Grade 7
South Range Middle School

I Am Lucky

I am lucky
For lots of things
Like having a Christmas tree
With tons of gifts on Christmas day
Having a roof over my head
A bedroom to myself
Where I can be alone
And parents who love me
Having parents who take me
Where I need to go
I am lucky
That I have soldiers fighting for our freedom
And that I can get together with my family
And have a great time
I am also lucky that Jesus died for me
It is incredible
Think of the poor who live in a box
Wow am I lucky

Amanda Hermann, Grade 7
Waterloo Middle School

War

I don't understand all of the fighting
Because all I hear is "Freedom ring"
Why do people have to die everyday
I just want some one to stand up and say
Why do we always have to fight
Please just think for a second and say "Is this right?"
I don't believe it is and I will never know why
Every night they have to hear their families stay up and cry
"Why" is such a small word but means so much

Jameson Sheely, Grade 8
Gesu Elementary School

If I Were a Soldier...

If I were a soldier, that defended everyone's life,
I would stand in honor, knowing I am respected.
If I were a soldier,
I would not want to be killed, knowing it was the end,
But that I let everyone down.
If I were a soldier,
I would tell many people to stand tall,
And be proud of our flag and what it represents.
If I were a soldier,
I would guard my fellow brother and sister's lives,
As if they were my own.
If I were a soldier,
I wouldn't fear losing my life,
But I would fear for losing my fellow people.
If I were a soldier,
I wouldn't take anything for granted,
But I would take everything I have
And cherish if forever.

Casey Mers, Grade 7
Gahanna Middle School East

Canada

I love to stand by the lake
And hear the sound of the calming wake.

One big Pike will put up a fight,
Just to not be dinner tonight.

When dinner is caught and all is done,
We go out tubing to have some fun.

We play cards all night,
Joke around, and get in silly, funny fights.

A week in Canada is always fun,
I always hope it's never done.

Briana Miller, Grade 7
J A Garfield Middle School

Truth and Lies

I'm 12 years old.
I'm a dog.
I play basketball
I'm six foot tall.
I play football.
I'm Shaquille O'Neil.
I go to school.
I'm a cheerleader.

Daniel Schmidt, Grade 7
Hamersville Elementary and Middle School

Eternity

Eternity means different things to everyone.
To some it is a blessing.
To others it is a curse.
To most it is the unachievable dream.

To me eternity means something else.
To me it is impossible.
A dream that doesn't exist,
To me eternity is made up,
A thing to people who are afraid of death.
To me death is not a fear.
To me eternity is the thing to fear.

Why would anyone want to live forever?
Having to sit by and watch everyone you ever knew die
Knowing you never will join them,
And it really is good-bye.

So if you live life like you should
Why wish for eternity?
And if you know that all things die
Why live forever?
And with all this knowledge
What good is eternity.

Michelle Blum, Grade 8
Springboro Jr High School

Life

Life is like going
to the movies after
it begins and leaving
before it ends.
Alex Radwanski, Grade 7
J A Garfield Middle School

From Christmas to the New Year

Christmas
family, trees
presents, joy, Jesus
happiness, prayers, food,
snow, peace, togetherness, harmony,
singing, ending, new year,
beginning, resolutions,
New Year
Emmi Abel-Rutter, Grade 7
St Gertrude School

Happiness

A smile as bright as the sun,
Laughing,
Giggling,
Friends,
Family,
God,
Love,
Children,
And many silly faces.
We are so happy,
You cannot bring us down.
Oh how hard it is to frown!
Christine Meadors, Grade 8
St Christopher Elementary School

The Epitome of Beauty

Horses so gracefully
Run and play around the pasture,
And beautifully they stride along,
As their manes and long, thick tails
Flow in the wind,
A wind they make from their gait,
Whether at a gallop,
Or an elegant trot,
Their power moves in a fiery burst
Of beauty and delicate sophistication.
In the bright sun they may come,
Or in a starry night they travel,
You see them, then they pass,
As fast and quick as can be.
They thrust their legs forward
With sheer power and strength,
The epitome of beauty,
The horse.
Will Rhoads, Grade 8
Pike Christian Academy

Lost

I look up, hands shaking
Black
Intense fear grips my soul
Black…I squint…
Desperate for a ray of hope
Black…the night is eerie and cold
A sea of darkness, and suddenly a ray of hope
Squinting, blinking, my eyes attempt focusing
A far off glint magnifies
Glitter reflects in my eyes, someone tells me
A light inside me magnifies, filling up some empty corner I didn't know existed
My focus zooms
The star shines brighter every second
Hope floods my heart
Maybe we will find our way out
Out of this place where we seemed so desperately
Lost
Maybe we aren't quite as lost as we think,
Just maybe
Molly Fitch, Grade 8
St Christopher Elementary School

Blue

Blue is
Vibrant, calm and dark.
The crash of the blue waves against the wall of rocks.
The loud pastel of a dark blue poster.
A cool cold winter night cuddled under the stars.
Fiji water and the clear blue sky on a cold winter day after a storm.
Serenity of a moonlit dinner on the beach.
The smell of burning tires on a drag strip making the blue body shakes.
The peaceful blue lucky charm with a light marshmallow taste.
Rachel Considder, Grade 8
Chardon Middle School

Morphing of Seasons

Nights are cool.
Days are short.
The leaves are shedding their ancient colors, transforming to red and gold.
The petals are hibernating,
The birds are now migrating,
To the south where the fresh warm air will be in their grasp

I'm excited for when white blankets of fluff will engulf the Earth,
And tell stories with every beautiful flake,
Painting a picture of life in a fantasy world.
The mentors are gliding to search for mementos,
Looking for extravagant remembrances of this year for their blossoming children.

The temperature gauge is attempting to freeze at zero for this season,
And presently the moving picture of fall is being painted.
Now the skies are attempting to paint the awesome overhead of autumn.
I am also ready for the incarnation of the winter holidays to come,
But right now I rest my head for my alarm clock has fallen behind.
Jake Pelini, Grade 8
Sacred Heart School

Go Out and Have a Ball

No matter who you are, go out and have a ball.
Short and tall, big and small, go out and have a ball.

Go to a harvest, go to a fair, go to a dance, anywhere!
As long as it's something of traditional fall, I don't care!

I don't know why you wouldn't because it's a wonderful season.
I don't know if there's a valid reason.

Go out and have a ball

Kalen Banks, Grade 7
Gesu Catholic School

Wind

Today there is no wind.
No blowing leaves,
No trees swaying high in the air.
There are no clouds,
Driving along the big blue highway.
There is no wind.
Pushing the acorns of the oak.
Propelling the little boy's kite.
There is no wind whispering in my ear.
There is no wind whistling through the tunnel.
There is no wind for the birds.
There is no wind.
Creating the waves in the ocean.
Creating the fresh breeze in your hair
Everything is motionless.
Without the wind.

Ryan Bannan, Grade 8
Chardon Middle School

Hearts Don't

Hearts don't get broken,
   only bruised.
Hearts don't mend themselves
   without a little help.
Hearts can't be worn on your sleeve —
   they beat in your chest with every breath you breathe.
Hearts aren't meant to be alone;
   they need a little socialization.
Hearts don't die,
   only stop beating.
Hearts don't lie,
   they tell the truth no matter how much it hurts.
Hearts aren't annoying,
   just mildly frustrating.
Hearts don't know love
   until they are introduced.
Hearts don't fall in love,
   they drown.
Hearts don't represent love,
   they are simply messengers.

Haleigh Hart, Grade 8
Chardon Middle School

Childhood Is…

Childhood is watching *Spongebob* for countless hours.
Childhood is wishing you had super powers.
Childhood is dropping a penny into a wishing well.
Childhood is ringing that tiny Christmas bell.
Childhood is making your first finger painting masterpiece.
Childhood is accidentally letting your dog off the leash.
Childhood is your older cousin making you go to bed at seven.
Childhood is when you first learn about heaven.
Childhood is working together to put up the Christmas tree.
Childhood is feeling happy and free.

Andrew Bucur, Grade 7
St Monica Elementary School

Sonnet to a Cookie

See that cookie in the distance yonder?
In the window, from sun's rays it dost shine;
Golden brown, baked with loving care and time.
Should I take it and eat it? I ponder.
Lo! What will he do? the cookie wonders.
To steal it, would it be such a great crime?
I decide nay and so stand up supine.
My arm reaches out; forward I saunter.
I grasp the cookie in my eager hands.
I count the chips and note the perfect shape.
I toss it up and in my mouth it lands.
It is delicious, much like a French crepe!
I swallow; it crumbles like soft, sweet, sand.
'Twas the best cookie that I ever ate!

Ignatius Chad Kringen, Grade 9
Beavercreek High School

Where I'm From

I am from hide-and-seek,
From parents who aren't perfect.
I am from survivors and casualties,
From a war long fought.
I am from starry summer nights,
From two little sisters who follow me everywhere.

I am from Jovan musk and poker,
From dogs and cats.
I am from computers and mp3 players,
From a home built by my grandfather.
I am from baskets of books and stuffed animals,
From rock to country.

I am from the smell of candles burning,
From staying up until midnight in the summer.
I am from sleeping until one in the afternoon,
From autumn leaves all around me.
I am from snow covering my boots,
From gardening in the spring.
I am from Middletown, Ohio.

Deanna Swem, Grade 8
Verity Middle School

The Jack-o'-Lantern Smile
The jack-o'-lantern
Glowed in the cold dark night sky
With a smiling face

Ashley Rouhier, Grade 7
St Paschal Baylon School

Was It Me?
I didn't do it
I know it wasn't me
I don't understand why people do this
How can they be so hateful?
I don't know what to do
Should I run?
Was it me?

I didn't do it
I know it wasn't me
He was young and short
But old and wise inside
Why must the good die young?
He didn't do anything wrong
Was it me?

I didn't do it
I know it wasn't me
I was sleeping when it happened
How could it be me?
He was my best friend
But I must say goodbye
Was it me?

Corey Deal, Grade 7
South Range Middle School

War!!!
Guns billowing smoke,
Surrounding trees blazing,
Children's screaming faces,
Friends and family,
Crying their hearts out,
This is the pain of war!
A crimson red ground,
A brown broken tree,
Large rattling machines,
Bombs booming as they go,
This is the war!
Many dead, many dying,
Wounds a bleeding,
These are the people,
Who protect their loved ones,
These are the wounded of war!
The Army, the Air force,
The Navy, the Marines,
All protecting,
These are the people of war!

Rebekah Eller, Grade 9
Westerville South High School

Eye on the Ball
Take your time, give a nice pass
Swing all the way through
Smiling, trying to do what my coach said
I watch the ball go over the net and contact the ground
I hear the crowd cheering like I won the game
I see my coach jump up
She says "good job"

The next serve goes over
They bump, set, and spike the ball over
I dive across the gym, saving it as I'm on the floor
The setter sets the ball up, I make the kill
I spike the ball to the floor
I see my coach jump up
She says "good job"

As I look at the score I see 25 to 10
I feel the rush of excitement go through me
As we show respect to each opponent with a shake and a "good game"
Our team huddles together
We discuss how well we did and the mistakes
I feel the pain on the outside but happy on the inside
Our coach says "good job"

Sarah Bradford, Grade 8
Licking Valley Middle School

Fall
A favored season among all,
With its warm weather
And its crisp, clean air.
Plus all the changes that it brings.

Take a look out the window,
What do you see?
Leaves dancing to the ground,
Children running around.

Soon come the decorations,
Pumpkins, corn stalks,
Witches, ghosts.
Neighborly contests to see who attracts the most.

One night at the end of October.
The children dress up along with adults, up and down the street they parade.
Going up to every door, saying, "Trick or Treat"
Candy is given on the night of Halloween

Winter approaches.
Trees are bare and down come the decorations,
Making room for the new season. Chilly now and frost falls at night.
Then comes the snow. Then, all at once, fall's over.

Rian Lees, Grade 8
Licking Valley Middle School

Alone in the World Again
Little David is three years old
He usually sleeps out in the cold
But his mother told him to go pack
But all he has now are the clothes on his back
He met a girl on the street
Who barely had enough to eat
While searching for food, they found a canoe
But when she leaned over the edge to get her shoe
She fell off the boat
Only she did not float
She sunk to the floor
Now David is four
If you ask him how he's been, he'll reply
I'm alone in the world again

Kaycee Kuhn, Grade 7
Waterloo Middle School

Be All That You Can Be
Be like the water, so pure and refined,
Take the right path, though the path will wind
Be like the wind, so swift and divine,
Be like the flower, it's beauty does shine,
Be like the mountain, strong and high,
Be all that you can, just give it a try,
You can be like a leaf, float soft to the ground,
You can be soft and kind, and show love you have found.

Nathan Wilkins, Grade 9
BOSS Buckeye On-Line School for Success

Blue
What is blue?
  Blue is relaxing and calm,
  Blue is the color of a sad song
  Blue is a newborn baby's eyes
  Blue is the ocean of tears after someone dies
  Blue is the sky — full of endless possibilities
  Blue is the color that gives us a sense of tranquility
That is blue.

Emily Thomas, Grade 7
Pike Delta York Middle School

Normal
We're all normal inside
It is something you can't hide
Even Batman is a regular guy
Some people run, some can fly
Just be normal on the inside
You don't have to be special
Don't have to be cool
I see the grayness in eyes
Just hang on, I have a surprise
It's not cool, and it won't make you cry
Just always remember, you're normal inside

Levi Milko, Grade 7
J A Garfield Middle School

I Am Allie
My favorite color is pink.
I am a good listener, I think.
I struggle with formulas, but am okay with math.
Maybe I resemble a dog, dogs are rarely in a wrath.
I love mashed potatoes, my grandma's are the best.
Becoming a doctor would put me to the test.
Kanye West is my favorite, he has very good songs.
I prefer to ride on airplanes, they don't take as long.
I get that I'm short, you don't have to remind me.
When you sing, get the words right, I will plea.
If I see a snake, you might as well tell me goodbye.
I will be gone in a blink of an eye.
Basketball and soccer are what I like to play,
But I am not up for it every day.
If you need me, I'll be at the mall.
I always have my cell phone, just call.
You have just read a little about me.
I am Allie, can't you see?!

Alexandra Pirrone, Grade 8
St Monica Elementary School

Fall
Fall is so beautiful!
The trees are losing their leaves
and getting new beautiful, bright colored leaves,
greens, yellows, oranges and browns.
Every yard you see there's a beautiful pile of leaves.
You see kids jumping in the piles again and again,
with a smile and it's so joyful and fun.

Karlee Bates, Grade 7
Meadowbrook Middle School

I Am From
I am from an old green house
From a big backyard and a swing set
I am from the sand in a sandbox
(White, all shinny it looked like snow)
I am from grumpy old men and their dogs
And their sweet old wives
From grandparents around the corner
I'm from Christmas presents in the wagon
And from the porch swings
I am from too much food
And loud talking
From making up dances
And long car rides
Wishing we would hurry up and get there
I am from the little kitchen
From vanilla sandwich cookies
And cranberry juice
And missing them
When Grandpa was gone
All my friends and family
In my memory forever

Jessica Whalen, Grade 8
Logan Hocking Middle School

The White Coffin
December comes 'round.
And brings a coffin of ice
To seal off the Earth.
Matt Tischler, Grade 7
St Brendan Elementary School

So Many Things and Ways
Sit, don't sit
Stand, don't stand
So many things to do

Left or right
North or south
Some many ways to go

So many ways and things to feel
Love or hate
Don't differentiate
It's better to collaborate
In the end it all turns out the same

So many things and ways
Choose the right things
Choose the right ways
And you'll turn out okay
Maria Lopez, Grade 9
Westlake High School

Veterans' Day
V ietnam
E lite fighting core
T rained American soldiers
E nthusiastic war heroes
R etreating German soldiers in WWII
A ttacking the flanks
N ational Guard
S quads fighting battles

D -Day
A merica's army fighting for freedom
Y ears of service in the army
Greg Gambone, Grade 8
Western Reserve Middle School

July
Marches in audibly
With a stagger.
It shoves away
The rainy weather.
July dances in,
Full of heat.
It saunters in,
Then limps away,
Leaving everyone wilted.
Cortnee Marchese, Grade 7
Wooster Christian School

The Last Vestiges of Summer
Pull…Breathe…Pull…Breathe…
Moving fluidly, endlessly, back and forth.
When will it end?
The minutes, seeming like hours, move ever so slowly.
Finally, it is over, and the vast waters wait for me to return another day.

Bounce…Bounce…
The sound of a ball,
Bounce…Bounce…
I am in my backyard
Working diligently to break records, entertain,
Becoming better at what I love.

"Take Cover!"
Voices shouting in my ear, from unknown places.
As I play a game, from the cybernetic world,
The anonymous voices give me commands,
To ensure victory.

It soon becomes late.
I spend time with my family,
No thoughts of homework or due dates,
The last vestiges of my summer are spent lazily,
Wishing it would never end.
Nico Zullo, Grade 8
Mayfield High School

I Remember
I remember…
Like pages in a volleyball instruction booklet
Words like referee, no earrings, and have fun
Two famous people Jill Colleymore and Flo Hyaman
Anybody's ball, spike, or set
The place in the story when the going gets tough, the tough get going
The injury when I broke my arm playing volleyball
Our house was a big gym in Greenford, Ohio
And outside it is a huge, sweaty gym
The sound of everyone saying "mine" or "got it"
Anyone who play's volleyball should think of victory
Allison Turnbull, Grade 7
South Range Middle School

Childhood Is
Childhood is getting money every time your grandparents see you.
Childhood is hating to get clothes for Christmas presents.
Childhood is playing from dawn to dusk outside with your friends.
Childhood is thinking that a dollar is a lot of money.
Childhood is having candy, pop, chips, and cookies hidden away under your bed.
Childhood is being too small for roller coasters.
Childhood is being scared to go to the doctor's office.
Childhood is not worrying about tests.
Childhood is spending hours on video games.
Childhood is playing house with your friends.
Childhood is the best time of your life!
Maria Bonvissuto, Grade 7
St Monica Elementary School

Sunburst Orange

Sunburst orange is pumpkins,
leaves, and trees.
Sunburst oranges is the smell of pumpkin pie
on a winter day.
Orange is the mums popping
out of the ground.
Orange is the zesty citrus all around.
Orange is shy and orange is quiet
but when you get inside orange is a riot.
Orange is happy like kids on a cold winter day,
Orange is the Halloween holiday.
Orange can walk and orange can run
and orange can have all the fun.
Orange is in a bouquet of poppies.
Orange is my color through and through
and forever always will I love you.

Hannah Satterfield, Grade 7
West Branch Middle School

Childhood Is

Childhood is doing bad things and going to your room.
Childhood is having snowball fights.
Childhood is being in bed by 8:30.
Childhood is eating ice cream all the time.
Childhood is drawing pictures for mom.
Childhood is playing Nintendo 64.
Childhood is not caring about anything.
Childhood is coloring on the walls.
Childhood is not being able to drink coffee.
Childhood is wanting to be a grown-up.

Justin Puma, Grade 7
St Monica Elementary School

I Am

I am an athlete in training.
I wonder if there is actually life out there.
I hear the ocean even in the silence of night.
I see people for who they are and not what they appear.
I want to be someone.
I am an athlete in training.

I pretend I score the winning goal at the FIFA world cup.
I feel like I am in a sea of voices.
I touch the bat even when I am not up to the plate.
I worry that I will be a no one, a nothing.
I cry when in the midst of failure.
I am an athlete in training.

I understand why we go to war, but not why we stay.
I say the words and hope they come true.
I dream of fame and my name in lights.
I try to forgive when they may not need forgiveness.
I hope to be a professional athlete in many different sports.
I am an athlete in training.

Kevin Coppus, Grade 7
Hopewell Loudon Local Elementary School

Sadness

Sadness is an ocean blue.
Blue like a teardrop
And like a clear, empty sea.
It scurries in and out of my life without warning.
It reminds me of a friend that passed away.
Sadness makes me feel sorry.

Elise Bleser, Grade 7
Incarnation School

Where I'm From

I'm from the smell of cookies and a black couch.
I'm from money don't grow on trees.
I'm from Karen and Earl.
I'm from rock and metal like Disturbed and Slipknot.

I'm from my friend next door and across the street.
I'm from watermelon, apples and grapes.
I'm from the half pipe to the basketball hoop.
From swimming and fishing to biking and skateboarding.
I'm from TV, music and movies.
I'm from my brother and me fighting.
I'm from my cat, dog and gecko.

I'm from my friends Quan, Greg, Corey.
I'm from brothers and two sisters.
I'm from technology being important.

Phillip Glass, Grade 8
Verity Middle School

Is This It?

The buses rolling down the hot summer street
Soldiers standing one by one in a straight line
Stepping up and saying good-bye
Families cry as they say good-bye
Husbands and wives getting one last kiss
For their loved one they'll terribly miss
So they leave just one kiss

Off and down the buss goes
It's time to grow up and fight
For this is it
It's time to fight so our country will shine
Smoking bombs and blasting guns
As a bunch of troops painfully die
One by one

It's sad to say
This may be the last breath that you take
For this is war and never forget it
Goodbyes, the dead cannot say,
But they hear the families cry as they get the news
Their broken hearts go around and around
They simply start to lose their hope.

Nicole Mossor, Grade 7
South Range Middle School

Choices

I had to make a choice
but it seemed no matter what
I had no voice.

I realized it was the smart thing to do.
It's worse than a blister
but better than the flu.

I guess I had to accept her
since she is my little sister.
Keegan Scott, Grade 8
Pike Delta York Middle School

I Do Too

I can't sleep
The trains are racing
The geese are flying
The leaves are falling

I dart out of the cabin
The cold wind stings my face
There is laughter in the background

The water is still…
then the world goes to sleep,
and I do too.
Austin Borton, Grade 7
Incarnation School

My Sorrow

Sweet scented flowers
Among the empty field
Through sunshine, through rain
My sorrow has healed
Courtney Klein, Grade 7
Reed Middle School

Inside This Bike…

Inside this bike,
there is a heart beating.

When you wreck,
it starts crying and weeping,
just like a baby,
when it needs a changing.

When you jump a ramp,
it prays that you won't wreck,
and die that day.

When you get off,
it laughs and plays,
the rest of the day.
William "Andrew" Flynn, Grade 8
Riverview East Academy

Childhood Is

Childhood is eating ice cream until you get sick.
Childhood is not having any responsibility.
Childhood is coloring outside the lines, and not caring.
Childhood is wearing crazy and funky clothes.
Childhood is sneaking candy wrappers under your bed.
Childhood is having a care free life.
Childhood is having long peaceful naps.
Childhood is trying to stay up for New Year's Day.
Childhood is making a mess and not cleaning it up.
Childhood is getting tons of toys for your birthday and not playing with them.
Rayanna Hinkle, Grade 7
St Monica Elementary School

In the Shoes of an Arabian Child

Full of confusion and fear
What's happening, what's going on here?
As I sit in a corner, trying to think happy
But my mind keeps flashing back to war.
The blood, the pain
Screaming in vain.
I just sit there, helpless, not knowing what is next
Then an American soldier comes up and says,
"What is your name?"
I took his waist and hugged him and said,
"Thank you, my name is Sadie, and I've seen bad things, please help me."
And he says, to me; "I will, it's my job."
Riley Chafin, Grade 7
J A Garfield Middle School

As the Rain Comes Down

A storm begins and dark clouds appear all around
And soon much healing goes on as the rain comes down
The beggar sits in the street
A person no one cares to meet
Huddled in a ball, chin to his knees
When the rain begins he turns up his face and cries "Please!
Oh Lord! Why me?"
The thug waiting when a man walks by
He begins to tail the man he sees
When the rain and the wind rustles a tree's leaves
He looks to the sky and goes home, no one knows why
The prisoner sitting in his iron cage
The sinner sees not but rage
With anger at those by which he was caught
And anger at those on whom his dark deeds he wrought
When the steady rain begins with a calming rustle of the leaves,
And through clear smoke he sees
He should point the anger at himself and not at others' deeds
The scholar studying late in the college preparing for a life wrought with knowledge
When he hears the rain and looks up to see
He chuckles to himself I remember when it saved me.
Jacob Broida, Grade 7
Birchwood School

God

You are bright and warm like a dancing flame,
Magnificent to the wandering eye,
But when too close, you scorch my tender flesh,
You bring warmth to those who are oh so cold.
You're rough all around like a jagged rock,
But you get worn from the flowing river,
You have a look of toughness about you,
But you crumble underneath the pressure.
You are brilliant like the burning sun,
Bringing light to the lives of so many,
But when looked at directly, blinds one's eyes.
You are the center of the galaxy,
But you are more distant than ever now.
You are everything I am not.

Joe Fluegemann, Grade 8
St Aloysius Gonzaga School

Day at the Beach

Lying on the warm sand
I listen to the oceans soft roar,
so soothing and calm.
The birds singing off in the distance.
Slowly the sun melts through the sky,
the soft pink and orange meet with the glistening blue water.
The day turns into night
and the sun drifts away,
slowly turning the sky into a dark place
waiting for the sun to come back again
and light up the world with its vibrant rays.

Kiera Wing, Grade 7
Gahanna Middle School East

The Moon Night

The night
Sweeps in
And tickles the air
Seeping inward
Until the air is completely black
The purple black of night
That comes to know and love everything
In a suffering sad silence
That sees all
Knows all
Is a part of all
But is not considered part of all life
The night is the light of all knowledge
That sees more than the sun
For the sunlight is arrogant
And the moon night is timid
The night is shy and humble
It will consume the light in a forceful move
But only when the time is right

Riza Miklowski, Grade 8
Birchwood School

The Cage

I leave here young and bold
Ready to die for my country.
Holding the weapon in my hands,
The cold steel, the smooth wood.
Prowling through the jungle
Silently stalking them with cruel thoughts.
The enemy is in my sights, helpless
I pull the trigger with no regret.

I lay here now in my old age
Feeling so alone, helpless.
Their blood on my hands,
Their faces tattooed in my mind.
Why did I pull the trigger?
The guilt builds up like a wall,
Caging me in.
My heart aches for the widow.
I cry myself to sleep.

Ross Stoffer, Grade 7
South Range Middle School

The Hike

Tramping across hill and prairie,
Climbing cliffs steep and scary.
On a winding path like a snake,
Stopping briefly to eat by the lake.

Walking through intimidating pines,
All the while looking for animal signs.
Watching deer jump across the trail,
While we startle resting quail.

Gulping water from our jugs,
And swatting at annoying bugs.
Finding the campsite after wandering around,
Gratefully plopping our backpacks down.

Setting up camp before it is night,
Eating dinner in the evening's light.
Sitting quietly near the campfire,
Recalling God's beauty before we retire.

Colin Lamprecht, Grade 8
St Christopher Elementary School

What Is Faith?

Faith is…
    the trust that is given
        from one to believe in you.
Faith is…
    a great amount of caring
        and the love you show.
Faith is…
    the greatest amount of trust you will ever
        put into anyone.

Nicole Fields, Grade 7
Hamersville Elementary and Middle School

Inside the Earth
Inside the Earth
Is an indignant spirit
Shocked at how
Its inhabitants
Have soiled and disfigured
Its beautiful face
From its snowcap eyes
To its green, forest hair
To its soft, tan desert skin
It winces every time someone digs a hole
Or brings coal out of the ground
The Earth cries out
When buildings pop up on its face
Like acne
And when it's oceanic tears
Are filled with trash
And pollutants
The Earth is an indignant tortured spirit
Matt Bernert, Grade 7
Gahanna Middle School East

Autumnal Pyre
A spurt of wind
Brushes the discarded leaves
And transfigures them
Into whirling, spinning dervishes.

Not yet browned,
The freshly sown leaves
Roar up like a bonfire
Their glowing hues dancing like flames

As the gust departs
The dance dies down
And the leaves
Become still, fiery coals.
Jacob Dennis, Grade 7
Birchwood School

Next in Line
Their eyes are wide.
Never blinking,
Never moving to the side,
They're always staring … Staring.

Their hands are entrenched.
No one is talking.
Their teeth are clenched
As they're slowly walking … walking.

As I look at their fear,
Etched into their eye,
The truth strikes me like a spear.
Soon I … soon I.
Levi Callicoat, Grade 8
Hopewell Jr High School

Martin Luther King Jr.
I am Martin Luther King Jr.
Come to my home of equal rights.
I am a hero for the blacks. Hear me speak for the rights of the colored.
See my marches for the rights of colors.
See my speeches of having a dream.
See my proud face as I stand up for my rights of color.
I am an ordinary person. Watch me fight for what I believe in.
Watch me make progress for all colors.
I am a believer, hear me, see me, speak of me, and
One day you will understand what I have done.
Amy Link, Grade 7
Fort Recovery Middle School

Where I'm From
I am from climbing trees, skipping rope,
And going swimming in the lake.
From going to Grandma Dot's house to a smell
of fresh baked cookies.
I am from a car wreck that changed my father's life. And my family's too.
From my two dogs Spike and Minnie,
And my two rats Nikki and Samantha.
I am from my older sister Erin who I love very much
From my niece Mandy who calls me Brit-Brit.
From my two best friends Brittany and Kourtnie
Who I'm with every day all day!
I am from Monday Night Raw from Saturday Night movies
From the WEBN fireworks I go see every year.
From writing my own stories, reading books, and listening to music.
I am from an old stuffed Pooh Bear that my
Sister gave me when she left the house.
I am from a mother that left me when I was young.
From first loves to heartbreaks and all From family losses and new births love them all
I am from happy times, from sad times.
But no matter what kind of time it is
I know that my friends and family will always be there when I need them!
Brittany Woodward, Grade 8
Verity Middle School

Looking Out
I'm on the inside looking out.
I see little kids wanting to be like us.
I see their jaws drop and eyes widen in amazement as we fly through the air.
I see kids acting like high level gymnasts, toes and fingers pointed like a
straight compass arrow pointing north and south…all at Emeth Gymnastics.
I'm on the inside looking out.
I hear them gasping, taking such a breath as if it were their last.
I hear them applauding as loud as thunder.
I hear them whispering, "I wish, I wish, I could be like them."
I'm on the inside looking out.
I can feel their intense and awed gaze following like a lion watching his prey.
I feel the overload of admiration that they have and show for us as we do
and show for Carly Patterson and Dominique Moceanu.
I feel the excitement they have when they come to Emeth Gymnastics and watch us.
I'm glad I'm on the inside looking out.
Kristen Heslop, Grade 8
Chardon Middle School

An Average Teen

I sit in my room,
easily distracted by the surrounding commotion,
between the radio playing and the occasional daydream taking my mind into another world,
I find it hard to concentrate.
Mother calls me to put away the dishes,
Dad tells me to set the table.
After supper, I finally have time to write.
My name is Brian, and I'm a fairly normal teenage boy.
I love sports, music, and of course, girls.
Hanging out with friends and going to concerts are some of my favorite things to do.
If my family and friends weren't there for me, I don't know what I would do.
I do not know where I want to live or what I want to do when I grow up.
I guess those are just some of the mysteries I am going to face in life.
I don't have any crazy dreams or wants;
I just try to live one day at a time.
If I can be grateful for what I have been given and am not focused on material things, I will live a great life.

Brian Skladany, Grade 8
St Monica Elementary School

Childhood Is

Childhood is jumping and playing in the freezing snow.
Childhood is eating all you can eat on Thanksgiving.
Childhood is raking the bright-colored leaves and jumping into them.
Childhood is waking up from bed and running downstairs to see your presents on Christmas.
Childhood is going to school to meet or make new friends.
Childhood is having friends come over in the summer and playing football in the front yard.
Childhood is waking up on Easter Day and running around the house to find the hidden eggs.
Childhood is eating all the cake that you get for your birthday.
Childhood is baking cookies with your mom then eating them all.
Childhood is going to baseball games and eating nachos and ice cream.

Allan Medovic, Grade 7
St Monica Elementary School

My Life Inside and Out

My name is Allyson, standing tall and proud.
Unique and outgoing, shining through the crowd.
My favorite color is sky blue, like on a clear spring day.
I'm talkative and loud, but sometimes having not much to say.
I love to play all sorts of sports, especially volleyball out on the court.
I'm mostly like a killer whale, fast, wild, and free; every day; yep that's me.
When I grow up I plan on being a veterinarian, in a hospital is where I'll be.
For my later career, I would like to be a marine biologist and work with the killer whales, which are fast, wild, and free.
My mom and dad are the people I admire, I would keep them forever and they would never expire.
I have blue eyes that match the sky, brownish, blondish hair like a teddy bear, and my skin is a slight tan just like the sand.
In my spare time, I am in Tae Kwon Do.
It teaches us how to fight so we don't have to.
Sometimes, I fear the darkness in many spaces, but I know my home is one of the safest places.
My strongest character trait is helping people out, because I hate to see them pout.
Sometimes, I picture myself as a sunflower, strong like King Kong.
Maybe tall like a tree in the fall.
Yet sometimes delicate, because not everyone is always tough and strong.
I am known as Xena Princess Warrior because of my great strength and spirit in Tae Kwon Do.
I may not be the most popular in my school, but my friends and I are cool.
I love being me, because I know that that is the key!

Allyson Mitchell, Grade 8
St Monica Elementary School

Wind

Wide and open
So open it blows everything
Hugs you when you're standing
Then you fall forward
From the wind tackling you
Just like football
Whistles to warn you
Warn you that it's coming
Blows through the grass
Singing while the grass sways
Rapidly flying over the wings of a bird
Lifting the bird high in the sky
The bird soaring through the arms
The arms of the
Wind

Abby Hersey, Grade 7
Gahanna Middle School East

Wet Leaves

Wet leaves on the ground,
Were pushed around by a jump,
Then floated back down.

Amanda Zbinovec, Grade 7
St Paschal Baylon School

44460

The moo of the cows
The rumbling of the tractor
Nice cut grass
Perfectly mixed grain
The splashing of the creek
The stereo banging
But not so close to the road
The sight of the big red barn
   The night
   The peace
   The sunlight
My home

Tyler Pidgeon, Grade 7
West Branch Middle School

Oh Sun

Oh sun so bright,
Oh sun so might,
Why do you not shine at night?
For such a wonderful sight,
You never seem to fright.
For so bright you are,
You'll never find a matching star.

Oh sun so bright,
Oh sun so might,
Why do you not shine at night?

Dustin Duling, Grade 8
Columbus Grove Middle School

Fear

I watch the clear, vast night sky, wondering what will become of me
I stare into the darkness, my fear rising.
As it comes closer, my fear, I don't understand.
How does it expect me to realize how it sees?
We always fear what we don't understand.
Thus is the human way, to fear.
And to love. To feel in a way none other can.
Or so we think.
My fear rising. Coming closer. Closer.
My understanding fading as I see more.
I gaze into the clear night sky once more,
as I fear what's to come.

Karissa Payne, Grade 8
Glenwood Middle School

Veteran's Day

The veterans stand so straight and tall.
They all remember friends and soldiers that died in combat.
They remember the sacrifices they made.
The dedication and hard work paid off when we won the wars.

Uncle Marty is a veteran from the marines.
So is my cousin Matt but he is in the war now on stand by.
Matt can get called any minute of any day to go battle across the seas.
They understand what it is like to battle and fight.

Soldiers could die and leave their families alone at home without them.
The bombs bursting in air before them gives them the chills.
It's the scariest thing in life for them.

I love you Matt.
Be careful out there.
I pray for you like the rest of the family.
You have a son arriving soon.
He will look up to you,
So be careful and come home safely.

Haley Moore, Grade 7
South Range Middle School

Mozart

Rain patters on the ground, driving relentlessly,
I walk along the sidewalk as the storm grows,
Trudging on through the driving rain,
The storm grows as I move forward.
It seems as if the sky has opened up, letting out all rain,
I am soaked to the bone, drenched, sodden.
Suddenly the clouds part and I feel the warmth of the sun on my shoulders,
A rainbow appears in the sky,
I move onward through a mixture of emerging beauty and a retreating tempest.
The birds chirp, the dogs bark,
I am home at last, the storm is gone.

Brian Clark, Grade 8
Incarnation School

A Place to Go

I dream of peace
A place to go
A place to be myself
Where the wind sweeps me off my feet
Where the grass sways to the winds song
A place to sit and think
Where the flowers dance from the sun's happiness
And the rain comes down to see me smile
I can lay there watching
The clouds make shapes for me
Where the snow comes down to make me shiver
And forms blankets so I can sleep
A place to call my own
Where the stars shine to make me laugh
And the moon sings me to sleep
Where the trees grow branches to bring me up to climb
And animals come to keep me company
A place where no one can interfere
Where love is sprinkled through the air
I can go and nothing will stop me
Because they know I belong

Ginelle Reed, Grade 7
Gahanna Middle School East

True Love

I liked you at first sight,
but I loved you in the water fight.
I loved you more when you gave me a hug
and my heart was soaring through the sky,
but I loved you even more when I had to say,
"Good-bye."

Angelica Pifer, Grade 8
Labrae Middle School

It's Not Fair

It's not fair he had to go
It's not fair I miss him so
It's not fair it happened so fast
It's not fair I can't change the past
It's not fair the memories fade
It's not fair he couldn't stay
It's not fair I was only four
It's not fair my heart was so sore
It's not fair he had to suffer so long
It's not fair he can't sing me my favorite song
It's not fair he passed so long ago
It's not fair sometimes I feel low
It's not fair he couldn't win
It's not fair when I get married he won't be there
It's not fair he can't be here
It's not fair people stop and stare at his grave
It's not fair I have to go when I want to stay
It's not fair he had to go
It's not fair I miss him so

Miranda Bennett, Grade 7
Waterloo Middle School

Ocean

Walking on a sandy beach
Cool water splashes my feet
Sounds of ocean
Calm and peaceful
Dolphins jumping
Fish swimming
Beautiful sight
Clear blue water
Wavy calm ripples
Perfect place to relax

Amber Camp, Grade 7
St Clement Elementary School

About Me

Hi my name is Billy;
My friends call me Billy Bob Joe.
I consider myself very silly,
And I'm afraid of tornadoes.

My greatest talent is baseball,
Even though I like basketball.
I play them in the summer, winter, and fall.
Though I love sports so much, I can't play them all.

When I grow up I want to be a cop;
My job right now is cutting grass.
My favorite restaurant is IHOP,
I also like to fish for bass.

Video games are my passion,
To me they are a big deal.
I'm not so great when it comes to fashion.
Every night I like to have a big meal.

Overall, I think I'm a good guy,
Because I'm a child of God.
He made me not too social, but not too shy,
And I'm a unique, special gift from God.

William Hendrock, Grade 8
St Monica Elementary School

Pink Is…

Soft and elegant like a ballet slipper,
The warm pinkish feeling of a baby blanket,
The mellow pink of a sunset,
The pink chirp of a bird in the morning,
The silky pink of a child's ballet skirt,
The sweet pink taste of Smarties,
The lovely pink of love and marriage,
The soft pink whistle of the wind,
The twinkle pink of the stars at night, and
The sweet tickle-me-pink of a father and a daughter.

Abby Fairbanks, Grade 8
Chardon Middle School

Death

Death is hurtful, scary,
confusing and unexpected
People ask why,
they want to know why it had
to happen to them but they'll
never know,
cause death is a mystery
no one will ever understand
Until they die themselves and
meet death
Death is a person no one
knows until they die
Most people don't want to
meet death
I know I don't

Jessie Raisor, Grade 7
J A Garfield Middle School

Off Road

4x4
Trails
Jumps
Tires humming
Mud flinging
Engines roaring
Trucks crashing
Steel bending
Clouds of smoke
Snapping limbs
Bang!!

Samuel Gearhart, Grade 8
Licking Valley Middle School

Ridin' My Tractor

Ridin' my tractor
Going down the road,
Feeling like an actor,
Breaking a code.
Riding on my tractor
With the wind in my hair,
Faced with a factor
Of my hair ruined from the air.
Going up the field
With hay on a wagon,
Making sure I yield,
So the hay doesn't fall off the wagon.
Sun so bright,
Burning down on me,
Such a vivid light,
I felt like a steamy tea.
Then when I look up,
I see the bright blue sky,
I see the big airplanes going up so high,
And I take a glance and watch them fly.

Tracey Teichman, Grade 8
Chardon Middle School

A Cold Winter's Day

The winter snow falls like stars from the heavens.
Each flake a precious jewel, no two like each other.
The snow can put a smile on our face.
Or trap us in a solitary place.
Winter ice glows in the midday sun.
Sledding in the winter is always fun.
After all of the snow's fun,
You can enjoy a fire and some hot chocolate, then your day will be done.

Will Hartman, Grade 7
Gesu Elementary School

No Resent

My paws pad softly across the well-worn path,
Whose destination I know not.
The scent of man close behind,
I break into my swiftest run.
Enamel white teeth, obsidian black claws,
Neither are good against his silver metal rounds.
I skid to a stop,
Icy rocky barrier standing before me.
Knowing my fate, I turn around, waiting.
His silhouette approaches on the glistening snow.
My amber eyes meet his,
But all I see are two black, never ending holes.
I go cross-eyed, focusing on the red dot now centered on my face.
he whispers, "I'm sorry," and gently edged the trigger back.
As my legs buckle, I look back and reply,
"It's too late to apologize."
I lie down, and take a final look toward the sky,
And a single snow flake floats down and closes my eyes.
he went and collected his prize,
The majestic wolf.

Kim Savides, Grade 8
Chardon Middle School

Myself

Some might say I'm "weird" and some might say,
I'm "crazy," but I think I'm a great person.
My favorite color is black, and I'm most like a cat.
My favorite food is Japanese and I'm cool with that.
My crush is a cartoon,
Boy do the kids laugh at that.
Some people say my true passion is drawing, but they got it all wrong.
My true passion is writing, though poetry isn't really my call.
Someday, I hope to meet my hero, the comic artist Rumiko Takahashi.
I hope to be a graphic artist like her and go the distance.
I truly dislike getting up early, especially on school days,
But I got eight years of this left, so I've got to face that.
Volleyball is my favorite sport, and I love to bump the ball around with my cousin.
My favorite instrument is the guitar. If only I knew how to play it!
I'm not a ballerina, but I walk on my toes.
I love to play with my hair, especially when I'm bored.
My friends call me "Hikaru" and sometimes "Alyssa."
But I settle for Alli, because that's truly me.

Allison Ford, Grade 8
St Monica Elementary School

The Mountain Cat
The she-devil screams madly a bloodthirsty call
It echoes through the mountains as a warning to all
That this land is hers; a wooded abode
And on all who enter will her wrath be bestowed
This beast is the queen, the empress, the goddess
Navigating the mountains with a skillful prowess
Only prowling and assiduous well after dusk
Moving swiftly and silently; every paw step hushed
As she stalks the impotent, we hear two sounds alone:
A startled yelp cut short and the crunching of bone
Alert through the night, constantly on the prowl
Bearing the permanent expression of a vindictive scowl
Sculpted muscles rippling beneath a pelt of amber
Glowing eyes of topaz, both malicious and somber
And to all who to question her awful power dare:
Take heed, take caution and of the mountain cat beware!
Alexa Urbanic, Grade 8
Incarnation School

Halloween Is
Halloween is hearing kids having fun,
Jumping in puddles,
Diving in a pile of crunchy leaves like dolphins,
Seeing the kids run from the haunted house
Seeing my dad Julius Caesar on Halloween
For the first time in a long time

Halloween is
Holding my pet cat Bologna in my arms
Holding Save my pet bird
Seeing my step-dad Terry
Watching my sister carve the pumpkin

Halloween is
The smell of the pumpkin pie coming from the oven
And having a nice family to share it with
That's what
HALLOWEEN IS
Catherine Flynn, Grade 7
West Branch Middle School

Train Wreck
Yell, scream, cry, sob
Rage, burning deep down inside
Why don't the understand, why don't they care
All the pain, and frustration
It's all just so confusing
Talk to friends the ones who care
Pain, suffering
More outrage, more crying
My life's a train wreck, a crazy mess
Where's the light at the tunnel's end?
Kindle Crossley, Grade 8
Licking Valley Middle School

Choices
Sometimes it's hard to see
The light that's guiding me,
To travel down this path,
Or face society's wrath.
Numerous choices yet to make,
Still, there will be many a mistake.
You could follow your heart,
And everything falls apart,
Or even be headstrong,
Yet it all turns out so wrong.
Should I take the gate, attractive and wide,
Brought forth by sloth, anger, and pride?
Or perhaps the road, narrow and torn,
Given through ignoring distasteful scorn.
So, have you merely tried your best?
Will you surpass your final test?
An easy life is yours to choose,
All you've got is your soul to lose.
A life full of suffering may not seem fine,
But trust me when I tell you such life is divine.
Jennifer Knippenberg, Grade 8
Little Miami Jr High School

More Than Average Me
I am alone in a horde of people,
Invisible but always around.
A simple greeting would bring me out
Of the everlasting, bleak background.
People never notice,
Never care to see
Past the average appearance
And see the more than average me.

I stand alone, watching the world pass by,
Wishing someone could see me.
Then the boy who has everything, and
Says nothing, mutters a simple hi
And I pour my heart and soul into the one
Who looked past the average appearance
And saw the more than average me.
I am no longer alone as I walk into the setting sun.
Paige Smearman, Grade 8
Chardon Middle School

Splash! Splash! Splash!
Splash, splash, splash!
I heard the rain smash.
I ran out to the rain,
And looked up to the sky,
Tiny raindrops landed on my eyes.
I held out my hands and grabbed him,
Then I saw a mirror of him on the ground,
I took my tiny boots and jumped,
Splash, splash, splash!
Isaac Yeh, Grade 7
Birchwood School

What Should My Poem Be?
What should my poem be?
It must stop at the 21st line
I hope that it's not too hard
To write a poem real fine.
Should it be of the old?
The mysteries that lie in the past
Their stories which were untold
But, the memories still last.
Should it be of the present?
There are many interesting things
Everyone has their own story
Some as precious as rings.
Should it be of the future?
To think of what it might bring.
We'll be able to make new stories
That we'll be able to sing.
What should my poem be?
I still have to write one.
I still have many ideas
As for this one, it's done.
Dominick Kessler, Grade 8
Pike Christian Academy

Liar
Liar, liar, pants on fire.
Start a spark or start fire.
Thinks that it will make you better,
Fake trend setter, fake friend getter,
Manipulating's like a game.
Grabbing for that fake lied fame.
Climbing up the breaking ladder,
Watch them fall and watch them shatter,
Watch them all go up in flames,
Playing risky lying games.
Climbing dangerously higher,
Liar, liar, pants on fire.
Alana Friedman, Grade 8
Agnon School

Davy Jones' Beans
A sailors' life is in my genes,
Walk the plank, eat your beans!
Fragmentation, crow's nest and more,
I shall swab the poop deck nevermore!
Land Lubbin' is against the code,
No whinin', cryin', or it's Keel Haul!
Many things and sights to see,
It usually ends in a brawl.
We are such a motley bunch,
Yo first mate, grab me my lunch!
Cold nights, a cold hard bed,
On my crew, you might end up dead.
Jesse Eckert, Grade 7
Glenwood Middle School

Soon
Soon the day will end.
Soon the night will fall.
Soon we will discover,
What is hidden behind that wall.

Soon everything will change.
Soon the stars will fade away.
Soon we will discover,
What we need right now today.
Zoe Berns, Grade 8
Agnon School

Time
Time is like a road in the night,
Slowly unfolding its treasures.
Time is like a bad decision,
There is no going back.
Time is an unknown pleasure,
That brings us joy.
Time is like a lightning bolt,
It goes away fast.
They think you can go back and
Fix things when broken.
No, they can't.
All the time spent making mistakes,
Gone.
5 minutes of their lives,
Gone.
That is time.
Kendal Elder, Grade 7
Incarnation School

A Forest
A forest
Big
  Colorful
Full of life
A beautiful place
  The animals,
Losing their lives in a heartbeat
Their habitat being destroyed
  Humans
Making that building or house
Destroying vast amounts of the forests
  Oxygen
Made by trees and plants
Decreasing every second of every day
  Without trees
There is no oxygen
  Without oxygen
There is no life
Think before cutting
Alex Crognale, Grade 7
Gahanna Middle School East

Frozen Lake
Skating down the frozen lake
Snow is in my face.
I pass the puck to Jake
He slips and falls
He starts to really ache.

Skating down the frozen lake
Heading towards the net.
I make a move and shoot top shelf
What a crazy play.
Colin Suter, Grade 7
Gesu Elementary School

In…
In my house —
free, calm, lounged,
having fun,
cooking food —
the procrastinator.

In school —
challenged, confused, participating
having knowledge,
learning a lot —
a questioner.
Dean Iacianci, Grade 7
St Michael School

Higher and Better
Climbing to the top,
when's it going to stop?
Rocks keep sliding beneath my feet,
I don't want to retreat.
I feel I must get to the top.

I reach the peak,
A way down I seek.
The key to get down,
Is to turn around,
But that involves letting go.

This is starting to become a scare
Let go, I do not dare.
Now I need assistance,
But my dad is in the distance,
And my legs are starting to shake.

He finally comes to my aid,
Good-bye to the top I bade,
And at last to my relief
With my fears my dad was a thief
As I slid back down the mountain.
Ryan O'Connor, Grade 8
Hopewell Jr High School

Halloween

Halloween is all about
witches and bats, goblins and ghouls
The time for haunted hay rides
And haunted houses
To watch scary movies that make you jump
And scream 'til you lose your voice
To decorate your yard with gravestones and spider webs
So that no one will dare to take even one step on the drive
The day to go trick-or-treating in your best costume yet
That makes everyone in sight stop as if in a trance
To eat candy all night long until you feel like Santa Claus
From al those Snickers and Milky Ways
To finish the night at a traditional costume party
With all your witch friends to talk about the historical day of
HALLOWEEN!

Caitlyn McNeil, Grade 8
Incarnation School

Soldiers

All soldiers fight for our right.
So that other people may sleep at night
Bombs, guns, and grenades make
People die in vain. Up early, out late.
all the things that make our soldiers shake.
All and all let's show our love
So soldiers know all is well.

Randy Jenkins, Grade 7
J A Garfield Middle School

Running

Running from something but
You don't recognize what it might be
You better not stop or else it might capture you
So you do the only smart thing you can
And that is to mislay whatever is following you
No mater what it takes
So that it can't find you so after you lose it you're secure
At your house with your loving family

Charlie Schaefer, Grade 8
Incarnation School

On the Balcony

On the balcony,
The wonderful leaves.
The colors of the rainbow.
On the balcony,
The rustling sound of leaves in the wind.
On the balcony,
The hamburger scent of my dad's sizzling grill.
On the balcony,
The feel of wind in my face.
On the balcony,
The taste of that fresh air in my mouth.
If only I could do this more often.

Spencer Wells, Grade 7
Incarnation School

Winter

Sparkling snowflakes floating from the sky,
Down to the cold white ground below.
Your glove falls off, and your hand, touches the cold icy snow.
The cold wind whips your cheeks and nose,
The wind, and evil ice demon attacking your whole body
All the way down to your toes.
Your house like a penguin protecting its egg from the cold,
It will protect you from the demon until you grow old.
The sound of snowflakes pitter-pat, pitter-pat
Fall from the sky onto your hat.
The smell of hot cocoa,
Can drive you loco,
The season after fall,
Is winter, the best season of all.

Rachel Zavakos, Grade 7
Incarnation School

Fall

Trees turning red and orange
as the sunlight fades away.
Leaves lazily falling as I'm calling
my sister in from play.
To share a meal with a family
to which we owe so much.
As the sky is turning red and orange
from the sun's golden touch.

Quinn Hosler, Grade 8
Logan Hocking Middle School

The Special Moment

For a moment,
You sit by a lake.
Listening attentively to the birds.
You sense the breeze,
It whistles in you ears.
You spy the trees,
They sway back and forth,
Side to side.
The weeping willow cries,
The sound of the brushing leaves calms you.
You glance around,
All you see are flowers blooming,
In the vast country field.
You sit alone, wishing you were with someone.
You begin a prayer,
Thanking the Creator
For all the special gifts,
Natures embraces and gathers,
Places, animals, lakes, flowers,
And, of course, for
The special moment,
With Him.

Maura McKenna, Grade 8
Incarnation School

Chico y Chica

The boy —
tough, cool, class clown,
cracking jokes,
playing rough —
a wolf!

The girl —
quiet, creative, smart,
having fun,
being there for each other —
a fox!

Colin Maloney, Grade 7
St Michael School

Campfire

Flames licking
the black night.

Sparks exploding
into the blanket of darkness.

Tasting gooey smores
and crunchy hot dogs.

Roasted
over the open fire.

Hear fire's
snap, crackle, and pop.

Sticky smores
and hard wood sticks.

As smoke
and melting chocolate
fills my nose!

Christine Zavakos, Grade 7
Incarnation School

I Once Knew a Truck

I once knew a truck
That was all in one piece.
The fenders stayed on without any help
The cab was tight on the frame.
The doors shut tight

But now that truck is gone...
Now the fenders are bolted on
There are rust holes in the bed
Big enough for the cats to fit through.
The cab is getting loose off the frame,
The doors don't shut tight anymore.
That other truck is gone.

Jamie Malcomson, Grade 7
West Branch Middle School

Football

In the huddle receiving the play down by 4
Running up to the line with time running low
Trouble hearing the count with the load uproar of the crowd
The nerves and the excitement ready for the play

The sound of you deep breathing in and out catching your last breaths
Flashes of lights from cameras of spectators watching you play
The intimidating glare from the opponent's eyes causing fright
The taste of victory with this one last chance

Set and ready checking the line making sure everyone is set
Starting the count "Ready Set HUT"
Now with the ball in hand ready to throw your search for a receiver
Your eyes scavenge for an open play but you feel the defensive rush coming close

Knowing this is the last chance he hurls the leather football into the dark sky
As the ball moves through the air the prayer and hope that it is caught
The ball finally reaches the hands of number 83 who dove in the end zone
He has caught the ball and victory at last for you and the team

Ted Schoen, Grade 8
Christ the King Catholic School

Best Friends

There's this girl and she's my best friend.
Even though we sometimes fight we'll always be tight till the end.
She's there for me through thick and thin.
I love how I can tell her everything and she won't tell anyone my secrets.
She's the best friend a girl can ask for.
I wouldn't trade her for money even if I were poor.
She's my world.
If it wasn't for her I don't know how I would survive.
She's my best friend alive.
I swear we're the greatest pair.
She's there for me when I have a bad day.
You couldn't trade me to give her away.
A friendship like this you could never peel.
Her name's Sarah Wills and she's pretty much a big deal.

Summer Cline, Grade 8
Licking Valley Middle School

Friends

Friends are the companions who allow me to be strong
Even at my weakest times.
Friends are the loving people close to my heart that I can trust with all my
secrets I bury inside.
Friends are the siblings that accept me for myself,
allowing all my faults to shine.
Friends are the people that teach me how to have a good time
without spending a dime.
Friends are the ones I cherish in my heart
all throughout my life.

Maggie Williams, Grade 8
Chardon Middle School

I Was Raised By

"It's time to get up" is what I heard.
Pancakes, bacon, and toast is what I smelled.
A beautiful woman is what I saw.
A wonderful day is what I remember.
I was taught, "Let me do your hair." I feared the most.
"I wish I had hair like yours," I dreaded the most.
"Stand up straight," I did the most.
A beautiful woman singing,
I remember the most.
"Do your best," is what I heard.
Roses and lotion is what I smelled.
A beautiful mother is what I saw.
Another wonderful day
Is what I remember.

Abigail Stryffeler, Grade 8
Nordonia Middle School

Our Mother

We live in this humble place,
as our world revolves in endless space.
A wonder to see this world of ours,
too marvelous not to gaze at for hours.

No Martian is worthy to discover
this place — our home— that's like no other.
We are blessed with nature and life,
an extravagant place with little strife.

This wonderful place is our home,
with plenty of room to grow and to roam.
This is our home, our place of birth.
What a beautiful thing, our Mother Earth.

Naomi Jean Taylor, Grade 7
Evergreen Middle School

The Perfect Snow Day

The joy on little kids' faces,
When they see a snow day.
They play around all day long,
In the beautiful white colored snow.

They sled down the hill,
With laughter coming from their faces.
Falling off the sled one by one,
Into the white puffiness.

The warm hot cocoa waiting for them,
While they come in with bright red cheeks.
Their numb fingers around the cup,
Makes them dream of a warm winter's nap.

And that's a perfect snow day.

Leah Yodzis, Grade 7
Gesu Elementary School

The Fallen Tree

The Fallen Tree
It stood tall and strong
My dear friend all the way to the end
For when his time had come it had
Shone in the light from the
Storm as I watched and
Listened
To the
Fate of
Poor
Friend
He came
Down with
A thud the one
I would talk to when no one else would he was my friend.

Matthew Stroh, Grade 8
St Brendan Elementary School

When I Picture a Farm…

I see a nice little house, all pretty and white,
And a fiery red barn, filled up quite tight
With ripe fruits and vegetables ready to eat
From the small, fenced-in garden, so prim and neat.
Past the cornfields where the wild bunny plays,
The distant hills stand in a weird, grayish glaze.
The cows in the pasture are grazing in peace
While the sheep in the barnyard are nipping their fleece.
The curious kitten is chasing a mouse
While the great German shepherd stands guard of the house.
I see a beautiful pony for the children's delight.
The chickens are clucking in the dim morning light.
There is a mud pit where the pig likes to wallow —
Under the eye of a watchful barn swallow.
The farmer stands with his watering hose
While his wife is inside, where she bakes and she sews.
The little white farmhouse is made up of boards,
But the home is made strong by invisible cords.
The little white farmhouse has no spire or dome,
But love makes this farmhouse truly a home.

Edith Howell, Grade 7
Zanesville Christian School

I Remember

I remember…
Like pages in a journal
Words like passion, romance, secrets
Two famous people Romeo, and Juliet
Anybody's tears, fears, death
The place in the story where they fall in love
The injury when Romeo drinks poison
Our house was as quiet as mice on a cold day
And outside it was raining like tears from Juliet's beautiful eyes
The sound of panic, terror, and fright
Anyone who had loved and lost

Destinie Pazel, Grade 7
South Range Middle School

Sunset on the Beach
Half a ball floating on the surface
Orange and yellow like a peach
With me sitting on the beach
Watching it sink below the horizon
Getting ready for a new day
Chris Huls, Grade 8
St Christopher Elementary School

The Secret
Who knows?
Anyone?
Why did I tell them?

The secret is mine.

Secrets
Kept
Secrets
Told
Secrets
Sealed
Secrets
Revealed

Whispers
All over
Give me *shivers*
Down
My spine

Why did I tell…
The secret of my life?
Tori Montgomery, Grade 8
Licking Valley Middle School

Hunter's Dream
Buck!
Heart pounding
Gun shaking
He's coming…
Nervous
Ranged at 30 yards
Pulling slowly
10 yards…
Safety off
Squeezing the trigger
POW!!
Gun fires
He's running
Boom!!
Crashes!
Deer down
Yes!!
My trophy!
Travis Morehouse, Grade 8
Licking Valley Middle School

Hunting
Hunting is a streak of black, green, and an electrifying brown!
Hunting sounds like an explosion of ice cream trucks singing a tune.
Hunting tastes like hot cocoa with white marshmallows on a cold winter's morning.
Hunting smells like fresh maple syrup running down a maple tree.
Hunting looks like a horse drawn sleigh with shiny bells!
Hunting makes me feel like I want to do it again!
T.J. Zimmerman, Grade 8
Chardon Middle School

My Cabin
I spot the colorful leaves tumbling across the ground.
I catch the sound of chainsaws clearing the quad trails deep in the forest.
I wipe the mist in the moist dull sky from my forehead.
I get wind of the fresh cut grass skidding across the damp yard.
I watch the morning sun slowly creep the cool morning fog.
I watch little squirrels spring along the windy gravel road.
I listen to horses galloping alongside of their trainers.
I pick the thorns out of my hand as I crawl out of a thorn bush I tripped into.
The smell of grilled chicken on the charcoal grill.
The frames in my mind of what might happen the next day.
The cold side of the pillow at night.
The wonderful odor of homemade flapjacks at sunrise.
The sound of loose children running around the log cabin.
Rustling leaves beneath your feet as you walk through the woods.
The spine tingling scent of race gas in the shed.
The mud covered recreation vehicles.
The black-and-white TV with 4 channels, and poor sound.
The exhaustion at the end of the day. Not wanting to leave.
Getting in the car thinking of going back to school. Feeling sad.
Vinnie Petrella, Grade 7
South Range Middle School

These Streetz
These streets is cold, young men can barely make it to 18 years old.
You can't go nowhere without hearing gunshots.
Man, it's really crazy on this block.
Gang fights. Loud nights.
If you don't claim a set, you ain't that tight.
Everywhere I go "Gang this," "Gang that."
Don't bring that stuff to me. Cause I ain't on that.
Police chases, street races, yeah — that's cool to see.
But it just ain't for me.
Dice game. Shots rang.
I can't believe they killed my cousin.
That stuff is insane.
Now I look back
and remember how he rolled.
Man, he was young. 25 years old.
I miss my cousin.
I love him dearly.
I would've took the bullet for him.
I'm serious, really.
The only thing left to do is pray.
And know I'll see my cousin another day.
William Wheatt, Grade 7
Hope Academy Cathedral Campus

Jazzy Destiny

A day in my shoes,
Sometimes the blues,
With limited clues,
To show the right thing to do.
I hear a sound in the midst,
The sweet sound, my saxophone's kiss,
To reassure, my destiny door is ahead.
I rock as the sounds grows louder,
Du-duu, Du-duu
The clouds start to clear, as I come near,
My so dear, fear
But as the clouds clear, my fear disappears.
Then I see my destiny, is to be, the one and only me.

Ryan Brooks, Grade 9
Fairfield Freshman High School

Those Summer Times

Walking outside barefoot,
In the soft green grass,
The sun greets you with warmth,
Enjoy it while it lasts,
Hear the noises all around you,
The neighbors having a blast,
People diving into the water,
Others floating gently on rafts,
The smell of lawns being mowed,
Flying through the air are blades of grass,
Getting together with family and friends,
Barbecuing chicken with loads of laughs,
Nothing can take the place of,
Warm, summer days!

Taylor Niese, Grade 8
Miller City-New Cleveland School

Undiscovered Rock Star

Lives fly by like birds in the sky,
Some days all you want to do is cry.
Even though you have someone to help you when you're down,
It seems to me that they're really never around.

Through the confusion that I see,
The pain that runs in thee,
The drama between you and me.
It's not working out and I need to be me.

When I close my eyes days and weeks pass by.
It's so easy to find what's wrong.
And so hard to find what's right.

The ups, the downs, spinning round and round,
That's just a rock star's life.
As for me I'm undiscovered, but I'll stay undercover,
So I can live my life free.
Because that's the way it's supposed to be.

Aja Johnson, Grade 8
Alexander Graham Bell Academy

Ode to the Broken Crayons

Thanks to the broken crayons
Who gave creativity to me
Thanks to the broken crayons
Who shattered my sullen being
You set me free
Thanks to the broken crayons
Who taught me to read and write
For it was you who brought me through it
The fear and all the fright
Thanks to the broken crayons
Who once were to sharp and new
But slowly, as I became better,
Turned a duller shade of blue
Thanks to the broken crayons
For sharing with me
For showing me the rainbow
And the colors of the sea
Thanks to the broken crayons
Who brought me here today
If not for your lovely art
Many a vibrant memories would time fade

Dawn Musil, Grade 9
BOSS Buckeye On-Line School for Success

Blue

Blue is the sadness I see in his eyes,
Blue is the wondering I seek inside,
Blue is the soft sweet touch of his tear,
The blue whisper of his sorrowful voice in my ear.

The numbness I feel inside is blue,
Blue is the color of his cold dead face,
Blue is the smell of his gallant cologne,
Blue was his favorite color when he was here.

The eternal sadness I feel is blue,
Blue is the one thing I remember about him,
Blue is the funeral procession that occurred,
It was the grinding blue of his solemn funeral.

Morgan Stephenson, Grade 9
Eastern High School

Snow Leopard

There is a snow leopard inside me
It has jaws that make my enemies cringe
But a smile that makes my friends laugh
It bounds across fields like an unstoppable blur
It pursues its prey with open jaws
Padding silently through the grass of a wintery tundra
It abides in my mind
A figment of imagination
It makes me want to dream

Alex Roesch, Grade 7
Incarnation School

Live Laugh Learn

Sometimes you wish you could be in two places at once,
Other times you could disappear when you're needed the most.
You wish you could save the world from any harm there is out there,
Other times you wish that you could just sit on the sidelines and watch the world pass you by.
Some things come to an end, and are never seen again,
Others live forever, maybe just not where you thought they would.
When someone you hold dear to you and love so much passes away,
You think that you can't move on in your life,
But through all the tears and memories, you live, you laugh, you learn.

Angela Penza, Grade 7
South Range Middle School

Friends

Friends are people that understand you for who you really are.
Friends are people who you can trust with your secrets.
Friends are people who stand up for you when you get in to some tight spaces.
Friends help you when you fall down or when you get hurt.
Friends are people who hang around you even when nobody else will.
Friends cheer you up when you are down.
Friends are people you sometimes get mad at, but they'll always be your friends no matter what.
Friends are people you never get tired of, because your friends are always there.

Jordan Scott Eugene Lammers, Grade 7
Miller City-New Cleveland School

Late Fall Stargazing

Oh in the dawning of the eve when the moon was in it's full
When crickets sung their nightly songs all across the knoll

The forest was dark, devoid of hue: the leaves had long since left
Two forms withdrew from the deepening shadows, the midnight their presence cleft

One strode upright, the other on fours as they made their way to a field
Beyond the woods, where they lifted their eyes to see what the night sky would yield

Together they marveled at Orion; Lacerta, and Hyiades,
They drank in the vastness of the Milky Way, they wondered at the Pleiades

The twosome were awed by the great expanse, the stars in their vast array
They looked up, confounded by the heaven's greatness and, oh, how they longed to stay

But night and sleep are a couple, so with a sigh and sleep filled groan
The pair vanished back into the forest: A girl and her cat went home

Mayim Moore, Grade 7
South Range Middle School

Broken Living

When you're living with a broken heart every day is the hardest
You wake up still dreaming in a world of long-full pain
Your day is a routine you perform like malfunctioning machinery
Your hope fades with the color in your cheeks, and the life in your eyes hide behind a corner
You scurry away from lost happiness, trying to subdue the wave of
remembrance seeping through the locked doors of your mind like air from a balloon
You've changed the way you view the world, for even this is a threat to your stability
When you finally awake from your walking slumber all is lost to the winds of cruel thunder

Hannah Niehaus, Grade 8
Western Reserve Middle School

High Merit Poems – Grades 7, 8, and 9

Friday Nights in Chardon

The crowd is a wave of red and black,
School spirit is not something that we lack.

The action on the field contains extremely hard-hitting,
That ensures that nobody is sitting.

I see many a deep throw,
They just seem to go and go.

Out of nowhere, interception!
All because of defensive deception.

The referee throws the yellow flag,
The fans know this game is in the bag.

The visitors call a hail mary,
And our defender picked it off and started a carry.

Victory!
This game will definitely go down in history.

Jeff Seufer, Grade 8
Chardon Middle School

Ode to Music

You soothe my mind,
no matter if you are rock, pop, or even alternative,
You are the sound of happiness on a successful day.
Every beat you play, I listen carefully,
Every word you say, it lingers in my mind,
Taking me to a place that is free
of all negative things…
You soothe my mind
You make my day.

Julie Colaianni, Grade 7
St Brendan Elementary School

Christmas

Time to give a time to share
Time to appreciate all that's there
Time to gather with friends and family
Time for happiness and prosperity
Time for love
Time for everything that is good
Time when Jesus was born
Time to remember special memories spent together

Green, red everywhere
Colorful, Christmas lights fill the air
People running here, there
Houses which we live are no longer bare
Smells of good food are no longer rare
Cause that time of year is finally here

Lauren Richardson, Grade 8
Licking Valley Middle School

Racing Against the Clock

Racing against the clock.
Will time ever stop for me?
'Cause the days fly by,
and the weeks fly by.
And still, I'm waiting here.
And there's no time
to stop and think.
There's no time
to smile and laugh.
Because we've come to fear that ticking sound.
It's the sound of passing time.
We're racing against the clock.
Will time ever stop?
To let us take in the beauty, let us see the world.
Let us smile and laugh,
And not worry, for once.
I've waited and waited,
And yet still, the clock ticks.
As a constant reminder, and our greatest fear.
We're racing against the clock.
Will time ever stop?

Shoshi Bieler, Grade 8
Agnon School

The Navy

Sailors on deck.
They fight bravely and with courage.
They know the risk they take.
My pap flying a plane to the carrier.
I know the sailors have lots of training.
Is it enough?
They refuel the plane and it flies away.
They know. They know. They have done well.

Tom Cole, Grade 7
South Range Middle School

One Small Jump

So many things to remember for just
    one small jump

Keep the same rhythm,
    count out the strides,
    all in preparation for just
    one small jump.

Heels down, toes in,
    steady contact on the reins,
    land on the correct lead, look where you're going,
    all the things to remember over just
    one small jump.

Land and canter away because
    finally, it's over, that
    one small jump.

Carita Haverlock, Grade 8
Chardon Middle School

I Was Raised with Family

I was raised with camping vacations,
Fishing off the boat at six a.m.,
Diving for dimes and pennies in the pool,
Staying up late and waking up early family.

A wild birthday party throwing,
Kids yelling and running in the yard,
Burgers nearly burned on the grill,
"Catch me if you can" sort of family.

A "Shut your face,"
A few punches in the arm,
"You don't want to pick a fight with me,"
Kind of independent family.

The "Say it loud and say it proud,"
"Don't let no one pick on you,"
Polish, Italian, Slovenian, German
Mutt of a family.

A smoke quitter,
Cancer fighter,
Standin' out in the crowd
Kinda family.

I was raised with family.

Megan Zangara, Grade 8
Nordonia Middle School

Where I'm From

I am from the hills seen around you.
From the sweet smell of pine behind the house.
I am from the flames that swirl in the wind.

I am from the lakeside where my uncle and I used to fish.
I am from the memories of cold nights under the stars,
From slips in the water everywhere I went.
I am from the adrenaline of catching a big fish,
And from helping my uncle land a large catfish.

I am from laughs at Christmastime, they arise from childish jokes.
I am from the family squabbles, and quick make ups.
I am from the paper and boxes scattered across the floor.
From the grateful smiles of children with what they wanted.

I am from the smell of steak fresh off the grill.
From picnic tables and potato salad.
I am from full stomachs, and hearty meals,
And from the leftovers that still taste great.

Those are the moments I am from.
Where my mind thrives, and feels calm again.
They are what keep me here, every year, and every day.
As everything else seems to fade away.

Garrett Mount, Grade 8
Logan Hocking Middle School

I Have a Headache

I have a headache
And it won't go away.
I have a headache
And it just wants to stay.

My dad gave me a pill
And I drank some water.
I leaned out the sill,
But my head just got hotter.

I turned out the lights;
Turned off the sound,
But this really bites —
I still hear that "pound, pound!"

I ate a small snack;
It didn't do a thing.
I laid on my back —
But my ears still, "ring, ring!"

I have a headache
And it just wants to stay.
I have a headache —
Can you take it away?

Katie Klassen, Grade 9
School for Creative and Performing Arts

When We Met

From the first time we met, I thought you were an angel from above
And for the first time in my life I felt a thing called love

I want to share my life with you
No one else will ever do

Love is about the truth, not lies
I should not bring you down, but lift you up high

Love never gives up
No matter if you're down on your luck

From the beautiful way you look
My breath away you took

In my hand you hold my heart
Right where you had it from the start

You lift me up on the darkest day
You made my day bright before it was gray

You stand by my side through thick and thin
Though you don't know how it will end

Tim King, Grade 8
Logan Hocking Middle School

Fredrick

Freaky Fredrick Foony follows frequently
Sitting shallowly in the shadows
Swinging swiftly and soaring silently somewhere
Stalking, standing, waiting, watching
Tammy trembles terribly foreseeing Fredrick following fastly
Sandra sees oh scary Fredrick following her female friend
Persnickety Polly Porter phones the Piersonville Police,
Seeing someone being stalked, a.k.a. her sister
Sirens Roaring 'round Rainly Road, recklessly arriving
Every second clearly counts, contagious fear fills her friends
Peoples hearts begin to pound, Piersonville Police unpleasily frown
Sweet Tammy still trembling is truly in deep trouble
Fredrick's face fills with fear, his future is fading fastly
Police swarm shouting, "Save the sweet sweet girl!"
Still the sirens screaming, still police surrounding
Suddenly smiling, sprinting soundlessly toward the trembling Tammy
He grabs her frightened hand, not fierce but friendly
She sounding not so scared says "Thank you Sirs and Madams, sorry if we scared you."
The Audience stands straight up, applauding their astonishing act

Erin McNamara, Grade 8
St Jude School

Who Is the Little Girl?

I ask myself who I truly am.
Am I that person I have always wanted to be?
Will I grow up to be that pro,
that is dedicated to give 110%?
Who puts her everything into trying to be best?
Do I love that sport that I used to love
when I get out there on that field and put on that glove?
To see the reflection of that uniform in the mirror,
and say to myself, "I'm a sponsor of this team right here!"
When I get that bat into the palms of my hands, I feel the everlasting power.
The power of love, dedication and stress that it takes to be a true athlete and to truly do the best.
I am that girl that puts pain and power into the games she has learned over the years.
I am that girl I wanted to be!
The hard working girl that has softball written all over her dream.

Gina Tosti, Grade 8
Chardon Middle School

The Day the Sun Fell

I saw it hurtling down to Earth.
It was like a basketball on fire.
So luminous that no pair of sunglasses could help fight the rays of light.
The ball of fire fell so fast that I blinked and it was almost to the ground.
The screams of the people were heard all over but I just stood there like a curious child.
It hit the ground without a sound.
Things started blazing with fire all around me.
I stood there in total awe.
While people ran somewhere far!
I walked up to it and let me say it is not as big as the scientists say.
With a smile I picked up the flaming marble sized ball.
Standing on my toes I reached up high
And put the sun back in the sky!

Leah Castelaz, Grade 8
Gesu Catholic School

My Problem

I never knew how hard writing a poem was
Until I was assigned to write one
It had to be a maximum of 21 lines
I could write about anything under the sun

As easy as that sounds
It was quite a challenge you see
I sat around, thinking of ideas
But nothing ever came to me

I had several thoughts
Baseball? Life? The night?
I typed a little of each
But then I decided that none seemed right!

I was starting to get frustrated
This assignment seemed too tricky
But I guess I should have expected that
If I was going to be so picky

But then the idea came to me
It was right under my nose
A poem about my problem!
That is what I chose.

Rachel Kraus, Grade 8
Agnon School

Flying

Ever since I was a little boy,
I have always dreamed to fly.

I watch out my window,
To see my willow littered in birds,
Little do I know, I have learned to fly.
the birds take off; so do I;
Flying above the tree tops,
I soon feel free,
Free, free, to fly away.

I follow the birds and the birds follow me.
I flow from movement to movement.
To stay in the moment,
The moment with a great sensation to fly.

As I soar the heavens,
I plea to descend,
I send my prayers,
To let it all end,
I miss my family, so deep inside.

It all ends as soon as it came,
I wake in my bed.

Benjamin Leach, Grade 8
Clinton Massie Middle School

Heartbreak

The seasons began knocking teams down
Making them look like fools, their coach, a clown
Moving up the ranks to number one
Making the game just look like fun.

We were number one still, when the season started coming to an end
Next was our rival, the utterly horrible Michigan
Forty-two to thirty-nine by just a few
We went to our cars like nothing was new

The long break enters. Until we find our competitor.
It's Florida a fierce predator.
We hit the fields for weeks of practicing rough
Florida, we hope to out tough.

They kickoff to us to start the game
Teddy Ginn running it back, what a shame
But then a turning point in the match
Teddy limping off, our eyes all catched.

The Gators soon prevailed
countless rants soon became stale.
A great season we couldn't fake
But it ended with a heartbreak.

Ben Dumler, Grade 8
St Christopher Elementary School

Spring Night

A thin mist covers the rain, moistened land,
Clouds drift away, setting the sky ablaze with stars,
The moon rises, pouring silver light over tree, grass and flower,
A pool of water, shimmers and trembles as life rises to land,
Crickets awaken, to sing their hearts out,
Frogs climb to earth, to seduce any that hear their voices,
Birds and squirrels nestle down in their warm, dry homes for sleep,
Foxes hurry out of dens, to be seen as dancing silhouettes on the hills,
But as the sun slowly rises and the moon falls,
All life returns to how it was,
Bright and dry,
Birds and squirrels,
All life of the dark gone,
Until again, the sun sleeps and the moon wakens.

Bekah Eller, Grade 9
Westerville South High School

This Is for the Soldiers

This is for the soldiers who are fighting for our country.
This is for the soldiers who are risking their lives for us.
This is for the soldiers who don't see their family every day.
This is for the soldiers who eat beef jerky, even if they don't like it.
This is for the soldiers who spend the holidays without their loved ones.
This is for the soldiers who lost their friends.
This is for the soldiers who are wishing to be home.
Thank you.

Erin Stiner, Grade 7
Austintown Middle School

I'm Not Gonna Cry for You

Why should I try for you,
    when I'm just going to end up crying about you.
No offense to you,
    but you're just not worth it.
you want to see me cry,
    you're gonna have to wait til the day I die.
Even then it won't matter,
    I'm still not gonna get sadder.
I think I should do us both a favor,
    and say "Hey, guess what it's over!"
Yes you guessed it, I'm not done yet,
    I still have some things to say.
I know you don't care about me,
    but that doesn't matter to me.
I bet you'll never be able to leave,
    I'm gonna tell you what I'll do.
I'll break up with you so you can have her,
    now that I know I don't matter.

Alix Lansing, Grade 8
Fairfield Local High School

The Stars

Many think they're wished upon
many say they're pointed
But what they truly are
leaves nobody disappointed
They're as hot as the fires of hell
and as dangerous as thunder
But even though they're really bright
they are an immense and vast wonder
Even though they can bring danger
they bring wonder to the skies
Their smile is the smile of God
and it never ever dies
The number depends on point of view
however few know them all
They look as though they're tiny specks
but they're anything but small
Even in the saddest days
they will twinkle in the night
Because they are God's way of watching us
and our way to light

Tim Flinn, Grade 8
St Christopher Elementary School

Thanksgiving

Thanksgiving is a time for giving.
A time for sharing and a time for living.
At Thanksgiving we always swear,
that these family members will always be there.
We eat the turkey, we may make a toast,
some families may even eat roast.
So now that Thanksgiving is done,
I hope we have all had some fun.

Dana Kropp, Grade 7
J A Garfield Middle School

Oak Leaf

Drifting down, the last to fall.
It was once on a limb that stood so tall.
Out in a forest with crooked bare tees,
Great, dreamy fields with grass blowing in the breeze.
Spinning and spiraling, gliding towards the ground.
The sun peeking out from a patch of gray clouds.
Crispy and crunchy from autumn's cool wind,
The life of the oak leaf had come to an end.

Hannah Saunders, Grade 8
Logan Hocking Middle School

The Fourth of July

I come when the Earth is warm and gold
I come when all are free
In me there are sparks and booms
There are crackles and flares
During my nights the sky is light and burning
First there are flashes and cracks of light
Next there is a boom of explosion
Finally I come back in a roaring echo of thunder
I start many parties in the warm summer sun
I bring fun and happiness into the air
I only last one day but sometimes start before I start
And end after I've ended
I am bright flashes over a dark lake in a warm cove
I am the fire from the island and the echoes in the hills
I am the height of the summer that everyone waits for
But I mean none of this
I represent freedom
I represent independence
I am part of the U.S.A.

Wade Rich, Grade 7
Gahanna Middle School East

Jakub

Red is a color,
Like bittersweet love.
Skiing is my passion.
It is my tie for all time.
Soccer is the sport no one dares talk to me about.
A cheetah is most like me,
Because like a cheetah I'm smart.
I go to a restaurant, and I must have a steak,
If I don't, I'm deeply saddened.
My dreams are full of hope,
And wonder, but the one thing that sticks out —
Is the unforgiving urge
To become a pilot.
A role model is
Someone that cares
My role model is my mom
Because she is always there
To help me.
People make fun of me,
Mostly because of my glasses.
That's my poem for English B.

Jakub Blazejewski, Grade 8
St Monica Elementary School

Imaginary Light

I hide in fields of paper flowers,
Shying away from my long forgotten powers
Living in the past of lost glory
Watching raindrops fall, holding all the stories
I lie in silence for many hours,

I linger in the luminous moonlight
Frightened by the fear of a silent night
Deafened by the sound of my own screaming
The ghost of my past haunting my dreaming
Its a clear full mooned sight

Staring into the eyes of utter regret
Hiding the things I wish they would accept
The moonlight is slowly dying
Everyone is grievingly crying
Over the memories no one will ever forget

A starry night, I feel so free
But inside the pain is killing me
All alone in the darkness of the night
Searching for the illusion of imaginary light
Trying to find what no one can see

Shannon Graf, Grade 9
Western Reserve High School

Life Is a Highway

Life is a highway
I've been following all my life.
Sometimes there are potholes,
sometimes some dead ends
but I take a detour and get back on the highway.
I see my life staying on the highway,
but probably with a few more potholes.
I also see myself hitting some rough weather
which may slow me down
but I'll get back up to speed.

Rob Ackerman, Grade 7
West Branch Middle School

Paint the Town Red

In kindergarten you learn to share,
In first grade you learn to be fair,
In second grade you learn to be friends,
In third grade you become a friend,
In fourth grade you are working towards your goal,
In fifth grade you are ready for the world
In sixth grade you are trying not to slack,
In seventh grade you start to give back,
In eighth grade you meet new faces,
In ninth grade you meet new races,
In tenth grade you do your best,
In eleventh grade you are almost ready to rest,
In twelfth grade you paint the town red.

Aamna Aziz, Grade 9
Hilliard Davidson High School

About Me

My name is Anthony Corsi, an 8th grader, at St. Monica school.
I love playing baseball, basketball, and swimming in my pool.
I am a kind boy and I get good grades.
Some say my mind is as sharp as a blade.
I love working around the house and helping my dad.
When he says "No," it makes me very sad.
I love the outdoors and God's beautiful creation.
I'm just so happy that God created this nation.
I love hanging out and playing football with my friends.
We hike together, camp and search in dens.
My friends are awesome and very important to me.
But when I make a new friend, I am happy with glee.
I also love to hunt, fish, drive my aunt's go cart, and swim in the sea.
Well, it looks like I just told you a poem about me.

Anthony Corsi, Grade 8
St Monica Elementary School

Trees

They have always lived and breathed.
They swayed in the breeze as I walked outside.
The sun was in perfect alignment with their leaves.
They are beautiful.

They sent their crisp scent through my nose.
As their leaves start to fall, my eyes love what they see.
They fall…fall…fall…
They hit the ground with nothing more than their beauty.

The colors change with the days.
The crunch beneath my feet is my favorite sound in the world.
They are now bare; the branches all covered in snow.
They are in a new section of their life cycle.

In a few months, they will have blossoms.
Then, they will provide fruit and air for me.
After, they will be at the same stage that seemed like only yesterday.
The most marvelous creation made by God: the trees.

Jessica Grilliot, Grade 7
Incarnation School

Childhood Is

Childhood is sleeping in every day.
Childhood is taking naps when your parents tell you to.
Childhood is making a big pile of leaves and then jumping into them.
Childhood is playing board games with your friends.
Childhood is going to school even though you don't want to.
Childhood is having a baby-sitter when no one is home.
Childhood is going on merry-go-rounds at Cedar Point.
Childhood is being read bedtime stories before bedtime.
Childhood is building a snowman and then watching it melt.
Childhood is waking up every day and learning something new.

Blake Warrington, Grade 7
St Monica Elementary School

Color

Green is like my garden hose.
Red is like a funny clown's nose.

Purple suckers dye my tongue.
Gray is for a smoker's lung.

Black shadows in the night.
Pink flowers in the light.

Blue ink stained my shirt.
Yellow angry bees really hurt.

White ghosts on the run.
Orange pumpkins carved for fun.

What color do you think you are?
Emma Raulinaitis, Grade 7
St Michael School

Prayer of the Mouse

In this open field
Of animals and grass
I must run for shelter
From screeching hawks
And hopping bunnies
Devon Nelson, Grade 7
St Michael School

Come Back

On the outside I look fine
but on the inside I'm crying.
I wish that you could come back
To the place you belong.
Here in my arms
Is where I want you to stay.
Allison Hohman, Grade 8
Danbury Jr/Sr High School

Man of the Hour

Do you know what you expected
When you spoke to me.
Sorry to disappoint you,
But I feel no obligation
To join your charade.
Go ahead and be the man of the hour
If that is what this is about.
I have no interest in her.
Watching you tell lies,
In attempt to win the respect of others.
Maybe you will get some attention,
You may even fool the spectators.
But at least when I go home,
I can look in my mirror.
Casey Laughter, Grade 8
St Christopher Elementary School

The Prayer of the Bunny Rabbit

In my burrow
of silence and safety
I scamper away
from fierce wolves
and two legged beasts.
Carey Artrip, Grade 7
St Michael School

Dark

The smell of sulfur fills the air
Mingling with the smoke
Ringing won't leave my ears
Torturing me with a pound

Crimson and olive surround me
Masses are running past
Shouts and blasts add to the bang
A heavy object weighs my arms

Clutching tight to the heaviness
Holding closely to my sanity
Unfamiliar blur rushes at me
The ring is larger then back to norm

Falling, eyes growing blank, black sea
Run on, knowing not to hesitate
Banging slows, all sounds going
An immense burst comes from the sky
Kathleen Pedigo, Grade 8
Gesu Elementary School

You'll See

One day,
Some day,
You'll see,
  Regret,
  Remorse,
  None from me,
  Just wait,
  You'll see,
    Living my dreams,
    Is what I did,
    Never again,
    Will I let them win?
      No way,
      No how,
      Is what you said,
      Just look at me now,
      On top of the world. Wow!
        Now I'm here,
        Sure showed you,
        On top of the world,
        With a great view.
Callie Staggers, Grade 8
Licking Valley Middle School

Go Inside a Closet

Go inside a closet,
See its darkness.
It's like a bind.
Perhaps you'll find eternal doom.
Leave if you wish.
Alan Suhr, Grade 7
Incarnation School

She's the One

There before me, a goddess
standing there with much perfection
shining as the best selection
though she acts so modest

well, where to start?
from her long brown hair
to the blue in her stare
yes, she put the arrow in my heart

next comes her smile
she proudly shows her teeth, so white
no darkness can stop that light
I sure hope it stays awhile

she has a heart of gold
she really shines above
for this you'll truly love
she shows it strong and bold

I'll count the days 'till she comes to me
side by side we'll walk together
no matter the harshness of the weather
oh how strong our love will be.
Michael C. O'Connor, Grade 8
Columbus Grove Middle School

Tears

Silent tears of feeling
no one can see or hear.
Tears of feelings locked inside and
held away.
Tears of hate and
Tears of fear.
Tears of sorrow and sadness.
Tears that want to be let go
but can't and won't.
Tears of one who is
scared to cry.
To show her feelings
from deep down inside.
Tears of one who everyone
Yet no one knows.
Tears of one,
named me.
Jasmine Dickerson, Grade 8
Alexander Graham Bell Academy

Heavenly
Angel
Heaven, harmonious
Relaxing, calm, soothing
Clean spirited, greedy, mean
Tasteless, hurtful, harmful
Villainous, rude
Devil
Taylor Wendel, Grade 7
Fort Recovery Middle School

Secret Silent War*
Through thick and thin
No matter what, they got my back
My two best friends are like that
We talk with our eyes
Never to say — goodbye
Friends I would die for
Care and love, more and more
Both cut too deep
One won't eat…
They think no one cares
They are living in a nightmare,
It's like a bullet going through my heart
Razor blades, glass
It's cutting me too, so upset…
HEY!!! Don't you see me standing here?
Don't give up
I don't know what I would do
If I ever lost a friend like you
You ask me who?
All I can say…
They mean more to me than anything!!!
Tamara Melrose, Grade 8
Licking Valley Middle School
*Dedicated to Brittany Cox
and Jessica Newman.

Daddy
My Country 'tis of thee
My dad's on his way to Germany,
To help soldiers in need,
He took the Navy creed,
While I stand proud of his good deeds.
Ally Gallaway, Grade 8
St Michael School

Hero
Hero
Courageous, fun
Working, thinking, loving
Always outside doing something
Caring, owning, uplifting
Nice, happy
Dad
Peter Blake, Grade 7
St Jude School

I Am…
I am a funny girl who loves her friends and sports.
I wonder what it is like to be famous.
I hear the plinking of raindrops on a window pane.
I see the world revolving around sports.
I want to be the best I can be.
I am a funny girl who loves her friends and sports.

I pretend that I will rule the world.
I feel mad when I am ignored.
I touch the distant stars sparkling in the night sky.
I worry when I am all alone in my big frightening house.
I sob when someone dies.
I am a funny girl who loves her friends and sports.

I understand that one plus one is two.
I say that everyone should express their feelings.
I dream that my friends and I will go on an unlimited shopping spree.
I try to do excellent in school.
I hope that my sports teams will succeed.
I am a funny girl who loves her friends and sports.
Marissa Reinhart, Grade 7
Hopewell Loudon Local Jr/Sr High School

She'd Never Tell
She thought she'd fallen in love,
He was the perfect one, she thought
Day by day it got worse, his anger just came out on her
Her friends saw the marks and knew something was wrong
But she'd never tell, and they would never say anything
Her pain got worse and she tried to hide it all
But she'd never tell
Her parents were too busy to listen anyway
She wanted to tell someone but couldn't she wanted the pain to leave
She finally took matters into her own hands and told him to leave
But he didn't listen, he just started to swing
The last words she ever heard were
"I love you and if I can't have you no one can"
Torey Frame, Grade 7
Waterloo Middle School

Fairytales Aren't Just for Little Girls You Know…
Every little girl wants to be a princess,
But do they ever tell stories about young adults or women who want to be princesses or queens?
I mean we all know that they aren't that cute since they are "older" but come on.
Every girl, young or old, wants that fairytale ending,
With the knights, princes, trolls, giants, wizards, witches, and talking animals.
And their best friends are those talking animals.
We usually don't take time to think about these things anymore,
But isn't it good too?
Maybe it will get hopes up and maybe it won't.
But just once, there should be one story with,
"Once upon a time, there once lived a woman who wanted to be a Queen…"
And the rest is for you to tell.
Gina Horvat, Grade 8
Chardon Middle School

Childhood Is…

Childhood is playing in the snow.
Childhood is eating ice cream.
Childhood is looking for your basket on Easter.
Childhood is playing video games.
Childhood is having fun on Christmas.
Childhood is swimming in the summer.
Childhood is skateboarding.
Childhood is playing sports.
Childhood is going to amusement parks.
Childhood is having friendships.

Matthew Wendling, Grade 7
St Monica Elementary School

Write a Poem?

Write a poem?
Is it truly as simple as they say?
I'm 13, 14 in June and go to this here
school in Garfield Heights.
It's not easy growing up,
going through friends, trying to fit in.
It seems I can't do much with being short.
and jump rope is the worst.
As I write this poem,
three crumbled up papers,
and then I start with a brand new sheet.
Blue eyes, brown hair?
No more to say?
The thoughts go through my head,
asking to be put on paper.
Anything else? I begin to ask myself.
So this is me? I guess it is.

Rachel Upholz, Grade 8
St Monica Elementary School

Speeding

My brother Jake is learning how to drive,
It will make him feel so alive.
He likes going way too fast,
He doesn't like to be last!

He thought speeding would be fine,
It's not like he committed a crime.
That's not what the cop said,
He got caught and sent to bed.

He will not drive fast anymore,
Even though it will be such a bore.
He will have no more fun,
Now that the car feels like it weighs a ton.

He has no more car,
So he can't go that far,
Now he feels dead,
So he'll have to take turns riding his friends instead!

Kayla Brosko, Grade 7
South Range Middle School

Man of War

When you are riding on a bus
Toward a camp with barb wire all around
And do push-ups on your pointer finger
Then you think it's cool

Until you get a call
You get onto a plane
Then they drop you and your friends off
And…
They say you're on the front line

And every night is like a thunderstorm
The night scattered with explosions and lights
And machine guns ring like rain drops on your tent
And now you think is that so bad
To give your little daughter piggyback rides again

But after a year or so you get the call
That you are going home
And you still have the nerve to say
"Well that was cool"
Well after all this you come a battered man
But you still give your little girl a…
Piggyback ride

Patrick Petit, Grade 7
Waterloo Middle School

I Once Knew a Country

I once knew a country that was my home
So hot and dry all the time
Many women who dressed in abayas
Didn't grow very many plants, palm trees
A king ruled over all his land, passing the throne
Down to his son or brother
Many compounds were throughout its land
Camels were being watched by their caretakers
Mosques are people's religious base
Its people speak Arabic
Keeps girls and boys separated

Now

My country has many seasons
Speaks English
Its people dress as they wish
Church on Sundays
Has many holidays
Presidents are elected every four years
Has many different things to do
Lets girls and boys blend

For me, that other country is now gone

Leila Katabi, Grade 7
West Branch Middle School

Movies

I love to watch movies
With no lights on
Watching X-men
Drawing them with a pen.

With lots of blood
Like Halloween 4 Return of Michael Myers
A bowl of popcorn in one hand
and one foot on the TV stand.

I watch them all night long
In my room with the door closed
Sitting in my chair
Sometimes even scared.

Brandon Derr, Grade 7
South Range Middle School

About Me

I am a wacky girl who loves cats
I wonder what will happen tomorrow
I hear the rain against my roof
I see snow drifting to the ground
I want there to be world peace
I am a wacky girl who loves cats

I pretend not to hear hurtful comments
I feel the soft fur of a kitten
I touch the stars
I worry about what will come
I cry when people get hurt by others
I am a wacky girl who loves cats

I understand that things won't always go my way
I say that you should be yourself
I dream of sitting on a cloud
I try to be kind to other people
I hope someday there will be peace
I am a wacky girl who loves cats

Jenna Gosche, Grade 7
Hopewell Loudon Local Jr/Sr High School

It's Snowing Outside…

It's snowing outside,
And I don't know why.
It's snowing outside,
And I want to cry.
It is getting too cold.
The basements start to mold.
Why can't we hibernate like a bear,
All cozy and warm inside his lair?
Winter is the only season that comes twice a year.
Which makes my eye drop a tear.
Why can't we have spring, summer, and fall?
It's snowing outside and it's hard for us all.

Eileen Mangan, Grade 7
J A Garfield Middle School

Grandpa

To me my grandpa was the best.
A few years ago he was laid to rest.
I think of him each night and day.
I don't know why he had to go away,

A grandpa, like mine, is hard to find.
To me, my grandpa was one of a kind.
He was helpful, funny, kind, and smart.
He was a great person with lot of love in his heart.

He helped all the family and neighbors too,
I can't think of anything that he couldn't do.
He helped many people in the cold and snow.
It didn't matter if they were people that he didn't even know.

He helped people in the sunshine or in the rain.
No matter what the problem was, you didn't hear him complain.
Whether it was human or animal my grandpa helped them all.
He didn't care what the weather was: Spring, Summer, Winter or Fall.

I saw my grandpa every day because he lived next door.
It's just still hard for me to believe that he's not here anymore.
A considerate, thoughtful person was he.
I loved my grandpa and he loved me.

Jen Hinkle, Grade 7
J A Garfield Middle School

Farm Life

I am from the hay bales, wooden walls and dirt floors,
from feathers flying and cows mooing.
I am from baby chicks hatching out, and baby goats being born.

I am from the hay in the field,
the pine trees whose pine sap stuck on my fingers.
I am from gardens and dirt
I'm from cookies and rings
From Opal and Charles.

I'm from dinner tables and turkeys and potatoes on ham.
From corn on the cob and carrots.
I'm from the stable with a wooden cradle
And have presents all wrapped up for me.

I'm from my dad's broken neck and my grandmother's death
from the cards I played to the chickens I've lost
My brother's cursed knee.
In my room is a suitcase.

Recovering my memories a vast number of thoughts a difficult process
But here I would rather be remembering my past.

Joseph Watrous, Grade 8
Logan Hocking Middle School

High Merit Poems – Grades 7, 8, and 9

Music

Whispering in the mid-summer's drift
Flowing like rich, creamy chocolate
So, so, sweet and satisfying
You can never get enough

The beat of your heart thumps with the music
Every movement of your body is corresponding
The feeling is almost like being enslaved
Enslaved by the emotions of the music

Devin Shanahan, Grade 8
St Christopher Elementary School

There's No Escape

It was late.
So late that you could see the darkness
Pushing down on my emotions,
Reminding me of what was soon to come.
He locked his arms around my body,
Calming the fire of fear inside of it.
I am disappearing,
Trembling in my skin.
The shadow peeks out of the door.
The deep, dark words,
Tell me enough.
I have run out of time.
A quick good-bye to him.
The momentary seconds of terror
Would seem like forever.
The screams will pierce through me,
Leaving scars of depression on my heart.
I am melting into the ground.
I feel so scared ... so helpless.
I can't get away.
There is no escape

Amanda Long, Grade 8
Hopewell Jr High School

Where Chuck's From

He's from eating take out at Red Barn.
To eating his favorite candy Mounds.
He's from building forts and climbing trees.
From his parents encouraging him to be a pilot.
He's from wearing his Converses and Lee jeans
and T shirts with sayings on them to school.
He's from never being inside.
To jumping ramps and riding his bicycle.
He's from loving and waiting for Halloween.
He's from saving up ten cents to buy Balsa gliders.
He's from a time of trustworthy people.
From building model airplanes when he wasn't outside.
He's from getting up on the weekends at 8 A.M. to do chores.
He's from saying "That was a simpler time back then."

Rusty Williams, Grade 7
West Branch Middle School

Winter Time Is Coming

The glistening snow beneath my feet.
The warm hot chocolate that tastes so sweet.
The green grass trampled underground.
Unique snowmen all through the town.
The downtown lights they shine so bright.
Santa and his reindeer all take flight.
All of the little ones tucked in bed.
While visions of sugarplums dance through their heads.

Karley Sullivan, Grade 8
Labrae Middle School

Imagination

The first wave went up as I shivered in fright,
For I knew that this would be a long sleepless night.
The boat seemed to sink as the pressure increased,
And the whole world shook as the first sail ceased.
There was no where to go, nothing ahead,
Just some high waves and lightning and thunder, stone dead.
The boat slipped forward and my rubber boots slid.
It came to me quickly, what the wave did.
The front of the boat was gone, and I was going in,
In fact, the last thing I saw was a sharp pointy fin.
Alas, I fell to the ground at the base of my swing set
And looked over to see my mom who was really upset.

Jenny Stamberger, Grade 8
Chardon Middle School

The Night Before Battle

The night before battle Joby was very afraid,
He was scared because he had no gun to his aid,
Joby feared death and never returning home,
Not ever to roam the states he called home.
He was worried and nervous that they could lose,
And that it all rested on his shoulders for them to pull through.
For enlisting in the army he is very sorry,
Because he may never live to be forty.
Possibly he may never have a child,
That will make his brain go wild.
All this runs through Joby's head,
As he lies in the peach field ready for the battle ahead.

Charles Hagler, Grade 8
Gesu Elementary School

Inside Looking Out

I am on the inside looking out
I see colorful leaves blowing through the cold brisk wind
I am on the inside looking out
I hear the wind whistling all around the outside
I am on the inside looking out
I feel as happy as a little kid eating a chocolate candy bar
when they are excited
I am on the inside looking out
I wish I were outside playing in all the colorful leaves
that are stacked in little tiny piles.

Morgan Rowe, Grade 8
Chardon Middle School

I Use To

I use to walk around with my head
Hung low
I use to cry
Every night, cutting, wanting to die
I use to not think
I could ever love again
But boy was I wrong
I think of you
And a smile comes to my face
I walk the streets
With my head up high
And every night
I thank God for
The person that
Finally came into my life

Krista Osenbaugh, Grade 8
Aurora Academy

It's Not Fair

It's not fair I have a twin brother
And it's all because of my mother
She just had to have him too
So now I don't know what to do.

He's annoying and lazy
And sometimes he's crazy
He always thinks he's the best
But he's just being a pest.

He always likes to eavesdrop
And I really wish he would stop
He thinks it's just a game
And he's the one to blame.

He always gets into my notes
Making it all seem like a joke
He never lets me have any alone time
I think he acts as sour as a lime.

He always gets in my way
But there's one thing I have to say
I love my twin brother
And I never want another.

Emily Luli, Grade 7
Waterloo Middle School

Advent

Rusty colored leaves
As the world waits for winter
All the world is bare
Shedding its green summer coat
Waiting for snowflakes to fall

Forde Ripich, Grade 8
Birchwood School

44634

Rain falling down
On tall, thick trees, big, empty fields
Dogs barking
Red and white, wood-built barns
But not the tractors running all the time
This is where I'm at
Quiet
Calm
And I like it

Jake Logorda, Grade 7
West Branch Middle School

Grandpa

Grandpa
Thoughtful, responsible,
Offering, understanding, thinking,
Veteran, Doctor, friend, father
Providing, inspiring, observing
Brave, logical
Idol

Maria Tony, Grade 7
St Jude School

Light from Shadows

At times the world is a desolate place,
Filled with crime and war.
Most people don't even show their face,
When kindness knocks at our door.

If we look hard enough,
We all may see light.
The world is not too rough,
When we get out of the blight.

Some people will see the tiniest flickers,
Of hope in the dark.
They will avoid all of the Devil's snickers,
And open God's heart.

Patrick Davet, Grade 8
Gesu Catholic School

Thank You God

Thank you God from up above
and everything you do with your love.
Thank you God for making me
now I'm as happy as can be.
Thank you God for flowers and trees,
frogs, roses, and bumble bees.
So many beautiful sights
football games under the lights.
Thank you God for flags waving in the air
Just to show freedom is what we share.

Tiffany Eden Jennings, Grade 7
J A Garfield Middle School

Inside Outside

Inside I am a mouse in the woods,
Swift, quiet, scurrying about
Outside I am a chart in a planner,
Always organizing important information

Inside I am an eagle in the mountains,
Soaring high in my thoughts
Outside I am sticky Scotch tape,
Always keeping things together

Monica Patrick, Grade 7
South Range Middle School

Veterans

They are sent away
To fight in a war
For our country
We pray for them

As they are fighting
They help our country
Stay free like it is today
They give up their lives

To save others
We love them all
Those who fight

Neil Allen, Grade 7
South Range Middle School

October Leaves

The colorful leaves.
Flying through the sky like planes.
As the wind goes by.

Alex Baele, Grade 7
St Paschal Baylon School

Inside This Paintbrush

Inside this paintbrush;
Is life.
New drawings anxious
To get out and belong
On their very own paper.
Inside this paintbrush
Are different colors,
Waiting to burst out
And become as colorful
As a rainbow.
Inside this paintbrush
Is hidden talent.
Inside this paintbrush
Is a Picasso waiting,
To become.

Madison Marquez, Grade 7
Gahanna Middle School East

No Life to Live

I'm caught in a corner
I don't know what to do
No one can understand what I'm possibly going through
I can't explain it
I don't know where to go
I'm no longer important
I'm but a memory in time
There's no one here who truly loves me
The life I live is not my own
The things I do are what people are better at
Where do I go?
Who do I turn to?
I'm, I'm, I'm gone.

Kaleigh Gilmer, Grade 7
J A Garfield Middle School

On the Inside Looking Out By: A Criminal

I'm on the inside looking out,
Children are about,
I once had a family,
Now I've only doubt.
Yes I broke the rules,
But then I was a fool,
Living in a dream,
That's all I could see.
Now I have a view,
Of a cold dreary room.
Bars chain me in,
This is punishment for my sin.
So now I sit and pout,
I'm on the inside looking out.

Taylor Johnson, Grade 8
Chardon Middle School

On the Inside

The pierced heart can always ache,
When someone hurts you bad.
You might not have a bruise or scar,
But memories never fade.
You might feel all better,
But then the mind plays again.

So when upset,
Don't take it out
On someone precious and dear.
Because hurt can't be taken back,
like taking clothes back to a store.

If you have ever been hurt real bad,
Try to face the facts and live.
If you never let the moment fade,
Then your troubles will never leave.
But make sure to tell someone you love,
So they can help you get through the pain.

Riley Lannon, Grade 8
Chardon Middle School

Elephants

E normous in size
L ays down roads for others to walk
E legant in the water like a swan in a pond
P lows through trees like a bulldozer in dirt
H eads as thick as rocks
A n amazing creation of God
N urture their young
T rample anything in their path
S tronger than Superman

Joey Kemper, Grade 8
St Christopher Elementary School

The Respected

Lieutenants, captains, sergeants, generals, officers
The respected men and women who serve in the army
The brave men and women who protect this country
The strong, mighty, brave, and respected

Heavy loads on their backs
Traveling on dry land
The fear of getting killed
The remembrance of their families
Oh the sorrow and the pains

I would not dare go out there
I would not like the risk of losing my life
I would be home sick and never go to sleep at night

Even in these sorrows
These men and women push on

Curtis Schaffer, Grade 7
South Range Middle School

A Child's Christmas

Leaping
Out of bed, and running
Downstairs.
I didn't know what to open
First, or even
What to expect. No one
Had awoken yet, so I knew I had
To wait. I glanced over
And saw half eaten cookies,
And an empty cup. I wonder when that guy's going to go
On a diet. Next to the table
Was our tree. It was bright, and covered
In eye opening
Ornaments, while a warm glow came
From it. Only once a year
Was our living room ever like this.
It was almost magical, the feeling
You get. Pondering in that thought
I heard a noise. Now I knew the rest were up.
Time to open the presents, and
Have a very Merry Christmas

Kelly Cavanaugh, Grade 8
St Aloysius Gonzaga School

Blue Waves
The fast, gusting wind
Pushes the waves throughout time
In the blue ocean
Alexandra Calabrese, Grade 7
St Paschal Baylon School

One Shot
One shot, one chance
One shot at glory
Thirty seconds left
29…28…27…
Clock ticking down
The score scorching me
54-53 THEM
Dribble…dribble…pass
20…19…
Defense tight, offense right
Looking, seeking, THERE
A hole, a gap, an alley
Running, moving, focusing
10…9…
Panic rushing in
8…7…
Looking, teammate cuts off the defender
Last shot coming into view
Pass…then…SWISH!
The championship was ours!
55-54!
Billy Lee, Grade 8
Licking Valley Middle School

Why Do People Smoke?
Some people smoke because
they think it's a game
What a shame!
It will only cause you pain
to play the Smoking game

Some people smoke to be cool
Well they're fools
To ignore the surgeon general rule
Because smoking shortens your life
and that isn't right

Some people smoke to be popular
with their friends
But they will be lonely in the end
Dying of cancer ain't a good thing

There is really no good reason to pick
up that death stick

Save your life
Because you know smoking isn't right.
Christina Perry, Grade 7
Incarnation School

Seasons
The seasons come and they go with rain, heat and snow.

Spring, the time the flowers bloom, and thunder crackles and booms.
The heavy rain pours down, and the tree buds are all around.
The day light gets long, and in the wind there is a song.
The seasons come and they go with rain, heat and snow.

Summer, the time for fun and play, and it is warm every day.
The humidity is very high, and almost no clouds are in the sky.
The leaves are green and fully grown, and the fireworks are well-known.
The seasons come and they go with rain, heat and snow.

Fall, the time of luscious gold on all the trees young and old.
Pumpkins glowing in the night, and little kids flying a kite.
The days get cold and dark, the bon fires start burning bark.
The seasons come and they go with rain, heat and snow.

Winter, the time of slush and ice, but the snow is very nice.
It's the season to be jolly, while decking the halls with lots of holly.
The temperature is well below 32, and there is frost but no dew.
The seasons come and they go with rain, heat, and snow.
Zach Baierl, Grade 8
Chardon Middle School

The Joys of Christmas
Christmas time is very near.
It comes around this time of year.
Christmas is after a big feast at the end of November.
It is a day I will always remember.
Family and friends are built as one heart.
It beats so fine and it continues from the start.
The kaleidoscope of vivid hues mix and match on the decorative tree.
Candy canes and sugar plums are saved in a bowl for you and me.
The mistletoe hangs up on the ceiling.
Kisses and hugs are given in a warmhearted feeling.
Presents are hidden under the green pine.
They hide from the children who scream "That's mine!"
On Christmas Eve though, the children snug with hopes so bright.
They hope that Santa will be coming that night.
Christmas Day is on the 25th of December.
It is a day I will always remember.
Stephanie Hoover, Grade 8
Chardon Middle School

These Are the Moments
Sweat falls down my face like the beginning of a light April rain
I move down the field despite the pain
Dribbling the ball through the defenders towards the other end
Passing to my open player, the ball slightly bends
The opponents race towards her, crowding her like a swarm of bees
She kicks the ball back to me; someone misses and knocks her knees
I tap the ball right past the goal keeper
We won the game; we rush off the field like dust being pulled up by a sweeper
These are the moments that make the season worth the effort.
Morgan Porter, Grade 8
St Christopher Elementary School

Sunny Day

Calm blue sky.
Still warm air.
The sun is bright.
The sound of birds singing softly.
The trees are green.
The sound of kites gliding smoothly in the air.
Birds soaring through the soft blue sky.
Suddenly clouds gather.
And rain begins to fall all through the sky.

Faith Bryant, Grade 7
Hamersville Elementary and Middle School

The Winning Goal

Thoughts racing, this is it! This is for the glory!
Mind blank except one thought,
Did I score
The referee points to the goal and blows the whistle
My hands shoot up
the crowd roars.
We won! We won!
They pile on me
The winning breakaway
The winning shot
The winning goal

Christian Hayden, Grade 8
Licking Valley Middle School

For This Is a Special Season!

Seasons
It is blazing hot outside,
for which we all have to abide,
The children run out of school,
to go to the refreshing pool.
For this is a special season!

I waddle slowly outside,
and feel the cold winter wind glide.
The trees sparkle with white snow,
covering both high and low.
For this is a special season!

The flowers blossom up,
and it becomes the day of the Irish luck.
I see in the pond the ducks,
and also the left over snow muck.
For this is a special season!

We hurry to meet,
for it's almost trick-or-treat.
As the graceful leaves fall,
the school begins to call.
For this is a special season!

Connie Hodge, Grade 8
Chardon Middle School

And a Song So Sweet

A thousand stars glimmered and the moon shined.
Carefully opening the door,
I crept outside.
Onto my balcony,
All alone.
My skin caressed by the wind's soft blow.

My pain slowly swallowed.
Providing guidance with a song so sweet,
Healing wounds that feel so deep.
The night sang its song, my mind's dance followed.

Tingles of cold slunk up my spine,
Lying on the floor, alone in the sky.
We spoke for a while, the moon and I.
The bright orb smiled, as I cried.
A refreshing newness flooded my mind,
And I knew I could go on,
At least for a while.

Rows of stars rolled over me.
The song went on and the wind blew tenderly,
The lullaby played as my eyes slowly set,
Flowers closing, sealed for the night.

Sahar Atassi, Grade 8
Birchwood School

Anger

Anger is red like a cardinal.
It creeps into my head.
It reminds me of the time I yelled at my sister.
It makes me feel the adrenaline racing to my anger.
Ready to use it, to do something extraordinary.

Steven Cady, Grade 7
Incarnation School

The Pressures of Growing Up

Remember the days when you were a child
Full of energy and ready for life
Now gone, all of your days of being mild
You need to take care of your nagging wife

There's no more playing and joking around
The high expectations you have to meet
This may have you hiding under the ground
Climbing the corporate ladders under your feet

Growing up is not that easy at all
When you were young you wished you could be old
When you were a child you would start to bawl
When you're an adult you're out in the cold

The truth is I'm excited to grow up
It's not that bad so why don't you perk up!

Leah Streeter, Grade 8
Gesu Elementary School

Touchdown

Rough, tough, and ready to go
Look at that amazing throw
Way to go, Jake fought right through
Fans, players, and cheerleaders to
All stand up and scream, Go Gold!
Fight tonight, be so bold.
There goes the boys there goes the ball
Football, that's what I love about fall.

Taylor DeBee, Grade 8
Regina Coeli/St. Joseph's Elementary School

The Chase

Beyond earthly experiences,
The birds go on a chase
Through the mountains and above trees,
Never ending is their race.

In the heavens, they chase each other,
Hoping to finally catch one another
Skimming the water and touching the clouds,
Interrupting gatherings and disturbing large crowds.

Reaching the limits,
They slow it down.
Each one is getting tired,
They are homeward bound.

Now flying side by side,
They try not to collide.
The chase is now completed.
Neither is defeated.

They fly together without despise.
Until the next sunrise…

Joseph Zimmerman, Grade 8
Incarnation School

World of Music

Music flutters around my head
As I plug the headphones in my ears
All I can feel is the pounding
Of the drum's feet
And the guitar wails in my ear
Sending messages of excitement
Straight through the speaker
The bass hums a melody subtly in my ear
And makes sure I can't get it out of my head
The microphone reaches out
And grabs the perfect notes from the singer's throat
Words from the lyricist's notebook
Jump at me without warning
And strike me with their meaning
I relax in the unusual world
That the music has created for me

Angie Stewart, Grade 7
Gahanna Middle School East

The Championship Game

As the scoreboard counts down, we're down by two.
I look in the stands I see the whole town.
The opponents point guard drives in for a lay-up; two points for them.
Our point guard takes it out; the other team decides to press.
We manage to get the ball through with all of the stress.
I get the ball a half court and turn around.
I pass down low and an easy two points for us; 34 to 32.

Thirty seconds count down, 30…29…28…27…26…25…
They dribble around to stall.
They pass the ball and it goes out of bounds; our ball.
As the time runs, the point guard calls out a play.
Our heart pound louder than the ball hitting the ground.
We know it all comes down to this last play.

I get open at half-court.
I pass to a teammate open as could be.
She turns to the basket.
At that moment she knew she had to shoot.
The clock only had 2 seconds left.
She shot…
She missed!
We hear the last buzzer of the game.

Tricia Norris, Grade 8
Chardon Middle School

Magic of a Snowflake

I sleepily gaze upon the window,
It is frosted with ice and has glittering icicles hanging from its sill.
I hear the young children giggling and laughing,
Ecstatic, for being released early from the schoolhouse.
I race down the stairs, quickly gathering my warm layers.
I must be the first to arrive at the hill,
For being first, means leaving my legacy on the Earth,
Until it is wiped clean again.

I make it to the top then quickly race to the bottom,
I feel the sleigh vibrate beneath me,
And the blistery winds create a cherry upon my face.
I shrill with laughter, as I reach the end of my journey.
All the day was spent there,
Only disappearing to get a quick sip of cocoa.
At the end, the sunset appeared to be painted on the horizon,
As the sun fell the moon and stars rose into the darkness.

We were brought together for dinner,
Sitting near the blazing fire.
We fell into a deep sleep,
As the Earth was coated with a new blanket.
This is the magic of the snowflake

Sydney Scribner, Grade 7
Gesu Elementary School

Memories

I remember the times that we used to share. The times that I would look in the dark sky and just stare. You were a big influence on my life. When you died it felt like someone stabbed me with a knife left and right. I didn't know where to turn. I was thinking about whether I should give up or get through this next day. So every night I would pray like maybe this is a dream and hoping it wasn't as real as it seemed. But now I know all because I let you go on your journey. You are now where I wanted you to be and where you wanted to be, in Heaven, and I am down here on Earth just filled with memories.

Brandon Davis-Pearl, Grade 9
Roger Bacon High School

A Mother

A mother is as sweet as chocolate covered cherries.
Mothers know how to brighten up every day like sunshine entering a dark room.
Mothers know everything from healing cuts and bruises to kissing it and making it better.
Mothers do all this but what she does the best is love you.
No matter what you do or say she will be there to take your hand and lead you out of the darkness.

Miranda Roe, Grade 7
Buckeye North Middle School

Hockey

It is an hour before the game; the ice looks as smooth as a sheet of paper. You look into the stand and see a lot of people sitting down. Then, the coach says, "It's game time!" So we march out of the locker room like an army. Next, we get into our lines for our warm up drill. When the puck is shot it looks like a bullet coming out of the gun. Coach calls us over and gives us a talk. Then the referee blows his whistle, we line up, and he drops the puck. The game begins.

Martin Clancy, Grade 8
St Brendan Elementary School

Childhood Is…

Childhood is catching lightning bugs until the sun goes down.
Childhood is being excited and wanting to go to school.
Childhood is not caring who's cool.
Childhood is not going to bed until you read a bedtime story.
Childhood is sitting in time-out for coloring on the wall.
Childhood is racing your dog and playing fetch with his ball.
Childhood is swimming and splashing in a pool that's only two feet deep.
Childhood is being afraid of monsters that live in the dark.
Childhood is putting out cookies and milk for Santa.
Childhood is a time for dressing up on Halloween night.
Childhood is going to the store and wanting to buy everything.
Childhood is a time for pillow fights and jumping on beds.
Childhood is cutting, coloring, and painting everything you see.
Childhood is having mountains of stuffed animals to comfort you on those dark scary nights.
Childhood is the greatest time in the world.

Ryan Sobel, Grade 7
St Monica Elementary School

Mountain Climbing

While I gaze upon the mountain I get a sense of astonishment.
As I step foot onto the trail I think to myself, "Why am I about to do this?"
I start to climb, higher and higher.
Finally I get to the top. I look over the edge to see how far I've come.
But now I have to go back down.
I trip and slide over the tiny rocks, almost falling off the side.
Only minutes away from the bottom I feel as if a giant boulder has fallen off my shoulders.
I set my foot back on the same land where I started.
A feeling of relief comes across me as once more I gaze upon the mountain.

Jake Kopronica, Grade 8
St Christopher Elementary School

Name

My name is George,
It is a Greek name.
People make fun of it
So long I can understand why:
For it's only a silly name.

I was named after my Grandpa,
A very good man.
All I have left is my name,
Now that he is gone.

As a name is a name,
I'd rather go by Michael:
My confirmation name it is.
Any name would work,
But George is the one for me.

George Carleton, Grade 7
St Brendan Elementary School

When Will This Talent Show End?

Magic tricks and children singing,
Instruments playing, bells a-ringing,
Dance routines and poems recited,
Baton twirlers, the crowds excited!

Gymnastic moves, funny skits,
Ballerinas performing splits,
Comedians making jokes,
Funny costumes, long dark cloaks.

Guitars playing classic cords,
Karate masters chopping boards,
The last act's just around the bend,
When will this talent show ever end?

Natalie Santoro, Grade 7
South Range Middle School

I Miss You

I used to have you.
But now I only have me.
I always think of you.
But I never forget what we had.
I once had you to hold me.
But no one holds me now.
If I could fix things.
I would have stopped you.
I never blame myself.
But I might one day.
I can't get your memory to fade.
But I can just for a second.
I won't lose someone like you again.
But I will always want you back.
I used to have you hold me.
But now I hold my pillow.

Anna DeAngelis, Grade 7
Waterloo Middle School

The Voice

Her voice, her stabbing words echoed in my head with distinct discouragement
that had passed unnoticed in the negative atmosphere which we all had lived.
You can't. You won't. You never will.
The words tore at my insides like a vicious guard dog with a piece of raw meat.
I tried to brush them off as I brushed the white dust off my arms.
Maybe it's just not your thing.
No. It was my thing. I had to prove it to her. I had to prove it to myself.
I couldn't let her be right.
She could never be right.
I pushed myself harder. Almost there. Still failing.
She took over my mind, my soul, and taunted me.
Letting her take over would ruin everything I had worked for, everything I changed,
Everything I had become.
I squeezed tight and let go, letting go of the past along with it.
I had gone against all odds before. I was willing to do it again.
I pushed myself against the past, against her words.
This time a triumph.
Her voice slowly faded, and mine was heard once again.
I can. I have. I always will.

Mariah Quick, Grade 8
St Christopher Elementary School

About Me

Alexis is her name.
Gym class is her shame.
Purple is the color she prefers.
Her eyes are as brown as a chocolate sundae,
her hair as silky as the women on Broadway,
and her skin is as golden as gold.
She's also known by her mother as Lexaphena,
her friends say she laughs as much as a hyena.
Her special talent is to cheer for her school sports teams all year.
She plans on becoming a doctor,
and her favorite food is pizza.
The car she mostly resembles is a Camaro,
laid back and cool.
She gets teased for being organized,
maybe too in line.
She thoroughly hates the dark,
and her walk has bounce and spark.
Her mother says she blossoms like an African Violet,
keeps growing without ceasing.
Always pleasing other people.
Alexis is her name and she is all that she can be.

Alexis Marino, Grade 8
St Monica Elementary School

Opening a Door

I've lost belief in the Easter Bunny, the Tooth Fairy and Santa Claus
I've gained the true meaning to Christmas and Easter
I've lost best friends and the city of my parents and where my family lives
But I gained new friends and a town of my own
I've lost a passion and gained a new dream
Opportunities will rain down as I enter the door of success

Tim Cooper, Grade 7
Western Reserve Middle School

High Merit Poems – Grades 7, 8, and 9

It's Not Fair
It's not fair
That he makes me cry
To get that sting in my eye
It's not fair
That he is not here
But his spirit is still near
It's not fair
That I never got to meet him
Even though I heard he was really neat
It's not fair
He would have been a good grandfather
That I could have sat on one knee then the other
It's not fair
That he is gone
Although it has been so long
It's not fair
But life goes on
I think that he is still my hero
It's not fair he had to go
And I miss him so
It's not fair

Lani Gregory, Grade 7
Waterloo Middle School

I Blinked and Fall Was Here
Feeling the sudden urge to go outside
"I'm not going to fight it," I told myself
Strutting through my dead yard
The gentle whistling of the wind was disturbed
By the soft chimes coming from the chimes on a nearby tree
The distant hum of an airplane was floating through the air
Behind the glass door, the family puppy was barking at me
Because I wasn't inside
Gazing out over the dead yard
The swings were swaying
The drip drop of the water splashing into the hot tub
From the cover was very distant for I had zoned out,
Mesmerized by the leaves that were quickly changing color
"Fall is almost here," I whispered as I went back inside
I turned around
The yard looked the same
Then I blinked and it was fall…

Caroline Hoffmann, Grade 7
Incarnation School

Ice Cream
Life is an ice cream cone.
You eat it on a hot summer day.
It is cool and refreshing.
It has many different flavors to pick from.
Sometimes it is hard to choose what flavor.
Also if you don't eat it fast enough it could melt.
Also if you don't have a proper grip on it
you can lose the whole thing.

Joe Gyorky, Grade 7
St Brendan Elementary School

Alone
Alone in the night I lay crying.
Now, afraid of you.
Every move I make, pains me more,
Numb inside,
Inside this core.

Dark within a burning heart.
You've destroyed my love, ripped me apart.
I thought you loved me,
That's what you said,
Another moment,
Gone and dead.

Afraid of you,
Afraid of time,
Weeping my issue,
For all lifetime.

Alone in the night I lay crying.
Now, afraid of you,
Afraid of trying.
Every move I make pains me more,
Numb inside,
Inside this core.

Sarah McCartney, Grade 7
Wooster Christian School

All That I Am
My name is Mackenzie you've got that right,
But please don't tease me because of my height.
I'm a life-size Barbie with my blue eyes and blonde hair,
Sweatshirts and jeans are what I love to wear.

I'm most like a train I can't function off track,
If there is a spider near you I may never come back.
I'm like a kangaroo with my bouncy walk
Stay for the night and in my sleep I will talk

When I listen to music, I tend to lip sync.
When it comes to colors, I choose blue over pink.
If you tell me to be quiet, I might not listen,
Even if there is something important I'm missing.

I have to say I'm a big fan of french fries.
I really don't like it when people spread lies.
Yes, I'm a dancer, but I'm somewhat clumsy,
I guess I can say I got it from my mumsy.

Fifteen years from now I wish to be an M.D.,
But until you're my patient, you'll just have to wait and see.
Well, this is my poem, I gave it all I've got.
This is me whether you like it or not.

Mackenzie Duale, Grade 8
St Monica Elementary School

Happiness

Happiness
Is like the wind
It comes and it goes
It grows strong
And then very weak
It never stays for long
But when it is here
You think of it as normal
Something that's with us
Every day
But yet when it is gone
Life seems but unchanging
Dull
Pointless
So, my advice to you
Is to appreciate the presence of
Happiness
And to enjoy every second of it.

Abby Linson, Grade 7
Gahanna Middle School East

Dragon of Hope

The dragon has came to save my soul,
from what has been lost forever.
The dragon has also came to help me
defeat the devil from eating my soul.
One alone, I can't defeat him.
But, with the dragon of hope,
and my own hope,
I might stand a chance
to stand up to him and fight.

Ashley Mann, Grade 7
Fairfield Local High School

Feelings

The feeling of *courage*
gains for you determination and nerve.
The feeling of *loneliness*
brings on solitude and withdrawal.
The feeling of *excitement*
aims for adventure and hullabaloo.
The feeling of *hatred*
causes evil glares and ugly stares.
The feeling of *happiness*
blesses you with laughter and prosperity.
The feeling of *sorrow*
brings you tears and heartache.
The feeling of *bravery*
is the foundation of fortitude and spunk.
The feeling of *pain*
causes hurt and wrong-doing.
The feeling of *love*
keeps the world turning!

Marissa Schroeder, Grade 8
Miller City-New Cleveland School

I Remember

I remember...
Like pages in a horror story
Words like frighten, beware, and stay away
Two famous people Johnny Depp and Orlando Bloom
Anybody's family, necklace, furry pets
Place in a story where Cassie gets kissed by Burnie
The injury when I fell off my new bike and cut my kneecap on the rocks
Our house was small in a small down
And outside it was a big yard with space to see the sunset
The sound of crickets cherpin' while my mom and I watchin' the sunset on the grass
Anyone who can hear it, is in for a treat.

Natalie Peace, Grade 7
South Range Middle School

A Devastating Day in American History: A Tribute to 9-11 Victims

Every day rolls by people wondering if there's terrorist around
All because of that devastating September day.
We lost many American people that worked in the Twin Towers
And it's hard on the anniversary of September 11 not to cry.

It's something that we need not to ever forget
For if we do it's a shame that we would be forgetting all those who died.
Many people have already started to forget
And we need to remind them about September 11
Because it's a day in history that needs never to be forgotten.

So when anniversary of September 11 comes around
Don't be afraid to wear red, white, and blue to honor
The people who lost their lives, do to the terrorist attacks on the Twin Towers.

Kelsey Golec, Grade 9
Claymont High School

Sorrow of a Veteran

A teardrop slides down a porcelain cheek.
A warrior carries a heart heavier than a sack of flour.
He has a badge for bravery that he displays with pride.
But recounting the details of war aren't easy for him
War was filled with hate and sorrow.
Some time ago, there was so much killing.
But the slaughtered were innocent.
Guilty of only wishing to make our country a better place.
As they ran and hid, trying to survive.
And the deafening silence and cause fear to ripple through their bodies.
Will the next bomb hit them?
It's a war against position and destiny.
Being at the right or wrong place at the right or wrong time.
And his memories hurt like glass in skin.
But his pride is so strong, the hurt becomes numb.
And he smiles at what he's done.
And he thinks, "I am a Veteran!"

Ravyn Taylor, Grade 8
Western Reserve Middle School

Canceled

They wake with anticipation,
With a general optimistic notion,
That Mother Nature has began to function,
To make their world frozen.

They celebrate with much glee,
And run around aimlessly,
Preparing to play freely,
In the outdoors quite chilly.

They frolic through the yard happily,
Making snowmen quickly,
For they know what is coming swiftly,
They know that it cannot remain peacefully.

They make the deduction,
This to them is more like an assumption,
And with an expected motion,
They prepare for explosion.

They increase base fortification,
And use a shovel as a snow cannon,
Preparing to defend their new faction,
The first snowball falls from the horizon.

Tyler Koester, Grade 9
Delphos St John High School

Hiding from the Wind

Cara and I, lying on the floor,
Playing *Life* our favorite summertime game.
The wind rustles the plastic on the walls more and more,
We hear footsteps, though no one else is home.

We run from the shadows,
There is no place for us to hide.
The house seemed safe until now.
We escape to the outside, racing to our neighbor's yard.

Hearts beating fast,
Both of us turn to look behind our backs —
Neither Cara nor I want to get to the trampoline last,
We don't want to find out what beast made those sounds.

Our nerves shivering inside —
Our breaths fast and short,
I'm not scared — I lie.
We gather up courage to go back to the house.

We laugh at our fear —
The wind is just playing tricks on us.
Our ears and our minds don't agree on what we hear,
We relax, and continue our summer fun.

Nikki Kaine, Grade 8
Hopewell Jr High School

Peer Pressure

My mind is a war zone,
Should I do it? Should I not?
It's my choice right or wrong
I can't be sure for what I long
My parents trust I've had since birth
Or a "friendship" to someone who couldn't care less about me?
I know what to say…
But that little voice inside me is telling me otherwise
Should I do it? Should I not?

Brandon Paul, Grade 8
Licking Valley Middle School

Rain

I look outside my window and I see the pounding rain.
Its monotonous tone so sweet to me,
but to others, it will bring pain.
Rain is a blessing.
Rain is a curse.
It's joyous, but it's sad.
Rain brings life.
Rain brings death.
It's good but also bad.
Your mind will tell you what rain is.
There's no right or wrong way.
Your mind will tell you what you see,
on a rainy day.

Jonathan Sylak, Grade 8
Chardon Middle School

Autumn Is…

Autumn is…
Dead leaves rustling on the ground
Cold mornings and nights
Candy corn
Mashed potatoes
Turkey on Thanksgiving
Fog and frost settle in on a cold morning
Geese overhead looking like an arrow pointing south
Autumn is saying hello to school
And saying good-bye to summer vacation
Saying hello to coldness
Hearing crunching leaves as I go outside
That's what fall means to me.

Tyler Kerpsack, Grade 7
West Branch Middle School

Love

Love is pure, love is gold,
But can break your heart to mourn and be cold.
Powerful, maddening, sweet as a cherry pie.
Juvenile, troublesome, addicting as it may be,
Love is a handsome thing, not to be seen.
Quietly touching one another's hearts,
Love is a sacred possession of art.

Rachel Huehner, Grade 7
J A Garfield Middle School

My Best Friend

I have a best friend
Whom I love more than life,
He makes me smile
By holding me tight.
When we're on the phone,
He makes me laugh,
And when I'm mad,
He calms my wrath.
My best friend is amazing.
he is unbeatable.
And the things he says
Are unbelievable.
My best friend is like a big brother to me
He takes me to another world
And makes me feel free.
He makes me feel weightless,
As if I could fly;
He understands me completely
And makes me happy inside.
He is my friend,
From now 'til the end.

Ashley Karcic, Grade 8
Chardon Middle School

October Sky

The October sky
Looks like cotton candy swirls
Bringing me great joy.

Mike Vala, Grade 7
St Paschal Baylon School

Hold on Tight

Only one leaf left,
Who's holding on for its life,
Avoiding its death.

Jenna Consolo, Grade 7
St Paschal Baylon School

Houses

Our houses are like our blankets
They keep us warm at night
It protects us from the dangers outside.
Houses are a part of our families
It has been through everything with you
And it is hard to let go of them.
When you walk inside
The floors creak
It is trying to smile.
Houses hold memories
Many great, but some bad
Our houses will always be there for us
Even if we move out
It will be sad
As if the creaks become tears.

Bianca Brutovski, Grade 7
Gahanna Middle School East

Life Is a Guitar

Life is a guitar.
Sometimes it can be out of tune.
Sometimes you might not play how you want.
The strings might snap.
You might want to play something but not know how to play it.
You might perform in front of a group of people and do really well.
Playing well lets you know that the practice and the dedication pay off.

Jack FitzGerald, Grade 7
St Brendan Elementary School

Advice on the World

Is it love?
Who knows anymore? Love is so disguised anymore.
Open your eyes, or you'll be deceived.
Love ain't what it seems to be.
It's not just boy vs girl…it's girl vs world.
Your friends won't be there when you need them the most,
And all boys that you'll date will be cocky and boast.
The boys that told you they loved you and cared
Are probably not even there…
They probably left you for some other girl.
They're all just the same; they think they own this whole world.
The girls are all just so catty and fake.
Some of us get lucky and see that two-faced girls don't get what they think.
All they do is start drama; make a scene.
They honestly think that they mean something.
So, you see little girl, this world is a joke.
The word we used as "love" is only a hoax.
So trust only yourself, and you'll do just fine.
Just don't put your heart on the trusting line.
Oh, little girl, open your eyes, try to see…
Don't trust in this world, or you'll end up like me.

Tia Sowers, Grade 9
Washington Sr High School

Horses

Click-Click-Click Horses gallop off into the sunset,
on a warm summer's night.
Through the cool sand and over the crabs.
What a beautiful sight.

As dawn hits the next morning,
Swish-Swish-Swish along the ocean as the waves pound the sand
Shhh-Shhh-Shhh The wind starts to blow as a storm comes to the land.

The horses trot to the barn. *Boom-Boom-Boom*
The thunder shakes the ground.
When the thunder, wind, and rain stop
the horses *Nay* and start to trot around.

A great way to end the day
is with a herd of horses.
I love to watch the horses on the other side of the bay, *Whoosh-Whoosh-Whoosh*,
and with a rainbow in the blue sky.

Kali Stivison, Grade 7
Logan Hocking Middle School

Sad Is Gray

It tastes like rain,
It smells like a coffin,
It sounds like thunder,
It feels like being depressed,
It looks like tears,
Sadness is the death of a person you love.

Taylor Ogden, Grade 7
Hamersville Elementary and Middle School

This Is Me

This is me, a dancer at heart.
I love to let the music move my soul.
When I dance, I dance freely to the music.
My flexibility and smallness,
makes it easier for me to move with the music.
Dancing makes me feel free and at peace.
It is my escape when I am upset.
Being shy and quiet,
dancing is an easy way for me to express myself.

My other passions are gymnastics and cheerleading.
These help my aggressive side.
Yes, I do have one of those, but it doesn't show very often.
I may be quiet and fragile,
but I love to yell as loudly as I can,
for my cheerleading squad.
Tumbling helps to release my anger,
not that I need much help, because I'm not usually angry.

I am a shy athletic dancer.
I love to let the music move my soul.
This is me, Mya Erickson!

Mya Erickson, Grade 8
St Monica Elementary School

Sailing It All in the Fall

I set sail on the Pacific Ocean, but before I leave,
I observed the waves crash and fall.
When I set sail
I have no fear at all.
My best friend is coming with me
because he is visiting for the fall.
We watch our last wave tumble as
we take off to sea.
As we see the land recede
into the thick and foggy air,
the wind is picking up, pushing
our sail and blowing our hair.
We will be back in December,
just in time for the cold, cold, air.
Our stock of food is chips,
fish, salad, deer, and bear.
We have only 5 plaid, plain pairs
of clothes to wear.

Tanner Dovsek, Grade 8
Chardon Middle School

Snow Day

As night draws near
A storm is looming.
But have no fear
There will be no booming.

For this storm that is arriving,
It will have the children thriving.
Because when they awake,
They will see their first snow flake.

They will put on mittens and their boots
To keep them warm while they go play.
On this very cold and snowy day.

They will build snowmen and have snowball fights,
As they prance and dance around the lights.
They will make snow angels and slide on ice.
This day home from school has been very nice.

As the children come in from their very fun day,
In hopes that tomorrow will be the same way.
As another stormy night begins,
Tomorrow will leave us home again.

Dakota Frank, Grade 7
J A Garfield Middle School

My Big Brother

My brother is eighteen years old
He is very smart and bold

I look up to him in every way
And miss him tons when he's away

We do often get in fights
But we'll have made up by the end of the night

I love my brother off and on
But we will always have that special bond

Madyson Stephens, Grade 7
Union Local Middle School

Veterans' Day

V ery important Americans
E very person should always remember them
T hey are remembered as heroes
E ven they had hard times
R emembered forever and ever
A lways thinking bout what happened in war
N ever will forget all the friends they lost
S aviors to everyone in America

D ad's and mom's to kids
A person you can always look up to
Y ours and my grandparents

Tyler Powell, Grade 8
Western Reserve Middle School

Where I'm From...

I am from the country, from homemade meals and chores.
From our farm in Tennessee, (the animals I loved to feed).
I am from the great big oak, in which my cousin and I got stuck.
I am from a great big family, whose love always grows.
I'm from love and laughter, that seems to fill the room.
I am from the support of friends, who are the best in the world.
I am from the heartbreak of my father, to the love of my mother. From Sylvia and Brenda, my grandmas so dear.
I'm from the loss of loved ones, to the love they left behind.
I am from my little brothers and sisters, who are all a little bratty.
From my two baby sisters, I hardly ever see.
I am from a large family, to the ones of my friends.
From living and laughing, to crying and hurting.
From living at home, to living at Angela's.
I am from the house I used to live in, to the one I live in now.
From my grandma's house, in which I lived for a year. I am from good people, which will always be true.
I am from working parents, to caring friends.
I'm from people who love me, and others who don't.
I'm from working hard in school, and the same at home.
I am from the Germans, and the Irish as well.
I'm from my family, mixed up as it is.
I'm from knowing, they'll always love me.

Brittany Butler, Grade 8
Verity Middle School

Intelligence

Intelligence
To know when to stop arguing with your sister and start agreeing on sharing
To know what is important in life and letting the feeble things go
To decipher good from bad in friendship
To live with your faults like being small and try to improve in the future by eating your veggies
To always give your mother a good-bye kiss even when your friends are around
To be kind to everybody because you will meet them again in life
To never procrastinate while working on a big project
To follow your dream of becoming an architect and make it happen
To know when to ask Miss Pepple for help on integers
This is to have intelligence.

Jacob Pfeifer, Grade 7
South Range Middle School

What I Saw in the Mist

I wandered near a noisy pond, covered completely by mist.
I heard frogs, birds, and animals of such sort, but one sound was distinct.
It sounded like a harp, beautiful and heavenly, so I wandered into the mist.
There, before my eye, I saw a lady, dressed in light blue, with a golden harp in her hands.
She did not stop playing when she looked at me, and I just stared in awe.
She told me, "Only one with a pure heart and soul can enter into my pond."
I told her my name and asked her hers, and she told me with a smile.
My name is Elena, Goddess of Pure Hearts, and I will ask you, what brought you here?
I told her about her beautiful music and her ethereal face lightened up.
The gods have sent me to Earth, to bring joy to all and mend broken hearts,
as long as you keep this place a secret, I will permit you to visit again.
I swore on my honor to never tell and she continued to play her song.
I listened and listened until the sun downed and hurried in time to get home.
And I kept my promise, never to tell of what I saw in the mist.

Ilona Kereki, Grade 7
Birchwood School

A Walk in the Secret Garden
The secret dahlias surrounding me with clarity,
The buzzing of bees, working around the garden,
A drop of blood from a rose thorn on my finger,
The fresh aroma of honey from a nearby hive,
The cushiony and smooth red rose petal between my bare toes,
The secret garden.
Cassandra Molocea, Grade 7
South Range Middle School

A Hopeful Wish
A nine year old girl born to a world barely known,
Her parents' "secret" jobs were not to be shown.
Meeting with strange people and whispering to make sure they aren't loud.
Coming from their mouths is a puff-like cloud.
The girl watches from the street and looks terribly afraid,
Then notices with an exchange of items her parents get paid.

So much arguing and fighting with fists,
It appears as if they don't realize that she exists.
Soon cars show up with blinking lights,
And a strong young man assures her she'll be all right.
To her he's an angel that saved her from fear,
And she feels a new life for her is near.

A caring young couple shows her a new home,
They tell her that here she is safe and free to roam.
The darkness of night appeared and she fell asleep in her new, warm bed,
And felt it comforting to finally have a pillow under her head.
She woke up the next morning cold, but happy she seemed,
Until she saw beneath her the street, and discovered it was all just a dream.
Tiffany Geise, Grade 9
Delphos St John High School

Who I Am
I am a shepherd, who likes wildlife.
I wonder if our universe is on a person's shoulder in a larger universe.
I hear a wolf's howl in the black of night.
I see a polar bear roll over in its nightly home.
I want to own a wild life preserve.
I am a shepherd, who likes wildlife.

I pretend to be in Montana.
I feel the pain of my sheep.
I touch the soft wool of newborn lambs.
I worry about my sheep day and night.
I cry when a lamb that I've watched since birth dies.
I am a shepherd, who likes wildlife.

I understand the way animals think.
I say, save endangered species.
I dream to be a vet on a ranch out west.
I try to always be my best.
I hope to live on a beautiful Montana mountain.
I am a shepherd, who likes wildlife.
Dave Beleny, Grade 7
Hopewell Loudon Local Jr/Sr High School

Life
We live a life like no other,
No one can feel our pain
It's not a life of misery
But not a life of fame,
It's a life of freedom
But freedom with restraints,
Our life comes with independence
But independence with rules
We all may be able to see
But are blind to the truth
A life where we can hear
But a life where we are deaf to the music.
It's a life of color
But a life of black and white.

It's just life!!!
Nathan Denton, Grade 8
Incarnation School

The Vampire
Their eyes are hot as a December day
Sometimes they spread their wings and fly away
They all mutate into a savage beast
They look at you then they plan their big feast
Their skin as white as January snow
They pull out their so darkening crossbow
The bow puts you into a horrible trance
If you walk at night you're taking a chance
Jet-black hair but is yet so wirey
Wretched breath that is oh so fiery
They wear clothes that are ripped and raggedy
If you spot one it's a bad tragedy
If you're walking and hear a spooky sound
Don't have a second thought just turn around
Keith Spille, Grade 8
St Aloysius Gonzaga School

Things I Didn't Know Were There
Freezing in my back yard,
And I plopped into my chair.
I sat there viewing the world I had
Outside my house.
I spotted things I didn't know were there.
The birds playing,
The wonderful yard I had
And the houses my friends lived in.
Hearing things in the cold breeze and
Feeling the wind against my face.
My pen against the paper.
Sometimes the wind was so strong
I could taste it, even smell it.
I finished what I came out to do
And then went inside and stayed
Next to the fire.
Nick Godfrey, Grade 7
Incarnation School

How Much I Love You
Every time I see you,
My knees get weak,
I go to open my mouth,
Yet, I can't seem to speak.

The feeling I get when I'm with you
Leaves me short of breath,
Every time you turn to leave
I feel a part of me has left.

I miss you when I'm with you
I need you when I'm not,
Every time you touch me
I can feel my heart get hot.

I try to find a way
To tell you how I feel,
But the words, they got lost
And the feelings, they're too real.

Without you, I'd be lost
With you, I know who I am,
I love you, I mean it
I'll forever hold your hand.
Elayna Brizendine, Grade 8
Jackson Middle School

Shark
Shark
Bloodthirsty, mindless
Hunting, ripping, crunching
Enemy, threat, cooperation, ally
Gathering, splashing, swimming
Swift, smart,
Dolphin
Alex Thien, Grade 7
Fort Recovery Middle School

Hero
Hero
Helpful, caring,
Life-giving, loving, offering,
Idol, fireman, policeman, friend,
Leading, honoring, dedicating,
Compassionate, gracious,
Grandpa
Leah Karlie, Grade 7
St Jude School

Winter
Snow falls from the sky
It blankets the ground and trees
It sparkles in the light
Josh Streicher, Grade 8
St Aloysius Gonzaga School

Fight…Fight…Fight
One for the books
Amazing fight
Punch to the left
Now to the right
Upper cut, he's down
1…
2…
Oh, he's up
Almost out for the count
Filled with determination
Taking a powerful swing…
His opponent awestruck
Like time stood still
Almost falling down completely
He grabbed the rope…
Now we have a fight
Jordan Moore, Grade 8
Licking Valley Middle School

The Desert
My school is like a desert
Ever moving in the wind
Never in the same place,

Always shifting
going in the wind
Then separating
A million grains of sand
Easily moved by the wind
Never in the same place
Grains are the people always scattering

They can be deceiving
They can be deadly
But sand is sand
Justin Jordan, Grade 7
Gahanna Middle School East

Change/Familiarity
Change
Dangerous, seductive
Thrilling, endangering, enthralling
Interesting, scary, comforting, safe
Calming, mellowing, understanding
Aware, relaxed
Familiarity
Elizabeth Guilbert, Grade 8
Incarnation School

Trees
Leafless extensions
Blowing, raking, climbing high
Windy, chilled, mists come forth
Chris Samborsky, Grade 8
Incarnation School

Wind
Blowing through branches
Disrupting placid oceans
Pounding Mother Earth
Ben Brabender, Grade 8
Incarnation School

A Softball Game
Playing a softball game
Is like dancing
To an unknown beat,
You don't know
What move to make
Until you hear the beat,
But once you start
It is impossible to stop,
You get caught up
In the game,
Like flies get caught
In a spider's web.
Amanda Miggo, Grade 7
Gahanna Middle School East

In the City, on the Farm
In the city —
hectic, loud, busy
crowded with people,
lights, traffic,
buildings and pollution.

On the farm —
relaxing, peaceful, quiet,
lots of stars, animals,
open fields, trees, wildlife,
and clear skies!
Julius Sorma, Grade 7
St Michael School

Volleyball
Stepping onto the court
Red-hot uniforms
Warming up
Starting the game
Sweat trickling down my face
The gym is scorching
Setting up to serve
The crowd is peaceful
Then I erupt!
The serve is good
Then the crowd erupts!
Their applause sounding like thunder
I'm drenched with excitement
I'm overflowing with happiness
We won the game
Anna Shepherd, Grade 7
St Clement Elementary School

High Merit Poems – Grades 7, 8, and 9

Man in Black
On a dreary day, my brother and I are on the driveway,
A man in black, drives up in his car, and gets out.
From afar, he coaxes us, trying to lead us astray.

He moves closer and closer to us. My brother starts making a fuss.
The menacing man advances, his next words, piercing, like lances,
"Come with me," he says to us.

My brother and I move away. "Gabe, go get mom," I quietly say.
Gabe runs inside while I try to hide
From this man who tries to lead me astray.

He takes a careful step toward me saying, "It will be all right, you'll see."
I start to retreat from his advancing feet,
But I stumble into a tree.

Then my brother and mom came both having looks of the same,
Angry and annoyed by the man. This intruder rose up and ran,
Showing no hint of shame.

Swiftly he drove over the road, oh, who knows what next person he'll goad?
Yet deep inside me I know that he will never show up
Ever again at my abode.

Ian West, Grade 8
Hopewell Jr High School

Morning Miracle
Waking to the bright light of the morning sun.
As you look out the window the gleaming dew catches your eye.
Watching it sparkle and shine another morning miracle captures your attention.
A young white tail buck prances along a long tree line in the distance.
As more does follow a young spotted fawn lags behind.
Finally evaporation from a nearby pond drifts away.
Just another morning miracle,
God's miracle.

Misty Miller, Grade 8
Continental Middle School

As the Sun Sets
As the sun sets in the West, two lovers hold hands.
They watch the wondrous haze of fiery reds, yellows and purples.

As the sun sets in the East, weak and slowly dying soldiers are rewarded with
the cool breath of the night air.
They slowly drag their tired bodies back to the base to rest for the night,
hoping their fighting will end in days to come.

As the sun sets in the West, little kids are tucked in gently,
While teenagers are doing homework plenty.

If only if only the West could see, how terrible the mighty East can be.

If only if only the East could come home,
then no more wives, sons or daughters would be crying alone.

Garret Szalay, Grade 8
Chardon Middle School

Love
Love is light pink.
It sounds like relaxing music,
and it tastes like Dove dark chocolate.
Love smells like beautiful red roses.
It looks like hearts on cards.
Love makes me feel great.

Brianna Huston, Grade 8
Chardon Middle School

They Don't Understand
People don't understand.
They think I'm sick with something bad.
I am sick,
Sick of all the unnecessary attention.
People think I'm a boy.
I'm a girl, A GIRL!!
Sometimes they make fun of me.
I tell them, "I'm a girl!"
They laugh.
It's sad, people can't be nice.

Some people understand.
My friend has the same situation.
Alopecia, no hair.
Her friends like her.
My friends like me.
Just for who I am.
Don't you see?

People get me frustrated.
They make me feel all alone.
I want to be recognized,
Just as a normal kid.

Kaitlin Kilbane, Grade 7
St Mary Elementary School

Who Are You?
God took the strength of a mountain,
the majesty of a tree,
the warmth of a summer sun,
the calm of a quiet sea,
the generous soul of nature,
the comforting arm of night,
the wisdom of the ages,
the power of the eagles flight,
the joy of a morning in spring,
the faith of a mustard seed,
the patience of eternity,
the depth of a family need.

Then God took these qualities,
when there was nothing more to add.
He knew his masterpiece was complete,
and so he called it Dad.

Marie Cheeseman, Grade 7
Clinton Middle School

The Trees

 Oh the trees. The trees. They understand me. They always understand. They see my problems. They know how I feel. Yet they can't help. Oh if only humans understood. If only.

 Oh the trees. The trees. They know me. They try to help me. If only they could. They reach, they try. Yet they can't reach out with their long branches. Oh if only. If only.

 Oh the trees. The trees. How close you are to me. If only God, made you like me then we could share our problems. Oh tree, if only you could come to me. If only. If only.

Matthew Haber, Grade 7
Incarnation School

Life's Lesson

Love is a prayer that needs to be heard.
Life is a message that needs to be read.
The inside of your heart can hold only so much.
You can scream so loud and no one can hear.
Your standing chained up so tight inside and out, and you don't have one word to say.
Love is a roller coaster it has its ups and downs.
Life is a hill — you'll sooner or later find the top.
You never know what will become of you.
Love is only a prayer that needs to be heard, and you can be the one to say it.
Life is only a message that needs to be read — so read it.
Never let one person stop you from moving on, and never let the fear of striking out keep you from playing the game.
Go straight for home and never turn back.
Win the game not only for us but for yourself.

Amber Udell, Grade 8
Lakeside Jr High School

I Am From…

I am from bunk beds, from my Uncle Cookie, from a blanket that was squares of green and pink.
I am from Barney, and the song off his show (clean up), from the color pink.
I am from coloring pictures, from fighting with my brothers and getting along with my sisters.
I am from family reunions, from fishing and camping at Cowan Lake.
I am from the saying, "treat others how you want to be treated," from family all over the states.
I am from Oreos and chocolate chip cookies dipped in milk, from Jesus loves me
I am from country to rap, from scary movies to funny.
I am from speaking English, from home movies.
I am from cats, dogs, fish, duck, rabbit, turtles, and kittens.
I am from playing with my cousins, from being an aunt my whole life.
I am from a clean backyard to dirty, from car races in Indiana.
I am from watching old westerns with my dad, from 4 different schools.
I am from baby-sitting, from a merry-go-round in my backyard.
I am from cell phone, from Pepsi.

Audrey Puckett, Grade 8
Verity Middle School

Out and In

As I step outside my mouth immediately starts watering because of my neighbor's BBQ
The sound of my neighbor's voice screaming at his TV because the Bengals are losing rings in my ears
I step into the cool grass and it is still damp from the early rain
I open our shed door and the mice scatter all over
I pull my bike out the door but to my surprise the tires are squishy and flat
I drag my bike up to the garage and right after I put it down my muscles start aching
I open the fridge and grab a nice cold refreshing Gatorade
I take a sip and the juiciness rushes into my mouth
I set the drink on the bumper of my mom's car and walk inside

Nick Wanamaker, Grade 7
Incarnation School

Sun and Wind

The sun refulgent
It beats on my heated back
But I do not mind

Time seems almost still
I hear the soft whistle of
The very strong wind
McKenzie Wills, Grade 8
St Aloysius Gonzaga School

Years to Come

I often think of years to come,
The later years of my life,
Will I sit around and get tan in the sun?
Or will I marry and take a wife?

In the upcoming years,
Will growing up be easy for me?
Will I shed many tears?
What kind of person will people see?

When I grow up, I will be outgoing,
And all my friends I will still be knowing.
Joshua Hoffman, Grade 8
Gesu Elementary School

Football

The referee blows the whistle
Football flies through the air
Helmets smacking
BAM, the ball lands in the receiver's arm
Touchdown, the crowd goes wild
Taste the hot-dogs
Smell the sweaty body parts
Hear the cheering
Feel the cold air
Hear the jumping defense
Smacking the ball carrier
Autumn is football fun.
Austin Davenport, Grade 7
West Branch Middle School

Depression

I am depression.
You know me
For all the pain
The loss of care,
Not caring about your family and school.
My one enemy is hope
Of someday being free.
I am depression.
You know me.
Melissa Masimore, Grade 8
Reed Middle School

Veteran's Day

I hear the screams,
They shot of a gun,
The Air Force
Overhead.

The terror of
Watching people die,
Soldiers dying,
This is definitely a war.

Strangers getting shot,
People watching on the television
Hoping their loved one is okay
Hoping anyone is okay.
Dakota DeAmicis, Grade 7
South Range Middle School

Shapes

Circle
Endless, Side-less
Everlasting, continuing, rounding
Loop, ring, quadrilateral, box
Corners, terminating, angles
Pointed, varieties
Square
Ariel Ligman, Grade 8
Wooster Christian School

Rain Drops

The falling rain drops
Look just like little soldiers
Dropping into war
Alec Arunski, Grade 7
St Paschal Baylon School

God's Tapestry

Autumn is God's tapestry
Of sights, the pumpkins,
And jack-o'-lanterns,
Grinning in bright vibrant oranges,
The scarecrow's patched clothes
Look so real with the
Miniature stitches
On the side of the patches
Look so small, the reds,
oranges, greens, yellows,
And brown on the leaves
And the scarecrow's clothes
On a deep, dark blue background
It seems like
I'm in a fairy tale of
God's tapestry.
Mary Matuszak, Grade 7
West Branch Middle School

Star Thoughts

As the night starts to fall
And the people drift off to sleep
I think about the dreams
That people just won't keep

As the stars dance by
I think about the laughter
And I think about the tears
The laughter that makes me smile
And the tears that make me weep

As the sun fades away
And dawn starts to break
I promise the dreams
That people just won't keep
The laughter that makes me smile
And the tears that make me weep

I promise to hold onto dreams
To smile when I hear laughter
And to cry when I see tears.
Shining promises.
Lina Wiley, Grade 8
Birchwood School

Puddles

Lying on the ground
Glistening in the sunshine
The giver of life
Emilia Zywot, Grade 8
Incarnation School

Wolf

On the hill
Howling loud
To the moon
Obscure by cloud

In the woods
Standing tall
This is his home
All and all

On the plains
Hunting together
As a pack
They do better

All alone.
Away from home.
Cast away.
From his throne.
Landon Adrian, Grade 8
Licking Valley Middle School

Split in Two

I'm on the outside looking in
A cold winter day, watching a family drink hot cocoa
Wishing I was there, instead of shivering outside
Smelling that pungent smell,
I'm on the outside looking in
Don't know how much time has passed
Hoping they're not fake, to make me sad
Wishing I was with my family,
But work takes over them
Hoping one day they'll rescue me
Maybe one day we can be a real family
I'm on the outside looking in.

Monika Lovric, Grade 8
Chardon Middle School

Hurricane

Hurricane comes in a whirlwind of terror.
Like a panther it comes in
Stealing pride and joy with it.
From the deep depths of the ocean it rises up in power.
Claiming the lives of everyone and everything.
Surprising all who come into its path.
Chomping down on houses and cities.
When all is over,
Silently, on cat feet, it gradually walks away.

Caitlin Curtis, Grade 7
Wooster Christian School

I Am From

I am from the city
From cars and loud noises,
I am from the concrete woods.

I am from Dave and Lori
And the horse racing business
Who love each other through thick and thin
And as if they were my best friends.

I'm from the city folk
And the city life
And never the country way
I'm from the church bells
To rock music.

I'm from the horse wreck
That changed my life
And from the heart attack
Of my grandpa.

Digging through pictures
I see old lost faces
This is my life
Of family and friends.

Tyler Myers, Grade 8
Logan Hocking Middle School

The Game

My heart is thumping,
Sweat is racing down my face,
As I watch the green ball,
Coming at me like a bullet,
My eyes focus,
As my racquet forms its position,
Like it is ready to attack,
As if I am in slow motion,
My heart slows down,
My eyes watch carefully,
As I stroke the ball with power,
Watching, waiting,
Suddenly I am at normal speed just in time to see,
The little green ball rise over the net,
I jump in victory,
As if I had just won an Olympic gold metal,
I love this game,
I love to play,
The game called Tennis!!

Stephanie Vandergriff, Grade 7
Gahanna Middle School East

We're Not Alone

The somber darkness
Shades our faces
Speeding and letting go of time
As the summer breeze whispers its hello in my hair …
Alone, or so we think.
Faster and faster
Sweaty palms, and hearts racing …
We drive faster
We aren't the only ones out here …
Our phones read 9:45 P.M.
Help!
Overwhelmed!
We make the slightest turn for the safety of the house
I feel throbbing.
My face is as pale as sheer porcelain
My heart relaxes.
The darkness recedes, and we embrace the reassuring light.
Only now can this word "safety" fall from these trembling lips.
Home.

Alex Green, Grade 8
Hopewell Jr High School

Tiger in Me

There is a tiger in me.
With nails that can be sharp.
With fur that is brown.
Its eyes, big and round with brown in them.
It roars like there's no tomorrow.
It runs like there's something delicious near it.
It lives in my heart.
It just makes me want to run
and scream things out.

Beka Hart, Grade 7
Incarnation School

Young Poets
Grades 4-5-6

Note: The Top Ten poems were finalized through an online voting system. Creative Communication's judges first picked out the top poems. These poems were then posted online. The final step involved thousands of students and teachers who registered as online judges and voted for the Top Ten poems. We hope you enjoy these selections.

Top Poem Grades 4-5-6

Life

Life is not a circle,
It doesn't go round and round,
You can't replace the times,
You made a mistake or fell down.

It's not always a straight line,
It has its points and bumps,
And even if I'm 99,
I was a preschooler once.

Life sometime seems like a road,
That has so many turns,
And even if that happens to you,
From your mistakes you will learn.

Life isn't simple,
It's not steps to a dance,
So make life worthwhile,
There is no second chance!

Olivia Balcerzak, Grade 5
Tremont Elementary School

Top Poem Grades 4-5-6

A Thousand

Slipping through your grasp,
Flying in the clouds,
Your desperate moaning echoes,
For you'd climb a thousand mounds.

You jump as high as possible,
She soars with graceful ease,
You cannot stop her ascending soul,
Not with a thousand pleas.

Her milky, satin dress,
Billows in the breeze,
You beg her to come back,
That you'd cross a thousand seas.

Her glowing halo emerges,
A tear slides down your cheek,
Then suddenly she's gone,
But there is nothing more to seek.

Sophie DeRosa, Grade 6
School for Creative and Performing Arts

Top Poem Grades 4-5-6

The Dance of Dawn and Night

Night's black ballet slippers dance upon her floor, the forest,
Dawn's gold slippers are cast upon a luminescent hill.
Night's shadowy hair twists around her pearl white eyes,
Her sister's ruby hair is vibrant upon the calm blue sky.
Night brings sleep to the Earth, her comfort angelic,
Dawn wakes the Earth with a gentle light.
Stars and Moon accompany Night,
Dawn is followed by light and the waking sounds of all creatures.
Night's black, glittery gown swirls around her legs,
Dawn's fiery crimson dress crackles
As the dew nestles into the cracks between her toes,
Fresh morning air radiates and becomes her perfume.
Night's skin is bathed in moonlight, ebony eyes sparkle like stars.
Both sisters share the dance,
But each dances alone.

Andrianna DiMasso, Grade 6
EH Greene Intermediate School

Top Poem Grades 4-5-6

Veteran's Day

A day to celebrate world peace
Parades and flags
Eleventh day, eleventh month, eleventh hour
To honor veterans
Some died in Flanders Field
Some died raising the flag
Honored armed forces
Blue stars for living.
Remember.

David Esarco, Grade 4
Dobbins Elementary School

Top Poem Grades 4-5-6

A Lovely Winter

A sparkle in the snow
Where the sun shines
Where it will blow
Will change over time

A simple amount of heat
Will make the snow disappear
Where the hot weather fleets
The snow will be clear

Every snowflake different then each other
All waiting to hit the ground
When they hit the ground they all will smother
As they hit they make the slightest bit of sound

Wonderful times
A wonderful place
The most peaceful times
Not always the case

Loud and deep
Or soft and meek
You will always keep
These memories that are so unique

Brenna Gates, Grade 5
Logan Christian School

Top Poem Grades 4-5-6

The 7th Book

One book
Takes you everywhere
You wait with baited breath
Reading faster and faster
As the book gets thinner and thinner
You gasp
When you realize what's true
Who was good
And who was bad
The things you overlooked
How could they have been important?
You cry
Over the characters
Who died
Your eyes dart quickly over the page
Words become sentences
Sentences
Are the story
Your eyes widen with shock
As you finish
The 7th book

Arona Mostov, Grade 5
Akiva Academy

Top Poem Grades 4-5-6

Slipped Away

The room was dark with bitterness
As she was diagnosed with the sickness
Please don't slip away

She was always so numb
And tired every single day
Please don't slip away

She was very brave and bold
But the doctor still foretold
That she would slip away

She cried all night long
And so she wrote a song
That she would slip away

She was exhausted from all of the chemo
And so she decided to go
And slip away

That night she cried herself to sleep
That's when the buzzer beeped
That she had slipped away

Alesha Vovk, Grade 6
Harding Middle School

Top Poem Grades 4-5-6

Strength

Strength is the season of fall.
When the leaves hold to trees with their all.
Strength is the touch of rain.
It keeps dripping on the window pane.
Strength is shaped like the wind.
It hits you and you never cringe.
Strength is the month of December.
The animals try to stay warm, remember?
Strength is like air.
It has no stop when people stare.
Strength is a pocket of hope.
You shall never mope.
Strength is like a rope.
You never want to let it go.
Strength is the song of a hawk.
It never travels in flocks.

Lea Wilczynski, Grade 6
Old Fort Elementary School

Top Poem Grades 4-5-6

Nature's Gift

The wind whistles through the trees,
Like the mist upon the seven seas,
As raindrops fall from the sky,
The wolves howl a lullaby,
And as the world falls fast asleep,
The only things awake are the ghosts that creep,
And then the sun says to the moon,
Don't worry for I'll be back soon,

Ashley Zimmer, Grade 5
Waynesville Elementary School

Top Poem Grades 4-5-6

A Day at the Beach

I step on the sun-baked sand
That burns beneath my feet
As I run to the ocean's edge
I breathe in the salty air, so sweet.

The waves are high, the water's clear
The breeze is blowing smooth
And with the seashells all around
It's so beautiful I forget to move.

Then I remember why I came
As I watch the waves roll in
I run back through the warm, smooth sand
And that's where the fun begins.

I grab my wave board and run back
To the ocean's side
Something calls me to the water
It's the waves, big and wide.

Suddenly a heartbreaking sound calls
And though I beg and plea,
I have no choice I must obey
For it is time to leave.

Alaina Zorzi, Grade 5
Copley-Fairlawn Middle School

Stop and Think
We all say "freedom" without a thought
We never stop to think,
about the ones who bravely fought
and were killed in a blink.

The soldiers risked their lives,
They battled for a cause,
They fought for freedom just for us,
And still, we never pause.

Because of them we're free,
In what we do or say
And still we go to work or school,
Without thinking every day.

But now we finally stop,
To applaud them and to cheer,
To thank them for their work and heart,
On this day every year.
Taylor Combs, Grade 6
EH Greene Intermediate School

Summers
So hot and muggy
Doing whatever I want
No school for three months!
Cole Dargavell, Grade 6
Tippecanoe Middle School

Seasonal
Ah, sweet summer!
How good it shall be
to have all the sun's light
shining on me.

Oh, quiet autumn!
With crisp clear air,
and all nature's colors
sitting right there.

Oh, bleak winter,
with white glistening snow!
It provides me release
with snowballs to throw!

Ah, brisk spring!
When flowers do bloom,
with radiant colors
that break up the gloom!

This poem describes
rather well, actually,
when you look into nature,
the beauties you'll see.
Will Spallino, Grade 6
Rocky River Middle School

Snow
Snow is a wonderful
thing about Christmas
It is like a soft marshmallow that
runs down into the ground
It falls into a pillow of snow
With much more softness of
More soft marshmallows
  Snow
Miriam Avila, Grade 6
Woodward Park Middle School

Halloween
H orror
A wesome
L ate
L aughing
O utstanding
W et
E ager
E njoying
N oisy
John Cika, Grade 4
Sts Joseph and John School

My Imagination
I sit and gaze at the sky so dark blue;
looking to see what goes on
upon the stars and the moon
still wondering without a clue
when the owl will hoo
Charlotte Smith, Grade 4
Greenfield Elementary School

Marshmallows
Marshmallows are squishy and sweet
and stick to your feet.
They smell like candy
and better than my Aunt Mandy.
And they bounce good on my dad's hood
and on his head if I could.
Makayla Ammon, Grade 5
Stanton Middle School

The Worm
Damp skin
Slimy rings
Mixing soil
Decomposing leaves
Tunneling in the dark
Clitellum for an adult
Girl and boy
Some setae segments
Feel enemies coming
Stretchy invertebrate.
Kailah Vargo, Grade 4
Dobbins Elementary School

Snow
When you see snow,
you see a sparkling glow.
When snow fall from the sky,
it looks like it can fly.
I love the snow, it's fun to play in,
and you can go sleddin'.
Hannah Hunter, Grade 5
Stanton Middle School

Kodie
A California pound dog
Waiting in his kennel
To find a loving home
To sleep in and be fed
Now this California dog
Is sleeping in my bed
Waiting for morning
So he can wake me up
And so he can be fed.
We named this pound dog
  Kodie
Like a Kodiak bear
The California pound dog
Is now 15 years old
And has moved from
California to Connecticut,
To Michigan and now
He is an old pound dog
Who will always be loved
In my heart.
Ellie Wood, Grade 5
Tremont Elementary School

This Is Me
I am tall and athletic.
I wonder what I'll get for Christmas.
I hear reindeer.
I see snow.
I want a Philadelphia Eagle jersey #20.
I am happy.

I pretend to fly.
I feel good.
I touch the Christmas tree.
I worry about the war.
I cry when it rains.
I am tall and athletic.

I understand that Santa is real.
I say the National Anthem.
I dream to go to the NFL.
I try to do my best.
I hope I get mashed potatoes.
I am tall and athletic.
Corey Grindle, Grade 6
St Clement Elementary School

Whatifs*

Yesterday I was dreaming,
when some thoughts popped in my head
all bright and gleaming…
Whatif my house burned down?
Whatif all my food was brown?
Whatif I don't have a family to go home to?
Whatif my parents got married out of the blue?
Whatif I die in my sleep?
Whatif I have to eat sheep?
Whatif I trip in front of the school?
Whatif I am no longer cool?
Everything goes well in my school,
until those whatifs start to make me look like a fool.

Wyatt Bronson, Grade 6
Pike Delta York Middle School
**Inspired by Shel Silverstein's poem "Whatif"*

Intriguing Iguana

With its piercing eyes as it is in disguise
And a crest of scales all down its back
The movement is motionless, quite a lack
Eats fruits, flowers, leaves, not bugs
And they certainly are big lugs
Since they're active at day and sleep at night
They are definitely not a fright
In tropical rain forests they lie all day
Never going out to play
Growing to be six feet long
This animal is obviously an iguana!

Jennifer Hill, Grade 6
EH Greene Intermediate School

Apart…

In a dream I seldom remember…
I walk through the trees with a long lost friend,
We told secrets not meant to be heard by others,
Standing across from each other,
Clapping hands in a steady beat,
We went to the park and sat in the midst of the sun,
You swayed in the swing when I pushed you,
You flew high and up into the world,
And now my dream is over.
Once I had a best friend,
No longer friends, never friends,
Meant best to stay that way,
I walked with you,
You walked with me
But now we push away,
I want to have it like before,
But it will never be the same,
You used to be my closest friend,
But now we are far away,
I used to know you now I don't
Only in an old dream never forgotten.

Stephanie Kley, Grade 6
EH Greene Intermediate School

An Ode to My Grandpa

My grandpa's biggest accomplishment
is becoming a judge for the county and elsewhere.

He always treated his wife and his family members
truly like he loves us.

He has so many friends that love him, too,
like he is part of their family.

He's always loved his kids and grandchildren,
— and most of all, his wife —
more than anything in the world.

Grandpa treats me with the respect I deserve,
and I treat him with the respect he deserves.

Kristian Frantom, Grade 6
Tippecanoe Middle School

A Winter Day

Snowing, snowing all around
Gently, softly hitting the ground
Walking through a winter wonderland,
My friends and I hand in hand,
We run, jump, skip, slide,
Sometimes we even run to hide,
"Snowball fight!!" We yell together,
Wow, these snowballs are as light as a feather,
We come inside, shut the door and lock it
Then end the day with some warm hot chocolate
Snowing, snowing all around
Hope you like my poem now.

Alyssa Kreider, Grade 5
Norwich Elementary School

Camp Y-Noah

Camp Y-Noah was really fun,
the weather was great, there was lots of sun.
We got out of the car and unpacked our bag,
then we played a game of tag.

We went to Kastner Hall and decided what to do,
it was hard to decide 'cause we could only pick two.
After that it was time to play,
whatever we wanted during the day.

There is a lake called "Noah,"
in the lake we saw a boa!
While we were swimming, we played baseball,
but we wished we could go to the mall.

At the end of the day we went to a bonfire,
it was hard to find my cabin so I had to inquire.
I made lots of new friends including Fred,
I've never been so tired — I went straight to bed!

Christopher Elliot, Grade 6
Kinsner Elementary School

A Lonely Street

As I sit in my room,
keeping cool with the fans
I listen…
And in the distance, I hear a
band.
My neighbor is whistling for her cat,
so I go outside and put on my
favorite hat.
I look down my lonely street
waiting for someone to meet
but then, my brother comes out…
He screams and shouts
away goes the quietness
and the rest of my day is
filled with loud happiness.

Emily Morrison, Grade 4
Indian Springs Elementary School

Fishing

We wait and wait
But oh!
We have a fish on
I reel and reel
But the fish does not budge
I try to reel some more
The fish is coming to the surface
We get him in the boat
And I realize that fishing is fun
But catching is better.

Jackson Pfister, Grade 5
Tremont Elementary School

Seasons

Fall is,
colorful,
stupendous, beautiful,
cold, amazing, fun,
gorgeous, warm fuzzy blankets,
leaves. Summer is,
warm,
pool, baseball,
sweat, air conditioning,
green leaves, humid, sunny,
nature. Spring is,
rain,
shorts, lacrosse,
short sleeve t-shirts,
flowers, green trees, pool,
warm. Winter is,
cold,
snow balls,
snow ball fights,
hot chocolate, heat vents,
winter coats, winter hats.

Scott Brooks, Grade 4
Norwich Elementary School

I Am

I am Peyton Luich adventurous and admirable,
I wonder a lot about what will befall in the future,
I hear many people vocalizing all around me everywhere I go,
I see numerous amounts of people every time I visit a location,
I desire to be a chef when I am an adult,
I am Peyton Luich adventurous and admirable.

I pretend I am a gourmet chef and deliberate on recipes,
I feel afraid when I witness a movie that is scary,
I touch the base when my teammates heave the baseball to me,
I worry about terrorists showing violent aggression in the U.S.,
I cry when I get a wound when I get in an accident,
I am Peyton Luich adventurous and admirable.

I understand how important it is to be responsible in preserving our environment,
I say that God is a genuine person and Heaven is a real place,
I dream of the day my sisters move out and not trouble me again,
I try to skateboard outside after school and attempt some tricks,
I hope that in the future I will do superior in school,
I am Peyton Luich adventurous and admirable.

Peyton Luich, Grade 6
Harmon Middle School

My Special Heart

My special heart has love and joy inside of it.
My special heart has care in it.
My special heart has my family inside of it.
My special heart has my memories inside of it.
My special heart has my friends inside of it.
My special heart has my favorites inside of it.
This is why I am thankful to have my special heart that Jesus made for me!

Nadia Paskert, Grade 4
Northfield Elementary School

Silver Drops of Rain

Silver drops of rain, fall quickly from the sky
Making everything wet so nothing is dry
Silver drops of rain make wishes come true
Making everything great so nothing is blue
Silver drops of rain pound on your window pane
Slicing and dicing to make the "pitter patter" that drives you insane.
Silver drops of rain fall quickly from the sky
Making everything wet so nothing is dry.

Keeley Williams, Grade 6
Rocky River Middle School

Friend

F riends are the people who are there for each other loving, caring, special too
R emember the days you spend together laughing, playing in the dreary weather
I n the darkest days they are together still playing on and on forever
E ven when they are in their beds at night they dream of playing again and again
N o one to stop them no one knows the peace between them ever grows
D on't you know that deep inside all of us stirs that peace
   our F.R.I.E.N.D

Eleanor Robinson, Grade 6
Olentangy Liberty Middle School

High Merit Poems – Grades 4, 5, and 6

Family

Family is someone there for you
No matter how hard it is to do.

When we go to get-togethers, I want to shout hooray
Because we are all unique and special in our own way.

Though sometimes we my fight,
We always find what's right.

We all fit together like a puzzle
All nice and snuggle.

Jordi Emrick, Grade 6
Holy Angels School

Fall

Fall is over it's getting cold,
More sweaters are being sold.

All the animals are hibernating,
For spring they are waiting.

In fall we have to close up the pool,
Because the weather is very cool.

I like to climb trees because they are bare,
At the neighbor's garden I stare.

Yitzi Rubinoff, Grade 4
Cincinnati Hebrew Day School

Christmas Memories

I wake up to my brothers yelling
When will they stop doing this?
Run down the stairs quickly STOP!
Dad has to videotape and take pictures
Christmas Memories

So many presents under the tree
A trinket-filled, very stuffed stocking
Tearing open colored paper Riiiiiiiip
Christmas Memories

Light floods the room through the windows
Of course we didn't light a fire
Don't want Santa Claus to burn
Christmas Memories

I feel warm like someone lit a fire in me
That Christmas feast tastes so good I feel like I'm in a dream
I don't want the day to end as I snuggle in my bed
When will Christmas come again?

Christmas Memories
Christmas Memories
Christmas Memories

Kathryn Tenbarge, Grade 5
EH Greene Intermediate School

Jodi/Grodi

Once upon a time I saw Jodi on a log in the lake
and I said, "Look at Jodi."
Then I swam out to the log
and she handed me a roasted frog
and I said "Jodi that's grodi."

Brady Barnett, Grade 4
Greenfield Elementary School

I Am No One But Me

I am no one but me, Shelby.
I am Shelby, not Cassie or Joe.
I'm not Daisy or Poe.
I'm not Silly or Willy, Frilly or Nilly.
I am no one but me, Shelby.
I love snakes and wizards, not pipes or sisters.
I like to play in the snow.
If there's a party somewhere I would like to go.
I like the color black.
My teeth have no plaque.
I am no one but me, Shelby.
I like to sing but not dance.
I like to play at beaches in the sand.
I am no one but me, Shelby.
Computers are fun.
Games are too.
Something that's not is the flu.
I will stay who I am and that is my plan.
I am no one but me, Shelby.

Shelby Swick, Grade 5
Frank Ohl Middle School

Skipping School Is Not Cool!

Today I woke up late for school. I thought it was pretty cool!
I missed the bus but did not fuss.
I wanted to have some fun. So I tanned in the sun.
I went to the mall and had a ball.
I shopped until I dropped.
I went to my favorite store which I adore.
I was looking at dresses for prom then I saw my mom!
I tried to flee then she looked up at me.
I felt like a fool because I was not in school.
She said "You are grounded," I didn't like how that sounded.
Not to mention my principle later said "Detention."
I no longer think it's cool to skip school.

Kayla Helleis, Grade 6
Rocky River Middle School

Wind

As silent as a butterfly flapping its wings.
As cold as an ice cube in my hand melting to its way.
Warmer than a mild summer coming my way.
Stronger than any eye of a tornado.
More gentle than leaves dragging on the ground.
And that is wind.

Reno Riha, Grade 4
Emerson Academy of Dayton

Princess
P retty
R eally sweet
I ntelligent
N ice puppy
C ould have been your first friend
E specially happy when I am around
S martest dog I have ever seen
S ad to see her go!!!!
Rachael June, Grade 5
Wintersville Elementary School

Astounding Mountains
Astounding mountains
Touching the sky with ridges
With their pointed peaks
With shimmering snow on top.

Amazing mountain beauty
They cut the clouds
So you can only see part
Of the amazing mountains!
Tori Shepherd, Grade 5
Westview Elementary School

A Raccoon Who Lived in a Cocoon
There once was a raccoon
who lived in a cocoon
everybody thought he was
weird because he had a beard
Breighton Hershiser, Grade 4
Greenfield Elementary School

All About Me!!!
My name is Halee,
I come from a big family,
My dad is one of ten,
When we all get together,
It's like we're all in a big pig pen.
I have a cat and three dogs,
I wish we could play ping-pong,
They are all really smart,
They even like sweet tarts.
I have an older sister Syd,
Sometimes she acts like a little kid,
I really really love her,
This I know for sure.
I really like to flip flop,
On the floor I have to hop,
Fly to the high bar,
And leap on the beam,
Halee is my name,
And gymnastics is my game.
Now you know a little of me,
Don't forget to tell your name!!!!
Halee Jones, Grade 6
Immaculate Conception School

Bike Riding
We go bike riding
Down a hill, then up a hill
Then I hear a crash!
Justin Dailey, Grade 5
Wintersville Elementary School

My Daddy
I love my dad
very much. He is always
there when I need him. I like
his hair but sometimes it needs a
trim. When he travels I hope it is
not far so I can call him in his
little car. Like I said before
I love him very much
but now I have
to go it's
lunch
Hannah Van Nuys, Grade 5
Stanton Middle School

Thank You
No one takes the time to stop
And thank you.
We often think it's expected
For you to care for us.
So now I thank you, Mom and Dad.

Mom, you make me dinner every day;
You educate me oh so much.
You always comfort me,
And I can't live without this,
So now I thank you.

Dad, you get the fire started
In the freezing cold;
You teach me almost everything,
And I can't live without this,
So now I thank you.

So now I stop
And recall all that you do,
But the list never ends.
I can't live without you.
So now…I thank you.
Nick Hershey, Grade 6
EH Greene Intermediate School

The Desert
Vast, dreadful desert.
Scorching hot under the sun.
Sharp cacti will poke.
Sandstorms blowing every day.
Astounding, but it's deadly.
Joseph Wines, Grade 5
Westview Elementary School

Winter
Snow
White, fluffy
Flying, freezing, deepening,
Sparkling in the cold winter air
Squishing, squashing, melting,
Cold, wet
Precipitation
Isaiah Kolb, Grade 5
Hylen Souders Elementary School

Snatched
My eyes are covered I cannot see
I was snatched by thievery
I uncover my eyes and look around
The room looked like a dog pound
The thieves come in
I pretend to be quiet
I hope I don't pay
They pull off their masks and yell
HAPPY BIRTHDAY!!!!
Logan Baker, Grade 6
Pike Delta York Middle School

Worms
Boy and girl
Clitellum segment
No backbone
Long muscles
Circular muscles
Tunnel in the ground
Help soil
Brown color
Hide from enemies
Earthworms.
Darren Goodin, Grade 4
Dobbins Elementary School

Summer
The sun shines bright
And gives the world light
Summer is the hot season
And it is hot for a reason
Swimming is very fun
Or you can lay out in the sun
We get so much ice cream
And at night we dream
Summer is great
And we stay out late
I like this season the best
And so do the rest
It is summer break
And no more leaves to rake
In the summer I have a blast
I knew the fun could never last
Jamie Gaillard, Grade 6
Kinsner Elementary School

The Farm

I gaze into the distance, looking at all of the animals,
wondering what it's like to be one.
Then, I see it: The Farm —
the one of my dreams, sitting there all empty,
just waiting for me!

Claire Benson, Grade 6
Melrose Elementary School

Orchestra

Orchestra
When we stepped up onstage,
the lights shining sharply as bright as the sun
We blushed, looking out into the crowded auditorium
Music played
Our bows piercing the air, like arrows shooting,
Shooting through the sky
We smiled at one another
Knowing, knowing it was beautiful
The song ended, we bowed,
people applauding then they were standing,
Cheering
We bent down once more, toward the floor,
Cameras flashing, people clapping, still.
We left the stage, with our teacher,
Our teacher, singing,
Singing praises.
Friend,
Did you think it was colorful?
The sounds painting the air?
I did, I know I did.

Nora Varcho, Grade 6
Harding Middle School

Christmas Time

I see a Christmas tree,
Like a guardian angel in every house,
I see my family,
Christmas is here, it's Christmas time.

The sun winks at me through the window,
There is light shining off the clean white snow,
Christmas is here, it's Christmas time.

I hear joyous laughter all day long,
I hear birds sing their touching song,
Christmas is here, it's Christmas time.

What do gingerbread men really have to say?
Why must there only be one Christmas day?
Christmas is here, it's Christmas time.

I cannot bear the very truth,
Christmas is no more after one measly day,
Christmas is gone, no more Christmas time.

Stephen Mills, Grade 5
EH Greene Intermediate School

White

White is the color of the shining snow.
White is the color of someone's hair I know.
White is the color of the sycamore tree.
White is the color of my cat can't you see?
White is the color of my mom's car.
White is the color of the stars afar.

Caleb Cornelius, Grade 6
St John the Baptist School

My Family

My family is sweet
They let me meet any friends I want to meet
If I'm bad they'll just get mad and yell
I don't want them to yell so I'll just sit there and not yell
I'm good like an angel and just find my dangles.

Cierra Plump, Grade 5
Emerson Academy of Dayton

Freedom

Freedom is the greatest thing of all.
It can't be chained or taken away.
Freedom walks among us every day.
But sometimes we don't let it into our hearts.
And giving it to someone, we sometimes don't do.
But one day everyone will be free,
And everyone will feel how good it can be.

Micah Morales, Grade 6
Woodward Park Middle School

White Magic

When the cold weather
bites at our hands
and nose;
when the wind blows
The white magic is on its way

It covers streets and rooftops
in a sparkling blanket of fluff
and some adults think Enough! Enough!
Let's move away, to Florida, they'd say,
But the white magic keeps on coming

White magic, oh white magic!
I'm delighted by your shine
and shimmer
You will always be mine in the winter
White magic, stay forever!

I'm afraid of the day
when I'll have to say goodbye,
and you won't return for a year
My heart will start to tear!
How I love my dear
White magic

Victoria Sullo, Grade 6
Rocky River Middle School

Swimming

Looks like glistening water
Sounds like kids playing
Taste like chlorine
Feels like flying
Smells like bleach

Myles Walker, Grade 5
Northfield Baptist Christian School

The Answer

I need the answer,
How do storms start?
How do you rip friendship apart?
Searching, wondering

What is the answer?
Why did she have to die?
What will I do to stay alive?
Searching, wondering

Why is the answer not so simple?
Is someone playing tricks with my life?
Held together by the string of a kite?
Searching, wondering

Where is the answer?
In the fluffy clouds of heaven above?
Or the fiery pits of hell below?
Searching, wondering

I need the answer,
What is the key to life?

Adrienne Jones, Grade 6
Harding Middle School

The Magician

The magician did magic
But some of his tricks were tragic
He made a boy disappear
Then he came back as a deer

Then he made some toys
With the magic he enjoys
But then he did something weird
He made a girl grow a beard

The man had no clue
What magic he was about to do
He made a coin go away
Then he found it in a bay

His tricks were crazy
He turned a lion into a daisy
Then he stepped out onto the lawn
The next thing I knew he was gone

Vasu Munjapara, Grade 6
Kinsner Elementary School

Winter's Night

Multicolored lights twinkling in the night,
a tiny glow from dimming candles,
there is no moon tonight.
One star brighter than all the rest
　Brighter,
　　Brighter,
　　　Brighter.
The ticking clock is a waiting man,
looking for Santa Claus.
While a looming green tree listens
for the midnight dong.
The world seems to be asking, "When will he come?"
And why tonight this cold, cold night was the Child born?
Why not summer with its warm flowers, or spring a time of rain?
With the snow drifting slowly down with all of its white wonder.
And close in tow of the glowing white snow lies joy for all the world.
Now with all people in their beds dreaming of all the toys,
the real meaning is not the toys, it's something more important.
Silent hooves and quiet bells
with a dong the wait is over.

Alex Toney, Grade 5
EH Greene Intermediate School

Creative and Inspiring

I am creative and inspiring
I wonder if there is a museum full of creative drawings
I hear my pencil connecting to the paper as I think of new drawings
I see a museum of art that inspires me to make a collage
I want to motivate the world with my creative drawings
I am creative and inspiring.

I pretend to be the painter of the *Mona Lisa*
I feel that I am one with my art
I touch the hearts of others with my creations
I worry that I cannot inspire others to feel the emotions of art
I cry if I do not give my dreams my best shot
I am creative and inspiring.

I understand that inspiring people with art is not easy
I say that an inspiration leads to another
I dream of having an art show with my creations
I try to be the best artist I can be
I hope that I will be able to inspire the country to see the passion of art
I am creative and inspiring.

Dezmon Gilbert, Grade 5
Sanderson Elementary School

Rain

Rain comes creeping like a little mouse.
Then the mouse starts jumping, it is shocked because the rain is pouring.
It jumps excitingly and a little nervous like the rain would.
The mouse is even more scared because it is in the country all alone.
Then suddenly BOOM! The rain stops and then the little mouse leaves, thumping
like a lion back to his home.

Sarah Patching, Grade 5
Wooster Christian School

Nature

In nature it is very fun.
In nature you can run.
Don't go to the mall.
Come outside and have a ball.

In nature you don't have to pay fees,
have fun with a tree.
Don't bother with the bees.
The tree says come outside and play with me.

In nature trees are very tall.
Watch out do not trip.
In nature it turns to fall,
Sometimes there is a mud pit.

When you're walking you don't have to pay a toll.
You can watch a friendly mole.
You should watch out for rats.
The good thing is you don't have to wipe your feet on the mats!

Tyler Wm. Young, Grade 6
Kinsner Elementary School

Mistletoe

I am way up high,
Above all of the love and joy,
People pass under me, and kiss their spouse,
Everyone shows a warm heart,
While eating cookies, and candy canes,
Everyone looks at me, and thinks of love,
And how wonderful I am,
I hope to be down from here soon,
Because I hurt from hanging way up high,
Though I will never come down,
Because I am a mistletoe.

Emily Peters, Grade 6
Glenwood Middle School

Be a Leader Not a Follower

Every day before I get to the bus
I get told to be a leader
Not a follower
Every day I'm glad to hear it —
It lets me know that they care

Being a leader not a follower means to me
Follow what you believe is right
And what I think is right
Is not following the crowd

Being a leader not a follower
Gives you a lot of responsibility
You need to have control of you
And make good choices
That's what being a leader means to me

Ciaran Guinn, Grade 6
Eastmoor Middle School

Kitty Kitty

Kitty Kitty, whose eyes are so bright,
They looks so much like a light;
Kitty Kitty, you are so cute,
But sometimes I wish I could put you on mute!

Sabrina Marshall, Grade 5
Stanton Middle School

God's Miraculous Hand

When you have a bad day,
You think of nothing, but black and gray.
But when you go outside,
And see the light, you know
You have seen a miraculous sight.
You look at the sky, you look at the ground,
You know everything has been turned around.
You think of God when
You see the earth,
But then you think,
How did it work?
You open your Bible
To Genesis chapter one,
And then you know how it is done.
God made the heavens,
God made the earth,
He made you and me and all the birds.
He made the water from the stream,
He made the whales from the deep blue sea.
God's wonderful hand is here every day,
He's always with you far or astray.

Madison Parsons, Grade 5
Pike Christian Academy

Mother to Daughter*

Well, girl, I'll tell you:
Life for me ain't been no Hollywood movie.
It's had terrible actors in it,
And disappointing endings,
And horrible scripts,
And directors with no sense of humor —
Outrageous.
But all the time
I'se been a-waitin' for that perfect part,
And practicin' my lines,
And takin' on the fans,
And sometimes the paparazzi are out of control
Where they just don't leave you alone.
So, girl you stop actin' out those parts.
Don't stop livin' your life
'Cause you find it's kinder hard to go on.
Don't you give up now —
For I'se still believe in you, honey',
I'se still actin',
And life for me ain't been no Hollywood movie.

Danielle Diersing, Grade 5
St Ignatius School
*Inspired by Langston Hughes

Color Me Gold
Color me gold
Like the shining sun in the sky,
Or golden coins everybody wants.
Color me gold
Like a school bus,
Reflecting the sun.
Gold is such a fluorescent color
It blinds us if it's in the sky,
but is gorgeous at the same time!
Coty Burnette, Grade 5
Westview Elementary School

Stars
Stars
Dazzling, giants
Dancing, twinkling, whistling
The past and future
Spectators
Coburn Gillies, Grade 5
Norwich Elementary School

Pirates
Demons of the sea
Taking everything with glee
Merciless they will be
David Sturges, Grade 5
Barrington Elementary School

Love
Love is in the air.
You can't see it,
but you can
find it anywhere.
Thomaz Lewis, Grade 6
Prospect Elementary School

Fifth Grade Is a Zoo
Fifth grade is a zoo!
Kids are always up and down
Screaming and shouting
Acting like wild creatures
Shoving food in their faces
Acting as though they're caged
Fifth grade is a zoo!
Brittanie Thompson, Grade 5
Westview Elementary School

Friends
Friends are so special to me
We are like one big family
We run, and we play,
Each and every day.
Friends, friends so special, so nice,
You never have to roll the dice.
Caleigh Weeter, Grade 6
Pike Christian Academy

I'm Chris
Hello! I'm Chris
I love outdoors
and airsoft wars.
Football is my sport,
I can make cool forts

I like war games
and getting good grades.
I like hunting
and eating pudding.

My friends are:
Ian, Joey and Cameron.
We play together at school,
they are really cool!
Christopher Weaver, Grade 6
Immaculate Conception School

I'm Not a Poet
Anyone can write
poetry well, except for me.
I try really hard, but that's
obviously not the key.
Poetry is hard, but I have to
face it because good poetry
equals a good grade and a
good grade equals a happy me.
Now I really really
want a good grade, but so
far this poem's a bit dry.
I try and try although
its coming out thin,
but I know in the end the
good grade will sink right in.
So as you can see I'm not a
poet I'm just Natasha Niese.
Natasha Niese, Grade 6
Miller City-New Cleveland School

Gymnastics
Gymnastics
On vault you fly and come to a halt
On bars you swing all over the place
On beam you leap from end to end
On floor you flip then do a backbend
Finally your score
Then there's no more
Lauren Vanderhorst, Grade 6
Holy Angels School

Komodo Dragon
Deadly and vicious,
stalking animals all day,
waiting to attack.
Morgan Silvers, Grade 6
Roosevelt Elementary School

My Brother Bryan
Bryan is two years old,
To me he is worth gold,
He cut his palm,
He was not very calm

Sometimes he is cold,
Sometimes he is bold,
He plays with our dog,
And he plays with a frog

He is good most of the time,
His words never rhyme,
He likes chocolate cake,
But he doesn't know how to bake

His feet are so small,
For his age he is tall,
He says "do do" for down,
He always acts like a clown
Tyler Borges, Grade 6
Kinsner Elementary School

Ode to My Bike
It's a red bike
that looks like a dirt bike.
It's traveled with me
to places I need to go.
I have fun with my friends
when we ride our bikes to the park.
I always show off when doing tricks,
but I have to be careful not to crash!
When my bike needs to be repaired,
I ask my dad to help me fix it.
Everybody wishes they had my bike.
I've told them, "You won't find one
as special as mine."
My bike is more than a bike to me.
I love my bike and take good care of it.
and I believe
it loves me.
Brendon Dix, Grade 6
Tippecanoe Middle School

Sports
Sports are awesome,
Sports are fun!
Sports are everything
I have done!
There's basketball and softball,
and there's hockey too.
There's volleyball and football,
Let me think, what are some others I do?
I can't think of any more,
But I'll think of some I'm sure!
Emily Ward, Grade 5
West Elementary School

Little White Pillow

A little mini pillow that sounds like a squishy bug.
Sticky, squishy, gooey describes the present from above.
Smells like a sugar cookie.
Looks like a spring moving up and down,
Just like a heart beat.
Sweet sugar with a tiny sound.

Kaylee LaRue, Grade 5
Wintersville Elementary School

Fall's Music

As the dry leaves scamper across the road,
And the wind blows in perfect tune,
It is a beautiful sound like the summer days,
In the wonderful, mid-June.

The trees blow and swing with the wind,
And the flowers hide from view,
The birds will chirp in the sun's rays,
As though it was saying, I miss you.

The fall's music is nature, and nature itself,
The trees, flowers, and blustery weather,
The beauty is there and all by itself,
As a feminine, delicate, feather.

Lindsay Stone, Grade 6
Monroe Elementary School

School

School's a super, spectacular space
With books and binders and bunches of papers,
Crowded, cramped kids,
Teachers and tests and talking too.
Detention, discipline, and disappointments, too.
All are wrapped up into
My magnificent, marvelous middle school.

Harley Humbert, Grade 6
Tippecanoe Middle School

A Savior's Birth

A Savior's born on Christmas day
lying there in a manger bed.

The shepherds journeyed far
to find that special Child in the stable barn.

A Savior's born on Christmas day
lying there in a manger bed.

All the animals stood and watched
the Savior's birth,
without a peep or squeak.

A Savior's born on Christmas day
lying there in a manger bed.

Zachary Zemrock-van der Meer, Grade 5
Wooster Christian School

The Wolves

The wolves dominate the night,
Their echoing howls flow through the moon lights
They have eyes that glisten bright,
That leads to that strong powerful bite,
They catch animals mid-flight.

Sierra Hickok, Grade 6
Woodward Park Middle School

Star Wars

In Star Wars there are many characters.
They are no more than actors.
Harrison Ford played Han Solo.
Here's something I bet you didn't know —
All his friends were Wookies,
Only because they baked him cookies.
Mark Hammel played Luke Skywalker.
Man, that guy is a talker!
He never really owned a light saber;
he just borrowed one from his neighbor.
Princess Leia was played by Carrie Fisher.
She was as pretty as a picture.
She wore cinnamon buns stuck to her head;
too bad she's allergic to bread.
Obi-Wan was played by what's his face.
I bet he's never been up in space.
His apprentice, Anacin, is so resentful,
I hear his light saber is a rental.
That's pretty much everyone,
So I think I'm done.

Joshua Bellas, Grade 6
Tippecanoe Middle School

Chinese New Year

Lots of people lots of fun
So much commotion
So many delicious snacks

Either dark or either bright
So many shadows
Dancing about

Screaming, shouting exploding crackling
Fire sticks smelling like smoke
Booming with energetic music

Why is there a soft, smooth dragon prancing about
Why is there so much glee why is it so enjoyable
And so much fun

So much like a crowded mall
Or like a circus act
With so many people crowded together

Boom Boom Boom

Gloria Hu, Grade 5
EH Greene Intermediate School

I Am
I am
Family Friends Pets
I like basketball and dance.
Honesty is important to me.
Happiness is important to me.
Caring is important to me.
Flowers make me feel good.
Being dishonest is bad but you can become honest.
Stealing is not good.
Dogs are fun.
Butterflies are cool.
I am
Krista Korsnack.
Krista Korsnack, Grade 6
St Clement Elementary School

Will I Ever See You Again?
When you get on that bus,
Will I ever see you again?

When we hang up the phone,
Will I ever hear you again?

When we have a fight,
Will I ever know you again?

I never want to lose you,
My friend.

You are the comfort for my soul,
Will I ever lose you?

When we part to our own ways,
Will I ever see you again, my friend?
Kaleigh May, Grade 6
Rocky River Middle School

Goodbye
You're leaving today,
But this is what I want to say,
You've been a great friend
From beginning to end
You are there through thin and thick
Even when I tend to kick

You make me smile every day
And with you leaving I want to say
I'll miss you very much
Especially not sitting by you at lunch
School will not be the same,
In fact it will be very lame
Goodbye and farewell
Be sure to give me a ring on my cell.
Abby Greco, Grade 5
Wintersville Elementary School

My Dog
I have a little dog.
She's a little morky,
And half Yorkie

She likes to go on walks and play.
She likes to go with me every day.

She will sleep and not make a peep.
I love my dog,
I don't know what we'd do without her.
Tanner Haas, Grade 6
Trilby Elementary School

Capture Your Dream
A dream is waiting for you somewhere.
Whatever it may be,
You capture it, you cherish it,
Maybe you set it free.
What is your dream?
Make it happen.
Courtney Turner, Grade 5
Spaulding Elementary School

The Inchworm
An inchworm crawled down the leaf,
he was the Commander in Chief.

He wore a little hat,
on the top it was flat.

He was in charge of the brigade,
and he organized the parade.

His name was Neal,
and he had great appeal.

Neal's mother's name was Glow,
but she wasn't all that slow.

Neal's father's name was Paul,
he was extremely tall.

Now you know the deal,
of an inchworm named Neal.
Meredith Coughlin, Grade 6
Tippecanoe Middle School

Fall
Yellow, gold
The leaves fall off the old trees
Orange, brown
All of the trees frown
But I smile because it is
Fall
Alex Hoey, Grade 5
Barrington Elementary School

The Ocean
The ocean is blue.
My friend is too.
I ask her why.
She just turns and says bye.

There are many huge waves.
On the beach there are caves.
Drawn in the sand a note.
It talks about a billy goat.

I fly a kite.
And hang on with all my might.
The wind picks up and I run.
I am having fun in the sun.

I'm at the beach and have a wish.
To enjoy some fish.
On the cool refreshing land.
I feel the wet sand.
Julia McGregor, Grade 6
Kinsner Elementary School

Sailing
Anchor in the water,
Sailboat at the dock:
Not knowing what time it is
I rush to check the clock.

Noticing I'm late
I dash aboard my sloop.
I run to blow the horn
With an awful "Toot!"

I feel really good
Out on the open lake.
When I see the dock
I think "Piece of cake."

I see a ship in front of me
I can't stop, so I hit her.
Water washes over the deck.
It tastes very bitter.

It's now or never. With my life jacket,
I have to jump ship.
Now that I have, I'm glad I did.
The sailboat took a dip.
Jacob Bash, Grade 5
St Joseph Parish School

Winter
White and puffy snow
Gently making its way down
Small specks on my nose
Emma Warner, Grade 6
Tippecanoe Middle School

The Flying Dutchman

Weeheeheehee! Hooooooo! Wissshhh!
The best Halloween is Halloween on the beach!
Building haunted houses out of sand,
Have a Halloween party with lots of candy and fun,
Then, the party is interrupted by shrieks and howls,
Wolves and owls,
But worst of all, torturing terror, brain bursting badness, THE FLYING DUTCHMAN!!!!
No wait, it can't be, cracks, torn sails and, Uh, and GHOSTS!!
Everybody scattering to get back in the cabin! Ghosts on their tails!
Back and forth, rocking back and forth, the sight is sea sickening but in a ghostly sort of way.
Then, CRASH! Against the shore,
Out come the ghosts,
Hopefully the city is not a ghost city now.

Sally Squires, Grade 4
St Joseph Montessori School

I Remember

I remember my summer vacations:
I remember being so excited while driving to Dale Hollow Lake in Tennessee;
I remember how excited I was when I learned how to water-ski;
I remember how fun it was swimming in the crystal clear lake water.
I remember how much fun I had camping at Ohiopyle in Pennsylvania;
I remember white water rafting with my family on the Youghiogheny River;
I remember when we got stuck in a big storm on our bikes.
I remember when we left to go to Hilton Head Island at three o'clock in the morning;
I remember my sister and my dad getting stung by jelly fish;
I remember getting bit by a lot of misquotes when I went putt-putting.
I remember being so anxious when I was going to Paramount Kings Island;
I remember I went on five big roller coasters while at Kings Island;
I remember going down a lot of water slides and going on the lazy river at the water park.
I remember going to the Ohio State Fair with my family and grandparents;
I remember seeing all kinds of animals and getting to pet them;
I remember eating fair fries, which are the best fries ever.
I remember my summer vacations this year.

Kristin Oliphant, Grade 6
Harmon Middle School

I Remember

I remember Hawaii:
I remember swimming in the Pacific Ocean and the pool at the Kahala Hotel;
I remember the Kahala Hotel pool because I could swim up to the bar and order food and drinks;
I remember finding a shark tooth for my dad when I was swimming in the ocean.
I remember the Kahala Hotel and how cool it was to be in a five star hotel; they had an awesome Jacuzzi;
I remember being on the seventh floor because my friends were right next door to our room;
I remember the buffet at the hotel, and it had a chocolate fountain.
I remember visiting my auntie Brenda's house; she had us take off our shoes before entering the house;
I remember a flower called a Hibiscus and it was beautiful;
I remember a mango tree and how I got to pick one.
I remember a coconut tree and I got to peal it;
I remember a mangene flower and how wonderful it smelled;
I remember the flight home and it took 13 hours to get back from Hawaii.
I remember how nice the plane was because they had pillows, blankets, and TVs to watch;
I remember when we got back to Ohio Airport my mom couldn't find her bag, so they had to bring it to the house;
I remember Hawaii.

Taylor Young, Grade 6
Harmon Middle School

A Busy Day
It's time to get up.
I hop out of bed.
I pet my pup,
His name is Ted.
I brush my teeth
With my brother Keith.
I jump in the shower.
It takes 'bout an hour.
I fill my cup,
and feed my gup.
Now time for school.
This is so uncool!
After working math sums,
The end of the day comes.
I ride home on the bus
With my best friend Gus.
Haleigh McKibben, Grade 6
Tippecanoe Middle School

My Brother
I have a brother named Garrett
he never will eat a carrot
he makes lots of noise
he has lots of toys
sometimes he smells like a ferret
Connor Formick, Grade 5
Rootstown Elementary School

Fall
With the howling and coldness of fall,
Trick-or-treaters are
Getting ready for Halloween night.

The crunching and falling of the leaves
And the colors are
Vivid to me

The colors of the trees
Tell me
That fall is here.

When the trees are bare and
The reds, yellows and oranges are here
The migration of animals is beginning.
Andrew Cline, Grade 5
Immaculate Conception School

Autumn
Autumn is the most colorful of the year
where the leaves drop from trees yet tall.
People do work with rakes and shears
to clean up what has fallen in the fall.
But lazy people use machines with gears
So they do no work at all.
Brian Oldenburgh, Grade 6
Birchwood School

Cloaked in Red He Comes
Wake up, wake up, it's finally Christmas Day!
Oh, how many presents await me under the tree?
I run into the living room,

I am greeted by glitter covered ornaments smiling at me,
And by pastries in the pantry that smell like flaky cream-filled breads.
The snow is like a fountain of jewels filtering through the clouds,

The sun from afar makes a twinkling light.
On the table platters of sugary sweetness awaits me.
Presents wrapped in paper, give me paper cuts.

"Thank you," that is all I hear today,
Then a deep bass voice rings through the room,
Happiness fills the air.

Laugh, shout, jump for joy,
Because Santa's here;
And he's cloaked in red.
Gian Carlo Valli, Grade 5
EH Greene Intermediate School

A Day at the Beach
As I'm there, sitting — sand between my toes —
the water swishing up on the shore, making a white foam,
I hear a flock of birds go by, making little tweeting noises.
Kids make sandcastles and sand pies.
Babies are being held in the water, toddlers wearing floaties, crying.
Children try to run in the water like whales, splashing everyone in sight:
a day at the beach.
Tiffany Townsend, Grade 6
Melrose Elementary School

My Family
My passion is participating in sports:
I love playing soccer, catching softballs and dribbling down the courts.

My brother, Clay, is a high school sophomore with a job and a car.
The 1985 Bonneville from Grandma is the coolest by far!

My mom is in a new account relationship role.
Keeping EVERYONE happy is her number one goal!

My dad keeps extremely busy with everything going on with the clan.
Healthy family…lots of laughter…he is a very blessed man!

My Granny loves to clean.
She works so hard, she's better than any machine.

My Grandpa loves pretzels and chili.
He has been married for over 50 years to my Grandma Lilly.

My Grandma loves to sew all day and night.
She is so peaceful that she would never take part in a fight.
Kara Johanson, Grade 6
Rocky River Middle School

High Merit Poems – Grades 4, 5, and 6

Most Sincerely, Erie
Dear Lake Erie, the lake by my home,
The lake of the mountains, the crevices, the domes,
I play on your beaches, and splash in your waters.
I am among many friends, families, sons and daughters.
Though someday, far from now, your beauty will go.
No one admits it, but they all know.
They know how we've treated you, unfair and unjust.
Instead of hugs and kisses, we've given you silt and dust.
Sure, it's great that our technology has advanced,
But people aren't looking; they haven't even glanced.
If they had, they would've seen the changes every day:
The gentle, rolling waves replaced by large ships at bay.
Whenever I see you, so many memories are revealed:
Splashing, sand castles, a banana being peeled.
In my lifetime, you'll be here, though I'm not sure what amount,
So as the clock ticks, I'll let every moment count.
Your fate is a blur, and its answer is query.
But for today, most sincerely…most sincerely, Erie.
Alex Manoloff, Grade 6
Rocky River Middle School

Beaches!
The waves roll in and out.
Waves are crashing all about.
I surf all day.
In the sand and water I like to play.

The sun beats down on my skin.
Out in the ocean, is that a fin?
We had a picnic on the beach.
I got sand on my peach.

The sand feels good on my feet.
I think it feels really neat.
I sunbathe on my chair.
The wind blows in my hair.

I've had a great day.
Now I watch the sun fade away.
The ocean and beach have a mystical power.
Now it's time to go home and take a shower.
Elizabeth Vidoli, Grade 6
Kinsner Elementary School

Friendship
Friendship is a box of emotions.
Friendship is the month of September.
Friendship remembers first sleepovers and tastes bittersweet.
Friendship is like receiving a box of chocolate.
Friendship is a spongy ball that soaks up good qualities.
Friendship is the season of Fall.
Friendship is a pocketful of uniqueness.
Friendship is like a trip to the beach and has no secrets.
Also, joy is found in a friend.
Lynette Kelbley, Grade 6
Old Fort Elementary School

Marshmallows
Of all the things I like to eat,
A marshmallow just can't be beat,
There are many reasons I've come to this,
and some of them I'll try to list.
First of all they taste so sweet,
there's nothing more I like to eat.
I also think they're fun to roast,
over a fire turning brown like toast.
Their cylinder shape is also grand,
just another reason they're in high demand!
There are many things that make them cool,
but one thing's for sure, marshmallows rule!
Maddie Billick, Grade 5
Wintersville Elementary School

School Lunch Last Friday
Friday's lunch was a simple school lunch — BORING!
So I pretended that my lunch was having fun.
Soon my water was spinning like a twister.
I was so amazed!
Next, my French fries were flipping in the air.
I could not believe my eyes!
Then my pudding and my sandwich were dancing.
All of a sudden, I saw my peaches singing to the beat
While my bread was playing the drums.
Uhhh…I guess I dozed off.
Oh, man! It was all a dream?
Oh, my boring school lunch was back.
My school lunch on Friday.
Leslie Keene, Grade 6
Tippecanoe Middle School

That First Curtain Call
Rushing, hurrying, thinking
Everyone going over their lines and song
Excited, nervous, and happy all at the same time
Darkness all around me
But when a door is opened the stage floods with light
Excited, nervous, and happy all at the same time
Laughing every minute singing too
Talking, screaming, and whispering
Excited, nervous, and happy all at the same time
I want to ask if anyone else feels the way I do
Is it just me that feels
Excited, nervous, and happy all at the same time?
On this day I feel as if I'm on top of the world
This is the day that I live for. I feel so
Excited, nervous, and happy all at the same time
All of the talking, screaming, and whispering
Suddenly stops, with one flick of a wrist
That is our cue to be silent
Then you see light, like the sunrise
Then a full audience
Excited, nervous, and happy all at the same time
Katie Amster, Grade 5
EH Greene Intermediate School

What Is a Brother?
What is a brother?
   an annoying jerk
   a dummy to beat up
   a couch potato
   a person to hug
That is a brother.
Skyler Baker, Grade 4
York Elementary School

Hope
Hope is a box of happiness
and has a song of joy.
Hope is the month of January
and dreams of light.
Hope is a dance of love
and the season of spring.
Hope has a pocketful of peace
and sounds like a bird singing spring.
Hope remembers your loved ones that
went to war.
Molly Cleveland, Grade 6
Old Fort Elementary School

The Big Tree
The cat was running,
The dog was chasing.
The cat ran up a tree.
The dog tried and tried,
but just could not get the cat.
He could have gotten the cat
if it weren't for that big tree.
Brooke Spence, Grade 5
Wintersville Elementary School

What Would I Do Without Music?
What would I do without music?
I wouldn't be able to play guitar
On the hood of my car
My fiddle, I wouldn't be able to hear
Even if I put it up to my ear
What would I do without music?
Haley Ferguson, Grade 4
Hylen Souders Elementary School

Christmas
C hrist's birthday.
H oliday cookies galore.
R eally fun with family.
I s on the twenty fifth.
S nows sometimes.
T oo cold to wear shorts.
M ittens are perfect for this day.
A lways is very festive.
S nowflakes fall on my windows.
Kristen Robarge, Grade 6
Pike Christian Academy

The Sun Going Down
Such a beautiful thing
Glowing in the air
So red and yellow
And so very hot
You can see from many miles away
But sadly the day is ending
When the day was just getting fun
But sadly the sun is going down
With the day
Alex Stepanishchev, Grade 6
EH Greene Intermediate School

Flowers
My favorite flower is a rose,
I water it with a hose.
We pick it for someone dear,
Because in our hearts they are near.
The petals are red,
They look pretty by your bed.
Whenever you are down or felling blue,
A red rose may be the medicine for you.
Kylie Ford, Grade 6
Roosevelt Elementary School

Penguins
All black, orange, and white
But not too big in height
Their favorite dish
Is fish
They waddle around
They slide on the ground
They swim
Till the light goes dim
Watch out for seals
They will be on their heels
If they don't take care
Sharks will be there.
Grant Girten, Grade 6
EH Greene Intermediate School

Richie Blough
Richie Blough
Intelligent, short
Talking, swimming, reading
He loves to play.
Student
Richard Blough, Grade 6
Jefferson Elementary School

Nature
The moon listens to the stars messages.
The morning takes us to the night.
The mountains bring us to the sea.
The sky is blue when it's not snowing.
Myriam Milor, Grade 6
Woodward Park Middle School

Hot Chocolate
Hot chocolate
Is warm
And cozy
Hot chocolate
Is tasty
There is nothing better
Hot chocolate
Takes you in
On a cold, cold day
And warms you up
Hot chocolate.
Erin Eastwood, Grade 5
Tremont Elementary School

The Tempest's Fury
Beyond a pane of frosted glass
A tempest turned and tumbled
A rising din that ever last
Through dark of night, rumbled
In the winter gale

As snow clung to tempest swirling
A fire shield from frozen fang
Of cold wind howling, scowling, whirling
And night rang with tempest's roar
In the winter gale

And shadows cast of fire bright
Dancing in the flickering light
Swept away into the night
As tempest flung them out of sight
In the winter gale

So here I sit warm and cozy
Here with the fire in tow
Safe from tempest that turn cheeks rosy
Secure within my fire's glow
In the winter gale
Hayden Bish, Grade 6
Harding Middle School

Fish
Sparkled with color
Shining from light
Their scales are all
Very
Bright
Some you
Can't catch
Some you
Can't see
Some I don't like
Swimming with me.
Samantha Good, Grade 5
Tremont Elementary School

High Merit Poems – Grades 4, 5, and 6

Monkeys! Monkeys! Monkeys!
A monkey looks like an ape
And it can stay in good shape
Lives in many tropical places
It can have many different faces
Some are sent to space
That might look for a landing place
They are worshiped in Japan
But soon it will be the fall of man
One day monkeys will rule
And will learn how to go to grammar school.
Aneesh Jain, Grade 6
EH Greene Intermediate School

A Season Full of Excitement
A favorite time of year is here dumping leaves on the ground,
Soon it will be time for a ghoul to freak you out,
A cool breeze blowing in your face,
Be thankful for all you have today,
Now it is colder and snow is falling,
It is a holiday for joy and giving,
And last but not least we have a new year!
Christopher Ford, Grade 4
Licking Valley Intermediate School

Leaves Fall with Grace
Fall comes, and has peace in loyal
All the colors change into royal.
The wind can howl and we have lots of fun.
Please royal fall don't be done.
I dance and sing and have a ball
My excitement for fall is enormously tall.
Zoe R. Gallagher, Grade 5
Sanderson Elementary School

Amusement Parks
There are a lot of things to do
At an amusement park.
You get there in the morning
And stay till it gets dark.

There are a lot of rides you can go on
But you have to wait in line.
Or you can go to a restaurant
Where you can dine.

You can play games
And win cool prizes
Like stuffed animals
Or fun disguises.

You can also see a play or a show.
They usually take place in the middle of the day.
Amusement Parks are great places.
There you can always have fun in more than one way.
Melissa Kling, Grade 6
Kinsner Elementary School

Memory
A year ago I went to Mexico.
In the plane I could see the ocean flow.
At Mexico there was a lot of fish.
You could see them in the water or eat them on a dish.
There was a big hotel pool.
Inside the water was very cool.
I was mad when we had to go.
When we got home it was weird having snow.
Ryan Maraldo, Grade 6
St Clement Elementary School

The Flood
One morning and night it rained and rained.
All of the water into the river, drained.
As the day went on the river kept rising.
The destruction it would cause I found surprising.

A town nearby was in the flood's path.
On the news I watched to hear of the wrath.
The rainwater caused my family and friends.
Even sandbags and rescue boats couldn't defend.

When we first drove through the town and saw the mess.
It made me sad and I felt depressed.
Unimaginable damage to all our friends owned.
They lost a lot, maybe even their home.

The kindness of people changed the bad to good.
Cleaning, raising money, doing all that we could.
After the water went down and the damage was done.
The whole town worked as a team and won.
Ellie Wenzinger, Grade 6
Miller City-New Cleveland School

Seasons
The sky is blue
A wonderful hue
The shadow in the air is a kite
Made beautiful by the sun shining bright

I anticipate the summer
A time where school is out
And my friends and I are romping about
The next year, awaiting us is a newcomer

I long for the winter
It seems so far
Yet it is pretty near
The bad thing is the chimney will be filled with soot and tar

I yearn for spring
You won't need a sweater
Of all seasons it's the king
No season is better
Shaffan Mustafa, Grade 6
Kinsner Elementary School

Pencil

Pencil
I write with this
It is sharp and yellow
I really love my number 2
Pencil.

Alex Zink, Grade 5
Wintersville Elementary School

Hayley Mayer

H elpful to friends
A ccomplishes my homework
Y ounger sister
L azy at home
E nergetic at school
Y outhful female

E ntertaining person
L oud mouth
I nspiring to younger brother
Z ealous about learning
A thletic in spirit
B eautiful little girl
E legant reader
T rustworthy friend
H appy with life

M essy room
A mbitious, achieves goals
Y oung at heart
E nchanted story reader
R ight handed writer

Hayley Elizabeth Mayer, Grade 5
Frank Ohl Middle School

Prissy

Prissy
Playful, cute
Smiling, barking, running
Tail wagger
My dog

Shelby McVay, Grade 6
Melrose Elementary School

Winter

Winter is a time,
When snow is on the way,
Adults shovel snow,
While children glow in the snow,
Winter is a time to play,
So when you get the chance,
Go out in the snow and dance,
Now come in,
In the house,
And have some hot chocolate.

Drew Kauffman, Grade 5
Norwich Elementary School

Shepherds' Story

The shepherds sat in the fields; nothing was stirring.
Shining lights appeared and angels were flying in the fields!
They sang and told them about Jesus' birth.
The shepherds were petrified.
They may have been scared but they went to the place of Jesus' birth.
They went and saw Jesus and offered them what they had.
It may not have been much but they offered what they had.
The shepherds gave what they had
And were brave which was the best thing they could do that night.

Eric Buehler, Grade 5
Wooster Christian School

Christmas Meaning

The dark green tree wrapped with silver decorations,
Round, heavy ornaments weighing the tree down.
A clear window from where you can see snow,
Like a huge cloud covering everything.
A tray of mouthwatering chunky chocolate chip cookies
Wait inside the kitchen to be eaten.

There's a bright blinding light —
As bright as a shining star,
And flickering lights of all colors —
Lighting up the room like a rainbow.

The ripping of the smooth present wrappings
Is followed by laughing and excited squeals.
And yet, the soft whispery "whoosh" of the snow is still heard.

There are many questions to be asked during this wonderful holiday:
Is the tree tired of carrying such a heavy weight?
Are the ornaments tired of hanging?
But perhaps this is the biggest question of all:
What is Christmas really about?
Happiness.
Happiness.
Happiness.

Jonathan Weng, Grade 5
EH Greene Intermediate School

The Sky Watcher

In the cool of the sallow night, you can hear the crickets chirping,
Orion's belt bundled up with clusters of the twinklers,
A fleeing boleide always excited the eye,
Beginning to feel the zest for the obscurity,
An immense luna joins you as your eye is glued to the vast welkin,
Being hopeful you see Cassiopeia disguised as an M,
The stars are like marbles lined up in a Chinese checker game,
Never having the ability to see the Andromeda Galaxy,
Getting irate because it never can gape on the Aurora Borealis,
Spica stars looking resplendent against the firmament,
Billions of quasars adorning like a Christmas tree in the sky,
The pulsars decreasing as the sun rays flee up to the sky,
All types of stars, Spica, Sirius, Sun, Arcturus, and Betelgeuse, vanished into obscurity.

Ashley Rau, Grade 5
Cline Elementary School

Diving

Diving is my life to some day go to the Olympics to
stand on the board and jump into the cool water below
to share my gold medal that shines in the light above
this is my biggest dream.

Emily Jones, Grade 5
Barrington Elementary School

Halloween!

Halloween is my favorite time of year
Everyone has something to fear!

Up and down, left and right,
All the spooks will give you a fright.

Vampires, goblins, witches too
And ghosts that jump out and say, "Boo!"

That is why Halloween is so much fun…
But if you get scared, just scream and run!

Alysha Kunz, Grade 5
Westview Elementary School

My Sister

Sometimes she's nice and cool.
Sometimes she's mean and cruel.

Sometimes she lets me borrow things.
Oh you don't want to hear when she sings!

She is not a mister.
She is my big sister.

When she moves out I might be sad.
But then again I might be glad.

Brock Whalen, Grade 6
Trilby Elementary School

Mike Robert Hood

M essy kid
I nteresting person
K ind to others
E ntertained by TV and computers

R eally good with computers
O pen-minded friend
B ig head
E nergetic at gym
R esponsive student
T iny person

H elpful friend
O rganized desk
O ld for my size
D etermined to become a computer programmer

Mike Robert Hood, Grade 5
Frank Ohl Middle School

Have You Ever?

Have you ever had someone
where you just felt comfortable
around? Where you could laugh,
play and have fun? Well I have
two groups of these people. Family
and friends. Family I know will have
my back. Friends are very
unpredictable. I love my family
and my family loves me. When
friends turn their back you will
know your family won't.
My friends are cool. Have you
ever felt like nothing could go
wrong, then BAM the script changes?
I have had those same feelings.
But I have people to comfort me.
Have you ever had someone who, when
you needed to cry they were there,
and when you need to talk they heard you?
I have. But have you ever?

Sarai Tyson, Grade 6
Eastmoor Middle School

The Last Snowman

They have all gone, away from me,
I, the one they will never see,
Their warmth is good but mine is not,
They put me together, have they forgot,
Here come new ones, can they help me,
They gave me a hat and scarf, they can see,
I can be happy because they helped me,
I may be melting but I am happy.

Lionel Johnson, Grade 6
Glenwood Middle School

Brothers

Big brother
Mean, quiet
Yelling, hitting, biking
Basketball, television, swim team, videogames
Running, kicking, batting
Gentle, squirmy
Little brother

Zachary Evans, Grade 6
Tippecanoe Middle School

Halloween Scares

You'll see creepy masks
As laughs and screams fill the air
Little kids get candy for Halloween.
Pretty costumes…witches, ghosts, ghouls…
You'll see fake R.I.P. stones
And dead people walking.
Halloween is the scariest time of the year.

Katelyn Perdue, Grade 5
Westview Elementary School

Snow

Snow, it's wild like a wolf
Foaming at the mouth it growls
At the child. Staring quiet but
Getting louder, it lunges but wait
The child ducks there is nothing
There, he swore he saw a wolf.
He runs in the house then POOF
He wakes up, he runs down stairs,
He tells his mother. Her child
Said it went as quiet and as calm
As a mouse. His mother said that
It was just a dream and to go get
Dressed, so he went up stairs and
Put on his clothes only to find
That his boots are covered in snow.
Mariah Tiano, Grade 5
Wooster Christian School

Fall Is Here

Fall is when the leaves meet the ground
and become warm shades of red, yellow
and orange.

With it's howling winds and
cool air, fall is good to sit
around a nice warm fire.

School begins, can you hear
the school bells right, summer's
over, fall is here.
Nick Reineck, Grade 5
Immaculate Conception School

What a Little Girl Dreams Of

Flowers
Lolly pops
Their mommy
When they are going to school
Rainbows
Ponies
A candy land
Her mom getting her a new kitten
Puppies
Babies
Baby dolls
Her and her friend watching a sunset
Running through a grassy field
Cotton candy
Going to the fair
All the snacks a girl could ever want
Drawing a picture
Christmas
Her birthday
Getting their parents gifts at the store
Ashley Richardson, Grade 5
Sanderson Elementary School

Goldie

Goldie is a fish that likes to wish.
The orange fish likes to swim.
But never needs a trim.
He is a fish.

His fin almost broke.
He dropped his food.
Goldie thought it was a joke.
And was in a bad mood.

His best friend was Kelly.
She ate a piece of toast.
Also has a big belly.
And they saw a ghost.

Goldie cried because he was scared.
He was a dummy.
Finally he cared.
And also found a chummy.
Kelly Peskura, Grade 6
Kinsner Elementary School

The Spirit Lingers

Before your birth,
After your death,
The time you spent together,
It feels like a year is a minute,
Two is a day,
Three is a week,
And four is only a month.
Yes, they're gone,
But their spirit still lingers,
Looking down on you,
Smiling when you accomplish,
Comforting you when you're blue.
You can dream that one day,
You will be together,
Talking and laughing,
And that will happen,
After your death,
Your spirits will be together.
Scott Bentley, Grade 5
Dr John Hole Elementary School

Fall

When the leaves fall,
And the trees change colors,
That's when Fall starts it all.
Have some fun with sisters and brothers.

Make a leaf pile here and there.
Jump in on the count of three.
Breathe in the nice smelling air.
Have a great time with your family.
Megan York, Grade 5
Spaulding Elementary School

Halloween Night

Halloween is coming
Friends are near
Lots of different costumes here
Family sitting passing out candy
Dogs and cats you can hear
The six-wheeler starting
Finally we get pictures (smile)
It smells so good inside
I know it is the vegetable soup
Awaiting me to come
Spooky things on the front porch
Sometimes freak me OUT
Out the door
Out the window
Ahh ahh and ahh
Across the yard
Across the road
On the six-wheeler
Here we go
Grace Goodin, Grade 4
Licking Valley Intermediate School

Almost Out

It's 2:45 and school's almost out.
I just want to scream and shout,
When I hear that bell
I know school is out.
Justin Caniff, Grade 5
Wintersville Elementary School

Season Story

The snow lands softly
Looks like a marshmallow land
So I go outside
The snow is so soft
I touch it very gently
The frost bites my nose

What is that I hear?
It is the sound of the birds
They make me happy
I see her wings flap
It is a delighting sight
Silently she flies
The sun shines brightly
Down on my face it is warm
I see a storm come

Can you feel the wind?
It is pushing at my back
The wind goes away
The leaves on the ground
The colors are red and brown
But there is no sound
Maria Carioti, Grade 5
Hylen Souders Elementary School

About Myself!
My Sports:
A football player at heart
Enjoys going to Tribe games
Likes to play basketball pickup games
I wish to play football when I grow up.
My Pastime:
When bored, I listen to music, Billy Ray Cyrus
I sit outside looking at the sun
I play on the dinghy in the backyard
I pretend to be a fisherman.
My Favorites:
My favorite word is "awesome"
I like the Cleveland Indians most
Red is a great color, I think
Sports Center is my favorite show.
My life:
My parents are awesome, Thad and Jennifer
I have many great family members
I am smart, and lucky
I have a great life!

Cameron King, Grade 6
Immaculate Conception School

Black Hole
The black hole comes from nowhere
Like a bat in the darkness, it darkens everything in its path,
By sucking things up into the never ending hole of nothing
It is everywhere it wants to be
Then vanishes into thin air

Kyle Fishburn, Grade 6
Wooster Christian School

How Do I Forgive
How can I forgive when I have been hurt so many times?
If my heart has been broken so many times,
It is shattered,
Unusable,
Why do I even have a heart?
Just wait Dominique I will get myself together,
But I can't wait any longer
I have waited too long already
What am I supposed to do father?
Wait?
I am tired of waiting
Don't make me wait for you.
I want to have a life of my own
Not to take the path you choose
I am trying to heal the bruises in my heart.
Once you get it together call me
But I cannot wait
I want no more scars in my heart.
So I ask…how do I forgive after what you did
Once you know, tell me
How to forgive.

Dominique Forrest, Grade 5
The Intergenerational School

Guilt
Like a shadow that holds on tight,
Like a bad dream that hunts you at night.

It makes you sad, it makes you hurt,
Like a cut filled with dirt.

The only thing that treats guilt is not a shot,
But to tell the truth!

Kara Jobe, Grade 5
Dr John Hole Elementary School

Christmas
Christmas is coming, there's so much to do,
for Pete, Johnny, and oh me too!
We'll play and sing.
There's gifts to wrap, and tinsel to string.
I've got to be sure I don't miss the ding.
Christmas is exciting, I know what I'll do,
I will sneak down the stairs to see if Santa was there.
I'll play with my toys, and visit with my friends.
I can't wait until next year to do it all over again.
We'll take down the tree, sweep all of the floors,
And think, what will we do with presents galore?
I've got to be sure I don't miss a thing.

Cody Adams, Grade 5
Wintersville Elementary School

My Older Sister Ashley
Ashley is my sister
She's a really close friend
She always does my hair
We have contest of stare
We always listen to music and sing and dance
We like to sleep all day long
She has to do her make-up or she'll panic
We shoot some hoops
That is our favorite game
I always look up to her
So she can teach me to be the best
She just got her license
So get out of her road

Bethany Rutherford, Grade 4
Licking Valley Intermediate School

Springtime
I love spring,
When the robins sing.
I get to go out to play.
There are flowers popping out of the ground,
Like rabbits coming out of their holes.
Some people say spring is the love season,
But I say it is the birth of summer.
All the animals come out from hiding.
This is why spring is so great!

Todd Kinderdine, Grade 5
Dr John Hole Elementary School

September's Moon
The moon looks like a spirit
That is leading us in the midnight sky
With the stars hanging there like lights
Twinkling with the moon
In the darkened sky
With nothing in its way
To the race in space
With the stars guiding the moon
For victory

Brianna Blackmore, Grade 5
Cline Elementary School

Phases
The phases of the lunar
Crescent phase is flaky
And buttery
New phase is black
And ashy
   The phases of the lunar
   Make crazy and zany thoughts
   Fill your mind
   As if forcing you
   To think and imagine
      To think and imagine
      What the phases of the lunar
      Could be
      Compared to.

Jordan Henghold, Grade 5
Cline Elementary School

Happy Days
H appy days
A wesome days
P ast days
P erfect days
Y esterdays

D one days
A ll days
Y eah days
S weet days

Jaritt Louthan, Grade 4
Northfield Elementary School

Sunset
Hot bright sun
Big and round
Sometimes it's yellow
Sometimes it's orange
The sun makes the sky
So beautiful and young
When the moon comes up
The sun kisses the sky
'Good Night.'

Alexandra Greene, Grade 6
St Clement Elementary School

Fairies
The tiny fireworks display of these amazing little creatures
float like glowing balloons.
They frolic and dance amongst the petals of tree flowers and leaves.
The tiny sparks of light leave astounding jeweled gold sparkles
on the emerald leaves and pearl-lilac petals.
Up they soar like the wind,
carrying a tornado of leaves,
up into the midnight sky.

Samantha Schabitzer, Grade 6
Melrose Elementary School

I Am
I am Kyle Pasqualone energetic and a baseball player.
I wonder how many daring runs I will score by sliding into home plate.
I hear my fans roaring in the crowd and cheering me on.
I see the confident pitcher about to hurl a ball over the plate.
I want to smack the ball over the gigantic fence.
I am Kyle Pasqualone energetic and a baseball player.

I pretend I am winning the World Series and scoring the astonishing home run.
I feel someone helping me throw the ball and swing my bat.
I touch the end of the bat as I start to choke up on it.
I worry I will strike out on full count; that would be terrible.
I cry when I get thrashed in my face, or get struck in my gut.
I am Kyle Pasqualone energetic and a baseball player.

I understand if I hit the ball to sprint to 1st base.
I say if I try hard enough I can smack the ball over the fence.
I dream I am in the World Series about to hit an astounding line drive.
I try to hit an astonishing home run over the fence.
I hope I catch the baseball going at a super sonic speed.
I am Kyle Pasqualone energetic and a baseball player.

Kyle Pasqualone, Grade 6
Harmon Middle School

My Favorite Place
Quiet, peaceful
Sunny, humid
Soon after I get off the bus

Water running slowly
Wind blowing softly
Leaves drifting quietly over the smooth wet surface

Salamanders sleeping on the soft muddy sand
Crayfish slowly coming out from under their hiding places
Water moving over the rocky but smooth surface

Schools of fish swimming slowly in the calm pool of water
Squirrels running through the trees fighting over acorns
Birds singing softly overhead while I catch something moving by my feet

Tomorrow I will come here yet again
To be feeling great and be time to have fun

Aaron Myers, Grade 6
EH Greene Intermediate School

True Friends

True friends are with you until the end.
They help you with homework.
They talk to you when you are sad.
You can count on them for anything.
They are your friends.
True friends are always there for you
through thick and through thin.
They will be there forever.
You love them like a brother or sister.
You celebrate holidays together.
Best friends can be anyone
from a sibling to a cousin.
It could even be a parent.
True friends will never leave you, no matter what.
They will always be there for you.
Even when you're sad.
Like a book that I used to have,
they will love you forever.

Marni Altman, Grade 5
Akiva Academy

Dream Flight

As it flies on light wind it drifts and sways
through the seconds, minutes, hours and days.
Its white feathered wings carry it high,
above the clouds and beyond the sky.
It seems so hopeless, so small and weak
as it flies through the woods and above the flowing creek.
We also wish we could fly above the clouds, beyond the sky, yes.
Maybe someday.
Past the seconds, minutes, hours and days.

Elise Leonard, Grade 6
Rocky River Middle School

The Soccer Game

I woke up one morning and got in the car,
We drove to the field which wasn't far,
I walked on the field and practiced with my team,
I was so excited I wanted to scream!

I was ready to play a huge soccer game,
I hoped I would play good and not look lame.
I started to play with all my might,
I knew we wouldn't lose without a fight.

I would dribble, and pass, and shoot, and score,
I kicked and fought and knew this was war!
I ran so much I got a cramp,
But I fought it off, I needed to be champ.

The game was over and we had won,
My team had did it and it was done.
I put my trophy in its case,
And went to bed with a smile on my face.

Andrea Larsen, Grade 6
Kinsner Elementary School

Rainbow

Rainbow is the best color I've ever seen,
I like it much better than blue or green.
It makes me feel happy or sad and joyful or mad.
On some bad days when I feel torn,
It's nice to see a rainbow after a storm.
There are many kinds of different colors,
But the ones in the rainbow are better than others.
Some are green as leaves or as yellow as wheat.
Out of all the colors, rainbow is the best;
It raises above the rest.

Tyler Rutz, Grade 6
St John the Baptist School

Wonderful Winter

W inter is my favorite season
O h, look at all the snow gleaming
N aughty or nice, he'll put you down
D own on the list, so don't make a frown
E nter my house and see a tree
R eindeer, all 8, I really see
F ull of spirit and some joy
U sually on Christmas we get a toy
L oving the holiday and your family

W atching the Christmas movies, it's so nice
I sit by the fireplace and hear no mice
N ever hear a sound at night
T here I see a lot of light
E ither in the morning or when I lay
R ed and green are our colors for Christmas day

Nikki Wortman, Grade 5
Frank Ohl Middle School

Friends Are Like…

Friends are like stars that shine in the night,
They are gleaming and glowing and they are so bright!

Friends are like chocolate, they are so sweet,
And when it comes to singing they are upbeat!

Friends are like diamonds so precious and rare,
And don't forget one thing, they always love to share!!

Melis Gjergo, Grade 6
Rocky River Middle School

Blue

Blue is the color of the sky.
You're blue when you're sad.
Some people's eyes are blue.
Your walls in your room might be blue.
It's possible some people's hair might be blue.
Blue can be the color of your shoes.
Blue is my favorite color.
How about you?

Olivia Justice, Grade 6
St John the Baptist School

My Teddy Bear
When I am sad and all alone
and have no one to call my own
When a hug is what I need
or just to help me to sleep
My teddy bear I can depend
to be right there until the end
A hug a kiss a laugh or cry
or just to help me through the night
Bailey Jones, Grade 4
Monroe Elementary School

The Locker
No!
Don't open that locker!
It's horribly cursed!
What!?!? You want to open it?!?!
There's a horrible monster inside!!!
You'll be gone forever!
What? It's just an ordinary locker?!?
Oops, my mistake.
Michael Dick, Grade 5
Tremont Elementary School

What Is Anger?
What is anger?
the feeling of hatred
ferociousness
throwing toys across the room
punching the pillow to tiny bits
That is anger.
Matthew Albring, Grade 5
York Elementary School

Things That Are Quiet
Bark on a tree
chalk on the board
car on the rocks
sitting like a fly
staring at the clouds
butterflies in the sky
books on a shelf
turtle walking slowly
driving down the road
clocks ticking
going down the slide
sitting in the chair
birds flying through the sky
flying like a ladybug
napping on the couch
in the library
grass in the yard
snowflakes falling
reading a book
flowers on a bush
Kevin Sheets, Grade 5
Sanderson Elementary School

Me
M y nickname is Munchkin
A lways hear loud people
R ainbow colors I love
I ce cream I love
S tuffed animal collection
A t the store all the time

N ile blue is my favorite color
I mpressive at making ideas
C ongo red is my second
O ver to my friends house I go
L ikes to get good grades
E xercises every Wednesday

D addy's baby girl
E xcellent at my grades
S panish numbers 1-20, I do know
A rt lover
L oves animals
V olleyball is my third favorite sport
O ver at my grandma's all the time
Marisa Nicole DeSalvo, Grade 5
Frank Ohl Middle School

Groceries
Apples and Oranges
— sweet and round
Broccoli and Carrots
— make a crunchy sound
Brownies, Cookies
Chips and Sprite
— not very healthy,
— but taste just right
Sydney Carroll, Grade 6
EH Greene Intermediate School

A Rainbow
A beautiful rainbow in the sun
Is always shining
In the light blue sky
Like mostly every day…
But you never know
When a beautiful rainbow
Might come your way
In your heart one day.
Asianna White, Grade 4
Matthew Duvall Elementary School

How to Build a Sand Castle
Starting from scratch,
You build up, up, and up,
Till the day is done at the beach,
Put the windows in,
Up on top goes the flag.
Lindsey Sturwold, Grade 6
Holy Angels School

Halloween
We see lots of birds on Halloween
Like crows when they flew
When the wind blows
The candy wrappers blew

Trick or treat
Smell my feet
Give me something good to eat
Like a treat

I saw a bat
When I sat
On a mat
Then I saw a cat

I got to meet
On Halloween night
I share a fright
I get to greet
Emily Jones, Grade 6
Kinsner Elementary School

Rose
Soft and prickly,
petals falling off of stem
sticking to the ground.
Jordan Fortune, Grade 6
Roosevelt Elementary School

Horses
When horses walk,
You feel the love and faith in your horse.
When they trot,
you feel alive with passion.
When horses gallop,
you feel freedom as the wind
blows through their hair.
But when they run,
it's like nothing else exists.
Alone in the world,
just you and your horse.
Stephanie Carpenter, Grade 5
West Elementary School

My Sister
My sister is such a pest.
She always thinks that she's the best.
My friends think that she is cute.
But I want to put her mouth on mute.

She is scared of Mrs. Drees.
And she likes to climb our trees.
Abby is the craziest girl.
But I wouldn't trade her for the world.
Hannah Monroe, Grade 5
Spaulding Elementary School

Special Holidays to Me

It is a new time and a special time because it is a new year.
Now it is Easter Jesus had died and then came alive. We thank Him for that and all He has done.
But now is the time where fireworks are fired that brighten the sky because now we are free that has not been true this whole time.
Now it is Halloween the night before All Saints Day, we all go out and go get candy. Trick-or-Treat.
Now it is Thanksgiving the time for thanks. The time the pilgrims had that big long feast for three days. And still today we give thanks on that special day.
The year is almost over but there is still one holiday that I celebrate it is Christmas the time for giving and also time for thanks for the gifts we have received and for everything too.
Now we are done we are back where we've started, but do not be sad because there is a new coming year around the corner so don't be sad.
These were all the special days to me I enjoy them so much I would like to write more but like I said the new year has come again to start all over again.

Cassie Hamker, Grade 6
Rocky River Middle School

Christmas Wonders

Outside, the snow sits like a blanket, a blanket never losing its grip.
The cold, frozen world is eerie and still, with only the flutter of wings to break the silence.

The harsh, winter light, hitting the snow, makes it bright and dazzling as it dances.
But inside, it's cozy and warm and snug. Everything is just right.

It's Christmas morning, so you know what to expect. Brightly wrapped packages in green, gold, and red.
Rich, crispy gingerbread with a minty aftertaste, a Christmas tree with twinkling lights, and a shimmering star on top.
The fragrant candles of cinnamon and pine, light up even the darkest corners.

There is a child on the staircase, wondering…wondering…if the presents suffocate when they are wrapped.
She is wondering…wondering…until her sister knocks her over, impatient to be off.

They tore down the stairs at an incredible clip, and start opening presents one by one.
Their happy shouts of joy and surprise, can be heard from the end of the block,
And their delighted grins can be seen from at least a mile away.

Megan Jiang, Grade 5
EH Greene Intermediate School

The Star Tree

Dad brings up the annual tree, its pine needles so fresh and fragrant,
a savory smell that fills the room.
Mom gets the ornaments. We start to decorate.

"Heres" and "theres" ring out over the clanging of ornaments knocking together.
As Allison and I circle our tree, the rustling of sharp needles brushing against our shirts
sounds like a cat's claws against a sofa. The TV blares from the family room.

Soon, our tree stands like a giant in a dark cave, his lanterns blinking red, yellow, blue, and green.
Ornaments turn like a top and sway like a reed.
"O tree," I ask him, "Are you trapped within your woody stem?"

But the tree just stands there, powerfully, majestically,
but the star on top winks at me!
Stars twinkling, glittering, gleaming,
Stars twinkling, glittering, gleaming,
Stars twinkling, glittering, gleaming…
The Star Tree.

Megan Hsu, Grade 5
EH Greene Intermediate School

My Adorable Sister
I love her a lot

L oves me
O pen minded
V ery funny
E nergetic

E rika
R eally good
I s my sister Erika
K ind
A dorable
Ashlee Miller, Grade 5
Stanton Middle School

The Butterfly
When you look upon a butterfly,
you don't think of the caterpillar,
instead the butterfly.
As the wind carries it,
it's wings spread out and fly.
And no more may you see,
for it is in the sky.
Sarah Dresbach, Grade 5
Pike Christian Academy

Animals
Animals are good creations.
People should respect them.
Cruelty is not right.
I don't like their skins being sold.
People should protect them.
What do they think they're doing,
Hurting these beautiful animals!
Animals are good creations.
Natalee Landel, Grade 4
St Mary's School

Spare Time
Done with homework —
Strum my guitar —
A two hour task.

Lots of fun —
Humming to myself —
Fingers hurt badly.

Trust me —
I know —
So does Corey.

Corey loves it —
Josh loves it —
Really good fun!
Aaron Bachelder, Grade 5
St Joseph Parish School

Books
Books scream with
excitement. Whisper
with knowledge.

When you open
them up the words
bounce in your
head. Like when
you jump out of bed.
Phoebe Mesecher, Grade 6
Woodward Park Middle School

Winter
In the winter I see white
There are such cold nights
I like to drink hot cocoa
It makes my brother go loco
The trees are covered in snow
It shows a pretty glow
I like to have snowball fights
They are not pretty sights
Santa is at the mall
Decorations down the hall
Yelling, screaming "Christmas is here"
Santa is on his sleigh I know he is near
Sitting by the fire warms your toes
Everyone has a red nose
Snow angels, snowmen
They will be there until the end
Michelle Watson, Grade 6
Kinsner Elementary School

Thanksgiving
Thanksgiving, Thanksgiving
Is a special time.
We mumble and grumble
And cheer all day.

When I sit at the table
It is very loud. That's why
We get yelled at on
Thanksgiving Day.

When we go to bed
We say "Good Bye"
And that's what happens
On Thanksgiving Day.
Julia Helke, Grade 4
Demmitt Elementary School

Tiger
Prowling and stalking,
black stripes with silent footsteps,
growling then purring.
Jenna Matheny, Grade 6
Roosevelt Elementary School

Airplanes
Airplanes zoom,
Airplanes glide,
Airplanes flying everywhere,
Carrying cargo,
Carrying passengers,
Flying high in the sky,
Airplanes big,
Airplanes small
Alexander Baron, Grade 4
Norwich Elementary School

Things That Are Quiet
Angels helping you out step by step
The sun waiting to rise the next morning
Footsteps of a baby's first walk
The silence of love inside
Leaves blowing in the October breeze
People praying to the Lord
Clouds flowing in the sky
Deer eating in the fields
Birds gliding through the sky
Tigers sleeping in the shade
The wind blowing through the grass
Leaves falling from the tree
Vultures waiting for something to eat
When bucks are roaming the fields
When you're lonely and nothing to do
Reading a book
A shooting star in the sky
Using sign language
And just a breath
Jessica Grubb, Grade 5
Sanderson Elementary School

Time
Time, the forever whirling,
Forever curling void.
The past is filled with
Giant sharp-toothed lizards
The present with us,
Cars and cities.
The future, who knows what lies ahead,
Time,
The forever whirling,
And forever curling void.
Noah Marquand, Grade 5
Indian Springs Elementary School

Dusti Pilkington
Dusti Pilkington
Musical, intelligent
Talking, reading, rocking
He loves playing guitar.
Guitarist
Dusti Pilkington, Grade 6
Jefferson Elementary School

High Merit Poems – Grades 4, 5, and 6

Snow

Snow is falling everywhere
As long as it's winter.
Every snowflake has a different
Shape.
Used for snowballs, sledding, and snowmen.
Equivalent to water,
Comes in tiny snowflakes,
Covering up lots of places,
Leaving almost no spaces,
So fun to play with,
Snow.

Jungho Lee, Grade 5
Tremont Elementary School

Christmas Story

Following the star,
3 wise men and shepherds
meet the Son of God.

Wise men bring myrrh, frankincense, and silver
for the Baby just born.
We wonder what the baby is thinking and seeing.

Following the star,
3 wise men and shepherds
meet the Son of God.

Mary, what was she thinking
giving birth to the Son of God?

Following the star,
3 wise men and shepherds
meet the Son of God.

Nick Runyan, Grade 5
Wooster Christian School

A Bond Made to Last

You are the one that I depend on
When I was weak, you made me feel strong
You're the best friend I'll ever know
I never want to let you go
You're the fire that burns and the light that shines
You've helped and encouraged me
So many times
All the amazing things you have done
Because you have always been the one
Who makes me feel like I am free
Free to be what I want to be
In times of love, and deep pain too,
I can always turn to you.
You ease my mind, give me time to breathe
If I want to go, you let me leave
I know it's okay if I want to scream
Because you're the one who believes in me.

Krittika Chatterjee, Grade 6
EH Greene Intermediate School

Pixies

Flying, glistening in the dark, sparkling and gleaming,
as I watch in a gasp of wonder, pixies soar like dragonflies.
A streak of light flitters past me and
I yearn to play and dance in the never-ending black sky.

Patience Wentz, Grade 6
Melrose Elementary School

Sun

The sun is up when I'm up.
It's asleep when I'm asleep.
We go through the same cycle every day.
I love the sun, as it lights up the beautiful day.
I love the sun, as much as I love my Mom.
The sun is the best thing I've seen all day.
It's like lights on a Christmas tree.
The sun follows me every day.

Destinee Hill, Grade 6
Woodward Park Middle School

I Remember

I remember.
I remember the way your smile made my day.

I remember.
I remember the way you would say, "check the tent for snakes."

I remember.
I remember the way you would wake me up just to bond.

I remember.
I remember Dad, the day I found out you died.

Casondra Paul, Grade 6
Trilby Elementary School

Spring

Spring is my favorite time of year
With the cherry blossoms and the deer
I'm happy that I'm not cold
Because the sun is shining brighter than gold

Put away your snow gear
The weather is not cool
This is the time of year
You play in the pool

This is the time for ice cream
Vanilla flavor so it seems
Noon is the time of day
The time everyone wants to play

Spring is the time of year
Going into the forest
Logging the wildlife
And putting your hunting skills to the test

Austin Roberts, Grade 6
Kinsner Elementary School

Windy Leaves
Shining leaves glow
Ants crawling on gray fossils
Flowing leaves above
Kelli Worrell, Grade 4
Normandy Elementary School

The Elf
There is a little elf.
He lives upon my shelf.
He's getting me in trouble.
And now I'm seeing double!
He likes to chew pink gum.
But he is such a bum.
He blows a great big bubble.
And it's getting me in trouble.
My, my, my that little elf
That lives upon my shelf.
Zach Harp, Grade 5
Spaulding Elementary School

Winter
Cold days a comin'
leaves a crumblin'
Trees a tumblin'
Power lines a troublin'
People mumbling'
Football players tumblin' and fumblin'
Summer's a comin'
Riley Lees, Grade 4
Licking Valley Intermediate School

The Selfless Sharpshooter
Soaring over his head,
Whizzing past his ears,
Cracking in a terrible rhythmic pattern

Horses fleeing,
Maniacally trying to get away,
Stumbling over the dead,
Cannons blasting,
Shaking Earth as it,
Descends heavy blows upon its foes,

One wrong turn and it's over,
Shooting and shouting,
More casualties along the way,

He dives for a wounded soldier,
Shooting all around them,
His arm around the woeful man,

Excruciating pain,
Darkness,
He is in a better place.
Lydia Barner, Grade 5
St Joseph Parish School

Fall
The leaves are leaving the trees this time of year.
They are red, brown and different varieties.
We are having candy apples and Grandma is baking the pumpkin pie.
The wind blows the smell of cinnamon throughout the house.
It sounds like my family is laughing outside.
The wolves are howling like the wind in the trees.
Andrew Dillhoff, Grade 5
Logan Christian School

I Am
I am Benjamin Butcher independent and athletic.
I wonder if my baseball team will do fantastic this year.
I see my sister on her mobile cellular communication device.
I want a data processing unit this year for Christmas or my birthday.
I am Benjamin Butcher independent and athletic.

I pretend that I Ben Butcher am the smartest genius in the world and universe.
I feel someone extraordinary pushing me on in this exciting life.
I touch the extraordinary aluminum big barrel baseball bat today with my right hand.
I worry that this fantastic life and world will come to an end.
I cry that my fantastic grandfather died, and did not get to see me play baseball.
I am Benjamin Butcher independent and athletic.

I understand the importance of latitude and longitude in social studies in class.
I say that Babe Ruth was the greatest and most fantastic baseball player ever.
I dream about me being the most energetic baseball player ever.
I try to be really good at the exciting sport of baseball.
I hope that I will get a PlayStation 3 gaming system for Christmas
I am Benjamin Butcher independent and athletic.
Benjamin Butcher, Grade 6
Harmon Middle School

Rip, Crinkle, Crunch
Flash,
The camera strikes.
Family sitting around with a bright tree in the corner.
Huge mountains of gift wrap with small dogs excavating inside.
Rip, crinkle, crunch.
We hear everyone open up their gifts,
Chuckling and giggling fill the air.
The gifts are shouting, "Pick me!"
Rip, crinkle, crunch.
What will I get?
Will my family like their gifts?
Will I get the Uggs I want?
So many random questions running through my head.
Rip, crinkle, crunch.
The lights are glittering snowflakes glistening on a dark winter backdrop.
The ornaments sparkling like twinkling stars in a night sky.
The presents are a rainbow with many hues of colors.
Rip, crinkle, crunch.
At the end of the night, I drift to sleep,
Waiting 'till morning for more Christmas fun and warmth.
Rip — Crinkle — Crunch
Sammy Ciricillo, Grade 5
EH Greene Intermediate School

Cavs Basketball

Sounds like a roaring crowd at the swish of a ball
Looks like five maroon uniforms running across the court
Feels like an exciting rush as points add up
Tastes like salty snacks and large fountain drinks
Smells like snacks and excited, sweaty players
Madeline Lukehart, Grade 5
Northfield Baptist Christian School

Book

A book is a square shape,
it has a lot of words.
A book also has lots of things that happened
like Lord of the Rings.
Books are sometimes heavy,
but mostly not.
Michael J. Mates, Grade 4
Northfield Elementary School

Fall

Fall is fun and cool,
But I'd rather be hanging out at the pool.
I like going to the mall
And playing with my soccer ball.
I smell the scent of pumpkin pie.
The sun is so bright in the sky.
We go trick-or-treating door to door
And eat so much candy we fall to the floor.
Chelsea Clawson, Grade 6
Tippecanoe Middle School

Fall

Pumpkin pies, crunching leaves
Howling times three every week
Before Halloween you see pretty warm colors.
It starts to get colder.

Leaves become green,
Red, yellow, and orange.
Some are brown,
And some aren't.
Lauren Greider, Grade 5
Immaculate Conception School

Always Moving

When I'm awake I can never sit down.
If I don't have to run I will anyway.
On a bike, I'm always speeding.
In a car I want to accelerate.
When I'm typing on a keyboard I want to type faster and faster.
In a baseball game I want to swing harder and stronger.
When I'm in school, I never want to sit still.
On my couch I'm always trying to find a more comfortable spot.
I'm always shaking people's hands harder.
It seems like I'm always moving and I never want to stop.
Nick Tamarkin, Grade 5
Akiva Academy

Life

Life is an adventure, that is true,
there are hard and bright times that we all go through.

You can't let little things get you down,
nobody likes to see a frown.

Life is a challenge where everyone belongs,
but you can make it move along.

Many people take it as something they have to do.
Others know that it's a privilege too.

When you're doing great, but then you get stuck,
and you don't know what happened to your luck.

Always keep your heart faithful and true,
cause' it can definitely help you too.

It's a roller coaster ride, and a merry-go-round as well,
but someone will help you if you ever fall down.

But, when you ask yourself "What am I going to do?"
Turn to God and He will help you through.
Kayla Horning, Grade 6
Waterloo Middle School

Goldey's World

I am an adorable hamster named Goldey.
You know me for my super fluffy fur.
My mother is cream colored with patches of tan, just like me.
My father is a golden hamster with huge, pink, speckled ears.
I was born in a pet store, large and brown.
I live in a cage in a humongous, lavender room with my owner.
My best friend is a dwarf hamster named Snowball,
Because we both love to run.
We like to play hamster ball together.
My enemy is a horrible hawk,
Because he will rip me to shreds.
I fear my owner's frightening dog,
Because it will gobble me up.
I love being scratched on my head right between my ears,
Because it feels wonderful.
I wish to meet my brothers and sisters once again!
Jacquelyn Ravlin, Grade 5
Dr John Hole Elementary School

Shoes

You can walk with them or run,
You can kick with them or jump,
They can smell good or bad,
You can march with them or dance,
You can take them off and put them on,
You can stomp with them and get them muddy,
I love shoes!!!
Jack Strahm, Grade 5
Tremont Elementary School

Christmas
Christmas is a time to love.
It is a time to grow in Jesus' love.
The snow is falling,
the cookies are done,
it's time to go to bed.
just waiting to celebrate,
The birth of Jesus.
Christmas.
Madison Herman, Grade 4
St Mary's School

Love/Hate
I love pens but I hate pencils.
I love free-draw, but I hate stencils.

I love my name but I hate yours.
I love games but I hate chores.

I love markers but I hate crayons.
I love A.C. but I hate fans.

I love A+'s but I hate F's.
I love no rules but I hate refs.
Keely Edwards, Grade 5
York Elementary School

Monkeys
Monkeys are always swinging from vines.
All day long and grab a bite.
Fall to the ground.
Wait till morn to wake again
Darian Sapp, Grade 4
Norwich Elementary School

The Interception
I threw the ball up
I burst into tears
I threw an interception.
My first in three years.

I am a sub
For our star QB,
After he broke his arm
On a sack from their D.

Our third string quarterback
Was our first round pick.
We gave him some time.
He is the son of Mike Vick.

My dad was screaming,
He is the head coach,
And I felt worthless
As a brown cockroach.
Ryne Poli, Grade 5
St Ignatius School

Trees
Tall oaks wave to you
Strong winds make leaves fall around
The branches reach out.
Jimmy McGuire, Grade 6
Roosevelt Elementary School

Nature
Rays of glitter
forming in the sun.

Snow
touching my skin.

Water
in a deep sleep.

The smell of flowers
filling the air.

Hard tree bark
crunching under my feet.
Madison Short, Grade 4
Normandy Elementary School

Otters
Otters swimming everywhere
Going under collecting clams,
Laying on the smooth water
Breaking open their shellfish,
Eating all their food,
Having fun playing around on the shore,
Otters are the best,
The cutest in the world.
Hannah Romie, Grade 5
Tremont Elementary School

Seasons
There are
many seasons

Some are
cold some
are warm
and some
are windy

They come
in many different
forms such as
snow, leaves, and
flowers.

There are
many seasons
Joanna Darby, Grade 5
Charles A Mooney Middle School

The Feel of Christmas
Every year around this time
There is always something special
A feeling that you love to have,
And always want to share
Putting up lights on the Christmas tree,
And decorating around the house
To give to others with joy and love,
Is the best time of the year
Kate Blossey, Grade 6
Rocky River Middle School

Make It Happen
Think of a world
where joy is infinite
and loathing is no more.
A place where unscrupulous behavior
is shunned
and kindness, is highly taught.
Take a look at this world.
Although it seems wonderful
it is a facade.
And is contrary to the real one.
it is a wish,
a dream,
and it will stay this way
until we work to make it happen.
Calla Gilson, Grade 6
Pike Delta York Middle School

Ocean
As dark as the night sky
Lifeless all is quiet
Not one beam of light
Motionless all is still
That is the bottom of the ocean
Alex Hinkle, Grade 6
EH Greene Intermediate School

Life
Life is a joyful ride
up, down
down, up
But when it goes down
it's like a door closes on your dreams
But when it goes up
It's like a baby getting candy
Doors are closing everywhere
closing dreams
chances everything
Happy
Happy
Happy
Everyone enjoying life as we know it.
Enjoy it while you can.
Kelsey Gugel, Grade 6
Trinity Lutheran School

The Journey to Bethlehem

One night an angel came to Mary.
"Go to Bethlehem with Joseph."

Mary went to the house of Joseph
And told him what had happened.

One night an angel came to Mary.
"Go to Bethlehem with Joseph."

They started on their long journey
With Mary on a shaggy donkey.

One night an angel came to Mary.
"Go to Bethlehem with Joseph."

Both came to an inn in Bethlehem.
There was no room in that small, crowded inn.

One night an angel came to Mary.
"Go to Bethlehem with Joseph."

That very night the Babe was born.
What a wonderful night for Christ to be born!

Jocelyn Hunyadi, Grade 5
Wooster Christian School

Blue

The sky is blue.
An eye is blue.
When I feel bad I'm blue.
When you feel bad you're blue.
When I cry boo hoo I'm blue.
When I'm the new kid in school I'm blue.
The sky, an eye, a polka dot, a paint blot.
Any time you're not happy you're blue.
And for me when I feel blue is when I can't go outside.
Every day you can feel all the colors of the rainbow.
But almost all the time I feel blue.

Garret MacFarland, Grade 6
St John the Baptist School

Basketball

Basketball is the best
Because you cannot rest
If you do, you will be on the bench
And that is worse than being stuck in a trench.
I love when players do a slam-dunk
Then try to show off but look like a chipmunk.
I also like it when I shoot a three
Then buzz up the court like a bee.
Then I normally get a block
Because I'm flying like a hawk.
Then I sometimes get a steal
I can't believe this is all real.

Ben Stucke, Grade 6
Tippecanoe Middle School

School Day

As night approaches, I go to bed
I pull the sheets over my head.
And lying there I think of schemes
Then I close my eyes and in come the dreams.

I awake to my alarm, ringing in my head.
'It's time to get ready for school' I think as I jump out of bed.
I get a quick bite to eat as I head out the door
As the bus pulls up, I hear the engine's roar.

Then I get on the bus, and sit in my chair
While the static spikes up my hair.
After a bus ride that seemed like an hour we thought
The bus finally pulled up to the school parking lot.

Once inside my classroom, and I put my books away
I already start to think about the end of the day.
And then my teacher comes in and school starts
That is when we begin language arts.

Brad Hall, Grade 6
Harmon Middle School

Christmas

Christmas is a special time of year
A time to spread good will and good cheer

When all the little good girls and boys
Open presents, rejoice, and pray…

Because Christ was born on this very day.

Joshua Ginley, Grade 6
Rocky River Middle School

Skiing

In cold Canada on mighty mountains so tall,
Speeding, swooshing, swerving on snow,
Skiing is fun for all.
Take the chilly chair lift
To the precise point of the peak,
Go zooming, zigzagging, and straight down the mountain,
Your trip won't be bleak.
Back at your cozy, comfortable condominium,
The fantastic flames of fire keep you warm.
Practice, perfecting your every move,
You soon will have fabulous form.
Skiing in Canada is so much fun!

Jay Schairbaum, Grade 6
Tippecanoe Middle School

9-11-2001

9-11-2001 was a terrible day.
When innocent people had to pay for things they didn't do.
When many others thought, "Why did it have to be you?"
That is why we celebrate today with a moment of silence.

Carlee Griffey, Grade 6
Trilby Elementary School

Grandparents

All grandparents
Are friendly
All grandparents
Are kind
All grandparents
Are very nice
But none so much
As mine.

Aaron Payne, Grade 5
Indian Springs Elementary School

In the Sun

Roses are red
Violets are blue.
I like the sunlight,
How about you?
The sunlight is beautiful,
I wish, I could be just like you.
The sun is bright,
It has light, are you feeling all right?
We can play with a toy
The sun is filling us up with some joy.
I go running and playing,
Come on everybody
Let's have some fun.

Wesley Amaniampong, Grade 4
Monroe Elementary School

Football

Football is the greatest game of all.
You play it with an egg-shaped ball.
The quarterback makes the calls.
you know it's football season
When the leaves start to fall.
football season is near
When you hear the crowds start to cheer.
so come make some noise
For all those football boys.
cheer very loud
To make our town proud.

Dalton Allen, Grade 6
Tippecanoe Middle School

Gray

Gray is a nature color
A dark gray cloud
A little gray squirrel
Running swiftly on the
Gray clouded horizon
Sometimes the
Bark of the tree is grayish
Old gray crumbled up leaves
The moon
Gray is a nature color

Zach Brooks, Grade 5
Cline Elementary School

Blue

Blue is the color of gloom.
When you feel really sad you're blue.
Sapphires are blue and so is the sky.
Navy and royal are also blue.
Aqua, aquamarine, azure, cobalt, turquoise,
And wedgewood, are all examples of blue.
Water is blue, birds are blue, pens are blue, and even flags are blue.
Sky blue shirts, navy shorts, royal shoes, and sapphire socks.
When I think blue, I get a clue.

Jason Schuler, Grade 6
St John the Baptist School

Dance

I love to move. Especially to a beat.
The music has a special flow. When I dance I look sweet!

Dancing is great exercise. You can turn, slide, and jump.
It really makes you tired. But dance helps you not look like a lump.

I always liked to be in dance competitions. They always are so fun.
And my dance team does so good. But I am always glad when we are done!

Dance takes a lot of practice. Every part of your body has to be in the right position.
A key to dance is always remembering to smile. Dance is a true mission.

Kaitlin Rizk, Grade 6
Kinsner Elementary School

It Is Christmas Time

Tearing open packages. Ripping, plucking, crumbling.
Feeling pleased and happy. It is Christmas time.

Music racing in my ears. The smell of fire,
Warm and cozy. I am with my family.
Joy and Christmas spirit fill the room.
It is Christmas time.

Dim light pouring through the window.
Touching bows, ribbon, gift wrap and packages.
The sweet taste of hot chocolate fills my mouth.
It is Christmas time.

Gasps and ohhs and ahhs.
"Wow" and "Thank you" pop around the room like popcorn.
Ornaments sparkle in my eyes. I am as happy as a millionaire.
It is Christmas time.

Questions race through my head.
Does the fireplace have to expand for Santa to fit through?
Does the tree feel naked without ornaments?
Do the reindeer run out of breath?
It is Christmas time.

The savory smell of Christmas air fades as the day and the snow melt away.
Christmas Day is done.

Abby Miller, Grade 5
EH Greene Intermediate School

High Merit Poems – Grades 4, 5, and 6

The Frog in Summer
The frog can be found
in the pond
leaping up onto the bank
and sitting and croaking until the mud sank
under its toes
and away he goes
to another rainy spot
as the rain lightly drops

Yun Lu Sun, Grade 6
Birchwood School

Football
It is a sport with smashing and crashing,
And sometimes you can get hurt.
If you are not very careful you might lose the ball,
Then the other team can score.

Brad Montgomery, Grade 6
Holy Angels School

United Pride*
O'er the bodies of the fallen,
The hopes, the dreams, the tears.
We'll fight, we'll fight, with all our might,
In many battles through the years
Korea, 'Nam, or Iraq we'll always have your back.
Support our troops, even when our death rate droops.
We love our country and we always will.
So let us climb that final hill.
Finish the fight. No more leash.
Do what's right. Let's live in peace.

Keon Mullins, Grade 6
Lake Middle School
*In honor of the U.S. Military

Swim
Swim is a powerful sport.
You don't have a lot of time to rest,
Swimming laps, relays and dives,
Remember to do your best.

There's butterfly and backstroke,
Freestyle and breast,
While you're swimming all those strokes,
Remember to do your best.

While you swim you go really fast.
The people on deck have to guess,
Who are you because you're going so fast,
Remember to do your best.

You will grow really tired,
While you swim under the sun,
Here's a tip from me, your friend,
Remember to have fun!

Bernadette Rowe, Grade 6
Kinsner Elementary School

The Beach
The warm golden sand seeping through
the spaces in between your toes.
The crystal teal water crashing against the soft shore.
The saltwater aroma going through your head.
And the gorgeous sunset in the corner of your eye.

Alyssa Tedesco, Grade 5
Barrington Elementary School

Baseball
I step up to the plate
My bat in my hand.
The most confident person in the world!
The ball comes in;
I hit it high and deep.
The ball flies with the birds.
Suddenly gravity rips the ball over fence to the ground.
As my teammates cheer.
I feel a sense of joy!
Rounding third my team's cheers fade out,
And I can only hear my own thoughts.
As I step on home I think
"This is what it's all about!"

Joshua Keller, Grade 6
St Joseph Parish School

Ode to Mom1
I love the way you boost me up
because you can tell when it's needed.
I love the way you keep me safe.
I love the way you are able to do everything yourself;
you don't need a man!
I love the way you serve at church,
the way you sing and praise.
I love the way you get involved.
I love the way you don't have to hear it from me;
you already know that I love you.
I love the way you goof around and play,
but always serious.
I love the look you give to tell us we're crazy.
I love the smile you give to summarize that you're proud.
Thanks for the way you go to work every day
to give our family what we need.
I truly honor you for always being my mother and father.
I really appreciate your support, Mom.
You make me feel like I'm where I belong.

Gabbi Atwell, Grade 6
Tippecanoe Middle School

Angels
Peaceful, graceful things glowing in the dark night,
telling all, telling all, "Jesus is born!"
Guarding, helping, granting, they bring peace on glowing wings.
They glitter and fly, giving the message from God:
Let peace be within.

Kelsey Aukerman, Grade 6
Melrose Elementary School

Our Flag

Pledge of allegiance,
Promise to be loyal,
Red, white, and blue,
Our flag.
Made in 1776,
Flown at the Lincoln Memorial,
Might be flying halfway down the pole,
To honor the dead,
Fifty stars for fifty states,
Our flag.

Michael Angelilli, Grade 4
Dobbins Elementary School

The Moon

The moon of many shapes
As it changes
From phase to phase
The moon of joyfulness
As it puts joy
Into your life
With its smile
The moon of memories
As it reminds you
Of those special times
When the moon was up.

Garrett Fisher, Grade 5
Cline Elementary School

Our School

School is cool, I'm pretty sure!
　Math is facts that are fun!
I'm pretty sure school is cool,
　Cause math facts rock!
I think this is pretty cool,
　Being in school.
Although I'm in fifth, that is kinda hard,
　I think it's ok though.
Well you know what I mean,
　About school and math.

Marla Nikki Nelson, Grade 5
West Elementary School

The Pond

The pond has flowing water
When the wind blows
Through the air
The pond can rise,
The pond can fall,
When it rains from the sky
Or when it evaporates above
The pond is swishing,
Splashing, swirling
When the fish move
Up and down.

Tyler Holsopple, Grade 5
Tremont Elementary School

10 Seconds

10 seconds…need to score.
9, 8, 7…need a touchdown.
Need six points to win.
6, 5, 4…need just six points
3, 2, 1…ball in the air.
0 seconds…
Score! We win!!!

Brenden Gubala, Grade 6
Trilby Elementary School

Fall

Fall is so pretty,
　vivid colors everywhere,
　trickling down from the trees.

Kids playing in the crunching leaves.
　Time is changing now,
　daylight is running short.

Pumpkin pie smells in the air,
　howling noises everywhere.
　Fall's the time for me!

McKenzie Stine, Grade 5
Immaculate Conception School

My Cat

My cat, Joe, is great,
Purring…
Like an engine,
Curls up on my bed
He is my favorite pet.

Lily Morris, Grade 4
Indian Springs Elementary School

Thanksgiving Day

When it's Thanksgiving Day,
All the turkeys run away.
When the leaves keep falling down,
Everyone throws the football around.

When we eat the turkey beast,
We all enjoy the holiday feast.
After dinner is pumpkin pie,
It tastes so good my oh my.

We went outside to rake the leaves,
We saw there weren't many on the trees.
When we saw leaves on the ground,
Everyone started throwing them around.

We went inside and sat down,
When we said bye, we had a frown.
Now it's time to go to bed,
I laid right down and rest my head.

Jessica Vonderau, Grade 6
Kinsner Elementary School

Alive and Real

Tigers sleep in their den.
Then they come out.
Their fur is so cool.
Tigers go hunting.
Hide in a clump of grass.
Be very quiet.
Then POUNCE!
The prey goes down.

Jake Adkins, Grade 6
Woodward Park Middle School

The Ocean Blue

The sun is on my face,
There are butterflies to chase,
Today is great in every way.

Watching the clock,
I was on the dock,
When the trees started to sway.

Although I tried,
To watch the tide,
This was a game I couldn't play.

Bethany Haggy, Grade 6
Harmon Middle School

John

John
Cheerful, kind
Telling, talking, annoying
I love video games
Loving

John Lesneski, Grade 6
Jefferson Elementary School

Blaze Burr

Blaze Burr
Silent, cold
Looking, listening, freezing
He loves the woods.
Hunter

Blaze Burr, Grade 6
Jefferson Elementary School

Shadows

Shadows creep,
Shadows crawl,
Shadows walk upon the wall,
Without fear of taking a fall.

When the sun sets,
At the end of each day,
They must leave,
Unable to play.

Alex Hannah, Grade 5
Norwich Elementary School

I Don't Want to Go to School

I don't want to go to school. Not one bit.
I don't want to go to school. I have a big zit.
But if you don't go you will not grow.
And if you don't go it won't show.
But what about gym?
I'll go take a swim.
But what about art?
I'll paint a colorful dart.
What about social studies, science or language arts?
I'll make up a story and study about carts.
If you really don't want to go that's o.k.
And just to let you know it's Saturday.

Jack Plasket, Grade 5
Barrington Elementary School

Trees

The perfect, genteel machine, you can rely on is a tree.
A tree is an active, delicate calendar:
spring is here when tiny buds peek out,
and when snow is terrified of perishing
A tree welcomes summer as it whispers to its flowers,
to bloom and its leaves to turn emerald green
Autumn gains its fame by painting a tree's leaves,
ruby red, straw gold, and tangerine
It is winter when a tree is inactive and still,
and when it wears ornaments and is cloaked with lights
A tree is a rich, magnificent creator:
Living things feast on its flavorful fruits
It produces advantageous wood used for copious situations
We couldn't live without the clean, fresh air a tree makes.
A tree is an inspiration for artists:
Its beauty encourages them to paint admirable paintings.
The factory of Earth would not manufacture, would not work,
without the most marvelous machines:
Trees.

Sam Kang, Grade 5
Cline Elementary School

Color

Purple is cool as can be,
Grey is spiffy, if you ask me.

Red shows love and longtime peace,
White is the color of Christmas fleece.

If you care for me, send flowers of pink,
Black is not a color, or so you may think.

Shocking hair is that of bright blue,
Yet, silver doesn't have a clue!

Gold is a lovely ring,
Brown is quite odd, the poor thing.
Colors bring imagination to life.

Laura West, Grade 6
Roosevelt Elementary School

Thanksgiving

When it is Thanksgiving,
I thank God that I am living.
We go over our cousin's house to celebrate,
We eat tons of turkey, it is great.

After the turkey we eat pumpkin pie,
It is so good, I swear I can fly.
We always watch football after we eat,
And watch one team get beat.

When leaves rustle on the ground,
You know it's very cheerful all around.
Every Thanksgiving turkeys get sad,
And think what a life they had.

Seeing your family is always so nice,
We play lots of games that include dice.
Thanksgiving is always so fun,
Till next year, I will miss it a ton.

Jordan Sedivy, Grade 6
Kinsner Elementary School

Cookie Moon

The moon is like a cookie
Some times on a plate with crumbs
Sometimes almost gone
Sometimes being dipped in milk
Sometimes he disappears
Sometimes he goes away for a night
Coming back a little silver
There are so many types of cookies and moons
But there's only one, cookie moon.

Brian Urbanic, Grade 5
Cline Elementary School

Fall

Leaves fall like rain on a stormy day
All stacked up for kids to play.
Reds, oranges, browns, and golds
All the leaves begin to blow in the wind all so cold.
Fall is fun with friends and family.

Bonfires flames are all so bright
Families gather around the light.
Its smoke is a stormy cloud,
The crowd's laughter is also loud.
Fall is fun with friends and family.

Every smell is oh so sweet
Pulling your nose over to see
Turkey, pie, candy, and burning leaves.
Sipping sweet cider that smells like apple pie,
Fall is fun with friends and family.

Tyler Vermilion, Grade 4
Fairfield Elementary School

The Spelling Bee

Spell ignition,
Can I have a definition?
Setting on fire,
Hard word,
I am no liar,
I-g-n-i-t-i-o-n,
Yes!
I am the best!

My turn again,
Spell hypothesis,
I know what this is,
H-y-p-o-t-h-i-s-i-s,
Ding!
Oh no!
E-s not i-s,
This is a mess,
But have no fear,
There is always next year!

Emily Hoersten, Grade 6
Holy Angels School

Gerbils

Oh, gerbils,
You're fun to keep.
You're soft and cute
And you don't make a peep!

Long whiskers and
A fluffy tail
Some are dark and
Some are pale!

Timidly, you eat
From my hand.
You run on your wheel;
You don't hear commands!

You nibble and chew
And build a nest.
You frolic and sleep.
Truly, you're the best!

Juliet Freed, Grade 6
Melrose Elementary School

Mistletoe

I hang above the people below,
They come in tracking snow,
They look at each other with a glance,
Then it is a big romance,
The next boy and girl look up and smile,
Their eyes meet and then beguile,
I am the mistletoe hanging above,
Who will bring everyone love!

Anna Schumm, Grade 6
Glenwood Middle School

The Haunted House

There's a haunted house at the end of Logan Lane.
(That's what locals say.)
I don't know what to think — whether the house is haunted or not.
As I scamper down the damp street, I stop to pick a sunflower —
some big flower, indeed. I play "Haunted or Not."
Why? I don't know which to choose.
The flower says, "Not" to me, so why can't I drop in?
As I spring into Logan Lane, my heart thumps, my brain gets lost,
but my rubbery body keeps frolicking.
The door of the haunted house was very close, indeed.
I tell myself, "Don't get scared."
But my brain is just not listening.
As I slowly open doors, a peculiar creaking sound is heard.
My heart is racing faster, I think I have a headache.
Someone, please do something.
Why did I stagger into this mess anyway?
Then, I feel a sudden chill as I walk into the great room.
Something tugs at my shoulder —
Augh! And I'm gone.
Too bad I didn't look back — it was just the neighbor's cat.

Seokhyeon Ryu, Grade 6
Melrose Elementary School

The Warrior Spirit of the Moon

The new moon a pitch black marble that sets in the dark night sky
With a shining glare until the darkness disappears
The phases are evolving as a powerful warrior
With new shining and flaring armor
Increasing with each phase, it goes through the phases
Then fierce waxing crescent, 1 quarter, and waxing gibbous
Develop its wings with flaring and armor shining
Then the waning crescent, 3 quarter, and gibbous
And develops its sword with hot lava oozing on the sword
Then success the ultimate phase the FULL MOON!
When all the phases are completed
The power that was waited to be unleashed unleashes
With invincible power for great leadership
Also for the common good of the world!

Arnold Vo, Grade 5
Cline Elementary School

Cheerleading

C ompete like nobody's watching you
H erkie, varsity, pike just jump high
E ven stunt and fly to the sky
E xtension double-down you get a 10
R eally tumble like never before, don't do a back flip do a back full
L ayouts are good too let's just see what you can do
E very day going to practice really pays off
A t every practice and every competition make sure you give 115%
D on't ever slack off and get hurt
I love the sport it is very fun
N ever ever do less than your best
G et a 10 on stunts, tumbling, dance, and cheer!!

Taylor Reidel, Grade 6
Harmon Middle School

July Fourth
It starts like an ordinary summer day.
Hot, sunny, humid
Not much to do
Just hang around and cool off under the fan
Near nighttime, we are in a hurry to eat and go.
We drive through the traffic
Lots of slow moving cars
Like a turtle race.
Playing hide and seek, looking for a parking space near the area we want to be.
Dashing through the parking lot searching for a patch of soft grass
To roll out our blanket to wait and watch
Sometimes we listen to music and toss our inflatable beach ball while we wait.
All near and far gather around to watch this show
And then it starts with a bang and boom with red, blue, and yellow in the dark sky.
The colors are like rockets which explode, shower and sparkle down…
We celebrate this holiday for many reasons,
But we rejoice for this day for freedom.
Boom! Ka-bam!
Freedom!

Greg Ota, Grade 5
EH Greene Intermediate School

Christmas Dance
Every snowy Christmas Eve
With white powder on my window,
I hopefully press my head against my door in the lonely pitch-black
To maybe catch a snip of a song, a glance of a dance,
For Christmas has come
So it's time for the Christmas dance,
The branches sway, twinkling in the light,
Teetering in anticipation, laughing softly and playing with my senses
Telling me that they're alive,
The ornaments surfaces are hard and cold
Why? I ponder, I don't get an answer,
But instead a feeling that they, too have fun,
Doing a dance so strong and clear. I hear the rhythm in my head, in sweet 3/4 time.
Then, spinning and grinning they invite me to join in their holiday merriment
But I refuse, instead turning to the shining gifts,
They ever so quietly sing, uttering soft falsetto notes
That tell me of that night in a tiny stable.
They, too invite me to join their caroling, and this time I accept
I twirl and whirl, rejoicing for what occurred this night so many years ago,
When my Savior was born, was born,
Was born.

Allison Rogge, Grade 5
EH Greene Intermediate School

A Comfy Day
What makes a comfy day? Laying on the coach, sun, beaming out my windows. What makes a comfy day? A pet, crawling into my arms, begging for a kiss and affection. What makes a comfy day? A family member, lighting scented candles. Smelling berries, oils, and maybe even pine. What makes a comfy day? Ending with taking a hot bubble bath. Your bed calling you to lie down. Your eyes may just close, but not yet asleep. You listen to all the noises around you. Soon enough, you have had that comfy day.

Julia Deems, Grade 6
Rocky River Middle School

Tall and Small
Tall and small
Very different,
Yet very much the same.
Tall is large,
And small is tiny
But if you put 'em together
They can turn out smart
It doesn't matter which
It just matters about the brain,
And the heart, and the care
Of a person,
Not their height.
William Gray, Grade 5
Tremont Elementary School

A Dog Named Chewie
I have a dog named Chewie,
He fell down and went "Kablewie,"
Nothing broke his fall,
Except a brick wall
And now his name is broken Louie!
Erika Irwin, Grade 6
Roosevelt Elementary School

Count on Me
Count on me
As I guide you
To strength and courage
Trustworthy and honesty
To see cause and effect

Count on me
As I help you
Reach out and find
Passion and heart
be brave to stand up
Be bold and obey
Count on me.
Ben Corr, Grade 5
Cline Elementary School

My First Basketball Game
I love basketball
The sound of the ball hitting the floor
The sound of the locker room door
The feeling I feel right now
Is the best one around town
The smell of candy and chips
Cheerleaders shaking their hips
And when the clock hits zero
There can only be one hero
The game is over by my love isn't
I want to go to another game
Maybe even the Hall of Fame
Colt Caughenbaugh, Grade 4
Licking Valley Intermediate School

Fall
The fall breeze is brisk
When I go outside to play
I play in the leaves
I never wear a jacket
But I will never catch a cold
Austin Walker, Grade 5
Harmon Middle School

Bubblegum
Bubblegum
Pink, sticky
Chewing, Blowing, popping
Small, delicious, tasty treat
Bubble Yum
Paige Green, Grade 6
Pike Delta York Middle School

Trumpet
T ransformed
R hythms of your life
U ntempted to
M atch up to
P ersonal
E nchanted
T houghts.
Logan Miller, Grade 6
Melrose Elementary School

Freedom Isn't Free
Freedom isn't free,
People fight for us every day.
We sit down and then we see
Why freedom isn't free.

We walk on and buy,
Buy things we don't need.
Then we sit down and wonder why,
Why freedom isn't free.

But I walk on and pray.
For this land and others.
For the troops every day.
I then pray that freedom becomes free.
Sean Cannon, Grade 6
Woodward Park Middle School

Winter and Summer
Winter
cold, frigid
snowing, sledding, skiing
ice, snow, flowers, trees
swimming, playing, jumping
warm, torrid
Summer
Aislynn Stocks, Grade 5
Northfield Baptist Christian School

Parts of Speech
A sport,
interesting and exciting,
harms and fulfills,
physically.
Entertainment.
Caden White, Grade 6
Harmon Middle School

Love Yourself
Down the street children shout hey,
And you sit there, still as clay.
Gloomy times will wash away,
Let go of the past, that's what I say.
Love will come.

Some are sorrowful, like you, not me,
Maybe you won't be tomorrow.
Just calm down, emerge from your shell.
Try and find love, reach for the stars.
Love will come.

Come follow me, and find your destiny.
Love the world, it will love you back
Love will come

Full of feeling, some call me coward,
But I'm sensitive, never sour.
Dreary days will drift away.
Love will come, love will come.
Rachael Bucey Leopold, Grade 6
Harding Middle School

New Year's Day
The neighborhood is full,
Of excited, impatient, eager people.
People waiting for
The new year, the new start.
It's finally come,
The night of New Year's Eve.
New York is dark,
But Times Square is bright and full,
Of horns and whistles,
Ringing in the new year, the new start.
And all the people,
Like little children sitting around
A Christmas tree,
Eagerly wait for a glistening sphere
To drop…
It's here,
New Year's day.
The tired, sleepy, overstuffed people
Write their resolutions.
For it is finally
The new year, the new start.
Joseph Ahn, Grade 5
EH Greene Intermediate School

Sleigh Horse

Clip-clop, clip-clop, clip-clop,
My hooves make a merry sound,
Stepping across the sparkling snow,
The bells are ringing, the rascals are singing,
Flakes in flurries, floating to the forest,
My fuzzy coat is cold, but I don't care,
This is the time for me.

Emily Nesbitt, Grade 6
Glenwood Middle School

Autumn

In autumn when leaves fall
They are bright as a disco ball
I like to rake all the leaves
And there is always a nice cold breeze
I wonder if there is a leaf that is blue
I'll just ask my teacher tomorrow at school
It's fun to play during autumn at recess
You find all kinds of things, even leaf pieces
Autumn is when the report cards come
If my parents see bad grades I may have to run!

Anthony Georgopoulos, Grade 6
Akiva Academy

Goodbye

Best of luck, my dear friend.
Please don't fear things aren't the end.
It doesn't matter if you'll be
A noble king or here with me.
Yes, no more walking side by side.
And to you I've never lied.
Here's a lesson. Don't forget.
For if you do you'll soon regret.
Joy, a giver brings,
To those who look on the bright side of things.
Always look for the silver lining.
Come on my friend, there's no denying.
Best of luck, may you be bright joy
I think I've even begun to cry.
For these are words that I will wish I had never said,
Goodbye.

Madalyn Rymer, Grade 6
Kinsner Elementary School

Terrific Thanksgiving Day

I wake up and think Thanksgiving thoughts
I smell some turkey and tater tots
Deviled eggs and seasoned dressing
Gravy, green beans — what a blessing.
Pecan, pumpkin, and apple pie,
Can't decide which delectable dish to try.
Family, friends — oh, so fun
Don't want this delightful day to be done.

John Weldon, Grade 6
Tippecanoe Middle School

Seal

Look at the baby seal,
Out there in the cold.
Did he have a nice meal,
Or was it full of mold.

Here comes his friend,
Sliding out on the ice.
With big flippers and a smile,
He looks very nice.

It looks like they're having fun,
Swimming and playing out in the sun.
They played until night,
And not once did they fight.

Outside is now dark,
And the day is done.
They went to bed,
And tomorrow they'll have even more fun!

Michael Yanetta, Grade 6
Kinsner Elementary School

Tinkerbell

My dog thinks she's a kid like me
But she's as furry as can be
While we're walking she bites our toes
She has the cutest nose
She's the sweetest dog you ever could see.

Erin Housley, Grade 5
Rootstown Elementary School

Waterfall

Shimmering in the morning's sun,
you are there to greet me when I awake.
I swim and splash in you
whenever I can and drink from your glistening water.
I cry when I have to leave you,
but you help me fall asleep
when the moon's light shines on your calming water.
The next morning comes and the cycle is reborn.

Micayla Carafelli, Grade 6
Melrose Elementary School

Warm Front

W andering owls during the night
A feeling of summer
R unning gracefully
M arching in lines

F un in the night
R ecord breaking temperatures in the day and night
O wls like the warmer temperatures
N ot until
T he cold front comes through

Michael Wing, Grade 5
Sanderson Elementary School

The Smallest Bird
Flying like a hawk
Speeding like the fastest plane
Is the humming bird
Dylan Reis, Grade 5
Elyria Community School

Repetition
Oh, repetition
Repetition, repetition,
It's words, words, words,
That are always, always,
Repeating, repeating, repeating,
Oh! Oh! Oh! Oh! Oh!
It it makes my very, very,
Confused, confused,
Head, head, head,
Begin to spin, spin, spin,
Oh! Repetition,
And this poem, poem will just
Keep repeating, repeating, repeating,
Until I stop, stop, stop it, so
I will just dot, dot, dot it…
Eliza Steffen, Grade 4
Indian Springs Elementary School

Little Mouse
Pumpkin
Pumpkin,
Lighting the house,
For that single but little gray mouse.
He scurries the house,
In his little white blouse.
When skeletons pop out,
He scurries on out.
Pumpkin
Pumpkin.
Michael Dolan, Grade 5
Elyria Community School

Fred the Hip Hop Zombie
Fred the hip hop zombie
Is the nicest zombie you'll meet.
Whenever you make him happy
Just look down at his feet.

He will do the Electric Slide
He will do the Floppy Worm
He will do the Funky Chicken
You just gotta watch him squirm.

He will go dancing through the night.
He will go dancing through the day.
His dancing is enchanting.
But he always makes you pay.
Alexander Pairan, Grade 5
Spaulding Elementary School

Cookies
Looks like round dough smiley faces
Sounds like the oven dinging
Taste like chocolaty sugary things
Smells delicious and chocolaty
Feels squishy, soft, and chewy
Halle Sobiech, Grade 5
Northfield Baptist Christian School

Me
N ickname is Pumpkin
I nvincible I feel
C omforts people when lonely
O utstanding effort at math
L ikes oranges
E xtraordinary girl

A bstract at art
N ever the girl you hope for
N icest girl you ever met

D addy's baby girl
E xcellent at drawing
S hopping is my favorite
A nimals are cute
N icest teacher I have
T rying is a good thing, never stop
I like to ride my bike
S anta's helper
Nicole Ann DeSantis, Grade 5
Frank Ohl Middle School

Fish
Fishes swimming in the water
Around and around.
They are so colorful,
They make no sound.
Orange, black, brown and blue
There are so many things they can do.
Purple, gray, yellow and red
They are fragile just like thread.
Liz Makley, Grade 4
Northfield Elementary School

Apples
Apples are red, yellow, and green.
They pull out teeth.
They are so good.
Taylor Pelsoczi, Grade 4
Northfield Elementary School

Starlight
Stars shine bright at night
Shimmering high up in space
Lightening the path
Gabrielle Mahuet, Grade 6
EH Greene Intermediate School

Can You Imagine
A world without school
No water in a pool

A naked mole rat with hair
Lambs lying down with a bear

Rabbits that can bark
Cars that can't park

A party with no double dippers
Horses wearing four slippers

Musical scales without doe
Winter without snow?
Derek Stallard, Grade 6
Wooster Christian School

Anger
Anger is a box of abhorrence.
Anger is a memory of dislike.
Anger is the season of winter.
Anger remembers everything.
Anger is the touch of death.
Anger tastes sour.
Anger dreams of hate.
Anger is the shape of a broken heart.
Maison Steyer, Grade 6
Old Fort Elementary School

Nature's Like Us
The night sky has the moon
as our head has a brain.
The moon is shining like
the knowledge we know.
Our knowledge is like our
personality coming to life.
Kaylynn King, Grade 6
Woodward Park Middle School

I Don't Understand
I don't understand…
Why it's cold outside
Why is the sky blue
Why do we have animals.

But most of all…
Why does it get dark
Why do we get old
Why do we die.

What I understand most is…
Why we go to school
Why it rains
Why we have rules.
Thomas Iha, Grade 5
Becker Elementary School

High Merit Poems – Grades 4, 5, and 6

Chuck and the Christmas Leprechaun

Chuck was opening present on Christmas day.
Inside the box was a game he could play.
It was a magical game that only he could see.
He had to wear special glasses and a hat.
So he put them on and counted to three.

All of a sudden he got very cold.
And the next thing he knew he was very old.
He found himself in a shop that was not ordinary.
It was Santa's shop and was extraordinary.

He saw a weird person.
Dressed in green.
He was short and jolly
And holding a hot tamale.

The short green man asked Chuck some questions.
Do you like Snickers or Skittles?
He didn't get most of them.
Because they were all riddles.

He let Chuck go home.
With a present that was very cool.
He got home with plenty to tell.
Nobody believed him and they thought he was a fool.

Anthony Rubino, Grade 6
Rocky River Middle School

Red

Red is everywhere yo go
There's rosy when your cheeks are aglow
I see auburn from leaves falling through the sky
I see scarlet when I watch the beloved Buckeyes

There is cherry-red and berry
The color of red can vary
There's maroon, ruby, and wine
That shows that red is so divine

If you swim in the ocean you can see coral red
You may like crimson red instead
You see cardinal red above
Red is the color of true love

Kamryn Ross, Grade 6
Harmon Middle School

Go Tribe!

Indians
Tribe time, winners
Scoring, beating, hardworking
World Series, Jacobs Field, Sizemore, Sabathia
Winning, sliding, jumping,
Awesome, beat team
Winners

Nina Nardi, Grade 4
Northfield Elementary School

Fall Is Here

The leaves rustle in the air,
You can tell that fall is here!

You hear the wind blow through the trees,
Say good-bye to bumblebees!

So much color everywhere,
You can tell that fall is here!

All the leaves fall, one by one,
Let's jump in them; it's so much fun!

We're getting close to a new year,
You can tell that fall is here!

It's time to Trick-or-Treat tonight,
The full moon looks very bright!

Is it scary? I don't care!
All I know is, fall is here!

Lexi McCormick, Grade 6
Tippecanoe Middle School

Cheerleading

When you cheer you have fun
You have to get exercise and run

When you jump and do pikes
There is a show that everyone likes

Everyone on the team likes to tumble
This makes the floor give a rumble

There is a mount called a bow and arrow
You wear a uniform and a cute hair bow

I like to make up cheers somehow
After I show my friends and take a bow

Taylor Lachey, Grade 6
Holy Angels School

Midnight Mystery

I hear the sound of footsteps downstairs.
The scratching and banging
Running and climbing coming up the stairs.
The breathing so heavy and getting so near.
I start to whimper and my eyes fill with tear,
Afraid of the shadow that will soon appear.
It's getting closer, the running is faster,
I tremble with fear as I face disaster.
I hide under the covers only to discover,
The object I fear jumps on my bed,
And turns out to be, my little dog Fred.

Elizabeth Johnson, Grade 6
EH Greene Intermediate School

Spring Is Here!
Birds are chirping in my ear,
Letting me know spring is here!
I'm running around with the sun in my face,
Without the snow, there's so much more space!
I see kids riding their bikes in the woods,
And along the roads of my neighborhood.
I look up at the blue sky — it's so clear,
That lets me know that spring is here!
Meghan Murphy, Grade 5
Norwich Elementary School

When Winter Is Fun
Winter is a time of fun
When the snow is white like crystals
We get on our sleds and then run
As the snow shines like silver pistols

Please don't eat the snow when it's yellow
That wouldn't be good
Because you won't be a lucky fellow

Find a hill that's high and fast
Your sled will run as smooth as a whistle
Push your sled, don't be last
As the snow shines like silver pistols.
Jenna Callahan, Grade 5
Wintersville Elementary School

Yellow
When I am yellow I feel mellow.
Yellow feels like it's just a happy normal day.
Yellow makes me feel like a simple young fellow.
Yellow is a cello.
A cello is quite peaceful just like yellow.
Yellow is the sun.
The sun is fun but also silent.
A yield sign is yellow.
Yield means slow and pay attention.
Yellow is slow just like the flow.
Jorge Naciff, Grade 6
St John the Baptist School

Wind Blew Hard
The wind whispers to my ear
as the sun
shone down
the grass
is so green
the wind
blew hard
and I felt
it was a
dream.
Estella Martinez, Grade 6
Woodward Park Middle School

The Pumpkin Lady
There was a lady who lived in a mill
She watered her pumpkins at quarter 'til.
Her pumpkins were the best in town,
And if you ate her pumpkin pie you'd never frown.
She was growing very old.
"She'll die this year," her kids were told.
Her daughter Ann was very sad.
She thought "This will be the last pie I ever had."
Then had a wonderful dream.
"We'll sell her pies and yummy whipped cream!"
The lady and Ann worked for weeks
Making pies that were so fine and sleek.
At last their hard labor was done,
And they had a big party just for fun.
Those were the best days of her life, but we knew she would die,
So when you eat pumpkin pie, think of the old lady named Mrs. Nye.
Bailey Flora, Grade 6
Tippecanoe Middle School

Vermont
I love you Vermont
You have clean air and mountains.
You have the most beautiful mountains and creatures.
You have miniature animals, but huge ones too.
Yes, you have it all.
You are one of the best states in the USA.
I still love you, even though a bear broke into Uncle Sean's house
And chipmunks invaded Grandma's house.

It makes me delighted to be in such a beautiful environment.
You also receive enormous amounts of snow each winter.
We can play in it and do anything.
Finally, you have my mom's family.

The top reasons I love you are because every time I come
You create new memories.
Despite your small size, you have the best things —
Dunkin Donuts, "The Wurst Place in Town," sledding hills,
The Green Mountain Railroad,
And family.
Thomas Gaier, Grade 6
Tippecanoe Middle School

The Indigo Sky
The pearl white moon against the dark indigo sky.
The gold shimmering stars surrounding the moon.
The house lights going off to state that it is officially nighttime,
The bats, the owls, and the raccoons coming outside
saying that it is officially their daytime, and going to catch their prey.
The noisy wind keeps blowing as if never out of breath.
The soft pitter patter of the rain helps all of the people get to sleep.
Slowly the bright sun rises out of the horizon, and the moon goes to bed.
The owls, the bats, and the raccoons go into their nesting area,
as the people come out of theirs ready for a new day to come!
Cara McCarthy, Grade 5
Cline Elementary School

High Merit Poems – Grades 4, 5, and 6

Memories

Memories are precious times spent with
people held close to you
like a small baby toy

Memories are like a window
you look through and you remember
all of the great times spent with friends and family

Memories are important times to remember
a memory is something from long ago
something warm like a cup of soup
something special
a memory can be something silly
something that makes you laugh
memories can also be sad or disappointing
like someone close to you passing away

Memories can also be exciting and cheerful
like getting together with your friends
or having a birthday surrounded by people
that care for you

All these precious times in your life called
MEMORIES

Emily Whittaker, Grade 5
Cline Elementary School

While the Candles Burn

While the candles burn and flicker,
As the fire faintly crackles,
Dad and I try to spin dreidels upside-down
Trying to win the sugary chocolate coins,
As we also eat them,
Joyful songs being sung being joined by
Gasping and laughter while the lighting was
As dim as dusk from the candles glimmering in
The window.

Why, Oh, why can't this joyful holiday last longer?
While the candles burn
While the candles burn
While the candles burn.

Allison Nemoff, Grade 5
EH Greene Intermediate School

Halloween to Easter

Halloween
Pumpkins, beggars' night
Scaring, trick-or-treating, exciting
Costumes, candy, Easter bunny, chocolate
Coloring eggs, hunting, eating
Chicks, lambs
Easter

Kayla Rinker, Grade 6
Tippecanoe Middle School

Jingles

A little stuffed cat in a raggedy purple shirt
sleeps on my shoulder.

Feeling the worn white fur on her small paws
comforts me when I'm scared.

When it is time for bed,
together we walk up stairs and jump under the covers.

We talk for awhile,
then I whisper "good night."

I fall asleep thinking how lucky I am
to have a furry friend like Jingles

Emily Sewall, Grade 5
Cline Elementary School

Be Thankful

You are lucky.
You may not think so,
but you are.
Think hard
of what you have.

What don't other people have?
A house of warmth or food to eat
not even someone to visit with or to comfort them.
Be thankful for what you have.
It could be worse.

Todd Miller, Grade 6
Pike Delta York Middle School

Jesus Is Our Christmas

After all the events that happen every year,
Comes a special holiday full of happiness and cheer.
Upon this night a baby was born,
Jesus we call him — our Savior, our Lord.
We think of Christmas as a present giving time,
And nothing but wrapping paper and rhyme.
Jesus came to save us,
From sin, the unwanted must,
And people everywhere have learned to trust.
Greeting family and friends are lots of fun,
Putting on plays and concerts that our teachers run.
They're sometimes about Santa, sometimes fictional stories,
But the ones I like to hear are about Jesus' glory.
So much can happen while in this state of mind,
Good things, like Jesus, are always the right kind.
Don't get me wrong about our artificial trees and lights,
But if you come to know Jesus, your life will be bright.
He'll save a place in Heaven for you,
And Christmas is the time to start over — become new.
So think about it, and pray with all your might,
"Merry Christmas to all, and to all a good night!"

Madison Wells, Grade 6
Canaan Middle School

The Listening of Peace
peace is a season of Spring,
peace sounds like
birds singing
smooth,
peace is the shape of a smile,
peace is the
month of
April,
peace feels like freedom,
peace is
a dance of
ballerina,
peace looks like flowers blooming
Taylor Miller, Grade 6
Old Fort Elementary School

Changes and Phases
Fly away
To the soul
Of Mother Nature
From one sky
To another sky
Through the clouds
And under the stars
From morning
To night
Always coming
Back from
The dream land
The moon
Filling our world
With more potential
Madeléine Sanders, Grade 5
Cline Elementary School

Autumn
Every fall we turn on FOX
It's the middle of football
Start of basketball
The fall classic is on
the leaves are different shades
Jumping in leaves
Autumn, Oh! What Fun!
Zaeem Mustafa, Grade 6
Birchwood School

Siblings
I'm in the middle
of a little sister
and older brother
sometimes we fight
sometimes we play
we put aside our differences
and have fun together!
Taylor Whitman, Grade 5
Tremont Elementary School

Phases and Changes
Phases
Are what the moon
Goes through
It changes
Night by night
Just like me
The cycle starts
On the right
And it grows
And grows
Until the moon
Is full
As round
As a bright
Yellow ball
But then
The moon
Gradually lessens
On the right
'Till it is nothing
But a hair
Monica Yen, Grade 5
Cline Elementary School

Blue
Blue is the color of the sky
Blue is the color in a rainbow
When I am sad I think of blue
When its cold outside I turn blue
Some eyes are the color of blue
Blue is on some shoes
Blue is the color of some pens
Blue is beautiful
Blue is the color of a swimming pool
This is why I think blue is cool
Carly Speed, Grade 6
St John the Baptist School

Beautiful Birds
Birds chirping loudly
Flying in the big blue sky
Landing for a worm
Dionte Hudson, Grade 6
EH Greene Intermediate School

Myrtle Beach
Windy, hot
First day of July
Afternoon
Calm, waves, kids splashing
Shells, suds, crabs
Swimming, running
This July
Happy, tired
Daniel Staub, Grade 6
Tippecanoe Middle School

Black
Black is the sky at night.
You get a *black* eye in a fight.
Black like a bat.
Bad luck with a *black* cat.
Black in your hair.
Black is everywhere.
Black ink is real nice.
Black dots are on dice.
Black in the dark.
Can you see *black* in the park?
Black crayons *black* hats.
You even see *black* mats.
We call it *black*.
French call it *noir*.
Can you think of any more?
Black with no light.
Black on a kite.
Evan Wethington, Grade 6
St John the Baptist School

Leslie*
When I first saw you
I thought you were weird.
At recess you raced with the boys
You certainly weren't coy!
When I got to know you
You were smart, imaginative, and fun.
We made Terabithia
Prince Terrian, Leslie and Me.
We swung on the rope
To get to our land.
Where we ruled happily
Till that terrible day.
You left to heaven
Where I will meet again someday.
Elina Huculak, Grade 6
EH Greene Intermediate School
**Inspired by the book*
"Bridge to Terabithia"
by Katherine Paterson

Summer Day
I run and I play out on a summer day.
I jump in the pool.

On a summer day there is only one rule:
Never, ever, ever go to school.
Sara Woika, Grade 5
Stanton Middle School

My Sister Is Crazy
My sister is the color blue
because she used the glue
to get the flu.
Callie Jones, Grade 4
Greenfield Elementary School

Freedom
F ree to make the decisions in your life
R ight to drink out of the same drinking fountain
E agle is our sign of freedom
E ducation that is provided
D ecisions you are able to make
O pportunities you have to make a better world
M emories of veterans and soldiers that fought for our freedom
Olivia Slater, Grade 5
Sanderson Elementary School

Dogs
Dogs are funny
Sometimes they chase a bunny
Dogs are a house pet
They don't like going to the vet.

Dogs are cool
Dogs can be big or small
Dogs can be short or tall
Dogs can go to doggy school

Dogs attract a crowd
People walk their dogs
Their barks are loud
Sometimes I see strays laying by logs.

Dogs have their own food
They learn tricks
And they give you licks
Sometimes they can be very rude.

Dogs are very smart
They love their owners with a big heart
Dogs have a wide variety of names
Owners even let their dogs play with games.
Kallie Wilson, Grade 6
Kinsner Elementary School

Blue
Blue is the color of the sky,
Blue is the color of the water,
And you ask me why.
Sapphire, turquoise, many different kinds of blue,
Aqua is my favorite, how about you?
Brown, purple, yellow, and white,
Those are all good colors,
But mine's just right.
Emily Richter, Grade 6
St John the Baptist School

My Step-Dad and My Cat
My step-dad's face was as pale as can be
as soon as he saw our cat in the top of a tree
and then my cat fell down how silly is he.
Evan Mesnard, Grade 4
Greenfield Elementary School

Kiwi
You're a small green golf ball.
With an old "raggy" feeling.
As I peel you, you sound like cheese melting in the oven.
Inside you look like fireworks bursting with black pencil points.
When I feel you, you're as slimy as a worm,
But you exploded in my mouth with a sweet and sour taste.
Stephanie Heimbach, Grade 5
Dr John Hole Elementary School

Strong and Agile
I am strong and agile
I wish to be a pro lacrosse player
I am engaged when the other team has the ball
I hear the crowd's thunderous roar
I can feel my legs throbbing because of exhaustion
I am strong and agile.

I pretend to intercept the ball
I feel as if my arms are on fire
I touch the crowd as they give me high fives
I worry that my team will not be in the finals
I cry when I get called a loser
I am strong and agile.

I understand that you do not win every time but I try too
I say I will be fair to my teammates and coaches
I dream to go pro and be famous
I try to play my hardest and to give one hundred percent
I hope the other team will be good sports
I am strong and agile.
Tyler Bieker, Grade 5
Sanderson Elementary School

Ohio State Buckeyes
O n task, all the time
H urls very fine
I ncites never let them down
O utstanding, I never have a doubt

S tate we live in
T ackle, it's perfection
A jersey was made every ten to thirteen years
T eam is cheered by lots of cheers
E veryone mostly loves 'em

B ecame a team in 1891
U nstoppable and ranked number one
C hocolate draped around peanut butter
K ept Michigan out of the end zone
E nters every game with good sportsmanship
Y ou should like them too
E arly teams wore varsity union suits
S ix Ohio State players have won seven Heisman trophies
Alexa L. Thompson, Grade 5
Frank Ohl Middle School

Secrets

Secrets are memories of a friend.
Secrets are the month of October.
Secrets are like a song and dance.
Secrets dream of people.
Secrets feel like and look like disasters.
Stephanie Simon, Grade 6
Old Fort Elementary School

Kaczmarczyk

K indly treat people
A mazing
C ool
Z ero bad people in the family
M any good times
A wesome
R ight every time
C alm family
Z ero drama people
Y ou can come anytime you want
K now how to be good
Nicoletta Kaczmarczyk, Grade 4
Northfield Elementary School

Football

Drops back to pass
He throws it very far
He finally caught it…goodbye
Touchdown!
Jordan Herald, Grade 5
Wintersville Elementary School

Autumn Orange

Color me orange
Like a jack-o'-lantern,
And the beautiful leaves in the front yard,
Like tasty apple cider
From the roadside produce stand.
Orange…the most beautiful color of fall!
Sara Weber, Grade 5
Westview Elementary School

Winter Dance

Freezing wind, blowing
On white, snowy days
Snowflakes are dancing.
Mayu Suzaki, Grade 6
Harmon Middle School

Stars

Stars so small
and how they twinkle.
They are bright
and look like big sprinkles.
I see them every night.
Abby Bevilacqua, Grade 5
Wintersville Elementary School

Happy Birthday, Granny!*

Here she is, resting in her favorite wicker chair in the sunroom
The warmth of the sun's rays fills the room and her rosy cheeks
I see a classy, wise woman, a historian, the keeper of our family history, the elder
As regal as a queen, sweet, but sometimes stubborn
She's popular, well-liked, trusted, because she is as real as the sun
Dad says she spoils my sister and me, her "angel children"
But I think it's a grandmother's job
She's full of memories
She's full of love
She's full of life and 85 years young.
Happy birthday Granny!
Michael Saxon, Grade 6
EH Greene Intermediate School
*Dedicated to my grandmother on her 85th birthday

Stars in the Night

Stars in the night, blink brightly.
Sometimes big, and sometimes small.
Sometimes they are dancing happily,
and sometimes still and sad.

When they are happy, they shine as crystals in the sky.
When they are gloomy, they show a dim light through the clouds.

My feelings are like stars; sometimes I am full of joy,
and sometimes I am just plain grumpy.
I stare at the stars, and they stare back at me,
like billions of eyes, wondering.
Jocelyn Liao, Grade 6
Birchwood School

Enjoying Christmas

The jolliest time of the year was here
It was the time when ornaments are shining like the sun
Rooms are bright and filled with cheer, Merry Christmas!
Time to eat Christmas breakfast we all felt excited
The warm yummy taste of cinnamon rolls filled my mouth
It was then time to open presents, Merry Christmas!
The colorful presents stood out of the huge pile
Gasps and laughter filled the room
The crinkling, crunching, shredding of paper filled my mind
The plucking of bows of presents were like crickets hopping
All the presents could fill an ocean, Merry Christmas!
In the background, Christmas carols played they were cheerful and happy
The songs filled my mind as I opened my last present
I was pleased this Christmas, Merry Christmas!
But still, questions were in my mind
Christmas tree, do you feel uncomfortable with ornaments hanging on you?
Chimney, can you feel Santa slowly trying to climb down you or can you not feel it?
No person could ever answer these
Just like that Christmas was over
It was done only once a year
Merry Christmas!!!!!
Ellen Martinson, Grade 5
EH Greene Intermediate School

High Merit Poems – Grades 4, 5, and 6

Ocean
As I walk along the beach, I gaze over my shoulder
and see the waves crashing up against the shore.
I turn to see a big whale flipping its tail to greet me.
But then I stop and stare at the sun setting, and I think:
What an amazingly beautiful sight!

Megan McCrossen, Grade 6
Melrose Elementary School

Christmas
Christmas is my favorite holiday
With the warm and soft cookies that crumble in my mouth
And the delicious, mouth watering ham
Also the squishy salty mashed potatoes
Christmas is my favorite holiday

With the green, red, and gold ornaments
And all the small, but bright lights
That shine as bright as 100 stars
But I wonder if they weigh too much for the tree
Christmas is my favorite holiday

I have on my fuzzy warm fleece
Wrapped in shiny, slippery wrapping paper
That makes me feel warm and cozy
Christmas is my favorite holiday

I feel joyful and happy inside
While I listen to the crackling of the fire
I can smell the savory, sweet ham roasting in the oven
Christmas is my favorite holiday

Olivia Wells, Grade 5
EH Greene Intermediate School

The Night Jesus Was Born
Jesus was born on Christmas night.
And all the animals were silent.

Mary was calm and content
With the babe in her arms.

Jesus was born on Christmas night.
And all the animals were silent.

Joseph was silently and proudly looking over the infant.

Jesus was born on Christmas night.
And all the animals were silent.

All the angels were rejoicing!
Singing songs of joy.

Jesus was born on Christmas night.
And all the animals were silent.

Alexis Webber, Grade 5
Wooster Christian School

Winter's at Bay
As Autumn diminishes and warmth finishes
we all come out and say, "winter's at bay, winter's at bay"
as the snow lay out on the icy bay
The sky is gray, the penguins play
as we all get ready for winter.

Zach Issa, Grade 6
Birchwood School

The Worst Year of School
It's the worst year of school in my life.
I don't know how I'm gonna survive
People are always being jerks
And I can't stand all of the work
At the end of the day when school is done
And people are all out having fun
I'm stuck here sitting in SACC
And I'm so bored that I might crack.

Stephen Davies, Grade 5
Tremont Elementary School

Mrs. Saltzman
Mrs. Saltzman is the nicest and the best teacher around
She still has time for fun, but we still have to learn.
She is the coolest, nicest, and the sweetest,
And she's the answer to my prayer.
She's kind of heart, and oh so pure.
She's the best above the rest.
She's a friend when I need her.
She's like the guardian angel I always wanted.
She's an angel on earth to me.
All I can say is, "THANK YOU."

Andrea Cole, Grade 5
Pike Christian Academy

School
Sometimes school is such a bore,
I could fall asleep and snore.
I watch and listen while learning,
And sometimes I am even yearning.

We do gym and music,
I may even get sick.
I sit in class in my chair,
The whole day I have to bear.

I can get in trouble,
I might get kind of mad.
I won't take it like a kid,
Because I won't be that bad.

I'm happy when the bell rings,
And go outside and hear when a bird sings.
I go home and then I'm glad,
But my homework makes me mad.

Brad Campbell, Grade 6
Kinsner Elementary School

Responsibility

Responsibility is including others,
Making your bed,
Doing your homework and
Not ripping
Your math test
To microscopic shreds
It's cooperating with friends
And helping
Your sibling in soccer camp
Responsibility is interdepending on
Your soccer team to defend
The goal
You need to be
Responsible by respecting
Yourself, others, and the world
And not smoking,
By not taking drugs,
And just saying NO!
At the right time
Responsibility is being bold
And standing up to bullies.

Christopher W. Jenkins, Grade 5
Cline Elementary School

My Favorite Season

My favorite season
Is summer
I like seeing races
of four-wheelers at
The fair
It feels warm outside
Which my mom likes
My rabbits that
Are special love the
Heat of the year
They play so much they
Can't play anymore

Rachel Welch, Grade 4
Licking Valley Intermediate School

Seasons Changing

Seasons are changing
With a chilly autumn breeze
To cold snowy months

Matt Bernstein, Grade 6
Harmon Middle School

Clouds

C razy little poof balls
L ike little hyper omplumps
O n and on floating away
U nable to stop
D rowning people in H2O
S ilently floating away

Mark Campbell, Grade 5
Sanderson Elementary School

Sky

The stars listen in on my dreams
The moon snores in his sleep
The sun takes a dip in the water too
They all live in the sky
The clouds float in the sky bouncy

McKenzie Thompson, Grade 6
Woodward Park Middle School

Friends

Friendly
With you when down
Forever there for you
Always looks out for you and pals
No price

Andrea Wiley, Grade 5
Stanton Middle School

Being Respectful

R eady to learn
E very day counts
S tupendous
P erfect
E xcellent
C oming to class on time
T alent

Antwan Robertson, Grade 6
Eastmoor Middle School

Cold Is Beauty

Talent singled into graphs,
Hanging in midair.
The new creation
Of gossamer silk,
Pleased by the
Eerie silence worshipping
The gate of death
For unfortunate insects.
A cold heart thumps
Within an ugly, creepy
Spider, alighting upon
A tender leaf to
Rest on the green victim
Who had fallen to the crisp, icy frost.
Gazing at her web,
Its silver streaks emphasized
By winter's purity, watching the world,
Menacing wicked beauty.

Hope Wang, Grade 6
EH Greene Intermediate School

Rainforest

I am a blue bird
in a large green rainforest
singing while it rains

Tyler Bowen, Grade 6
Harmon Middle School

My Pup, Princess

Princess is a wild pup.
Round and round she surely can run!
Chasing buses and having fun!
Princess is a white Jack Russell,
With Brett's dog, Nick, she tussles,
Coming and going, she strikes again,
Having great fun with her kin.

Devynne Eldridge, Grade 5
Westview Elementary School

Storms

Thunder makes me scared
Lightning lights the skies above
Storms come in the spring

Emma Bradbury, Grade 6
Harmon Middle School

The Great Hike

I see
the tall trees
with points
covering the sky.

I touch
crunchy leaves
and smell
fresh air and flowers.

I taste
fresh water
on my lips.

David Jason Day, Grade 4
Normandy Elementary School

Fall Is Here

Fall leaves are yellow
Fall leaves are brown.
What makes tree trunks
round and round?

A squirrel can climb a tree
a cat can climb a tree
but what makes the
birds sing and fly free?

Fall leaves are orange
Fall leaves are red.
The sun goes down earlier
and makes me want to go to bed.

The sky is getting cloudy
the wind is starting to blow.
It won't be very long till
we start seeing snow.

Courtney Remley, Grade 6
Miller City-New Cleveland School

A Neglected Tree

Me a tree who nobody sees, how wonderful I can be,
With bright lights, such a beautiful sight, ornaments near top, and string popcorn wrapping around top,
I can sit in a corner, I don't take up much room, for I am a small neglected tree
Who nobody imagines how wonderful I can be,
Me a tree who nobody sees cause to them, they see how wonderful I can't be,
Me a tree who nobody sees, when will somebody adopt me?
They could use me for decorations, that bring wonderful sensations,
And when I see Santa, Rudolph and Frosty,
I just can't wait cause the excitement has too much glee for maybe this is not all real,
But how will I know? How will I feel? Wait, for there is one more way, but it probably won't be
For all somebody has to do, is just adopt me.

Nicholas Goldacker, Grade 6
Glenwood Middle School

Cleveland Browns

I like football, I like the Cleveland Browns, but most the time they let me down.
I really like it when they win, but they seem to lose again and again.
Maybe this could be the year; maybe I'll have a reason to cheer.
It seems like whenever we get close, by the end of the season, there's no reason to boast.
But what can I do, but continue to root; I won't ever leave them or give them the boot.
I'll continue to watch them on the edge of my seat, always believing that we will never get beat.
That maybe someday, we will reach our goal, and will become NFL champions by winning the bowl.

Mitchell Shroyer, Grade 6
Holy Angels School

UD Arena

UD Arena is my second home. I love the roar of the fans before the game and the smell of hot dogs at the concession stand.
UD Arena is a place where all my troubles go away.

The energy and the excitement of the Flyer Faithful make this the best basketball arena in the country. When we win the game the fans go crazy when we lose a game we try another day. UD Arena is where my Flyers play.

Drew Westerheide, Grade 6
Holy Angels School

Joy

Joy sparkled like dancing snowflakes in everyone's eyes.
A lonesome tree twinkled with orbs of glass and colorful lights
The shimmering glass felt brittle in my hand.
Hugs and kisses are thrown around the room, love springs off the walls like a bouncing ball
Warmth covers the room like a blanket, and my dog curls up like a little kitten.
I rip a present open and the noise rings in my ears, the torn edge of the paper is rough and jagged
A delighted squeal flies out of my mouth when I see the toy.
The smell of pine spins and twists around me, a new aroma combines with the pine
The new smell is peppermint cookies.
I join my family for the delightful treat, the taste is sugary and it melts in my mouth.
While joy sparkles like dancing snowflakes in everyone's eyes.
As I enjoy this great holiday, I wonder,
"What would the world be like without Christmas?"
I am answered with a soft, "It's a mystery."
But inside me the question does not burn because the feeling of happiness will always remain in my heart.
My thoughts are stopped by the plinking of the tree's needles as they fall to the ground, a choir starts to sing Christmas carols.
When the carols stop the crackling of the candles can be heard, the dime light causes shadows to be thrown across the room.
Then there is a sudden giggle and laughter peals away the silence.
As joy sparkles like dancing snowflakes in everyone's eyes.

Rose Menyhert, Grade 5
EH Greene Intermediate School

Famous Player

Troy Aikman
is a great man
he's in the Hall of Fame
he's played a great game

Troy Sargeant, Grade 5
Stanton Middle School

The Sun and the Stars

I always like to watch the sun
Before every day is done
Looking at the stars puts me in a daze
Those are the things I like to gaze

I like to look up at the sky
The sun and stars are there
The thing I do not like to spy
Is a sky that is bare

I like to watch the sun
And look at the stars, too
They are o' so beautiful
In that sky of blue

I like the sun
Up in the sky
The stars fly by
When the day is done

Kristiana Federico, Grade 6
Kinsner Elementary School

Fall

Summer is over, fall is here,
Squirrels collect nuts everywhere.

Leaves are falling from the sky,
Red, orange and yellow they fly.

It's getting very cold,
Lots of coats are being sold.

While I'm raking leaves,
I feel the cool breeze.

It's fun to run and jump in the pile,
But first we rake for a while.

Bring your coats outside,
Because we're going for a ride.

Winter will be here soon,
It will get darker in the afternoon.

It's time to say goodbye,
Like the leaves, I've got to fly!

Hadas Schreiber, Grade 4
Cincinnati Hebrew Day School

The Little Creek

Flowing smoothly through small rocks,
Heading toward a small waterfall,
Gaining speed as it goes,
Pounding farther and farther down,
Fish squirm under the rushing water,
Sudden peacefulness as the water goes on,
As it goes down, the sun leaves the water shimmering,
Like millions of little floating gold diamonds,
Still it flows softly through the night,
HONK is the sound it hears as it gets pushed on by a steamboat in the morning,
The creek has flowed into the river,
Here it's waters shall become murky, polluted and icky,
But it still flows on,
Now this little bit of water is in the ocean,
Separated from it's other parts,
This is the eternal fate of a little creek.

Amy Burte, Grade 6
The New School

A Man's Best Friend

In the store I hear a snore, a puppy
He wakes up and is up and about
The puny fluff ball prances to the window
Staring, his eye on a particular customer, but soon he left and his hopes had gone
Scratching the window with all his might, hoping for a rescuer

Suddenly there came a click
The bell rang and the day began
Customers rushing in
Then I came
I said hello and how are you
He blinked and wagged his tail at me
His motoring tail was on maximum speed
His beige spot on his furry back made him unbearable
I finally decided to buy him
You could see a furry grin
Enthusiastically he set out into the world
His first time since he was born

Bengi, you frizzy puffball, you make me happy
One little friend to keep me company
For that I thank you

Irina Vatamanu, Grade 6
Harding Middle School

Blue

Blue is sometimes sad and sometimes happy.
But blue is the best.
Blue comes in different shades sapphire, steel, and peacock too.
But blue can be sad like navy blue.
Sometimes it's happy, sapphire blue.
Like the sea is turquoise.
The sky is royal.
There is always a shade for the color blue.

Morgan Willcox, Grade 6
St John the Baptist School

The Bus Ride

The bus ride home is a wonderful ride.
As we turn at the corner, we hear a "too-toot!"
It was the truck, coming to say hello.
Along the road, we hear a "woof, woof" and "arf, arf."
It's an owner walking her two dogs.
Then there is a big "whoosh" as we all hear
A car speed by like a race car.
As we drive to the next stop, we hear
A "peck, peck, peck" in the woods.
As we peer through the window.
It's a woodpecker, a lovely, beautiful woodpecker.
When we arrive at my bus stop,
It is peaceful and quiet.
It was an awesome bus ride.

Mariah Drake, Grade 6
Tippecanoe Middle School

Heaven

Heaven is a place people think in the sky.
Where you will never cry.
To get there you should do this thing.
Believe that Jesus is your king.
When you're there you will meet Adam and Paul.
But I'm not sure if you'll meet Saul.
In Heaven there will be lots of things.
Like golden streets and diamond rings.
Let me make this very clear.
Love the Lord for the end is near!

Michael Jayne, Grade 5
Pike Christian Academy

Squirrels

The squirrel in my hand holds a walnut,
With razor sharp teeth that munch and crunch,
Metal jaws that open and spread wide,
The jaws squeeze together
While the teeth chew.
It cracks open the shell,
Then SNAP!
Out comes the tasty snack.

Tara Boehringer, Grade 6
Tippecanoe Middle School

Ode to My Grandparents

My grandparents make me feel very happy.
They love me and help me.
I like to go to their house and play.
They help me play tennis and I enjoy that.
I also enjoy spending the night at their house.
When we go camping we do all kinds of things.
We go swimming and tubing in the lake.
When I am around my grandparents
They make me feel safe.
I love them so much!

Taylor Sutton, Grade 6
Tippecanoe Middle School

Shandrea Veal

Shandrea
Who is happy, pretty and truthful.
Who wishes of becoming a famous singer.
Who loves to sing, play, dance, and shop.
Who dreams of having an album come out.
Who wonders what will I be when I grow up.
Who fears spiders and my brother.
Who likes to write and draw.
Who believes in God and Jesus.
Who plans to live large.
Who is a resident of Sagamore Hills.
Veal

Shandrea Veal, Grade 4
Northfield Elementary School

Fall

Fall is here,
Summer is gone.
Days are shorter,
Nights are longer.

Leaves are falling,
Trees will be bare.
Skies will be gray, most of the day.

Holidays will be coming around the bend.
Thanksgiving and Christmas
with holiday fun.

John Ross Vallance, Grade 5
Immaculate Conception School

Snow

Dizzy
Dizzy
Tumbling
Down
Old Jack Frost has come to town
Dizzy
Dizzy
Tumbling
Down
Through the streets and through the towns
Through the school yard, through the park
Glittering when it gets dark
Snowflakes falling through the air
Falling
Falling
Everywhere
Dizzy
Dizzy
Tumbling
Down
Old Jack Frost has come to town.

Lizzie Cahill, Grade 6
Rocky River Middle School

Hohos
H ilarious shape
O utstanding filling
H ypnotic color
O ut of control taste
S ensationally amazing
Trent Newby, Grade 6
Rocky River Middle School

Marshmallow
Marshmallow, marshmallow
You are so white and fluffy
You really are so yummy
In my little tummy.
Christian Durbin, Grade 5
Stanton Middle School

Soccer
S wiftly they move
O ut toward the goal,
C utting through people
C razily,
E scaping the goalie then,
R ejoicing in victory.
Gabrielle Sibilia, Grade 6
Melrose Elementary School

Johnnie
Johnnie
Stylish, Awesome
Loving, Caring, Funny
She loves to laugh.
Unique
Johnnie Zerucha, Grade 6
Jefferson Elementary School

Angels
Angels are guardians of life;
they watch over you,
protecting you from danger and
guiding you to heaven.
Alyssa Bevington, Grade 6
Melrose Elementary School

Snow
Snow falls on me,
It lingers in the air
Dreaming and dancing
Balancing in the air

Snow it falls on us
Like a white crisp
Blanket whispering,
Whispering, leaving a tear of
Cold wafting in the air
Vanessa Maya, Grade 6
Woodward Park Middle School

Love
What is love?
Is it like a dove?
Soaring and flying through the air,
without any care?
Is it some infection?
Or is it affection,
That you have for somebody
That very special someone
That some day you'll call Hun?
Is it a disease?
That puts you right at ease
Or is it some desire
That just lights up like fire
Is it something you ignore?
Or is it something more
So come and tell me
What is love?
Breanna Baldwin, Grade 6
Fairbanks Middle School

Responsibility
R espectful
E fficient
S mart
P ush self to do right
O n the go, right on time
N ever give up
S elf-efficient
I n many ways intelligent
B est at anything you try
I n all problems stays away
L ikes doing active things
I ntelligent
T akes care of house and self
Y es to everything that's right
Jazmin Vinson, Grade 6
Eastmoor Middle School

Volcano
Black smoke turns day to night
Rocks explode into the sky like rockets
An eruption of molten lava
Engulfs the houses
Plows over the forest trees
Red rivers run down the volcano
Turning what was grass to black rock
Stewart Barnes, Grade 6
St Clement Elementary School

Robots Dead
Robots are dead,
'Cause of lack of grease,
the person said:
"Please *rust in peace*"
Chandler Batey, Grade 5
West Elementary School

Tom
There once was a boy named Tom,
who tried to set off a bomb.
It didn't quite work,
'cause he sat on a fork.
Oh, poor, poor Tom.
Tori Greene, Grade 6
Pike Christian Academy

Opposites
Chihuahua's shrill yap,
Trying hard to fend off foes;
The mountain dog's hulk.
Lydia Fang, Grade 6
EH Greene Intermediate School

The First Bomb!
When the first bomb falls from the sky,
The soldiers line up in the field.
And then they begin to yield.
The American flag is held high.
A gun is shot into the sky.
And the helicopters land in the field,
As they drop off soldiers nearby,
They keep shooting their guns.
Blood is scattered everywhere,
Out in the middle of nowhere.
Kirsten Oliver, Grade 5
Spaulding Elementary School

A Home Run
That baseball will go so far,
(No one knows where lost ones are!)
It may be caught…
That happens a lot…
Sometimes it goes out,
And a home run's scored, no doubt.
Ben Rice-Hawkins, Grade 5
Westview Elementary School

Seasons
As the snow falls from the sky
In the house the heat goes high

When the snow melts from the ground
I start to hear the bird's soothing sound

As I walk along the shore
I see the seagulls begin to soar

Now the leaves are on the grass
I know summer has surely passed

The seasons surely are not done
But I'll live well in anyone
Gabrielle O'Neill, Grade 6
Waterloo Middle School

High Merit Poems – Grades 4, 5, and 6

Halloween Night
Monster
Creepy, sinister
Hiding, lurking, stalking
Vampires, mummies, werewolves, and more
Chasing, pouncing, eating
Hungry, scary
Creatures

John Osburn, Grade 5
Hylen Souders Elementary School

Lay Krathong
I set my krathong on the water
I won't wish wrong
I close my eyes
What's my wish?
I can't tell you, can I?

Candles off at sea
Twinkling and winking at me
It's a pitch black night and the time is right
To set my lantern free

People wishing
Bubbly silence

What will I wish?
For a doll? For a fish?
Will it come true?
Oh, what do I, what do I, what do I do?

Like a bird, up so far
Like the stars
Wish, wish, wish

MacKenzie Boyd, Grade 5
EH Greene Intermediate School

The Military
My dad's friend Tary was killed in the military.
His wife Cary was very sad.
Mom, Dad, brother, and me still love Tary
for fighting in the military.

Wade Winland, Grade 4
Licking Valley Intermediate School

Someday
Someday I will get every game system.
Someday I will graduate from high school.
Someday I will have my own video store.
Someday I will get a car.
Someday I will be a doctor.
Someday I will propose to my girlfriend on the beach.
Someday I will be a father.
Someday I will be president.

Sean Steele, Grade 5
Becker Elementary School

A Startling Scene
I went scuba diving one day.
The scene I saw was startling.
The fish were frightened when they saw me.
The swordfish were scampering.
Other fish were hiding in an old hull.
I saw a sea snake slithering toward me.
I saw the clown fish clowning around.
The hammerhead shark was shimmering
As it swam toward the rising reef.

Haley Cook, Grade 6
Tippecanoe Middle School

Polar Bear Swim
With my cousins, aunts, and uncles,
We rip off our clothes down to our black, bathing suits,
And dive into the forty-degree river.
Dunking our heads, we scream and slosh in
The water that's as frigid as February.

We scatter from the water
And then we seize our towels.
In the cold breeze we hurriedly dry our shivering skin.
Everybody's bundled up in sopping wet towels,
Except Foxy — he doesn't seem wet.

How dare you Foxy not to dunk.
And then you grab a towel!
You pretend to go in,
But you only submerge your knees!
YOU CHEATER!!!!

Danny Toner, Grade 6
Harding Middle School

Bosnia
Bloodshed
My campaign eventuates vanward towards my birth
Minefields, weapon fire, manifest in girth
Family of mine, oh so loving, oh so caring, only gain their faith
To contest through illimitable confrontations on this Earth

Pacifism
Days before my "magnificent" bearing
Within an acreage
The earsplitting barrage of gunfire is no longer tearing
Though the filthy life of refuge takes its toll
The case of faith do they keep wearing

Accord
The struggle has ceased
But this country is a shell
For only now can we move to America, the economic beast
Life here is marvelous — no threats to our lives
No need for displeasing dives
Life here is gratifying, life here is great, but it requires haste

Edvin Rosic, Grade 6
Harding Middle School

I Can't Write a Poem Today!
This poem is very hard to write,
It looked easy at first sight.
My brain is getting very swollen,
It feels like all the words were stolen.
My poetry skills have gotten worse,
Ever since I got this curse.
I have to go and all I can say,
Is that I can't write a poem today!
Christina Cupple, Grade 6
Rocky River Middle School

Black
Black to me is everything.
It is also my favorite thing.
Black is the absence of light not the sky.
But it is the color of the sky.
But still it will not lie.
Maybe to you but not me.
Black is the color of the sea.
Jonathan Moeller, Grade 6
St John the Baptist School

Thanksgiving List
The warm scent
Of my house,
The family members
Who take care of me
Wherever I go,
And the world beyond us,
Which provide our needs.

Teachers,
Who help us cogitate,
Learn,
And take care of ourselves.

The cawing of raven,
The love
From my parents,
The joyous shriek from my neighbor.
The beauty of nature,
That surrounds us all.

But especially,
My life,
The one that keeps my alive,
For all these days.
Heather Wang, Grade 5
Cline Elementary School

The End
The end of all life
probably won't be that fun
so enjoy it now.
John Currie, Grade 6
Leetonia Middle School

Sad
Shadows fill my heart with blackness,
My heart is turning cold.

I tried for happiness,
But had success like mold.

I'm falling down, down, down.
How can I ever be happy again?

I've tried a million years,
For the laughter and the cheeriness,
Although I know I can't find the light.
Yijia Liang, Grade 5
Tremont Elementary School

Beach
There are waves foaming at the top.
People drink lots of pop.
Pelicans are diving into the water.
A dad is yelling at his daughter.

The fish are swimming.
In the sand I am digging.
The boats are racing.
I am pacing.

The palm trees are big.
The lady wears a wig.
The crabs are mean.
I saw a bean.

Kids are playing in the soft white sand.
Across the sea I see land.
The sea is cool.
It is better than the pool.
Alex Boyd, Grade 6
Kinsner Elementary School

Wind
It is powerful
It is blowing leaves around
It roars in my ear

It's invisible
It destroys, comforts, and chills
It can sway the trees

In Autumn it starts
In winter it grows stronger
In spring it's a beast

It blows through my hair
Flowing through my veins wildly
It's the mighty wind
Matt Bumpus, Grade 5
St Ignatius School

Things That Scare You
The creaking of a door,
The squeaking of the floor.

The flapping of a bat,
The hissing of a cat!

The groaning of a stair,
The snapping of a chair.

The howling of a coyote,
The wind whistling a note.

The creeping of a spider,
The galloping of a midnight rider!
Jonathan Carpenter, Grade 6
Wooster Christian School

Hockey
The center face off,
The awesome score,
The dangling move,
The slapshot goal,
The huge check.
The sweet fight,
Super sport!
Ethan Black, Grade 4
Dobbins Elementary School

What Is Fear?
What is fear?
It is the bloody coldness
that you feel before the moment.
It is the dark demon under your bed.
Fear is what rules us out
one by one by one…
What is fear?
Brett Grassan, Grade 5
Emerson Academy of Dayton

Flying in the Air
I want to fly in the air
so I can feel the breeze in my hair.
Oh, how much fun that would be
flying over the open sea.
Brandon O'Brien, Grade 5
Stanton Middle School

Red
Red comes in many shades.
It is my favorite *color*.
It comes in many shades
like pink, rose, and wine.
It is a very special color
because it is on our flag.
Jessica Flamm, Grade 6
St John the Baptist School

Christmas

Waking up and seeing all the present under the tree.
Opening all the wonderful gifts.
Eating breakfast and talking about all the gifts we got.
Getting the dog something like a dog bed and she looks so cute.
Going to my grandma's and grandpa's and seeing them.
I love eating my grandma's hot, sweet potatoes and
Seeing my cousins and
laughing about what we did when we were little.
Giving nice big hugs when it's time to leave.

Paige Kreager, Grade 4
Licking Valley Intermediate School

Tonight

The night is dark.
There is no sound.
I dream of an art.
I feel as if I'm going round.

There is no such thing as the Boogey Man.
I feel as if I should have ran.
My nightmares are deep.
Tonight I cannot sleep.

I am now laying.
I hear a sound.
Now I am praying,
Looking around.

Tonight I will sleep.
Trying not to weep.
I look at my cat,
She is chasing a rat.

Stephen A. Supanich, Grade 6
Kinsner Elementary School

Orange

You feel like a piece of wood,
Freshly cut and smoothed on the outside.
On the inside you feel like a slimy slug
crawling in a sand bucket at the beach.
The inside of you looks like
a very squishy sun becoming a white dwarf.
It smells like a rotten pumpkin on the inside,
and you taste like an apple
that has been sitting in lemon juice all day.

Caitlyn Tobin, Grade 5
Dr John Hole Elementary School

Marshmallow

Mushy, gushy, creamy, and toasty
cooking on the fire under the moonlight.
Taste so great
up so late
because I can't get enough of those toasted marshmallows.

Russell Shannon, Grade 5
Stanton Middle School

Halloween Night

In the dark night,
Children yelling,
Laughing, talking, running.
The ground shaking underneath the loud clatter of feet.
Moonlight spilling through the trees like
Water falling from a waterfall.
Children getting home
With truckloads of sweet candy.
Children singing and eating
Tasty Hershey bars and candy corn.
Jack-o'-lanterns
Glowing in the night
With tiny ladybugs crawling over them like
Berries crawling over bushes.
Is the candy nervous?
Is it happy?
Whatever it is,
    Trick-or-treat.
        Trick-or-treat.
            Trick-or-treat.

Nakul Narendran, Grade 5
EH Greene Intermediate School

Public Eye

If the Public Eye could run for presidency,
the whole system would fail.

If the Public Eye would hand out food,
we would have none to spare.

If the Public Eye gave out money,
we would all be poor.

The Public Eye is not always right.
One person can make a difference.

Nicholas Jones, Grade 6
Pike Delta York Middle School

God's Wonderful Creation

Beautiful butterflies flapping their wings.
Watch and listen as the pretty bird sings
Look at the doe and fawn come and feed.
Notice how God fulfills every need.

The horses are trotting in the meadow so green
Feeding on grass where not a soul can be seen
The squirrels are gathering nuts for cold weather
God's creation all works together.

Look at the leaves that fall in the wind
And when the birds sing the animals attend
All God's nature is such an inspiration
And it's all part of God's wonderful creation.

Bailey Patrick, Grade 5
Pike Christian Academy

The Moon

The Moon
is
like a balloon
glowing in the
nighttime sky

It doesn't
always give us
light if the sun
isn't by its
side

Some moons
are
half full
and some are
half empty

So you
should always
say
Sweet Dreams Moon
before you sleep
away

Ella Koscher, Grade 5
Tremont Elementary School

Winter

Snow in the winter
falls gently in the ground
to form a blanket.

Michael Reed, Grade 6
Tippecanoe Middle School

Oceans

Pretty waves going by
The sun is glowing
Birds are crowing
I have to leave with a sigh

Playing fun games
Swimming in the ocean
Throw the ball to James
Don't forget suntan lotion

Playing in the sand
Picnicking at the beach
Give me your peach
Listening to a good band

Looking for treasure
Building stuff
With nothing to measure
So don't bluff

Gabi D'Abato, Grade 6
Kinsner Elementary School

Eerie Halloween

Creepy shadows, flying arrows, everyone is trick or treating
Oh, so much fun, everyone loves to run
Banging on doors, getting some butterscotch candy
Yelling Trick-or-treat to Mrs. Mandy
Then run to the next house, fill your bags full
Then let the gnomes and goblins try a pull.

If it will be a trick, it will be some peat (YUCK!)
It it's some candy, it will be a treat
If the witches don't get you, the Jack-o'-lantern will
Chasing you all the way down the hill
Boo boo boo
You will say "Abradakedabra" and the poor old Jack-o'-lantern will vanish!
Are you not glad it's going to be banished?
After a few moments, I see a suspicious face
It might be on my trace, I can already feel the taste!

Now that we are almost done with our adventure
We will to last-minute houses venture
"Thud thud" That was a mean trick
The Jack-o'-lantern threw a brick
"Run for your life with all your might!"
Into the wee hours of the night

Naveen Viswanath, Grade 5
EH Greene Intermediate School

Halloween

Tonight is dark, house lights on, pumpkins lit with smelly candles by each walk
Not much brightness this time of day.

Kids running around in bright colored costumes
Carrying sacks filled with yummy candy
From house to house, collecting more squishy gummies and hard lollipops.

Hear their voices yelling, "Trick or treat!"
Hear the music playing at a few houses.

Where did your name come from, oh great Halloween?
May I have more candy, oh great Halloween?
You are as joyful as Christmas, oh great Halloween.
Your memories come alive in my head, telling me that you miss me.
Trick or treat, trick or treat, trick or treat.

Jeff Wagner, Grade 5
EH Greene Intermediate School

Freedom

F lags waving through the air
R especting our country by saying the Pledge of Allegiance before school
E agles reminding us of our free country
E veryone at the age of eighteen and older can vote
D eveloping a better place for us to live
O pportunities for people to make their own choices in life
M any soldiers risking their lives for us

Colin Hietikko, Grade 5
Sanderson Elementary School

High Merit Poems – Grades 4, 5, and 6

Chocolate
Chocolate is my most favorite candy.
It's always mine, fine and dandy.
When I am sad, it comes in handy.

I love chocolate, it makes me so glad.
But my mom takes it away and that makes me sad.
MOM! I am so MAD!
I Love CHOCOLATE!

Tommy Saylor, Grade 5
Spaulding Elementary School

Space
I like to look at the sky at night,
And pretend that I am an astronaut in flight.
God gave us Mars so red,
So that everyone can watch it from their bed.

We have our sun that is bright,
We depend on it for our light.
The Big Dipper can lead us the way,
But you cannot see it during the day.

I love the constellation Orion,
There should be one about a lion.
The Seven Sisters and Sirius too,
He's a dog and his star is blue.

Black holes such a mysterious sight.
Is it true that they can suck up light?
Space, space it doesn't drool,
You'll find that it's kind of cool.

Nicky Stewart, Grade 6
Kinsner Elementary School

Things That Are Quiet
A ladybug sitting on a tree
Clouds rolling in the sky on a hot summer day
Wild flowers swaying in a field
Wind whistling in the air
Ants hunting for food on the ground
Worms slithering through the mud
Trees blowing in the wind
Water reflecting in a puddle
Leaves on a tree
The smell of cut grass in the air
Rocks on a porch
Apples on the ground
Bugs trying to find shelter
Rocking chairs outside
Umbrella in the ground
Dogs sleeping in the yard
Chairs on a patio
Swing set outside

Blaike Frazier, Grade 5
Sanderson Elementary School

Veterans
Veterans were soldiers,
who worked with determination.
"A — ten — hut" "at ease" and "salute,"
are things they learned.

They fought for freedom with bravery,
and hoped that they would make it home.

Freedom with a lot of courage in their hearts.
They fought for the rights of the U.S.A.!
They fought for the red, white, and blue!
For FREEDOM!

Keisha Martin, Grade 6
Waterloo Middle School

All About Me!
R espects everybody
E xcellent
S mart
P retty
h **O** nesty
N ice
S ocial Studies is my least favorite subject
I ntelligent
B est person
I 'm entertaining
L opez is my last name
I ce cream is my favorite dessert
T ruthful
Y asmin is my sister's name

Deisy Lopez, Grade 6
Eastmoor Middle School

Christmas Tonight
The moment is silent.
Gingerbread fills the air
In which my lungs take in.
The sensation of sweetness and snap of spice
At the end, startles me.
The Christmas tree gives off a scent
That feels like nature's kindness.
Lumpy presents sitting under the tree sit and stare at me.
The gifts are the Rocky Mountains covered in striped paper.
What is really inside?
The twinkling lights light up the room
And their shadow dances on the wall.
Outside the window there is a fresh, new blanket of snow.
Snow is as cold as the Arctic Ocean.
It goes up; it goes down; like an emotion.
Up, up, up. Down, down, down.
Full of happiness, cheerfulness, and joy,
I turn on the little drummer boy.
Christmas is what makes my day just right.
No sadness will be seen on this wonderful night.

Megan Schroeder, Grade 5
EH Greene Intermediate School

The Amusement Park
As I walked into the amusement park
I heard people talking.
Blah, blah, blah
As I walked to the roller coaster
I heard it running.
Vroom, vroom, vroom
As I climbed into my seat
I heard the latch bar come down.
C-r-r, c-r-r, crack
As we started up the hill
I heard everyone screaming.
Aaahhhhhhhh!
When the ride was over
I heard a baby crying.
Wah, wah, wah
Then my brother got sick
So we had to go home.
What a fun day at the amusement park!
Jonathan Pfister, Grade 6
Tippecanoe Middle School

Mysterious Creatures
Cheetahs are:
Firecrackers that light
up the night.
Teardrops of pure,
golden honey.
Beautiful, noble
warriors.
Sleek, lightning
bolts.
Mysterious gems.
Ruthless killers.
Swift hawks that
fly as they run.
Brave soldiers that
fight to the death.
Kings of the plains.
Corinne Engber, Grade 5
Normandy Elementary School

Chubacobra
I'm a chubacobra,
you know me for my legend.
My friend is a vampire bat,
but I fear the giant squid,
I wish to be a giant someday.
Nick Fayette, Grade 5
Dr John Hole Elementary School

A Summer's Day
A warm summer day
Goes away, cold winds blow in,
And then fall comes in.
Alex Demers, Grade 6
Tippecanoe Middle School

Friendship
Friendship is a beautiful thing
Like a flower
It blooms on a sunny day
Rainbows, like friends,
Have all different colors.

Friendship is a beautiful thing
It is a doorway
When you walk through
You find someone new
As if a rainbow could bloom
In the sky.
Elijah Rice, Grade 4
Matthew Duvall Elementary School

Waterfall
Wind blowing gently
Motion flowing all around
Water rushing down
Richard Grieshop, Grade 6
Tippecanoe Middle School

Snowy Mountain Tops
Snowy mountain tops
Fresh pine forest
Cold snow melting
Frozen water streams
Cold wind blowing
A beautiful winter day
Ally Zeigler, Grade 6
St Clement Elementary School

Christmas
Christmas is a time of sharing,
hoping, loving, and caring.
Sleigh bells ring all around,
while we love people in our town.
Emma Gabor, Grade 4
Northfield Elementary School

Run
Past the big houses,
around the huge lake,
across the rocks,
onto a curvy street,
over the hills,
into the school yard,
out of the neighborhood,
by the highway roads,
about to get hit,
dodge every car,
up the hill to grandma's house,
outside I waited, till she came out.
"I run"
Justin Meyer, Grade 6
Harmon Middle School

Music
Beat, tempo, rhythm.
All these things go with music.
But the best is rock.
Korey Barr, Grade 6
Leetonia Middle School

Dreams
Captured in my fantasies,
Ensnared within my made-up magic,
Spiraling through the sky.
Skimming over streams,
Flying with the blue jays,
Lying under the sunset,
Nothing can go wrong.
This is my own world.
in my head,
I can only visit it,
As I sleep
As I dream.
Kathleen Turner, Grade 6
Harding Middle School

Ohio State Michigan Game
Two teams, such big rivals,
They will fight to win.
One scarlet and gray,
The other maize and blue.
Both will want victory,
But there can only be one winner.
I would want OSU to win,
Don't you agree?
Austin Buczkowski, Grade 6
Trilby Elementary School

Rivers
It is very soothing,
The way the river is moving.
Bending like a snake,
It runs into a lake.
The water is very clear,
This is not something to fear.
The banks are very sandy,
It looks like sugar candy.
Matt Manna, Grade 6
Roosevelt Elementary School

Dance
Dance is fun to do
Spin, twirl, jump
Many things to do
From jazz to ballet, children play
To leaps, jumps, and splits
We learn many things to do
We put on shows for you!
Jenna Mahood, Grade 5
Rootstown Elementary School

Doubt

Never doubt a thing or it will eat you,
And before you know it there will be nothing left.
You will be a whole different you.
You may look in a mirror and think you see yourself,
But tell me when you look in someone's eyes you won't see,
YOU!!

Jay Schulte, Grade 5
Dr John Hole Elementary School

My School Dragon

My school bus is a dragon.
It eats little kids for breakfast.
It flies through neighborhoods
And then it spits me out at school.
Then it comes back to eat me for a snack.
Then finally it spits me back at home.

Nick Hudson, Grade 6
Tippecanoe Middle School

Why I Don't Have My Homework

I SWEAR!
 My dog ate my homework!
 He ate it in one big chew!
 He almost ate my science paper too!
 He ground it in his teeth,
 And it went beneath my feet,
I reached down to grab it,
 I tripped —
 It ripped —
And that is why I don't have my homework.

Anna Grumman, Grade 5
Tremont Elementary School

Nature's Fury

I am coming as darkness seeps,
You will hear me as you sleep,
Fury looms in my cloud,
I will warn you, I am loud,
My ally fog, drifts below,
As I hit my hurtful blow,
Upon the Earth my rain will fall,
Hail, I bring, will hit you all,
Tornadoes spread throughout the land,
All the power in my hand,
Watch the wind blow the trees,
You will be at my knees,
The sun will run and I'll be free,
To make my history,
The way it is suppose to be,
…for me,
Alas, my rain will die,
So I will slip into my cloud and sigh,
Until my rains fall upon the Earth again,
For I am nature's Fury and I will strike now and then.

Teagan Storch, Grade 5
Black River Education Center

That Special Night

It was the middle of the night
It was very, very white
When I saw something bright
A chubby old man with a cookie in his hand
As he laughed ho, ho, it was time for him to go
Under the tree presents galore
As I looked at the plate there were cookies no more
I will never forget that night
It was very, very bright

Paige Geanangel, Grade 5
Wintersville Elementary School

The First White Christmas

Snow is falling to the ground,
Children watching all around,
They have never seen the snow,
Only on a Christmas show,
Although I wish I were there to see,
The faces of children just like me,
They are waiting for Santa's sleigh,
Which will come the night before Christmas Day,
On Christmas morning they hope to see,
Lots of presents and gifts under the tree,
Then they will play in the snow,
Next they'll make cookie dough,
After they'll bake,
Perhaps a white chocolate cake,
Finally they will put on a show
About the first time it ever snowed.

Shannon R. Calhoun, Grade 5
Frank Ohl Middle School

Fight Night

You walk through the crowd
People screaming
It's fighting time
Take your robe off
Put your mouth guard in
And drink your water
All you think about is the
First punch and how hard
You can push yourself
It's fight night
Losing is not an option
Never give up
You can always change your fate
It doesn't matter where you came from
Or where you made your first punch
All that matters is that if you get knocked down you can
KEEP MOVING FORWARD
Wait for the bell
Ding-Ding
Let the punches begin

Cali Titmas, Grade 6
Rocky River Middle School

Winter

Winter is blowing in the air
The snow is falling at the fair.
Winds are reaching 50 miles an hour,
Let's build a snowman in the yard of ours.
Birds migrated south, bears are sleeping,
winter is so exciting.

Mohammed Munim, Grade 6
Birchwood School

Sports

Hearing the cheering of the home field crowd.
Feeling good and very proud.
Trying to make the last second shot.
Or hitting one out of the park.
Big players making cash.
Or making it look easy like Steve Nash.
Hockey players slashing down for the Power Play.
Or waiting for the Super Bowl at the end of the day.
Sports what a great thing.

Marquis Flowers, Grade 6
Harmon Middle School

Be Yourself

Be kind to those you loathe,
Help those in turbulent situations,
Abduct all unscrupulous thoughts,
Tout what you believe in,
Have infinite thoughts,
Be yourself,
Don't let facade be a word to describe you,
Love everyone,
And if you need someone to help you
Pick me.

Megan Lantz, Grade 6
Pike Delta York Middle School

Christmas Is Here!

When dawn arrives on Christmas morn
It's family time when Christmas is here
Christmas music and Christmas shopping
Christmas is here!

Hot apple cider with a cinnamon stick
Everyone waits for jolly St. Nick
Many presents under the tree
Decorations are red and green
Christmas is here!

The ground is covered with a blanket of snow
The frosty wind starts to blow
Bells are ringing
Children singing
At last, Christmas is here!

Lisa Peterson, Grade 5
EH Greene Intermediate School

She's Ready

Her eyes twinkle like brilliant stars in the sky,
Her smile shines like an iridescent ornament,
Her skin glows as if she had just gotten a tan.

Her personality is still blooming, like a peony in late May,
But she knows how to treat people, she shows it every day,
And she is not conceited, she just knows that she is meant for great things.

So say good-bye to the little girl you knew,
And say hello to the little girl that grew,
Thank her for the times you've had,
And cherish them until she takes her path.

Because she just needs a push, to put her into place,
To guide her along her way, to hurry her pace.
So there you have it, you now know that she is ready,
Ready to explore and venture forever more.

Harmonie Coleman, Grade 6
Northwestern Middle School

What Is Money?

it is a big part of my life
it takes place in an important role
this is something that helps me in life
it can get me a lot of stuff
this comes in when I need to pay for something
it will not get me that far in life
the money that can give me a lot of willing and forgiveness
the money that is a part of my life that helps me find my meaning for it
that is my money

Isaiah Williams, Grade 5
Emerson Academy of Dayton

Competitive and Athletic

I am competitive and athletic
I wonder if I will ever be remembered as a baseball legend
I see my fellow teammates beside me saying good job
I see players trying to strike me out so I won't hit the ball up the middle
I want to be in the winner's circle
I am competitive and athletic.

I pretend to bunt the ball in the batter's box
I feel myself crushing the ball
I touch the ball with confidence
I worry that I will not do my best
I cry when I mess up a play
I am competitive and athletic.

I understand what I am supposed to do on the field
I say that I will try as hard as I can
I dream that I will be the best player in MLB history
I try to play 110% each game
I hope that I will reach my dreams of becoming a great player in the MLB
I am competitive and athletic.

Mac Starkey, Grade 5
Sanderson Elementary School

I Am

I am a wonderful ballet dancer who has the potential to achieve her dreams of becoming famous one day. I wonder how famous people live their lives all day every day. I hear the sounds of my floor creaking as I lay in my bed all night. I see my beautiful grandma looking out for me every day no matter what. I want Angela, Breanna, Joy and I to be in each other's lives forever no matter what. I am a wonderful ballet dancer who has the potential to achieve her dreams of becoming famous one day.

I pretend that I'm on stage dancing in front of everyone. I feel joy and a bright sunshine shining inside of me when I dance. I touch my grandma's soft face when she's full of sorrow. I worry having to leave my grandma just for screwing up. I cry every time my mom promises me she's going to be in my life but breaks it. I am a wonderful ballet dancer who has the potential to achieve her dreams of becoming famous one day.

I understand that it's hard for my mom to keep those promises. I say mom I believe you I know you would never lie to me does she yeah. I dream of me growing up and turning into a nice young lady like my grandma. I try to believe my mom no matter what she says but can I no. I hope when I grow up my kids will want to know how wonderful their Great Grandma is.

KiKi Green, Grade 6
Harmon Middle School

It's a Wonderful Feeling

A sparkling tree lit with colors of the rainbow, with gifts neatly wrapped, at 11:00 p.m., it's a wonderful sight.
As we leave for midnight mass, we see a treat laid out for Santa, milk and cookies oh so delectable.
Dong, dong, dong, dong…sounded the church bells, calling people to mass.
I sing hymns and recite prayers, and it's kind of fun, too!
One hour has passed, and we head home to see even more gifts laid out around the tree.
The joy is clear on all of our faces (especially mine, since I'm as happy as a hungry sheep in an ocean of grass);
it's a wonderful feeling, it truly is, opening presents at 1:30 a.m.!
We go to bed since we are tired so very much, but we can hardly wait for morning to come!
Morning is here! While I play with my new toys, gadgets and gizmos, mom starts preparing for a big feast!
I gorge on turkey, mashed potatoes and stuffing galore (and also on some panettone); at the end of the day, I wish I had more!
Bedtime has come, so as I pull up the covers, I say "Merry Christmas to all, and to all a good night!"

Christian Emmanuel Fernandez, Grade 5
E.H. Greene Intermediate School

I Am Michael Mallory

I am Michael Mallory humorous and athletic.
I wonder what occupation I will have in the near future.
I hear numerous people cheer when my team makes an exuberant play in football.
I want to be able to participate in sporting events and other activities.
I am Michael Mallory humorous and athletic.

I pretend I make a game winner that thrills everyone.
I feel like I am the greatest athlete everyone knows and play like I am the best.
I touch a basketball when I shoot a brilliant shot or pass.
I worry my arm won't heal and it will become paralyzed.
I cry when a family member dies or when my bones fracture or break and I feel an intense pain.
I am Michael Mallory humorous and athletic.

I understand how losing is harsh and winning is delightful.
I say I don't care when I do and it hurts numerous people.
I dream I will win many Super Bowls and other big events.
I try to be the best and exceed at everything I do.
I hope the buckeyes will win the championship and I will excel at everything I do.
I am Michael Mallory humorous and athletic.

Michael Mallory, Grade 6
Harmon Middle School

Kelly Pavlik
Oohs and aahs
Hits and dodges
Sold out crowds
Watching the champ
Working hard
We drink beverages
And eat hot dogs
While cheering the
   wins and losses
Knock out gets wins!
Brian Velasquez, Grade 4
Dobbins Elementary School

I Miss My Dad
I really miss my dad,
Because he was so rad.

He used to tell such funny jokes
I'd laugh so hard, I'd almost choke.

Cancer is such a nasty disease,
I'd rather have some nasty peas.

I just had to cry
When I had to say, "Good-bye."

It's almost been three years,
You can tell by my tears.

I really miss my dad
Because he was so rad.
Millie Ann Cartwright, Grade 6
Holy Angels School

Stingray
S harp barb
T errifying
I nch long tail
N ice
G ray
R ough
A nxious
Y ikes!
Sterling Smith, Grade 5
Stanton Middle School

Video Games/Board Games
Video games
Discs, round
Interesting, exciting, thrilling
Controller, wireless, dice, markers
Rolling, moving, rotating
Flat, square
Board games
Erick Collier, Grade 6
Holy Angels School

Sarah Rose Brook
Sarah Rose Brook
Kind, caring
Learning, imagining, helping
She loves fuzzy goats,
Goat-lover.
Sarah Rose Brook, Grade 6
Jefferson Elementary School

Kittens
Kittens are fun
Playing on the rug
They are nice and snug
Sure they're nice
And like mice
That is why they have no clue
Kittens are fluffy
While they are snuffy
Even though they're bad
Sometimes they are sad.
Samantha Mineweaser, Grade 4
Northfield Elementary School

Me
E nthusiastically I run.
R eliably I get the goal.
I ntelligent is the move I made.
C aring about the whole team.

E nergetic is my game.
D riven to do what's right.
W ise to pass the ball.
A thletic is the game I play
R esponsible I am.
D ifficult I can be.

E xcited about most things.
D iligently working on this poem.
W himsically picking up my pencil.
A rtist at the art.
R emarkable at drawing.
D emanding of those around me.
S illy in certain ways.

S uper in soccer.
E ric is my name.
T echnically I made this nickname.
H elpful all the time.
Eric Edward Edwards, Grade 5
Frank Ohl Middle School

Ode to a Snowflake
Your crystalline points,
they will melt on my lips like
warm, soft chocolate.
Grant Horvath, Grade 6
Leetonia Middle School

I Am
I am bright and helpful
I wonder if I'll ever go to space
I hear the sound of crickets at night
I see the future ahead of me
I want to go back to Chicago
I am bright and helpful

I pretend to sleep when I'm awake
I feel confident
I touch the juicy red watermelon
I worry about getting bad grades
I cry when I am sad
I am bright and helpful

I understand big math problems
I say anyone should have rights
I dream to be successful in life
I try to do my best in everything
I hope to travel around the world
I am bright and helpful

I am Matt Young
Matt Young, Grade 5
Sanderson Elementary School

My Three Cats
I have three cats
They love their food
They like to eat rats
They are never rude.

They're not in a bad mood
We have three mats
They're still not in a bad mood.

I love my three cats
They still like to eat their food
They still like to sleep on mats
They are never rude.
Miranda Miller, Grade 5
Stanton Middle School

Winter Days
On a snowy winter day
There are many games to play.
You can build a fort,
Play a sport,
Or even ski at the winter resort.
To go to the park, take a right
You better bundle up tight!
Thank the guard, be polite
Then you can have a snowball fight
But when the snow melts away
We'll have to make snowmen out of clay.
Bryan Waterhouse, Grade 6
EH Greene Intermediate School

High Merit Poems – Grades 4, 5, and 6

Twinkie
T errific taste
W orldly shape
I n commercials
N ot too big not too small
K rispy Kreme can't compete with the Twinkie
I n the height of the Great Depression the Twinkie was made
E xcellent filling

Ryan Lertzman, Grade 6
Rocky River Middle School

Friendship
Friendship is a bumpy road
That sometimes can be broken
One day I was with my friend,
When my other ex-best friend came along.
I did not know
That they were friends, too…
So when she came over,
She asked Janee if she could come play
With her!
"I was playing with her first," I said.
Then she acted like
She really didn't care,
So I walked away.
Friendship is a bumpy road…

Asia McKenzie, Grade 4
Matthew Duvall Elementary School

What Is Happiness?
What is happiness?
a volcano that does not erupt
an earthquake that does not happen
a plane crash that is avoided
an asteroid that was headed for earth but changes direction
That is happiness.

Michael Thomas, Grade 4
York Elementary School

Fall
Fall is colorful and cold,
If fall was a toy it would be sold.
The leaves are gone and they have no spare
So let's have fun this is not a dare.

The crunching leaves in the wind
Pumpkin in the bin
And outside it is drizzling so let's have some pumpkin pie
And we all sigh.

The kids are playing, they are having fun.
They are playing before fall is done.
When fall is gone we are so sad
Fall is gone that's too bad.

Alec Ochs, Grade 5
Immaculate Conception School

Seasons
Today is such a rainy day
I wanted to go outside and play
I wanted to play with my ball
But instead I had to play with my doll

Today is such a hot hot day
I really wanted to swim today
But instead I had to go to the store
And that was such a total bore.

Today is the first day of fall
I see the leaves begin to turn dull
I thought the leaves were supposed to be colorful
But they were still very wonderful

Today begins the first day of spring
When all of a sudden I heard the doorbell ring
It was my friend and she yelled it's finally spring
I love all of these seasons they are so much fun
I can't wait for the next one to come.

Emily M. Bevan, Grade 5
Frank Ohl Middle School

Kitty
Oh, kitty, so soft and fuzzy,
your eyes are so big and round.
You purr in my arms until you fall asleep.
You think everything is yours —
at least in your dreams.

Alicia Zimmerman, Grade 6
Melrose Elementary School

Shining Stars
It's done it's done
the sukkah is done,
chicken; grapes
I smell the sweet cakes.
Night has fallen,
good night.
I look through the clear roof,
beautiful sky.
The shining stars are as bright as flickering lights.
The moon is sparkling so much it looks like it is twirling.
Grape lights hanging on the roof.
Dad is snoring so loud, it is like a giant walking around.
Mice skittering; raccoons scattering
Owls hooting; bats flying
I feel the green grass on my feet.
Soft pillow; silky covers.
How, how do lemons feel to be hung on the roof?
Stars shining
Stars shining
Stars shining
Sukkot

Talia Bailes, Grade 5
EH Greene Intermediate School

Pets
Pets are big,
pets are small.
It doesn't matter,
you have them all.
They're fun to have,
and fun to keep.
Let's play a game
of hide-and-seek!
Peyton Tolley, Grade 5
West Elementary School

The Mall
Shop for anything you can imagine
Clothes, toys, food, a pet
Sales, clearance, free, you name it
Meet up with someone you just met

I love this one
But I want that
It costs a ton
And matches that hat

Eighty dollars, that's way too much
Probably because of the soft touch
I need a coat for the winter chill
Then T-shirts for the spring thrill

Abercrombie, Aero
That's where I'll go
I want this one, does it fit?
It's the mall and everyone knows it
Connie Morino, Grade 6
Kinsner Elementary School

Marshmallows
Marshmallows are gooey, soft, cloudy.
They taste good.
And they smell good.
You can put them in hot cocoa.
Aimee Merritt, Grade 5
Stanton Middle School

My Cat and Dog
Cat — lazy and tired
Sleeps four paws up
Runs quickly
But fast.
Chases walkers
Enjoys himself,

Dog — old and heavy
Naps a lot.
Finds snacks in the trash
And in the cat's dish.
Megan Elizabeth Weir, Grade 5
St Joseph Parish School

Christmas
Christmas is the time of year when everyone's filled with laughter and cheer.
Everybody's happy on Christmas day for when they go down stairs,
They see that Santa has come,
With their stockings stuffed with candy and treats,
And wonderful gifts stacked under the tree.
Once they open their gifts, it's off to eat,
With all at the table, staring at the marvelous feast,
All tummies are growling like small little beasts until they're finally able to eat.
When their stomachs are full, what happens next?
They all go out caroling, with heavy hearts in their chests.
When they come back from singing, when they finally return,
They take a long rest and that day is adjourned.
Then the very next morning they all could agree,
That Christmas is the best holiday, the very best holiday indeed.
Mackenzie Vining, Grade 6
Rocky River Middle School

Autumn Has Arrived
Leaves of brown and red and gold
are scattered on every inch of the yard.
The bare branches of every tree
swiftly sway to the hushed tune of the breeze.
The sun is shining brightly
as it casts the shadows of the trees.
The air is ringing with laughter
from children so lively and bright.
The leaves feel as coarse as sandpaper against my skin.
My cheeks turn crimson as the cold wind begins to howl against them.
I open my mouth and the air that rushes in tastes cool and crisp.
Can't you see?
Autumn has arrived.
Crunching,
Crunching,
Crunching,
as I step onto the grass.
The leaves are crunching, crunching,
as I run across the yard.
But why,
Why do you have to leave so soon?
Atiya Dosani, Grade 5
EH Greene Intermediate School

Mothers
Mothers are the guideline for Life
They make sure every waking moment in your life is filled with Joy
They check your homework and study with you
They make sure your clothes are clean
and that you have a lunch
They help you when you are sick
and stay with you until you are better
Mothers are the guidelines for life
and may God bless them
Elizabeth Bayer, Grade 6
St Gertrude School

High Merit Poems – Grades 4, 5, and 6

The Sharpener

The pencil sharpener is a stubborn monster.
It will eat your pencil away.
I crank and crank until my hand hurts,
Then give up and sit back down
Until another day.

It grinds and spits and glares at me
While the next kid gives it a try.
That is how he spends every day
Being so sneaky and sly.

Katherine Shirley, Grade 6
Tippecanoe Middle School

Riding Horses

The taste of dust in my mouth.
The smells of green grass in the field.
The sound of the horse's graceful whinny as we run.
As the horse runs across the bumpy ground
I feel good when I go up and down.
I feel the wind in my hair.
I see the horse's wavy mane flicker
as she throws her head.

Brooklyn Trout, Grade 4
Licking Valley Intermediate School

My Dog

My dog doesn't bite
My dog is afraid of kites,

She eats a lot
Of all the food she's got,

I love it when she wags her tail,
She loves when the guy comes with the mail,

She never barks,
Even at parks,

She always smiles
When she's in leaf piles,

And sometimes goes completely berserk
And once she ate my homework,

Overall she's really nice
Except to her least favorite animal, mice.

Michael Roberts, Grade 5
Tremont Elementary School

This Monkey

Beautiful brown fur and big black eyes
This monkey's energetic attitude is no surprise
Swinging through the tops of trees
This monkey is a sight to see

Genna Lukshus, Grade 6
EH Greene Intermediate School

Braces

Move back my front teeth
I feel them pushing
Not supposed to pick at them
Don't play with them.
Not allowed to chew gum, candy, or crunchy foods
Sometimes they hurt.
Go visit the dentist.

Randy Altman, Grade 4
Dobbins Elementary School

In the Shadows of Darkness

Oh light
Please shine so bright
For in the shadow lurks something dark
Something dangerous with more than a viscous bark
It crawls, creeps, and spies
And when you try to hide
It does nothing
For it can always see you with its evil eye
What this thing is I do not know
I believe it's a darkness that will not go
So cry and scream all you want
But all this dark thing will do is taunt
Although it won't hurt it'll mess with your mind
Until you feel like you need to unwind
Try as you might you're too filled with fear
Then eventually you'll shed many tears
But do not worry about this evil thing
Because there's an easy way to get a happy ending
For even the smallest light
Shines in the darkness so bright

Grace Rhodes, Grade 6
Central Intermediate School

Wish for Winter

Oh, how I wish winter would always stay.
Keeping it cool, unlike in May.
The Earth is blanketed with pearly, white snow.
And during the winter you always know,
Wear heavy clothes, just to stay warm,
Even in your college dorm.

Oh, how I wish winter was always here,
Cause then you know Christmas is near.
Your family comes closer to you,
Always wondering what to do.
Holidays come close and near,
You can spread Christmas cheer.

Oh, how I wish winter could always be around.
You can barely hear a sound.
You know there's much to do,
Don't you wish winter would stay too?

Cassie R. Wirtz, Grade 5
Frank Ohl Middle School

Snow

Snowy snow
Great and white
Playing all through the night
Having fun
You do too
You will want to everyday
You will want to play, play, play!

CJ Huang, Grade 5
Norwich Elementary School

Summer

Summer
scorching, exuberant
swimming, frolicking, biking
pool, slide, sled, coats
sledding, shivering, bundling
bitter, gloomy
Winter

Emily Jaskari, Grade 6
Harmon Middle School

Fall

You see warm colors.
You smell pumpkin pie all day long.
Time changes, the day is shorter.

You hear crunching leaves.
You feel the cool breeze.
You see the migrating animals.

You see all the vivid colors.
You hear the howling wind.
Last, but not least, you eat pumpkin pie.

Dennis Elias, Grade 5
Immaculate Conception School

Dogs in the Nature

Dogs make me feel
As if I have a 6th family member
In a big cabin in the country.

Ryan Cooper, Grade 6
Harmon Middle School

This Halloween

Candy, pumpkins
Ghouls and ghosts
Skeletons, witches
Who scares you the most?
Time's running out
So now we're all sad
If you got enough candy
Then you'll be glad
But some are mad.

Anelisa Vitucci, Grade 4
Dobbins Elementary School

Winter!

Winter almost here
Time to go sledding,
Snow boarding, too.
Receive presents
At Christmas
Spend time with family.
Celebrate birthdays
Go back to school
Playing with friends.

Kirsten Ensman, Grade 6
St Joseph Parish School

Wonderful Workers

W onderful toys
O r lots of noise
N aughty or nice
D og feet on ice
E ager to open gifts
R eindeer love to fly
F alling snow
U nhappy to get coal
L aughter in the North Pole

W onderful workers
O rnaments and decorations
R udolph is happy
K ids love Christmas
E lves make the toys
R udolph does too
S anta says ho ho ho!

Garrett Wycoff, Grade 5
Frank Ohl Middle School

O Why, O Why

O, why am I here?
O, why right now?
I hope someone can hear
My painful cry.

I'm tired and cold.
I wish I was inside.
I wish I was bold,
Or fierce, or strong.

This isn't fair,
I thought to myself
My cold feet.
My cold heart.

I wish I could go home.
I miss my family.
O, why am I here?
O, why am I here?

Morgan Nash, Grade 6
Ascension School

My Crazy Sister

My sister is a caged bear
Out of control!
When she is mad,
She is crazy and mean —
Always talking on her phone.
If I ask her a question she growls!
If I help her, she claws me!
My sister is a caged bear!

Kyle Shasteen, Grade 5
Westview Elementary School

Mom/Vivian

Mom
Funny, happy
Helping, running, laughing
She is really cool
Vivian

Corey Miles, Grade 5
Barrington Elementary School

Shoelace

Oh, shoelace, so long
And annoying
So why are you there —
Legs are what you are pulling.

Get outta here —
You're just kidding.
Hey, I bought you
And that's me you're hitting.

Fine, if that's the way
It's going to be.
I'll get the springy,
Glowy ones maybe.

So, if I were you,
I'd be a better shoelace.
So be very good, then
You'll help me win the race!

MaKayla Combs, Grade 6
Melrose Elementary School

My Mom

Gives me shelter
Feeds me
Cooks really well
Lots of fun, too.
Plays with me
Buys me stuff
Brown hair
Looks like me
The best ever!

Marsia Manna, Grade 4
Dobbins Elementary School

Star Gazing in the Pale Moonlight
When you look outside at night,
What do you see in the pale moonlight?
You will see little shimmers of light.

In the pale moonlight,
There are tons of those little shimmers.
They light up the sky most of night,
They light up the sky more than the pale moonlight.
Trinity D. Ankrom, Grade 5
West Elementary School

Marshmallow
This marshmallow looks like a fluffy cloud
This marshmallow makes me proud
This marshmallow makes me hyperactive and loud
This marshmallow is a very good tasting marshmallow
Kaitlyn Grimm, Grade 5
Stanton Middle School

Tubing
Sitting in the tube with a friend
Relaxing, enjoying the sun.
The green water moves slowly, rocking us gently.
We talk quietly so only we can hear.
Fish and ducks are floating near.

The engine roars like a lion.
The boat races around the lake.
My tube bounces up and down and side to side,
Which way we go, it doesn't matter.
Fish and ducks quickly scatter.

Sitting in the tube holding on tight,
Laughing and splashing behind the boat,
Having so much fun in the sun.
Cold water sprays in our faces.
Fish and ducks please stay in your places!
Jenna Bierly, Grade 5
Cline Elementary School

Best Friends
I was waiting for the school bus
And then I heard a chatter
I walked down to the sidewalk
To see what was the matter
I saw a girl who was wet and scared
And water dripping from her hair
I told her to come, come and get warm
Before you know it, there will be a storm
We went inside and drank some tea
We read a book called *The Princess and the Pea*
We stopped at the part about the prince
And we've been best friends ever since
Sydney Leigh Zebrasky, Grade 5
Frank Ohl Middle School

Fall Leaves
Fall leaves are lean,
Yellow, orange, red, brown, but not green.
Seeing them may make you quite keen,
But they won't be sheen 'till April the fourteen!
Haley Alishusky, Grade 6
Central Intermediate School

Fall
F is for fall, and the leaves falling down
A is for autumn, another word for fall
L is for leaves that turn red, brown and orange on the trees
L is for the leaves that I rake into piles and
    u   p
 j m
into.
Miranda Manimbo, Grade 6
Birchwood School

Night
At night sometimes the moon is bright.
When the sun goes down the time is right.
The nocturnal animals come out to play.
When the sun's out, they sleep all day.

Animals can see far at night.
An owl takes off into flight.
You can't see them but they can see you…
So you'd better watch out for them, too.

The animals, they search for food.
Don't go into the forest at night.
Because they might get you!
So don't go where there is no light.

At night, it is so very dark.
In the night you might hear a bark.
Those are sounds of animals now hunting,
So right now you best be running.

You might think there are things following you there,
But when you turn around, there is just air.
Don't go where you cannot see,
For you might run into a tree!
Karen Tan, Grade 6
Kinsner Elementary School

My Cat Named Sammy
Sammy snuggles,
As I fall asleep,
The black and white paws lying against me,
The blue-green eyes looking up at me,
The soft pointy ears touching my neck,
All his sharp teeth,
But Sammy is still my sleeping companion.
Brigid McKee, Grade 5
Tremont Elementary School

Chain

Breaking the chain is hard
to do. Especially when your
family's a zoo. Wrong decisions
here and there, what's a girl
like me to do. To keep this
chain from biting at me,
I guess I should take time for
me and then you'll see that
this chain won't be a burden on me.

Evin Moss, Grade 6
Woodward Park Middle School

Jakob

J ust shocking
A thletic
K ing of the field
O bnoxious
B rave in football pads

Jakob Brown, Grade 6
Louisville Middle School

Honoring My Hero

Honoring my hero.
Standing tall and proud.
Fighting for my freedom.
Protecting me from harm.
Praying for a safe return.
Coming through my door.
Hugging so tight.
Feeling so right.
Leaving me no more.

Kayla Stevenson, Grade 6
Harmon Middle School

Outside

Swings, basketball, monkey bars
basketball, monkey bars, baseball
monkey bars, baseball, soccer
baseball, soccer, kickball
soccer, kickball, fun
kickball, fun, toss
fun, toss, jump rope

Carleno Johnson, Grade 5
Becker Elementary School

Vroooooom!

Qualifying for a good spot!
On race day, it's a good thing,
Hearing those motors ring!
Being near the front,
Giving one big grunt,
I can just feel a win…
Can't wait for the race to begin!

Cameron Baker, Grade 5
Westview Elementary School

Summer

S uper season
U mbrellas at the beach
M any ways to have fun
M uch better than fall
E verything is happy
R arely dull

Adam Kopniske, Grade 4
Northfield Elementary School

Brothers

I have two older brothers
They are twins
They pick on me
They're not my biggest fans
I feel like a bug on their car
Being squashed by the windshield
Sometimes they hate me and
Sometimes they like me
I will be living
With them for a while
So I better get used to it.

Caroline Shisler, Grade 5
Tremont Elementary School

Animals

Animals
Soft and sweet
See them at the zoo
Play with them all day
Makes me happy
Joy

Marla Schroeder, Grade 6
Holy Angels School

Jonathan

J umping
O utstanding
N oble
A chiever
T errific
H appy
A wesome
N ice

Jonathan Resnik, Grade 4
Sts Joseph and John School

The Sea

What is the sea said a young girl
Her dad said many things
A place you can sit down and just watch
A place to forget all your thoughts
As you can see it runs then walks
Then he said what is the sea for you

Jasmine Winston, Grade 6
Woodward Park Middle School

A Walk in the Woods

Clouds
like cotton candy
swirling at a fair.

Air feeling
like a creek
flowing with water.

Air smelling
like falling leaves.

Rocks
Under my feet
like glaciers
in the middle of the ocean.

Makenzie Ward, Grade 4
Normandy Elementary School

Mom

My mom is cool
And she's no fool.
She's the best
Because she helps me study for tests!
She cleans and cooks
And loves to read books.
Now that is my mom!

Jordan Young, Grade 6
St Clement Elementary School

Jack-O-Lantern

J ack-O-Lantern, the pumpkin
A scary face you carve
C ackling evilly
K nives are what you use to sculpt it

O h, my gosh, that's scary!

L antern of Hallows Eve
A candle you stick in it
N ight is its time
T ime to light the candle
E ver will it haunt
R un while you can
N ow, I've got you, mhuahahaha…

Daniel Pacheco, Grade 5
Indian Springs Elementary School

Rain

Rain
Crystal, clear
Falling, splashing, jumping
Angel tears
Fun

Brooke Drouhard, Grade 6
Melrose Elementary School

Soldiers

As I pray for our soldiers
I think how they carry others on their shoulders
Every day and night
How they have to fight
I can't believe how brave
As they dedicate their lives to save

Cody Donohoue, Grade 6
EH Greene Intermediate School

The Holiday

Every year I walk downstairs to a room full of presents.
Christmas is definitely the best holiday of them all no question,
From the gifts to the best food ever.
The dim light outside makes it seem so warm inside.
Our Christmas tree lights shine
Like glowing stars among the entire room,
Only making it more fun to open presents.
The fancy music that is always on
Floats throughout the entire house,
Making it impossible to escape.
The RRRIIIPPP of the gift wrap
Just means that people are receiving their wishes.
Why does this day have to ever end?
Who would ever get tired of all these gifts?
How will I get to sleep on Christmas Eve?!
I can't wait until next year!
"It's the most wonderful time of the year"
Is the first thing that comes to mind
When Christmas comes up in my head.
Merry Christmas, Merry Christmas, Merry Christmas!

Reese Allison, Grade 5
EH Greene Intermediate School

Thank You to the Soldiers

People say that there was a time
When the grass was always green
The sky was a beautiful bright blue
A perfect picture scene.
But I completely disagree
Things don't always go right
Now all we have is the pride of our country
As we continue to fight.
The brave soldiers put their lives on the line
No matter what they have to do
And you never really think
That they do it all for you.
But why do we need to go through this?
I am sure you will agree
There's too much suffering in this war
Way too much for me.
Although the war has been a long, bloody fight
I just have to say
Thank you to the soldiers
That fight for us every day.

Christina Shebata, Grade 6
EH Greene Intermediate School

The Starlit Sky

The immense black sky, full of incredible stars
shimmering as bright as a blazing light.
Mother moon so much bigger than the stars,
watching over them like her babies.
Down on Earth everyone is slowly dozing off.
The sun has gone to sleep for the night.
In the morning, people on Earth are waking up.
The sun is happy to be awake and warming the Earth.
Every last nocturnal animal has just said good night.
The moon slowly fades, and stars do the same.
"Goodbye, and farewell!
We will be back tonight" they all say!

Mandy Mazzola, Grade 5
Cline Elementary School

Grandma's House!

Grandma's house is a wonderful place,
With a lot of joy and grace.
Grandma's house is a wonderful place
with the sweet smell of cookies in your face.
Grandma's house is a wonderful place.
I love it a lot, and you better come quick
While the cookies are hot!

Isaac Q. Lee, Grade 4
Licking Valley Intermediate School

Space

Flying, flying ever so high
You're in space, not in the sky
Stars and moons are all you can see
It's truly a wonderful place to be
Space is ready to be explored
Astronauts in rockets see more and more
I have always wanted to go to space
I thought it was an amazing place
When up there you don't know where you are
You fly so long, so far
Martians on mars, aliens everywhere
We think they're not, but I think they're there.

Brian Hirschl, Grade 5
Akiva Academy

Truth

The morning baby
at the garden pool
saw a boy and girl
walking together on the glowing wing
of a whispering owl —

She jumped into the mirror lake and started to swim,
She could imagine her brother and sister
talking of a story so sad that it could not be told —
She gently cried of the truth

Erin Lescinsky, Grade 4
Hylen Souders Elementary School

Dancing

I am dancing,
Dancing so gracefully,
Like a beautiful little flower,
With its petals twirling in the wind.

I am dancing,
With my hair flying like a bird,
My feet barely touch the floor,
And my hands are moving,
Like a leaf falling to the floor.

I am dancing,
Everything stops to look and listen,
The world stands still,
Except for me,
I am dancing.

Judy Daboul, Grade 6
West Side Montessori Center

Sunshine

Sunshine,
So divine,
It makes me
Feel warm and nice.
If someday,
It went away,
I would
Think about it twice.
Sunshine
Very bright,
How I love
The warm, warm light.
How sunshine
Makes me feel
Just so, so
Real!

Meryl Schor, Grade 5
Akiva Academy

Seasons

Seasons are fun
In the summer sun.

In the winter with all the snow
There goes Santa Claus saying Ho Ho Ho.

In the spring where the big sky is blue
You won't be saying boo hoo.

In the fall with all the leaves
You will love the cool breeze.

In the summer with lots of fun
A brand new school year's just begun.

Alexis Morley, Grade 4
Northfield Elementary School

Autumn

Hearing leaves go crunch, crunch, crunch
Walking through the rustling leaves
Remembering when I was a little girl
Rolling through the huge piles
This makes autumn.

Watching children delight in sweet, sticky candy corn
Seeing them walk home with overflowing treat bags
The look in each child's eyes says, "I want more candy, please"
Chocolaty, caramel, smooth, heavenly tasting candy
This makes autumn.

Trying to find the perfect pumpkin to carve
Huge, tall, small, and round
Wishing I had the biggest one there
Giggling at all the funny faces I have carved
This makes autumn.

Jumping in piles of colorful leaves
Tossing leaves in the air making them look like they are flying
As they soar through the air, I imagine what it would be like without fall
Beautiful colors are being brushed upon my face
This makes autumn.

Megan Allen, Grade 5
Sanderson Elementary School

The Snowy Penguin

T his is about a snow penguin.
H e is well made with a snow body, button eyes, and a carrot beak.
E xcellent at making snowballs.

S now forts are easy for him to make.
N yalas are his favorite animals.
O wls are his least favorite animals.
W ar bonnets are his favorite thing to wear.
Y o-yos are his favorite type of toys to play with.

P eople dislike him.
E nemies are snow vultures and snow leopards.
N ipa palms are his favorite type of trees.
G enius at science.
U nlike most penguins he can fly.
I nsects are his favorite things to study
N obody likes him.

Nick Crawford, Grade 5
Frank Ohl Middle School

Tangerine

On the outside you look like a little orange sun rising in the morning,
You feel like a basketball with little bumps,
When I peel you, you sound like a paper gently being torn,
Then you look like bright orange burning hot lava,
You feel like extremely slick butter,
Tell me tangerine, can I eat you and fulfill my hunger with your fabulous taste?

Ty Wheeler, Grade 5
Dr John Hole Elementary School

High Merit Poems – Grades 4, 5, and 6

Gold
Gold is the color of dark yellow.
Gold is everywhere.
If you look around you will find gold.
There is no gold in mold.
There is nothing in gold that is bold.
Gold is also the color of yellow.
There are some kinds of gold — dark, light, and yellow.
Some things that are gold can be very bold to you.
You don't see gold in clothes anymore because it is old.

Mason Stanton, Grade 6
St John the Baptist School

About Me
I am happy and awesome
I wonder what will happen when I'm older
I hear in my head lots of sounds of the forest
I see a big rainbow in my dreams
I want a boat and a jet
I am happy and awesome

I pretend to be a pirate
I feel happy and glad
I touch a pan and it burns
I worry if there will be a war
I cry if my mom dies
I am happy an awesome

I understand that a war will come
I say I will never get hurt
I dream a big rainbow
I try to get better grades
I hope there will never be a war
I am happy and awesome

I am Nikki Mansberger

Elizabeth Mansberger, Grade 5
Sanderson Elementary School

Walking Home from School
I was walking home from school,
On a cold fall afternoon,
When all of a sudden, I heard CRUNCH!
Seems I have just stepped in a pile of leaves.
Then I hear RUFF! RUFF!
I look around; it's just my neighbor's dog.
I walk inside my house.
WHAM! I slam the door.
I run upstairs.
HUH, HUH, HUH!
I'm totally out of breath.
I sit on my bed to take a nap.
Under my bed, my cat meows.
I'm awake again.

Zoe Mendenhall, Grade 6
Tippecanoe Middle School

Opening Night
On opening night of every play,
All you can see is bright, shimmering lights,
Bright, shimmering lights,
Bright, shimmering lights,
That seem deeper than all of the oceans,

You can feel the excitement of opening night all over,
It makes you tingle, like your whole body is numb.
The occasion is as joyful as kids in a candy shop.
You can taste the joy and pride of the actors in the air.

Center stage is shining on opening night,
With colorful props abound everywhere you see,
It is empty though,
Not one soul is on it,
You can hear the magical music,
Of the orchestra tuning up,
Violins, cellos, flutes, and clarinets
Is the sound that fills the air, they make enchanting music,

"Will the show ever start?" we wonder,
The audience lights turn dark…
The stage lights turn brighter…
3…2…1 the magical show begins.

Ilana Frankel, Grade 5
EH Greene Intermediate School

Music
Music is one of my favorite things
Especially the bells' dongs and dings.

Music just drives on and on
Until the music just is gone.

I love music oh so much
It gives my life a jubilant touch.

These reasons why and so much more say
That music is my best forte!

Jayce Fryman, Grade 6
Woodward Park Middle School

I Live in a Game
The board game "Risk" is a lot like life.
To win the game, one must plan ahead.
You must start small and slowly grow bigger.
You have to beware of people trying to trick you.
You should always have some reserve resources.
Always be prepared to protect what you've gained.
Try to learn from your mistakes.
Learn to choose the best course of action
when presented with options
Anticipate what others are attempting to accomplish.
And remember: the goal is to have fun.

Josh Dunn, Grade 6
Tippecanoe Middle School

Fall
Fall is pretty. Fall is bright.
I just like the bright fall light,
Come upon howling winds,
crunching leaves and taking a spin.

Migrating butterflies soar across the sea,
And one stopped by to play with me.
When I see them all go away,
I like to smile and wave good day.

I like pies, cakes and strudels
And when I find warm bright colors,
It's the end, it's through,
It's time to say goodbye to you.
Emily Ashley, Grade 5
Immaculate Conception School

Leaves
Leaves swishing swirling
All fall down into
A carpet across the grass
Full of
Fire like color.
Megan Wheeler, Grade 5
Tremont Elementary School

My Book
My book tells me stories
Every night before bed
It dances and sings
And stands on its head
It likes to sing
Annoying songs
And they make
Me join along
Then it starts
To dance and toot
On a little horn
Before I know it
I'm running out
My bedroom door
Brianne Frederick, Grade 6
Leetonia Middle School

About Me
E xpert
R uler
I nteresting
K ing

L ast
E xcellent
E ducated
Erik Lee, Grade 5
Stanton Middle School

My Dog
My dog's name is Dollar
He likes to play with his bone
He always wears a collar
When he's talking on the phone!

He eats meals out of a bowl
Just until he's full
He tries to jump
But he lands on his rump.

He likes to chase cattle
It is always a good battle
He will fall in the pool
The splash looks very cool.

He always likes to play
He rolls his ball to the door
He will have a long day
After, he will want to play more.
Nicolette Griesinger, Grade 6
Kinsner Elementary School

Blue
Blue is the color of the sky.
Blue is also the color of the sea.
I see the sea every year on the beach.
I walk with the sky and the sea.
I see a blue dolphin.
It jumps freely out of the blue sea.
Meggie Roettker, Grade 6
St John the Baptist School

Stimulation!
Slipping, Slashing
Curving, Dashing

Then CRASH!

I'm riding down the hill
Swerving, what a thrill

Then CRASH!

Jumping over a pile
I slowly grow a smile

Then CRASH!

I get back up and strap back in
Better than I've ever been

Then CRASH!
That's snowboarding for you.
Nathan Christian, Grade 6
Birchwood School

Homework
Oh, dear homework,
I truly do
Think I'm in
Love with you.

You keep me up
All night long.
You make me want
To sing a song.

Homework, you are
Of course, the best
Especially when
You are a test.

It's not at all
That I am lazy
It's just that, see,
I think I'm crazy!
Ian Mount, Grade 6
Melrose Elementary School

Winter
Winter is a lot of fun,
even though there isn't much sun.
We play in the snow
and watch it blow.

As the days grow colder,
I feel I'm getting older
I can't wait for the sun,
so I'll be able to run.

I'll slide down a hill,
seeking a thrill,
but I'll hit a bump
and hurt my rump.

We throw snowballs,
but not in school halls,
we throw at our friends,
the fun never ends.
Ryan Frank, Grade 6
Kinsner Elementary School

Tennis and Soccer
Tennis
Racket, court
Hitting, passing, serving
Overhand, underhand, defense, offense
Kicking, scoring, running
Midfield, outside
Soccer
Patrick Pudlewski, Grade 6
Holy Angels School

I Am

I am Zach, athletic and knowledgeable,
I wonder why people fight and argue every day and shoot people for no reason,
I hear on the news about killings, maulings and kidnappings,
I see every day at school and at home people fighting and arguing for silly reasons,
I want all wars to end along with terrorist groups and world hunger so we can all get along well.
I am Zach, athletic and knowledgeable.

I pretend not to pay attention to all the world's problems so I'm not so stressed,
I feel very good about a perfect, non-crisis world,
I touch people's hearts with my friendliness and niceness,
I worry that I might never see a better world than it is now,
I cry when I see someone who has lost a loved one in the war,
I am Zach, athletic and knowledgeable.

I understand that I cannot end world hunger and terrorism all by myself,
I say to myself "there's got to be a solution, we've just got to make an effort to find it somehow some way,"
I dream that all of us all over the world will get along and live together in harmony,
I try to make a difference in the world by donating to the homeless and poor,
I hope that someday we will find a solution to this madness and insaneness so that everyone can live together in peace,
I am Zach, athletic and knowledgeable.

Zachary Trainer, Grade 6
Harmon Middle School

Christmas Day

What's in that gift, I ponder?
Does she like it, I ask?
All of these questions fill the pool of curiosity inside me.
Spread about the holiday room,
People are thanking, talking
Giggling and walking.
As I slowly pace around the room
I notice the light is dim, with one lanky lamp lighting the space.
The cramped people in the room look as jolly as Old St. Nick himself.
The room is bouncing with laughter from jokes, presents, and gifts.
The aroma of the precious cakes, melted cookies, cooked ham and cold pudding fills me with joy.
I tasted almost everything; the whole buffet, against my warm, moist tongue.
My excited and trembling hand was next to the smooth and slippery gift wrapping.
All of this happens…
On Christmas Day
On Christmas Day
On Christmas Day

Jessica Hobart, Grade 5
EH Greene Intermediate School

Hope

Hope is a box of wishes just waiting to be opened.
Hope is the song that the birds are chirping, that only the happy and merry can dance to.
Hope is shaped like a heart and is inside of everyone.
Hope is the memory of good times that will live on forever and ever.

Hope dreams of happiness, but not only at night.
Hope feels like joy and always lifts your spirits and keeps them high.
Hope looks like courage and allows you to do anything you put your heart to.
Hope is the touch of love that reaches everyone and effects who it touches.

Miranda McIntyre, Grade 6
Old Fort Elementary School

Soccer

Soccer is a ruling game,
I will tell you how.
Over your head the ball goes,
coming together we win.

Catching defender off guard,
Every goal we keep,
Roars filling the stadium,
Because we shot a goal.

Sumaya Alkatib, Grade 4
Norwich Elementary School

Sometimes I Feel Like a Frog

My dog purrs and meows all night long,
When I wake up my cat's whining and
Barking in my ear.
To get my brother up his rooster moos.
When I go outside to feed the horses
They're laying eggs.
At school, students teach
And the teachers learn.
Sometimes I even feel like a frog!

Samantha Pawliski, Grade 6
Trilby Elementary School

Wonder

Wonder,
Why life
Is so difficult,
But yet very beautiful
To you.

Kaitlin Park, Grade 6
Harmon Middle School

The Sky

The sky is blue
The moon is glue
Old bird flew
With a shoe

The clouds are gray
With such dismay
A view of oceans bay
Like a grape soufflé

The sun is hot
In a burning spot
In the sky there is a dot
That looks like a pot

The stars are gleaming bright
All through the night
Planets are a pretty sight
I see them with all my might

Ky Pace, Grade 6
Kinsner Elementary School

The Devil's Cupid

I hide my real self, so you don't see. You see a person, that isn't me.
A hollow person, full of pain and hate. With a heart, that has no fate.
I look so happy, like life's a breeze. But I cry to god and say please, please.
A lost love, that I hate and desire. My heart burns like an inner fire.
He tells me that I am his. But there's only one answer, to the Quiz
He say's I'm gone, I am no more. But he's not the only one, I will adore.
Now I'm back and filled with such glee. But I can't stop the pain I see.
I see him with another girl. I stop and stare because I know she's in his world.
I need to stop this and clear my mind. But I can't because I know he is behind.
A love I lost and still adore. He tells me, he loves me. Doe's he really care.
He tells me, he wants me. Is he really there.

Damieshia Ash, Grade 6
Forest Park Elementary School

Pink

Pink keeps me feeling perfect,
In every single possible way.
Then I don't care what other people say.
I can just go about my day.
Pink is the color of strawberry milk, my favorite drink.
Pink is the color in my mind when I think.
Pink is the color of my cheeks when I come in from playing in the snow.
Pink is the color of my favorite bow.
Pink is my favorite color.
There is no doubt about that.
That's just a fact.

Hannah Wolterman, Grade 6
St John the Baptist School

I Remember Friends and Family Times

I remember friends and family times:
I remember the inflatable my parents rented for my ninth birthday;
I remember my friends and I boxing each other with huge boxing gloves;
I remember playing tag and wrestling with my friends in the ring.

I remember the awesome moving party I had at my friend's house;
I remember the dry ice in the punch that made it look spooky;
I remember all my friends going on a snipe hunt in the dark.

I remember living in a hotel for a while when we moved to Ohio;
I remember playing basketball with my dad on the hotel court;
I remember the thrill of finally moving into our new house.

I remember the first Christmas we had in our new house;
I remember the huge tree we cut down and put in the living room;
I remember the little tree I cut down and decorated for the loft.

I remember my 11th birthday party at Fort Rapids indoor water park;
I remember playing basketball and winning the race down the racing slide;
I remember sliding down slides, and playing in the arcade room.

I remember many fun times with family and friends!

Jacob Gividen, Grade 6
Harmon Middle School

Dancing with the Bengals

Have you ever imagined Houshmanzadeh in tights?
Carson Palmer with taps on his shoes every night?

Can you picture Chad Johnson with a rose in his teeth?
Or doing the Salsa with someone named Keith?

Madieu Williams, it would be a hoot
If we could see him do the Boot Scoot.

Rudi Johnson, man, I'd sure shout Aye Carumba
To see him dress up and dance a fast Rhumba.

Now picture them entering a quick stepping contest.
Where they have to be great and are put to the test
At something that they have never done before.
But it would be hilarious, that's for sure.

Too bad that Sabrina was unable to win.
But the Bengals? Just maybe. Can you just imagine?

Brandi Steele, Grade 5
Spaulding Elementary School

Changing Eyes

My sister Kiersten is the best to me.
She helps me feel joyous when I'm down in the dumps.
Kiersten is a very good writer.
Poems and books are her strongest words.

Her voice is like angels singing in your ears,
So pure and beautiful.
She can sing to sleep with no problem.

Her looks are awesome,
Even if she doesn't own up to it.
Her red hair and her changing eye color are amazing.

Kiersten and I are almost the same person inside.
We both love to write and can read all day.

When I need some advice or someone else does,
I will go to her and ask away because I know
She will tell me the truth.

I love my sister with all my heart.

Kendra Fields, Grade 6
Tippecanoe Middle School

Tigers

Tigers are big.
Tigers are smart.
Tigers have orange fur with black stripes.
Tigers are great animals.
Tigers are our basketball mascot.
Tigers.

Gunnar Siebenaler, Grade 4
St Mary's School

Wise Men

The wise men were on an extraordinary voyage
Looking for the new born King.
They may have some clues,
Clues where He may be.
They probably traveled for 1,000 miles,
Searching for Emanuel.
Traveling by camel
They got there after a while.
What a journey they had been through.
But finally they got there,
And they saw the King.
Even though it was in a stable,
He was Emmanuel,
The new born King.

Blaine Hamilton, Grade 5
Wooster Christian School

My Computer

My computer is very frustrating,
And it is very time consuming.
This simple machine always keeps me waiting,
This piece of junk just waits there looming.
After all this computer dispute,
I told myself, "This thing isn't a lever or a pulley."
I should not think this is very cute,
This PC is the office's new bully.
I'll give it one more shot,
If it freezes it won't be there,
Oh no! It's getting hot.
It's smoking like a smoke affair.
It's making freaky sounds,
The room is turning grey.
How many more rounds?
I shall give this thing away.
Other people must suffer,
And accept their fair share.
And make their lives tougher,
For people everywhere.

Cameron Perisutti, Grade 6
Kinsner Elementary School

What I Like About Me!!!!

In the summer I like to play in the sand.
I'm in 4-H which stands for Head, Heart, Health, and Hand.
And I play in the Middle School band.

I have a wild imagination you can explore.
A cute little doggie you will adore.
But I hate when my mom makes me do a chore.

A country music lover, that's who I am.
I'm not fond of ham.
I show goats not lambs.

Ericka Castillo, Grade 6
Immaculate Conception School

Peaceful White Winter
Peaceful white winter
Snowmen sitting in quiet yards
Ice-covered treetops
Traffic moving so slowly,
Icy, frigid weather comes.
Gaige Roe, Grade 5
Westview Elementary School

Nature
The sky is like someone's
big, blue eyes

The sea waves gently
pushes on us

The sun watches us
during the day

And the moon and
stars watch us
at night

Hurricanes remind us
that mother nature
can be mean

Dawn is saying hello

While dusk is saying
good bye
Mariah SanFillipo, Grade 6
Woodward Park Middle School

Opposite Seasons
Summer,
Hot, humid,
Scorching, blazing, relaxing,
Swim, sun, sled, snow,
Snowing, caroling, freezing,
Chilly, icy,
Winter
Scot Sapp, Grade 6
Harmon Middle School

My Favorite Place
Relaxing, sunny
The third day
Early in the morning
Ducks quacking, people laughing
The mountains, gift shops, bumper cars
Walking, laughing
Next July
Happy
Mallory Reynolds, Grade 6
Tippecanoe Middle School

Holiday Season
Snow is falling.
Christmas is coming.
Going to get a Christmas tree.
The lights on the houses.
Decorating the Christmas tree.
Winter break from school.
Smell of a Christmas tree.
Hearing Christmas songs.
Presents under the tree.
Feeling snowflakes falling on your head.
Hockey season.
Taste of Christmas cookies.
Going sled riding.
Bailey Hayden, Grade 4
Licking Valley Intermediate School

Hot Dog
H owever yummy
O ut of this world
T asty

D oes have ketchup
O nions
G ood
Brandon Pearl, Grade 4
Northfield Elementary School

Your Song
Creativity is a burst of thought
music, art even things we weren't taught
It's awesome it's sweet, move to the beat
whistle sing tap your feet
open up
  look up
    find yourself
      upon the shelf
        glide along like the dawn
      find your song
Alice Leach, Grade 6
Woodward Park Middle School

Halloween
One day on Halloween.
I heard a loud scream.

I met a guy that was fat.
He said he wanted a bat.

After that I went to get candy.
That went just dandy.

When I got home.
I had to write a poem.
Mykal Howard, Grade 6
Roosevelt Elementary School

Why I Like Animals
I like animals because they
Have lots of energy
Are fun to play with
Funny sometimes
Hearing them make their own sounds
Seeing them be active
Feeling them lick you
Naming them
Raegan Donchess, Grade 4
Licking Valley Intermediate School

The Stable Horse
There once was a stable horse
Who ran the jumping course
One day he lay in the hay
And awoke in Massachusetts Bay
Now the stable has no horse!
Samantha Oliveri, Grade 5
Rootstown Elementary School

Fall
If fall leaves
are crunching, the wind
is howling, and there are
vivid colors everywhere.

The leaves have
beautiful colors like
oranges, yellows, and
reds.

The days are
changing and there
are pumpkin pies
everywhere.
David Leone, Grade 5
Immaculate Conception School

A Nature Walk
The sky looks
like a big sea filled with marshmallows.

The air feels
like cold water touching me.

The creek sounds
like when you slide over paper.

The air smells
like tree bark and animals.

My feet feel
soft grasses growing.
Emi Nobuoka, Grade 4
Normandy Elementary School

High Merit Poems – Grades 4, 5, and 6

A Christmas Morn

In the morning, as I run downstairs,
The snow outside reflects sliver light,
Almost like a frozen miracle,
Many cool crystals, melting with time
Warmth inside, warmth inside,
A quiet Christmas morn.
I see presents under the tree,
Looks like Santa was here!
Waiting for mother and brother to rise,
This beautiful Christmas morn.
The fire crackles, I drink warm cocoa,
Its scent like melted chocolate,
As it warms me from head to toe.
The sun peeks through the blinds,
Creating a perfect patch of light.
I twirl trough, a merry, joyful sight.
I tear open colorful gift wrap, when everyone is up
Wondering if I was naughty or nice,
Presents are wonderful, I shout for grateful joy
On this blessed Christmas morn.

Natalie Miller, Grade 5
EH Greene Intermediate School

My Teacher

M erry is she
R oses are her favorite flower
S haring and giving is a daily deed

L oving her job is what she shows
I t comes through in her smile right from her toes
S mart kids grow in her class
K ind words always flow from her mouth
O pen minded is what she encourages
V ery happy 24/7
E legant she always dresses
C aring she shows to each student

Lauren Ihnot, Grade 6
Rocky River Middle School

Blue

Blue is the color of the sky.
I wonder why?
Sometimes it makes me cry.
Blue is the color of my school.
it's also the color of the water in the pool.
It's true I love *blue*.
Some people like the color pink.
But it's obvious that they didn't think.
There are other colors of *blue*…
Like aquamarine sky and royal too.
Remember *blue* is the best.
Better than all of the rest.

Ally Engel, Grade 6
St John the Baptist School

Moon Phases

From the invisible new moon to the gargantuan full moon
There are many phases in between
The minuscule crescent roll comes first
Then the waxing semicircle comes along
Next comes the lima bean gibbous moon
The monstrous full moon is the biggest of them all
Then the moon starts waning
Next comes a slice of cheese with a bite missing
The waning midway moon is next
Next the watermelon rind is here
Lastly there is no moon
How does the mysterious moon do it all?

Ronald Knapp, Grade 5
Cline Elementary School

Freedom

You have the freedom of speech,
Religion and more
You are free to come and go
Whether you're rich or you're poor
We can go to school and learn,
So we can be whatever we want to be
We can assemble and vote and protest and just be free!
Freedom in America can't be beat!

Jani Bailey, Grade 6
Central Intermediate School

Snowflakes

Snowflakes come in all different shapes
Snowflakes come in all different sizes
They come in the winter, and some people despise them
No two snowflakes are ever the same,
But some people claim they are the same.

Sara Connelly, Grade 6
Rocky River Middle School

The Moon

Crystal ball in the sable hole,
Your face is the highlighted fall leaf,
A golden egg, your mouth,
Your eyes a shiny, sparkling apricot.
Glittering, gray clouds, your hair,
Your ears a rust that glows,
A clear frozen ice block, your nose,

Your habitat the perfect astronomical picture,
Small moonlings so beautiful,
Your neighbors the best ones,
Asteroid belt zooming past you,
Your shooting star granting wishes,
A comet flying through space

Your man on the moon
That smiles and whispers goodnight.

April Arellano, Grade 5
Cline Elementary School

Christmas

C is for carolers that sing door to door.
H is for holly that decorates the stores.
R is for reindeer that prance on my roof.
I is for icicles that form on my gutters.
S is for Santa Claus who wear white and red.
T is for tinsel all over my Christmas tree.
M is for mass that we go to on Christmas day.
A is for angels that sing the good news.
S is for sleigh rides in the snow.

Greg Ginley, Grade 6
Rocky River Middle School

Baseball

I run to first as I hit the ball
I hit it so far it went off the wall
I ran to second base
Now it is just a foot race

The game is fun
When you know how to play
You can run
Day after day

There are singles, doubles, triples, and home runs
You need to run at a fast rate
To get to home plate
At the stadium you can eat hotdogs with buns

The game is very cool
But it is fun to play
Baseball is the best
When you hit a home run people say hooray

Cory Tibbits, Grade 6
Kinsner Elementary School

I, the Man

If I were in charge of the world,
I would bring global warming to an end,
All friends would remain true friends,
Dogs would have longer lives,
And meat would have to be eaten every day.

If I were in charge of the world,
All wars would end,
No Marine would die at war,
And everyone would have a home.

If I were in charge of the world,
Storms would not harm the environment
And everyone will be equal.
If I were in charge of the world,
Cars would fly.

Clayton Hutton, Grade 5
Sanderson Elementary School

The Feast

I ring the doorbell; I hear a faint ring,
The door opens wide, and the smell flows to me,
The sweet smell of the juicy fruit and the spices of the stuffing
together make a glorious smell,
But then I smell it, the savory smell of the turkey!

I step inside and hear a faint noise,
I get a bit closer and hear soft, soothing music
along with the chatters of people getting the food ready,
I start to pour the soda,
I see the fizz like waves crashing on the shoreline,
Careful not to spill, I walk cautiously into the dining
room holding the cup like they're $100.

The light reflecting off the china cabinet blinds my eyes,
I jerk my head out of the light and see it, the FOOD!
First, I see a mountain of mashed potatoes heaved with gravy,
Next, I see the stuffing,
And I finally see it, the turkey!

Yes, we finally sit down,
We all say grace and the feast begins, the feast being, the feast begins!

Doug Hoffmeister, Grade 5
EH Greene Intermediate School

I Am

I am Keegan creative and intuitive.
I wonder if global warming will destroy the Earth in 70 years.
I hear my cowardly dog viciously barking at the neighborly deer.
I see the morning sun happily shining into my window.
I want to be a lot taller than I am now.
I am Keegan creative and intuitive.

I pretend to like football because it's fun to go to the games.
I feel like it would be fun to fly without planes.
I touch my 5 year old Australian Shepherd's fluffy black fur.
I worry about sudden death of a favorite relative happening soon.
I cry when I get cut and I need stitches.
I am Keegan creative and intuitive.

I understand that war is no way to solve a problem.
I say world peace is what we need instead of fighting.
I dream of soaring over the clouds with my arms wide.
I hope that I will be successful in getting a job.
I am Keegan creative and intuitive.

Keegan Orr, Grade 6
Harmon Middle School

Dew

Dew comes in silently like a little mouse
It is a light protective blanket for the grass.
By waiting until night and peacefully and quietly covering the grass.
All across the field making its way along the town.
When the rooster crows and the sun is rising it creeps away like magic.

Shannon Garrison, Grade 5
Wooster Christian School

Friendship

Friendship is a box of chocolate,
friendship is the month of February,
friendship is the year of 2008,
friendship tastes like chocolate,
friendship is shaped like a heart,
friendship is the season of Spring,
friendship has a pocket of love,
friendship sounds like music.

Nick Mikovits, Grade 6
Old Fort Elementary School

Monkey

There's a monkey named Jim
He loved a monkey named Kim
He brought her bananas and candy
She thought he was dandy
So they had a boy named Tim.

Haley Whitacre, Grade 5
Rootstown Elementary School

Football Thrill

Football in fall
Fun for all

Put on our gear
The crowd will cheer

Friday nights
Under the lights

No one will frown
When we score a touchdown

Justin Stewart, Grade 6
Holy Angels School

Statue of Liberty

Oh, the Statue of Liberty,
Standing tall,
On an island so small.
As long as her torch is lit,
We shall not fail to succeed.
Her crown says we are free
   to be and have no fear.
Her book has the knowledge
   of our great leaders.
To let us have peace.

Zach Arnett, Grade 4
Dobbins Elementary School

Like the Sun

The color yellow
   is like the sun,
and the day
   has just begun.

Kaleb Rowe, Grade 4
Greenfield Elementary School

My Crazy Morning

When I rolled out of bed,
I hit my head.
I almost wound up dead.

When I went to the table to eat,
I fell right off my seat.

I think I'll just skip the food.
Hey! There's the bus!
I'll just go hang with Gus.
But I'm still in a terrible mood.

Davey Rose, Grade 6
Tippecanoe Middle School

Trees

Trees rustling leaves
That blow softly in the wind
Silent in the night.

Aubry Lindauer, Grade 6
Roosevelt Elementary School

College Football Game

The crowd is roaring
Fans are on their feet
Students scream a war chant
To a steady beat

As the game is ending
We won't accept defeat
As our kicker tries to win the game
With only using his feet

We won we won
Now the celebration begins
Now I turn and ask my dad
Can we come again?

Jacob Collier, Grade 6
EH Greene Intermediate School

Bread!!

Nobody ever writes about bread!
Yet… bread is healthy
And fills me with energy!
White bread, wheat bread.
Rye bread, pumpernickel…
All full of energy.
Bread doesn't get enough notice
People eat it
But never write about it!
Being bread would be bad,
To be eaten by strangers,
Unable to have fun!
Being drowned with butter and…
OH, NO! The toaster is coming!

Chandler Spriggs, Grade 5
Westview Elementary School

Animals

Tigers jump with a jump rope
Dogs are playing the bongos
Cats are napping with their blankets
Jaguars are running through the forest.

Jobby Kurian, Grade 6
Woodward Park Middle School

Rascal

Rascal is my pet poodle
He's fluffy and white
He's so full of energy
He can jump out of sight!

With pitiful brown eyes
And his cold, cold nose,
I love my Rascal
From his head to his toes.

Tess Remy-Davis, Grade 5
Westview Elementary School

Adventure

Out into the wild,
Along a bending trail,
Down by the bubbling stream,
Around the cautious minnows,
Past the playful deer,
Outside everything I know,
Beyond the thoughts of getting lost,
For every day I try to make,
An adventure.

Zachary Goodchild, Grade 6
Harmon Middle School

Can You Imagine?

An alarm that doesn't ring
A bell that doesn't ding?

Night lights that don't light
Princesses without a knight?

Computers without chips
People without lips?

Movies without clips
People without tips?

Basketballs without air
Children without care?

A book without an end
Money that you can't spend?

Cars that don't stop
The world without cops?

Colin Faulkner, Grade 6
Wooster Christian School

Locksmiths
We are the locksmiths,
We give you keys,
We'll be there in a jif
To help you out of a tight squeeze.

For your problems we bring ease,
High prices are just a myth,
Our advertisement doesn't tease.

So don't stay in a miff,
Just call us whenever you please.
We are recommended by the sheriff
To help you out of a tight squeeze.
Zach Thompson, Grade 5
Stanton Middle School

Night Fire
Crackle, crackle
Watch it go
Flames of destruction,
Immense sorrow
Burning bright,
Throughout the night,
Carrying destruction, misery, and fright
Spiting out sparks
In the dark
Spilling out hate
Throwing up misery,
Leaving nothing,
But burnt down history
Shine, shine
In the night
Living up humanity's fright
When all is burnt
When all is gone
It's time for you to say
So long.
Matt Degenhardt, Grade 6
EH Greene Intermediate School

All About Me
Athletic funny person I am,
And for Thanksgiving I have ham.
It may not be the most original thing
I play the flute I do not sing

All about me you want to know
I always stub my pinkie toe,
There is more you must know.

I do not have a favorite color
I bounce back from one to another
I have an awesome mother.
Claire Zielinski, Grade 6
Immaculate Conception School

Brothers and Sisters
Brothers and sisters can be annoying
They're not a thing to be enjoying
I think they're from someplace like Mars
Where all the kids are kept in jars
They argue
They fight
They ripped up my kite
Brothers and sisters are an ugly sight
Samuel Lehman, Grade 4
Licking Valley Intermediate School

Whispering Rain
Soft rain
Tapping softly
Whispering soft to me
Silently calms me down to rest
And sleep
Janie Moller, Grade 6
Harmon Middle School

Leaves
Leaves fall through the sky
Looking like butterflies
Many kinds of colors
Red, yellow, orange, and brown
Trees, bare of leaves
Kids running in piles
Of leaves to have some fun
Here comes spring
Where the leaves gleam
Unyime Usip, Grade 5
Akiva Academy

How Weird!
My friends and I
We like the same guy.
He plays sports like us
But he doesn't ride our bus.
He talks with us outside
But he doesn't know our other side.
He likes us all as a friend
But will that be the end?

How weird!
Brooke Edwards, Grade 5
Spaulding Elementary School

Wondrous Mountains
Wondrous mountain peaks
So tall and mysterious
Snowcapped tops amaze.
A falcon circles and dives...
Oh, the wonder of mountains!
Landon Montalto, Grade 5
Westview Elementary School

How to Behave in School
Say your teacher looks nice
Turn in all your homework
Raise your hand for questions
Never talk back
Say your teacher is the best
Always use your Sunday manners
Listen to your teacher
Do not be late for class
Never talk in class
Always behave in class
Do not say bad things about your teacher
Always say she smells nice
Buy her chocolate
Study for a test
Help her
Say thank you
Do what she says
Be kind
Be the best student you can
Kasia Bartram, Grade 5
Sanderson Elementary School

The Lone Comfort
Soaring high in the sky.
No one by my side.
The lone comfort.
Nobody knows the pain
I go through every day.
The lone comfort.
No reason to cry
Yet I do every night.
The lone comfort.
Shooting stars I see.
No wish for me.
The lone comfort.
The lone comfort comes for me.
Jesus is thee.
The lone comfort.
Hannah Smith, Grade 4
Buckeye Woods Elementary School

Joe's Puppy
Joe is getting a puppy
Instead of a guppy.

He named it Spot.
Because it has a dot.

He taught it tricks.
And spot jumps over bricks.

Joe likes to play.
With Spot all day.
Brian Kelzer, Grade 6
Roosevelt Elementary School

Winter Days

My favorite time of year is winter.
My grandma and grandpa come up to our house to visit.
I love going hunting with my dad.
I love to spend time with my family.
I like to play with my brother and sister.
The sound of deer stepping on the leaves.
I love getting up and going out and smelling the air.
Just feeling the cold rush of air.
The feeling of shooting a deer.
Going out to do a drive.

Jordyn Wood, Grade 4
Licking Valley Intermediate School

Fall

Fall is so much fun.
It is fun to catch the leaves as they fall.
It is cool to see the many colors.
Fall is sometimes boring
Like when your Dad makes you rake the leaves.
But, most of the time fall is fun.
A pine tree is lucky.
It doesn't have to lose its leaves.
Unlike some other tress
Who must.

Tyler Tamarkin, Grade 5
Akiva Academy

Wolf

Slowly stalking through the night
begins his hunt at first light.
In the forest it is cold
he passes by the trees so old.

The wind whispers secrets to him
it's getting late, the light is dim.
He hears the hooting of an owl
and lets out a mighty howl.

Slowly stalking through the night
quickly as a ray of light.
Walks so fast he could turn on a dime,
past the dark green evergreen as old as time.

He spies a rabbit, behind some flames
he gets ready to jump and slowly aims.
Bravely, courageously, leaps over the fire,
kills and eats the rabbit, because need for food is dire.

Slowly stalking through the night
under moonlight, oh so bright.
The night is done, the hunt is over,
gently lies down in his bed of clover.

Nicholas Rushlow, Grade 4
Fairfield Elementary School

I, the King

If I were in charge of the world,
I would ban all cigarettes,
There would be no pollution,
All video games would have no killing,
And guns would not be used.

If I were in charge of the world,
Nobody would every get sick or die from cancer,
People would not make fun of anyone,
And all cats would have owners.

If I were in charge of the world,
Potatoes, eggs, and bacon would be eaten every day
And candy would be free.

If I were in charge of the world,
Halloween would be 3X a month.

Andrew Redman, Grade 5
Sanderson Elementary School

Change

Change is something we fear,
and yet it comes every year.
For nothing is forever.
Change is bad never.

Change is always there.
It's just not always seen.
Many things change in the world.
Leaves turn brown from green.

Change is good for the soul.
Change makes things worth while.
Change is good for your mind
It always makes me smile.

Change always has to be.
Change brings people together.
Change will set you free.
Yet it is so strong for being lighter than a feather.

Lauren Miller, Grade 6
Kinsner Elementary School

Blue

Blue is the color of the sky, though I don't know why.
People can be blue too. Yes it's true.
Some flowers are blue and some houses too.
Blue can be turquoise, aqua, peacock, and sapphire, too.
The water is aqua, a greenish-blue.
A priceless gem is a sapphire.
Fire can also be blue.
Ouch!
That's hot!
Blue, blue, blue.

Adam Moeller, Grade 6
St John the Baptist School

Christmas Red and Gold

Christmas Day has finally come!
I'm as happy as a babbling baby
bouncing a blue ball.

Questions flooded my mind.
What will I receive this year?
Perhaps red and gold stockings.

Did Santa enjoy his warm sugar cookies?
I heard him laughing with delight
as he took his last bitty bite.

Singing family gathered around our
red and gold pine-scented tree,
gazing at the glowing star
perched up on the top, what glee.

Excited as a puppy
chasing a squirrel,
my little sister gasps as she
shakes the giggling gifts.
Red and gold holiday,
Red and gold holiday,
Red and gold holiday.
Kate Ammerman, Grade 5
EH Greene Intermediate School

Moonlight Shadows

The moonlight shadows
make you dream of ghostly hallows
as you sleep through the night.

There is no sound
or footsteps on the ground
just the street lights.

You lay awake
until dawn's break
and the day takes over the night.
Dylan Rouda, Grade 5
Barrington Elementary School

A Fly of a Lifetime

I'm ready for flight,
above the sky
the smell of the water,
makes me feel like I'm free
from the world
and everything that's mean.
So lets take off
and have the night of our
wonderful lives
of fun.
Sammantha Adams, Grade 5
Elyria Community School

Homework

The dog ate my homework last night
It really gave me a fright
My teacher was mad
I wasn't glad
Now I'm in detention all night
Betty Jo DelFratte, Grade 6
Roosevelt Elementary School

Hate Is Like a Broken Glass

Hate is like a broken glass
It's very sad…

Hate is like a broken glass,
Because it's wrong
Using those strong words
To hurt someone's feelings.
Brian Bailey, Grade 4
Matthew Duvall Elementary School

Halloween

H orror.
A lot of candy.
L oads of fun.
L awns are decorated.
O n October 31st.
W ho has the best costume?
E at lots of candy.
E njoy your walk.
N ever pass a house.
Katie Brown, Grade 4
Sts Joseph and John School

Night

Night
The blackness
Cooling, soothing, sweet, sorrowful,
The night is everything,
Yet nothing…
It is a treasure, but
Still an empty box
The blackness,
night
Clayton Peacock, Grade 4
Indian Springs Elementary School

Football

Running up the field
Twenty yard pass
Quarterback sneak
Run up the gut
Big hit
But if there's a touchdown
The crowd goes wild.
Eric White, Grade 4
Dobbins Elementary School

Thanksgiving

I am really thankful,
of everything, and everyone.
They care for me,
especially my one and only parents.
I also am thankful
of the soldiers that fought for us
and die to save their country.
I am really thankful for that rain
that continues to rain
because there are some states
such as Georgia,
that barely get rain every year.
Most of all, I am thankful
of everything, and everyone.
David Shon, Grade 5
Cline Elementary School

Little Bumble Bee

Oh little bumble bee!
Flying, stinging, buzzing, screaming.
Makes me want to cry.
Crying, hurting, painful, smarted,
Oh little bumble bee oh oh my.
Hannah Lawson, Grade 4
Monroe Elementary School

Snow

Outside, on a freezing,
snowy day, the leafless tree,
clothed in downy flakes.
Brent Hamre, Grade 6
EH Greene Intermediate School

My Cat Thai

You make me feel happy
'Cause you're always happy.
Your smooth, soft fur
Your blues eyes like mine
Softly purring
Rubbing against me
Winking at me every day
You're the only Siamese kitty I know
Thomas DeHays, Grade 6
Tippecanoe Middle School

Ocean to Desert

ocean
peaceful, powerful
enjoying, shivering, shining
Indian, water, Gobi, desert
sweating, torching, scorching
torrid, warm
desert
Morgan Sevel, Grade 5
Northfield Baptist Christian School

Blue

Blue is like the sky.
One of my favorite blues is marine.
I also like cobalt.
There is sky, sapphire, and turquoise too.
Blue reminds me of a King.
Because a kind of blue is royal.

Garret Liette, Grade 6
St John the Baptist School

Guinea Pig

I am a guinea pig.
You know me for my squeaky voice.
My mother is brown with specks of white.
My father is gray with a white belly.
I was born in a big pet store.
I live in a marvelous new house.
My best friend is a small hamster,
Because we are rodents.
We like to run in our balls together.
My enemy is a fast, sneaky dog,
Because he tries to eat me.
I fear the winter,
Because I don't want to freeze.
I love my caring owner,
Since she takes very good care of me.
I dream to lose weight.

Stephanie Greer, Grade 5
Dr John Hole Elementary School

Baseball

I like running the bases.
Also when I see all of the kids' faces.
It's fun in the day.
At night, in my bed, I get some rest and lay.

To warm up, we only play catch.
We wait for our teammates to attend.
We run laps, but some people fall on their rear ends.
With our teammates, we do a match.

After, we go out and play the game.
The pitcher threw some balls.
Then we came back with the fame.
Each one of us got one of the balls.

My team got trophies.
I put it next to my bed.
My mom took me to McD's, I got a McFlurry.
I came home, and "You're the champion!" everyone said.

Then in the summer I practiced.
"Are you going to play baseball?" a lot I hear.
My mom was looking at a magazine, I noticed.
She was looking at baseball for next year.

Zachary Batts, Grade 6
Kinsner Elementary School

Paradise

Paradise, paradise, beautiful paradise,
Paradise is nice and beautiful,
Paradise is very peaceful.
Allah made everything in paradise.
I will live in a castle where I can be,
Surrounded by nature and beautiful trees.
Paradise, paradise, beautiful paradise,
Whenever you think of something you want,
It will come to you from Allah's love.
Everyone loves paradise and so do I.
It's brighter than the sun, moon and the sky.
Thank you Allah for paradise,
It is better than the world.

Ramsha Rashid, Grade 5
Islamic School of Greater Toledo

Canoe Trip

On the water,
In a canoe,
The air so hot,
The water so blue.

Part of a troop of three canoes,
Some were yellow, some were green,
Some were of every sheen.

Four hours long was our tour,
We saw a great heron, so big, so pure,
It babbled, it talked, and was so loud,
We saw some minnows, as slick as butter,
They were butterflies, in mid flutter.

Paddle, stroke, left, right,
Every second the sun was so bright,
Paddle, stroke, right, left,
We stopped to rest upon a cleft.

Hour, hour, on we went,
Hour, hour, we were spent,
And then,
Finished! Land ho!
We were glad so.

Andrew Grever, Grade 6
OHDELA Academy

Tsunami

A Tsunami comes in very fast
Like a tiger grabbing its prey.
It starts out at sea when an earthquake creates a wave.
The wave grows big.
It crashes over land.
It snatches anything in its path and drags it out to sea.

Colin Reed, Grade 5
Wooster Christian School

Friends

When you're alone and have nothing to do,
Friends will come and help you.
If you're having trouble and you're scared,
Don't worry, your friends will be there.
Friends you should trust,
Friends you should love.
To help you get through all of the things you do.
If they help you,
You should help, too!
Just remember that friends are friends
And they will always be there.
Do you have a best friend?
I know I do!

Lorena Opris, Grade 6
Rocky River Middle School

Ramadan

Ramadan is a special month
When we all have to fast
I really can't wait
Until it all goes past
We fast from 6:00 am to 7:00 p.m.
It feels like you're being stabbed with a pen
I don't like it
But it's for the better
But I can't wait 'till it's time for dinner.

Hashem Anabtawi, Grade 5
Tremont Elementary School

Thanksgiving

Thanksgiving, Thanksgiving
What a wonderful day.

What I wouldn't do for a beautiful
Thanksgiving day.

I am thankful for the Pilgrims
Making Thanksgiving a wonderful holiday.

Collin Hanna, Grade 4
Demmitt Elementary School

Winter

Winter is cold
freezing cold
my nose is strawberry red
icicles growing on it — ouch
snowflakes in my eye
I catch snowflakes in my hand
watch them melt
the snow looks like a big white fluffy marshmallow
I hate winter
but I love winter.

Katherine Adams, Grade 5
Tremont Elementary School

A Summer Treat

One summer morning a boy was yearning for a treat.
He got ready and put socks on his feet while the birds were saying tweet.
He asked his mom if he could go with his friend Boe.
His mom said yes because he got an A on his test.
He jumped on his bike and went to Boe's house.
When Boe's mom opened the door she was wearing her pretty blouse.
They got on their bikes and went to the store.
When they opened the door the floor seemed to gleam.
They went down the aisle and got ice cream.
It took them a while but they ate it all.
Then they went back to Boe's house and played some ball.

Max Finnerty, Grade 6
Central Intermediate School

Autumn

The Fairfield County Fair covered with scent of funnel cakes
The Zero Gravity ride spinning very fast
My sister putting force on the wheel in the middle of the Twister ride
Playing for a new pet fish
This makes autumn.

Leaves change from green to yellow, orange, red, and brown
Children chasing leaves as they fall
And asking parents to rake the leaves
Making and hiding in forts made of leaves
This makes autumn.

Chanting, "Go Bucks"
Jumping up and down when a touchdown is scored
Putting on my Buckeye jersey
Booing at the Wolverines
This makes autumn.

Scary costumes at Krogers
Children singing about ghosts
Yards filled with blow up pumpkins
Parents buying lots of candy
This makes autumn.

Erin Jamison, Grade 5
Sanderson Elementary School

School

School is a place for learning new things.
School is a place for excellence and to do your best.
To get to the next grade you will have to pass the achievement test.
If you don't go to school you will be a mess.
Work your hardest don't guess.
Science, math, literacy, gym, play games for fun not to win.
Doesn't matter if you're popular or not cool
You will still rule if you follow the rules.
Doesn't matter how your dressed or what clothes you wore.
Stay in school, go to college you'll score

Cassidy Tennity, Grade 6
Monroe Elementary School

I Am

    I am Sara, energetic and appreciative.
I wonder what matters I will have to confront tomorrow, and 10 years from now.
I hear the squabbling of my parents, and myself wishing it could end soon.
I see the gladdening faces of my friends when we make each other laugh.
I want a jubilant life, but sometimes I feel as if it's too far away for me to reach.
    I am Sara, energetic and appreciative.
I pretend my life is filled with joyousness, but sometimes it really isn't.
I feel the softness of my dogs' coats when they nestle up against me when I am sad.
I touch the irregular tree bark when I climb a tree to get away from everything happening on the ground.
I worry that I will lose a member of my family in a devastating accident again.
I cry when everything in the world seems to despise me.
    I am Sara, energetic and appreciative.
I understand that most people don't have an ideal life, but we make the best of it.
I say, "Believe, and you can do anything!" because we are capable of doing mostly anything!
I dream that the world will one day become a more cleaner, relaxed place to live.
I try to be the most optimum person I can be, no matter what.
I hope that one day I will become an extraordinary author like Jack London, or Judy Bloom!
    I am Sara, energetic and appreciative.

Sara Defibaugh, Grade 6
Harmon Middle School

Veterans…A Thrilling Retelling of Some of the Amazing Acts of Veterans in the Second World War

Fear plagues the Earth like a disease.
Nazi troops storm the planet like a raging wildfire.
People hide in basements, or attics, terrified of destruction, always unsure,
Unaware of what horrors the next moment will bring.
Tragedy lurks around every corner, awaiting its next victim.
But then, shining like a beacon of hope and promise, our soldiers appear,
Selflessly defending all that represents peace, nobility, and justice.
Many other every day people are risking their lives protecting strangers and family,
Always seeking to help.
The people themselves are showing great courage and skill.
We are forever grateful to all of those who gave their own lives to save others.
Thank you, amazing veterans in all wars, not just the second world war,
But all those that have come before and since.
It is you who have helped to build our glorious nation, defeating the British and
Freeing us from their tyranny in the Revolution.
It is you who have protected America from looming threats, serving in the Armed Forces.
Your great deeds are too innumerable to list.
Thank you once again.

John Carroll, Grade 6
EH Greene Intermediate School

I Am From

I am from the hard streets of crime, of gunfire, fights and murders in East Cleveland.
I am a priceless jewel with one diamond for my sister and one ruby for my brother.
I am from lots of community bus trips, to trips in a car daily to grandma's and many dazy cousins.
I am like a fly on the wall when it's holiday time, buzzing, tasting all the lemon cakes, dressing, and collard greens.
I am the music princess of the party, and they want to hear my jazzy tunes.
I am filled with lots of love, and Tweety bird cakes makes it even colorful to me.
I am closing up like a tulip, nights are quiet in my hood.
I am from a big dream of family and because they believe, SO DO I.

Kayla Lane, Grade 6
Prospect Elementary School

The Smithsonian Institution
More than three buildings
Our nation's attic
One museum just for airplanes
Lots of visitors
Paintings, sculptures
Artifacts everywhere!
Matt Duran, Grade 4
Dobbins Elementary School

Parachuting
flying high in the white sky
jumping off very fast
catching the wind
looking down at green grass
rushing down to land
screaming loud over blue ocean
hitting the ground very excitedly
bursting out with a great big laugh
Brian Tempel, Grade 6
St Clement Elementary School

All About Me
K ittens that cuddle
A dog named Cassie
I ce cream sundae
L ove to dance
A pple dumplings as treat

M ystery
A purple room
R oller skating is my pleasure
I love cats
E nglish muffins for breakfast

P ersian cat named Baby
A pple cider for a drink
U nderstanding friend
S hy person
C otton candy eater
H uskie's are the cutest dogs
E njoying having fun
R oot beer float explode
T rampoline limousine
Kaila Marie Pauschert, Grade 5
Frank Ohl Middle School

Basketball Game
Shoot the ball and make a basket.
Block someone to get the rebound.
Then pass the ball to your teammates.
Then jump when you win!!!

GO TEAM!
Aubrey Lincoln, Grade 4
Northfield Elementary School

Cobra
Cobra, Cobra, sly and fast
slinking slowly cross the grass
Cobra, Cobra, head above
a small mouse's grey blue fuzz
Cobra, Cobra, slithering
doing your own type of thing
Cobra, cobra camouflaged
creeping quickly past a lodge
Cobra, Cobra a predator
prowling past as a greenish blur
Cobra, Cobra tongue long and pink
moving fast as you can blink
Cobra, Cobra amazing
obviously fascinating
Kami Previte, Grade 6
EH Greene Intermediate School

The Cat
My cat
Looks like a huge puffball
He roams our house
So big and tall

He eats many varieties
Of cat food and treats
He moves quickly
On his four muscular feet

He can open doors
Without the help of us
He's the smartest cat
On the bus

And now you know
The story of a cool feline
So good-bye and remember
I tell no lies
Justin Van Wagenen, Grade 6
EH Greene Intermediate School

Basketball
I love basketball
However, sometimes you fall.
This sport is action packed,
And that's a fact!

You're put into groups
Then you shoot some hoops.
Even when you have to block,
Basketball rocks!

You get to jump and run
It's a whole lot of fun!
Abbigayle Hodge, Grade 6
Tippecanoe Middle School

Living Nature
The sky is like
little creatures
running through the wind.

Plants rush in
as wind and flowers
shout with cheer
waiting for a new adventure.
Melanie Engber, Grade 4
Normandy Elementary School

My Toad
I once had a toad.
Who played in the road.

One day a car went by
SPLAT! I watched him die

He was too small to put in a casket
So instead, I put him in a basket

When Toad died, I was really sad
But my mom seemed kinda glad
Liza Perry, Grade 6
Trilby Elementary School

Memories
Memories are
Humorous times with
Friends and family,
Telling jokes and
Wondrous secrets,
Memories are
Wonderful thoughts of
Sitting around
A burning campfire
Followed by a
Willowed breeze.
Nuha Wahdan, Grade 5
Cline Elementary School

My Dog Summer
I have a Golden Retriever
She is dumber
Than a drummer.

I bet we really need to get
My golden dog to the vet,
She isn't even 1 yet.

She is golden-red
And has a small head
And never goes to bed.
Tyler Ogle, Grade 6
Trilby Elementary School

Pumpkin Head

You have no head, but you sure are scary
When you walk through the woods on Halloween
Scaring little kids that are in there.
When they come through they will get a surprise
When you jump out at them with a pumpkin for your head!
Boo!!!

Phillip Mercer, Grade 5
Stanton Middle School

Skating

I put my wheels on the ground
Put on my music, turn up the sound
Take off down the street
Doing tricks to the beat.

The wood, metal the falling and pain
Without them we'd all be insane
Would we ride bikes or even rollerblade?
Or would we just hide ourselves in the shade.

Ollie, manual to treflip out.
But that's not what it's all about.
It's all about the liberty
Being able to ride freely.

On the street, at the park
Skating all day until after dark
Skating makes us all stand tall
About skating, that is all.

Bekka Barnett, Grade 6
Monroe Elementary School

Soccer

I like soccer it is fun
you have to work and run.
If you try to be the best
you can be better than the rest.

You have to run down the field
I shoot the ball at the goal
the goalie blocks the ball like a shield.
I hope it will land in the hole.

The goalie has to block the ball.
Offense is my favorite position
each one has a mission.
Even if they're short or tall.

Soccer is great
it is one of the many sports that uses a ball
soccer is the best sport
it is the best of them all!

Michael Congeni, Grade 6
Kinsner Elementary School

Fever Pitch

Spring, summer, winter, fall
Big league dreams of playing ball
Warm breezes bring spring training fever
Out of the park bombs, I'm a miracle believer

Summertime's here, it's getting so hot
I'm pitching so great and hitting the spot
Crack of the bat before the seventh inning stretch
Robbed at the wall by a spectacular catch
Home run Derby and the All-Star Break
Records are broken, history is made

Leaves are falling, the weather's getting colder
Monroe Swarm is in The Hunt for October
I swing with all my might and pray it stays fair
Cause we're bringing home the World Series hardware!

Winter is here and it's oh so cold
I'm dreaming of spring and what the new season holds

Josh McCready, Grade 4
Monroe Elementary School

Home

I know of a place, a place I called home.
Where you could wake to be reminded,
"Don't forget to comb!"
Where I used to sit all day,
and watch my favorite bluebird play.
Where I used to go to see my friend Matt,
Only to find I forgot to say "hi" to his cat.
Oh, what fun we had, taking long hikes,
or riding our really fast bikes.
Then, at the end of the day,
I would go to bed thinking, of new ways
I could have fun the next day.

Omar Yacteen, Grade 6
Islamic School of Greater Toledo

The Gingerbread Man

I'm a gingerbread so delicious and colorful,
Our town full of gingers are so wonderful,
Though many like Christmas,
Because of the warmth and cheer,
All the gingers hate this time of year,
People baking us is the only fun,
Hearing the buzzer and the words "It's done!"
Until Christmas Eve it is very jolly,
Looking around and see all the holly,
Its time for bed and without a sound,
Here comes Santa, big and round,
We all get scared and start to cry,
For he's going to take one of us just for a try,
Here comes his hand and we all start to shiver,
Whew not me, maybe next winter.

Stephanie Koch, Grade 6
Glenwood Middle School

Sammi
S illy
A mazing
M anners
M ysterious
I ntelligent
Sammi Calabrase, Grade 4
Sts Joseph and John School

Father
F atherhood:
A
T ime to be
H appy
E ven when it gets
R ough.
Sharon Arnold, Grade 6
Melrose Elementary School

Mosquito
Oh, mosquito, big pest,
You make me cry.
I just can't stop itching —
I think I'll die.

I've counted fifteen —
Just on my right hand.
There are millions more
Just waiting to land.

When you suck my blood,
I can't sleep all night.
It drives me nuts
When you start to bite.

I'm ready this time —
This is how it will be.
I smack you dead —
Yippee for me!
Lauren Miller, Grade 6
Melrose Elementary School

Spring
Spring is upon us
The birds sing and play
The air smells so sweet
Maddie Acklin, Grade 6
Harmon Middle School

Autumn Dean
Autumn Dean
Intelligent, lucky
Singing, talking, reading
She loves to learn.
Student
Autumn Dean, Grade 6
Jefferson Elementary School

Picking a Christmas Tree
The best time
of the year is when
Christmas is near. Families
pile into the truck to try their luck
at finding the best tree to cut. Look up
ahead at that tall, fat, green pine; don't you
agree it would be fine? We will need a chain saw
since it is 9 foot tall. I can't wait for the whistle of the
branches when it falls. The whole family grabs the trunk, to
drag it back to the truck. Into the bed it goes with straps so it does
not blow off on the trip back home. Everyone piles out and we drag it
into the house. Once it is in the stand, the whole family lends a hand to add
decorations and to end the fun day we have thought of a great way we decided
the tallest will
add the star.
Nick Elsner, Grade 6
Holy Angels School

Snow Day
It is the first day of snow,
All the kids are happy,
Laughing and yelling shouts of joy,
Playing in the bright white snow,
The sun is still shining,
The kids still playing,
Having snow ball fights and sledding,
You can hear the crunch of snow under foot,
The snow is like a blanket,
Covering a bed,
"Oh snow day, how much snow will you bring?"
After the kids are done,
Frolicking in the snow,
They go inside to find warmth and the smell of a warm sticky bun,
And drink their cinnamon hot cocoa,
Sitting by the fire,
It's muffled crackling behind the case,
And the soft whistle of a kettle brewing more warm cocoa,
The sun is glinting off the snow,
What a glorious day it is,
Snow, snow, snow!
Tyler Hegyesi, Grade 5
EH Greene Intermediate School

The Wind's Cries
The wind whispered in my ear sweet, gentle cries of help
Then they got fiercer, and it began to cry big, heavy weeps into the sky
And I don't know why
The wind just kept crying to me with gigantic yelps
It went on and on and it still didn't tell me why
So I repeatedly asked the sky
then the wind swirled in the air
As if it didn't have one single care
Then I knew the wind was crying
For the wind was nearly dying.
Mackenzie Pahren, Grade 6
Woodward Park Middle School

Winter Joy

The wind whispered
softly blowing the last leaf of the tree

It is winter now

Small, white flakes hit the ground
Silently I shiver and wrap my coat tightly around me

The winter beauty showing itself

The soft snow resting on the sturdy branches of the old oak
the red robins chirp loudly,
piercing the air with their rare, delightful song

The snow crunching under my heavy winter boots
The birth of the morning, waking the world

Life starts to flitter, and the sun
glittering and gleaming on the new fallen snow
The tops of the buildings illuminated with the tip of the sun

Anna Mackey, Grade 4
Hylen Souders Elementary School

I, the Smart One

If I were in charge of the world,
There would only be four hours of school,
Dogs would be allowed in stores,
Doing homework would be illegal,
And kids would be in charge of the adults.

If I were in charge of the world,
There would be no drugs,
Smoking would be prohibited,
And the war would end.

If I were in charge of the world,
Buses would be rollercoasters
And no one would be left out.

If I were in charge of the world,
Everyone would have a home.

Courtney Bernard, Grade 5
Sanderson Elementary School

Ode to My Dog Riley

My dog's name is Riley.
Riley and I like to play together.
She also likes to play with her dog friends.
Her fur is soft and smooth
And golden like the sun.
Riley loves to swim in the pool with us.
I feel safe when I feel her soft fur
Right up against me
When we sleep together at night.

Jenna Collins, Grade 6
Tippecanoe Middle School

The Sound of Snow

The sound of snow
Stops me from whatever I'm doing.
I look out the window.
I see sugar coating the grass.
The sky is as gray as a hippo.

I quickly put on my coat and boots,
Running not to get outside.
The door flings open.
I spring across the sidewalk as fast as a cheetah,
And jump in like a bunny.

Snow angels are now lined up across my lawn.
A line of snowmen are stretching down the driveway.
The cold doesn't seem to bother me.
I lay down in the blanket of snow.
It feels so wonderful.

All of a sudden, I hear my mother shouting from the distance.
I look up at the sky,
Now black as coal.
I slowly drift inside,
And hope tomorrow I'll wake to…
The sound of snow.

Faith Kaufman, Grade 6
EH Greene Intermediate School

Love Is Explanatory

Love is a box of joy.
You're so happy you can't express it.

Love is the song of your heart.
You feel like it's going to sing.

Love is the month of October.
It's colorful like your heart.

Love tastes like chocolate.
You feel like your heart's melting inside you.

Love is the touch of God
telling you it's that special someone.

Love is the season of Fall
when all the leaves come down and
you know they were meant for you.

Love feels like a touch of cupid.
When you see him, he shoots you and you find your someone.

Love sounds like a woodpecker.
Your heart beats against your chest trying to escape.

Madison Hammond, Grade 6
Old Fort Elementary School

Fall

Since fall has come,
I'm filled with fun.

When I rake the leaves,
I feel the breeze.

When I jump into the pile,
I laugh and always smile.

On Yom Kippur our parents fast,
And they can't wait till it has passed.

Fall, fall, don't go away,
I really want you to stay!

Rivka Lifshitz, Grade 4
Cincinnati Hebrew Day School

Cats

I have a cat,
she is my only love,
and yesterday she caught a dove.
My cat is black and that is a fact.

Sarah Smith, Grade 4
Greenfield Elementary School

Growing Together

Together we stand
Holding hand and hand
We come together
And grow
When we grow
It's not to slow
We are fast
To not stand last
At last we grown
Happily together
We had thrown
The holding back down.

Macy Smith, Grade 5
Elyria Community School

Grandma at Night

My grandma is a star.
I'm the night sky.
So cherished and wonderful.
She creates my dreams with warmth.
Grandma shoots out of the night sky.
And lands in the ocean.
Or wherever I need her.
Grandma is exciting.
And full of adventures!
My grandma is a great star.
In the night sky.

Kayla Rose, Grade 5
Westview Elementary School

Christmas Eve

Glittery fragile glowing snow
Falling from the bright blue sky
Kids excited for tomorrow, Christmas
The day every kid desires
Hoping Santa comes.

Nick Edison, Grade 6
EH Greene Intermediate School

I Can See Anything

On this late fall afternoon
I see purple
That is special to me!
I see kids way bigger than me
Finding their books
Then scattering to class
The exit sign is as red
As an apple
I always see Thomas,
My best friend's brother!
Now I see 8th graders talking
I don't know why
Everything is normal
Except those 8th graders!

Dakota Morris, Grade 5
Emerson Academy of Dayton

Mrs. Drees

My teacher's name is Mrs. Drees.
She just got stung by 20 bees.
She found out that her dog has fleas.
And then she fell onto her knees.

We've seen her fall at least three times.
We think that hurting her's a crime.
Every time she finds a dime.
She goes to the store to buy a lime.

My teacher's name is Mrs. Drees.
Her favorite plants are maple trees.
She loves to read us mysteries.
That's our crazy Mrs. Drees.

Shannon Harrington, Grade 5
Spaulding Elementary School

Worms

Worms, worms,
They help our soil.
Digging holes for water to get in.
On your driveway when it rains,
Please don't throw them in the drains.
But, be careful when you eat,
Because you don't want worms
In your treats.

Krista Nolfi, Grade 4
Dobbins Elementary School

Sports

The quarterback threw a pass
He threw the ball
He falls on the grass
You get in a brawl

In volleyball you slide
You pull a fake
If you don't get a hit you have a fit
You really ache

You get outs
You get hits
Singles, doubles, triples, homers
If you don't you have fits

You shoot the ball
Some people are tall
You get a block
You beat the clock

Zack Zatezalo, Grade 6
Kinsner Elementary School

As the World Turns

Day
Sunny, bright
Beautiful, amazing, wonderful
Shining, sun, dark, gloomy
Quiet, moon, sullen
Stars, silent
Night

Jill Berning, Grade 6
Harmon Middle School

Sweets

Ice cream is something that tastes great
Meaty things I do hate
Whenever I bite
It fills me with delight

Candy is a great one too
Either sweet or sour
Crunchy or chewy
I can eat it in less than an hour

I love apple pie
It's so sweet
Whenever I eat it it's a real treat
I could never sigh

Candy tastes so good
Yet it should
Like Candy Land
It's nothing like sand

Dana Gore, Grade 6
Kinsner Elementary School

Is He with You?

God is good all the time,
to every boy and girl!

He is with his children,
All around the world!

So when you weep,
And you have a broken heart!

Remember if you repent and believe Jesus is God's son,
Then you'll know the love of Christ that's there for everyone!

So if your life's not filled with Christ,
You need to make a sacrifice!

Mallory McIntosh, Grade 4
Monroe Elementary School

Love Faithfully

Love every part of them
Overlooking their past
Visualize them and no one else
Erase the pain and rewrite love

Forgive their mistakes
and accidents
Accept their apologies and make up
Impress them with you charm and romance
Teach them your talents, skills, and love
Help and have patience

Use your heart to guide them
through problems
Love how they look even when they feel low
listen to what they say
watch what they do
Yes!!
You will love faithfully.

Patrice Howard, Grade 6
Eastmoor Middle School

Orange

You look like an orange bouncy ball
that has yet to be bounced,
or like a not so bright sun shining at us.
You peel quietly, a faint grumpy sound,
like something being ground by a pestle.
If I slice just one slice,
You sound like cords being ripped apart
As silently as a cat creeping toward a mouse.
Inside you feel like a wet sponge
That has tons of water waiting to jump out!
You smell like a fragrant candle.

Alexa Jennings, Grade 5
Dr John Hole Elementary School

Midnight Moon

The fading blue sky slowly turns into
a huge charcoal black sea of stars.
In the middle of the sea
a pearly white moon sits,
giving off an eerie lunar glow as
bugs and nocturnal animals
tell each other good morning.
Humans taking one last yawn
their heads go hurdling toward the pillows,
"Good night," whispers Midnight Moon
"Good morning," whisper the raccoons.
The owls dance
as two rats leave for a little romance
The fox chases the mouse
as they try not to wake the people in the house.
Finally the animals go to sleep
The humans' alarm clocks go beep-beep-beep
"Good night," whisper the raccoons.
"Good night, Midnight Moon."

Emma Hofmann, Grade 5
Cline Elementary School

Things That You Tell Your Mother

Yes, Mother, I made my bed.
No, Mother, I'm not dead.

Yes, Mother, I ate my vegetables.
No, Mother, I didn't find them likable.

Yes, Mother, I washed the dishes.
No, Mother, the job was Trish's.

Yes, Mother, I brushed my teeth.
No, Mother, I did not skip the ones beneath.

Yes, Mother, I washed my clothes.
No, Mother, I didn't use the hose.

Yes, Mother, I fed the dog.
No, Mother, he's not a hog.

Yes, Mother, I fed the cat.
No, Mother, I didn't hit it with a bat.

Katherine Schmidle, Grade 6
Wooster Christian School

Candy

Skittles, Sweet Tarts, suckers galore.
So much candy we adore.
It's the stuff that makes everyone say, "Give me more."
Candy for all of us to enjoy.
Every single girl and boy.
So much candy to choose from and eat.
Who doesn't love this wonderful treat?

Madeline Pugh, Grade 6
Put-In-Bay Elementary School

Blue

Blue is so cool.
Blue is the color of the sky.
Even some people's eyes.
Blue is the ocean.
Wizards make blue potions.
Blue is my favorite color.
I wear it a lot in the summer.
BLUE IS THE BEST COLOR!!

Mariah Icard, Grade 6
St John the Baptist School

Happy Holidays

It's that time of year,
When people are full of cheer,
Parents get no rest
And children are on their best,
Sleigh bells are ringing,
The winds are singing
As we watch the snowflakes fall,
We wish Happy Holidays to all.

Patricia Crawley, Grade 6
Woodward Park Middle School

Snakes and Birds

Snake
Cold, sinister
Slithering, sneaking, hissing
Scales, asp, feathers, wings
Flying, chirping, singing,
Colorful, loud,
Bird

Franco Platania, Grade 6
Harmon Middle School

My Legs

My legs are flexible.
They help me jump and walk.
they help me ride horses.
They help me play games.
God gave them to me.
Thank you God,
For such wonderful legs!

Rachel Wickerham, Grade 4
St Mary's School

Stocking

I hang above the fireplace,
Just waiting for Santa to fill my face,
Until the morning I wait to see,
All of the children come run at me!
Then after that my fate will come,
Once Christmas Day is finally done,
I'll sit in the closet for a whole year,
Waiting for next year's holiday cheer!

Hannah Block, Grade 6
Glenwood Middle School

Anger

Anger is a box of madness waiting to explode.

It is a song of madness.
It's shaped like a broken heart.
It tastes sickening.
It is the dance of evil and it has a pocketful of meanness.
It's the touch of hatred.
It feels like the mean rushing and roaring wind blowing your hair,
picking up dust and blowing it in your eyes and face.
If you make it through all that then your anger will go away and you will
start to strengthen again and calm down.

Krista Ward, Grade 6
Old Fort Elementary School

Fireworks at Midnight

Laughter and joy surrounds me.
I check my watch,
Only one more minute till the New Year.
I wait and wait and wait.
Then, suddenly…

The countdown begins!
5, 4, 3, 2, 1 MIDNIGHT!
BOOM!
  BOOM!
    BOOM!
The fireworks shot up into the air.
People cheer for the New Year as the fireworks dance in the sky.
The fireworks are as bright as daylight, flashing up above.
They paint gorgeous rainbows of sparkly colors everywhere.

And I think to myself,
What will this year be like?
Better?
Worse?
That's for me to find out.

Alma Rechnitzer, Grade 5
EH Greene Intermediate School

Black

Black, a solemn, solid color.
The color of darkness, the color of failure.
But does it always mean bad times?
No, black can also mean many other feelings.
Such as anger, sadness, but sometimes even happiness.
What pops into your head when somebody says the word, "Black?"
Gloomy days that never end? A place where absolutely nothing turns out. Right?
All of these things are possible,
But do people ever come to mind?
Such as African-Americans? Maybe even gothics?
Or maybe the color black describes a personality,
Black, a feeling, a personality, but mostly a color.

Candisse Fejer, Grade 6
St John the Baptist School

Pastries

A good dessert is pastry,
It's yummy, delicious, and tasty.

Donuts, cookies, pies, and cakes,
They really are so fun to bake.

Made with jelly, icing, and sprinkles on top,
Once you start eating, it's hard to stop.

Full of sugar and oh, so sweet,
It's just the thing I love to eat.

Eating too many won't keep you lean,
So don't eat too many, if you know what I mean.

Ashley Bruce, Grade 6
Tippecanoe Middle School

Nick McAfee

Nick
hyper, smart, funny, confident
son of Jamie and Roger
lover of soccer and wrestling
who feels sad when grounded
and renewed at 8:00 in the morning

who needs to get grades up and eat more
who gives my fish food
who fears wrecking on my dirt bike
who would like to go to Kings Island
resident of Lancaster
McAfee

Nick McAfee, Grade 5
Sanderson Elementary School

Hate

Like the sting of a knife in the back.
Like the confusion of a needle in a hay stack.
But God's love you do not lack
the devil can still control you
just like that.

Alissa Colegrove, Grade 6
Fairbanks Middle School

Teacher's Pet

You raise your hand for everything and try not to let,
yourself turn into the teacher's pet.

You try to ignore when the kids make fun,
you think that's the worst they can be,
but really it has just begun.

You stop what you're doing,
and start slouching in your chair,
now all the kids really don't care.

Larken Temple, Grade 5
Monroe Elementary School

The Bad Girl

There once was a bad girl.
Her name was Breanna
She was 7 years old.
Breanna lived on a farm and let me tell you something —
Living on a farm with that girl was not good.
Breanna would let the pigs out and the cows and ducks.
Then Breanna would roll in the mud with the pigs.
She would put hay in her mouth like the horses did.
She would pull the feathers off the chickens.

Paige Workman, Grade 5
Stanton Middle School

Speaking My Own Language

Standing by myself independently,
Wondering why the others will not play with me.
Being in my phase of depression,
I have on my worst expression.
A girl walks by and ignores that I am here,
I quickly wipe away my tears.
What makes me different and makes me stand out,
Is hard to find, I have no doubt.
I want to be liked and I want to be loved,
I am tired of being pushed and shoved.
A friend is the top thing on my Christmas list,
Followed by some happiness.
The new girl then approaches me,
Making me have a moment of glee.
We start to play and joke around,
We even play on the playground.
I later realize that being myself and being happy,
Got me to where I want to be.

Ellen Corcoran, Grade 6
Rocky River Middle School

Me

Z apped with baseball talent
A nd I'm always valiant
C an achieve in math, science, and history too
H ere we go Indians in red and blue
A ssign me a spelling paper, I'll do it three times
R eally, I like Sprite, it is made of lemon and limes
Y ou'd never know that I like books

A lmost all of them, even with good guys and crooks
L ibrary is one of my favorite parts of school
A ny time, I'd follow the rules
N icholas is my brother, his baseball skills have landed

B ut me, I'm different, I'm left handed
U nthinkable wisdom, which I use often
S ometimes even when I'm sick and coughin'
H as a good time while watching Kenny Lofton

Zachary Alan Bush, Grade 5
Frank Ohl Middle School

Basketball and Football
basketball
dribble, shoot
bounce pass, chest pass, lay-up,
dunk, alley oop, tackle, running,
touchdown, pass, intercept,
fumble, pads
football
Zach Mason, Grade 6
Harmon Middle School

Halloween
H aunted house
A pple cider
L antern
L oads of candy
O ctober
W itches brew
E ek
E at lots of candy
N ighttime
Rachel Ullrich, Grade 4
Sts Joseph and John School

Reading
R ead books
E nrichment reading
A great way to learn
D ifferent point of view
I nteresting plots
N ight time stories
G reat authors
Kayla Boros, Grade 4
Sts Joseph and John School

Fight
Would you send a child to war?
drown them in desolation
Isolation
have them cling to the dark
and fear the light?
that's too bad
you already have.
The world is war
a war we all have to suffer.
We are all soldiers
we're fighting for a life
fighting to keep our sanity
But few fight the light
and let the moon kiss their skin
and the night to reflect in their eyes
this is our war
my war
a war we all have to suffer.
Eve Miller, Grade 6
Woodward Park Middle School

Home Run
As I get up to bat,
I tip my ball cap,
wondering what I will do.
I got into my stance,
and it was my chance,
next thing I knew the ball flew.
As I am running,
inside I feel funny,
going, going, gone.
As the crowd cheered,
my teammates just leered,
I had hit my first homerun!
Madisen Hunter, Grade 6
Stanton Middle School

The Horse That Knows No Owner
He rose in the air,
like a great bonfire.
Then raced around
Like his tail was on fire.
Pitching his rider off and away
As if he were just a tiny ant in the way.
Then he ran to the hillside
And hid away
until the search
for him was over.
Nicholas Kochanek, Grade 5
Tremont Elementary School

My Run
Legs bent, body ready,
Breathing steady, ready
To run

Stick in hand, eyes on
Goal, Pro!

Ready! Set! Go! Heart
Racing, adrenaline on
High gear

Pass thirty runners, sweat
Pouring down, coming
Closer

Sweat changing into dancing
Rain

One runner ahead of me
I could see me with the trophy

I pass the runner, in excitement
I threw my hands in the air, smiles.
Tayler Brewer, Grade 5
St Joseph Parish School

Musical ABCs
A B and **C** an **D** ance **E** very **F** riday.
G uitars **H** ammer **I** n **J** azz.
K im **L** oves **M** y **N** ew **O** boe!
P ianos **Q** uickly **R** ap.
S ongs **T** ell **U** nusual **V** erses.
W histling **X** -tols **Y** our **Z** aniness.
Shandock Jamiyansuren, Grade 5
Logan Christian School

Forgotten
I hate to feel forgotten
But I do feel forgotten
That nobody cares
As invisible as air
I feel forgotten
I hate to feel forgotten
But I do feel forgotten
Doing whatever I want
With no one telling me otherwise
I feel forgotten
I hate to feel forgotten
But I do feel forgotten
Making many mistakes
That nobody corrects
I feel forgotten
I hate to feel forgotten
But I do feel forgotten
Hanging out with the wrong crowd
But still feeling alone
I feel forgotten
Jade Borocz, Grade 6
Harding Middle School

The Soccer Moon
The crowd roars
As the moon sets off
Dodging stars along the way
It may take awhile,
But you must stay and watch
Crickets as cheerleaders
Keeping the moon going
A one against a million battle
Winner takes victory
The moon in it's off white shirt
Goes towards the goal:
The East
The game is near end
One final goal
Swoosh
Last goal
Moon scores
And wins
Hannah Wright, Grade 5
Cline Elementary School

Sports

I love sports,
Any kind, any sort.
Because I'm tall,
My favorite sport is basketball.
On the court, with my head held high,
I never end the game with less than a tie.
Pictures of Mia Hamm fill my locker,
Because I like to play soccer.
When I take the field with heart and soul,
I usually tend to make a goal.
Playing sports is like a test,
I practice and practice to do my very best.
So now you see why I love sports,
Of any kind, of any sort.

Brittany Clark, Grade 5
Spaulding Elementary School

Freedom

We still stand tall,
after all of the wars we fought;
we stand proud in a place called America.
We continue to fight for freedom 'til this day.
The deaths make us sad,
but we show pride in our country,
as the National Anthem says,
"O'er the land of the free and the home of the brave."

Mitch Miller, Grade 6
Melrose Elementary School

Fall

When you look outside
Colors of reds, yellows, oranges
Falling from the trees.

Pumpkin pie warms me up
When I come inside.
Howling winds stir up

The leaves as it chases the squirrel up the tree.
Picking pumpkins all day long.
Trying to carve funny faces.

Taylor Zink, Grade 5
Immaculate Conception School

Freedom

Fighting across the seas far away
Right to vote
Education for all children
Everyone having their own freedom of speech
Debate your own opinions with others
Opportunity to practice your own religion
Many memories of our fighting soldiers

James Herzog, Grade 5
Sanderson Elementary School

What the Bird Taught Me

I hear a little bird that sings tweet-tweet-tweet.
If I stay there long enough I'll think that it's so sweet.
The bird goes running up the tree.
I almost fell and hit my knee.
The bird flies off the branch and up into the sky.
Then I start to realize that I am beginning to cry.
Later in the year of 1833.
I look inside and find it in a little tree.
And see like the little birdie.
There is a God who really does love me!

Sable Kessler, Grade 6
Pike Christian Academy

Riding My Bike

I see water and children playing.
I hear water balloons splashing.
I hear people diving and splashing in the pool.
I smell Wonder Bread and Pizza Hut.
I taste popcorn home made and peanut butter and jelly.
I touch apples and leaves on the ground.

Briana Elliott, Grade 4
Licking Valley Intermediate School

Veteran Thank Yous

Right now we're honoring a special kind of people.
They are our country's great, big steeple,
That supports everything everywhere, anywhere.
They cradle our country like a mother bear,
And protect us from people who dare,
Try to harm us and also try to scare.
They are the people who our country owes huge debts.
For they are the ones that get back at threats
To those made against us.
And so they protect the country, thus,
We must honor these people who have fought,
The other people for freedom and brought,
A temporary peace that surrounds the world…
They have also very carefully unfurled,
The goods sides of people one and all,
They always stand straight and tall.
Like the tails of those proud wren.
So let's honor these people again,
Those who are fighting and have fought,
Those who have died and survived,
Even the soldiers that have revived.

Prativa Amom, Grade 6
EH Greene Intermediate School

A Story About King Arthur

There once was a castle so tall
that King Arthur was afraid it would fall
so he grabbed a big stick
and gave it a big kick
and laughed while he watched the wall fall.

Jared Englert, Grade 4
Greenfield Elementary School

What Is a Sister?
What is a sister?
   a guidance counselor
   bunch of love
   a cuddly teddy bear
   a teacher
That is a sister.
Dannica Culler, Grade 5
York Elementary School

Airplane
An airplane is like a dragon in the sky.
It soars and roars in the sky
breathing smoke out of its nose,
Releasing it into the air.
It launches from its lair
And comes back every night.
Jacob Belcher, Grade 6
Tippecanoe Middle School

Leaves
Colorful leaves,
Are nothing like bees
They can feel rough,
But they are tough

They are red, yellow, and green,
But they are not a bean,
They are bright,
But not like night

They fall to the ground,
But don't howl like a hound
Some are dark and some are light,
But none of them are bright

It is such a wonderful day,
When leaves fall in the bay
And there are people raking,
So they can go home and finish baking
Sarah Vapenik, Grade 6
Kinsner Elementary School

My Dad
Loves to cook,
Owns a restaurant,
Likes to have fun,
Makes really good food,
Helps me with anything,
Wants me to do my best,
Takes care of me,
Pays the bills,
Loves me.
Katie Berndt, Grade 4
Dobbins Elementary School

My Favorite Treat
Marshmallow, Marshmallow
in my mouth gooey, chewy
I like you because you're sweet
and you can't be beat
because you are my favorite treat.
Autumn Snyder, Grade 5
Stanton Middle School

Colors
Salmon is the color of a swimming fish,
Gold is the color of a shining dish.
Pink is the color of a beautiful flower,
Sea green has wonderful power.
Green is the color of grass,
Red has very much class.
Purple is the color of a grape,
Tan is the color of a crepe.
Brown is the color of a leaf,
Blue is the color of the sea's reef.
What colors would you use?
Victoria Ross, Grade 6
Roosevelt Elementary School

Voting Booth
So many
Choices on
The ballot
All very
Different
Representing
So many
Different
Ideas
Stickers
That say,
VOTE!
Electronic
Machine
Tallying
The votes
So…
Done!
Chase Maston, Grade 5
Indian Springs Elementary School

Friendship
Friendship is like a butterfly
Friendship is like a dream
Friendship is a love
A love you can count on
So grab a friend
Until the end
And be friends forever
Breane Thompson, Grade 6
Woodward Park Middle School

Ferrets at Halloween
My ferrets are so happy
At Halloween
They get to run outside
With leaves falling
On them all the time
They get to play in the leaves
Can't you hear the leaves
Falling all the time?
It's funny how every Halloween
my ferrets and I
Get to feel the morning's
Fresh air on Halloween
And the ferrets get to jump in leaves!
River Barnhart, Grade 4
Licking Valley Intermediate School

Oceans and Deserts
Ocean
Wet, warm
Swimming, fishing, boating
Fish, seashell, snakes, scorpions
Blazing, sweltering, burning
Barren, dunes
Desert
Christain Teague, Grade 6
Tippecanoe Middle School

Holiday Joy
Bright lights from the morning glow
Blue, silver, and gold
Shadows below the enormous presents
A dark, misty black

The peaceful sleep in the morning
The holiday music all day
The cardinals are all chirping
Like the bells on Santa's sleigh

Could it be that Santa has truly come?
Could it be, could it be, could it be
He has left his presents for all of us?
And brought his joy to me

Warm, delicious cinnamon rolls
Roasting in the oven
The smell of them has brought to us
The warm Christmas feeling

The day has almost ended
The sun is drifting down
That was a special Christmas
I'll have the memories forever
Isaac L.G. Goldstein, Grade 5
EH Greene Intermediate School

Season of Giving

Excited as ever, racing down the steps like a cheetah catching its prey.
There they are, a beautiful sight, presents perched under the tree.
Wondering, wondering, which one is for me?
The living room is as bright as the sun.
The twinkling, flashing lights on the tree glitter like the North Star in the night sky. Merry Christmas!

Dad films as if he is a Hollywood producer, aiming his camera and capturing memories.
The smiling faces of family opening presents gleefully.
The sweet aroma of fragrant candles and breakfast casserole fill the room.
I'm a little hungry, so I sneak a sample of Santa's leftover cookies set by the fireplace. Merry Christmas!

Talking, giggling and laughter pour through our home in perfect harmony.
Wrapping paper crinkles as we reveal thoughtful gifts.
Mom's favorite *Take 6 Christmas* CD flows through our speakers like water in a stream.
All of the sounds of the season. Merry Christmas!

When will everyone finish opening *their* presents, so my brother and I can play with ours?
Merry Christmas!
Merry Christmas!
Merry Christmas!

Lauren Saxon, Grade 5
EH Greene Intermediate School

Waterfall

Gentle water gliding through the rocks.
The water is crystal clear like a clean and polished diamond.
It's shifting this way and that way.
Then with full power it blasts off a cliff skydiving to the rocky earth.
The little droplets then come back together to form again another gently flowing stream.

Sam Fulwider, Grade 5
Barrington Elementary School

The Festival of Lights!

On Diwali morning, we wake up with our minds racing with joy. When I look outside, I see the sun and I see the leaves falling down. As I zoom downstairs, I start to hear many people talking and laughing. This is an ecstatic holiday of radiance, peace, and love.

We start to light candles all around the house, for it is the festival of lights. They are as bright and beautiful as amazing stars. Nothing can beat them. Yes, this is an ecstatic holiday of radiance, peace, and love.

Since I know that in India this festival is so much more busy and exciting, I try to do my best to equal that here. Even though we don't have parades and a few days off of school, we have the same amount of fun with our special activities.

As the bright day moves on into the dark night, the joyous fun doesn't stop. We head on outside for more celebrations, after a sumptuous dinner prepared by my mother and grandma.

Again, we light candles on the front step. I can smell the fire which gives me a calming, warm feeling. Do they get burned from the fire? But that's not all; we light fireworks and also hang lights upon bushes. Somewhere close by, I hear fireworks bursting, but as I look over, I see my family — they already started! I run over, eager to light some myself. This is an ecstatic holiday of radiance, peace, and love.

When we start to go inside, I really have mixed emotions. I'm sad that this holiday is over,
but happy that it went great. I glance to my left stopping to gaze at the bright lights. They were casting huge shadows on our brick house. Definitely, Diwali is an ecstatic holiday of radiance, peace, and love.

Sneha Rajagopal, Grade 5
EH Greene Intermediate School

At the Beach with My Family
My favorite time of the year
Summer
The nice hot air outside
Jumping in a nice cold pool
People laughing
Camping at Myrtle Beach
Spending time with family
Going to the nice cool ocean
Brrrr!
Javan Fogle, Grade 4
Licking Valley Intermediate School

Tears
T ears run down her face,
E nding slowly at her
A ching heart, her
R estricted mind
S lows down.
Jen Taylor, Grade 6
Melrose Elementary School

Maggie
She's as black as the night sky
She's cute, smart, lovable, and sly

She chases most everything she sees
That's why our cat is always in trees

She likes to catch those ugly moles
That's why our yard is full of holes

She eats so sloppy like a hog
Hey, it's Maggie and she's our dog
Lauren Goettemoeller, Grade 6
Holy Angels School

Goodnight, Dear God
The sun has gone down from the sky,
And peace of night is drawing nigh.

I pray, dear God, my soul you'll keep,
While in your loving arms I sleep.

Forgive the things I did today,
When from your glorious path I'd stray.

And as I slumber through the night,
Please take my hand and hold it tight.

And when I awake to a bright new morn,
Restored, refreshed, renewed, reborn.

I'll try again, dear God to be,
The person you would hope of me.
Lindsey Woelfl, Grade 6
Trilby Elementary School

Some Day
Some day I'll be a super star
Some day I'll be a dancer or a singer
Maybe some day I'll even be a famous doctor, maybe a teacher or a veteran
Maybe, just maybe
Many of my hopes are based on some of these
My future will always be my future and my dreams will stay my dreams
But now I will focus on being a kid and I'll enjoy the present time.
Lyric Harden, Grade 5
Akiva Academy

Love
My heart pounds while my feet travel faster.
I wonder about the marvelous feeling when I am zipping past you,
the boy my heart whispers when I'm in dreamland.
Alyssa Aukerman, Grade 6
Melrose Elementary School

Wind
The wind brings a sorrow cry
it sees who has listened as it passes by.
But everyone minds their own business and doesn't care.
Then the people hear the wind, they stop and stare.
The wind taps on the window and starts to dance.
Everyone is so amazed they're in a trance.
They wander outside and start joining in.
They get tired and night arrives, it's time to sleep so "goodnight" wind!!!
Bryan Quijada, Grade 6
Woodward Park Middle School

The Magic of Christmas
The magic of Christmas is rushing around,
People peeking inside frost covered windows,
Shimmering, glistening lights are hung on trees,
Smiling faces shining everywhere,
Wrapping paper on presents feels soft and smooth to the touch,
Twinkling lights and joyous people.

The dim-lighted room is bursting with life,
A brushed silver lamp is shedding light into the room,
The delightful smell of gingerbread cookies in the air,
The warm, sweet taste of them makes my senses tingle
Oh why does this glorious time have to end?
Twinkling lights and joyous people.

People of all shapes and sizes are busy as bees,
The cheerful sound of dogs barking and children laughing fills my ears,
Mistletoe being hung and wreaths everywhere,
Red bows standing proud and snowmen in the yard,
The feeling of Christmas fills me from head to toe,
Twinkling lights and joyous people.

But as always, the fun must come to an end,
Tired children climb sluggishly into bed but they will always remember…
The twinkling lights and joyous people of Christmas.
Prianka Kumar, Grade 5
EH Greene Intermediate School

High Merit Poems – Grades 4, 5, and 6

They Need Saving
Animals are in the pound looking for our help.
All night they are whining, or they yelp.
They all die if we don't save them; they have death dates!
I learned that from the TV I watched their rates
I felt horrible, I almost cried
but I knew I couldn't help them, then I sighed.
Maybe I couldn't, but others can
I am sure if you do, your new pet will be your
Number one fan!

Nardine Taleb, Grade 6
Birchwood School

Fall
Brown and red leaves everywhere,
When I take my step they crunch.
Then the wind blows the leaves.
They fall off the trees into my hair and everywhere.
The air outside smells like smoke from a fire and
Cinnamon from the candles in the house.
It's cool and brisk like the night air.

Ana Shepherd, Grade 6
Logan Christian School

The Ache in My Head
I got out of bed
With a severe ache in my head
So I went to my father
So I could stop the bother
To find the cure
For the ache in my head

I climbed up the stairs
To my father's lair
To find the magnificent cure to the ache in my head

Father, father please help
I don't think I can cope
With this unbearable pain
No, son it's simple and plain
You are obviously lying
So I went back to my room sighing
I was trying
And he wasn't buying

Cooper Brown, Grade 6
Harding Middle School

A Bird's Wings Flapping
A cardinal flies through the air.
The wings are going up and down like a tick-tock, tick-tock.
A chirp, chirp splits the air.
It's going so fast if it hit a tree there would be a splat.
Snapping at a worm, not slowing its wings.
Turns almost like a wedge in water.
The wings are going up and down like a tick-tock, tick-tock.

Kyle Moesle, Grade 4
Fairfield Elementary School

Orange
Orange is an awesome color.
It is the color of the Cincinnati Bengals
And my soccer team.
Orange is my favorite color.
On my "orange" days I am hyper.
The sun has orange
Which keeps us warm.
Orange has many different shades.
Red orange, neon orange, yellow orange,
Scarlet, and so many others.

Maddie Knecht, Grade 6
St John the Baptist School

Don't Back Down
Wherever you go or do,
I'll still love you.
But when you are in and out of that jail cell,
This is your 100 times making a mistake.
Not just with me,
But with everybody.
But now I just don't care, for what you do,
So just put it down and walk away,
From the stuff that you do.
Stand up and be with the people who you care for.
Be a real father to the kids that you love.
So don't back down, stand up and,
Show people who you really are.
And what you can actually do with your life.

Kalsea Wells, Grade 6
Trilby Elementary School

When I Think of You
Every time I think of you
My mind starts to race into the blue
Deep down inside you stole my pride
I wonder and wonder if I will love again

What I need is a true friend
Now I wonder if my heart is whole
Maybe I will find someone to fill that part you stole
I miss your smile I miss your laugh
Maybe someday I will get you back

Nick Isley, Grade 5
Fairfield Intermediate Elementary School

White
White, the color of the snow.
How I love it's sparkle and glow.
White, the color of a milky cream.
My mom puts in her coffee every morning.
White, the color of a platinum ring.
I got on Christmas morning.

Amanda Meiering, Grade 6
St John the Baptist School

Hmmmmmm…
Hmmmmmmm…Is a sound, a pause
When you can't think of
Anything
To say or do
Everyone says it,
Either now or later
You will say
Hmmmmm…
Victoria Van Benschoten, Grade 5
Tremont Elementary School

My Favorite Place
Cozy and warm
A cold wet day
About 10:00 o'clock in the evening

Low deep snoring
TV screaming random words
Dreams talking like I'm there

Cold dark shadows
Pitch black stillness
Clock's bright numbers

Feeling reborn with extra energy
Cuddly cat warming me up
Large comforter on top of me

The exact next day
I am tired and bored, yet happy
Victor Kurz, Grade 6
EH Greene Intermediate School

Little Creatures
Major Role
Spinnerets silk
None Antarctica
Paralyze to kill
Liquid tissues
German spinner
Widow venom
Dangerous recluse
Look out for spiders!
Juliana Kreatsoulas, Grade 4
Dobbins Elementary School

Chevy Chevelle
Chevy Chevelle
Jet, cherry
Thundering, sparkling, shimmering
Cool car
Hot rod
Zac Brugger, Grade 6
Melrose Elementary School

Football
I love football.
Sometimes I play it late.
In the dark or during the day,
No matter what, I think it's great.
I can play quarterback,
Running back, and safety too.
No matter what position I play,
I'm sure that I can beat you.
Chance Behymer, Grade 5
Spaulding Elementary School

Black
Alone in the pitch black night.
All alone till the dawns first light.
Black is the color of my pack
The only thing with me as I walk alone.
Black comes in many shades
Such as jet, ebony, and licorice.
As I leave you in the cold
Black night think about
Where your loved one are
Very far or near.
Alban Schneider, Grade 6
St John the Baptist School

Football
F un
O utstanding
O ut of this world
T ailback
B locker
A wesome
L ocker
L ocker room
Scout Aswad, Grade 4
Sts Joseph and John School

Footprints
Glitter forms from the sun
filling the sky.

The rush of wind
touches my skin.

Mud and tree roots
under my feet.

The creek is calm
and barely flowing.

Smells of pine and tree bark
fill the air.
Taylor Pearson, Grade 4
Normandy Elementary School

My Dog
Playing with my dog
Throwing her the ball
She gets it
Sometimes she comes back
Sometimes she doesn't
She runs through the grass like a horse
She looks like a big cat
Mariah Carr, Grade 4
Licking Valley Intermediate School

My Mom
My mom is generous and kind.
My mom cooks my dinners
and keeps shelter over my head.
My mom also washes my clothes.

She takes me on vacations
and other fun places.
I can rely on her
to take me to soccer practices.
I know I can count on her,
and she knows she can count on me.

She heals my sadness
when I have a frown.
She surprises me with colorful candy.
She plays games with me, too!

No matter where I go,
I always think of my mom and her love.
When I look into her eyes,
I always see love
and she loves me, no matter what.
Lonna Sedam, Grade 6
Tippecanoe Middle School

Barley
B arks a lot
A dventurous beyond belief
R eally rambunctious
L oves cheese
E ats a lot
Y ellowish gold
Madilyn Brown, Grade 6
Holy Angels School

Christmas
Looks like family, a tree, and presents
Feels like happiness, and warmth
Sounds like laughter, and songs
Tastes like breakfast, and cookies
Smells like a fire, and coffee
Samantha Marlowe, Grade 5
Northfield Baptist Christian School

High Merit Poems – Grades 4, 5, and 6

Read Between the Lines
Thank you book, for taking me,
On adventures very few can see.
Unless they read between the lines,
Of the pages that a cover binds.
The adventures range from near to far,
Even some places too far for car.
A witch infested fairyland,
To cities in a giant's hand.
The list just goes on and on,
You could read the list from dusk 'till dawn.
Not all people can read and see,
The between the lines, mystery.

Benjamin Goldschneider, Grade 6
EH Greene Intermediate School

The Sun and the Moon
The Sun is like a big bright orange in outer space.
When I see it, it puts a smile on my face.
When I see It's going down I frown.
The Moon is like a giant pearl that circles the Earth.
I love looking up and seeing it shine in the bright starry sky.
If I look at it long enough it doesn't seem so high.
And every every night before I go to bed
I always say, "Goodnight my dear friend."

Angela Fink, Grade 6
Leetonia Middle School

Dance
I love to dance, I love ballet
I twirl around all through the day
I raise my hands and point my toes
And with the music my body flows.

I love to dance, I love to tap
My shiny black shoes go clap clap clap
I hear the music, my feet follow the beat
and before you know it I'm out of my seat.

I love to dance, especially jazz
dance costumes full of razz a ma taz
I spin, and dip, and twirl around
the upbeat music, a wonderful sound.

I love to dance, to do hip hop
my hands start to clap, my feet start to stomp
the timely rhythm is a magical thing
while my feet do the dancing my heart starts to sing.

I love to dance, by now you can tell
from years of practice, I do it well
I hope I've made it perfectly clear
dancing I'll do it all through the year.

Ciara Gable, Grade 6
Miller City-New Cleveland School

Strings
All of my strings just sound so good.
And the rest of the instrument is made out of wood.
Except for the hairs of the bow that I use,
and other parts of the viola, which I never abuse.
The notes I play flow like a majestic stream,
and they help me to raise my self-esteem.
Even though it's never low,
I look inside of me and see a glow.

Mike Goldenberg, Grade 6
EH Greene Intermediate School

Decorating for Christmas
All before Christmas
We put up a tree
Hanging our stockings
On the mantel as a family
With lights and ornaments
Surrounding the tree
We can wrap all of the presents
So they are ready that morning
With the fireplace blazing
And warm cocoa too
We can have friends over
To sing Christmas carols
Then we put on our hats and gloves
And sing to our neighbors and friends
As Christmas is almost here
We see angels and stars everywhere above
As the snow continues to fall
I can't help but think that
Baby Jesus was the best gift of all

Nathan Hall, Grade 6
Holy Angels School

Pittsburgh Steelers
P ulverizing big hits
I n Pittsburgh is where they play home games
T hey are a terrific team
T roy Polamalu is their safety
S uper Bowl champions
B en Roethlesburger is their quarterback
U nstoppable in 1974
R odney Harrison used to be their end
G reat at football
H its they will give

S pecial to me
T hey always score touchdowns
E ven though they lose, I still like them
E nthusiastic players they have
L osers they will never be
E xperienced players they have
R ed is for one of the diamonds on their helmets
S teelers will always be my team

Kevin A. Ziegler, Grade 5
Frank Ohl Middle School

About Me

I am smart, and athletic
I wonder if I will play in the NFL
I hear the cracking of leaves with every step I take
I see a humming bird drinking nectar
I want to go to Arizona
I am smart and athletic

I pretend to be Vince Young
I feel mad when somebody calls me a name
I touch a dog's fur
I worry if somebody will break into the house
I cry when a pet or friend dies
I am smart and athletic

I understand I won't live forever
I say that God is real
I dream of going to Ohio State University
I try to get good grades in school
I hope I will see my aunt
I am smart and athletic

I am Alex Starkey

Alex Starkey, Grade 5
Sanderson Elementary School

Firecrackers

Firecrackers, firecrackers
burst in the sky
with brilliant colors up so high
baby blue and then orange

Firecrackers, firecrackers
up so high
a brilliant pink then silver
the sky lights up
and turns the dark into light

Firecrackers, firecrackers
oh, so magical
make the sky happy and beautiful
with a bang and a boom
burst and explode
light up the sky as the night goes and hides

Karen Gonzales, Grade 6
St Clement Elementary School

Black

Black is the color of space and it's whack.
Black can sometimes mean mad or sad.
Some people think there is lack in black.
Black can sometimes be called ebony,
licorice, or jet like the color of the sun set.
Most of all, black is my favorite color.
Don't think there is any lack in black.

Alex Maccarone, Grade 6
St John the Baptist School

The First Snow Day

A bright light is coming from behind my door.
Open the bedroom door,
The window is cold to the touch
I see snow and icicles galore!
The icicles are extremely long.
The birds are singing a song.
An aroma of pancakes fills the air.
This means on this marvelous Thursday, this day is an amazing snow day!

No need to turn on the lights,
the sun is very, very, bright.
The light reflects off of the snow.
It seemed like the sun made it glow.

The dogs are barking while eating snow.
Birds are chirping, icicles cracking.

What is the temperature?
When did it start snowing?

The snow looks as radiant as a fresh bouquet of roses.
The snow is sparkling, sparkling, sparking in the sunlight.

Eva Brod, Grade 5
EH Greene Intermediate School

Best Friends

Best friends are here to stay.
When they are together I know they will find the way.
Even though sometimes they argue and don't get along.
I know they will always find the way to stay strong.
Friends stand by your side when you are sad or mad.
They share your happiness when you are glad.
They understand your problems, and will always give you a helping hand.
They are someone you can tell a secret even when they don't understand.
Friends share their things every day.
No matter what comes their way.
This is why I call you my best friend.
I will always call you this, my best friend until the end.

Amanda C. Englebert, Grade 4
Monroe Elementary School

Christmas Angels

For we are the ones you've missed days, weeks, months, or years,
We weren't there to wipe your tears,
Now we come to ease your pain,
In your heart our love will remain,
Forever shall we live in your heart,
Even if we are far apart,
If you look up yonder and see the light,
That is where we live day and night,
For we are the angels,
Waiting for Christmas Day.

Kirstie Hans, Grade 6
Glenwood Middle School

High Merit Poems – Grades 4, 5, and 6

A Walk on the Beach
Taking a walk on the beach
Watching the sun set over the ocean
The colors of the sun are beautiful
The water has no motion.

Looking back I see my footprints
Seeing nobody on the shore.
Everything is still
Except my feet moving even more.

Looking out at the water
I see a whale;
Jumping high out of the sea
Down the whale dives. SPLASH! Leaving only a tail.

Kaitlyn Sutton, Grade 6
St Joseph Parish School

Santa
Santa
jolly, friendly,
exciting, loving, caring,
gives you toys, candy, a wink and a smile —
amazing, surprising, giving,
smiley, cheerful,
Saint Nick

MaryBeth Medley, Grade 5
Hylen Souders Elementary School

Pink
Pink is an ink.
I could just sink.
Some people call me fink.
Pink is not a bad day or a good day.
It is a so-so day.
So think about the color pink
"Oh my" there is a kink in the sink.
I hope I can fix it.
"WOW" that's a huge link.
"Hey" what's a link?
It is a connecting structure.
I hope no one's pinkie is pink that would stink.
My favorite color is pink.
So remember think pink.

Nick Finke, Grade 6
St John the Baptist School

Colors
Colors are a beautiful thing.
Just like a golden ring.
Green is like fresh cut grass.
Or red roses in a brand new glass.
Turquoise is the color of the Caribbean Sea.
White is the color of a new golf tee.
If you had to choose a favorite what would it be?

Lauren Demarchi, Grade 4
Northfield Elementary School

Miracle Child*
My child is the only one for me
He was born with problems, you see,
I prayed and prayed and then one day
By the grace of God, I heard the doctor say,
Life for this child has been very rough
But he has held on and been very tough,
I'm happy to say your child is healthy
But to pay for the surgery you must be very wealthy,
I didn't hope for the last part,
But I paid because I was smart.
I didn't hesitate to pay, my friend,
Because I will be with my son until the end.
My child has grown up to be a man with a heart
Because he believed from finish to start,
My prayers were answered by the angels who got together,
To decide whether to let my child be an angel
Or a miracle!

Julia Beitz, Grade 5
St Ignatius School
*Dedicated to Theresa Beitz

Magnificent Moonlight
If you look up in the sky at exactly midnight
You would see the beauty of the moonlight
I love it most if it is snowy white
With white and yellow against the black night
The light is a reflection from the great sun
Looking at constellations is a great deal of fun
Stars aren't the only ones who can move and run
For the moon can run too, around us and the sun
The moonlight is just so very great
I can stay up later than thirty past eight
Looking up into the peaceful and gorgeous sky
I can feel as if I can float and fly
But I have to go to bed and dream
Except that I feel as if it is a scheme
For me to see the beauty of the moonlight
Such a magnificent and extraordinary sight

Alyssa Spear, Grade 5
Frank Ohl Middle School

Me
I am
Life, family, animals
Christmas is important to me.
Life is important.
Peace is important to me.
Love is a good thing.
Meanness is bad but good at times.
I think we should stop global warming
And we should have peace.
Peace is GOOD.

Jared Vogel, Grade 6
St Clement Elementary School

Thanksgiving
Luscious roast turkey.
Smells so good with pumpkin pie.
Really yummy meal.
Mouthwatering, awesome yams!
The turkey is delicious!
Gavin Strong, Grade 5
Westview Elementary School

Buttons
Buttons are round
As they lay on the ground,
Most of them are small
And not very tall,
Now they are all found!
Kelly Whybrew, Grade 6
Tippecanoe Middle School

Christmas
Christmas,
A happy time.
The Savior is born.
My favorite holiday.
We all rejoice and celebrate.
Christmas.
Tayla Davis, Grade 4
St Mary's School

My Hero, Dad
Helps me with homework
Keeps me safe from danger
Works for money
Spends time
Fixes toys
Believes in me.
Nicole Ruse, Grade 4
Dobbins Elementary School

My Sister
My sister, Christine,
Helps me with homework
So fun, so cool
Makes lunch for me on weekends
And dinner too.
Jessica Colucci, Grade 4
Dobbins Elementary School

Old Man
There was an old man named Paul
Who seemed rather boring and dull
He was not very nice
He gave me his lice
And now I am scratching and all
Noelle Marva, Grade 5
Rootstown Elementary School

Wild Boy
He's an out-of-control tornado
With no "off" button,
Running down the halls
At a rampaging speed
Talking everyone's ear off
Bouncing off the walls
Rolling like tumbleweeds,
As he laughs wildly,
He's an out-of-control tornado.
Amy Smith, Grade 5
Westview Elementary School

Basketball
I love to play basketball
In the championship game.
I love to shoot
The last second shot.
It goes in
Nothing but net.
The crowd goes wild
And everybody cheers.
I jump up with glee
And yell
We are the champions!!!
Tommy Vetter, Grade 6
St Clement Elementary School

Presents
Shredding,
Clawing like a wild cat.
Ripping the thin barrier between
You and your gift.
Surprised faces,
Family and warm fire.

A chandelier floating,
Dimly lighting the room.
Twinkling stars placed gently on
The Christmas Tree.

Laughing and shouting,
Crackling fire,
Feasting on the buffet of presents.

The smell of pine,
Overjoyed hearts.
"Is Santa real?"
Children ask.
Parents just say
"Yes he is."
"Yes he is."
"Yes he is."
William Hobart, Grade 5
EH Greene Intermediate School

Danny Breeden
Danny Breeden
Elephant lover, confused
Flute-playing, horse-riding, laughing
I love Court T.V.
Forensic Detective
Danielle Breeden, Grade 6
Jefferson Elementary School

Crackerjack
C an do anything!!
R eally playful
A lert
C uddly
K ing of Wheaten Terriers
E xcellent
R eady to walk
J umpy
A nn loves him
C ute
K een
Marissa King, Grade 6
Rocky River Middle School

Invisible or Fly
I dream I am invisible,
But I'm not,
I try and try,
but I'm still not invisible,
So I changed my dream,
Now I want to fly,
I jumped from bed,
But I can't,
I try and try,
But I can't,
Now I have
The impossible dream
To be invisible and fly.
Ivan Pires, Grade 5
Tremont Elementary School

Fall
With fall here,
There are tons of deer.

Fall is fun,
Now it's time to run.

Now it is cold,
The trees look bare and old.

Winter will be here soon,
Then it will get dark in the afternoon.
Rochel Spetner, Grade 4
Cincinnati Hebrew Day School

Monster Dryer

The dryer is a monster.
It walks around the room.
Every night he pulls in my clothes
and blows hot air on them while they spin,
because they are flaming hot when they are done.

Sometimes he pulls clothes in
and, if he thinks they are ugly,
he changes them to a different color.
Sometimes in the laundry room
you can hear him roar,
but he roars only when you have put
a quarter or something in your pocket
and you don't take it out.

I think we should trade him for a puppy.
Dani Richards, Grade 6
Tippecanoe Middle School

Snow

Fresh new snow falls from the sky
telling animals to get ready for winter.
As tracks are forming because of active animals,
the snow starts to hide mysterious things.
In the morning it sits and waits
to be played in and then, the snow spreads on.
Samantha Schwab, Grade 6
Woodward Park Middle School

Roller Coaster

Up and down,
Around and around,
past some people amusedly waiting to ride,
Under the bright blue sky warmed by the scorching hot sun,
On that old shaky track I've ridden before,
With people of all ages young and old,
I ride.

Heather Blackwell, Grade 6
Harmon Middle School

Fall

Trickling leaves and howling winds.
This is what fall sounds like.
With the wind the leaves and the trees move.

The pretty colors and the cold leaf showers,
This is what fall looks like.
With the greens, reds, oranges and yellows.

Short fall days and the football games,
This is what happens in fall.
All these things are what make up fall.
Emily Zibert, Grade 5
Immaculate Conception School

Winter Dream

I step outside to notice my breath flowing white as can be,
Cold air sweeps around me like Cinderella sweeping the floor,
Then I see the snow falling, blowing as far as my eyes can see,
I run inside I am cold, shivering, and shaking,
But then I notice someone is waking me and this is all a dream.
Lexie Herron, Grade 6
Woodward Park Middle School

Soccer

The game of soccer is to score.
After you get a goal, you want more!

Running fast to the ball.
Hoping you will not fall!

Offsides, bad calls, and pushy players.
When you play in the cold, you want to wear layers!

Goalie, Defender, Midfields, and Forward.
you may just get a yellow card!

Throwing the ball over the defender.
Maybe your teammate can get a header!

Coaches running down the sideline.
Wanting you to use your minds!

Refs calling terrible calls.
When you are just playing the ball!

Shaking hands at the end of the game.
Telling them they played in an awesome way!
Madeline Franklin, Grade 6
Holy Angels School

Trees

Why cut down the trees,
When it provides shade?
Why cut down the trees,
When the paper will just be wasted?
Why cut down the trees for wood to keep us warm,
When it will soon be ashes?
Why cut down the trees,
When you are only cutting beauty?
Gassan Yacteen, Grade 5
Islamic School of Greater Toledo

Middle School

Middle school is boring everyone is snoring.
It is very lame everyone gets blamed.
All the teachers do is peck it's like you're on a pirate deck.
If you do something wrong they will make you walk the plank.
The plank will make you go blank.
While I was jumping off my heart sank.
Nick Gregg, Grade 5
Stanton Middle School

Sunset
Yellow sun
Shines so bright
As it ends in the night
Slides like an egg on a pan
Waits until tomorrow to rise again
Jenny Moeller, Grade 6
St Clement Elementary School

My Sister
My sister is a pest.
But she really is the best.
She has big brown eyes.
When she gets hurt, she cries.
She likes to play on WebKinz.
But she only likes the lil' Kinz.
She does really well in school.
And boy she loves my mammaw's pool.
Hanna Schafer, Grade 5
Spaulding Elementary School

Stampeding Elephants
The dark grey clouds were elephants
Stampeding through the sky.
Bringing fear wherever they went,
Roaring and flashing the heavens.
People scattered in disarray…
Running, running, running,
To escape the wrath.
The dark clouds were elephants
Noah McGhee, Grade 5
Westview Elementary School

She Is
Smooth brown hair
Bright blue eyes
Every time I
Hate good byes

She's funny and cool
As well as nice
She's so perfect
Not a single vice

She's not tall
She's not wide
But one thing's big
That's her pride

And she's got

Smooth brown hair
Bright blue eyes
And every time
I hate Good byes
Ben Wells, Grade 6
EH Greene Intermediate School

I Need to Leave
Tic-tock the clock strikes 2:00
Forty-five minutes till the I'm away from you
But why why do they have to torture us
With the windows that let us see the patiently waiting bus
So close, and yet so far
Why can't I run away to my car
I need to leave you school

Time to pack up I can taste summer
The times that I can play and play some more
Free at last, no more of you
No more of your pencils, pens, paper, or glue
No more cuts from your scissors
No more Yes Ma'am and Yes Sirs
I need to leave you school

As you can see I'm on the bus
So for the last time it's time to say good-bye to us
Say good-bye to our last-day smiles
Because trust me, you won't be seeing these for a while
I'm thinking that I might actually miss you these weeks
I'll miss the teachers, the kids, and the locker smashing my cheeks
But what I'll miss most is you why must I leave you school?
Alexis Corcoran, Grade 6
EH Greene Intermediate School

Poems
Dark poems, scary poems, passionate poems, all kinds of poems.
Follow your instincts and you will be great.
Use nature and follow the great valleys and rivers.
A lily petal flowing gracefully through roses and violets.
Like a beautiful island with palm trees and treasuries to find.
Poems can be fun, graceful and sweet. So in the end that is how it is meant to be.
Jake Sullivan, Grade 4
The New School

Christmas Joy
The sun is not up, but I'm awake eager to look under the tree.
The cookies are gone, the milk is drained, and there has been a note left for me.
I jump, I prance, I do a little dance for I'm so happy with joy!
A mountain of presents was left for us which makes my eyes grow wide.
I'm still in shock as I hear a ding and go to answer the door.
Relative pour in laughing with delight gifts are topping over them.
Come in! Come in! I greet at once eager to unwrap the surprises.

The presents are unwrapped, now the floor is decorate with bright holiday paper,
But the fun isn't done…we still have stockings.

Everyone gets treats, no one gets coal
We all find tasty chocolates and small gifts jammed inside the special sock.
Nobody gets the little thing everyone hates, a tiny small black rock.

Everyone is now tired, the guests start to head for the door
Such a joyful holiday that leaves you wishing it would go on forevermore.
Abigail Singer, Grade 5
EH Greene Intermediate School

High Merit Poems – Grades 4, 5, and 6

Christmas Eve Night
Trying
Not to fall asleep,
Lying on the couch,
Dim, colorful, blinking lights
Trying to keep me up all night.
The train is racing around the tree,
The sweet smell of warm cookies
Hanging in the air, finishing the scene.
      Hush.   Still.   Quiet.
All is still. Not a sound dare breaks the silence,
Only my shallow breath and the Hmmmmmmm —
Mmmmmmmmmmmmmmmmmmmmmm of the radiator.
      Hush.   Still.   Quiet.
My animals guard me, ready to fight.
My rabbit stays snug in the crook of my arm.
My eyes start to close. The atmosphere is perfect.
      Hush.   Still.   Quiet.
      Rustle!
Maria Beaucage, Grade 5
EH Greene Intermediate School

Spooky
On Halloween night, what gives you a fright?

S limy, slithering snakes at your feet
P iercing screams that make you leap
O wls screeching overhead!
O possums pretending to be dead
K ooky costumed witches flying through the air
Y ucky monsters messing up your hair

You've heard all of the possibilities,
Now you tell me, what is spooky?
Elli Schwartz, Grade 4
Indian Springs Elementary School

Christmas Morn
Jesus was born on Christmas morn
Mary was Jesus' mother; who fed and clothed him.

Jesus was born on Christmas morn
Joseph was His earthy father but God was number 1.

Jesus was born on Christmas morn
Shepherds visited by singing angels.

Jesus was born on Christmas morn
Wise men journeyed far, guided by a star.

Jesus was born on Christmas morn
Animals shouting for joy!

Jesus was born on Christmas morn
He lies in a manger soft with hay.
Valerie Harley, Grade 5
Wooster Christian School

Grandma
I miss Grandma
tasting her wonderful home made potatoes
Yumm!
remembering her warm hugs and kisses
ALL the time!
hearing her sweet voice calling me
in the kitchen to help her bake!
smelling the freshness in her house
vanilla and lavender
Ahh!
Always telling me that she loves me
and I love you too!
Kirsten Wills, Grade 4
Licking Valley Intermediate School

Education
Education is a roller coaster that helps you learn
Every time you ride it.
Education is a doorway to succeeding
And getting all of the incorrect answers to change
To correct answers.
And education is important to all,
Who really need it to learn.

Education is learning things in school
About different subjects
That the teacher has planned for the day
For all the students to do.
Adrianna Day, Grade 4
Matthew Duvall Elementary School

My Family
I love my brother.
But he can be very mean.
He's 17 and has a car.
He's weird, he keeps his room clean.

I love my mom so much
She's very good at sports.
Sometimes she can get mean.
But she's a monster on those tennis courts.

My dad rocks!
He's awesome at sports.
He is my basketball coach.
He rocks all the time when he's on the basketball courts.

Me and my sister get along great!
We do everything together.
We watch TV, play games and beat up our brother.
We'll always be together forever!
Amanda Riley, Grade 6
Kinsner Elementary School

Baseball

When you are swinging
The ball makes a noise that's dinging
Nice out when you play
Bright and shiny during the day

The sky is cloudless
The field is dry
Birds flying in the sky
The day will be great doubtless

Water and Gatorade
Propel and Powerade
Lots of running
Certain people are stunning

Bring gum to chew
Refreshments are there
Jerseys to wear
On the morning field is dew

Spencer Clarke, Grade 6
Kinsner Elementary School

Fall

The sound of crackling leaves,
Makes fall beautiful
Pumpkin pies are very delicious,
Vibrant colors are everywhere.

Coldness is in the air,
Migrations have birds on the go.
Howling breezes make it colder,
It makes leaves trickle down.

Times change with day and night,
Vivid colors turn to warm colors.
Fall is great for me and you,
Try to do what you can do.

Rebecca Chapman, Grade 5
Immaculate Conception School

Darkness

In the dark at night.
Comes a star so bright.

It sounds like many running mice.
Spinning around so very nice.

It comes to me so soon.
It takes to the moon.

Before all the animals moo.
Daylight comes to me and you.

Manahil Ismail, Grade 6
Trilby Elementary School

The Hike

Trees cover
the sky
with blue dots
between them.

Bumpy ground
below my feet
with leaves crunching
and birds singing.

Emily Fagan, Grade 4
Normandy Elementary School

My Hero

A great cook
Good with kids
Loves to shop
Like me!
Likes to help others
Talks for hours
Loves dogs
Likes red
My outstanding mom!

Gabriella Carbon, Grade 4
Dobbins Elementary School

Christmas

Christmas,
My favorite season.
I love Christmas.
This Christmas I want a lot.
But the most I want,
Is a kitten.
I am a cat lover.
I used to have another cat,
but, now I have only one.
When I was young,
I used to have one named Emma,
We had to give her to the shelter.
Now, I have one cat.
Her name is Boots.
Maybe this Christmas,
I'll get a new kitten.
Christmas.

Paige Richardson, Grade 4
St Mary's School

A Boy Named Nat

There once was a boy named Nat
One day he borrowed a bat
He lost the Louisville Slugger
To a man who was a mugger
Then his mom and him had a spat.

Josiah Lovejoy, Grade 6
Roosevelt Elementary School

Quidditch

Q uickly catch the snitch
U gly game quidditch
I ncredibly fast
D angerous
D odging bludgers
I tching to catch the snitch
T antalizingly fun
C areful not to get crushed by a bludger
H arry Potter is seeker

Christopher Haritos, Grade 4
Norwich Elementary School

Sky's Watching

As I watch the sky
It stares back at me
The big endless blank sable sky.

Becoming a big bright beautiful scene
The grasshoppers singing and dancing.

Lying in the dewy grass
Watching the night sky
People all around me gazing
At the amazing scene.

Humidity is picking up and
The summer sun is setting
But the night moon is rising.

Emma Kujawa, Grade 5
Cline Elementary School

Me

K it Kat is my nickname
A nimal lover
T akes care of my family
H igh School Musical lover
L oves my teachers
E mily Bevan is my best friend
E mily Dunn is my other friend
N ice to others

R are jewel
U nique worker and listener
T hinks about my grandma
H elps my grandma all the time

R upert is my last name
U nderstanding friend
P lays a lot
E ats healthy food
R eads genres
T aylor Nicole Lisk is my favorite friend

Kathleen Ruth Rupert, Grade 5
Frank Ohl Middle School

From…

I am from afternoons on the rope swing in my Poppa's backyard,
from the memories of that lovely woman I had the pleasure of calling Grandma.
I am from the stubborn and the headstrong,
from the loving and the kind.
From reading the adventures and misfortunes of my friends Harry, Hermione, and Ron.
I am from corn on the cob, yellow and juicy,
from ballet flats and football.
From the red, brown, and yellow layering the ground,
from the crisp air that is Fall.
I am from the cool sensation, so strong, when you dive into the pristine chlorine water.
From the braces I sported for over a year.
That special song I share with my father,
from sitting near the crackling fire on a cold winter's night,
sharing the day's events with Mom.
I am from my most complemented "bright blue" eyes,
and my frizzy, thick, and brown hair that aggravates me.
From sled riding down that mountain of a hill and screaming at the top of our lungs,
"Happy New Year!"

McKenna P. Moore, Grade 6
Genoa Middle School

I Remember

I remember going to Myrtle Beach:
I remember going to the Pavilion Amusement Park almost every year;
I remember riding a lot of rides and eating good food;
I remember two years ago, we went because they were tearing it down.
I remember eating dinner with my aunt, uncle, two baby cousins, and my immediate family;
I remember going to Nascar Cafe and having fun playing games and having a great dinner.
I remember swimming in the huge Atlantic Ocean and playing in the warm sand;
I remember riding the really fast yellow banana boat and not falling off;
I remember my sister finding seven hermit crabs and keeping them in our condo.
I remember going to the rectangular pool and having a great time;
I remember going to the pool almost every night after we got back from dinner;
I remember making six new friends at the pool and one of them I keep in touch with by e-mail.
I remember going mini golfing each year and having a great time;
I remember this year we went to Lost Treasure golf and had to ride a train to start golfing;
I remember that I came in last place, but I still had a lot of fun.
I remember going to Myrtle Beach.

Lea Fisher, Grade 6
Harmon Middle School

Snow Day Wish

"Snow day! Snow day! We want a snow day!" That's how it all starts, changing and wishing.
Nobody can ruin your spirits by telling you that there is no chance of snow as you go to bed.
"Oh my goodness!" you hear your mom cry from the window the next morning.
"Wow!" you say as you look down and see all the little white flakes resting on the ground.
Dad checks and sure enough, there is no school and you have your first snow day of the year.
"Awesome!" your sister screams as you both run outside ready to sled.
You're to excited that you just jump on and slide as far as it will take you.
When you come to the hill, you sled until you're finally frozen.
"I need hot chocolate!" you cry as you enter your house.
Sure enough, there's already some waiting for you.
Has the day really ended you ask yourself as you climb into bed hoping that soon there will be
another Snow Day Wish.

Lauren Thompson, Grade 6
EH Greene Intermediate School

Summer Day!
On a hot summer day
Heavy with heat
Westley ready to play
Wanted a treat

As the sun sets
Westley's energy lagged
My frisky pet
Sagged

Finally night
Done pink
Westley missed light
Mom drink
Michaela LaForest, Grade 6
St Joseph Parish School

I Love Nature
Big cotton balls
  fill the sky.

Air touching me
like stuffed animals.

Creek sounds
like butterflies over pebbles.

  Fresh air
  fills my nose.

As the ground around me
  turns and weaves.
Zoe Istas, Grade 4
Normandy Elementary School

Puppies
Scampering around,
Chewing,
Getting into things,
NO!
Not on the carpet!
McKenna Walquist, Grade 5
Tremont Elementary School

I'm Thankful
I'm thankful
for life,
thankful for money,
I'm thankful for the
people around me
You see
I'm thankful for almost everything!
Charles Hill, Grade 6
Caledonia Elementary School

Personality
Brown eyes
Black hair
That's all you

Brown skin
White skin
That's all you

Big lips
Small ears
That's all you

All you
All you
Always will be you.
Keleada Lipscomb, Grade 5
Prospect Elementary School

The Moon
The moon following all the
way to home tell me his
life in the sky.

The sun shines
Every morning the sun shines
out of my window saying
wake up it's morning time.
Adolfo Robles-Cruz, Grade 6
Woodward Park Middle School

Dogs
In the morning
She will wake me up
She will be my alarm clock
When I get home
She will bark until I let her out
She always wants a treat
In the afternoon
She is always ongoing with barking
Bark! Bark! Woof! Woof!
Kris Park, Grade 6
Woodward Park Middle School

Fish
Fish,
Squirmy, fun, and cool,
Sometimes green, pink, and white,
They're always in the water,
'Cause that is cold.
What I like about them most,
Is their small little eyes.
Fish!
Colin Etchen, Grade 4
St Mary's School

Strawberry
On the outside,
You look like a
Baby porcupine with
Very, very short spikes
Seeing the light for
The first time.
When I peel you,
You sound like a
Mouse creeping around
For some cheese.
When I slice you,
You sound like someone
With muddy shoes
Walking around the house.
Tell me, how does
It feel to be a fruit?
Brianna Carr, Grade 5
Dr John Hole Elementary School

Winter into Spring
Winter into spring
Drizzle, drizzle down
Falling on my head
Falling on the ground
Soon all the snow will stop
And it will become springtime
All the snow will be gone
And then there will be beautiful flowers
Roses and violets
Pink and red
Scents so good
I dream of them in bed
When I raise my head up; it goes wild
I see all of the beautiful flowers
Now you see winter into spring
Annie Hendricks, Grade 6
Akiva Academy

Nature
The sea dances while I'm asleep.
Morning brings joy to all.
The stars tell me a story.
The sun guides me throughout the day.
The rain makes me weep.
Jesse Bourgeois, Grade 6
Woodward Park Middle School

A Gust of Wind
A gust of wind almost threw me down,
A gust of wind went through my gown,
A gust of wind was full of sound,
A gust of wind fell to the ground.
Lauren Wagner, Grade 5
Tremont Elementary School

The Evening Sky
I watch as the sun slowly goes down, creating a beautiful hue.
Then, slowly, it turns darker and darker before turning black.
The stars come out along with the moon.
How lovely is the evening sky.
Vicki Anderson, Grade 6
Melrose Elementary School

Jesus Was Born in a Stable
Jesus was born in a stable
Because there was no room in the inn.
Mary was the mother of Jesus
God's own humble servant.

Jesus was born in a stable
Because there was no room in the inn.
Joseph was the father
Affectionate for Mary and Babe.

Jesus was born in a stable
Because there was no room in the inn.
Here come the shepherds followed by sheep
They were told to come by angels who said, "Go to Bethlehem."

Jesus was born in a stable
Because there was no room in the inn.
Last came the 3 wise men in robes
Bowing down to the baby holding out gifts.

Jesus was born in a stable
Because there was no room in the inn.
Tirzah Talampas, Grade 5
Wooster Christian School

Intelligent and Athletic
I am intelligent and athletic
I wonder if I will make the basketball team
I hear the squeaking of tennis shoes on the basketball court
I see the ball dropping through the net
I want to play for the Lady Gales basketball team
I am intelligent and athletic.

I pretend to shoot the ball to fake the other person out
I feel the pressure when I am shooting a foul shot
I touch the basketball lightly to dribble the basketball
I worry that I will not make the foul shot when the pressure is on
I cry when someone fouls me really hard
I am intelligent and athletic.

I understand all of the rules of a basketball game
I say I will try my best to make the Lady Gales basketball team
I dream that I will be a varsity basketball player when I am a freshman
I try to make my coaches happy about how good I play
I hope I will then make a college basketball team
I am intelligent and athletic.
Reilly Hennessy, Grade 5
Sanderson Elementary School

A Very Merry Christmas
Today is a very joyful day for me.
Family and friends gather under the tree.
Mounds of presents wrapped in colorful paper,
Wait for me and my family.

Bright lights surround the room, twinkling.
It glints off the ornaments, gleaming.
Sparkles in yellows, reds, and greens.

Cameras click and paper crunches.
Yipee! I shout as I open my presents.
Sleigh bells ringing outside.

How many presents do I have?
When was the first Christmas?
Is this a happy day for everybody?

The lights are like twinkling stars.
The tree is a tall mountain.
Ornaments like a tree's clothes.

This is a very merry Christmas;
Very merry Christmas;
Very merry Christmas.
Anthony H. Popenoe, Grade 5
EH Greene Intermediate School

The Moon
The moon is like a lighthouse beacon,
Lighting the darkened sea,
Casting a ghostly glow,
On the drifting waves.

Right now the moon is a banana,
With fireflies buzzing around,
Cotton balls are surrounding
The warm happy smile.

The moon has gotten bigger in the last few days,
A nice flat slice of watermelon in the sky,
The perfect semicircle,
Illuminates the ground.

The moon is swelling, growing bigger,
Bulging at its side,
Its shape like a football,
Ready to spiral into someone's hand.

Still the moon is growing bigger,
Until one day, the moon is full,
As vivid and yellow as the sun,
With its face beaming at us with joy.
Andrew Wang, Grade 5
Cline Elementary School

Night Sky
Stars so shiny in the night sky.
The night is filled with pitch, black sky.

The moon is full and high in the sky.
Here I lie watching the great, big sky.

I watch the sky with my big, brown eyes.
The stars are twinkling in my eyes.

Nature's wonder lights up my eyes.
Just then I realize
How lucky I am to have two eyes.
Chelsea Patton, Grade 6
Trilby Elementary School

My Dog Noelle
Her name is Noelle,
She is my dog.
She barks when she hears bells,
And she tends to eat like a hog.

She eats food bit by bit,
Until it's almost gone.
Then we have to refill it.
Before she's done it is dawn.

Then it is time for bed,
We think that it's the end.
We finally rest our heads,
But it was all pretend.
Kelsie Rhoads, Grade 5
Spaulding Elementary School

Fall
The leaves will fall,
The trees are tall.

"I can see red!"
My brother said.

Don't make a sound,
Look what the squirrel found.

It has an acorn in its mouth,
And look at his house.
Shalhevet Fox, Grade 4
Cincinnati Hebrew Day School

Ello
There was a young fellow
who dreamed he was eating his pillow.
He woke up in the night
With a terrible fright
and said "its just yellow jello"
Seth Bensman, Grade 6
Holy Angels School

What Is Halloween
A holiday
Going to get candy
Dress up in costumes
Say…Trick or treat
Ghosts are walking around
Bats are flying around
Carve pumpkins
Go to haunted houses
Dress up scare crows
That is Halloween!
Bailey Smith, Grade 6
Tippecanoe Middle School

In the Snow
Playing in the snow so white,
my snowsuit can be very tight.
Building snow forts ever so high,
wondering if they could touch the sky.
Making snowmen can be fun,
until it melts and then you're done.
Once you're cold enough out there,
sit by the fire and be as warm as a bear.
Bobby Johnson, Grade 6
Roosevelt Elementary School

Sue
There once was a girl named Sue,
And her school fees were really due,
She exclaimed in fright,
That she wouldn't sleep all night,
Because her school fees were due.
Sophia Sorboro, Grade 5
Rootstown Elementary School

Soldiers
Soldiers are brave.
Soldiers are willing,
To give their lives,
To their country.
Soldiers train a lot.
Soldiers are in Iraq.
Soldiers carry big guns there.
Soldiers should be,
Honored a lot more.
Soldiers.
Landon Thiel, Grade 4
St Mary's School

Cats
Cats
admirable, snugly
running, jumping, pouncing
tepid in the winter
sophisticated
Sophie Erieau, Grade 5
Hylen Souders Elementary School

Goblins/Spirits
Goblins
Clear and see-through
Moaning, groaning at you
Staring at you with a big Boo
Spirits
Miranda Morgan, Grade 6
Roosevelt Elementary School

Holiday Cheer
Paper tearing,
Gasps of surprise,
Loud clangs to get the feast ready

Munching on cookies,
Munching on cookies,
Munching on cookies

The cookies are coming,
From the best place on Earth,
My grandma's kitchen, now a bakery

Lights twinkling on trees,
Candles casting a beautiful glow,
The room is as golden as the sun

Precious ornaments dangling,
Candy canes in the front yard,
Baby Jesus in the window sill

"Will Santa come this year?"
"Will I get the gifts that I wanted?"

Christmas brings joy,
To every girl and boy,
Let's bow down and pray,
That it always stays that way.
Paige Henry, Grade 5
EH Greene Intermediate School

Horse
With its sleek fur coat
Running through the big thick grass,
It makes a scene
That will ever last.

They only take a few stops
To eat and to rest,
Then they're off again
On a quest.

They could go from Europe
To Asia at a simple trot,
Thinking of only one thought,
To get there.
Michaella Keyes, Grade 6
EH Greene Intermediate School

My Cat
I have a cat that's white and black,
She likes to be carried on my back.
When she jumps off, she jumps so high,
It almost looks like she can fly.
Emily Throckmorton, Grade 5
Wintersville Elementary School

Forest
So many animals you will find,
that it will boggle your mind.
So many different kinds of trees
their leaves move in the breeze.
Over by the peak,
there is a small creek.
In the creek there is a deer,
how I wish my mom was here.
Jarrod Ward, Grade 6
Roosevelt Elementary School

Halloween Is Coming!
Halloween is coming.
Grab your costume and go!
Tricking and treating
Here it is!
Halloween is coming,
And I don't fib.
Bring your lantern and basket.
But wear a black hat
With some ears and a tail
You'll make a fine cat.
Halloween is coming,
It's almost here!
In fact, it's tonight
So give a loud cheer!
Mackenzie Malmer, Grade 4
Dobbins Elementary School

Keith/Friend
Keith
Dark skin
Loves playing basketball
Love to be with
Friend
Kevin Schilling, Grade 5
Wooster Christian School

Dancing
Dancing
Twirling, jumping
Living life wildly
Your time to shine with joy and poise
Graceful
Margo Shininger, Grade 6
Tippecanoe Middle School

Fireflies
The firefly flies through the night
Bringing joy to everyone's sight.

Kid's showing ability
Catching them with curiosity.

These creatures are not out all day long
Living for who knows how long.
Anna Stanton, Grade 6
Rocky River Middle School

Red
Red is the color for blood.
But there is no red in mud.
Red is the color of your ties.
A red pillow is where your head lies.
Red could have so many features.
There's even some red on the creatures.
You could even have some red wine.
Or you can swing on that red vine.
Out of all the colors, the best is red.
Even my friend thinks so.
His name is Fred.
Kiley Sunderhaus, Grade 6
St John the Baptist School

Hair
Wavy
Stagger curly
Cutesy
Wet
Dry
Highlight
Colored ratty
Up in a pony tail
In bun braids
Colored black
White, Gray, Yellow,
Brown,
Black with highlights,
Woman's crowing glory.
Allison Babbs, Grade 5
St Joseph Parish School

My Life
My name, Ray'onna. My life, cool.
I get my emotions from my family like…

Dad, he's strong and I'm strong.
Mom, she's smart and I'm smart.
Grandma, she's pretty and I'm pretty.
Grandfather, he's fun and I'm fun.
Ray'onna Jernigan, Grade 5
Prospect Elementary School

Hockey
Play on ice
With a puck
Sharp skates
Padded gloves
Played with nets
Powerful shots
Toughest sport ever!
Nick Ryan, Grade 4
Dobbins Elementary School

Fall
Bright colorful leaves
flowing in the wind
crunching under feet
cool air
great taste
how fun
Alex Browne, Grade 6
St Clement Elementary School

Puzzle
Find the right piece
Put it in the puzzle
Force it to fit
Break the piece
Punch the wall
Throw a fit
Spill coffee all over it
Should've thought twice
Buy a new puzzle
OH NO
Alexander McEvoy, Grade 6
Harmon Middle School

Outside the Window
I look at the blue sky
out the window
and I wonder
what's below.
Wow.
I see the tops
of green, green trees,
buildings
as high as the eye could see,
a crane
as red as a rose.
I see a water tank
blacker than coal.
And that's what I see
on a wonderful day
in the middle
of a great great August day.
Austin Morris, Grade 5
Emerson Academy of Dayton

Life

Life is like a roller coaster; full of ups and downs,
But never let these obstacles put you in a frown.
Never give up and never quit, that is a great way to live;
It is not as good to take as it is to give.
Sometimes the world is cruel and destructive,
Sometimes it is kind and polite;
Just because everyone is doing wrong
Does not mean you should not do right.
We try to do right but we all sometimes sin,
But it is not an excuse to ever give in.
Love your neighbor and love the Lord
Because our God is the best award.
Life is the greatest thing you will get
No matter how good or bad;
If things get overwhelming, do not start getting mad.
Life is a strong ride; either wrong or right;
Love life with all your heart and do not forget to hold on tight!

Brandon Brown, Grade 6
The Calvary Academy

Chanukah Dreidle

Why does the dreidle spin so
Wildly?

A mountain of
Gifts sitting on the hearth,
Family waiting, watching,
Dreidle spinning wildly!

Soft light streaming from
Above shimmering off the hearth,
Dreidle spinning wildly!

A baby whinnying nearby,
The ripping of wrapping paper,
The laughter of family members,
Dreidle spinning wildly!
The hot wax drips from the menorah
But refuses to touch the counter. Why does it do that?
Dreidle spinning wildly!

The oil lasted for eight days not just one,
Dreidle spinning wildly…
GIMEL!

Spencer Mandell, Grade 5
EH Greene Intermediate School

Life

Life is what you go through every day.
Life is nature all around you.
Life is what you and others do.
When you grow up and get old.
But life is also your family and the people you care about.

Zenaye Sanchez, Grade 5
Dr John Hole Elementary School

A Chair

Oh, chair, oh chair,
You are so darn squeaky.
A screw must be loose
Because you're sounding creaky.

You're brown and
So ugly and weak
I cannot believe
I must sit on you all week.

Kyle Hoff, Grade 6
Melrose Elementary School

Patriotic

The patriotic moon
September is patriotic
It reminds me of New York
The World Trade Center tragedies
A full moon with great light
Lighting the darkness
Where the buildings once stood
That is the patriotic moon

Kyle Munn, Grade 5
Cline Elementary School

Black

Black is dark,
An unlucky cat ragging past,
Afraid of the jet black night,
Running through the black shadows.
Black cat, superstitious black cat,
Black is the emotion,
Black is the car coming down the newly paved road,
Black is the sight of the cat, black.

Lydia Gordon, Grade 6
Hilliard Tharp Sixth Grade School

Index

Abel-Rutter, Emmi 146
Abrams, Mark 21
Ackerman, Rob 172
Acklin, Maddie 294
Adams, Caitlyn 118
Adams, Cody 227
Adams, Katherine 290
Adams, Sammantha 288
Adkins, Jake 240
Adrian, Landon 195
Ahmed, Zeenet 139
Ahn, Joseph 244
Alam, Mohammad 42
Alberti, Lauren 79
Albi, Anna 58
Albring, Matthew 230
Alexander, Desiree 81
Ali, Osman 18
Alishusky, Haley 273
Alkatib, Sumaya 280
Allen, Dalton 238
Allen, Destynee 140
Allen, Megan 276
Allen, Neil 178
Allen, Tiffany 105
Allison, Reese 275
Alt, Jessica 25
Altman, Marni 229
Altman, Randy 271
Amaniampong, Wesley ...238
Ammerman, Kate 288
Ammon, Makayla 208
Amom, Prativa 301
Amster, Katie 221
Anabtawi, Hashem 290
Anderson, Katie 31
Anderson, Vicki 317
Anello, Joey 106
Anello, Maci 96
Angelilli, Michael 240
Ankrom, Trinity D. 273
Antypas, Eva 122
Apple, Sarah 24
Appleman, Monica 123
Archer, Ashley 143
Arellano, April 283
Armes, Samantha 80
Arnett, Zach 285
Arnold, Kayla 143
Arnold, Sharon 294
Artis, Dion 28
Artrip, Carey 173

Arunski, Alec 195
Ash, Damieshia 280
Ashford, Brianna 36
Ashley, Emily 278
Ashworth, Amy 43
Aswad, Scout 306
Atassi, Sahar 181
Atkinson, James 24
Atwell, Gabbi 239
Aufderbeck, Jami 84
Aukerman, Alyssa 304
Aukerman, Kelsey 239
Avila, Miriam 208
Aziz, Aamna 172
Babbs, Allison 319
Bachelder, Aaron 232
Baele, Alex 178
Baierl, Zach 180
Bailes, Talia 269
Bailey, Brian 288
Bailey, Jani 283
Bais, Monique 141
Baker, Cameron 274
Baker, Logan 212
Baker, Shelby Mae 104
Baker, Skyler 222
Balcerzak, Olivia 198
Baldwin, Breanna 258
Ballew, Kelsey 42
Banks, Kalen 147
Bannan, Ryan 147
Bao, Caroline 90
Baringer, Melissa 23
Barlow, Paige 76
Barner, Lydia 234
Barnes, Stewart 258
Barnett, Bekka 293
Barnett, Brady 211
Barnhart, River 302
Baron, Alexander 232
Barr, Korey 264
Barren, Billy 95
Barth, Jessica 132
Bartram, Kasia 286
Bash, Jacob 218
Bashour, George 81
Bates, Karlee 149
Batey, Chandler 258
Batts, Zachary 289
Bauer, Nathan 129
Bayer, Elizabeth 270
Baytos, Katie 87

Beard, Elisabeth 102
Beaucage, Maria 313
Bedacht, Brad 8
Beery, Dustin 41
Behymer, Chance 306
Beitz, Julia 309
Belcher, Jacob 302
Beleny, Dave 191
Bell, John 35
Bellas, Joshua 217
Bender, Autumn 56
Bennett, Alexandria ...142
Bennett, Joe 18
Bennett, Miranda 157
Bensman, Seth 318
Benson, Claire 213
Bentley, Scott 226
Berger, Ariel 111
Bernard, Courtney 295
Berndt, Katie 302
Bernert, Matt 154
Berning, Jill 296
Berns, Zoe 160
Bernstein, Matt 254
Berry, Luke 52
Bessey, Austin 48
Bevan, Emily M. 269
Bevilacqua, Abby 252
Bevington, Alyssa 258
Bieker, Tyler 251
Bieler, Shoshi 167
Bierly, Jenna 273
Billick, Maddie 221
Binius, Matthew 123
Bish, Hayden 222
Black, Ethan 260
Blackmore, Brianna ...228
Blackwell, Heather 311
Blake, Peter 174
Blankenship, Arielle 35
Blazejewski, Jakub 171
Bleser, Elise 151
Block, Hannah 298
Blomer, Molly 75
Blossey, Kate 236
Blough, Richard 222
Blubaugh, Jessica 88
Blum, Michelle 145
Bode, Rebecca 104
Boeckman, Katie 103
Boehringer, Tara 257
Boetcher, Lakota 114

Bohme, Alexandra 88
Bolen, Jessie 103
Bonfiglio, Carly 108
Bonvissuto, Maria 150
Borges, Tyler 216
Borocz, Jade 300
Boros, Kayla 300
Borton, Austin 152
Boudon, Andrew 102
Boughner, Danna 9
Bourgeois, Jesse 316
Bourst, Tyler 122
Bowen, Tyler 254
Bowers, Trent 74
Boyd, Alex 260
Boyd, MacKenzie 259
Brabender, Ben 192
Brackman, Eric 128
Bradbury, Emma 254
Bradford, Sarah 148
Breeden, Danielle 310
Brewer, Ken 82
Brewer, Tayler 300
Briggs, Nicole 20
Brizendine, Elayna 192
Brod, Eva 308
Broida, Jacob 152
Bronson, Wyatt 209
Brook, Sarah Rose 268
Brookover, Jacob 125
Brooks, Ryan 165
Brooks, Scott 210
Brooks, Zach 238
Brosko, Kayla 175
Brown, Abbie 89
Brown, Brandon 320
Brown, Cooper 305
Brown, Jacqueline 98
Brown, Jakob 274
Brown, Kate 57
Brown, Katie 288
Brown, Madilyn 306
Brown, Matthew 79
Brown, Sean 130
Brown Hicks, Dii'Azia ...119
Browne, Alex 319
Brownfield, Alexa 78
Brownlee, John 130
Bruce, Ashley 299
Bruening, Tamara 92
Brugger, Zac 306
Brutovski, Bianca 188

Bryant, Faith 181	Castelaz, Leah 169	Cooper, Tim 184	Deepe, Alaina 121
Bryant, Jay 81	Castillo, Ericka 281	Cope, Alex 119	Defibaugh, Sara 291
Bucey Leopold, Rachael ..244	Caughenbaugh, Colt 244	Copley, Kevin 93	Degenhardt, Matt 286
Buchenroth, Paige 117	Cavanaugh, Kelly 179	Coppus, Kevin 151	DeHays, Thomas 288
Bucur, Andrew 147	Chaffee, Ciera 110	Corcoran, Alexis 312	Deile, Breanne 36
Buczkowski, Austin 264	Chafin, Riley 152	Corcoran, Ellen 299	DelFratte, Betty Jo 288
Buehler, Eric 224	Chang, Serena 76	Corley, Ashley 125	Delp, Derek 125
Buettner, Eric 21	Chapman, Rebecca 314	Cornelius, Caleb 213	Demarchi, Lauren 309
Bumpus, Matt 260	Chatterjee, Krittika 233	Corr, Ben 244	Demers, Alex 264
Buratti, Brandon 134	Cheeseman, Marie 193	Corrigan, Dan 43	Demjanenko, Emily 137
Burgei, Olivia 93	Chef, Jonathan 114	Corsi, Anthony 172	Dennis, Codi 85
Burger, Nolan 47	Cherry, Jasmine 87	Coughlin, Meredith 218	Dennis, Jacob 154
Burnette, Coty 216	Chido, Mike 26	Coulson, Denver 55	Densmore, Jessica 43
Burns, Ariel 106	Christian, Nathan 278	Courter, Suzanne 133	Denton, Nathan 191
Burr, Blaze 240	Christmann, Nate 21	Covitch, Orly 57	DeRosa, Sophie 199
Burris, Amanda 115	Cika, John 208	Cowgill, Christy 75	DeRose, Carly 99
Burte, Amy 256	Ciricillo, Sammy 234	Cox, Nick 138	Derr, Brandon 176
Bush, Meghan 47	Clancy, Martin 183	Craft, Kira 25	DeSalvo, Marisa Nicole ...230
Bush, Zachary Alan 299	Clark, Brian 156	Crain, Sammy 82	DeSantis, Nicole Ann ...246
Bushnell, Amanda 130	Clark, Brittany 301	Crawford, Nick 276	Dexter, Kraig 112
Butcher, Benjamin 234	Clarke, Spencer 314	Crawley, Patricia 298	Dick, Michael 230
Butler, Brittany 190	Clawson, Chelsea 235	Creech, Steven 41	Dickerson, Jasmine 173
Butler, Sarah 21	Clepper, Erin 62	Crognale, Alex 160	Diersing, Danielle 215
Cady, Steven 181	Cleveland, Molly 222	Crossley, Kindle 159	DiGeronimo, Mary 110
Cahill, Lizzie 257	Cline, Andrew 220	Culler, Dannica 302	Dikowicz, Meghan 103
Cain, Kristina 113	Cline, Summer 162	Cunningham, Sarah 109	Dillhoff, Andrew 234
Calabrase, Sammi 294	Coccia, Beth 126	Cupito, Lauren 33	DiMasso, Andrianna 200
Calabrese, Alexandra 180	Cockrell, Evan 89	Cupple, Christina 260	Dix, Brendon 216
Calhoun, Shannon R. 265	Cohen, Morrisa 119	Curby, Laurna 87	Dober, Alexandra 36
Callahan, Jenna 248	Colaianni, Julie 167	Currie, John 260	Dolan, Michael 246
Callicoat, Levi 154	Colborn, Veronica 72	Curtis, Caitlin 196	Dona, Krista 132
Cameron, Lindsay 57	Cole, Andrea 253	D'Abato, Gabi 262	Dona, Nicole 109
Camp, Amber 157	Cole, Tom 167	Daboul, Judy 276	Donaldson, Chloe 24
Campbell, Brad 253	Colegrove, Alissa 299	Daboul, Lynn 129	Donchess, Raegan 282
Campbell, Dustin 88	Coleman, Harmonie 266	Dagg, Matt 80	Donohoue, Cody 275
Campbell, Mark 254	Coler, Rachel 103	Dagg, Shannon 105	Dosani, Atiya 270
Caniff, Justin 226	Collier, Erick 268	Daigle, Nick 42	Dotson, Melinda 78
Cannon, Sean 244	Collier, Jacob 285	Dailey, Justin 212	Dovsek, Tanner 189
Cappa, David 29	Collins, Jenna 295	Dandridge, Maya 137	Drake, Mariah 257
Carafelli, Micayla 245	Collins, Sadie 138	Darby, Joanna 236	Drenten, Deanna 25
Carbon, Gabriella 314	Colucci, Jessica 310	Dargavell, Cole 208	Dresbach, Sarah 232
Carioti, Maria 226	Combs, MaKayla 272	Davenport, Austin 195	Drouhard, Brooke 274
Carleton, George 184	Combs, Marcheri 46	Davet, Patrick 178	Drummond, Jessica 20
Carmosino, Jessica 31	Combs, Taylor 208	Davies, Stephen 253	Duale, Mackenzie......185
Carpenter, Jonathan 260	Concilla, Nicholas 88	Davis, Tayla 310	Dudas, Krystal 128
Carpenter, Stephanie 230	Condon, Reilly 90	Davis-Pearl, Brandon 183	Duling, Dustin 156
Carr, Brianna 316	Congeni, Michael 293	Day, Adrianna 313	Dumler, Ben 170
Carr, Kaitlynn 78	Connelly, Sara 283	Day, David Jason 254	Dunn, Josh 277
Carr, Mariah 306	Connolly, Colleen 114	de Villiers, Jacques 136	Duran, Matt 292
Carrington, Katelynn Elizabeth 23	Connolly, Megan 144	Deal, Corey 148	Durbin, Christian 258
Carroll, John 291	Considder, Rachel 146	Deall, Laura 88	Dyer, Jared 81
Carroll, Sydney 230	Consolo, Jenna 188	DeAmicis, Dakota 195	Dykstra, Matt 38
Carruthers, Jordan 97	Cook, Anna 140	Dean, Autumn 294	Eastwood, Erin 222
Cartwright, Millie Ann ...268	Cook, Haley 259	Deane, Becky 39	Eckert, Jesse 160
Carver, Aron 91	Cook, Peggy 28	DeAngelis, Anna 184	Edge, Stephanie 34
Carvour, Ava 20	Cooper, Cloe 89	DeBee, Taylor 182	Edison, Nick 296
Casper, Jordan 92	Cooper, Heather 117	Decipeda, Jonathan 80	Edmonds, Terrance 22
	Cooper, Ryan 272	Deems, Julia 243	Edwards, Brooke 286

Index

Edwards, Eric Edward ...268
Edwards, Keely 236
Edwards, Marcus Alan 38
Edwards, Tara 30
Egnor, Shayla 18
Elder, Kendal 160
Eldridge, Devynne 254
Elekonich, James 76
Elias, Dennis 272
Eller, Bekah 170
Eller, Rebekah 148
Elliot, Christopher 209
Elliott, Briana 301
Elsner, Nick 294
Emery, Kaitlyn 120
Emling, Erika 82
Emrick, Jordi 211
Engber, Corinne 264
Engber, Melanie 292
Engel, Ally 283
Englebert, Amanda C. 308
Englert, Jared 301
Enoch, Patrick 111
Ensman, Kirsten 272
Erdel, Dylan 137
Erickson, Mya 189
Erieau, Sophie 318
Erskin, Tyler 37
Ertle, Devon 138
Esarco, David 201
Espe, Kristen 26
Etchen, Colin 316
Evans, Zachary 225
Fagan, Emily 314
Fairbanks, Abby 157
Falorio, Maria 133
Fang, Lydia 258
Fantozzi, Angel 10
Fath, Abby 126
Faulkner, Colin 285
Fayette, Nick 264
Federico, Kristiana 256
Fejer, Candisse 298
Ferguson, Haley 222
Fernandez, Christian
    Emmanuel 267
Ferrell, Victoria 76
Fields, Kendra 281
Fields, Nicole 153
Fiely, Katarina 96
Fink, Angela 307
Finke, Nick 309
Finley, Rob 50
Finnerty, Max 290
Finney, Chelsea 91
Fishburn, Kyle 227
Fisher, Garrett 240
Fisher, Lea 315

Fitch, Molly 146
FitzGerald, Jack 188
Fitzgerald, Tyler 121
Flamm, Jessica 260
Flaugher, Nicole 144
Fleisher, Ana 53
Flinn, Tim 171
Flora, Bailey 248
Flowers, Marquis 266
Fluegemann, Joe 153
Flynn, Catherine 159
Flynn, William "Andrew" .152
Fogle, Javan 304
Forcier, Racheal 82
Ford, Allison 158
Ford, Christopher 223
Ford, Kylie 222
Formick, Connor 220
Forrest, Dominique 227
Fortune, Jordan 230
Fowler, Summer 59
Fox, Alyssa 98
Fox, Esther 19
Fox, Shalhevet 318
Frame, Torey 174
Frank, Dakota 189
Frank, Logan 90
Frank, Ryan 278
Frankart, Kaitlin 49
Frankel, Ilana 277
Franklin, Madeline 311
Frantom, Kristian 209
Franz, Chantal 48
Frazier, Blaike 263
Frederick, Brianne 278
Freed, Juliet 242
Freeman, Tearna 116
Friedman, Alana 160
Friley, Brian 124
Froimson, Kevin 138
Fromel, John 142
Fryman, Jayce 277
Fuerst, Abrielle 36
Fulwider, Sam 303
Gable, Ciara 307
Gabor, Emma 264
Gaier, Thomas 248
Gaillard, Jamie 212
Gallagher, Irene 11
Gallagher, Zoe R. 223
Gallaway, Ally 174
Gambone, Greg 150
Garber, Hannah 124
Garnek, Alexis 132
Garrison, Shannon 284
Garzony, Topher 75
Gates, Brenna 202
Geanangel, Paige 265

Gearhart, Samuel 158
Geise, Tiffany 191
Georgopoulos, Anthony ..245
Geresy, David 73
Gerschutz, Brandi 101
Getz, Alex 97
Giblin, Meagan 135
Gibson, Brittney 53
Gifford, Deanna 83
Gilbert, Dezmon 214
Gillies, Coburn 216
Gilmer, Kaleigh 179
Gilson, Calla 236
Ginley, Greg 284
Ginley, Joshua 237
Girten, Grant 222
Giuffre, Claudia 63
Giuliani, Kayla 77
Gividen, Jacob 280
Gjergo, Melis 229
Glass, Phillip 151
Gockel, Kristi 127
Goddard, Audrey 64
Goddard, Hannah 123
Godfrey, Nick 191
Goettemoeller, Lauren ..304
Goldacker, Ashley 76
Goldacker, Nicholas 255
Goldenberg, Mike 307
Goldschneider, Benjamin .307
Goldstein, Isaac L.G. 302
Golec, Kelsey 186
Golias, Lizy 101
Gonzales, Karen 308
Good, Samantha 222
Goodchild, Zachary 285
Goodin, Darren 212
Goodin, Grace 226
Gordon, Lydia 320
Gordon, Sara 77
Gore, Dana 296
Gosche, Jenna 176
Goydich, Chris 138
Graf, Shannon 172
Grassan, Brett 260
Graves, Seth 34
Gray, TyAnn 99
Gray, William 244
Grebenc, Billy 106
Greco, Abby 218
Green, Alex 196
Green, KiKi 267
Green, Paige 244
Greene, Alexandra 228
Greene, Tori 258
Greer, Stephanie 289
Gregg, Nick 311
Gregory, Lani 185

Gregory, Michael 60
Greider, Lauren 235
Grever, Andrew 289
Grieshop, Emily 97
Grieshop, Richard 264
Griesinger, Nicolette ..278
Griffey, Carlee 237
Griffin, Jasmine 134
Grilliot, Jessica 172
Grimm, Kaitlyn 273
Grindle, Corey 208
Groh, Christopher 119
Grubb, Jessica 232
Gruenwald, Darci 88
Grumman, Anna 265
Gubala, Brenden 240
Gugel, Kelsey 236
Guilbert, Elizabeth ...192
Guinn, Ciaran 215
Gushura, Allie 90
Gutierrez, Santiago ...107
Gyorky, Joe 185
Haas, Tanner 218
Haber, Matthew 194
Haber, Mitchell 100
Hadzinsky, Megan 83
Hagenbuch, Brynn 144
Haggy, Bethany 240
Hagler, Charles 177
Hain, Michael 40
Haines, Raegan 47
Hall, Brad 237
Hall, Jessika 106
Hall, Nathan 307
Haller, Lauren 100
Hamilton, Blaine 281
Hamker, Cassie 231
Hamlin, Allyson 115
Hammond, Kristie ...115
Hammond, Madison .295
Hammond, Stephanie ..50
Hamre, Brent 288
Hanna, Collin 290
Hannah, Alex 240
Hans, Kirstie 308
Harden, Lyric 304
Hardin, Kylie 119
Haritos, Christopher .314
Harley, Nathan 115
Harley, Valerie 313
Harp, Zach 234
Harper, Morgan 112
Harrington, Shannon .296
Hart, Adam 110
Hart, Beka 196
Hart, Haleigh 147
Hartfield, Taylor ...127
Hartman, Will 158

Hassett, Brialyn 132	Hoersten, Emily 242	Janezic, Alyssa 47	Kennard, Jenna 43
Hatcher, Riley 57	Hoey, Alex 218	Jansen, Jerry 101	Kennedy, Kalene 86
Haverlock, Carita 167	Hoff, Kyle 320	Jaskari, Emily 272	Kenney, Alexis 106
Hawthorne, Brian 74	Hoffman, Joshua 195	Jayne, Michael 257	Kenney, Jon 123
Hayden, Bailey 282	Hoffman, Ryan 54	Jenkins, Christopher W. . 254	Kereki, Ilona 190
Hayden, Christian 181	Hoffmann, Caroline 185	Jenkins, Randy 161	Kern, Jared 138
Hayes, Ben 46	Hoffmeister, Doug 284	Jenkins, Shaun 131	Kerpsack, Tyler 187
Haygood, Sam 41	Hofmann, Emma 297	Jennings, Alexa 297	Kessler, Dominick 160
Haynes, Renae 121	Hohman, Allison 173	Jennings, Tiffany Eden .. 178	Kessler, Sable 301
Hegyesi, Tyler 294	Holland, Amber 50	Jernigan, Ray'onna 319	Keyes, Michaella 318
Hehemann, Evan 44	Hollis, Timmy 106	Jett, Ashley 91	Kilbane, Jason 124
Heigl, Jessica 142	Hollis, Tommy 104	Jewell, Dawnelle 51	Kilbane, Kaitlin 193
Heimann, Allison 51	Holsopple, Tyler 240	Jiang, Megan 231	Kilbarger, Candice 107
Heimbach, Stephanie ... 251	Honecker, Molly 96	Jobe, Kara 227	Kim, Seolah 13
Helke, Julia 232	Hood, Mike Robert 225	Johanni, Leah 54	Kinderdine, Todd 227
Helleis, Kayla 211	Hoover, Stephanie 180	Johanson, Kara 220	Kindle, Amanda 117
Helmke, Katrina 35	Horning, Kayla 235	Johnson, Aja 165	King, Cameron 227
Hemsink, Joseph 47	Horvat, Gina 174	Johnson, Bobby 318	King, John-Christopher .. 48
Henderson, Aykee 98	Horvath, Grant 268	Johnson, Carleno 274	King, Kaylynn 246
Henderson, George Alexander 75	Horvath, Tina 137	Johnson, Chelsa 65	King, Marissa 310
Hendricks, Annie 316	Hosler, Katie 114	Johnson, Elizabeth 247	King, Thomas 104
Hendrock, William 157	Hosler, Quinn 161	Johnson, Elizabeth Hope .. 73	King, Tim 168
Henghold, Jordan 228	House, Natalie 33	Johnson, Lionel 225	Kinman, Becca 130
Hennessey, Casey 33	Housley, Erin 245	Johnson, Matt 78	Kinser, Kiyara 77
Hennessy, Reilly 317	Howard, Mykal 282	Johnson, Taylor 179	Kirian, Robert 29
Henry, Paige 318	Howard, Patrice 297	Jones, Adrienne 214	Kirkendall, Kayla 131
Herald, Jordan 252	Howell, Edith 163	Jones, Bailey 230	Kirker, Caroline 37
Herbert, Maddie 24	Howell, Julie 81	Jones, Callie 250	Kitchens, Allison 120
Herman, Madison 236	Hsu, Megan 231	Jones, David 12	Klassen, Katie 168
Hermann, Amanda 145	Hu, Gloria 217	Jones, Deon 25	Klausing, Renee 53
Herringshaw, Halle 105	Huang, CJ 272	Jones, Emily 225	Klausner, Peter 112
Herron, Lexie 311	Huculak, Elina 250	Jones, Emily 230	Klein, Courtney 152
Hersey, Abby 156	Hudson, Dionte 250	Jones, Halee 212	Kleinmann, Sierra 136
Hersha, Matt 51	Hudson, Nick 265	Jones, Jessica 117	Kley, Stephanie 209
Hershey, Nick 212	Huehner, Rachel 187	Jones, Kayla 106	Kling, Melissa 223
Hershiser, Breighton ... 212	Huelskamp, Mark 18	Jones, Nicholas 261	Kmetz, A.J. 97
Herzog, James 301	Hughley, Quinten 143	Jordan, Justin 192	Knapp, Ronald 283
Heslop, Kristen 154	Huls, Chris 164	June, Rachael 212	Knecht, Maddie 305
Hess, Natasha 73	Humbert, Harley 217	Justice, Olivia 229	Knippenberg, Jennifer .. 159
Hickey, Cassandra 97	Hunter, Hannah 208	Kaczmarczyk, Nicoletta ... 252	Koch, Stephanie 293
Hickey, Sean 95	Hunter, Madisen 300	Kaine, Nikki 187	Kochanek, Nicholas 300
Hickok, Sierra 217	Hunyadi, Jocelyn 237	Kaiser, Jessica 84	Koenn, Ashley 53
Hietikko, Colin 262	Hurford, Kayla 45	Kang, Sam 241	Koester, Tyler 187
Hill, Charles 316	Huston, Brianna 193	Karcic, Ashley 188	Kogelnik, Elise 143
Hill, Destinee 233	Hutton, Clayton 284	Karlie, Leah 192	Kolb, Isaiah 212
Hill, Jennifer 209	Iacianci, Dean 160	Katabi, Leila 175	Kopniske, Adam 274
Hinkle, Alex 236	Icard, Mariah 298	Katzenmeyer, Jacob 94	Kopronica, Jake 183
Hinkle, Jen 176	Iha, Thomas 246	Kauffman, Drew 224	Korsnack, Krista 218
Hinkle, Rayanna 152	Ihnot, Lauren 283	Kaufman, Faith 295	Koscher, Ella 262
Hinojosa, Amanda 23	Irwin, Erika 244	Kayser, Molly 24	Kover, Jaimie 41
Hirschl, Brian 275	Isley, Nick 305	Keaton, Katie 75	Kovich, Andrew 74
Hite, Shawna 36	Ismail, Manahil 314	Keene, Leslie 221	Kramer, Aleisha 121
Hobart, Jessica 279	Issa, Zach 253	Kelbley, Lynette 221	Kraus, Rachel 170
Hobart, William 310	Istas, Zoe 316	Keller, Joshua 239	Kreager, Paige 261
Hodge, Abbigayle 292	Jain, Aneesh 223	Keller, Kylie 101	Kreatsoulas, Juliana ... 306
Hodge, Connie 181	James, Kylie 45	Kellum, Blake 55	Kreider, Alyssa 209
Hodgson, Nicole 144	Jamison, Erin 290	Kelzer, Brian 286	Kringen, Ignatius Chad .. 147
	Jamiyansuren, Shandock .300	Kemper, Joey 179	Kropp, Dana 171

Index

Krumpak, Cole 113
Kuebler, Megan 14
Kuharich, Elissa 88
Kuhn, Kaycee 149
Kujawa, Emma 314
Kula, Gregory 95
Kulakowski, Richard 27
Kumar, Prianka 304
Kunz, Alysha 225
Kurian, Jobby 285
Kurtz, Dalton 109
Kurtz, Haley 74
Kurz, Victor 306
Kuzmic, Samantha 104
Labhasetwar, Disha 20
Lachey, Taylor 247
LaForest, Michaela 316
Lagace, Jake 124
Lammers, Alison 117
Lammers, Jordan Scott
  Eugene 166
Lamprecht, Colin 153
Landel, Natalee 232
Lane, Kayla 291
Lang, Cody 116
Lannon, Riley 179
Lansing, Alix 171
Lantz, Megan 266
Larkin, Elizabeth 111
Larkin, Rickey 56
Larsen, Andrea 229
LaRue, Kaylee 217
Lash, Shane 110
Lashner, Molly 51
Laughter, Casey 173
Lavender, Hayley 95
Lawson, Hannah 288
Leach, Alice 282
Leach, Benjamin 170
Lee, Billy 180
Lee, Derek 124
Lee, Erik 278
Lee, Isaac Q. 275
Lee, Jungho 233
Lees, Rian 148
Lees, Riley 234
Leever, Megan 34
Leffler, Laura 134
Lehman, Samuel 286
Leonard, Elise 229
Leone, David 282
Lertzman, Ryan 269
Lescinsky, Erin 275
Lesneski, John 240
Lewis, Thomaz 216
Liang, Yijia 260
Liao, Jocelyn 252
Lieb, Alex 54

Liette, Garret 289
Lifshitz, Rivka 296
Ligman, Ariel 195
Likar, Daniel 141
Lincoln, Aubrey 292
Lindauer, Aubry 285
Link, Amy 154
Linson, Abby 186
Lintz, Taylor 88
Lipp, Cassie 89
Lipscomb, Keleada 316
Lockwood, Emily 18
Logorda, Jake 178
Lollo, Stephie 83
Lomax, Karlie 105
Long, Amanda 177
Looney, Haley 77
Looser, Lindsey 27
Lopez, Deisy 263
Lopez, Maria 150
Lott, Constance 27
Louthan, Jaritt 228
Lovejoy, Josiah 314
Lovric, Monika 196
Lowther, Kelsi 72
Loy, Marina 77
Lozen, Leah 51
Lucas, Sarah 72
Luich, Peyton 210
Lukehart, Madeline 235
Lukshus, Genna 271
Luli, Emily 178
Lyons, Bree 48
Maccarone, Alex 308
MacFarland, Garret 237
Mackall, Katie 124
MacKenzie, Camilla 86
Mackey, Anna 295
Mahood, Jenna 264
Mahuet, Gabrielle 246
Makley, Liz 246
Malcomson, Jamie 162
Mallory, Michael 267
Malmer, Mackenzie 319
Maloney, Colin 162
Manco, Anthony 44
Mandell, Spencer 320
Mangan, Eileen 176
Mangelluzzi, Johnathan . .132
Manimbo, Miranda 273
Mann, Ashley 186
Manna, Marsia 272
Manna, Matt 264
Manning, Thomas 106
Manoloff, Alex 221
Mansberger, Elizabeth . . .277
Maraldo, Ryan 223
Marchese, Cortnee 150

Marchese, Michelle 109
Marino, Alexis 184
Marino, Chris 92
Marlowe, Samantha 306
Marquand, Noah 232
Marquez, Madison 178
Marshall, Jane 66
Marshall, Megan 140
Marshall, Sabrina 215
Martin, Keisha 263
Martinez, Estella 248
Martinez, Wined 25
Martinson, Ellen 252
Marva, Noelle 310
Masimore, Melissa 195
Mason, Emily 92
Mason, Zach 300
Massa, Kelly 27
Massa, Lindsey 143
Massingill, Megan 130
Maston, Chase 302
Mates, Michael J. 235
Matheny, Jenna 232
Mathes, Mariah 86
Matuszak, Mary 195
Maurer, Cynthia Lynn . . .15
May, Kaleigh 218
Maya, Vanessa 258
Mayer, Hayley Elizabeth . .224
Mayo, Caroline 19
Mays, Emmy 131
Mazzei, Carolyn 38
Mazzola, Mandy 275
Mazzone, Christine 24
McAfee, Nick 299
McArtor, Drake 103
McBride, Matt 108
McCaleb, Jazmine 59
McCarthy, Cara 248
McCartney, Sarah 185
McConaha, Tyler 77
McCormick, Lexi 247
McCready, Josh 293
McCrory, Breslyn 108
McCrossen, Megan 253
McEvoy, Alexander 319
McFaul, Rory 138
McGee, Torez 116
McGhee, Noah 312
McGraw, Michael 80
McGregor, Julia 218
McGuire, Cody 35
McGuire, Jimmy 236
McHugh, Austin 107
McIntosh, Jade 114
McIntosh, Mallory 297
McIntyre, Emily 106
McIntyre, Miranda 279

McKee, Brigid 273
McKenna, Maura 161
McKenzie, Asia 269
McKenzie, Felicia 59
McKibben, Haleigh 220
McLoskey, Carly 96
McMahon, Allie 133
McNamara, Erin 169
McNeal, Brooke 78
McNeil, Caitlyn 161
McVay, Shelby 224
Mead, Tracy 30
Meadors, Christine 146
Mealick, Zane 133
Medley, MaryBeth 309
Medovic, Allan 155
Medvick, Jacob 31
Meier, Kyle 96
Meiering, Amanda 305
Meighen, Ariel 52
Melms, Connor 129
Melrose, Katelynn 73
Melrose, Tamara 174
Mendenhall, Zoe 277
Menyhert, Rose 255
Mercer, Phillip 293
Merriman, Alexandra 105
Merritt, Aimee 270
Mers, Casey 145
Mesecher, Phoebe 232
Mesnard, Evan 251
Meyer, Justin 264
Meyer, Tori 86
Miesle, Jackie 122
Miggo, Amanda 192
Mihaly, Eric 87
Miklowski, Riza 153
Mikovits, Nick 285
Miles, Chelsea 120
Miles, Corey 272
Milko, Levi 149
Miller, Abby 238
Miller, Amy 101
Miller, Ashlee 232
Miller, Briana 145
Miller, Brittany 34
Miller, Eve 300
Miller, Kate 82
Miller, Lauren 287
Miller, Lauren 294
Miller, Logan 244
Miller, Luke 129
Miller, Maddy 135
Miller, Mason 144
Miller, Miranda 268
Miller, Misty 193
Miller, Mitch 301
Miller, Natalie 283

Miller, Taylor 250	Munjapara, Vasu 214	Oddo, Jacquelyn 138	Perisutti, Cameron 281
Miller, Todd 249	Munn, Kyle 320	Ogden, Taylor 189	Perrault, Lexi 78
Mills, Aliesha 91	Murphy, Courtney Justine ..52	Ogle, Tyler 292	Perry, Austin 18
Mills, Stephen 213	Murphy, Meghan 248	Ohana, Lucksmi 19	Perry, Christina 180
Milor, Myriam 222	Murray, Marcus 86	Okyere, Robert 49	Perry, Liza 292
Mineweaser, Samantha ..268	Musil, Dawn 165	Oldenburgh, Brian 220	Peskura, Kelly 226
Mishler, Amber 74	Mustafa, Shaffan 223	Oliphant, Kristin 219	Peters, Emily 215
Mitchell, Allyson 155	Mustafa, Zaeem 250	Oliver, Allison 122	Peterson, Lisa 266
Mitchell, Jake 120	Myers, Aaron 228	Oliver, Kirsten 258	Petit, Patrick 175
Mixon, Jalisa 22	Myers, Sarah 32	Oliver, William 48	Petrella, Vinnie 164
Moeller, Adam 287	Myers, Stephanie 44	Oliveri, Samantha 282	Pettet, Megan 31
Moeller, Jenny 312	Myers, Tyler 196	Opris, Lorena 290	Pettibone, Andy 50
Moeller, Jonathan 260	Naciff, Jorge 248	Orr, Keegan 284	Pfeifer, Jacob 190
Moesle, Kyle 305	Nagy, Megan 69	Osburn, John 259	Pfister, Jackson 210
Mohd-Amir, Jannatun 67	Naiyer, Nada 32	Osenbaugh, Krista 178	Pfister, Jonathan 264
Moller, Janie 286	Nannah, Kyle 31	Ota, Greg 243	Phillips, Brad 136
Molnar, Camden 123	Napholz, Kaitlynn 39	Pace, Ky 280	Pidgeon, Tyler 156
Molnar, Stephanie 102	Napier, Shawn 98	Pacheco, Daniel 274	Pieper, Anna 56
Molocea, Cassandra 191	Nardi, Nina 247	Paez, Mandy 135	Pifer, Angelica 157
Monnin, Hillary 41	Narendran, Nakul 261	Pahren, Mackenzie 294	Pilkington, Dusti 232
Monroe, Hannah 230	Nash, Morgan 272	Pairan, Alexander 246	Pires, Ivan 310
Montalto, Landon 286	Neal, Monica 131	Palumbo, John 74	Pirrone, Alexandra 149
Montgomery, Brad 239	Nedzelski, Ted 106	Pangallo, Gabby 124	Pitsul, Yanna 30
Montgomery, Tori 164	Neiser, Cade 90	Panning, Seth 116	Plasket, Jack 241
Mooney, Terry 126	Nelson, Devon 173	Paquette, Marie 38	Platania, Franco 298
Moore, Alyssa 97	Nelson, Israelle 122	Pareja, Alvaro 72	Pleasant, Olivia 38
Moore, Ashley 57	Nelson, Marla Nikki 240	Parilla, Laura 72	Plumly, Jerrod 82
Moore, Elliott 39	Neltner, Rachel 29	Park, Kaitlin 280	Plump, Cierra 213
Moore, Haley 156	Nemoff, Allison 249	Park, Kris 316	Pohl, Nathan 135
Moore, Jordan 192	Nesbitt, Emily 245	Parker, Anna 140	Poli, Ryne 236
Moore, Mayim 166	Netto, Courtney 30	Parsons, Madison 215	Polverine, Olivia 124
Moore, McKenna P. 315	Neumeier, Katie 53	Paskert, Nadia 210	Popa, Alexis 100
Moore, Michael 55	Neumeister, Eddie 116	Pasqualone, Kyle 228	Popenoe, Anthony H. ...317
Moore, Trayvon 144	Newby, Trent 258	Patching, Sarah 214	Porcase, Nattalie 91
Morales, Micah 213	Newnam, Jacqueline 56	Patrick, Bailey 261	Porter, Morgan 180
Moran, Leigha 84	Ng, Amy 113	Patrick, Monica 178	Powell, Tyler 189
Morehouse, Travis 164	Nichols, Tim 94	Pattison, Gina 34	Prahl, Kristen 133
Moreland, Ashley 30	Nichols, Tyra 93	Patton, Chelsea 318	Previte, Kami 292
Morgan, Miranda 318	Niedermeyer, Linda 125	Paul, Brandon 187	Proverbs, Nicole 100
Morino, Connie 270	Niehaus, Hannah 166	Paul, Casondra 233	Puckett, Audrey 194
Morley, Alexis 276	Niehauser, Kelsey 102	Pauschert, Kaila Marie ...292	Pudlewski, Patrick 278
Morris, Austin 319	Niehoff, Joey 58	Pawliski, Samantha 280	Pugel, Ericka 80
Morris, Dakota 296	Niese, David 131	Payne, Aaron 238	Pugh, Madeline 297
Morris, Kelly 27	Niese, Natasha 216	Payne, Karissa 156	Pullins, Julia 100
Morris, Lily 240	Niese, Taylor 165	Pazel, Destinie 163	Puls, Jamie 27
Morrison, Emily 210	Nobuoka, Emi 282	Peace, Natalie 186	Puma, Justin 151
Morrow, Shala 20	Nolan, Emily 117	Peacock, Clayton 288	Quick, Mariah 184
Moss, Evin 274	Nolfi, Krista 296	Peake, Mariah 128	Quijada, Bryan 304
Mossing, Brittany 45	Norris, Tricia 182	Pearce, Carly 59	Quinn, Pat 107
Mossor, Nicole 151	O'Brien, Amanda 21	Pearl, Brandon 282	Quinones, Chelsea 120
Mostov, Arona 203	O'Brien, Ann 89	Pearson, Taylor 306	Rachovitsky, Daniel 35
Motter, Halie 52	O'Brien, Brandon 260	Pedigo, Kathleen 173	Radl, Lisa 99
Mount, Garrett 168	O'Connor, Lindsey 33	Peel, Rebecca 37	Radley, Sarah 142
Mount, Ian 278	O'Connor, Michael C. ...173	Pejsa, Jeff 59	Radwanski, Alex 146
Mowery, Hannah 109	O'Connor, Ryan 160	Pelini, Jake 146	Ragan, Eric 124
Mulay, Jackie 68	O'Donnell, Gabrielle 83	Pelsoczi, Taylor 246	Raisor, Jessie 158
Mullins, Keon 239	O'Neill, Gabrielle 258	Penza, Angela 166	Rajagopal, Sneha 303
Munim, Mohammed 266	Ochs, Alec 269	Perdue, Katelyn 225	Ramos, Carmen 111

Index

Ramos, Raymond 23
Randall, Erin 44
Randolph, Hannah 112
Rapp, Chris 37
Rashid, Ramsha 289
Raterman, Hayley 49
Rau, Ashley 224
Raulinaitis, Emma 173
Ravlin, Jacquelyn 235
Rayburn, Sara 127
Reaney, Olivia 60
Rechnitzer, Alma 298
Reck, Sean 108
Recker, Victoria 52
Redman, Andrew 287
Reed, Colin 289
Reed, Ginelle 157
Reed, Michael 262
Reidel, Taylor 242
Reidling, Tori 107
Reineck, Nick 226
Reinhart, Marissa 174
Reinhart-Anez, Erin 79
Reis, Dylan 246
Remley, Courtney 254
Remy-Davis, Tess 285
Resnik, Jonathan 274
Revels Jr., Allen 23
Reynolds, Mallory 282
Rhoads, Kelsie 318
Rhoads, Will 146
Rhodes, Grace 271
Ricco, Tasha 40
Rice, Elijah 264
Rice-Hawkins, Ben 258
Rich, Wade 171
Richards, Dani 311
Richardson, Ashley 226
Richardson, Lauren 167
Richardson, Paige 314
Richter, Emily 251
Rieser, Chris 102
Riha, Reno 211
Riley, Amanda 313
Rimmel, Maria 80
Rinker, Kayla 249
Ripich, Forde 178
Rizk, Kaitlin 238
Roach, Adriane 20
Robarge, Kristen 222
Roberts, Austin 233
Roberts, Michael 271
Roberts, Sherri 56
Robertson, Antwan 254
Robinson, Eleanor 210
Robinson, Tashina 34
Robles-Cruz, Adolfo 316
Rodriguez, Anthony 39

Roe, Gaige 282
Roe, Miranda 183
Roehm, Christian 79
Roesch, Alex 165
Roettker, Meggie 278
Rogge, Allison 243
Romie, Hannah 236
Rose, Davey 285
Rose, Kayla 296
Roseberry, Amanda 132
Rosic, Edvin 259
Ross, Elena 83
Ross, Kamryn 247
Ross, Savanna 125
Ross, Victoria 302
Roth, Bryan 115
Roth, Katy 26
Rouda, Dylan 288
Rouhier, Ashley 148
Roush, Breanna 120
Rowe, Bernadette 239
Rowe, Kaleb 285
Rowe, Morgan 177
Rowell, Alayna 79
Rubino, Anthony 247
Rubinoff, Yitzi 211
Ruble, Tyler 93
Ruff, Eddie 109
Ruffolo, Kara 143
Ruggles, Zach 88
Runyan, Nick 233
Rupert, Kathleen Ruth . . .314
Ruse, Nicole 310
Rushlow, Nicholas 287
Russell, Elizabeth 112
Russell, Kayla 48
Rutherford, Bethany 227
Rutz, Tyler 229
Ryan, Nick 319
Rybak, Emily 98
Rymer, Madalyn 245
Ryu, Seokhyeon 242
Sabol, Sarah 98
Samborsky, Chris 192
Sams, Miranda 73
Sanchez, Zenaye 320
Sanders, Madeléine 250
Sands, Jessica 139
SanFillipo, Mariah 282
Santoro, Natalie 184
Santos, Leslie 49
Sapp, Darian 236
Sapp, Scot 282
Sargeant, Troy 256
Satterfield, Hannah 151
Sauerwein, Anna 106
Saunders, Hannah 171
Saunders, Ryan G. 136

Savides, Kim 158
Sawicki, Caroline 42
Saxon, Lauren 303
Saxon, Michael 252
Saylor, Tommy 263
Schabitzer, Samantha 228
Schaefer, Charlie 161
Schafer, Hanna 312
Schaffer, Curtis 179
Schaffner, Laura 54
Schairbaum, Jay 237
Scheidenberger, Joe 54
Scheidler, Jessica 31
Schilling, Kevin 319
Schlagheck, Matthew 30
Schmidle, Katherine 297
Schmidt, Daniel 145
Schmuhl, Melissa 130
Schneider, Alban 306
Schneider, Brittany Ann . . .92
Schnipke, Stephanie 90
Schnupp, Ashley 136
Schockman, Kyle 83
Schoen, Natalie 129
Schoen, Ted 162
Schoenung, Ryan 122
Schor, Meryl 276
Schreiber, Hadas 256
Schroeder, Marissa 186
Schroeder, Marla 274
Schroeder, Megan 263
Schroer, Chad 86
Schuessler, Kat 32
Schuler, Jason 238
Schulte, Jay 265
Schulze, Paul 33
Schumm, Anna 242
Schumm, Rachael 121
Schwab, Samantha 311
Schwartz, Elli 313
Scott, Keegan 152
Scowden, Becca 139
Scribner, Sydney 182
Sedam, Lonna 306
Sedivy, Jordan 241
Seger, Caitlyn 79
Seitz, Ashlynn 134
Seitz, Katya 91
Seufer, Jeff 167
Sevel, Morgan 288
Sewall, Emily 249
Shanahan, Devin 177
Shannon, Russell 261
Shasteen, Kyle 272
Sheely, Jameson 145
Sheets, Kevin 230
Shehata, Christina 275
Sheller, Andrea 134

Shepherd, Ana 305
Shepherd, Anna 192
Shepherd, Jasmaine 45
Shepherd, Tori 212
Shepka, Amanda 92
Shifflett, Sarah 59
Shininger, Margo 319
Shirley, Katherine 271
Shisler, Caroline 274
Shon, David 288
Short, Madison 236
Shrake, Laura 108
Shroyer, Mitchell 255
Shtyrkalo, Nataliya 55
Sibilia, Gabrielle 258
Siclari, Carly 141
Siebenaler, Gunnar 281
Silvers, Morgan 216
Simokov, Victoria 40
Simon, Stephanie 252
Singer, Abigail 312
Sitch, Mark 84
Sizemore, Staci 39
Skedel, Rachael 106
Skladany, Brian 155
Skyllingstad, Brooke 32
Slamka, Sadie 136
Slater, Olivia 251
Slomski, Kayla 54
Slone, Ashdon 24
Smearman, Paige 159
Smith, Amy 310
Smith, Andrew 29
Smith, Bailey 318
Smith, Charlotte 208
Smith, Danica 111
Smith, Hannah 286
Smith, Kevin T. 55
Smith, Macy 296
Smith, Sarah 296
Smith, Scott 105
Smith, Sterling 268
Smith, Tara 75
Snow, Shelby 86
Snowden, Robbie 121
Snyder, Alyssa 90
Snyder, Autumn 302
Sobel, Ryan 183
Sobiech, Halle 246
Sobole, Holly 110
Sorboro, Sophia 318
Sorma, Julius 192
Souders, Kyle 101
Sowers, Tia 188
Spader, Tommy 80
Spallino, Will 208
Sparks, Markie 33
Spaulding, Vonnie 108

Page 327

Name	Page	Name	Page	Name	Page	Name	Page
Spear, Alyssa	309	Sturges, David	216	Titmas, Cali	265	Vonderau, Jessica	240
Speed, Carly	250	Sturwold, Lindsey	230	Tobin, Caitlyn	261	Voss, Rachel	45
Spence, Brooke	222	Suhr, Alan	173	Tolerton, Will	42	Vovk, Alesha	204
Spetner, Rochel	310	Sullivan, Jake	312	Tolle, Haley	74	Wagner, Erica	110
Spille, Keith	191	Sullivan, Karley	177	Tolley, Peyton	270	Wagner, Jeff	262
Sposetta, Kimberly	138	Sullo, Victoria	213	Toner, Danny	259	Wagner, Lauren	316
Spriggs, Chandler	285	Sun, Yun Lu	239	Toney, Alex	214	Wagner, Samantha	95
Squires, Sally	219	Sunderhaus, Kiley	319	Tony, Maria	178	Wahdan, Nuha	292
Stachowski, Paige	93	Supanich, Stephen A.	261	Tosti, Gina	169	Wahl, Emma	125
Staggers, Callie	173	Suter, Colin	160	Tournoux, Erica	49	Walker, Austin	244
Stainer, Megan	126	Sutton, Kaitlyn	309	Townsend, Tiffany	220	Walker, Myles	214
Stallard, Derek	246	Sutton, Taylor	257	Trainer, Zachary	279	Wallenhorst, Jacob	89
Stalnaker, Alexia	128	Suzaki, Mayu	252	Trimble, Tara	26	Walquist, McKenna	316
Stamberger, Jenny	177	Swem, Deanna	147	Trout, Brooklyn	271	Wanamaker, Nick	194
Stankiewicz, Catherine	118	Swick, Shelby	211	Trudeau, Leandra	70	Wang, Andrew	317
Stanley, Karene	19	Swint, Taylor	93	Truex, Matthew	81	Wang, Heather	260
Stanton, Anna	319	Switala, Mary	126	Turnbull, Allison	150	Wang, Hope	254
Stanton, Mason	277	Sylak, Jonathan	187	Turner, Courtney	218	Wang, Oliver	133
Stark, Savannah	115	Szalay, Garret	193	Turner, Kathleen	264	Ward, Briel	100
Starkey, Alex	308	Tabet, Aline	28	Turner, Michael	102	Ward, Emily	216
Starkey, Mac	266	Talampas, Tirzah	317	Tyler, Caroline	114	Ward, Jarrod	319
Staub, Daniel	250	Taleb, Nardine	305	Tyson, Sarai	225	Ward, Krista	298
Steele, Brandi	281	Tamarkin, Nick	235	Udell, Amber	194	Ward, Makenzie	274
Steele, Sean	259	Tamarkin, Tyler	287	Ullrich, Rachel	300	Warner, Emma	218
Steffen, Eliza	246	Tan, Karen	273	Ungruhe, Hannah	96	Warrington, Blake	172
Stein, Clay	46	Taphous, Beth	102	Upholz, Rachel	175	Waterhouse, Bryan	268
Steingass, Nate	140	Taylor, Anthony	95	Urbanic, Alexa	159	Watrous, Joseph	176
Stepanishchev, Alex	222	Taylor, Jen	304	Urbanic, Brian	241	Watson, Michelle	232
Stephens, Madyson	189	Taylor, Naomi Jean	163	Urbanic, John	135	Weakley, Paige	144
Stephens, Michael	16	Taylor, Nicole	58	Usip, Unyime	286	Weaver, Christopher	216
Stephenson, Caitlin	87	Taylor, Ravyn	186	Vala, Mike	188	Webb, Ashley	139
Stephenson, Morgan	165	Taylor, Sam	25	Vallance, John Ross	257	Webber, Alexis	253
Stevens, Rachel	22	Teague, Christain	302	Valli, Gian Carlo	220	Weber, Sara	252
Stevenson, Kayla	274	Tedesco, Alyssa	239	Van Benschoten, Victoria	306	Weeter, Caleigh	216
Stewart, Angie	182	Teichman, Tracey	158	Van Nuys, Hannah	212	Wehr, Evan	85
Stewart, Justin	285	Tejeda, Jennifer	87	Van Wagenen, Justin	292	Weiner, Julie	52
Stewart, Nicky	263	Tempel, Brian	292	VanCamp, Ashley	94	Weingart, Valerie	71
Steyer, Maison	246	Temple, Larken	299	Vandergriff, Stephanie	196	Weir, J.T.	26
Stine, McKenzie	240	Temple, Nicole	19	Vanderhorst, Lauren	216	Weir, Megan Elizabeth	270
Stiner, Erin	170	Tenbarge, Kathryn	211	VanOss, Shiloh	84	Welch, Rachel	254
Stivison, Kali	188	Tennity, Cassidy	290	Vapenik, Sarah	302	Weldon, John	245
Stocks, Aislynn	244	Tewksbury, Gregory	128	Varcho, Nora	213	Wells, Ben	312
Stoffer, Ross	153	Thiel, Landon	318	Vargo, Kailah	208	Wells, Cath	37
Stolte, Shayna	126	Thien, Alex	192	Vatamanu, Irina	256	Wells, Kalsea	305
Stone, Lindsay	217	Thomas, Emily	149	Veal, Shandrea	257	Wells, Lauren	107
Storch, Teagan	265	Thomas, Michael	269	Velasquez, Brian	268	Wells, Madison	249
Strahm, Jack	235	Thompsen, Kristina	73	Vermilion, Tyler	241	Wells, Olivia	253
Streeter, Leah	181	Thompson, Alexa L.	251	Vetter, Tommy	310	Wells, Spencer	161
Streicher, Josh	192	Thompson, Breane	302	Vidoli, Elizabeth	221	Wendel, Taylor	174
Strenk, Jennifer	29	Thompson, Brittanie	216	Villacres, Alyssa	81	Wendling, Matthew	175
Stricker, Becca	104	Thompson, Lauren	315	Vining, Mackenzie	270	Weng, Jonathan	224
Stroh, Matthew	163	Thompson, McKenzie	254	Vinson, Jazmin	258	Wentz, Patience	233
Strong, Emilee	129	Thompson, Zach	286	Vissing, Jessica	17	Wenzinger, Ellie	223
Strong, Gavin	310	Throckmorton, Emily	319	Viswanath, Naveen	262	West, Ian	193
Stroup, Katie	104	Tiano, Mariah	226	Vitucci, Anelisa	272	West, Laura	241
Stryffeler, Abigail	163	Tibbits, Cory	284	Vo, Arnold	242	West, Naomi Grace	50
Stuart, Tina	23	Tigner, Johna	104	Vogel, Jared	309	Westerheide, Drew	255
Stucke, Ben	237	Tischler, Matt	150	Volpe, Tori	134	Westphal, Christen	117

Index

Wethington, Evan 250
Whalen, Brock 225
Whalen, Jessica 149
Wheatt, William 164
Wheeler, Megan 278
Wheeler, Ty 276
Whelpley, Hannah 44
Whitacre, Haley 285
White, Arnisha 139
White, Asianna 230
White, Caden 244
White, Eric 288
White, Katie 111
White, Kim 87
White, Meeco 42
Whitman, Taylor 250
Whitney, Mary Margaret . . .93
Whittaker, Emily 249
Whybrew, Kelly 310
Wickerham, Rachel 298
Wilczynski, Lea 205
Wiley, Andrea 254
Wiley, Lina 195
Wilimitis, Blake 116
Wilkins, Nathan 149
Willcox, Morgan 256
Williams, Isaiah 266
Williams, Kara 131
Williams, Keeley 210
Williams, Laura 34
Williams, Maggie 162
Williams, Rusty 177
Williams, Sarah 35
Willis, Jamie 135
Wills, Kirsten 313
Wills, McKenzie 195
Wilson, Kallie 251
Wilson, Lauren 139
Wilson, Zeb 29
Wines, Joseph 212
Wing, Kiera 153
Wing, Michael 245
Winkel, Parker 121
Winkler, Matt 43
Winland, Wade 259
Winston, Jasmine 274
Winterhalter, Heather 41
Winters, Ashley 84
Winters, Lauren 21
Wirtz, Cassie R. 271
Wisniewski, Stephanie
    Marie 128
Woelfl, Lindsey 304
Woika, Sara 250
Wolking, Garrett 124
Wolterman, Hannah 280
Wong, Christine 36
Wood, Ellie 208
Wood, Jacob 123
Wood, Jordyn 287
Woodward, Brittany 154
Wooten, DJ 105
Workman, Paige 299
Worrell, Kelli 234
Worthing, Sara 76
Wortman, Nikki 229
Wright, Emily 118
Wright, Hannah 300
Wyatt, Ianna N. 72
Wycoff, Garrett 272
Yacteen, Gassan 311
Yacteen, Omar 293
Yanetta, Michael 245
Yeckley, Kayla 119
Yedid, Evette 137
Yeh, Isaac 159
Yehl, Sarah 126
Yen, Monica 250
Yodzis, Leah 163
Yoon, Jooheon 111
York, Megan 226
Young, Jessica 103
Young, Jordan 274
Young, Matt 268
Young, Taylor 219
Young, Tyler Wm. 215
Yutzy, Caleb 32
Zangara, Megan 168
Zatezalo, Zack 296
Zavakos, Christine 162
Zavakos, Rachel 161
Zbinovec, Amanda 156
Zbinovec, Kendra 140
Zebrasky, Sydney Leigh . . .273
Zeigler, Ally 264
Zemrock-van der Meer,
    Zachary 217
Zerucha, Johnnie 258
Zibert, Emily 311
Ziegler, Kevin A. 307
Ziclinski, Claire 286
Zilke, Scott 94
Zimmer, Ashley 206
Zimmerman, Alicia 269
Zimmerman, Crystal 19
Zimmerman, Joseph 182
Zimmerman, Roy 112
Zimmerman, T.J. 164
Zink, Alex 224
Zink, Taylor 301
Zorzi, Alaina 207
Zullo, Nico 150
Zumwald, Sheridan 137
Zywot, Emilia 195